W9-CIB-857

Mitsubishi Eclipse Plymouth Laser Eagle Talon Automotive Repair Manual

by Mike Stubblefield and John H Haynes

Member of the Guild of Motoring Writers

Models covered:
All models
1990 through 1994

(4B6 - 68030)
(2097)

ABCDE
FG

Haynes Publishing Group
Sparkford Nr Yeovil
Somerset BA22 7JJ England

Haynes North America, Inc
861 Lawrence Drive
Newbury Park
California 91320 USA

About this manual

Its purpose

The purpose of this manual is to help you get the best value from your vehicle. It can do so in several ways. It can help you decide what work must be done, even if you choose to have it done by a dealer service department or a repair shop; it provides information and procedures for routine maintenance and servicing; and it offers diagnostic and repair procedures to follow when trouble occurs.

We hope you use the manual to tackle the work yourself. For many simpler jobs, doing it yourself may be quicker than arranging an appointment to get the vehicle into a shop and making the trips to leave it and pick it up. More importantly, a lot of money can be saved by avoiding the expense the shop must pass on to you to cover its labor and overhead costs. An added benefit is the sense of satisfaction and accomplishment that you feel after doing the job yourself.

Using the manual

The manual is divided into Chapters. Each Chapter is divided into numbered Sections, which are headed in bold type between horizontal lines. Each Section consists of consecutively numbered paragraphs.

At the beginning of each numbered Section you will be referred to any illustrations which apply to the procedures in that Section. The reference numbers used in illustration captions pinpoint the pertinent Section and the Step within that Section. That is, illustration 3.2 means the illustration refers to Section 3 and Step (or paragraph) 2 within that Section.

Procedures, once described in the text, are not normally repeated. When it's necessary to refer to another Chapter, the reference will be given as Chapter and Section number. Cross references given without use of the word "Chapter" apply to Sections and/or paragraphs in the same Chapter. For example, "see Section 8" means in the same Chapter.

References to the left or right side of the vehicle assume you are sitting in the driver's seat, facing forward.

Even though we have prepared this manual with extreme care, neither the publisher nor the author can accept responsibility for any errors in, or omissions from, the information given.

NOTE

A **Note** provides information necessary to properly complete a procedure or information which will make the procedure easier to understand.

CAUTION

A **Caution** provides a special procedure or special steps which must be taken while completing the procedure where the Caution is found. Not heeding a Caution can result in damage to the assembly being worked on.

WARNING

A **Warning** provides a special procedure or special steps which must be taken while completing the procedure where the Warning is found. Not heeding a Warning can result in personal injury.

Acknowledgements

We are grateful to the Chrysler Corporation for providing technical information and certain illustrations. Technical writers who contributed to this project include Larry Warren, Robert Maddox and Mark Ryan.

© **Haynes North America, Inc. 1994, 1998**

With permission from J.H. Haynes & Co. Ltd.

A book in the Haynes Automotive Repair Manual Series

Printed in the U.S.A.

ISBN 1 56392 097 2

Library of Congress Catalog Card Number 94-75569

Contents

Haynes author, mechanic and photographer with 1990 Eagle Talon

Introduction to the Plymouth Laser, Eagle Talon and Mitsubishi Eclipse

These models are available in two-door liftback body styles.

The transversely mounted inline four-cylinder engines used in these models are equipped with electronic fuel injection. Some models are turbocharged.

The engine drives the front wheels through either a five-speed manual or an automatic transaxle via independent driveaxles. Some models use a transfer case and driveshaft to send power to a rear differential and then to the rear wheels, with independent driveaxles to provide four-wheel drive (4WD).

Independent suspension, featuring coil spring/strut damper units, is used on all four wheels. The power-assisted rack-and-pinion steering unit is mounted behind the engine.

The brakes are disc at all four wheels, with power assist standard.

Vehicle identification numbers

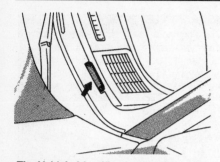

1st Digit	2nd Digit	3rd Digit	4th Digit	5th Digit	6th Digit	7th Digit	8th Digit	9th Digit	10th Digit	11th Digit	12th to 17th Digits
Country	Make	Vehicle type	Others	Line	Price class	Body	Engine	*Check digits	Model year	Plant	Serial number

The Vehicle Identification Number (VIN) is important for identifying the vehicle and engine type - it is on the front of the dash, visible from outside the vehicle, looking through the windshield on the driver's side

This chart shows the information conveyed by the VIN. Check Digits are used by the factory to verify the correct VIN. The eighth digit identifies the engine - see the text for further explanation.

Modifications are a continuing and unpublicized process in vehicle manufacturing. Since spare parts lists and manuals are compiled on a numerical basis, the individual vehicle numbers are necessary to correctly identify the component required.

Vehicle Identification Number (VIN)

This very important identification number is stamped on a plate attached to the dashboard inside the windshield on the driver's side of the vehicle (see illustration). The VIN also appears on the Vehicle Certificate of Title and Registration. It contains information such as where and when the vehicle was manufactured, the model year

and the body style.

The type of engine installed in the vehicle is indicated by the eighth digit of the VIN. On 1990 through 1992 models, a T indicates a 1.8L SOHC non-turbo engine, an R indicates a 2.0L DOHC non-turbo engine and a U indicates a 2.0L DOHC turbo engine. On 1993 and 1994 models, a B indicates a 1.8L SOHC non-turbo engine, an E indicates a 2.0L DOHC non-turbo engine and an F indicates a 2.0L DOHC turbo engine.

Vehicle Identification Code Plate

The Vehicle identification code plate is riveted to the engine compartment firewall (see illustration). The plate lists the model code, engine model, transaxle model and body code. Also listed is the paint and trim code.

Vehicle Certification Label

The Vehicle Certification Label is attached to the driver's side door pillar (see illustration). Information on this label includes the name of the manufacturer, the month and year of production, the Gross Vehicle Weight Rating (GVWR), the Gross Axle Weight Rating (GAWR) and the certification statement.

Engine model number

The engine model number is stamped onto a machined pad on the front (radiator) side of the engine block (see illustration). 1.8L SOHC non-turbo engines are designated by the model number 4G37. 2.0L DOHC turbo and non-turbo engines are designated by the model number 4G63.

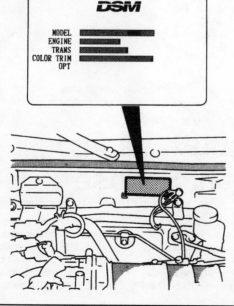

The Vehicle Identification Code Plate is on the engine compartment firewall - it is particularly useful in identifying paint and trim colors and types

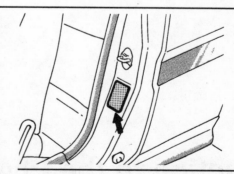

The Vehicle Certification Label is visible in the door jamb, after opening the driver's side door

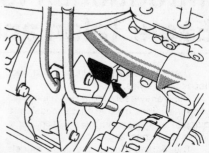

The engine model number is stamped onto a pad on the front side of the engine - see the text for an explanation of the number

Buying parts

Replacement parts are available from many sources, which generally fall into one of two categories - authorized dealer parts departments and independent retail auto parts stores. Our advice concerning these parts is as follows:

Retail auto parts stores: Good auto parts stores will stock frequently needed components which wear out relatively fast, such as clutch components, exhaust systems, brake parts, tune-up parts, etc. These stores often supply new or reconditioned parts on an exchange basis, which can save a considerable amount of money. Discount auto parts stores are often very good places to buy materials and parts needed for general vehicle maintenance such as oil, grease, filters, spark plugs, belts, touch-up paint, bulbs, etc. They also usually sell tools and general accessories, have convenient hours, charge lower prices and can often be found not far from home.

Authorized dealer parts department: This is the best source for parts which are unique to the vehicle and not generally available elsewhere (such as major engine parts, transmission parts, trim pieces, etc.).

Warranty information: If the vehicle is still covered under warranty, be sure that any replacement parts purchased - regardless of the source - do not invalidate the warranty!

To be sure of obtaining the correct parts, have engine and chassis numbers available and, if possible, take the old parts along for positive identification.

Maintenance techniques, tools and working facilities

Maintenance techniques

There are a number of techniques involved in maintenance and repair that will be referred to throughout this manual. Application of these techniques will enable the home mechanic to be more efficient, better organized and capable of performing the various tasks properly, which will ensure that the repair job is thorough and complete.

Fasteners

Fasteners are nuts, bolts, studs and screws used to hold two or more parts together. There are a few things to keep in mind when working with fasteners. Almost all of them use a locking device of some type, either a lockwasher, locknut, locking tab or thread adhesive. All threaded fasteners should be clean and straight, with undamaged threads and undamaged corners on the hex head where the wrench fits. Develop the habit of replacing all damaged nuts and bolts with new ones. Special locknuts with nylon or fiber inserts can only be used once. If they are removed, they lose their locking ability and must be replaced with new ones.

Rusted nuts and bolts should be treated with a penetrating fluid to ease removal and prevent breakage. Some mechanics use turpentine in a spout-type oil can, which works quite well. After applying the rust penetrant, let it work for a few minutes before trying to loosen the nut or bolt. Badly rusted fasteners may have to be chiseled or sawed off or removed with a special nut breaker, available at tool stores.

If a bolt or stud breaks off in an assembly, it can be drilled and removed with a special tool commonly available for this purpose. Most automotive machine shops can perform this task, as well as other repair procedures, such as the repair of threaded holes that have been stripped out.

Flat washers and lockwashers, when removed from an assembly, should always be replaced exactly as removed. Replace any damaged washers with new ones. Never use a lockwasher on any soft metal surface (such as aluminum), thin sheet metal or plastic.

Grade 1 or 2   Grade 5   Grade 8

Bolt strength marking (standard/SAE/USS; bottom - metric)

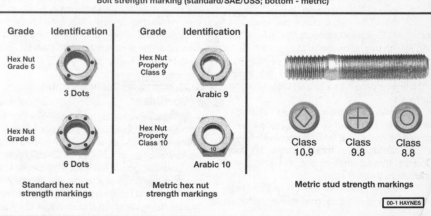

Grade	Identification	Grade	Identification
Hex Nut Grade 5	3 Dots	Hex Nut Property Class 9	Arabic 9
Hex Nut Grade 8	6 Dots	Hex Nut Property Class 10	Arabic 10

Standard hex nut strength markings

Metric hex nut strength markings

Class 10.9   Class 9.8   Class 8.8

Metric stud strength markings

00-1 HAYNES

Fastener sizes

For a number of reasons, automobile manufacturers are making wider and wider use of metric fasteners. Therefore, it is important to be able to tell the difference between standard (sometimes called U.S. or SAE) and metric hardware, since they cannot be interchanged.

All bolts, whether standard or metric, are sized according to diameter, thread pitch and length. For example, a standard 1/2 - 13 x 1 bolt is 1/2 inch in diameter, has 13 threads per inch and is 1 inch long. An M12 - 1.75 x 25 metric bolt is 12 mm in diameter, has a thread pitch of 1.75 mm (the distance between threads) and is 25 mm long. The two bolts are nearly identical, and easily confused, but they are not interchangeable.

In addition to the differences in diameter, thread pitch and length, metric and standard bolts can also be distinguished by examining the bolt heads. To begin with, the distance across the flats on a standard bolt head is measured in inches, while the same dimension on a metric bolt is sized in millimeters (the same is true for nuts). As a result, a standard wrench should not be used on a metric bolt and a metric wrench should not be used on a standard bolt. Also, most standard bolts have slashes radiating out from the center of the head to denote the grade or strength of the bolt, which is an indication of the amount of torque that can be applied to it. The greater the number of slashes, the greater the strength of the bolt. Grades 0 through 5 are commonly used on automobiles. Metric bolts have a property class (grade) number, rather than a slash, molded into their heads to indicate bolt strength. In this case, the higher the number, the stronger the bolt. Property class numbers 8.8, 9.8 and 10.9 are commonly used on automobiles.

Strength markings can also be used to distinguish standard hex nuts from metric hex nuts. Many standard nuts have dots stamped into one side, while metric nuts are marked with a number. The greater the number of dots, or the higher the number, the greater the strength of the nut.

Metric studs are also marked on their ends according to property class (grade). Larger studs are numbered (the same as metric bolts), while smaller studs carry a geometric code to denote grade.

It should be noted that many fasteners, especially Grades 0 through 2, have no distinguishing marks on them. When such is the case, the only way to determine whether it is standard or metric is to measure the thread pitch or compare it to a known fastener of the same size.

Standard fasteners are often referred to as SAE, as opposed to metric. However, it should be noted that SAE technically refers to a non-metric fine thread fastener only. Coarse thread non-metric fasteners are referred to as USS sizes.

Since fasteners of the same size (both standard and metric) may have different

Metric thread sizes	Ft-lbs	Nm
M-6	6 to 9	9 to 12
M-8	14 to 21	19 to 28
M-10	28 to 40	38 to 54
M-12	50 to 71	68 to 96
M-14	80 to 140	109 to 154

Pipe thread sizes	Ft-lbs	Nm
1/8	5 to 8	7 to 10
1/4	12 to 18	17 to 24
3/8	22 to 33	30 to 44
1/2	25 to 35	34 to 47

U.S. thread sizes	Ft-lbs	Nm
1/4 - 20	6 to 9	9 to 12
5/16 - 18	12 to 18	17 to 24
5/16 - 24	14 to 20	19 to 27
3/8 - 16	22 to 32	30 to 43
3/8 - 24	27 to 38	37 to 51
7/16 - 14	40 to 55	55 to 74
7/16 - 20	40 to 60	55 to 81
1/2 - 13	55 to 80	75 to 108

00-2 HAYNES

Standard (SAE and USS) bolt dimensions/grade marks

- G Grade marks (bolt strength)
- L Length (in inches)
- T Thread pitch (number of threads per inch)
- D Nominal diameter (in inches)

Metric bolt dimensions/grade marks

- P Property class (bolt strength)
- L Length (in millimeters)
- T Thread pitch (distance between threads in millimeters)
- D Diameter

strength ratings, be sure to reinstall any bolts, studs or nuts removed from your vehicle in their original locations. Also, when replacing a fastener with a new one, make sure that the new one has a strength rating equal to or greater than the original.

Tightening sequences and procedures

Most threaded fasteners should be tightened to a specific torque value (torque is the twisting force applied to a threaded component such as a nut or bolt). Overtightening the fastener can weaken it and cause it to break, while undertightening can cause it to eventually come loose. Bolts, screws and studs, depending on the material they are

made of and their thread diameters, have specific torque values, many of which are noted in the Specifications at the beginning of each Chapter. Be sure to follow the torque recommendations closely. For fasteners not assigned a specific torque, a general torque value chart is presented here as a guide. These torque values are for dry (unlubricated) fasteners threaded into steel or cast iron (not aluminum). As was previously mentioned, the size and grade of a fastener determine the amount of torque that can safely be applied to it. The figures listed here are approximate for Grade 2 and Grade 3 fasteners. Higher grades can tolerate higher torque values.

Fasteners laid out in a pattern, such as cylinder head bolts, oil pan bolts, differential cover bolts, etc., must be loosened or tight-

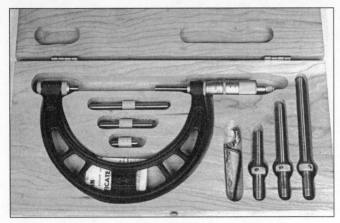

Micrometer set

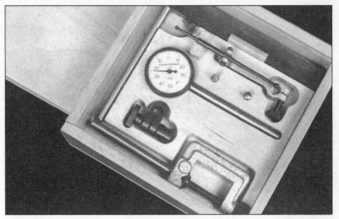

Dial indicator set

ened in sequence to avoid warping the component. This sequence will normally be shown in the appropriate Chapter. If a specific pattern is not given, the following procedures can be used to prevent warping.

Initially, the bolts or nuts should be assembled finger-tight only. Next, they should be tightened one full turn each, in a criss-cross or diagonal pattern. After each one has been tightened one full turn, return to the first one and tighten them all one-half turn, following the same pattern. Finally, tighten each of them one-quarter turn at a time until each fastener has been tightened to the proper torque. To loosen and remove the fasteners, the procedure would be reversed.

Component disassembly

Component disassembly should be done with care and purpose to help ensure that the parts go back together properly. Always keep track of the sequence in which parts are removed. Make note of special characteristics or marks on parts that can be installed more than one way, such as a grooved thrust washer on a shaft. It is a good idea to lay the disassembled parts out on a clean surface in the order that they were removed. It may also be helpful to make sketches or take instant photos of components before removal.

When removing fasteners from a component, keep track of their locations. Sometimes threading a bolt back in a part, or putting the washers and nut back on a stud, can prevent mix-ups later. If nuts and bolts cannot be returned to their original locations, they should be kept in a compartmented box or a series of small boxes. A cupcake or muffin tin is ideal for this purpose, since each cavity can hold the bolts and nuts from a particular area (i.e. oil pan bolts, valve cover bolts, engine mount bolts, etc.). A pan of this type is especially helpful when working on assemblies with very small parts, such as the carburetor, alternator, valve train or interior dash and trim pieces. The cavities can be marked with paint or tape to identify the contents.

Whenever wiring looms, harnesses or connectors are separated, it is a good idea to identify the two halves with numbered pieces of masking tape so they can be easily reconnected.

Gasket sealing surfaces

Throughout any vehicle, gaskets are used to seal the mating surfaces between two parts and keep lubricants, fluids, vacuum or pressure contained in an assembly.

Many times these gaskets are coated with a liquid or paste-type gasket sealing compound before assembly. Age, heat and pressure can sometimes cause the two parts to stick together so tightly that they are very difficult to separate. Often, the assembly can be loosened by striking it with a soft-face hammer near the mating surfaces. A regular hammer can be used if a block of wood is placed between the hammer and the part. Do not hammer on cast parts or parts that could be easily damaged. With any particularly stubborn part, always recheck to make sure that every fastener has been removed.

Avoid using a screwdriver or bar to pry apart an assembly, as they can easily mar the gasket sealing surfaces of the parts, which must remain smooth. If prying is absolutely necessary, use an old broom handle, but keep in mind that extra clean up will be necessary if the wood splinters.

After the parts are separated, the old gasket must be carefully scraped off and the gasket surfaces cleaned. Stubborn gasket material can be soaked with rust penetrant or treated with a special chemical to soften it so it can be easily scraped off. A scraper can be fashioned from a piece of copper tubing by flattening and sharpening one end. Copper is recommended because it is usually softer than the surfaces to be scraped, which reduces the chance of gouging the part. Some gaskets can be removed with a wire brush, but regardless of the method used, the mating surfaces must be left clean and smooth. If for some reason the gasket surface is gouged, then a gasket sealer thick enough to fill scratches will have to be used during reassembly of the components. For most applications, a non-drying (or semi-drying) gasket sealer should be used.

Hose removal tips

Warning: *If the vehicle is equipped with air conditioning, do not disconnect any of the A/C hoses without first having the system depressurized by a dealer service department or a service station.*

Hose removal precautions closely parallel gasket removal precautions. Avoid scratching or gouging the surface that the hose mates against or the connection may leak. This is especially true for radiator hoses. Because of various chemical reactions, the rubber in hoses can bond itself to the metal spigot that the hose fits over. To remove a hose, first loosen the hose clamps that secure it to the spigot. Then, with slip-joint pliers, grab the hose at the clamp and rotate it around the spigot. Work it back and forth until it is completely free, then pull it off. Silicone or other lubricants will ease removal if they can be applied between the hose and the outside of the spigot. Apply the same lubricant to the inside of the hose and the outside of the spigot to simplify installation.

As a last resort (and if the hose is to be replaced with a new one anyway), the rubber can be slit with a knife and the hose peeled from the spigot. If this must be done, be careful that the metal connection is not damaged.

If a hose clamp is broken or damaged, do not reuse it. Wire-type clamps usually weaken with age, so it is a good idea to replace them with screw-type clamps whenever a hose is removed.

Tools

A selection of good tools is a basic requirement for anyone who plans to maintain and repair his or her own vehicle. For the owner who has few tools, the initial investment might seem high, but when compared to the spiraling costs of professional auto maintenance and repair, it is a wise one.

To help the owner decide which tools are needed to perform the tasks detailed in this manual, the following tool lists are offered: *Maintenance and minor repair, Repair/overhaul* and *Special.*

The newcomer to practical mechanics

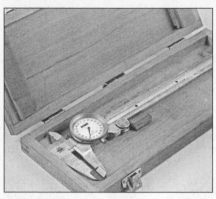

Dial caliper

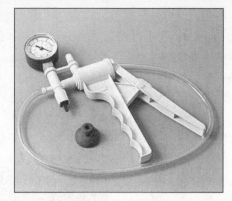

Hand-operated vacuum pump

Timing light

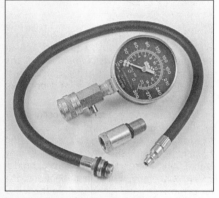

Compression gauge with spark plug
hole adapter

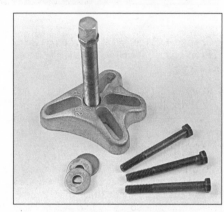

Damper/steering wheel puller

General purpose puller

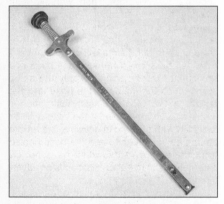

Hydraulic lifter removal tool

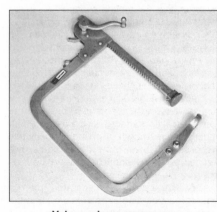

Valve spring compressor

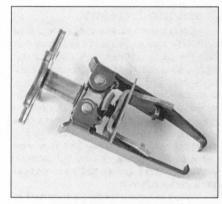

Valve spring compressor

Ridge reamer

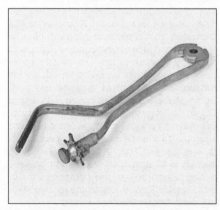

Piston ring groove cleaning tool

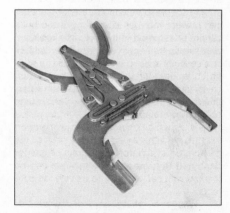

Ring removal/installation tool

Ring compressor

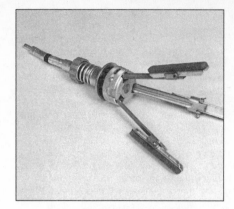

Cylinder hone

Brake hold-down spring tool

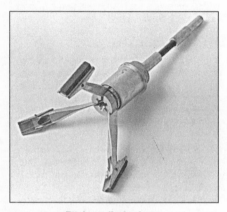

Brake cylinder hone

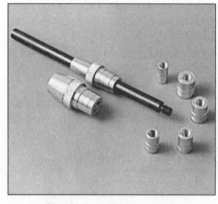

Clutch plate alignment tool

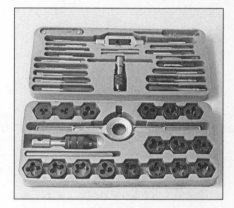

Tap and die set

should start off with the *maintenance and minor repair* tool kit, which is adequate for the simpler jobs performed on a vehicle. Then, as confidence and experience grow, the owner can tackle more difficult tasks, buying additional tools as they are needed. Eventually the basic kit will be expanded into the *repair and overhaul* tool set. Over a period of time, the experienced do-it-yourselfer will assemble a tool set complete enough for most repair and overhaul procedures and will add tools from the special category when it is felt that the expense is justified by the frequency of use.

Maintenance and minor repair tool kit

The tools in this list should be considered the minimum required for performance of routine maintenance, servicing and minor repair work. We recommend the purchase of combination wrenches (box-end and open-end combined in one wrench). While more expensive than open end wrenches, they offer the advantages of both types of wrench.

> *Combination wrench set (1/4-inch to*
> *1 inch or 6 mm to 19 mm)*
> *Adjustable wrench, 8 inch*
> *Spark plug wrench with rubber insert*
> *Spark plug gap adjusting tool*
> *Feeler gauge set*
> *Brake bleeder wrench*
> *Standard screwdriver (5/16-inch x*
> *6 inch)*

> *Phillips screwdriver (No. 2 x 6 inch)*
> *Combination pliers - 6 inch*
> *Hacksaw and assortment of blades*
> *Tire pressure gauge*
> *Grease gun*
> *Oil can*
> *Fine emery cloth*
> *Wire brush*
> *Battery post and cable cleaning tool*
> *Oil filter wrench*
> *Funnel (medium size)*
> *Safety goggles*
> *Jackstands (2)*
> *Drain pan*

Note: *If basic tune-ups are going to be part of routine maintenance, it will be necessary to purchase a good quality stroboscopic timing light and combination tachometer/dwell meter. Although they are included in the list of special tools, it is mentioned here because they are absolutely necessary for tuning most vehicles properly.*

Repair and overhaul tool set

These tools are essential for anyone who plans to perform major repairs and are in addition to those in the maintenance and minor repair tool kit. Included is a comprehensive set of sockets which, though expensive, are invaluable because of their versatility, especially when various extensions and drives are available. We recommend the 1/2-inch drive over the 3/8-inch drive. Although the larger drive is bulky and more expensive,

it has the capacity of accepting a very wide range of large sockets. Ideally, however, the mechanic should have a 3/8-inch drive set and a 1/2-inch drive set.

> *Socket set(s)*
> *Reversible ratchet*
> *Extension - 10 inch*
> *Universal joint*
> *Torque wrench (same size drive as*
> *sockets)*
> *Ball peen hammer - 8 ounce*
> *Soft-face hammer (plastic/rubber)*
> *Standard screwdriver (1/4-inch x 6 inch)*
> *Standard screwdriver (stubby -*
> *5/16-inch)*
> *Phillips screwdriver (No. 3 x 8 inch)*
> *Phillips screwdriver (stubby - No. 2)*
> *Pliers - vise grip*
> *Pliers - lineman's*
> *Pliers - needle nose*
> *Pliers - snap-ring (internal and external)*
> *Cold chisel - 1/2-inch*
> *Scribe*
> *Scraper (made from flattened copper*
> *tubing)*
> *Centerpunch*
> *Pin punches (1/16, 1/8, 3/16-inch)*
> *Steel rule/straightedge - 12 inch*
> *Allen wrench set (1/8 to 3/8-inch or*
> *4 mm to 10 mm)*
> *A selection of files*
> *Wire brush (large)*
> *Jackstands (second set)*
> *Jack (scissor or hydraulic type)*

Note: *Another tool which is often useful is an electric drill with a chuck capacity of 3/8-inch and a set of good quality drill bits.*

Special tools

The tools in this list include those which are not used regularly, are expensive to buy, or which need to be used in accordance with their manufacturer's instructions. Unless these tools will be used frequently, it is not very economical to purchase many of them. A consideration would be to split the cost and use between yourself and a friend or friends. In addition, most of these tools can be obtained from a tool rental shop on a temporary basis.

This list primarily contains only those tools and instruments widely available to the public, and not those special tools produced by the vehicle manufacturer for distribution to dealer service departments. Occasionally, references to the manufacturer's special tools are included in the text of this manual. Generally, an alternative method of doing the job without the special tool is offered. However, sometimes there is no alternative to their use. Where this is the case, and the tool cannot be purchased or borrowed, the work should be turned over to the dealer service department or an automotive repair shop.

Valve spring compressor
Piston ring groove cleaning tool
Piston ring compressor
Piston ring installation tool
Cylinder compression gauge
Cylinder ridge reamer
Cylinder surfacing hone
Cylinder bore gauge
Micrometers and/or dial calipers
Hydraulic lifter removal tool
Balljoint separator
Universal-type puller
Impact screwdriver
Dial indicator set
Stroboscopic timing light (inductive pick-up)
Hand operated vacuum/pressure pump
Tachometer/dwell meter
Universal electrical multimeter
Cable hoist
Brake spring removal and installation tools
Floor jack

Buying tools

For the do-it-yourselfer who is just starting to get involved in vehicle maintenance and repair, there are a number of options available when purchasing tools. If maintenance and minor repair is the extent of the work to be done, the purchase of individual tools is satisfactory. If, on the other hand, extensive work is planned, it would be a good idea to purchase a modest tool set from one of the large retail chain stores. A set can usually be bought at a substantial savings over the individual tool prices, and they often come with a tool box. As additional tools are

needed, add-on sets, individual tools and a larger tool box can be purchased to expand the tool selection. Building a tool set gradually allows the cost of the tools to be spread over a longer period of time and gives the mechanic the freedom to choose only those tools that will actually be used.

Tool stores will often be the only source of some of the special tools that are needed, but regardless of where tools are bought, try to avoid cheap ones, especially when buying screwdrivers and sockets, because they won't last very long. The expense involved in replacing cheap tools will eventually be greater than the initial cost of quality tools.

Care and maintenance of tools

Good tools are expensive, so it makes sense to treat them with respect. Keep them clean and in usable condition and store them properly when not in use. Always wipe off any dirt, grease or metal chips before putting them away. Never leave tools lying around in the work area. Upon completion of a job, always check closely under the hood for tools that may have been left there so they won't get lost during a test drive.

Some tools, such as screwdrivers, pliers, wrenches and sockets, can be hung on a panel mounted on the garage or workshop wall, while others should be kept in a tool box or tray. Measuring instruments, gauges, meters, etc. must be carefully stored where they cannot be damaged by weather or impact from other tools.

When tools are used with care and stored properly, they will last a very long time. Even with the best of care, though, tools will wear out if used frequently. When a tool is damaged or worn out, replace it. Subsequent jobs will be safer and more enjoyable if you do.

How to repair damaged threads

Sometimes, the internal threads of a nut or bolt hole can become stripped, usually from overtightening. Stripping threads is an all-too-common occurrence, especially when working with aluminum parts, because aluminum is so soft that it easily strips out.

Usually, external or internal threads are only partially stripped. After they've been cleaned up with a tap or die, they'll still work. Sometimes, however, threads are badly damaged. When this happens, you've got three choices:

1) *Drill and tap the hole to the next suitable oversize and install a larger diameter bolt, screw or stud.*

2) *Drill and tap the hole to accept a threaded plug, then drill and tap the plug to the original screw size. You can also buy a plug already threaded to the original size. Then you simply drill a hole to the specified size, then run the threaded plug into the hole with a bolt and jam*

nut. Once the plug is fully seated, remove the jam nut and bolt.

3) *The third method uses a patented thread repair kit like Heli-Coil or Slimsert. These easy-to-use kits are designed to repair damaged threads in straight-through holes and blind holes. Both are available as kits which can handle a variety of sizes and thread patterns. Drill the hole, then tap it with the special included tap. Install the Heli-Coil and the hole is back to its original diameter and thread pitch.*

Regardless of which method you use, be sure to proceed calmly and carefully. A little impatience or carelessness during one of these relatively simple procedures can ruin your whole day's work and cost you a bundle if you wreck an expensive part.

Working facilities

Not to be overlooked when discussing tools is the workshop. If anything more than routine maintenance is to be carried out, some sort of suitable work area is essential.

It is understood, and appreciated, that many home mechanics do not have a good workshop or garage available, and end up removing an engine or doing major repairs outside. It is recommended, however, that the overhaul or repair be completed under the cover of a roof.

A clean, flat workbench or table of comfortable working height is an absolute necessity. The workbench should be equipped with a vise that has a jaw opening of at least four inches.

As mentioned previously, some clean, dry storage space is also required for tools, as well as the lubricants, fluids, cleaning solvents, etc. which soon become necessary.

Sometimes waste oil and fluids, drained from the engine or cooling system during normal maintenance or repairs, present a disposal problem. To avoid pouring them on the ground or into a sewage system, pour the used fluids into large containers, seal them with caps and take them to an authorized disposal site or recycling center. Plastic jugs, such as old antifreeze containers, are ideal for this purpose.

Always keep a supply of old newspapers and clean rags available. Old towels are excellent for mopping up spills. Many mechanics use rolls of paper towels for most work because they are readily available and disposable. To help keep the area under the vehicle clean, a large cardboard box can be cut open and flattened to protect the garage or shop floor.

Whenever working over a painted surface, such as when leaning over a fender to service something under the hood, always cover it with an old blanket or bedspread to protect the finish. Vinyl covered pads, made especially for this purpose, are available at auto parts stores.

Jacking and towing

Jacking

Warning: *The jack supplied with the vehicle should only be used for changing a tire or placing jackstands under the frame. Never work under the vehicle or start the engine while this jack is being used as the only means of support.*

The vehicle should be on level ground. Place the shift lever in Park, if you have an automatic, or Reverse if you have a manual transaxle. Block the wheel diagonally opposite the wheel being changed. Set the parking brake.

Remove the spare tire and jack from stowage. Remove the wheel cover and trim ring (if so equipped) with the tapered end of the lug nut wrench by inserting and twisting the handle and then prying against the back of the wheel cover. Loosen, but do not remove, the lug nuts (one-half turn is sufficient).

Place the scissors-type jack under the side of the vehicle and adjust the jack height until it fits between the notches in the vertical rocker panel flange nearest the wheel to be changed. There is a front and rear jacking point on each side of the vehicle **(see illustration)**.

Turn the jack handle clockwise until the tire clears the ground. Remove the lug nuts and pull the wheel off. Replace it with the spare.

Install the lug nuts with the beveled edges facing in. Tighten them snugly. Don't attempt to tighten them completely until the vehicle is lowered or it could slip off the jack. Turn the jack handle counterclockwise to lower the vehicle. Remove the jack and tighten the lug nuts in a criss-cross pattern.

Install the cover (and trim ring, if used) and be sure it's snapped into place all the way around.

Stow the tire, jack and wrench. Unblock the wheels.

Towing

Two-wheel drive models should be towed with the front (drive) wheels off the ground. If a professional tow vehicle is not available, place the front wheels on an approved towing dolly. The ignition key must be in the OFF (not LOCK) position, since the steering lock mechanism isn't strong enough to hold the front wheels straight while towing.

Four-wheel drive vehicles must be towed with all four wheels off the ground; this

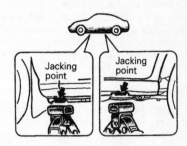

Jacking points

is a job for a professional.

Equipment specifically designed for towing should be used. It should be attached to the frame members of the vehicle; not the bumpers or brackets.

Safety is a major consideration when towing and all applicable state and local laws must be obeyed. A safety chain system must be used at all times. Remember that power steering and power brakes will not work with the engine off.

Booster battery (jump) starting

Observe these precautions when using a booster battery to start a vehicle:

a) *Before connecting the booster battery, make sure the ignition switch is in the Off position.*

b) *Turn off the lights, heater and other electrical loads.*

c) *Your eyes should be shielded. Safety goggles are a good idea.*

d) *Make sure the booster battery is the same voltage as the dead one in the vehicle.*

e) *The two vehicles MUST NOT TOUCH each other!*

f) *Make sure the transaxle is in Neutral (manual) or Park (automatic).*

g) *If the booster battery is not a maintenance-free type, remove the vent caps and lay a cloth over the vent holes.*

Connect the red jumper cable to the positive (+) terminals of each battery **(see illustration)**.

Connect one end of the black jumper cable to the negative (-) terminal of the booster battery. The other end of this cable should be connected to a good ground on the vehicle to be started, such as a bolt or bracket on the body.

Start the engine using the booster battery, then, with the engine running at idle speed, disconnect the jumper cables in the reverse order of connection.

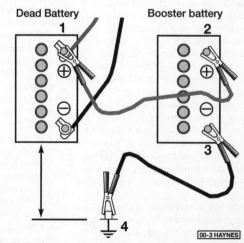

Make the booster battery cable connections in the numerical order shown (note that the negative cable of the booster battery is NOT attached to the negative terminal of the dead battery)

Automotive chemicals and lubricants

A number of automotive chemicals and lubricants are available for use during vehicle maintenance and repair. They include a wide variety of products ranging from cleaning solvents and degreasers to lubricants and protective sprays for rubber, plastic and vinyl.

Cleaners

Carburetor cleaner and choke cleaner is a strong solvent for gum, varnish and carbon. Most carburetor cleaners leave a dry-type lubricant film which will not harden or gum up. Because of this film it is not recommended for use on electrical components.

Brake system cleaner is used to remove grease and brake fluid from the brake system, where clean surfaces are absolutely necessary. It leaves no residue and often eliminates brake squeal caused by contaminants.

Electrical cleaner removes oxidation, corrosion and carbon deposits from electrical contacts, restoring full current flow. It can also be used to clean spark plugs, carburetor jets, voltage regulators and other parts where an oil-free surface is desired.

Demoisturants remove water and moisture from electrical components such as alternators, voltage regulators, electrical connectors and fuse blocks. They are non-conductive, non-corrosive and non-flammable.

Degreasers are heavy-duty solvents used to remove grease from the outside of the engine and from chassis components. They can be sprayed or brushed on and, depending on the type, are rinsed off either with water or solvent.

Lubricants

Motor oil is the lubricant formulated for use in engines. It normally contains a wide variety of additives to prevent corrosion and reduce foaming and wear. Motor oil comes in various weights (viscosity ratings) from 5 to 80. The recommended weight of the oil depends on the season, temperature and the demands on the engine. Light oil is used in cold climates and under light load conditions. Heavy oil is used in hot climates and where high loads are encountered. Multi-viscosity oils are designed to have characteristics of both light and heavy oils and are available in a number of weights from 5W-20 to 20W-50.

Gear oil is designed to be used in differentials, manual transmissions and other areas where high-temperature lubrication is required.

Chassis and wheel bearing grease is a heavy grease used where increased loads and friction are encountered, such as for wheel bearings, balljoints, tie-rod ends and universal joints.

High-temperature wheel bearing grease is designed to withstand the extreme temperatures encountered by wheel bearings in disc brake equipped vehicles. It usually contains molybdenum disulfide (moly), which is a dry-type lubricant.

White grease is a heavy grease for metal-to-metal applications where water is a problem. White grease stays soft under both low and high temperatures (usually from -100 to +190-degrees F), and will not wash off or dilute in the presence of water.

Assembly lube is a special extreme pressure lubricant, usually containing moly, used to lubricate high-load parts (such as main and rod bearings and cam lobes) for initial start-up of a new engine. The assembly lube lubricates the parts without being squeezed out or washed away until the engine oiling system begins to function.

Silicone lubricants are used to protect rubber, plastic, vinyl and nylon parts.

Graphite lubricants are used where oils cannot be used due to contamination problems, such as in locks. The dry graphite will lubricate metal parts while remaining uncontaminated by dirt, water, oil or acids. It is electrically conductive and will not foul electrical contacts in locks such as the ignition switch.

Moly penetrants loosen and lubricate frozen, rusted and corroded fasteners and prevent future rusting or freezing.

Heat-sink grease is a special electrically non-conductive grease that is used for mounting electronic ignition modules where it is essential that heat is transferred away from the module.

Sealants

RTV sealant is one of the most widely used gasket compounds. Made from silicone, RTV is air curing, it seals, bonds, waterproofs, fills surface irregularities, remains flexible, doesn't shrink, is relatively easy to remove, and is used as a supplementary sealer with almost all low and medium temperature gaskets.

Anaerobic sealant is much like RTV in that it can be used either to seal gaskets or to form gaskets by itself. It remains flexible, is solvent resistant and fills surface imperfections. The difference between an anaerobic sealant and an RTV-type sealant is in the curing. RTV cures when exposed to air, while an anaerobic sealant cures only in the absence of air. This means that an anaerobic sealant cures only after the assembly of parts, sealing them together.

Thread and pipe sealant is used for sealing hydraulic and pneumatic fittings and vacuum lines. It is usually made from a Teflon compound, and comes in a spray, a paint-on liquid and as a wrap-around tape.

Chemicals

Anti-seize compound prevents seizing, galling, cold welding, rust and corrosion in fasteners. High-temperature ant-seize, usually made with copper and graphite lubricants, is used for exhaust system and exhaust manifold bolts.

Anaerobic locking compounds are used to keep fasteners from vibrating or working loose and cure only after installation, in the absence of air. Medium strength locking compound is used for small nuts, bolts and screws that may be removed later. High-strength locking compound is for large nuts, bolts and studs which aren't removed on a regular basis.

Oil additives range from viscosity index improvers to chemical treatments that claim to reduce internal engine friction. It should be noted that most oil manufacturers caution against using additives with their oils.

Gas additives perform several functions, depending on their chemical makeup. They usually contain solvents that help dissolve gum and varnish that build up on carburetor, fuel injection and intake parts. They also serve to break down carbon deposits that form on the inside surfaces of the combustion chambers. Some additives contain upper cylinder lubricants for valves and piston rings, and others contain chemicals to remove condensation from the gas tank.

Miscellaneous

Brake fluid is specially formulated hydraulic fluid that can withstand the heat and pressure encountered in brake systems. Care must be taken so this fluid does not come in contact with painted surfaces or plastics. An opened container should always be resealed to prevent contamination by water or dirt.

Weatherstrip adhesive is used to bond weatherstripping around doors, windows and trunk lids. It is sometimes used to attach trim pieces.

Undercoating is a petroleum-based, tar-like substance that is designed to protect metal surfaces on the underside of the vehicle from corrosion. It also acts as a sound-deadening agent by insulating the bottom of the vehicle.

Waxes and polishes are used to help protect painted and plated surfaces from the weather. Different types of paint may require the use of different types of wax and polish. Some polishes utilize a chemical or abrasive cleaner to help remove the top layer of oxidized (dull) paint on older vehicles. In recent years many non-wax polishes that contain a wide variety of chemicals such as polymers and silicones have been introduced. These non-wax polishes are usually easier to apply and last longer than conventional waxes and polishes.

Conversion factors

Length (distance)
Inches (in)	X	25.4	= Millimetres (mm)	X 0.0394	= Inches (in)
Feet (ft)	X	0.305	= Metres (m)	X 3.281	= Feet (ft)
Miles	X	1.609	= Kilometres (km)	X 0.621	= Miles

Volume (capacity)
Cubic inches (cu in; in^3)	X	16.387	= Cubic centimetres (cc; cm^3)	X 0.061	= Cubic inches (cu in; in^3)
Imperial pints (Imp pt)	X	0.568	= Litres (l)	X 1.76	= Imperial pints (Imp pt)
Imperial quarts (Imp qt)	X	1.137	= Litres (l)	X 0.88	= Imperial quarts (Imp qt)
Imperial quarts (Imp qt)	X	1.201	= US quarts (US qt)	X 0.833	= Imperial quarts (Imp qt)
US quarts (US qt)	X	0.946	= Litres (l)	X 1.057	= US quarts (US qt)
Imperial gallons (Imp gal)	X	4.546	= Litres (l)	X 0.22	= Imperial gallons (Imp gal)
Imperial gallons (Imp gal)	X	1.201	= US gallons (US gal)	X 0.833	= Imperial gallons (Imp gal)
US gallons (US gal)	X	3.785	= Litres (l)	X 0.264	= US gallons (US gal)

Mass (weight)
Ounces (oz)	X	28.35	= Grams (g)	X 0.035	= Ounces (oz)
Pounds (lb)	X	0.454	= Kilograms (kg)	X 2.205	= Pounds (lb)

Force
Ounces-force (ozf; oz)	X	0.278	= Newtons (N)	X 3.6	= Ounces-force (ozf; oz)
Pounds-force (lbf; lb)	X	4.448	= Newtons (N)	X 0.225	= Pounds-force (lbf; lb)
Newtons (N)	X	0.1	= Kilograms-force (kgf; kg)	X 9.81	= Newtons (N)

Pressure
Pounds-force per square inch (psi; lbf/in^2; lb/in^2)	X	0.070	= Kilograms-force per square centimetre (kgf/cm^2; kg/cm^2)	X 14.223	= Pounds-force per square inch (psi; lbf/in^2; lb/in^2)
Pounds-force per square inch (psi; lbf/in^2; lb/in^2)	X	0.068	= Atmospheres (atm)	X 14.696	= Pounds-force per square inch (psi; lbf/in^2; lb/in^2)
Pounds-force per square inch (psi; lbf/in^2; lb/in^2)	X	0.069	= Bars	X 14.5	= Pounds-force per square inch (psi; lbf/in^2; lb/in^2)
Pounds-force per square inch (psi; lbf/in^2; lb/in^2)	X	6.895	= Kilopascals (kPa)	X 0.145	= Pounds-force per square inch (psi; lbf/in^2; lb/in^2)
Kilopascals (kPa)	X	0.01	= Kilograms-force per square centimetre (kgf/cm^2; kg/cm^2)	X 98.1	= Kilopascals (kPa)

Torque (moment of force)
Pounds-force inches (lbf in; lb in)	X	1.152	= Kilograms-force centimetre (kgf cm; kg cm)	X 0.868	= Pounds-force inches (lbf in; lb in)
Pounds-force inches (lbf in; lb in)	X	0.113	= Newton metres (Nm)	X 8.85	= Pounds-force inches (lbf in; lb in)
Pounds-force inches (lbf in; lb in)	X	0.083	= Pounds-force feet (lbf ft; lb ft)	X 12	= Pounds-force inches (lbf in; lb in)
Pounds-force feet (lbf ft; lb ft)	X	0.138	= Kilograms-force metres (kgf m; kg m)	X 7.233	= Pounds-force feet (lbf ft; lb ft)
Pounds-force feet (lbf ft; lb ft)	X	1.356	= Newton metres (Nm)	X 0.738	= Pounds-force feet (lbf ft; lb ft)
Newton metres (Nm)	X	0.102	= Kilograms-force metres (kgf m; kg m)	X 9.804	= Newton metres (Nm)

Vacuum
Inches mercury (in. Hg)	X	3.377	= Kilopascals (kPa)	X 0.2961	= Inches mercury
Inches mercury (in. Hg)	X	25.4	= Millimeters mercury (mm Hg)	X 0.0394	= Inches mercury

Power
Horsepower (hp)	X	745.7	= Watts (W)	X 0.0013	= Horsepower (hp)

Velocity (speed)
Miles per hour (miles/hr; mph)	X	1.609	= Kilometres per hour (km/hr; kph)	X 0.621	= Miles per hour (miles/hr; mph)

Fuel consumption*
Miles per gallon, Imperial (mpg)	X	0.354	= Kilometres per litre (km/l)	X 2.825	= Miles per gallon, Imperial (mpg)
Miles per gallon, US (mpg)	X	0.425	= Kilometres per litre (km/l)	X 2.352	= Miles per gallon, US (mpg)

Temperature
Degrees Fahrenheit = ($°$C x 1.8) + 32   Degrees Celsius (Degrees Centigrade; $°$C) = ($°$F - 32) x 0.56

*It is common practice to convert from miles per gallon (mpg) to litres/100 kilometres (l/100km),
where mpg (Imperial) x l/100 km = 282 and mpg (US) x l/100 km = 235

Safety first!

Regardless of how enthusiastic you may be about getting on with the job at hand, take the time to ensure that your safety is not jeopardized. A moment's lack of attention can result in an accident, as can failure to observe certain simple safety precautions. The possibility of an accident will always exist, and the following points should not be considered a comprehensive list of all dangers. Rather, they are intended to make you aware of the risks and to encourage a safety conscious approach to all work you carry out on your vehicle.

Essential DOs and DON'Ts

DON'T rely on a jack when working under the vehicle. Always use approved jackstands to support the weight of the vehicle and place them under the recommended lift or support points.

DON'T attempt to loosen extremely tight fasteners (i.e. wheel lug nuts) while the vehicle is on a jack - it may fall.

DON'T start the engine without first making sure that the transmission is in Neutral (or Park where applicable) and the parking brake is set.

DON'T remove the radiator cap from a hot cooling system - let it cool or cover it with a cloth and release the pressure gradually.

DON'T attempt to drain the engine oil until you are sure it has cooled to the point that it will not burn you.

DON'T touch any part of the engine or exhaust system until it has cooled sufficiently to avoid burns.

DON'T siphon toxic liquids such as gasoline, antifreeze and brake fluid by mouth, or allow them to remain on your skin.

DON'T inhale brake lining dust - it is potentially hazardous (see *Asbestos* below).

DON'T allow spilled oil or grease to remain on the floor - wipe it up before someone slips on it.

DON'T use loose fitting wrenches or other tools which may slip and cause injury.

DON'T push on wrenches when loosening or tightening nuts or bolts. Always try to pull the wrench toward you. If the situation calls for pushing the wrench away, push with an open hand to avoid scraped knuckles if the wrench should slip.

DON'T attempt to lift a heavy component alone - get someone to help you.

DON'T rush or take unsafe shortcuts to finish a job.

DON'T allow children or animals in or around the vehicle while you are working on it.

DO wear eye protection when using power tools such as a drill, sander, bench grinder, etc. and when working under a vehicle.

DO keep loose clothing and long hair well out of the way of moving parts.

DO make sure that any hoist used has a safe working load rating adequate for the job.

DO get someone to check on you periodically when working alone on a vehicle.

DO carry out work in a logical sequence and make sure that everything is correctly assembled and tightened.

DO keep chemicals and fluids tightly capped and out of the reach of children and pets.

DO remember that your vehicle's safety affects that of yourself and others. If in doubt on any point, get professional advice.

Asbestos

Certain friction, insulating, sealing, and other products - such as brake linings, brake bands, clutch linings, torque converters, gaskets, etc. - may contain asbestos. Extreme care must be taken to avoid inhalation of dust from such products, since it is hazardous to health. If in doubt, assume that they do contain asbestos.

Fire

Remember at all times that gasoline is highly flammable. Never smoke or have any kind of open flame around when working on a vehicle. But the risk does not end there. A spark caused by an electrical short circuit, by two metal surfaces contacting each other, or even by static electricity built up in your body under certain conditions, can ignite gasoline vapors, which in a confined space are highly explosive. Do not, under any circumstances, use gasoline for cleaning parts. Use an approved safety solvent.

Always disconnect the battery ground (-) cable at the battery before working on any part of the fuel system or electrical system. Never risk spilling fuel on a hot engine or exhaust component. It is strongly recommended that a fire extinguisher suitable for use on fuel and electrical fires be kept handy in the garage or workshop at all times. Never try to extinguish a fuel or electrical fire with water.

Fumes

Certain fumes are highly toxic and can quickly cause unconsciousness and even death if inhaled to any extent. Gasoline vapor falls into this category, as do the vapors from some cleaning solvents. Any draining or pouring of such volatile fluids should be done in a well ventilated area.

When using cleaning fluids and solvents, read the instructions on the container carefully. Never use materials from unmarked containers.

Never run the engine in an enclosed space, such as a garage. Exhaust fumes contain carbon monoxide, which is extremely poisonous. If you need to run the engine, always do so in the open air, or at least have the rear of the vehicle outside the work area.

If you are fortunate enough to have the use of an inspection pit, never drain or pour gasoline and never run the engine while the vehicle is over the pit. The fumes, being heavier than air, will concentrate in the pit with possibly lethal results.

The battery

Never create a spark or allow a bare light bulb near a battery. They normally give off a certain amount of hydrogen gas, which is highly explosive.

Always disconnect the battery ground (-) cable at the battery before working on the fuel or electrical systems.

If possible, loosen the filler caps or cover when charging the battery from an external source (this does not apply to sealed or maintenance-free batteries). Do not charge at an excessive rate or the battery may burst.

Take care when adding water to a non maintenance-free battery and when carrying a battery. The electrolyte, even when diluted, is very corrosive and should not be allowed to contact clothing or skin.

Always wear eye protection when cleaning the battery to prevent the caustic deposits from entering your eyes.

Household current

When using an electric power tool, inspection light, etc., which operates on household current, always make sure that the tool is correctly connected to its plug and that, where necessary, it is properly grounded. Do not use such items in damp conditions and, again, do not create a spark or apply excessive heat in the vicinity of fuel or fuel vapor.

Secondary ignition system voltage

A severe electric shock can result from touching certain parts of the ignition system (such as the spark plug wires) when the engine is running or being cranked, particularly if components are damp or the insulation is defective. In the case of an electronic ignition system, the secondary system voltage is much higher and could prove fatal.

Troubleshooting

Contents

This section provides an easy reference guide to the more common problems which may occur during the operation of your vehicle. These problems and their possible causes are grouped under headings denoting various components or systems, such as Engine, Cooling system, etc. They also refer you to the chapter and/or section which deals with the problem.

Remember that successful troubleshooting is not a mysterious "black art" practiced only by professional mechanics. It is simply the result of the right knowledge combined with an intelligent, systematic approach to the problem. Always work by a process of elimination, starting with the simplest solution and working through to the most complex - and never overlook the obvious. Anyone can run the gas tank dry or leave the lights on overnight, so don't assume that you are exempt from such oversights.

Finally, always establish a clear idea of why a problem has occurred and take steps to ensure that it doesn't happen again. If the electrical system fails because of a poor connection, check the other connections in the system to make sure that they don't fail as well. If a particular fuse continues to blow, find out why - don't just replace one fuse after another. Remember, failure of a small component can often be indicative of potential failure or incorrect functioning of a more important component or system.

Engine

1 Engine will not rotate when attempting to start

1   Battery terminal connections loose or corroded (Chapter 1).
2   Battery discharged or faulty (Chapter 1).
3   Automatic transmission not completely engaged in Park (Chapter 7) or clutch not completely depressed (Chapter 8).
4   Broken, loose or disconnected wiring in the starting circuit (Chapters 5 and 12).
5   Starter motor pinion jammed in flywheel ring gear (Chapter 5).
6   Starter solenoid faulty (Chapter 5).
7   Starter motor faulty (Chapter 5).
8   Ignition switch faulty (Chapter 12).
9   Starter pinion or flywheel teeth worn or broken (Chapter 5).

2 Engine rotates but will not start

1   Fuel tank empty.
2   Battery discharged (engine rotates slowly) (Chapter 5).
3   Battery terminal connections loose or corroded (Chapter 1).
4   Leaking fuel injector(s), faulty fuel pump, pressure regulator, etc. (Chapter 4).
5   Fuel not reaching fuel rail (Chapter 4).
6   Ignition components damp or damaged (Chapter 5).
7   Worn, faulty or incorrectly gapped spark plugs (Chapter 1).
8   Broken, loose or disconnected wiring in the starting circuit (Chapter 5).
9   Loose distributor or crank angle sensor is changing ignition timing (Chapter 5 or 6).
10   Broken, loose or disconnected wires at the ignition coil or faulty coil (Chapter 5).

3 Engine hard to start when cold

1   Battery discharged or low (Chapter 1).
2   Malfunctioning fuel system (Chapter 4).
3   Injector(s) leaking (Chapter 4).
4   Distributor rotor carbon tracked (Chapter 5).

4 Engine hard to start when hot

1   Air filter clogged (Chapter 1).
2   Fuel not reaching the fuel injection system (Chapter 4).
3   Corroded battery connections, especially ground (Chapter 1).

5 Starter motor noisy or excessively rough in engagement

1   Pinion or flywheel gear teeth worn or broken (Chapter 5).
2   Starter motor mounting bolts loose or missing (Chapter 5).

6 Engine starts but stops immediately

1   Loose or faulty electrical connections at distributor (or crank angle sensor), coil or alternator (Chapter 5).
2   Insufficient fuel reaching the fuel injector(s) (Chapters 1 and 4).
3   Vacuum leak at the gasket between the intake manifold and throttle body or between the intake manifold and engine (Chapters 2 and 4).

7 Oil puddle under engine

1   Oil pan gasket and/or oil pan drain bolt washer leaking (Chapter 2).
2   Oil pressure sending unit leaking (Chapter 2).
3   Cylinder head (valve) covers leaking (Chapter 2).
4   Engine oil seals leaking (Chapter 2).

8 Engine lopes while idling or idles erratically

1   Vacuum leakage. Check the mounting bolts/nuts at the throttle body and the air duct between the airflow meter and the throttle body for tightness, ensuring there's no possibility of air leaking at the gasket surface, at duct connections or through rips in the duct. Make sure that all vacuum hoses are connected properly and in good condition. Use a stethoscope of a length of fuel hose held against your ear to listen for vacuum leaks while the engine is running. A hissing sound will be heard. Especially check the throttle body and intake manifold gasket areas and also the points where the fuel injectors enter the engine (the O-rings sometimes harden and allow vacuum leaks).
2   Leaking EGR valve (Chapter 6).
3   Spark plug(s) fouled, spark plug wires damaged or shorted, distributor cap/rotor damaged or carbon tracked (Chapter 1).
4   Air filter clogged (Chapter 1).
5   Fuel pump not delivering sufficient fuel to the fuel injection system (Chapter 4).
6   Leaking head gasket (Chapter 2).
7   Timing belt and/or pulleys worn (Chapter 2).
8   Camshaft lobes worn (Chapter 2).

9 Engine misses at idle speed

1   Spark plugs worn or not gapped properly (Chapter 1).
2   Spark plug(s) fouled, spark plug wires damaged or shorted, distributor cap/rotor damaged or carbon tracked (Chapter 1).
3   Vacuum leaks (Section 8 of *Troubleshooting*; also *Vacuum gauge checks* in Chapter 2B).
4   Incorrect ignition timing (Chapter 5).
5   Uneven or low compression (Chapter 2).

10 Engine misses throughout driving speed range

1   Fuel filter clogged and/or impurities in the fuel system (Chapter 1).
2   Low fuel output at the injector(s) - first try cleaning the injectors - (Chapter 4).
3   Faulty or incorrectly gapped spark plugs (Chapter 1).
4   Incorrect ignition timing (Chapter 5).
5   Cracked distributor cap, disconnected distributor wires or damaged distributor components (Chapters 1 and 5).
6   Leaking spark plug wires (Chapters 1 or 5).
7   Faulty emission system components (Chapter 6).
8   Low or uneven cylinder compression pressures (Chapter 2).
9   Weak or faulty ignition system (Chapter 5).
10   Vacuum leaks (Section 8 of *Troubleshooting*; also *Vacuum gauge checks* in Chapter 2B).

11   Engine stumbles on acceleration

1   Spark plugs fouled (Chapter 1).
2   Fuel injection system component faulty (Chapter 4).
3   Fuel filter clogged (Chapters 1 and 4).
4   Incorrect ignition timing (Chapter 5).
5   Vacuum leaks (Section 8 of *Troubleshooting*; also *Vacuum gauge checks* in Chapter 2B).

12   Engine surges while holding accelerator steady

1   Vacuum leaks (Section 8 of *Troubleshooting*; also *Vacuum gauge checks* in Chapter 2B).
2   Fuel pump faulty (Chapter 4).
3   Loose fuel injector wire harness connectors (Chapter 4).
4   Defective computer or information sensor (Chapter 6).

13   Engine stalls

1   Idle speed incorrect (Chapter 1).
2   Fuel filter clogged and/or water and impurities in the fuel system (Chapters 1 and 4).
3   Distributor components damp or damaged (Chapter 5).
4   Faulty emissions system components (Chapter 6).
5   Faulty or incorrectly gapped spark plugs (Chapter 1).
6   Faulty spark plug wires (Chapter 1).
7   Vacuum leaks (Section 8 of *Troubleshooting*; also *Vacuum gauge checks* in Chapter 2B).

14   Engine lacks power

1   Incorrect ignition timing (Chapter 5).
2   Excessive play in distributor shaft (Chapter 5).
3   Worn rotor, distributor cap or wires (Chapters 1 and 5).
4   Faulty or incorrectly gapped spark plugs (Chapter 1).
5   Fuel injection system out of adjustment or excessively worn (Chapter 4).
6   Faulty coil (Chapter 5).
7   Brakes binding (Chapter 9).
8   Automatic transaxle fluid level incorrect (Chapter 1).
9   Clutch slipping (Chapter 8).
10   Fuel filter clogged and/or impurities in the fuel system (Chapters 1 and 4).
11   Emission control system not functioning properly (Chapter 6).
12   Low or uneven cylinder compression pressures (Chapter 2).
13   Obstructed exhaust system (Chapter 4).
14   Vacuum leaks (Section 8 of *Troubleshooting*; also *Vacuum gauge checks* in Chapter 2B).

15   Engine backfires

1   Emission control system not functioning properly (Chapter 6).
2   Ignition timing incorrect (Chapter 5).
3   Faulty secondary ignition system (cracked spark plug insulator, faulty plug wires, distributor cap and/or rotor) (Chapters 1 and 5).
4   Fuel injection system in need of adjustment or worn excessively (Chapter 4).
5   Vacuum leaks (Section 8 of *Troubleshooting*; also *Vacuum gauge checks* in Chapter 2B).
6   Damaged or worn lash adjuster and/or valves sticking (Chapter 2).

16   Pinging or knocking engine sounds during acceleration or uphill

1   Incorrect grade of fuel.
2   Ignition timing incorrect (Chapter 5).
3   Fuel injection system faulty (Chapter 4).
4   Improper or damaged spark plugs or wires (Chapter 1).
5   Worn or damaged distributor components (Chapter 5).
6   EGR valve not functioning (Chapter 6).
7   Vacuum leaks (Section 8 of *Troubleshooting*; also *Vacuum gauge checks* in Chapter 2B).

17   Engine runs with oil pressure light on

1   Low oil level (Chapter 1).
2   Short in wiring circuit (Chapter 12).
3   Faulty oil pressure sender (Chapter 2).
4   Worn engine bearings and/or oil pump (Chapter 2).

18   Engine diesels (continues to run) after switching off

1   Vacuum leaks (Section 8 of *Troubleshooting*; also *Vacuum gauge checks* in Chapter 2B).
2   Idle speed too high (Chapter 4).
3   Excessive engine operating temperature (Chapter 3).
4   Ignition timing in need of adjustment (Chapter 5).

Engine electrical system

19   Battery will not hold a charge

1   Alternator drivebelt defective or not adjusted properly (Chapter 1).
2   Battery electrolyte level low (Chapter 1).
3   Battery terminals loose or corroded (Chapter 1).
4   Alternator not charging properly (Chapter 5).
5   Loose, broken or faulty wiring in the charging circuit (Chapter 5).
6   Short in vehicle wiring (Chapter 12).
7   Internally defective battery (Chapters 1 and 5).

20   Alternator light fails to go out

1   Faulty alternator or charging circuit (Chapter 5).
2   Alternator drivebelt defective or out of adjustment (Chapter 1).
3   Alternator voltage regulator inoperative (Chapter 5).

21   Alternator light fails to come on when key is turned on

1   Warning light bulb defective (Chapter 12).
2   Fault in the printed circuit, dash wiring or bulb holder (Chapter 12).

Fuel system

22   Excessive fuel consumption

1   Dirty or clogged air filter element or engine in need of tune-up (Chapter 1).
2   Incorrectly set ignition timing (Chapter 5).
3   Emissions system not functioning properly (Chapter 6).
4   Fuel injection internal parts excessively worn or damaged (Chapter 4).
5   Low tire pressure or incorrect tire size (Chapter 1).

23   Fuel leakage and/or fuel odor

1   Leaking fuel feed or return line (Chapters 1 and 4).
2   Tank overfilled.
3   Evaporative canister filter clogged (Chapters 1 and 6).
4   Fuel injector internal parts excessively worn (Chapter 4).

Cooling system

24   Overheating

1   Insufficient coolant in system (Chapter 1).
2   Water pump faulty (Chapter 3).
3   Radiator core blocked or grille restricted (Chapter 3).

4   Thermostat faulty (Chapter 3).
5   Electric coolant fan blades broken or cracked (Chapter 3).
6   Radiator cap not maintaining proper pressure (Chapter 3).
7   Ignition timing incorrect (Chapter 5).

25 Overcooling

1   Faulty thermostat (Chapter 3).
2   Inaccurate temperature gauge sending unit (Chapter 3)

26 External coolant leakage

1   Deteriorated/damaged hoses; loose clamps (Chapters 1 and 3).
2   Water pump defective (Chapter 3).
3   Leakage from radiator core or coolant reservoir bottle (Chapter 3).
4   Engine drain or water jacket core plugs leaking (Chapter 2).

27 Internal coolant leakage

1   Leaking cylinder head gasket (Chapter 2).
2   Cracked or leaking cylinder sleeve or cylinder head (Chapter 2).

28 Coolant loss

1   Too much coolant in system (Chapter 1).
2   Coolant boiling away because of overheating (Chapter 3).
3   Internal or external leakage (Chapter 3).
4   Faulty radiator cap (Chapter 3).

29 Poor coolant circulation

1   Inoperative water pump (Chapter 3).
2   Restriction in cooling system (Chapters 1 and 3).
3   Water pump drivebelt defective/out of adjustment (Chapter 1).
4   Thermostat sticking (Chapter 3).

Clutch

30 Clutch release system problems

Malfunctions in the hydraulic clutch release system can cause a variety of problems. Listed here are problems with their most common causes.

Pedal travels to floor - no pressure or very little resistance
   a)   *Master or release cylinder faulty (Chapter 8)*
   b)   *Hose/pipe burst or leaking (Chapter 8)*

   c)   *Connections leaking (Chapter 8)*
   d)   *No fluid in reservoir (Chapter 1)*
   e)   *If fluid in reservoir rises as pedal is depressed, master cylinder center valve seal is faulty (Chapter 8)*
   f)   *If there is fluid on the dust seal at the master cylinder, the piston primary seal is leaking (Chapter 8)*
   g)   *Broken release bearing or fork (Chapter 8)*

Fluid in the area of the master cylinder dust cover and on the pedal
   Rear seal failure in the master cylinder (Chapter 8)

Fluid on the release cylinder
   Release cylinder piston seal faulty (Chapter 8)

Pedal feels spongy when depressed
   Air in system. Bleed the system (see Chapter 8)

31 Unable to select gears

1   Faulty transaxle (Chapter 7).
2   Faulty clutch disc (Chapter 8).
3   Release lever and bearing not assembled properly (Chapter 8).
4   Faulty pressure plate (Chapter 8).
5   Pressure plate-to-flywheel bolts loose (Chapter 8).

32 Clutch slips (engine speed increases with no increase in vehicle speed)

1   Clutch plate worn (Chapter 8).
2   Clutch plate is oil soaked by leaking rear main seal (Chapter 8).
3   Clutch plate not seated. It may take 30 or 40 normal starts for a new one to seat.
4   Warped pressure plate or flywheel (Chapter 8).
5   Weak diaphragm spring (Chapter 8).
6   Clutch plate overheated. Allow to cool.

33 Grabbing (chattering) as clutch is engaged

1   Oil on clutch plate lining, burned or glazed facings (Chapter 8).
2   Worn or loose engine or transaxle mounts (Chapters 2 and 7).
3   Worn splines on clutch plate hub (Chapter 8).
4   Warped pressure plate or flywheel (Chapter 8).
5   Burned or smeared resin on flywheel or pressure plate (Chapter 8).

34 Transaxle rattling (clicking)

1   Release lever loose (Chapter 8).
2   Clutch plate damper spring failure

(Chapter 8).
3   Low engine idle speed (Chapter 4).

35 Noise in clutch area

1   Fork shaft improperly installed (Chapter 8).
2   Faulty bearing (Chapter 8).

36 Clutch pedal stays on floor

1   Faulty or damaged clutch master or slave cylinder (Chapter 8).
2   Broken release bearing or fork (Chapter 8).

37 High pedal effort

1   Pedal mechanism binding (Chapter 8).
2   Pressure plate faulty (Chapter 8).
3   Incorrect size master or release cylinder (Chapter 8).

Manual transaxle

38 Knocking noise at low speeds

1   Worn driveaxle constant velocity (CV) joints (Chapter 8).
2   Worn side gear shaft counterbore in differential case (Chapter 7A).*

39 Noise most pronounced when turning

   Differential gear noise (Chapter 7A).*

40 Clunk on acceleration or deceleration

1   Loose engine or transaxle mounts (Chapters 2 and 7A).
2   Worn differential pinion shaft in case.*
3   Worn side gear shaft counterbore in differential case (Chapter 7A).*
4   Worn or damaged driveaxle inboard CV joints (Chapter 8).

41 Clicking noise in turns

   Worn or damaged outboard CV joint (Chapter 8).

42 Vibration

1   Rough wheel bearing (Chapter 10).
2   Damaged driveaxle or driveshaft (Chapter 8).
3   Out of round tires (Chapter 1).

4   Tire out of balance (Chapters 1 and 10).
5   Worn CV joint (Chapter 8).

43 Noisy in neutral with engine running

1   Damaged input gear bearing (Chapter 7A).*
2   Damaged clutch release bearing (Chapter 8).

44 Noisy in one particular gear

1   Damaged or worn constant mesh gears (Chapter 7A).*
2   Damaged or worn synchronizers (Chapter 7A).*
3   Bent reverse fork (Chapter 7A).*
4   Damaged fourth speed gear or output gear (Chapter 7A).*
5   Worn or damaged reverse idler gear or idler bushing (Chapter 7A).*

45 Noisy in all gears

1   Insufficient lubricant (Chapter 7A).
2   Damaged or worn bearings (Chapter 7A).*
3   Worn or damaged input gear shaft and/or output gear shaft (Chapter 7A).*

46 Slips out of gear

1   Worn or improperly adjusted linkage (Chapter 7A).
2   Transaxle loose on engine (Chapter 7A).
3   Shift linkage does not work freely, binds (Chapter 7A).
4   Input gear bearing retainer broken or loose (Chapter 7A).*
5   Dirt between clutch cover and engine housing (Chapter 7A).
6   Worn shift fork (Chapter 7A).*

47 Leaks lubricant

1   Side gear shaft seals worn (Chapter 7).
2   Excessive amount of lubricant in transaxle (Chapters 1 and 7).
3   Loose or broken input gear shaft bearing retainer (Chapter 7A).*
4   Input gear bearing retainer O-ring and/or lip seal damaged (Chapter 7A).*

48 Locked in gear

Lock pin or interlock pin missing (Chapter 7A).*

Although the corrective action necessary to remedy the symptoms described is beyond the scope of the home mechanic, the above information should be helpful in isolating the cause of the condition so that the owner can communicate clearly with a professional mechanic.

Automatic transaxle

Note: *Due to the complexity of the automatic transaxle, it is difficult for the home mechanic to properly diagnose and service this component. For problems other than the following, the vehicle should be taken to a dealer or transmission shop.*

49 Fluid leakage

1   Automatic transmission fluid is a deep red color. Fluid leaks should not be confused with engine oil, which can easily be blown onto the transaxle by air flow.
2   To pinpoint a leak, first remove all built-up dirt and grime from the transaxle housing with degreasing agents and/or steam cleaning. Then drive the vehicle at low speeds so air flow will not blow the leak far from its source. Raise the vehicle and determine where the leak is coming from. Common areas of leakage are:
    a) **Pan** (Chapters 1 and 7)
    b) **Dipstick tube** (Chapters 1 and 7)
    c) **Transaxle oil lines** (Chapter 7)
    d) **Speed sensor** (Chapter 7)

50 Transaxle fluid brown or has a burned smell

Transaxle fluid burned (Chapter 1).

51 General shift mechanism problems

1   Chapter 7, Part B, deals with checking and adjusting the shift linkage on automatic transaxles. Common problems which may be attributed to poorly adjusted linkage are:
    a) *Engine starting in gears other than Park or Neutral.*
    b) *Indicator on shifter pointing to a gear other than the one actually being used.*
    c) *Vehicle moves when in Park.*
2   Refer to Chapter 7B for the shift linkage adjustment procedure.

52 Transaxle will not downshift with accelerator pedal pressed to the floor

Throttle valve cable out of adjustment (Chapter 7B).

53 Engine will start in gears other than Park or Neutral

Neutral start switch malfunctioning (Chapter 7B).

54 Transaxle slips, shifts roughly, is noisy or has no drive in forward or reverse gears

There are many probable causes for the above problems, but the home mechanic should be concerned with only one possibility - fluid level. Before taking the vehicle to a repair shop, check the level and condition of the fluid as described in Chapter 1. Correct the fluid level as necessary or change the fluid and filter if needed. If the problem persists, have a professional diagnose the cause.

Driveaxles

55 Clicking noise in turns

Worn or damaged front outboard CV joint (Chapter 8).

56 Shudder or vibration during acceleration

1   Excessive toe-in (Chapter 10).
2   Incorrect spring heights (Chapter 10).
3   Worn or damaged inboard or outboard CV joints (Chapter 8).
4   Sticking inboard CV joint assembly (Chapter 8).

57 Vibration at highway speeds

1   Out of balance front wheels and/or tires (Chapters 1 and 10).
2   Out of round front tires (Chapters 1 and 10).
3   Worn CV joint(s) (Chapter 8).

Transfer case (4WD models)

58 Transfer case noisy

Insufficient or incorrect grade of lubricant. Drain and refill (Chapter 1).

59 Lubricant leaks from or output shaft seal

1   Transfer case is overfilled. Drain to proper level (Chapter 1).
2   Vent is clogged or jammed closed. Clear or replace the vent.
3   Driveshaft seal is incorrectly installed or damaged. Replace the seal and check surfaces for nicks and scoring (Chapter 8).

Driveshaft (4WD models)

60 Oil leak at seal end of driveshaft

Defective transfer case oil seal. See Chapter 7 for replacement procedures. While this is done, check the splined yoke for burrs or a rough condition which may be damaging the seal. Burrs can be removed with crocus cloth or a fine whetstone.

61 Knock or clunk when the transmission is under initial load (just after transmission is put in gear)

1 Loose or disconnected rear suspension components. Check all mounting bolts, nuts and bushings (See Chapter 10).
2 Loose driveshaft bolts. Inspect all mounting bolts and nuts and tighten them to the specified torque.
3 Worn or damaged universal joint bearings. Check as described in Chapter 8.

62 Metallic grinding sound consistent with vehicle speed

Pronounced wear in the universal joint bearings. Check as described in Chapter 8.

63 Vibration

Note: *Before assuming that the driveshaft is at fault, make sure the tires are perfectly balanced and perform the following test.*
1 Install a tachometer inside the vehicle and note the engine speed as the vehicle is driven. Drive the vehicle and note the engine speed at which the vibration (roughness) is most pronounced. Now shift the transaxle to a different gear and bring the engine speed to the same point.
2 If the vibration occurs at the same engine speed (rpm) regardless of which gear the transaxle is in, the driveshaft is NOT at fault since the driveshaft speed varies.
3 If the vibration decreases or is eliminated when the transaxle is in a different gear at the same engine speed, refer to the following probable causes.
4 Bent or dented driveshaft. Inspect or replace as necessary (See Chapter 8).
5 Undercoating or build-up dirt, etc. on the driveshaft. Clean the shaft thoroughly and recheck.
6 Worn universal joint bearings. Remove and inspect (Chapter 8).
7 Driveshaft and/or companion flange out of balance. Check for missing weights on the shaft. Remove the driveshaft (Chapter 8) and reinstall 180-degrees from original position, then retest. Have the driveshaft professionally balanced.

Rear axle (4WD models)

64 Noise

1 Road noise. No corrective procedures available.
2 Tire noise. Inspect the tires and check tire pressures (Chapter 1).
3 Rear axle bearings worn or damaged (Chapter 8 and 10).

65 Vibration

See probable causes under Driveshaft. Proceed under the guidelines listed for driveshaft. If the problem persists, check the axle bearings by raising the vehicle and spinning the rear wheels by hand. Listen for evidence of rough (noisy) bearings. Remove and inspect (Chapter 8).

66 Oil leakage

1 Pinion seal damaged (See Chapter 8).
2 Driveaxle output seals damaged (See Chapter 8).

Brakes

Note: *Before assuming that a brake problem exists, make sure that:*
a) The tires are in good condition and properly inflated (Chapter 1).
b) The front end alignment is correct (Chapter 10).
c) The vehicle is not loaded with weight in an unequal manner.

67 Vehicle pulls to one side during braking

1 Incorrect tire pressures (Chapter 1).
2 Front end out of line (have the front end aligned).
3 Front, or rear, tires not matched to one another.
4 Restricted brake lines or hoses (Chapter 9).
5 Malfunctioning caliper assembly (Chapter 9).
6 Loose suspension parts (Chapter 10).
7 Loose calipers (Chapter 9).
8 Excessive wear of brake pad on one side.

68 Noise (high-pitched squeal when the brakes are applied)

Front disc brake pads worn out. The noise comes from the wear sensor rubbing against the disc (does not apply to all vehicles). Replace pads with new ones immediately (Chapter 9).

69 Brake roughness or chatter (pedal pulsates)

1 Excessive lateral runout (Chapter 9).
2 Uneven pad wear (Chapter 9).
3 Defective disc (Chapter 9).

70 Excessive brake pedal effort required to stop vehicle

1 Malfunctioning power brake booster (Chapter 9).
2 Partial system failure (Chapter 9).
3 Excessively worn pads (Chapter 9).
4 Piston in caliper stuck or sluggish (Chapter 9).
5 Brake pads contaminated with oil or grease (Chapter 9).
6 New pads installed and not yet seated. It will take a while for the new material to seat against the disc.

71 Excessive brake pedal travel

1 Partial brake system failure (Chapter 9).
2 Insufficient fluid in master cylinder (Chapters 1 and 9).
3 Air trapped in system (Chapters 1 and 9).

72 Dragging brakes

1 Incorrect adjustment of brake light switch (Chapter 9).
2 Master cylinder pistons not returning correctly (Chapter 9).
3 Restricted brakes lines or hoses (Chapters 1 and 9).
4 Incorrect parking brake adjustment (Chapter 9).

73 Grabbing or uneven braking action

1 Malfunction of proportioning valve (Chapter 9).
2 Malfunction of power brake booster unit (Chapter 9).
3 Binding brake pedal mechanism (Chapter 9).

74 Brake pedal feels spongy when depressed

1 Air in hydraulic lines (Chapter 9).
2 Master cylinder mounting bolts loose (Chapter 9).
3 Master cylinder defective (Chapter 9).

75 Brake pedal travels to the floor with little resistance

1 Little or no fluid in the master cylinder

reservoir caused by leaking caliper piston(s) (Chapter 9).
2   Loose, damaged or disconnected brake lines (Chapter 9).

76 Parking brake does not hold

      Parking brake linkage improperly adjusted (Chapters 1 and 9).

Suspension and steering systems

Note: *Before attempting to diagnose the suspension and steering systems, perform the following preliminary checks:*

a) *Tires for wrong pressure and uneven wear.*
b) *Steering universal joints from the column to the rack-and-pinion for loose connectors or wear.*
c) *Front and rear suspension and the rack and pinion assembly for loose or damaged parts.*
d) *Out-of-round or out-of-balance tires, bent rims and loose and/or rough wheel bearings.*

77 Vehicle pulls to one side

1   Mismatched or uneven tires (Chapter 10).
2   Broken or sagging springs (Chapter 10).
3   Wheel alignment (Chapter 10).
4   Front brake dragging (Chapter 9).

78 Abnormal or excessive tire wear

1   Wheel alignment (Chapter 10).
2   Sagging or broken springs (Chapter 10).
3   Tire out of balance (Chapter 10).
4   Worn strut damper (Chapter 10).
5   Overloaded vehicle.
6   Tires not rotated regularly.

79 Wheel makes a thumping noise

1   Blister or bump on tire (Chapter 10).
2   Improper strut damper action (Chapter 10).

80 Shimmy, shake or vibration

1   Tire or wheel out-of-balance or out-of-round (Chapter 10).
2   Loose or worn front hub or wheel bearings (Chapters 1, 8 and 10).
3   Worn tie-rod ends (Chapter 10).
4   Worn lower balljoints (Chapters 1 and 10).

5   Excessive wheel runout (Chapter 10).
6   Blister or bump on tire (Chapter 10).

81 Hard steering

1   Lack of lubrication at balljoints, tie-rod ends and rack and pinion assembly (Chapter 10).
2   Front wheel alignment (Chapter 10).
3   Low tire pressure(s) (Chapters 1 and 10).

82 Poor returnability of steering to center

1   Lack of lubrication at balljoints and tie-rod ends (Chapter 10).
2   Binding in balljoints (Chapter 10).
3   Binding in steering column (Chapter 10).
4   Lack of lubricant in steering gear assembly (Chapter 10).
5   Front wheel alignment (Chapter 10).

83 Abnormal noise at the front end

1   Lack of lubrication at balljoints and tie-rod ends (Chapters 1 and 10).
2   Damaged strut mounting (Chapter 10).
3   Worn control arm bushings or tie-rod ends (Chapter 10).
4   Loose stabilizer bar (Chapter 10).
5   Loose wheel nuts (Chapters 1 and 10).
6   Loose suspension bolts (Chapter 10)

84 Wander or poor steering stability

1   Mismatched or uneven tires (Chapter 10).
2   Lack of lubrication at balljoints and tie-rod ends (Chapters 1 and 10).
3   Worn strut assemblies (Chapter 10).
4   Loose stabilizer bar (Chapter 10).
5   Broken or sagging springs (Chapter 10).
6   Wheels out of alignment (Chapter 10).

85 Erratic steering when braking

1   Front hub bearings worn (Chapter 10).
2   Broken or sagging springs (Chapter 10).
3   Leaking wheel cylinder or caliper (Chapter 10).
4   Warped rotor (Chapter 9).

86 Excessive pitching and/or rolling around corners or during braking

1   Loose stabilizer bar (Chapter 10).
2   Worn strut dampers or mountings (Chapter 10).
3   Broken or sagging springs (Chapter 10).
4   Overloaded vehicle.

87 Suspension bottoms

1   Overloaded vehicle.
2   Worn strut dampers (Chapter 10).
3   Incorrect, broken or sagging springs (Chapter 10).

88 Cupped tires

1   Front wheel or rear wheel alignment (Chapter 10).
2   Worn strut dampers (Chapter 10).
3   Wheel bearings worn (Chapter 10).
4   Excessive tire or wheel runout (Chapter 10).
5   Worn balljoints (Chapter 10).

89 Excessive tire wear on outside edge

1   Inflation pressures incorrect (Chapter 1).
2   Excessive speed in turns.
3   Front end alignment incorrect (excessive toe-in). Have professionally aligned.
4   Suspension arm bent or twisted (Chapter 10).

90 Excessive tire wear on inside edge

1   Inflation pressures incorrect (Chapter 1).
2   Front end alignment incorrect (toe-out). Have professionally aligned.
3   Loose or damaged steering or suspension components (Chapter 10).

91 Tire tread worn in one place

1   Tires out of balance.
2   Damaged or buckled wheel. Inspect and replace if necessary.
3   Defective tire (Chapter 1).

92 Excessive play or looseness in steering system

1   Front hub bearing(s) worn (Chapter 10).
2   Tie-rod end loose (Chapter 10).
3   Steering gear loose (Chapter 10).
4   Worn or loose steering intermediate shaft (Chapter 10).

93 Rattling or clicking noise in steering gear

1   Steering gear loose (Chapter 10).
2   Steering gear defective.

Chapter 1
Tune-up and routine maintenance

Contents

1

Specifications

Recommended lubricants and fluids

Note: *Listed here are manufacturer recommendations at the time this manual was written. Manufacturers occasionally upgrade their fluid and lubricant specifications, so check with your local auto parts store for current recommendations.*

Engine oil type	API grade SG or SG/CD multigrade and fuel-efficient oil
Viscosity	See accompanying chart
Automatic transaxle fluid type	MOPAR ATF + 3 TYPE 7176a, or equivalent, automatic transmission fluid
Manual transaxle lubricant type	API GL-5 SAE 75W-85W gear lubricant
Transfer case lubricant type (4WD models)	API GL-5 SAE 75W-85W gear lubricant
Rear differential lubricant type (4WD models)	API GL-5 SAE 90W* gear lubricant
Brake fluid type	DOT 3 brake fluid
Power steering system fluid	DEXRON II automatic transmission fluid

* Use 75W when anticipated temperatures are below -30-degrees F

Capacities*

Engine oil (including filter)
SOHC engine	4.1 qts
DOHC engine	4.6 qts
DOHC turbocharged engine	4.8 qts

Coolant
SOHC engine	6.6 qts
DOHC engine	7.6 qts

ENGINE OIL VISCOSITY CHART

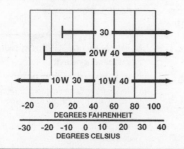

MANUAL TRANSAXLE LUBRICANT VISCOSITY CHART

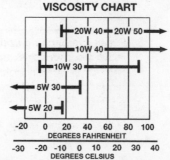

Engine oil viscosity chart - for best fuel economy and cold starting, select the lowest SAE viscosity grade for the expected temperature range

1-A1 HAYNES

Capacities* (continued)

Transaxle
  Automatic (when changing fluid in pan only**) .... 3.2 qts
    Manual .... 2 qts
Transfer case (4WD models) .... 0.3 qts
Rear axle (4WD models) .... 0.74 qts

* *All capacities approximate. Add as necessary to bring to appropriate level.*
** *This is an approximate capacity to be used after performing the drain-and-refill procedure described in Section 30 of this Chapter. Even after draining the pan, a large amount of fluid is retained in the torque converter, so, when filling the transaxle from "dry" (for example, after overhaul), approximately 3 to 3-1/2 more quarts of fluid will be required.*

Ignition system

Spark plug type and gap
  Non-turbo engine
    Type .... Champion RN9YC4 or equivalent
    Gap .... 0.044 inch
  Turbo engine
    Type .... Champion RN9YC or equivalent
    Gap .... 0.032 inch
Spark plug wire resistance .... 10,000 to 22,000 ohms
Engine firing order 1-3-4-2

1.8L engine

Cooling system

Thermostat rating
  Starts to open .... 190-degrees F
  Fully open .... 212-degrees F

Front ↓

2.0L engine

Clutch

Pedal height .... 7 inches
Pedal freeplay .... 1/2 inch

**Cylinder location
and distributor rotation**

*The blackened terminal shown on
the distributor cap indicates the
number one spark plug
wire position*

Brakes

Disc brake pad lining thickness (minimum) .... 1/16 inch
Parking brake adjustment .... 5 to 7 clicks

Suspension and steering

Steering wheel freeplay limit .... 1-3/16 inch
Balljoint allowable movement .... 0 inch

Torque specifications   **Ft-lbs** (unless otherwise indicated)

Automatic transaxle
  Pan bolts .... 84 to 108 in-lbs
  Filter bolt(s) .... 48 to 60 in-lbs
Manual transaxle drain and filler plugs 20
Transfer case (4WD models) drain and filler plugs .... 22 to 25
Differential (4WD models) drain and filler plugs 40
Spark plugs .... 14 to 22
Engine oil pan drain plug .... 26 to 32
Wheel lug nuts .... 87 to 101

1 Introduction

This Chapter is designed to help the home mechanic maintain the Plymouth Laser, Eagle Talon and Mitsubishi Eclipse for peak performance, economy, safety and long life.

On the following page is a master maintenance schedule, followed by sections dealing specifically with each item on the schedule. Visual checks, adjustments, component replacement and other helpful items are included. Refer to the accompanying illustrations of the engine compartment and the underside of the vehicle for the location of various components.

Servicing your vehicle in accordance with the mileage/time maintenance schedule and the following Sections will provide it with a planned maintenance program that should result in a long and reliable service life. This is a comprehensive plan, so maintaining some items but not others at the specified service intervals will not produce the same results.

As you service your vehicle, you will discover that many of the procedures can and should be grouped together because of the nature of the particular procedure you're performing or because of the close proximity of two otherwise unrelated components to one another.

For example, if the vehicle is raised for any reason, you should inspect the exhaust, suspension, steering and fuel systems while you're under the vehicle. When you're rotating the tires, it makes good sense to check the brakes and wheel bearings since the wheels are already removed.

Finally, let's suppose you have to borrow or rent a torque wrench. Even if you only need to tighten the spark plugs, you might as well check the torque of as many critical fasteners as time allows.

The first step of this maintenance program is to prepare yourself before the actual work begins. Read through all sections pertinent to the procedures you're planning to do, then make a list of and gather together all the parts and tools you will need to do the job. If it looks as if you might run into problems during a particular segment of some procedure, seek advice from your local parts man or dealer service department.

Engine compartment components (typical 2.0L DOHC turbo model)

1   Battery
2   Clutch fluid reservoir
3   Brake fluid reservoir
4   Air conditioning relay/fuse box
5   Power steering fluid reservoir
6   Windshield washer fluid reservoir
7   Engine oil dipstick
8   Engine oil filler cap
9   Coolant reservoir
10 Air filter housing
11 Fuse/relay/fusible link box
12 Radiator hose
13 Radiator cap

1

Engine compartment components (typical 1.8L SOHC non-turbo model)

1   Battery
2   Brake fluid reservoir
3   Air conditioning relay/fuse box
4   Power steering fluid reservoir
5   Windshield washer fluid reservoir
6   Engine oil dipstick
7   Engine oil filter cap
8   Coolant reservoir
9   Air filter housing
10 Fuse/relay/fusible link box
11 Radiator hose
12 Radiator cap
13 Spark plug wires
14 Distributor cap

Engine compartment underside components (1990 model shown, others similar)

1	Engine oil filter	3	Driveaxle outer boot	5	Exhaust pipe
2	Drivebelts	4	Engine oil drain plug	6	Brake caliper

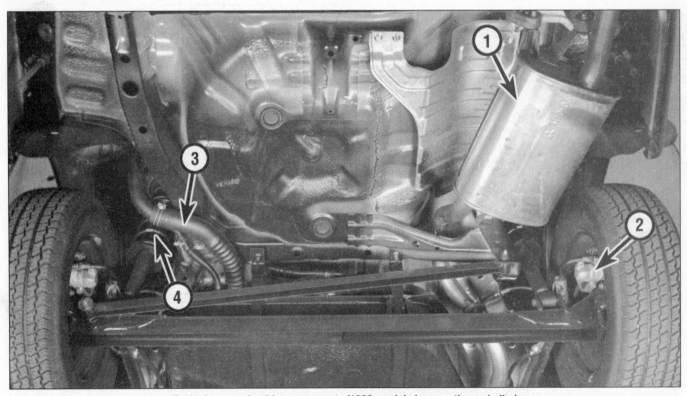

Typical rear underside components (1993 model shown, others similar)

1	Muffler	3	Fuel filler hose
2	Rear brake caliper	4	shock absorber assembly

2 Plymouth Laser/Eagle Talon/Mitsubishi Eclipse Maintenance schedule

The maintenance intervals in this manual are provided with the assumption that you, not the dealer, will be doing the work. These are the minimum maintenance intervals recommended by the factory for vehicles that are driven daily. If you wish to keep your vehicle in peak condition at all times, you may wish to perform some of these procedures even more often. Because frequent maintenance enhances the efficiency, performance and resale value of your car, we encourage you to do so. If you drive in dusty areas, tow a trailer, idle or drive at low speeds for extended periods or drive for short distances (less than four miles) in below-freezing temperatures, shorter intervals are also recommended.

When your vehicle is new, it should be serviced by a factory authorized dealer service department to protect the factory warranty. In many cases, the initial maintenance check is done at no cost to the owner.

Every 250 miles or weekly, whichever comes first

Check the engine oil level (Section 4)
Check the engine coolant level (Section 4)
Check the windshield washer fluid level (Section 4)
Check the brake fluid level (Section 4)
Check the tires and tire pressures (Section 5)

Every 3000 miles or 3 months, whichever comes first

All items listed above plus:
Check the power steering fluid level (Section 6)
Check the automatic transaxle fluid level (Section 7)
Change the engine oil and oil filter (Section 8)

Every 6000 miles or 6 months, whichever comes first

All items listed above, plus:
Inspect and replace, if necessary, the windshield wiper blades (Section 9)
Check the clutch pedal for proper freeplay (Section 10)
Check and service the battery (Section 11)
Check and adjust or replace, if necessary, the engine drivebelts (Section 12)
Inspect and replace, if necessary, the underhood hoses (Section 13)
Check the cooling system (Section 14)

Every 15,000 miles or 12 months, whichever comes first

Rotate the tires (Section 15)
Inspect the brake system (Section 16)*
Replace the air filter (Section 17)*
Inspect the fuel system (Section 18)
Check the manual transaxle lubricant level (Section 19)

Check the transfer case lubricant level (4WD models) (Section 20)
Check the differential lubricant level (4WD models) (Section 21)
Inspect the suspension and steering components (Section 22)
Check the driveaxle boots (Section 23)

Every 30,000 miles or 24 months, whichever comes first

All items listed above plus:
Replace the fuel filter (Section 24)
Replace the spark plugs (Section 25)*
Inspect and replace, if necessary, the spark plug wires, distributor cap and rotor (Section 26)
Service the cooling system (drain, flush and refill) (Section 27)
Inspect the evaporative emissions control system (Section 28)
Inspect the exhaust system (Section 29)
Change the automatic transaxle fluid and filter (Section 30)
Change the manual transaxle lubricant (Section 31)
Change the transfer case lubricant (4WD models) (Section 32)
Change the differential lubricant (4WD models) (Section 33)
Check and replace, if necessary, the PCV valve (1.8L engine only) (Section 34)

Every 60,000 miles or 48 months, whichever comes first

Replace the timing and balance-shaft belts (Chapter 2A)

> * If your vehicle tows a trailer frequently, is operated at idle for extended periods, is operated at low speeds and/or is used for short trips at freezing temperatures, replace the spark plugs at 15,000 -mile/12-month intervals and check the brakes more frequently. If your vehicle is driven in sandy, dusty or salty areas, check the brakes and air filter more frequently than indicated.

4.2 The engine oil dipstick (arrow) is located on the front of the engine, toward the driver's side

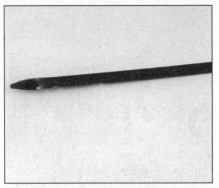

4.4 The oil level should be at or near the upper notch on the dipstick - if it isn't, add enough oil to bring the level to near the upper notch (it takes one quart of oil to raise the level from the lower to upper notch)

4.6 The oil filler cap is located on the valve cover - always make sure the area around the opening is clean before unscrewing the cap to prevent dirt from contaminating the engine

3   Tune-up general information

The term tune-up is used in this manual to represent a combination of individual operations rather than one specific procedure.

If, from the time the vehicle is new, the routine maintenance schedule is followed closely and frequent checks are made of fluid levels and high wear items, as suggested throughout this manual, the engine will be kept in relatively good running condition and the need for additional work will be minimized.

More likely than not, however, there will be times when the engine is running poorly due to lack of regular maintenance. This is even more likely if a used vehicle, which has not received regular and frequent maintenance checks, is purchased. In such cases, an engine tune-up will be needed outside of the regular routine maintenance intervals.

The first step in any tune-up or engine diagnosis to help correct a poor running engine would be a cylinder compression check. A check of the engine compression and vacuum (Chapter 2 Part B) will give valuable information regarding the overall performance of many internal components and should be used as a basis for tune-up and repair procedures. If, for instance, a compression check indicates serious internal engine wear, a conventional tune-up will not help the running condition of the engine and would be a waste of time and money.

The following series of operations are those most often needed to bring a generally poor running engine back into a proper state of tune.

Minor tune-up

Clean, inspect and test the battery (Section 11)
Check all engine-related fluids (Section 4)
Check and adjust the drivebelts (Section 12)
Replace the spark plugs (Section 25)
Inspect the distributor cap and rotor (1.8L engine only) (Section 26)

Inspect the spark plug wires and, if equipped, coil wire (Section 26)
Check the air filter (Section 17)
Check the cooling system (Section 14)
Check all underhood hoses (Section 13)

Major tune-up

All items listed under Minor tune-up, plus . . .
Check the charging system (Chapter 5)
Check the fuel system (Section 18)
Replace the air filter (Section 17)
Replace the distributor cap and rotor (1.8L engine only) (Section 26)
Replace the spark plug wires (Section 26)

4   Fluid level checks (every 250 miles or weekly)

1   Fluids are an essential part of the lubrication, cooling, brake, clutch and other systems. Because these fluids gradually become depleted and/or contaminated during normal operation of the vehicle, they must be periodically replenished. See *Recommended lubricants and fluids* and *Capacities* at the beginning of this Chapter before adding fluid to any of the following components. **Note:** *The vehicle must be on level ground before fluid levels can be checked.*

Engine oil

Refer to illustrations 4.2, 4.4 and 4.6

2   The engine oil level is checked with a dipstick located at the front side of the engine **(see illustration)**. The dipstick extends through a metal tube from which it protrudes down into the engine oil pan.

3   The oil level should be checked before the vehicle has been driven, or about 15 minutes after the engine has been shut off. If the oil is checked immediately after driving the vehicle, some of the oil will remain in the upper engine components, producing an inaccurate reading on the dipstick.

4   Pull the dipstick from the tube and wipe all the oil from the end with a clean rag or

paper towel. Insert the clean dipstick all the way back into its metal tube and pull it out again. Observe the oil at the end of the dipstick. At its highest point, the level should be between the two notches **(see illustration)**.

5   It takes one quart of oil to raise the level from the L notch to the F notch on the dipstick. Do not allow the level to drop below the L mark or oil starvation may cause engine damage. Conversely, overfilling the engine (adding oil above the F mark) may cause oil-fouled spark plugs, oil leaks or oil seal failures.

6   Remove the threaded cap from the valve cover to add oil **(see illustration)**. Use a funnel to prevent spills. After adding the oil, install the filler cap hand tight. Start the engine and look carefully for any small leaks around the oil filter or drain plug. Stop the engine and check the oil level again after it has had sufficient time to drain from the upper block and cylinder head galleys.

7   Checking the oil level is an important preventive maintenance step. A continually dropping oil level indicates oil leakage through damaged seals, from loose connections, or past worn rings or valve guides. If the oil looks milky in color or has water droplets in it, a cylinder head gasket may be blown. The engine should be checked immediately. The condition of the oil should also be checked. Each time you check the oil level, slide your thumb and index finger up the dipstick before wiping off the oil. If you see small dirt or metal particles clinging to the dipstick, the oil should be changed (see Section 8).

Engine coolant

Refer to illustration 4.8

Warning: *Do not allow antifreeze to come in contact with your skin or painted surfaces of the vehicle. Flush contaminated areas immediately with plenty of water. Don't store new coolant or leave old coolant lying around where it's accessible to children or pets - they're attracted by its sweet smell. Ingestion*

4.8 The coolant reservoir is located in the right front corner of the engine compartment - keep the level between the MAX and MIN lines

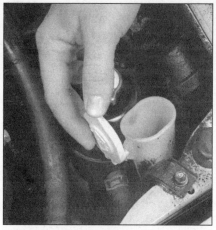

4.14a The windshield washer fluid reservoir is located at the left front corner of the engine compartment - fluid can be added after flipping up the cap

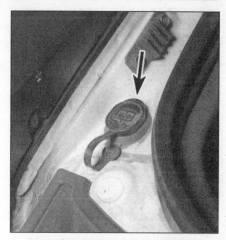

4.14b The rear window washer fluid reservoir is located in the rear compartment on the left side

4.15 Remove the cell caps to check the electrolyte level in the battery - if the level is low, add distilled water only

of even a small amount of coolant can be fatal! Wipe up garage floor and drip pan spills immediately. Keep antifreeze containers covered and repair cooling system leaks as soon as they're noticed.

8   All vehicles covered by this manual are equipped with a pressurized coolant recovery system. A white coolant reservoir located in the right (passenger side) front corner of the engine compartment is connected by a hose to the base of the coolant filler cap **(see illustration)**. If the coolant heats up during engine operation, coolant can escape through a pressurized filler cap, then through a connecting hose into the reservoir. As the engine cools, the coolant is automatically drawn back into the cooling system to maintain the correct level.

9   The coolant level should be checked regularly. It must be between the MAX and MIN lines on the reservoir. The level will vary with the temperature of the engine. When the engine is cold, the coolant level should be at or slightly above the MIN mark on the tank. Once the engine has warmed up, the level should be at or near the MAX mark. If it isn't, allow the fluid in the tank to cool, then remove the cap from the reservoir and add coolant to bring the level up to the MAX mark. Use only ethylene/glycol type coolant and water in the mixture ratio recommended by your owner's manual. Do not use supplemental inhibitors or additives. If only a small amount of coolant is required to bring the system up to the proper level, water can be used. However, repeated additions of water will dilute the recommended antifreeze and water solution. In order to maintain the proper ratio of antifreeze and water, it is advisable to top up the coolant level with the correct mixture. Refer to your owner's manual for the recommended ratio.

10   If the coolant level drops within a short time after replenishment, there may be a leak in the system. Inspect the radiator, hoses, engine coolant filler cap, drain plugs, air

bleeder plugs and water pump. If no leak is evident, have the radiator cap pressure tested by your dealer. **Warning:** Never remove the radiator cap or the coolant recovery reservoir cap when the engine is running or has just been shut down, because the cooling system is hot. Escaping steam and scalding liquid could cause serious injury.

11   If it is necessary to open the radiator cap, wait until the system has cooled completely, then wrap a thick cloth around the cap and turn it to the first stop. If any steam escapes, wait until the system has cooled further, then remove the cap.

12   When checking the coolant level, always note its condition. It should be relatively clear. If it is brown or rust colored, the system should be drained, flushed and refilled. Even if the coolant appears to be normal, the corrosion inhibitors wear out with use, so it must be replaced at the specified intervals.

13   Do not allow antifreeze to come in contact with your skin or painted surfaces of the vehicle. Flush contacted areas immediately with plenty of water.

Washer fluid

Refer to illustrations 4.14a and 4.14b

14   Fluid for the windshield washer system is stored in a plastic reservoir which is located at the left front corner of the engine compartment **(see illustration)**. The rear window washer reservoir is located in the rear compartment **(see illustration)**. In milder climates, plain water can be used to top up the reservoir, but the reservoir should be kept no more than two-thirds full to allow for expansion should the water freeze. In colder climates, the use of a specially designed windshield washer fluid, available at your dealer and any auto parts store, will help lower the freezing point of the fluid. Mix the solution with water in accordance with the manufacturer's directions on the container. Do not use regular antifreeze. It will damage the vehicle's paint.

Battery electrolyte

Refer to illustration 4.15

15   On models not equipped with a sealed battery, check the electrolyte level of all six battery cells. Remove the filler caps and check the level **(see illustration)** - it must be at or near the split ring. If the level is low, add distilled water. Install and securely retighten the cap. **Caution:** *Overfilling the cells may cause electrolyte to spill over during periods of heavy charging, causing corrosion or damage.*

Brake and clutch fluid

Refer to illustration 4.17

16   The brake master cylinder is mounted on the front of the power booster unit in the engine compartment. The clutch master cylinder used on manual transaxles is mounted on the firewall next to it.

17   To check the fluid level of the brake master cylinder or clutch reservoir, simply look at the MAX and MIN marks on the translucent plastic reservoir. The level inside should be visible and should be between the MAX and

1

4.17 The brake fluid (right) and clutch (if equipped) fluid level should be kept between the MIN and MAX marks on the translucent plastic reservoir(s) - unscrew the cap to add fluid

MIN lines, but close to the MAX line **(see illustration).**

18   If the level is low for either reservoir, wipe the top of the reservoir cover with a clean rag to prevent contamination of the brake or clutch system before lifting the cover.

19   Add only the specified brake fluid to the brake or clutch reservoir (refer to *Recommended lubricants and fluids* at the front of this chapter or to your owner's manual). Mixing different types of brake fluid can damage the system. **Warning:** *Use caution when filling either reservoir - brake fluid can harm your eyes and damage painted surfaces. Do not use brake fluid that has been opened for more than one year or has been left open. Brake fluid absorbs moisture from the air. Excess moisture can cause a dangerous loss of braking.*

20   While the reservoir cap is removed, inspect the master cylinder reservoir for contamination. If deposits, dirt particles or water droplets are present, the system should be drained and refilled (see Chapter 9).

21   After filling the reservoir to the proper level, make sure the lid is properly seated to prevent fluid leakage and/or system pressure loss.

22   The brake fluid in the master cylinder will drop slightly as the brake pads at each wheel wear down during normal operation. If the master cylinder requires repeated replenishing to keep it at the proper level, this is an indication of leakage in the brake system, which should be corrected immediately. Check all brake lines and connections, along with the wheel cylinders and booster (see Section 16 for more information).

23   If, upon checking the master cylinder fluid level, you discover one or both reservoirs empty or nearly empty, the brake system should be bled (see Chapter 9).

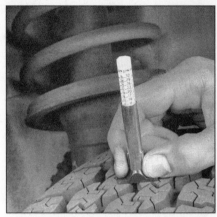

5.2 Use a tire tread depth indicator to monitor tire wear - they are available at auto parts stores and service stations and cost very little

5   Tire and tire pressure checks (every 250 miles or weekly)

Refer to illustrations 5.2, 5.3, 5.4a, 5.4b and 5.8

1   Periodic inspection of the tires may spare you from the inconvenience of being stranded with a flat tire. It can also provide you with vital information regarding possible problems in the steering and suspension sys-

UNDERINFLATION

CUPPING

Cupping may be caused by:
- Underinflation and/or mechanical irregularities such as out-of-balance condition of wheel and/or tire, and bent or damaged wheel.
- Loose or worn steering tie-rod or steering idler arm.
- Loose, damaged or worn front suspension parts.

OVERINFLATION

INCORRECT TOE-IN OR EXTREME CAMBER

FEATHERING DUE TO MISALIGNMENT

5.3 This chart will help you determine the condition of the tires, the probable cause(s) of abnormal wear and the corrective action necessary

5.4a If a tire loses air on a steady basis, check the valve stem core first to make sure it's snug (special inexpensive wrenches are commonly available at auto parts stores)

5.4b If the valve stem core is tight, raise the corner of the vehicle with the low tire and spray a soapy water solution onto the tread as the tire is turned slowly - leaks will cause small bubbles to appear

5.8 To extend the life of the tires, check the air pressure at least once a week with an accurate gauge (don't forget the spare!)

1

tems before major damage occurs.

2   Normal tread wear can be monitored with a simple, inexpensive device known as a tread depth indicator **(see illustration)**. When the tread depth reaches the specified minimum, replace the tire(s).

3   Note any abnormal tread wear **(see illustration)**. Tread pattern irregularities such as cupping, flat spots and more wear on one side than the other are indications of front end alignment and/or balance problems. If any of these conditions are noted, take the vehicle to a tire shop or service station to correct the problem.

4   Look closely for cuts, punctures and embedded nails or tacks. Sometimes a tire will hold its air pressure for a short time or leak down very slowly even after a nail has embedded itself into the tread. If a slow leak persists, check the valve stem core to make sure it is tight **(see illustration)**. Examine the tread for an object that may have embedded itself into the tire or for a "plug" that may have begun to leak (radial tire punctures are repaired with a plug that is installed in a puncture). If a puncture is suspected, it can be easily verified by spraying a solution of soapy water onto the puncture area **(see illustration)**. The soapy solution will bubble if there is a leak. Unless the puncture is inordinately large, a tire shop or gas station can usually repair the punctured tire.

5   Carefully inspect the inner sidewall of each tire for evidence of brake fluid leakage. If you see any, inspect the brakes immediately.

6   Correct tire air pressure adds miles to the life span of the tires, improves mileage and enhances overall ride quality. Tire pressure cannot be accurately estimated by looking at a tire, particularly if it is a radial. A tire pressure gauge is therefore essential. Keep an accurate gauge in the glove box. The pressure gauges fitted to the nozzles of air hoses at gas stations are often inaccurate.

7   Always check tire pressure when the tires are cold. "Cold," in this case, means the

vehicle has not been driven over a mile in the three hours preceding a tire pressure check. A pressure rise of four to eight pounds is not uncommon once the tires are warm.

8   Unscrew the valve stem cap protruding from the wheel or hubcap and push the gauge firmly onto the valve **(see illustration)**. Note the reading on the gauge and compare this figure to the recommended tire pressure shown on the tire placard on the left door. Be sure to reinstall the valve cap to keep dirt and moisture out of the valve stem mechanism. Check all four tires and, if necessary, add enough air to bring them up to the recommended pressure levels.

9   Don't forget to keep the spare tire inflated to the specified pressure (consult your owner's manual). Note that the air pressure specified for the compact spare is significantly higher than the pressure of the regular tires.

6   Power steering fluid level check (every 3000 miles or 3 months)

Refer to illustrations 6.5 and 6.6

1   Unlike manual steering, the power steering system relies on fluid which may, over a period of time, require replenishing.

2   The fluid reservoir for the power steering pump is located on the inner fender panel at the left (driver) side of the engine compartment.

3   For the check, the front wheels should be pointed forward and the engine should be off.

4   Use a clean rag to wipe off the area around the cap. This will help prevent any foreign matter from entering the reservoir during the check.

5   Twist off the cap and withdraw the dipstick from the reservoir **(see illustration)**.

6   Wipe off the fluid with a clean rag, reinsert the dipstick, the withdraw it and read the fluid level. The fluid level should be kept

6.5 Twist the cap off the power steering fluid reservoir and check the level on the dipstick

between the MIN and MAX marks on the reservoir **(see illustration)**.

7   If additional fluid is required, pour the specified type directly into the reservoir, using a funnel to prevent spills.

8   If the reservoir requires frequent fluid additions, all power steering hoses, hose connections, the power steering pump and

6.6 The fluid level should be kept near the MAX mark on the dipstick

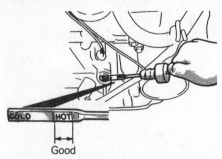

7.4 Check the fluid with the transaxle at normal operating temperature - the level should be kept in the HOT range with the transaxle at normal operating temperature

the rack-and-pinion assembly should be carefully checked for leaks.

7 Automatic transaxle fluid level check (every 3000 miles or 3 months)

Refer to illustration 7.4

1   The level of the automatic transaxle fluid should be carefully maintained. Low fluid level can lead to slipping or loss of drive, while overfilling can cause foaming, loss of fluid and transaxle damage.

2   For greatest accuracy, the transaxle fluid level should be checked when the transaxle is hot (at its normal operating temperature). If the vehicle has just been driven over 10 miles (15 miles in a frigid climate) and the fluid temperature is 160 to 175-degrees F, the transaxle is hot. **Caution:** *If the vehicle has just been driven for a long time at high speed or in city traffic in hot weather, or if it has been pulling a trailer, an accurate fluid level reading cannot be obtained. Allow the fluid to cool down for about 30 minutes.*

3   If the vehicle has not just been driven, park the vehicle on level ground, set the parking brake and start the engine. While the engine is idling, depress the brake pedal and

8.7 Use a proper-size box-end wrench or socket to remove the oil drain plug and avoid rounding it off

move the selector lever through all the gear ranges, beginning and ending in Park.

4   With the engine still idling, remove the dipstick from its tube, located at the right (passenger's) side of the engine compartment, below the air cleaner housing. Check the level of the fluid on the dipstick **(see illustration)** and note its condition.

5   Wipe the fluid from the dipstick with a clean rag and reinsert it back into the filler tube until the cap seats.

6   Pull the dipstick out again and note the fluid level. If the transaxle is cold, the level should be in the COLD range on the dipstick. If it is hot, the fluid level should be in the HOT range. If the level is at the low side of either range, add the specified automatic transmission fluid through the dipstick tube with a funnel.

7   Add just enough of the recommended fluid to fill the transaxle to the proper level. It takes about one pint to raise the level from the low mark to the high mark when the fluid is hot, so add the fluid a little at a time and keep checking the level until it is correct.

8   The condition of the fluid should also be checked along with the level. If the fluid at the end of the dipstick is black or a dark reddish brown color, or if it emits a burned smell, the fluid should be changed (see Section 30). If you are in doubt about the condition of the fluid, purchase some new fluid and compare the two for color and smell.

8 Engine oil and oil filter change (every 3000 miles or 3 months)

Refer to illustrations 8.2, 8.7, 8.13 and 8.15

1   Frequent oil changes are the best preventive maintenance the home mechanic can give the engine, because aging oil becomes diluted and contaminated, which leads to premature engine wear.

2   Make sure that you have all the necessary tools before you begin this procedure **(see illustration).** You should also have plenty of rags or newspapers handy for mopping up any spills.

3   Access to the underside of the vehicle is greatly improved if the vehicle can be lifted on a hoist, driven onto ramps or supported by jackstands. **Warning:** *Do not work under a vehicle which is supported only by a bumper, hydraulic or scissors-type jack.*

4   If this is your first oil change, get under the vehicle and familiarize yourself with the location of the oil drain plug. The engine and exhaust components will be warm during the actual work, so try to anticipate any potential problems before the engine and accessories are hot.

5   Park the vehicle on a level spot. Start the engine and allow it to reach its normal operating temperature (the needle on the temperature gauge should be at least above the bottom mark). Warm oil and sludge will flow out more easily. Turn off the engine when it's warmed up. Remove the filler cap in

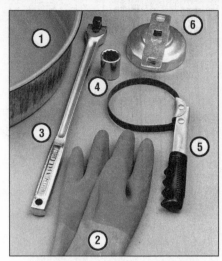

8.2 These tools are required when changing the engine oil and filter

1   ***Drain pan*** *- It should be fairly shallow in depth, but wide to prevent spills*

2   ***Rubber gloves*** *- When removing the drain plug and filter, you will get oil on your hands (the gloves will prevent burns)*

3   ***Breaker bar*** *- Sometimes the oil drain plug is tight, and a long breaker bar is needed to loosen it*

4   ***Socket*** *– To be used with the breaker bar or a ratchet (must be the correct size to fit the drain plug - six-point preferred)*

5   ***Filter wrench*** *- This is a metal band-type wrench, which requires clearance around the filter to be effective*

6   ***Filter wrench*** *- This type fits on the bottom of the filter and can be turned with a ratchet or breaker bar (different-size wrenches are available for different types of filters)*

the rear cam cover.

6   Raise the vehicle and support it on jackstands. **Warning:** *To avoid personal injury, never get beneath the vehicle when it is supported by only by a jack. The jack provided with your vehicle is designed solely for raising the vehicle to remove and replace the wheels. Always use jackstands to support the vehicle when it becomes necessary to place your body underneath the vehicle.*

7   Being careful not to touch the hot exhaust components, place the drain pan under the drain plug in the bottom of the pan and remove the plug **(see illustration).** You may want to wear gloves while unscrewing the plug the final few turns if the engine is really hot.

8   Allow the old oil to drain into the pan. It may be necessary to move the pan farther under the engine as the oil flow slows to a trickle. Inspect the old oil for the presence of metal shavings and chips.

9   After all the oil has drained, wipe off the drain plug with a clean rag. Even minute metal particles clinging to the plug would immediately contaminate the new oil.

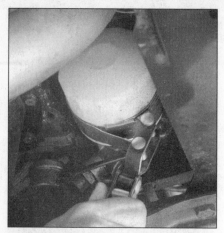

8.13 Since the oil filter (accessible from below) is on very tight, you'll need a special wrench for removal - DO NOT use the wrench to tighten the new filter

8.15 Lubricate the oil filter gasket with clean engine oil before installing the filter on the engine

oil pan drain plug and around the oil filter. If either is leaking, stop the engine and tighten the plug or filter slightly.

18 Wait a few minutes to allow the oil to trickle down into the pan, then recheck the level on the dipstick and, if necessary, add enough oil to bring the level to the upper mark.

19 During the first few trips after an oil change, make it a point to check frequently for leaks and proper oil level.

20 The old oil drained from the engine cannot be reused in its present state and should be discarded. Oil reclamation centers, auto repair shops and gas stations will normally accept the oil, which can be refined and used again. After the oil has cooled, it can be drained into a suitable container (capped plastic jugs, topped bottles, milk cartons, etc.) for transport to one of these disposal sites.

10 Clean the area around the drain plug opening, reinstall the plug and tighten it securely, but do not strip the threads.

11 Move the drain pan into position under the oil filter.

12 Remove all tools, rags, etc. from under the vehicle, being careful not to spill the oil in the drain pan, then lower the vehicle.

13 Loosen the oil filter **(see illustration)** by turning it counterclockwise with the filter wrench. Any standard filter wrench will work. Sometimes the oil filter is screwed on so tightly that it cannot be loosened. If this situation occurs, punch a metal bar or long screwdriver directly through the side of the canister and use it as a T-bar to turn the filter. Be prepared for oil to spurt out of the canister as it is punctured. Once the filter is loose, use your hands to unscrew it from the block. Just as the filter is detached from the block, immediately tilt the open end up to prevent the oil inside the filter from spilling out. **Warning:** *The engine exhaust manifold will still be hot, so be careful.*

14 With a clean rag, wipe off the mounting surface on the block. If a residue of old oil is allowed to remain, it will smoke when the

block is heated up. It will also prevent the new filter from seating properly. Also make sure that the none of the old gasket remains stuck to the mounting surface. It can be removed with a scraper if necessary.

15 Compare the old filter with the new one to make sure they are the same type. Smear some engine oil on the rubber gasket of the new filter and screw it into place **(see illustration)**. Because overtightening the filter will damage the gasket, do not use a filter wrench to tighten the filter. Tighten it by hand until the gasket contacts the seating surface. Then seat the filter by giving it an additional 3/4-turn.

16 Add new oil to the engine through the oil filler cap in the valve cover. Use a spout or funnel to prevent oil from spilling onto the top of the engine. Pour three quarts of fresh oil into the engine. Wait a few minutes to allow the oil to drain into the pan, then check the level on the oil dipstick (see Section 4 if necessary). If the oil level is at or near the F mark, install the filler cap hand tight, start the engine and allow the new oil to circulate.

17 Allow the engine to run for about a minute. While the engine is running, look under the vehicle and check for leaks at the

1

9 Windshield wiper blade inspection and replacement (every 6000 miles or 6 months)

Refer to illustrations 9.6 and 9.7

1 The wiper and blade assembly should be inspected periodically for damage, loose components and cracked or worn blade elements.

2 Road film can build up on the wiper blades and affect their efficiency, so they should be washed regularly with a mild detergent solution.

3 The action of the wiping mechanism can loosen bolts, nuts and fasteners, so they should be checked and tightened, as necessary, at the same time the wiper blades are checked.

4 If the wiper blade elements are cracked, worn or warped, or no longer clean adequately, they should be replaced with new ones.

5 Lift the arm assembly away from the glass for clearance.

6 Remove the two screws and detach the blade assembly from the wiper arm **(see illustration)**.

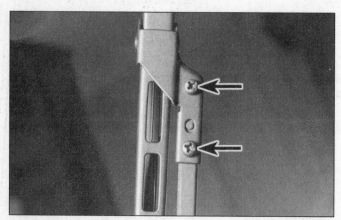

9.6 Remove the two screws (arrows) to detach the wiper arm

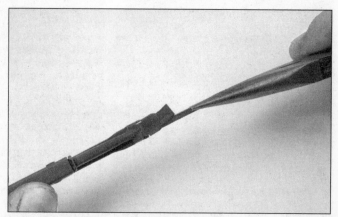

9.7 Use needle-nose pliers to pull the support rods out of the wiper blade element

10.1 Clutch pedal height is measured from the floor to the top of the pedal pad

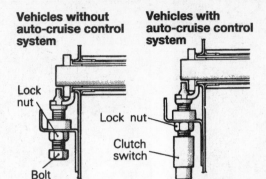

Vehicles without auto-cruise control system

Vehicles with auto-cruise control system

Lock nut

Bolt

Lock nut

Clutch switch

10.2 To adjust clutch pedal height, loosen the locknut and turn the bolt or clutch switch until the height is correct, then tighten the locknut

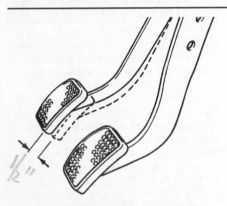

10.3 To determine the clutch pedal freeplay, depress the pedal, stop the moment clutch resistance is felt, then measure the distance

Lock nut

Push rod

10.4 Adjust clutch pedal freeplay by loosening the locknut, rotating the pushrod until the freeplay is correct, then tightening the locknut

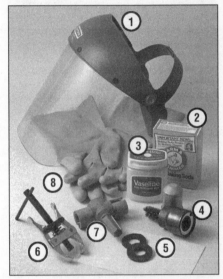

11.1 Tools and materials required for battery maintenance

7   Bend the end of the wiper element out of the way and use needle-nose pliers to pull the two support rods out of the element **(see illustration)**.
8   With the support rods removed, slide the element out of the blade assembly.
9   Slide the new element into place and insert the support rods.

10   Clutch pedal height and freeplay - check and adjustment (every 6000 miles or 6 months)

Refer to illustrations 10.1, 10.2, 10.3 and 10.4
1   Measure the clutch pedal height (the distance from the top of the clutch pedal to the floor) **(see illustration)**. The distance should be as listed in this Chapter's Specifications.
2   If the pedal height is not correct, reach under the dash and loosen the locknut until the adjusting bolt (non-cruise control) or clutch switch (cruise control) turns freely. Turn the adjusting bolt or the switch to achieve the specified pedal height **(see illustration)**.
3   Press down lightly on the clutch pedal and, with a small steel ruler, measure the distance that it moves freely before the clutch resistance is felt **(see illustration)**. The

freeplay should be within the limits listed in this Chapter's Specifications. If it isn't, it must be adjusted.
4   To adjust the freeplay, reach up under the dash, loosen the locknut and adjust the clutch pedal pushrod until the freeplay is correct, then tighten the locknut securely **(see illustration)**.

11   Battery check, maintenance and charging (every 6000 miles or 6 months)

Refer to illustrations 11.1, 11.6a, 11.6b, 11.7a, 11.7b and 11.8
Warning: *Certain precautions must be followed when checking and servicing the battery. Hydrogen gas, which is highly flammable, is always present in the battery cells, so keep lighted tobacco and all other open flames and sparks away from the battery. The electrolyte inside the battery is actually dilute sulfuric acid, which will cause injury if splashed on your skin or in your eyes. It will also ruin clothes and painted surfaces. When removing the battery cables, always detach the negative cable first and hook it up last!*

Check and maintenance

1   A routine preventive maintenance program for the battery in your vehicle is the only

1   *Face shield/safety goggles - When removing corrosion with a brush, the acidic particles can easily fly up into your eyes*
2   *Baking soda - A solution of baking soda and water can be used to neutralize corrosion*
3   *Petroleum jelly - A layer of this on the battery posts will help prevent corrosion*
4   *Battery post/cable cleaner - This wire-brush cleaning tool will remove all traces of corrosion from the battery posts and cable clamps*
5   *Treated felt washers - Placing one of these on each post, directly under the cable clamps, will help prevent corrosion*
6   *Puller - Sometimes the cable clamps are very difficult to pull off the posts, even after the nut/bolt has been completely loosened. This tool pulls the clamp straight up and off the post without damage*
7   *Battery post/cable cleaner - Here is another cleaning tool which is a slightly different version of Number 4 above, but it does the same thing*
8   *Rubber gloves - Be sure to wear these; remember, that's acid inside the battery!*

11.6a Battery terminal corrosion usually appears as light, fluffy powder

11.6b Removing the cable from a battery post with a wrench - sometimes special battery pliers are required for this procedure if corrosion has caused deterioration of the nut hex (always remove the ground cable first and hook it up last!)

11.7a When cleaning the cable clamps, all corrosion must be removed (the inside of the clamp is tapered to match the taper on the post, so don't remove too much material)

1

way to ensure quick and reliable starts. But before performing any battery maintenance, make sure that you have the proper equipment necessary to work safely around the battery **(see illustration).**

2 There are also several precautions that should be taken whenever battery maintenance is performed. Before servicing the battery, always turn the engine and all accessories off and disconnect the cable from the negative terminal of the battery.

3 The battery produces hydrogen gas, which is both flammable and explosive. Never create a spark, smoke or light a match around the battery. Always charge the battery in a ventilated area.

4 Electrolyte contains poisonous and corrosive sulfuric acid. Do not allow it to get in your eyes, on your skin on your clothes. Never ingest it. Wear protective safety glasses when working near the battery. Keep children away from the battery.

5 Note the external condition of the battery. If the positive terminal and cable clamp on your vehicle's battery is equipped with a rubber protector, make sure that it's not torn or damaged. It should completely cover the terminal. Look for any corroded or loose connections, cracks in the case or cover or loose hold-down clamps. Also check the entire length of each cable for cracks and frayed conductors.

6 If corrosion, which looks like white, fluffy deposits (see illustration) is evident, particularly around the terminals, the battery should be removed for cleaning. Loosen the cable clamp bolts with a wrench, being careful to remove the ground cable first, and slide them off the terminals (see illustration). Then disconnect the hold-down clamp bolt and nut, remove the clamp and lift the battery from the engine compartment.

7 Clean the cable clamps thoroughly with a battery brush or a terminal cleaner and a solution of warm water and baking soda **(see illustration).** Wash the terminals and the top of the battery case with the same solution but make sure that the solution doesn't get into the battery. When cleaning the cables, terminals and battery top, wear safety goggles and rubber gloves to prevent any solution from coming in contact with your eyes or hands. Wear old clothes too - even diluted, sulfuric acid splashed onto clothes will burn holes in them. If the terminals have been extensively corroded, clean them up with a terminal cleaner **(see illustration).** Thoroughly wash all cleaned areas with plain water.

8 Make sure that the battery tray is in good condition and the hold-down clamp bolts are tight **(see illustration).** If the battery is removed from the tray, make sure no parts remain in the bottom of the tray when the battery is reinstalled. When reinstalling the hold-down clamp bolts, do not overtighten them.

9 Information on removing and installing the battery can be found in Chapter 5. Information on jump starting can be found at the front of this manual. For more detailed battery checking procedures, refer to the *Haynes Automotive Electrical Manual.*

Cleaning

10 Corrosion on the hold-down components, battery case and surrounding areas

11.7b Regardless of the type of tool used on the battery posts, a clean, shiny surface should be the result

11.8 Make sure the battery clamp bolts (arrows) are tight

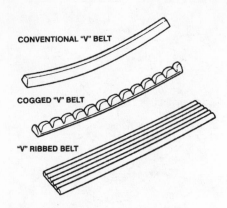

CONVENTIONAL "V" BELT

COGGED "V" BELT

"V" RIBBED BELT

12.1 Different types of drivebelts are used to power the accessories mounted on the engine - the water pump, alternator and air-conditioning compressor (if equipped) are driven by V-ribbed belts; the power steering pump (if equipped) is driven by a conventional or cogged V-belt

can be removed with a solution of water and baking soda. Thoroughly rinse all cleaned areas with plain water.

11   Any metal parts of the vehicle damaged by corrosion should be covered with a zinc-based primer, then painted.

Charging

Warning: *When batteries are being charged, hydrogen gas, which is very explosive and flammable, is produced. Do not smoke or allow open flames near a charging or a recently charged battery. Wear eye protection when near the battery during charging. Also, make sure the charger is unplugged before connecting or disconnecting the battery from the charger.*

12   Slow-rate charging is the best way to restore a battery that's discharged to the point where it will not start the engine. It's also a good way to maintain the battery charge in a vehicle that's only driven a few miles between starts. Maintaining the battery charge is particularly important in the winter when the battery must work harder to start the engine and electrical accessories that drain the battery are in greater use.

13   It's best to use a one or two-amp battery charger (sometimes called a "trickle" charger). They are the safest and put the least strain on the battery. They are also the least expensive. For a faster charge, you can use a higher amperage charger, but don't use one rated more than 1/10th the amp/hour rating of the battery. Rapid boost chargers that claim to restore the power of the battery in one to two hours are hardest on the battery and can damage batteries not in good condition; this type of charging should only be used in emergency situations.

14   The average time necessary to charge a battery should be listed in the instructions that come with the charger. As a general rule,

a trickle charger will charge a battery in 12 to 16 hours.

15   Remove all the cell caps (if equipped) and cover the holes with a clean cloth to prevent spattering electrolyte. Disconnect the negative battery cable and hook the battery charger leads to the battery posts (positive to positive, negative to negative), then plug in the charger. Make sure it is set at 12 volts if it has a selector switch.

16   If you're using a charger with a rate higher than two amps, check the battery regularly during charging to make sure it doesn't overheat. If you're using a trickle charger, you can safely let the battery charge overnight after you've checked it regularly for the first couple of hours.

17   If the battery has removable cell caps, measure the specific gravity with a hydrometer every hour during the last few hours of the charging cycle. Hydrometers are available inexpensively from auto parts stores - follow the instructions that come with the hydrometer. Consider the battery charged when there's no change in the specific gravity reading for two hours and the electrolyte in the cells is gassing (bubbling) freely. The specific gravity reading from each cell should be very close to the others. If not, the battery probably has a bad cell(s).

18   Some batteries with sealed tops have built-in hydrometers on the top that indicate the state of charge by the color displayed in the hydrometer window. Normally, a bright-colored hydrometer indicates a full charge and a dark hydrometer indicates the battery still needs charging. Check the battery manufacturer's instructions to be sure you know what the colors mean.

19   If the battery has a sealed top and no built-in hydrometer, you can hook up a digital voltmeter across the battery terminals to check the charge. A fully charged battery should read 12.6 volts or higher.

20   Further information on the battery and jump starting can be found in Chapter 5 and at the front of this manual.

12   Drivebelt check, adjustment and replacement (every 6000 miles or 6 months)

Refer to illustrations 12.1, 12.3, 12.4, 12.5a, 12.5b, 12.6a, 12.6b and 12.9

Check

1   The drivebelts, also referred to as V-belts, V-ribbed belts or simply "fan" belts, are located at the left (driver's side) end of the engine **(see illustration)**. The good condition and proper adjustment of belts is critical to the operation of the engine, electrical system and power steering and air conditioning (if equipped). Because of their composition and the high stresses to which they are subjected, drivebelts stretch and deteriorate as they get older. They must therefore be periodically inspected.

2   The number of belts used on a particular vehicle depends on the accessories installed. One belt transmits power from the crankshaft to the water pump and alternator. If equipped, the power steering pump and air conditioning compressor are each driven by a separate belt.

3   With the engine off, open the hood and locate the drivebelts at the left end of the engine. With a flashlight, check each belt for separation of the adhesive rubber on both sides of the core, core separation from the belt side and a severed core. On V-ribbed belts, also check for separation of the ribs from the adhesive rubber, cracking or separation of the ribs, and torn or worn ribs or cracks in the inner ridges of the ribs. On all belts, also check for fraying and glazing, which gives the belt a shiny appearance. Both sides of the belt should be inspected, which means you will have to twist the belt to check the underside **(see illustration)**. Use your fingers to feel the belt where you can't see it. If any of the above conditions are evident, replace the belt.

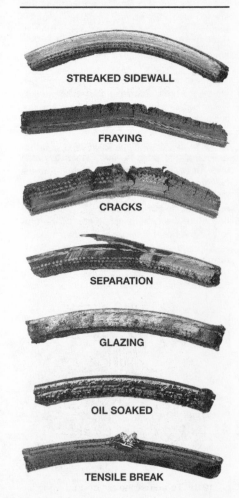

STREAKED SIDEWALL

FRAYING

CRACKS

SEPARATION

GLAZING

OIL SOAKED

TENSILE BREAK

12.3 Here are some of the more common problems associated with drivebelts (check the belts very carefully to prevent an untimely breakdown)

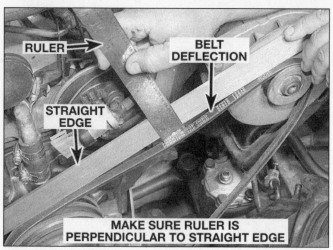

12.4 Measuring drivebelt deflection with a straightedge and ruler

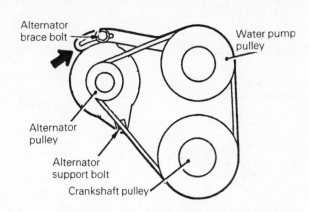

12.5a Loosen the adjustment bolt (arrow) and move the alternator in-or-out to adjust the drivebelt tension (1.8L models)

1

Adjustment

4   To check the tension of the drivebelts, push firmly on the belt with your thumb at a distance halfway between the pulleys and note how far the belt can be pushed (deflected). Measure this deflection with a ruler **(see illustration)**. The belt should deflect 1/4-inch if the distance from pulley

1.8L SOHC engine

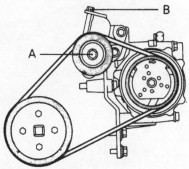

2.0L DOHC engine

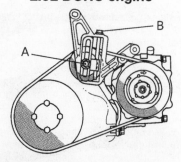

12.6a To adjust the air-conditioning compressor belt, loosen the lock bolt (1.8L models) or nut (2.0L models) at the center of the tension pulley (A), turn the adjust bolt (B) to tighten or loosen the belt, then re-tighten the lock bolt or nut

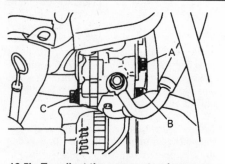

12.5b To adjust the power steering pump drivebelt tension, loosen bolts A, B and C, then move the pump in or out and tighten the bolts (all models equipped with power steering)

center to pulley center is between 7 and 11 inches; the belt should deflect 1/2-inch if the distance from pulley center to pulley center is between 12 and 16 inches.

5   To adjust the alternator on 1.8L (SOHC) engines and the power-steering pump on all engines, loosen the bolts holding the component to the bracket and carefully pry the component away from the engine (to tighten the belt) or toward the engine (to loosen the belt); then tighten the bolts **(see illustrations)**.

6   To adjust the alternator on 2.0L (DOHC) engines or the A/C compressor belt on all engines, loosen the lock bolt, then turn the adjust bolt until the tension is correct **(see illustrations)**. When the tension is correct, tighten the lock bolt.

Replacement

7   To replace a belt, follow the above procedures for drivebelt adjustment to loosen

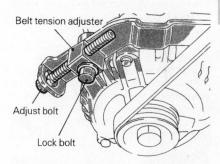

12.6b To adjust the alternator belt on a 2.0L model, loosen the lock bolt, turn the adjust bolt until the tension is correct, then tighten the lock bolt

the belt, but, when it's sufficiently loose, slip the belt off the crankshaft pulley and remove it. Since some belts may be installed outside of the belt you're trying to remove, you may have to remove other belts before you can get to the belt you're removing. Because of this and because belts tend to wear out more or less together, it is a good idea to replace all belts at the same time. Mark each belt and its appropriate pulley groove so the replacement belts can be installed in their proper positions.

8   Take the old belts to the parts store in order to make a direct comparison for length, width and design.

9   After replacing a V-ribbed drivebelt, make sure that it fits properly in the pulley or ribbed grooves in the pulleys **(see illustration)**. It is essential that the belt be properly centered.

 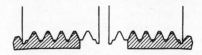

CORRECT   WRONG   WRONG

12.9 When installing a V-ribbed belt, make sure it is centered - it must not overlap either edge of the pulley

10   Adjust the belt(s) in accordance with the procedure outlined above.

13   Underhood hose check and replacement (every 6000 miles or 6 months)

Warning: *Replacement of air conditioning hoses must be left to a dealer service department or air conditioning shop that has the equipment to depressurize the system safely. Never remove air conditioning components or hoses until the system has been depressurized.*

General

1   High temperatures in the engine compartment can cause the deterioration of the rubber and plastic hoses used for engine, accessory and emission systems operation. Periodic inspection should be made for cracks, loose clamps, material hardening and leaks.

2   Information specific to the cooling system hoses can be found in Section 14.

3   Some, but not all, hoses are secured to the fittings with clamps. Where clamps are used, check to be sure they haven't lost their tension, allowing the hose to leak. If clamps aren't used, make sure the hose has not expanded and/or hardened where it slips over the fitting, allowing it to leak.

Vacuum hoses

4   It's quite common for vacuum hoses, especially those in the emissions system, to be color coded or identified by colored stripes molded into them. Various systems require hoses with different wall thicknesses, collapse resistance and temperature resistance. When replacing hoses, be sure the new ones are made of the same material.

5   Often the only effective way to check a hose is to remove it completely from the vehicle. If more than one hose is removed, be sure to label the hoses and fittings to ensure correct installation.

6   When checking vacuum hoses, be sure to include any plastic T-fittings in the check. Inspect the fittings for cracks and the hose where it fits over the fitting for distortion, which could cause leakage.

7   A small piece of vacuum hose (1/4-inch inside diameter) can be used as a stethoscope to detect vacuum leaks. Hold one end of the hose to your ear and probe around vacuum hoses and fittings, listening for the "hissing" sound characteristic of a vacuum leak. **Warning:** *When probing with the vacuum hose stethoscope, be very careful not to come into contact with moving engine components such as the drivebelts, cooling fan, etc.*

Fuel hose

Warning: *Gasoline is extremely flammable, so take extra precautions when you work on any part of the fuel system. Don't smoke or allow open flames or bare light bulbs near the*

Check for a chafed area that could fail prematurely.

Check for a soft area indicating the hose has deteriorated inside.

Overtightening the clamp on a hardened hose will damage the hose and cause a leak.

Check each hose for swelling and oil-soaked ends. Cracks and breaks can be located by squeezing the hose.

14.4 Hoses, like drivebelts, have a habit of failing at the worst possible time - to prevent the inconvenience of a blown radiator or heater hose, inspect them carefully, as shown here

---

work area, and don't work in a garage where a natural gas-type appliance (such as a water heater or a clothes dryer) with a pilot light is present. Since gasoline is carcinogenic, wear latex gloves when there's a possibility of being exposed to fuel, and, if you spill any fuel on your skin, rinse it off immediately with soap and water. Mop up any spills immediately and do not store fuel-soaked rags where they could ignite. The fuel system is under constant pressure, so, if any fuel lines are to be disconnected, the fuel pressure in the system must be relieved first (see Chapter 4 for more information). When you perform any kind of work on the fuel system, wear safety glasses and have a Class B type fire extinguisher on hand.

8   Check all rubber fuel lines for deterioration and chafing. Check especially for cracks in areas where the hose bends and just before fittings, such as where a hose

---

attaches to the fuel filter.

9   When replacing a hose, use only hose that is specifically designed for your fuel-injection system.

Metal lines

10   Sections of metal line are often used for fuel line between the fuel pump and fuel rail. Check carefully to be sure the line has not been bent or crimped and that cracks have not started in the line.

11   If a section of metal fuel line must be replaced, only seamless steel tubing should be used, since copper and aluminum tubing don't have the strength necessary to withstand normal engine vibration.

12   Check the metal brake lines where they enter the master cylinder and brake proportioning unit (if used) for cracks in the lines or loose fittings. Any sign of brake fluid leakage calls for an immediate thorough inspection of the brake system.

14   Cooling system check (every 6000 miles or 6 months)

Refer to illustration 14.4

1   Many major engine failures can be attributed to a faulty cooling system. If the vehicle is equipped with an automatic transaxle, the cooling system also cools the transaxle fluid and thus plays an important role in prolonging transaxle life.

2   The cooling system should be checked with the engine cold. Do this before the vehicle is driven for the day or after the engine has been shut off for at least three hours.

3   Remove the radiator cap by turning it to the left until it reaches a stop. If you hear a hissing sound (indicating there is still pressure in the system), wait until it stops. Now press down on the cap with the palm of your hand and continue turning to the left until the cap can be removed. Thoroughly clean the cap, inside and out, with clean water. Also clean the filler neck on the radiator. All traces of corrosion should be removed. The coolant inside the radiator should be relatively transparent. If it's rust colored, the system should be drained and refilled (see Section 27). If the coolant level isn't up to the top, add additional antifreeze/coolant mixture (see Section 4).

4   Carefully check the large upper and lower radiator hoses along with the smaller diameter heater hoses which run from the engine to the firewall. Inspect each hose along its entire length, replacing any hose which is cracked, swollen or shows signs of deterioration. Cracks may become more apparent if the hose is squeezed **(see illustration)**. Regardless of condition, it's a good idea to replace hoses with new ones every two years.

5   Make sure that all hose connections are tight. A leak in the cooling system will usually show up as white or rust colored deposits on the areas adjoining the leak. If wire-type

clamps are used at the ends of the hoses, it may be a good idea to replace them with more secure screw-type clamps.

6   Use compressed air or a soft brush to remove bugs, leaves, etc. from the front of the radiator or air conditioning condenser. Be careful not to damage the delicate cooling fins or cut yourself on them.

7   Every other inspection, or at the first indication of cooling system problems, have the cap and system pressure tested. If you don't have a pressure tester, most gas stations and repair shops will do this for a minimal charge.

15   Tire rotation (every 6000 miles or 6 months)

Refer to illustration 15.2

1   The tires should be rotated at the specified intervals and whenever uneven wear is noticed. Since the vehicle will be raised and the tires removed anyway, check the brakes (see Section 16) at this time.

2   Radial tires must be rotated in a specific pattern **(see illustration)**.

3   Refer to the information in *Jacking and towing* at the front of this manual for the proper procedures to follow when raising the vehicle and changing a tire. If the brakes are to be checked, do not apply the parking brake as stated. Make sure the tires are blocked to prevent the vehicle from rolling.

4   Preferably, the entire vehicle should be raised at the same time. This can be done on a hoist or by jacking up each corner and then lowering the vehicle onto jackstands placed under the frame rails. Always use four jackstands and make sure the vehicle is firmly supported.

5   After rotation, check and adjust the tire pressures as necessary and be sure to check the lug nut tightness.

6   For further information on the wheels and tires, refer to Chapter 10.

16   Brake check (every 15,000 miles or 12 months)

Warning: *Dust produced by lining wear and deposited on brake components may contain asbestos, which is hazardous to your health. DO NOT blow it out with compressed air and DO NOT inhale it! DO NOT use gasoline or solvents to remove the dust. Brake system cleaner should be used to flush the dust into a drain pan. After the brake components are wiped with a damp rag, dispose of the contaminated rag(s) and brake cleaner in a covered and labeled container. Try to use non-asbestos replacement parts whenever possible.*

Note: *For detailed photographs of the brake system, refer to Chapter 9.*

1   In addition to the specified intervals, the brakes should be inspected every time the

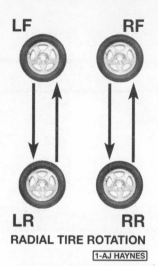

RADIAL TIRE ROTATION

1-AJ HAYNES

15.2   The recommended tire rotation pattern for these vehicles

wheels are removed or whenever a defect is suspected. Any of the following symptoms could indicate a potential brake system defect: The vehicle pulls to one side when the brake pedal is depressed; the brakes make squealing or dragging noises when applied; brake travel is excessive; the pedal pulsates; brake fluid leaks, usually onto the inside of the tire or wheel.

2   These models are equipped with disc brakes on all four wheels. The front disc brake pads have built-in wear indicators which should make a high-pitched squealing or scraping noise when they are worn to the replacement point. When you hear this noise, replace the pads immediately or expensive damage to the discs can result.

3   Loosen the wheel lug nuts.

4   Raise the vehicle and place it securely on jackstands.

5   Remove the wheels (see *Jacking and towing* at the front of this book, or your owner's manual, if necessary).

Disc brake pad/caliper check

Refer to illustration 16.6

6   There are two pads - an outer and an inner - in each caliper. The pads are visible through an inspection hole at the top of each caliper **(see illustration)**.

7   Check the pad thickness by looking at each end of the caliper and through the inspection hole in the caliper body. If the lining material is less than the thickness listed in this Chapter's Specifications, replace the pads. **Note:** *Keep in mind that the lining material is riveted or bonded to a metal backing plate and the metal portion is not included in this measurement.*

8   If it is difficult to determine the exact thickness of the remaining pad material by the above method, or if you are at all concerned about the condition of the pads, remove the caliper(s), then remove the pads from the calipers for further inspection (refer

16.6 You will find an inspection hole like this in each caliper (arrow) - placing a ruler across the hole should enable you to determine the thickness of remaining pad material for both inner and outer pads

to Chapter 9).

9   Once the pads are removed from the calipers, clean them with brake cleaner and re-measure them with a small steel pocket ruler or a vernier caliper.

10   Measure the disc thickness with a micrometer to make sure that it still has service life remaining. If any disc is thinner than the specified minimum thickness, replace it (refer to Chapter 9). Even if the disc has service life remaining, check its condition. Look for scoring, gouging and burned spots. If these conditions exist, remove the disc and have it resurfaced (see Chapter 9).

11   Before installing the wheels, check all brake lines and hoses for damage, wear, deformation, cracks, corrosion, leakage, bends and twists, particularly in the vicinity of the rubber hoses at the calipers. Check the clamps for tightness and the connections for leakage. Make sure that all hoses and lines are clear of sharp edges, moving parts and the exhaust system. If any of the above conditions are noted, repair, reroute or replace the lines and/or fittings as necessary (see Chapter 9).

Brake booster check

12   Sit in the driver's seat and perform the following sequence of tests.

13   With the engine stopped, depress the brake pedal several times - the travel distance should not change.

14   With the brake fully depressed, start the engine - the pedal should move down a little when the engine starts.

15   Depress the brake pedal, stop the engine and hold the pedal in for about 30 seconds - the pedal should neither sink nor rise.

16   Restart the engine, run it for about a minute and turn it off. Then firmly depress the brake several times - the pedal travel should decrease with each application.

17   If your brakes do not operate as described above when the preceding tests are performed, the brake booster is either in

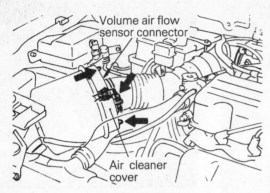

17.2 On non-turbo models, detach the volume air flow sensor connector and air duct, then unfasten the clips and lift off the air cleaner cover - be very careful not to damage the volume air flow sensor attached to the inside of the cover. The air filter is inside the air cleaner housing

17.3 On turbo models, detach the clips . . .

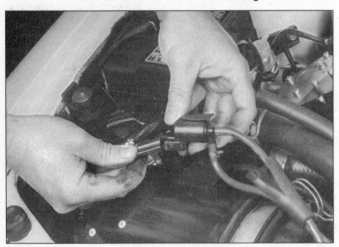

17.4 . . . unplug the connectors . . .

17.5 . . . use a socket and extension to remove the air cleaner housing bolts and nut . . .

need of repair or has failed. Refer to Chapter 9 for the removal procedure.

Parking brake check

18 Slowly pull up on the parking brake and count the number of clicks you hear until the handle is up as far as it will go. The adjustment is correct if you hear the number of clicks listed in this Chapter's Specifications. If you hear more or fewer clicks, it's time to adjust the parking brake (refer to Chapter 9).

19 An alternative method of checking the parking brake is to park the vehicle on a steep hill with the parking brake set and the transmission in Neutral. If the parking brake cannot prevent the vehicle from rolling, it is in need of adjustment (see Chapter 9).

---

17 Air filter replacement (every 15,000 miles or 12 months)

Refer to illustrations 17.2, 17.3, 17.4, 17.5 and 17.6

1   The air filter is located inside a housing at the right (passenger's) side of the engine compartment.

Non-turbo models

2   Unplug the volume air flow sensor electrical connector, disconnect the air duct, release the spring clips, then remove the cover (taking care with the volume air flow sensor inside) and lift the filter element out **(see illustration)**.

Turbo models

3   Detach the spring clips **(see illustration)**.

4   Unplug the vacuum and electrical connectors **(see illustration)**.

5   Remove the two air cleaner housing bolts and one nut **(see illustration)**.

6   Detach the cover (taking care with the volume air flow sensor inside), move it to one side, then push the radiator hose out of the way and remove the air filter element **(see illustration)**.

All models

7   Inspect the outer surface of the filter element. If it is dirty, replace it. If it is only moderately dusty, it can be reused by blowing it clean from the back to the front surface with

compressed air. Because it is a pleated paper type filter, it cannot be washed or oiled. If it cannot be cleaned satisfactorily with compressed air, discard and replace it.

8   Installation is the reverse of removal.

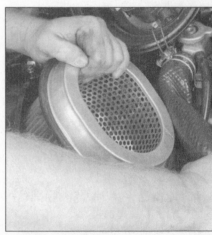

17.6 . . . then hold the radiator hose out of the way and lift the filter out of the housing

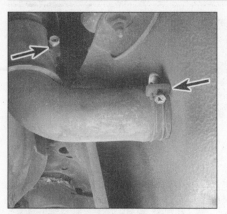

18.5 Check the condition of fuel filler hose and make sure the clamps (arrows) are tight

19.1 Remove the fill plug (arrow) from the transaxle and use your finger to make sure the lubricant level is even with the bottom of the plug hole

20.1 Remove the transfer case fill plug (arrow) and make sure the lubricant level is even with the bottom of the plug hole

18 Fuel system check (every 15,000 miles or 12 months)

Refer to illustration 18.5
Warning: *Gasoline is extremely flammable, so take extra precautions when you work on any part of the fuel system. Don't smoke or allow open flames or bare light bulbs near the work area, and don't work in a garage where a natural gas-type appliance (such as a water heater or a clothes dryer) with a pilot light is present. Since gasoline is carcinogenic, wear latex gloves when there's a possibility of being exposed to fuel, and, if you spill any fuel on your skin, rinse it off immediately with soap and water. Mop up any spills immediately and do not store fuel-soaked rags where they could ignite. The fuel system is under constant pressure, so, if any fuel lines are to be disconnected, the fuel pressure in the system must be relieved first (see Chapter 4 for more information). When you perform any kind of work on the fuel system, wear safety glasses and have a Class B type fire extinguisher on hand.*

1   If you smell gasoline while driving or after the vehicle has been sitting in the sun, inspect the fuel system immediately.

21.1 Rear differential fill plug location (arrow) - lubricant level must be even with the bottom of the plug hole

2   Remove the gas filler cap and inspect it for damage and corrosion. The gasket should have an unbroken sealing imprint. If the gasket is damaged or corroded, remove it and install a new one.

3   Inspect the fuel feed and return lines for cracks. Make sure that the threaded flare-nut-type connectors which secure the metal fuel lines to the fuel injection system and the banjo bolts which secure the banjo fittings to the in-line fuel filter are tight.

4   Since some components of the fuel system - the fuel tank and part of the fuel feed and return lines, for example - are underneath the vehicle, they can be inspected more easily with the vehicle raised on a hoist. If that's not possible, raise the vehicle and support it securely on jackstands.

5   With the vehicle raised and safely supported, inspect the fuel tank and filler neck for punctures, cracks and other damage **(see illustration)**. The connection between the filler neck and the tank is particularly critical. Sometimes, a rubber filler neck will leak because of loose clamps or deteriorated rubber. These are problems a home mechanic can usually rectify. **Warning:** *Do not, under any circumstances, try to repair a fuel tank (except rubber components). A welding torch or any open flame can easily cause fuel vapors inside the tank to explode.*

6   Carefully check all rubber hoses and metal lines leading away from the fuel tank. Check for loose connections, deteriorated hoses, crimped lines and other damage. Carefully inspect the lines from the tank to the fuel injection system. Repair or replace damaged sections as necessary (see Chapter 4).

19 Manual transaxle lubricant level check (every 15,000 miles or 12 months)

Refer to illustration 19.1
1   The manual transaxle does not have a dipstick. To check the fluid level, raise the

vehicle and support it securely on jackstands. On the lower front side of the transaxle housing, you will see a threaded plug **(see illustration)**. Unscrew and remove it. If the lubricant level is correct, it should be up to the lower edge of the hole.

2   If the transaxle needs more lubricant (if the level is not up to the hole), use a syringe or pump to add more of the specified lubricant (see this Chapter's Specifications). Stop filling the transaxle when the lubricant begins to run out the hole.

3   Install the plug and tighten it securely. Drive the vehicle a short distance, then check for leaks.

20 Transfer case lubricant level check (4WD models only) (every 15,000 miles or 12 months)

Refer to illustration 20.1
1   Raise the vehicle and support it securely on jackstands. On the side of the transfer case housing, you will see a plug **(see illustration)**. Unscrew and remove it. If the lubricant level is correct, it should be up to the lower edge of the hole.

2   If the transfer case needs more lubricant (if the level is not up to the hole), use a syringe or pump to add more. Stop filling the transaxle when the lubricant begins to run out the hole.

3   Install the plug and tighten it securely. Drive the vehicle a short distance, then check for leaks.

21 Rear differential lubricant level check (4WD models only) (every 15,000 miles or 12 months)

Refer to illustration 21.1
1   To check the fluid level, raise the vehicle and support it securely on jackstands. On the rear differential cover, you will see a plug **(see illustration)**. Remove it. If the lubricant level is correct, it should be up to the lower edge of the hole.

23.2 Flex the driveaxle boots by hand to check for cracks and/or leaking grease

24.3 Secure the filter with a backup wrench on the filter hex that's directly beneath the upper hose fitting, then unscrew the banjo bolt (arrow) - use a flare-nut wrench to disconnect the fuel line fitting at the bottom of the filter

2   If the differential needs more lubricant (if the level is not up to the hole), use a syringe or a gear oil pump to add more. Stop filling the differential housing when the lubricant begins to run out the hole.

3   Install the plug and tighten it securely. Drive the vehicle a short distance, then check for leaks.

22   Steering and suspension check (every 15,000 miles or 12 months)

Note: *For detailed illustrations of the steering and suspension components, refer to Chapter 10.*

With the wheels on the ground

1   With the vehicle stopped and the front wheels pointed straight ahead, rock the steering wheel gently back and forth. If freeplay is excessive, a front wheel bearing, intermediate shaft U-joint, control arm balljoint or tie-rod end is worn or the steering gear is out of adjustment or broken. Refer to Chapter 10 for the appropriate repair procedure.

2   Other symptoms, such as excessive vehicle body movement over rough roads, swaying (leaning) around corners and binding as the steering wheel is turned, may indicate faulty steering and/or suspension components.

3   Check the shock absorbers by pushing down and releasing the vehicle several times at each corner. If the vehicle does not come back to a level position within one or two bounces, the shocks/struts are worn and must be replaced. When bouncing the vehicle up and down, listen for squeaks and noises from the suspension components. Additional information on suspension components can be found in Chapter 10.

Under the vehicle

4   Raise the vehicle with a floor jack and support it securely on jackstands. See *Jack-*

ing and towing at the front of this book for the proper jacking points.

5   Check the tires for irregular wear patterns and proper inflation. See Section 5 in this Chapter for information regarding tire wear and Chapter 10 for the wheel bearing replacement procedures.

6   Inspect the universal joint between the steering shaft and the steering gear housing. Check the rack-and-pinion housing for fluid leakage or oozing. Make sure the dust seals and boots are not damaged and that the boot clamps are not loose. Check the steering linkage for looseness or damage. Check the tie-rod ends for excessive play. Look for loose bolts, broken or disconnected parts and deteriorated rubber bushings on all suspension and steering components. While an assistant turns the steering wheel from side to side, check the steering components for free movement, chafing and binding. If the steering components do not seem to be reacting with the movement of the steering wheel, try to determine where the slack is located.

7   Check each front wheel's balljoint for wear by grasping the wheel securely and moving it in-and-out to ensure there is no play. If any balljoint does have play, replace it. See Chapter 10 for the front balljoint replacement procedure.

8   Inspect the balljoint boots for damage and leaking grease. Replace the balljoints with new ones if they are damaged (see Chapter 10).

23   Driveaxle boot check (every 15,000 miles or 12 months)

Refer to illustration 23.2

1   The driveaxle boots are very important because they prevent dirt, water and foreign material from entering and damaging the constant velocity (CV) joints. Oil and grease can cause the boot material to deteriorate prematurely, so it's a good idea to wash the

boots with soap and water.

2   Inspect the boots for tears and cracks as well as loose clamps **(see illustration)**. If there is any evidence of cracks or leaking lubricant, they must be replaced as described in Chapter 8.

24   Fuel filter replacement (every 30,000 miles or 24 months)

Refer to illustration 24.3

Warning: *Gasoline is extremely flammable, so take extra precautions when you work on any part of the fuel system. Don't smoke or allow open flames or bare light bulbs near the work area, and don't work in a garage where a natural gas-type appliance (such as a water heater or a clothes dryer) with a pilot light is present. Since gasoline is carcinogenic, wear latex gloves when there's a possibility of being exposed to fuel, and, if you spill any fuel on your skin, rinse it off immediately with soap and water. Mop up any spills immediately and do not store fuel-soaked rags where they could ignite. The fuel system is under constant pressure, so, if any fuel lines are to be disconnected, the fuel pressure in the system must be relieved first (see Chapter 4 for more information). When you perform any kind of work on the fuel system, wear safety glasses and have a Class B type fire extinguisher on hand.*

1   Relieve the fuel system pressure (see Chapter 4). The fuel filter is located in the pressure line running from the fuel tank to the fuel rail in the engine compartment. On most models, it is located on the engine compartment firewall, toward the passenger's side

2   If necessary for access to the lower fuel filter fitting, raise the vehicle and support it securely on jackstands.

3   Using a back-up wrench to steady the filter, unscrew the banjo bolt at the top fuel fitting, removing the bolt and the two copper sealing washers, which are often called "crush" washers **(see illustration)**.

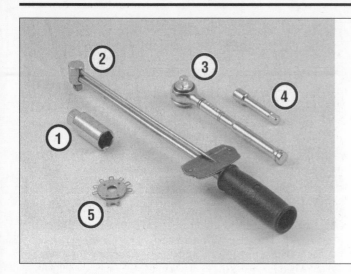

25.1 Tools required for changing spark plugs

1 **Spark plug socket** - *This will have special padding inside to protect the spark plug's porcelain insulator*
2 **Torque wrench** - *Although not mandatory, using this tool is the best way to ensure the plugs are tightened properly*
3 **Ratchet** - *Standard hand tool to fit the spark plug socket*
4 **Extension** - *A longer one is usually necessary on 2.0L (DOHC) models, since the spark plugs are set deeply into the cylinder head*
5 **Spark plug gap gauge** - *This gauge for checking the gap comes in a variety of styles. Make sure the gap for your engine is included*

4 Remove the two bolts securing the filter bracket to the firewall.

5 Again securing the filter with a back-up wrench, use a flare-nut wrench to unscrew the flare-nut fitting at the bottom of the filter.

6 Remove the clamp bolt and detach the filter from the bracket. Install the new filter in the bracket, making sure it faces the same way as the old filter.

7 Thread the lower flare-nut fitting into the filter by hand. **Note:** *This is done first to allow you to move the filter, as necessary, to align the threads when screwing in the flare-nut fitting; this is often more difficult with the filter bracket attached to the vehicle.*

8 Steadying the filter with a back-up wrench, tighten the lower flare-nut fitting securely.

9 Install and tighten the two bolts that secure the filter bracket to the vehicle.

10 Install the upper banjo bolt (using a new sealing washer on each side of the hose fitting) and, using a back-up wrench, tighten the bolt securely.

11 Run the engine and check for fuel leaks.

25 Spark plug check and replacement (every 30,000 miles or 24 months)

Refer to illustrations 25.1, 25.4a, 25.4b, 25.6a, 25.6b, 25.8a, 25.8b, 25.10a and 25.10b

1 Spark plug replacement requires a spark plug socket which fits onto a ratchet wrench. This socket is lined with a rubber grommet to protect the porcelain insulator of the spark plug and to hold the plug while you insert it into the spark plug hole. You will also need a wire-type feeler gauge to check and adjust the spark plug gap and a torque wrench to tighten the new plugs to the specified torque **(see illustration)**.

2 If you are replacing the plugs, purchase the new plugs, adjust them to the proper gap and then replace each plug one at a time. **Note:** *When buying new spark plugs, it's essential that you obtain the correct plugs for your specific vehicle. This information can be found in the Specifications Section at the* beginning of this Chapter, on the Vehicle Emissions Control Information (VECI) label located on the underside of the hood or in the owner's manual. If these sources specify different plugs, purchase the spark plug type specified on the VECI label because that information is provided specifically for your engine.

3 Inspect each of the new plugs for defects. If there are any signs of cracks in the porcelain insulator of a plug, don't use it.

4 Check the electrode gaps of the new plugs. Check the gap by inserting the wire gauge of the proper thickness between the electrodes at the tip of the plug **(see illustration)**. The gap between the electrodes should be identical to that listed in this Chapter's Specifications or on the VECI label. If the gap is incorrect, use the notched adjuster on the feeler gauge body to bend the curved side electrode slightly **(see illustration)**.

5 If the side electrode is not exactly over the center electrode, use the notched adjuster to align them. **Caution:** *If the gap of a new plug must be adjusted, bend only the base of the side electrode – do not touch the tip.*

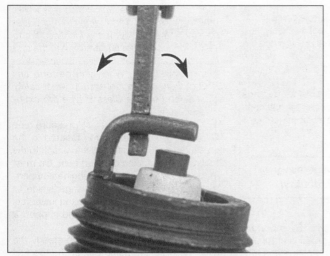

25.4b To change the gap, bend the side electrode only, as indicated by the arrows, and be very careful not to crack or chip the porcelain insulator surrounding the center electrode

25.4a Spark plug manufacturers recommend using a wire-type gauge when checking the gap - if the wire does not slide between the electrodes with a slight drag, adjustment is required

25.6a On 2.0L (DOHC) engines, remove the bolts, then liftoff the cover

25.6b When removing the spark plug wires, pull only on the boot and twist it back-and-forth

25.8a Use a socket wrench with a long extension to unscrew the spark plugs on 2.0L (DOHC) engines

25.8b On 2.0L (DOHC) engines, be sure to use a spark plug socket with a rubber insert to hold the plug as it is withdrawn from the engine

Removal

6   On DOHC models, remove the spark plug cover (see illustration). To prevent the possibility of mixing up spark plug wires, work on one spark plug at a time. Remove the wire and boot from one spark plug. Grasp the boot - not the cable - as shown, give it a half twist and pull straight up (see illustration).

7   If compressed air is available, blow any dirt or foreign material away from the spark plug area before proceeding (a common bicycle pump will also work).

8   Remove the spark plug (see illustrations).

9   Whether you are replacing the plugs at this time or intend to re-use the old plugs, compare each old spark plug with those shown in the color photos on the inside back cover of this manual to determine the overall running condition of the engine.

Installation

10   Prior to installation, apply a coat of anti-seize compound to the spark plug threads (see illustration). It's often difficult to insert spark plugs into their holes without cross-threading them. To avoid this possibility, fit a short piece of 3/8-inch ID rubber hose over the end of the spark plug (see illustration).

25.10a Apply a coat of anti-seize compound to the spark plug threads

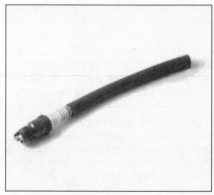

25.10b A length of 3/8-inch ID rubber hose will save time and prevent damaged threads when installing the spark plugs

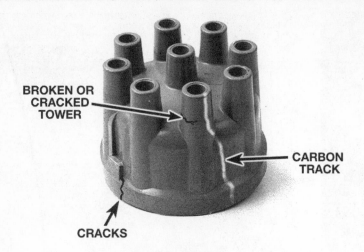

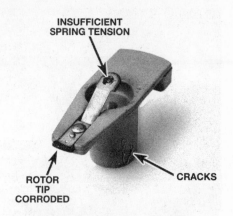

26.12 The ignition rotor should be checked for wear and corrosion, as indicated here (if in doubt about its condition, buy a new one)

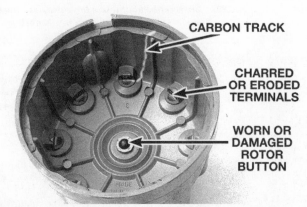

26.11 Shown here are some of the common defects to look for when inspecting the distributor cap (if in doubt about its condition, install a new one)

The flexible hose acts as a universal joint to help align the plug with the plug hole. Should the plug begin to cross-thread, the hose will slip on the spark plug, preventing thread damage. Tighten the plug to the torque listed in this Chapter's Specifications.

11 Attach the plug wire to the new spark plug, again using a twisting motion on the boot until it is firmly seated on the end of the spark plug.

12 Follow the above procedure for the remaining spark plugs, replacing them one at a time to prevent mixing up the spark plug wires.

26 Spark plug wire, distributor cap and rotor check and replacement (every 30,000 miles or 24 months)

Refer to illustrations 26.11 and 26.12
Note: *Only 1.8L (SOHC) engines require a distributor cap and rotor check. 2.0L (DOHC) engines are equipped with a direct ignition system that does not use a distributor.*

All engines

1 The spark plug wires should be checked whenever new spark plugs are installed.

2 Begin this procedure by making a visual check of the spark plug wires while the engine is running. In a darkened garage (make sure there is ventilation) start the engine and observe each plug wire. Be careful not to come into contact with any moving engine parts. If there is a break in the wire, you will see arcing or a small spark at the damaged area. If arcing is noticed, make a note to obtain new wires, then allow the engine to cool and check the distributor cap and rotor (if equipped).

3 The spark plug wires should be inspected one at a time to prevent mixing up the order, which is essential for proper engine operation. Each original plug wire should be numbered to help identify its location. If the number is illegible, a piece of tape can be marked with the correct number and wrapped around the plug wire.

4 Disconnect the plug wire from the spark plug. A removal tool can be used for this purpose or you can grasp the rubber boot, twist the boot half a turn and pull the boot free. Do not pull on the wire itself.

5 Check inside the boot for corrosion, which will look like a white crusty powder.

6 Push the wire and boot back onto the end of the spark plug. It should fit tightly onto the end of the plug. If it doesn't, remove the wire and use pliers to carefully crimp the metal connector inside the wire boot until the fit is snug.

7 Using a clean rag, wipe the entire length of the wire to remove built-up dirt and grease. Once the wire is clean, check for burns, cracks and other damage. Do not bend the wire sharply, because the conductor might break.

8 Disconnect the wire from the distributor or coil pack. Again, pull only on the rubber boot. Check for corrosion and a tight fit. Replace the wire in the distributor.

9 Inspect the remaining spark plug wires, making sure that each one is securely fastened at the distributor or coil pack and spark plug when the check is complete.

10 If new spark plug wires are required, purchase a set for your specific engine model. Pre-cut wire sets with the boots already installed are available. Remove and replace the wires one at a time to avoid mix-ups in the firing order.

1.8L (SOHC) engines only

11 Detach the distributor cap by removing the two cap retaining screws. Look inside it for cracks, carbon tracks and worn, burned or loose contacts **(see illustration)**.

12 Pull the rotor off the distributor shaft and examine it for cracks and carbon tracks **(see illustration)**. Replace the cap and rotor if any damage or defects are noted.

13 It is common practice to install a new cap and rotor whenever new spark plug wires are installed, but if you wish to continue using the old cap, check the resistance between the spark plug wires and the cap first. If the indicated resistance is more than the maximum value listed in this Chapter's Specifications, replace the cap and/or wires.

14 When installing a new cap, remove the wires from the old cap one at a time and attach them to the new cap in the exact same location – do not simultaneously remove all the wires from the old cap or firing order mix-ups may occur.

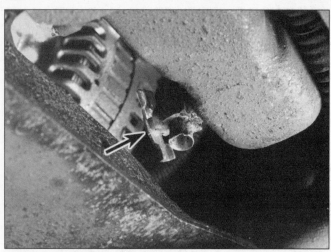

27.4 The drain fitting (arrow) is located at the lower corner of the radiator - turn it counterclockwise to loosen it

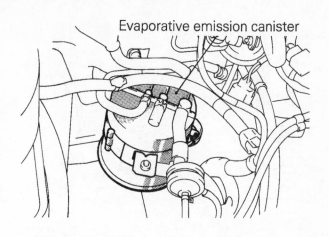

28.2 Check the evaporative emission (charcoal) canister for damage and the hose connections for cracks and damage

27   Cooling system servicing (draining, flushing and refilling) (every 30,000 miles or 24 months)

Warning: *Do not allow engine coolant (antifreeze) to come in contact with your skin or painted surfaces of the vehicle, since it will irritate your skin or damage the paint. Rinse off spills immediately with plenty of water. Antifreeze is highly toxic if ingested. Never leave antifreeze lying around in an open container or in puddles on the floor; children and pets are attracted by it's sweet smell and may drink it. Check with local authorities about disposing of used antifreeze. Many communities have collection centers which will see that antifreeze is disposed of safely.*

1   Periodically, the cooling system should be drained, flushed and refilled to replenish the antifreeze mixture and prevent formation of rust and corrosion, which can impair the performance of the cooling system and cause engine damage. When the cooling system is serviced, all hoses and the radiator cap should be checked and replaced if necessary.

Draining

Refer to illustration 27.4

2   Apply the parking brake and block the wheels. If the vehicle has just been driven, wait several hours to allow the engine to cool down before beginning this procedure.
3   Once the engine is completely cool, remove the radiator cap and inspect it, as described in Section 14.
4   Move a large container under the radiator drain to catch the coolant. Open the drain fitting (a pair of pliers may be required to turn it) **(see illustration)**.
5   While the coolant is draining, check the condition of the radiator hoses, heater hoses and clamps (refer to Section 14 if necessary).

6   Replace any damaged clamps or hoses (see Chapter 3).

Flushing

7   Once the system is completely drained, flush the radiator with fresh water from a garden hose until water runs clear at the drain. The flushing action of the water will remove sediments from the radiator but will not remove rust and scale from the engine and cooling tube surfaces.
8   These deposits can be removed by the chemical action of a cleaner. Follow the procedure outlined in the manufacturer's instructions. If the radiator is severely corroded, damaged or leaking, it should be removed (see Chapter 3) and taken to a radiator repair shop.
9   Remove the overflow hose from the coolant recovery reservoir. Drain the reservoir and flush it with clean water, then reconnect the hose.

Refilling

10   Close and tighten the radiator drain.
11   Place the heater temperature control in the maximum heat position.
12   Slowly add new coolant (a 50/50 mixture of water and antifreeze) to the radiator until it's full. Add coolant to the reservoir up to the lower mark.
13   Leave the radiator cap off and run the engine in a well-ventilated area until the thermostat opens (coolant will begin flowing through the radiator and the upper radiator hose will become hot).
14   Turn the engine off and let it cool. Add more coolant mixture to bring the level back up to the lip on the radiator filler neck.
15   Squeeze the upper radiator hose to expel air, then add more coolant mixture, if necessary. Replace the radiator cap.
16   Start the engine, allow it to reach normal operating temperature and check for leaks.

28   Evaporative emissions control system check (every 30,000 miles or 24 months)

Refer to illustration 28.2

1   The function of the evaporative emissions control system is to draw fuel vapors from the gas tank and fuel system, store them in a charcoal canister and then burn them during normal engine operation.
2   The most common symptom of a fault in the evaporative emissions system is a strong fuel odor in the engine compartment. If a fuel odor is detected, inspect the charcoal canister, located on the firewall on the right (passenger's) side of the engine compartment. Check the canister and all hoses for damage and deterioration **(see illustration)**.
3   The evaporative emissions control system is explained in more detail in Chapter 6.

29   Exhaust system check (every 30,000 miles or 24 months)

1   With the engine cold (at least three hours after the vehicle has been driven), check the complete exhaust system from its starting point at the engine to the end of the tailpipe. This should be done on a hoist where unrestricted access is available.
2   Check the pipes and connections for evidence of leaks, severe corrosion or damage. Make sure that all brackets and hangers are in good condition and tight.
3   At the same time, inspect the underside of the body for holes, corrosion, open seams, etc. which may allow exhaust gases to enter the passenger compartment. Seal all body openings with silicone or body putty.
4   Rattles and other noises can often be traced to the exhaust system, especially the mounts and hangers. Try to move the pipes,

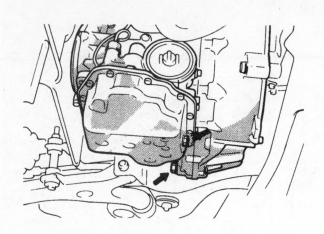

30.7 Remove both drain plugs to drain the automatic transmission/differential fluid

31.1 The manual transaxle drain plug (arrow) is located at the lower edge of the case

muffler and catalytic converter. If the components can come in contact with the body or suspension parts, secure the exhaust system with new mounts.
5   Check the running condition of the engine by inspecting inside the end of the tailpipe. The exhaust deposits here are an indication of engine state-of-tune. If the pipe is black and sooty or coated with white deposits, the engine is in need of a tune-up, including a thorough fuel system inspection.

30 Automatic transaxle fluid and filter change (every 30,000 miles or 24 months)

Refer to illustration 30.7
1   At the specified time intervals, the automatic transaxle fluid should be drained and replaced.
2   Before beginning work, purchase the specified transmission fluid (see *Recommended fluids and lubricants* at the front of this Chapter).

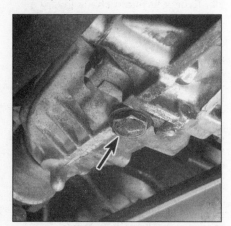

32.1 The transfer case drain plug (arrow) is located at the bottom of the case

3   Other tools necessary for this job include jackstands to support the vehicle in a raised position, a wrench, a drain pan capable of holding at least eight pints, newspapers and clean rags.
4   The fluid should be drained immediately after the vehicle has been driven. Hot fluid is more effective than cold fluid at removing built up sediment. **Warning:** *Fluid temperature can exceed 350-degrees F in a hot transaxle. Wear protective gloves and make sure the fluid cannot spill on you!*
5   After the vehicle has been driven to warm up the fluid, raise it and place it on jackstands for access to the transaxle and differential drain plugs.
6   Move the necessary equipment under the vehicle, being careful not to touch any of the hot exhaust components.
7   With the drain pan in place, remove the drain plugs and allow the fluid to drain **(see illustration)**. Once the fluid has drained, remove the bolts and lower the pan. **Warning:** *There is hot fluid in the pan that often splashes out, so position yourself out of the way!*
8   Remove the filter retaining bolt(s) and lower the filter from the transaxle. Be careful when lowering the filter as it contains residual fluid.
9   Place the new filter in position and install the bolt(s). Tighten the bolts to the torque listed in the Specifications Section at the beginning of this Chapter.
10   Carefully clean the gasket surfaces of the fluid pan, removing all traces of old gasket material. Noting the location, remove the magnet, wash the pan in clean solvent and dry it with compressed air. Be sure to clean and reinstall the magnets.
11   Install a new gasket, place the fluid pan in position and install the bolts in their original positions. Tighten the bolts to the torque listed in the Specifications Section at the beginning of this Chapter.
12   Reinstall the drain plugs and lower the vehicle.

13   With the engine off, add new fluid to the transaxle through the dipstick tube (see *Recommended fluids and lubricants* for the recommended fluid type and capacity). Use a funnel to prevent spills. It is best to add a little fluid at a time, continually checking the level with the dipstick (see Section 7). Allow the fluid time to drain into the pan.
14   Start the engine and shift the selector into all positions from P through L, then shift into P and apply the parking brake.
15   With the engine idling, check the fluid level. Add fluid up to the Cold level on the dipstick.

31 Manual transaxle lubricant change (every 30,000 miles or 24 months)

Refer to illustration 31.1
1   Remove the transaxle filler plug (see Section 19), then unscrew and remove the drain plug and drain the fluid **(see illustration)**.
2   Reinstall the drain plug and tighten it securely.
3   Add new fluid until it begins to run out of the filler hole (Section 19). See *Recommended lubricants and fluids* for the specified lubricant type.

32 Transfer case lubricant change (4WD models only) (every 30,000 miles or 24 months)

Refer to illustration 32.1
1   Remove the transfer case filler plug (see Section 20), then remove the drain plug and drain the fluid **(see illustration)**.
2   Reinstall the drain plug securely.
3   Add new fluid until it begins to run out of the filler hole (Section 20). See *Recommended lubricants and fluids* for the specified lubricant type.

33.1 You will need a thin-wall socket to remove the differential drain plug on 4WD models (arrow)

34.2a Pull the hose off the PCV valve . . .

34.2b . . . then unscrew the valve with a wrench

33 Rear differential lubricant change (4WD models only) (every 30,000 miles or 24 months)

Refer to illustration 33.1

1   Remove the differential filler plug (see Section 21), then unscrew and remove the drain plug and drain the fluid. **(see illustration).**

2   Reinstall the drain plug securely.

3   Add new fluid until it begins to run out of the filler hole (Section 21). See *Recommended lubricants and fluids* for the specified lubricant type.

34 Positive Crankcase Ventilation (PCV) valve and hose check and replacement (every 30,000 miles or 24 months)

Refer to illustrations 34.2a and 34.2b

1   The PCV valve and hose are located in the valve cover.

2   Disconnect the hose, unscrew the PCV valve from the cover, then reconnect the hose **(see illustrations)**.

3   With the engine idling at normal operating temperature, place your finger over the valve opening. If there's no vacuum at the valve, check for a plugged hose or valve. Replace any plugged or deteriorated hoses.

4   Turn off the engine and insert a small rod into the valve from the threaded side and make sure the plunger inside the valve moves. If the valve doesn't move, replace it with a new one.

5   When purchasing a replacement PCV valve, make sure it's for your particular vehicle and engine size. Compare the old valve with the new one to make sure they're the same.

Chapter 2 Part A Engines

Contents

2A

Specifications

General

Firing order	1-3-4-2
Cylinder numbers (drivebelt end-to-transaxle end)	1-2-3-4

Camshaft

Camshaft endplay (all engines)	0.004 to 0.008 inch

Lobe height
  1.8L SOHC engine (all years)
    Standard (intake and exhaust) ... 1.4138 inches
    Service limit (intake and exhaust) ... 1.3941 inches
  2.0L DOHC engine
    1990 through 1992
      Intake
        Standard ... 1.3974 inches
        Service limit ... 1.3777 inches
      Exhaust
        Standard ... 1.3858 inches
        Service limit ... 1.3661 inches

Lobe height (continued)
  2.0L DOHC engine
    1993 and later
      Intake
        Non-turbo and turbo with manual transmission
          Standard ... 1.3974 inches
          Service limit ... 1.3777 inches
        Turbo with automatic transmission
          Standard ... 1.3858 inches
          Service limit ... 1.3661 inches
      Exhaust
        Non-turbo and turbo with automatic transmission
          Standard ... 1.3858 inches
          Service limit ... 1.3661 inches
        Turbo with manual transmission
          Standard ... 1.3974 inches
          Service limit ... 1.3777 inches

Camshaft journal diameter (all years)
  1.8L SOHC engine ... 1.3360 to 1.3366 inches
  2.0L DOHC engine ... 1.0217 to 1.0224 inches
Camshaft bearing oil clearance ... 0.002 to 0.0035 inch

1.8L engine
0764H

Front

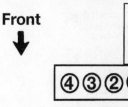
2.0L engine
0764H

Cylinder location and distributor rotation

The blackened terminal shown on the distributor cap indicates the number one spark plug wire position

Cylinder head
Warpage limit (all engines)
    Standard.. 0.0020 inch
    Service limit .... 0.008 inch

Intake and exhaust manifolds
Warpage limit (all engines)
    Standard.. 0.006 inch
    Service limit .... 0.012 inch

Rocker arm shaft assemblies (1.8L SOHC engine only)
Rocker arm shaft
    Diameter.. 0.7445 to 0.7440 inch
    Runout... Not available
Rocker arm
    Inside diameter
        Standard .... 0.7445 to 0.7452 inch
        Service limit .... Not available
    Rocker arm-to-shaft clearance
        Standard .... 0.0004 to 0.0016 inch
        Service limit .... 0.004 inch
Rocker arm shaft spring
    Free length
        Intake .... 2.098 inches
        Exhaust... 2.098 inches

Timing belt
Timing belt deflection .... Tension automatically adjusted
Balance shaft belt deflection 1/4-inch
Timing belt-to-cover clearance .... 0.40 inch minimum
Projection of 2.0L engine tensioner rod (on the bench) .... 0.047 inch
Projection of 2.0L engine tensioner rod (assembled)..................... 0.15 to 0.18 inch

Oil pump
Clearances
    1.8L SOHC engine
        Tip clearance
            Drive gear
                Standard .... 0.0024 to 0.0047 inch
                Service limit... 0.0079 inch
            Driven gear
                Standard .... 0.0016 to 0.0047 inch
                Service limit... 0.0071 inch
        Side clearance
            Drive gear
                Standard .... 0.0039 to 0.0063 inch
                Service limit... 0.0079 inch
            Driven gear
                Standard .... 0.0008 to 0.0020 inch
                Service limit... 0.0059 inch
    2.0L DOHC engine
        Tip clearance
            Drive gear
                Standard .... 0.0063 to 0.0083 inch
                Service limit... 0.0098 inch
            Driven gear
                Standard .... 0.0051 to 0.0071 inch
                Service limit... 0.0098 inch
        Side clearance
            Drive gear
                Standard .... 0.0031 to 0.0055 inch
                Service limit... 0.0098 inch
            Driven gear
                Standard .... 0.0024 to 0.0047 inch
                Service limit... 0.0098 inch

Pressure relief spring
    Free length
        1.8L SOHC engine .... 1.724 inches
        2.0L DOHC engine .... 1.835 inches
    Load (all engines) .... 13.4 lb. @ 1.579 inches

Torque specifications*   Ft-lbs (unless otherwise noted)

Both engines

Balance shaft belt tensioner bolt	11 to 16
Camshaft sprocket bolt	58 to 72
Crankshaft sprocket bolt	80 to 94
Flywheel or driveplate bolts	94 to 101
Intake manifold-to-engine nuts/bolts	
1.8L SOHC engine	11 to 14
2.0L DOHC engine	
8 mm bolts	11 to 14
10 mm nuts	22 to 30
Oil filter bracket bolts	11 to 16
Oil pan bolts/nuts	60 in-lbs
Oil pick-up tube and screen mounting bolts	15
Oil pressure switch	6 to 9
Oil pump cover bolts	29 to 36
Oil pump relief valve plug	11 to 13
Rear main oil seal retainer bolts	84 to 144 in-lbs
Timing belt front cover bolts	7 to 9
Water pump pulley bolts	6 to 7

1.8L SOHC Engine

Balance shaft sprocket nut	25 to 29
Camshaft bearing cap bolts	
Two front (small) bolts	48 to 60 in-lbs
Ten large bolts	14 to 20
Crankshaft pulley bolts	11 to 13
Cylinder head bolts	51 to 54
Front case bolts	11 to 13
Intake manifold stay bolt	13 to 18
Intake plenum-to-manifold bolts/nuts	11 to 14
Oil pump driven gear bolt	25 to 29
Oil pump sprocket nut	26 to 29
Timing belt cover bolts	9
Timing belt tensioner nut/bolt	16 to 22
Valve cover bolts	60 in-lbs

2.0L DOHC Engine

Balance shaft sprocket nut	31 to 35
Camshaft bearing cap bolts	14 to 15
Crankshaft pulley bolts	14 to 22
Cylinder head bolts	65 to 72
Exhaust pipe-to-exhaust manifold bolts/nuts	29 to 43

Refer to Part B for additional torque specifications

Front case bolts	14 to 16
Heat shield-to-exhaust manifold bolts	9 to 11
Oil pump driven gear bolt	25 to 29
Oil pump sprocket nut	36 to 43
Timing belt cover bolts	7 to 9
Timing belt tensioner mounting bolts	14 to 20
Timing belt tensioner pulley bolt/nut	31 to 40
Valve cover bolts	
Cover-to-cylinder head bolts	36 in-lbs
Center cover bolts	24 to 36 in-lbs

Refer to Part B for additional torque specifications

2A

1　General information

This Part of Chapter 2 is devoted to in-vehicle engine repair procedures. Information concerning engine removal and installation and engine block and cylinder head overhaul can be found in Part B of this Chapter.

The following repair procedures are based on the assumption that the engine is installed in the vehicle. If the engine has been removed from the vehicle and mounted on a stand, many of the steps outlined in this Part of Chapter 2 will not apply.

The Specifications included in this Part of Chapter 2 apply only to the procedures contained in this Part. Part B of Chapter 2 contains the Specifications necessary for cylinder head and engine block rebuilding.

There are two types of four-cylinder engines installed in the models covered in this book: The 1.8L Single Overhead Camshaft (SOHC) engine and the 2.0L Double Overhead Camshaft (DOHC) engine, which comes in *turbo* and *non-turbo* versions.

2　Repair operations possible with the engine in the vehicle

Many major repair operations can be accomplished without removing the engine from the vehicle.

Clean the engine compartment and the exterior of the engine with some type of degreaser before any work is done. It will make the job easier and help keep dirt out of the internal areas of the engine.

Depending on the components involved, it may be helpful to remove the hood to improve access to the engine as repairs are performed (refer to Chapter 11 if necessary). Cover the fenders to prevent damage to the paint. Special pads are available, but an old bedspread or blanket will also work.

If vacuum, exhaust, oil or coolant leaks develop, indicating a need for gasket or seal replacement, the repairs can generally be made with the engine in the vehicle. The intake and exhaust manifold gaskets, oil pan gasket, crankshaft oil seals and cylinder head gasket are all accessible with the engine in place.

Exterior engine components, such as the intake and exhaust manifolds, the oil pan, the oil pump, the water pump, the starter motor, the alternator, the distributor and the fuel system components can be removed for repair with the engine in place.

Since the camshaft(s) and cylinder head can be removed without pulling the engine, valve component servicing can also be accomplished with the engine in the vehicle. Replacement of the timing belt(s) and sprockets is also possible with the engine in the vehicle.

In extreme cases caused by a lack of necessary equipment, repair or replacement of piston rings, pistons, connecting rods and rod bearings is possible with the engine in the vehicle. However, this practice is not recommended because of the cleaning and preparation work that must be done to the components involved.

3　Top Dead Center (TDC) for number one piston - locating

Refer to illustrations 3.4, 3.6 and 3.7
Note: *The following procedure is based on the assumption that the spark plug wires and distributor are correctly installed. If you are trying to locate TDC to install the distributor correctly, piston position must be determined by feeling for compression at the number one spark plug hole, then aligning the ignition timing marks as described in Step 6.*

1　Top Dead Center (TDC) is the highest point in the cylinder that each piston reaches as it travels up-and-down when the crankshaft turns. Each piston reaches TDC on the compression stroke and again on the exhaust stroke, but TDC generally refers to piston position on the compression stroke.

2　Positioning the piston(s) at TDC is an essential part of many procedures such as rocker arm removal, camshaft and timing belt/sprocket removal and distributor or crankshaft/camshaft position sensor removal.

3　Before beginning this procedure, be sure to place the transmission in Neutral and apply the parking brake or block the rear wheels. Also, disable the ignition system by detaching the coil wire from the center terminal of the distributor cap and grounding it on the block with a jumper wire (non-DIS models). On models equipped with a Direct Ignition System (DIS), disconnect the electrical connector at the ignition coil pack (see Chapter 5). Remove the spark plugs (see Chapter 1).

4　In order to bring any piston to TDC, the crankshaft must be turned using one of the methods outlined below. When looking at the drivebelt end of the engine, normal crankshaft rotation is clockwise.

a) *The preferred method is to turn the crankshaft with a ratchet and an extension inserted into the drivebelt end of the crankshaft* **(see illustration)**.

b) *A remote starter switch, which may save some time, can also be used. These switches are available inexpensively from auto parts stores. Follow the instructions included with the switch. Once the piston is close to TDC, use a socket and ratchet as described in the previous paragraph.*

c) *If an assistant is available to turn the ignition switch to the Start position in short bursts, you can get the piston close to TDC without a remote starter switch. Make sure your assistant is out of the vehicle, away from the ignition switch, then use a socket and ratchet as described in Paragraph a) to complete the procedure.*

5　On 1.8L models, detach the cap from the distributor and set it aside (see Chapter 1 if necessary). On 2.0L models, remove the valve cover (see Section 4).

3.4　To rotate the crankshaft by hand, insert a 1/2-inch drive extension and breaker bar into this square hole in the crankshaft pulley bolt

3.6　Align the notch (arrow) on the crankshaft pulley with the "T" mark on the timing plate

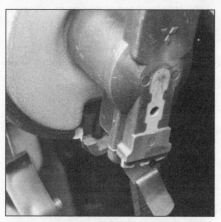

3.7 On 1.8L models, when the number one piston is at Top Dead Center (TDC) on the compression stroke, the distributor rotor should point straight down (Notice there is a paint mark on the cylinder head and distributor that is used to designate the position of the number one piston for purposes of correct reassembly)

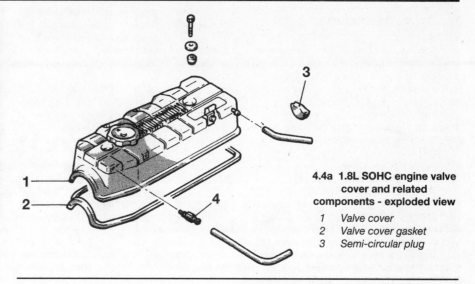

4.4a 1.8L SOHC engine valve cover and related components - exploded view

1   *Valve cover*
2   *Valve cover gasket*
3   *Semi-circular plug*

6   Turn the crankshaft (see Paragraph 3 above) until the notch in the crankshaft pulley is aligned with the T on the timing plate (located at the front of the engine) **(see illustration)**.

7   On 1.8L models, look at the distributor rotor - it should be pointing straight down **(see illustration)**. On 2.0L models, check the rocker arms for the number one cylinder - they should be loose, not applying any pressure to the valves.

8   If the rotor is 180-degrees off, or the rocker arms are not loose, the number one piston is at TDC on the exhaust stroke. Go to Step 9.

9   To get the piston to TDC on the compression stroke, turn the crankshaft one complete turn (360-degrees) clockwise. The rotor should now be pointing straight down or the rocker arms should be loose. When the rotor is pointing at the number one spark plug wire terminal in the distributor cap or the rocker arms are loose and the ignition timing marks are aligned, the number one piston is at TDC

on the compression stroke.

10   After the number one piston has been positioned at TDC on the compression stroke, TDC for any of the remaining pistons can be located by turning the crankshaft and following the firing order. On 1.8L models, with the distributor cap installed, use a felt-tip pen or chalk to make a mark on the distributor body directly beneath each of the terminals on the distributor cap. Then number the marks to correspond with the cylinder numbers. As you turn the crankshaft, the rotor will also turn. When it's pointing directly at one of the marks on the distributor, the piston for that particular cylinder is at TDC on the compression stroke. On 2.0L models, make a mark on the crankshaft pulley exactly 180-degrees opposite the notch. Rotate the crankshaft 180-degrees clockwise from the number-one-cylinder TDC position: this is the number-three-cylinder TDC position. Then rotate the crankshaft clockwise another 180-degrees, back to where the notch is aligned with the T mark on the pulley: this is the number-four-cylinder TDC position. Finally, rotate the crankshaft another 180-degrees clockwise: this is the number-two-cylinder TDC position.

4   Valve cover - removal and installation

Refer to illustrations 4.4a, 4.4b, 4.4c, 4.4d and 4.6

1   Disconnect the battery cable from the negative battery terminal. On 2.0L DOHC engines, remove the upper timing belt cover (see Section 8).

2   Detach the spark plug wires and cable brackets from the valve cover (see Chapter 1). On 2.0L DOHC engines, remove the center cover and disconnect the wires from the spark plugs (see Chapter 1). Use numbered pieces of tape to label the wires so they can be returned to their original locations on reassembly.

3   Clearly label and then disconnect any emission hoses and cables which connect to or cross over the valve cover.

4   Remove the valve cover bolts **(see illustrations)** and lift the cover off. If the cover sticks to the cylinder head, tap on it with a soft-face hammer or place a block of wood against the cover and tap on the wood with a hammer. **Caution:** *If you have to pry between the valve cover and the cylinder head, be*

2A

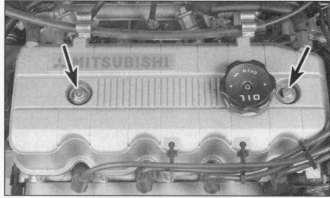

4.4b The 1.8L valve cover is held in place with two bolts through the center of the valve cover (arrows)

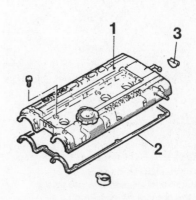

4.4c 2.0L DOHC engine valve cover and related components - exploded view

1   *Valve cover*
2   *Valve cover gasket*
3   *Semi-circular plug*

4.4d 14 bolts (arrows) secure the 2.0L engine valve cover to the cylinder head - the upper timing belt cover is shown installed in this illustration, but it must be removed before the valve cover will come off

4.6 Be sure to install a new semi-circular seal into the cylinder head. Apply a small amount of sealant to the bottom of the seal and, after it has been installed, to the top of the seal, at the seal-to-cylinder head joint

extremely careful not to gouge or nick the gasket surfaces of either part. A leak could develop after reassembly.

5   Thoroughly clean the valve cover and remove all traces of old gasket material. Gasket removal solvents are available from auto parts stores and may prove helpful. After cleaning the surfaces, degrease them with a rag soaked in lacquer thinner or acetone.

6   Install a new gasket on the cover, using RTV to hold it in place. Place the cover on the engine and install the cover bolts. **Note:** *Be sure to install a new semi-circular seal* **(see illustration)** *into the cylinder head. Apply a small amount of sealant to the bottom of the seal and, after it has been installed, to the top of the seal, at the seal-to-valve cover joints.*

7   Tighten the bolts to the torque listed in this Chapter's Specifications. The remaining steps are the reverse of removal. When finished, run the engine and check for oil leaks.

5   Rocker arm assembly - removal, inspection and installation

Removal

1.8L SOHC engine

Refer to illustrations 5.6, 5.7a and 5.7b

1   Position the number one piston at Top Dead Center (see Section 3).

2   Disconnect the negative cable from the battery.

3   Remove the valve cover (see Section 4).

4   Remove the distributor (see Chapter 5).

5   Remove the timing belt (see Section 8). **Note:** *If you're only removing the rocker arms and/or cylinder head and/or camshaft, you may be able to save time by not removing and installing the timing belt. Remove the upper timing belt cover (see Section 8), then try removing the camshaft sprocket center bolt and unfastening the camshaft sprocket from the camshaft. Next, suspend the camshaft sprocket out of the way - with the belt still attached - by a piece of rope. Be sure the rope keeps firm tension on the belt so the belt won't become disengaged from any of the sprockets.*

6   Remove the two small bolts at the left (driver's side) end of the engine, then loosen the ten larger bolts 1/4-turn at a time each until the spring pressure is relieved **(see illustration)**. Completely loosen the bolts, but do not remove them, since leaving them in place will prevent the assembly from falling apart when it is lifted off the engine.

7   Lift the rocker arms and shaft assembly from the cylinder head **(see illustration)**. Be

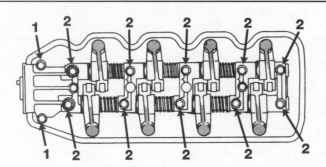

5.6 First remove the two small bolts (1), then loosen the large bolts (2), 1/4 turn at a time, working in a circular pattern from the outside bolts towards the center, until the spring pressure is relieved (1.8L SOHC engine)

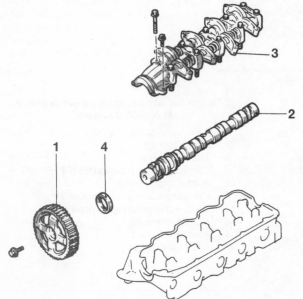

5.7a 1.8L SOHC engine camshaft and rocker arm assembly - exploded view

1   Camshaft sprocket
2   Camshaft
3   Rocker arm and shaft assembly
4   Camshaft front oil seal

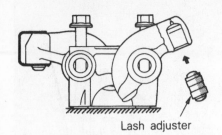

Lash adjuster

5.7b On 1.8L engines, the lash adjusters are inserted into the valve-stem ends of the rocker arms

sure not to let the lash adjusters fall out of the rocker arms. Wrap pieces of tape around the ends of the rocker arms to keep the adjusters in place **(see illustration)**. See Section 7 to inspect the lash adjusters.

2.0L DOHC engine

Refer to illustrations 5.9, 5.10, 5.11a, 5.11b and 5.14

8   Remove the camshafts (see Section 10).

9   Once the camshafts have been removed, the rocker arms can be lifted off **(see illustration)**. **Caution:** *Each rocker arm must be placed back in the same location it was removed from, so mark each rocker arm or place them in a container (such as an egg carton) so they won't get mixed up.* The lash adjusters can remain in the head at this time, unless they are being replaced (see Section 7).

Inspection

10   On 1.8L SOHC engines, disassemble the rocker arm shaft components **(see illustration)**. **Caution:** *Before disassembly, mark the rocker arm shafts, springs rocker arms and lash adjusters so all the parts are reassembled in the same locations they were removed from. To keep the rocker arms, springs and spacers in order, it's a good idea to remove them and put them onto two lengths of wire (such as unbent coat hangers) in the same order as they're removed, marking each wire (which simulates the rocker shaft) as to which end would be the front of the engine.*

5.9 On 2.0L engines, once the camshaft have been removed, the rocker arms can be lifted off. If necessary, the lash adjuster below the rocker arm can also be removed - be sure to keep the rocker arms and lash adjusters in order so they can be returned to their original locations!

2A

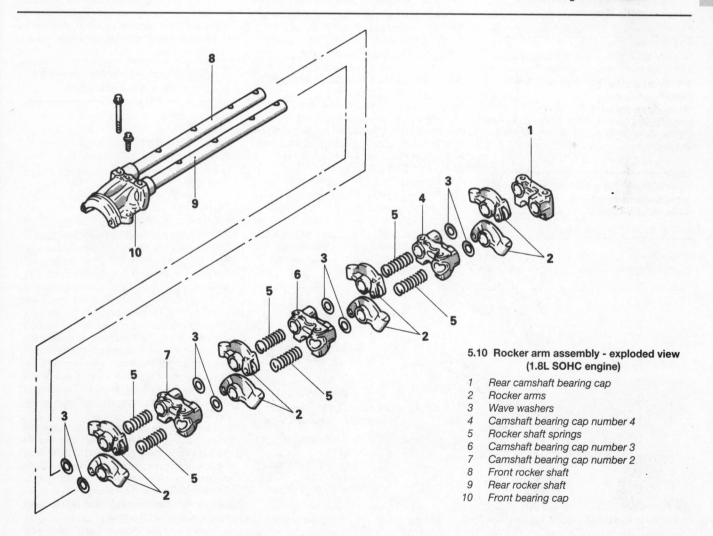

5.10 Rocker arm assembly - exploded view (1.8L SOHC engine)

1   *Rear camshaft bearing cap*
2   *Rocker arms*
3   *Wave washers*
4   *Camshaft bearing cap number 4*
5   *Rocker shaft springs*
6   *Camshaft bearing cap number 3*
7   *Camshaft bearing cap number 2*
8   *Front rocker shaft*
9   *Rear rocker shaft*
10   *Front bearing cap*

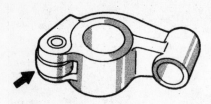

5.11a   Visually check the rocker-arm-shaft bore and roller (arrow) for score marks, pitting and evidence of overheating (blue, discolored areas) (1.8L SOHC engine)

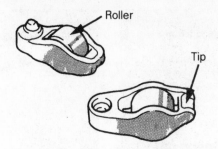

5.11b   On 2.0L DOHC engines, check the roller, tip and lash-adjuster contact area for score marks and pitting

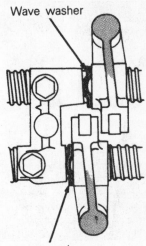

5.14   Make sure the wave tensioner washers (1.8L engines only) are installed on the shaft in the location and direction shown

11   Visually check the rocker arms for wear **(see illustrations)**. Replace them if evidence of wear or damage is found.

12   On 1.8L SOHC engines, check all the rocker shaft components **(see illustration 5.10)**. Look for broken springs, worn or scored shafts, etc. and replace any of the parts found to be damaged.

Installation

13   When reassembling the parts, be sure they all go back on in the same locations they were removed from.

14   Make sure the wave tensioner washers (1.8L engines only) is installed on the shaft in the location and direction shown **(see illustration)**.

15   The remainder of the reassembly is in the reverse order of disassembly. Run the engine and check for oil leaks and proper operation.

6   Valve springs, retainers and seals - replacement

Refer to illustrations 6.4, 6.9, 6.10, 6.15 and 6.17
Note: *Broken valve springs and defective valve stem seals can be replaced without*

removing the cylinder heads. Two special tools and a compressed air source are normally required to perform this operation, so read through this Section carefully and rent or buy the tools before beginning the job. If compressed air isn't available, a length of nylon rope can be used to keep the valves from falling into the cylinder during this procedure.

1   Remove the valve cover (see Section 4).

2   Remove the spark plug from the cylinder which has the defective component. If all of the valve stem seals are being replaced, all of the spark plugs should be removed.

3   Turn the crankshaft until the piston in the affected cylinder is at top dead center on the compression stroke (refer to Chapter 2B for instructions). If you're replacing all of the valve stem seals, begin with cylinder number one and work on the valves for one cylinder at a time. Move from cylinder-to-cylinder following the firing order sequence (see this Chapter's Specifications).

4   Thread an adapter into the spark plug hole **(see illustration)** and connect an air hose from a compressed air source to it. Most auto parts stores can supply the air hose adapter. **Note:** *Many cylinder compression gauges utilize a screw-in fitting that may work with your air hose quick-disconnect fitting.*

5   Remove the rocker arm assembly (see Section 7). On 1.8L engines, if you plan to use a lever-type tool, remove the assembly, remove the rocker arms from the shafts, then reinstall the shafts (the tool uses the rocker shaft as leverage).

6   Apply compressed air to the cylinder. **Warning:** *The piston may be forced down by compressed air, causing the crankshaft to turn suddenly. If the wrench used when positioning the number one piston at TDC is still attached to the bolt in the crankshaft nose, it could cause damage or injury when the crankshaft moves.*

7   The valves should be held in place by the air pressure. If the valve faces or seats are in poor condition, leaks may prevent air pressure from retaining the valves - refer to the alternative procedure below.

8   If you don't have access to compressed air, an alternative method can be used. Posi-

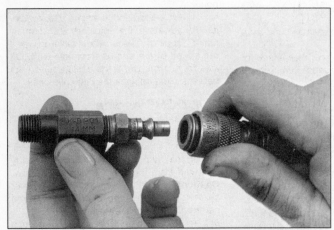

6.4   This is what the air hose adapter that threads into the spark plug hole looks like - they're commonly available from auto parts stores

6.9   Use needle-nose pliers (shown) or a small magnet to remove the valve spring keepers - be careful not to drop them down into the engine!

6.10 Remove the valve guide seal with a pair of pliers

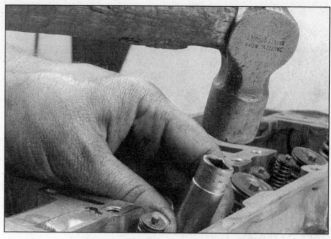

6.15 Gently tap the new seal into place with a hammer and a deep socket

tion the piston at a point a few degrees before TDC on the compression stroke, then feed a long piece of nylon rope through the spark plug hole until it fills the combustion chamber. BE SURE TO LEAVE THE END OF THE ROPE HANGING OUT of the engine so it can be removed easily. Use a large ratchet and socket to rotate the crankshaft in the normal direction of rotation until slight resistance is felt.

9   Stuff shop rags into the cylinder head holes above and below the valves to prevent parts and tools from falling into the engine, then use a valve spring compressor to compress the spring. Remove the keepers with small needle-nose pliers or a magnet (see illustration). Note: *A couple of different types of tools are available for compressing the valve springs with the head in place. One type, shown here, grips the lower spring coils and presses on the retainer as the knob is turned, while the other type utilizes the rocker arm shaft for leverage. Both types work very well, although the lever type is usually less expensive.*

10   Remove the spring retainer and valve spring, then remove the guide seal (see illustration). Caution: *If air pressure fails to hold the valve in the closed position during this operation, the valve face and/or seat is probably damaged. If so, the cylinder head will have to be removed for additional repair operations.*

11   Wrap a rubber band or tape around the top of the valve stem so the valve won't fall into the combustion chamber, then release the air pressure. Note: *If a rope was used instead of air pressure, turn the crankshaft slightly in the direction opposite normal rotation.*

12   Inspect the valve stem for damage. Rotate the valve in the guide and check the end for eccentric movement, which would indicate that the valve is bent.

13   Move the valve up-and-down in the guide and make sure it doesn't bind. If the valve stem binds, either the valve is bent or the guide is damaged. In either case, the

head will have to be removed for repair.

14   Reapply air pressure to the cylinder to retain the valve in the closed position, then remove the tape or rubber band from the valve stem. If a rope was used instead of air pressure, rotate the crankshaft in the normal direction of rotation until slight resistance is felt.

15   Lubricate the valve stem with engine oil and install a new guide seal (see illustration).

16   Install the spring in position over the valve.

17   Install the valve spring retainer. Compress the valve spring and carefully position the keepers in the groove. Apply a small dab of grease to the inside of each keeper to hold it in place if necessary (see illustration).

18   Remove the pressure from the spring tool and make sure the keepers are seated.

19   Disconnect the air hose and remove the adapter from the spark plug hole. If a rope was used in place of air pressure, pull it out of the cylinder.

20   Refer to Section 5 and install the rocker arms and shafts.

21   Install the spark plug(s) and connect the wire(s).

22   Refer to Section 4 and install the valve cover.

23   Start and run the engine, then check for oil leaks and unusual sounds coming from the valve cover area.

---

7   Valve lash adjusters - removal, inspection and installation

1.8L SOHC engine

1   Remove the rocker arm shafts (see Section 5) and pull the adjusters from the rocker arms (see illustration 5.7b). Be sure to keep them in order so they can be returned to their original positions.

2   Inspect each lash adjuster carefully for signs of wear and damage, particularly on the surface that contacts the valve tip. Since the

6.17 Apply a small dab of grease to each keeper before installation to hold it in place on the valve stem until the spring is released

lash adjusters frequently become clogged, we recommend replacing them if you're concerned about their condition or if the engine is exhibiting valve "tapping" noises.

3   Assemble the adjusters into the rocker arms. Install the valve cover and related components.

4   When re-starting the engine after replacing the adjusters, the adjusters will normally make "tapping" noises. After warm-up, raise the speed of the engine from idle to 3,000 rpm for one minute. If the adjuster(s) do not become silent, replace the defective ones.

2.0L DOHC engine

5   Remove the camshaft(s) (see Section 10).

6   Remove the rocker arms (see Section 5).

7   If the hydraulic lifters aren't already removed from the head, lift them out now. Caution: *Be sure to keep the lifters in order so they can be placed back on the same camshaft lobe it was removed from.*

8   Inspect each adjuster carefully for signs of wear and damage, particularly on the ball tip that contacts the rocker arm. Since the lash adjusters frequently become clogged, we recommend replacing them if you're con-

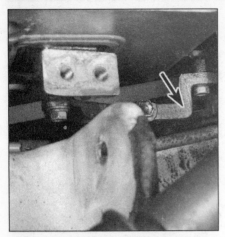

8.9 Unbolt and remove the tensioner pulley assembly (arrow)

8.12a Remove the four bolts that attach the pulleys to the crankshaft (arrows)

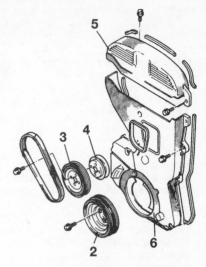

8.12b An exploded view of the tensioner, pulleys and timing belt covers (2.0L DOHC engine)

1   *Tensioner pulley bracket*
2   *Crankshaft pulley*
3   *Water pump pulley*
4   *Water pump pulley (power steering)*
5   *Timing belt upper cover*
6   *Timing belt lower cover*

cerned about their condition or if the engine is exhibiting valve "tapping" noises.

9   When re-starting the engine after replacing the adjusters, the adjusters will normally make "tapping" noises. After warm-up, raise the speed of the engine from idle to 3,000 rpm for one minute. If the adjuster(s) do not become silent, replace the defective ones.

8   Timing belt, balance shaft belt and sprockets - removal, inspection and installation

Removal

Caution: *Do not try to turn the crankshaft with the camshaft sprocket bolt and do not rotate the crankshaft counterclockwise. Also, don't turn the crankshaft or camshaft after the timing belt has been removed.*

1   Position the number one piston at Top Dead Center (see Section 3).
2   Disconnect the battery cable from the negative battery terminal.

3   Remove the air cleaner assembly and associated hoses (see Chapter 4).
4   Set the parking brake and block the rear wheels. Raise the front of the vehicle and support it securely on jackstands.
5   Remove the left engine mount and bracket (see Section 19). **Note:** *Make sure the engine is supported with a piece of wood and a floor jack placed under the oil pan. The wood will prevent the floor jack from denting or damaging the oil pan.*

Main timing belt

2.0L DOHC engines

Refer to illustrations 8.9, 8.12a, 8.12b, 8.13a, 8.13b, 8.14a, 8.14b, 8.15, 8.16a, 8.16b, 8.17a and 8.17b

6   Be sure to support the engine with a block of wood placed between the floor jack and the engine oil pan.
7   Remove the clamp and bracket for the power steering pressure hose (if equipped) and the clamp for the air conditioning hose, if equipped.
8   Remove the drivebelts (see Chapter 1)

and the tensioner pulley bracket.
9   Remove the tensioner pulley assembly **(see illustration)**.
10   Remove the splash pan from beneath the drivebelt end of the engine.
11   Remove the water pump pulleys. **Note:** *The smaller of the two pulleys runs the power steering pump.*
12   Loosen the large crankshaft sprocket bolt in the center of the crankshaft pulley. It might be very tight, so, to break it loose, wrap a rag around the pulley and attach a chain wrench. Slip a 1/2-inch drive extension through the hole in the inner fender and into

8.13a One bolt here (arrow), as well as two bolts at the top, secure the upper timing belt cover (2.0L DOHC engine)

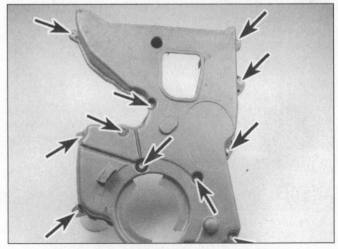

8.13b Remove the bolts (arrows) and remove the lower timing belt cover

8.14a An exploded view of the 2.0L DOHC timing belt assembly

1	Timing belt rear left cover (lower)	10	Inner belt guide
2	Timing belt rear left cover (upper)	11	Crankshaft sprocket "A"
3	Timing belt rear right cover	12	Special washer
4	Left engine support bracket	13	Crankshaft sprocket bolt
5	Crankshaft sprocket "B"	14	Oil pump sprocket
6	Spacer	15	Camshaft sprocket(s)
7	Balance shaft sprocket	16	Idler pulley
8	Balance shaft belt	17	Auto tensioner
9	Balance shaft tensioner	18	Tensioner arm
		19	Tensioner pulley
		20	Timing belt

the sprocket bolt head **(see illustration 3.4)**. Turn the extension with a breaker bar. If you are unable to loosen the bolt due to the chain wrench slipping, you can prevent the crankshaft from turning by having an assistant wedge a flat-blade screwdriver in the flywheel/driveplate ring gear teeth. To do this, you must first remove the flywheel/driveplate cover. Next, remove the bolts and remove the crankshaft pulley **(see illustrations)**.

13   Remove the retaining bolts from the upper and lower timing belt covers **(see illustration 8.12)** and remove the covers and gaskets **(see illustrations)**.

14   Remove the two bolts and lift off the automatic tensioner **(see illustrations)**.

15   Make a mark on the timing belt in the direction of rotation **(see illustration)** so it may be reinstalled in the same direction in the event the timing belt is reused. Remove the tensioner arm bolts and the tensioner, then remove the timing belt. **Caution:** *Be sure that the timing marks are correctly aligned before removing the timing belt* **(see illustration 8.39)**

16   If you plan to replace to remove the camshaft(s) or camshaft oil seal(s), remove

8.14b To remove the automatic tensioner, remove the two bolts indicated by the arrows - also, note the locations of the crankshaft and oil pump sprocket timing marks (circled areas) (2.0L DOHC engine)

8.15 If you'll be reusing the timing belt, mark an arrow on the belt in the direction of rotation so it may be reinstalled in the same direction - also, note the locations of the camshaft timing marks (circled area) and the dowel pins (arrows), which must face up (2.0L DOHC engine)

2A

8.16a When loosening the camshaft sprocket bolt, hold the camshaft at the hexagon with an open-end wrench . . .

8.16b . . . and, if the bolt is very tight, position a wood block, as shown, to prevent damaging the cylinder head when the bolt breaks loose

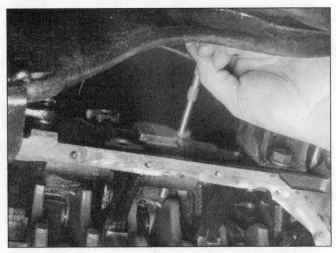

8.17a Remove the plug on the side of the engine block and insert a Phillips screwdriver to prevent the balance shaft from turning (oil pan removed for clarity)

8.17b Remove the oil pump sprocket nut (arrow) with a socket and a breaker bar and remove the oil pump sprocket

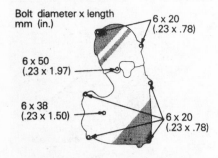

8.23 Remove the bolts that secure the timing belt upper and lower covers and lift off the covers and the gaskets (1.8L SOHC engine)

the camshaft sprocket(s). Using an adjustable wrench or an open-end wrench, hold the camshaft at the hexagon and remove the camshaft sprocket bolt **(see illustration)**. If the sprocket bolt cannot be loosened easily, place a block of wood between the head and the wrench **(see illustration)** to prevent damage to the head so more force can be used on the camshaft sprocket bolt. Remove the bolt and slide the sprocket off the camshaft.

17   If it's necessary to remove the balance shaft sprocket or oil pump, remove the plug on the side of the engine block and insert a Phillips screwdriver to prevent the shaft from turning **(see illustration)**. Remove the oil pump sprocket nut with a socket and a breaker bar and remove the oil pump sprocket **(see illustration)**.

1.8L SOHC engines

Refer to illustrations 8.23, 8.24, 8.25 and 8.26

18   Follow steps 1 through 5 of this Section. Be sure to support the engine with a block of wood placed between the floor jack and the engine oil pan.

19   Loosen the water pump pulley bolts and remove the drivebelts (see Chapter 1).

20   Unbolt and remove the water pump pulleys. **Note:** *The smaller of the two pulleys drives the power steering.*

21   If equipped, unbolt the bracket that secures the power steering/air conditioning hose bracket so the hoses will be out of the way when the timing belt is removed. Also, unbolt and remove the drivebelt tensioner pulley assembly.

22   Remove the four small bolts at the crankshaft pulley and remove the crankshaft pulley and adapter.

23   Remove the bolts that secure the timing belt upper and lower covers **(see illustration)** and lift off the covers and the gaskets.

24   Be sure the camshaft gear and the timing mark on the upper rear cover **(see illustration)** line up before removal of the timing belt. **Note:** *If you plan to reuse the timing belt, paint an arrow on it* **(see illustration 8.15)** *to*

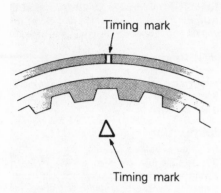

8.24 Be sure the camshaft sprocket mark and the mark on the rear cover line up before removing the timing belt (1.8L SOHC engine)

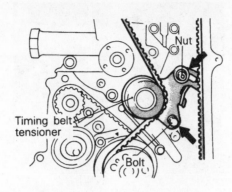

8.25 Loosen the bolt and nut and move the timing belt tensioner towards the water pump as far as possible to relieve the belt tension (1.8L SOHC engine)

indicate the direction of rotation (clockwise).

25 Loosen the adjusting bolt and nut and move the timing belt tensioner towards the water pump as far as possible (**see illustration**). Temporarily secure the tensioner by tightening the nut once the tension has been removed from the belt.

26 Remove the splash pan from beneath the drivebelt end of the engine, then remove the large center bolt from the crankshaft pulley (**see illustration**). It might be very tight, so, to break it loose, wrap a rag around the pulley and attach a chain wrench.

27 If you are unable to loosen the bolt due to the chain wrench slipping, you can prevent the crankshaft from turning by having an assistant wedge a flat-blade screwdriver in the flywheel/driveplate ring gear teeth. To do this, you must first remove the flywheel/driveplate cover.

28 Slip the timing belt off the sprockets and set it aside.

29 If you intend to remove the camshaft or camshaft oil seal, unscrew the camshaft sprocket bolt and slide the sprocket off - a large screwdriver inserted through a hole in the sprocket will keep it from turning while you remove the bolt. To remove the crankshaft sprocket, pull it off - it may be necessary to use a bolt-type puller.

30 Inspect the oil pump seal for leaks. If there are leaks or if you need to remove the oil pump for any other reason, remove the oil pump sprocket, as follows: Remove the plug on the side of the engine block and insert a Phillips screwdriver to prevent the shaft from turning (**see illustration 8.17a and 8.17b**). Remove the oil pump sprocket nut with a socket and a breaker bar.

Balance shaft belt (all engines)

Refer to illustrations 8.31a, 8.31b and 8.31c

31 If you're planning to install the same belt, mark the direction of rotation on the belt (**see illustration**). If you're planning to remove the balance shaft sprocket, loosen the bolt before you remove the belt. Be sure the alignment marks are positioned correctly before removing the belt (**see illustrations**).

2A

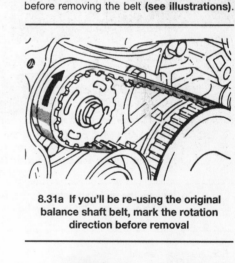

8.31a If you'll be re-using the original balance shaft belt, mark the rotation direction before removal

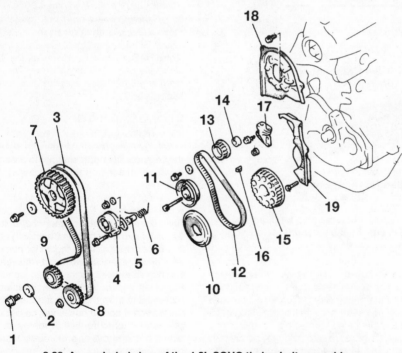

8.26 An exploded view of the 1.8L SOHC timing belt assembly

1 Crankshaft sprocket bolt	11 Balance shaft belt tensioner
2 Special washer	12 Balance shaft belt
3 Timing belt	13 Right balance shaft sprocket
4 Timing belt tensioner	14 Spacer
5 Tensioner spacer	15 Crankshaft sprocket
6 Tensioner spring	16 Key
7 Camshaft sprocket	17 Left engine support bracket
8 Oil pump sprocket	18 Timing belt rear upper cover
9 Crankshaft sprocket	19 Timing belt rear lower cover
10 Belt guide	

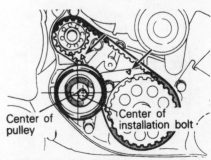

8.31b Be sure the alignment marks are positioned correctly before removing the belt (arrows) (1.8L SOHC engine)

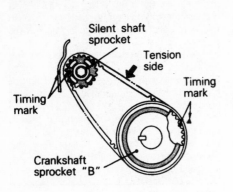

8.31c The timing marks are in different locations on the 2.0L DOHC engine

8.33a Carefully inspect the timing belt - bending it backwards will often make wear or damage more apparent

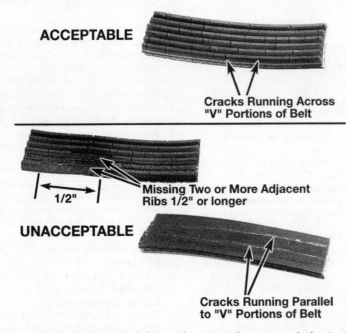

8.33b Inspect the timing belt for cracks, separation, wear, missing teeth and oil contamination. Replace the belt if it's in questionable condition

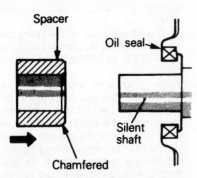

8.35 Be sure to properly install the spacer on the balance shaft sprocket. The chamfered edge must face toward the oil seal

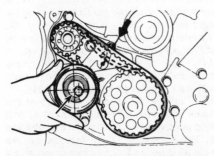

8.38 Make sure the tension sprocket for balance shaft belt has the center located just to the left side of the mounting bolt before you lift up on it to tension the belt - tension should be checked where indicated by the top arrow

Note: *The timing marks for the balance shaft belt are located in different places on the engine and sprockets for the DOHC and the SOHC engines, but the procedure is the same.* Remove the bolt from the center of the tensioner pulley, remove the pulley, then remove the belt. To remove the crankshaft sprocket, pull it off - it may be necessary to use a bolt-type puller.

Inspection

Refer to illustrations 8.33a, 8.33b

32   Rotate the tensioner pulleys by hand and move them side-to-side to detect roughness and excess play. Visually inspect the sprockets for any signs of damage and wear. Replace parts as necessary. Also, replace the pulley if there is a lubricant leak.

33   Inspect the timing belts for cracks, separation, wear, missing teeth and oil contamination. Replace the belt if it's in questionable condition **(see illustrations)**.

34   Check the automatic tensioner for leaks or any obvious damage to the body. Also, check the rod end for wear or damage. Measure the rod protrusion for the correct length - it should extend 15/32-inch (12 mm) beyond the body of the tensioner.

Installation

Refer to illustrations 8.35 and 8.38

35   Reinstall the timing belt sprockets, if they were removed. Tighten the bolts to the values listed in this Chapter's Specifications. **Note:** *Be sure to properly install the spacer under the balance shaft sprocket. The chamfered edge must face toward the oil seal* **(see illustration)**.

Balance shaft belt

36   Install the balance shaft belt. Be sure the timing mark on the crankshaft sprocket and the balance shaft sprocket are aligned properly **(see illustration 8.31b or 8.31c)**. **Note:** *The timing marks on DOHC engines are located in different places, but the procedure is the same.* Install the tensioner and bolt, but don't tighten the bolt completely at this time.

37   After installing the balance shaft belt, make sure the tension side has no slack.

38   Make sure the tension sprocket for the balance shaft belt has the center located just to the left side of the mounting bolt with the pulley directed to the front of the engine. Lift the tensioner up with one finger to tighten the belt **(see illustration)** and tighten the tensioner bolt and the balance shaft bolt to the torque listed in this Chapter's Specifications. **Note:** *Use your index finger and press firmly on the timing belt. The belt deflection should be 1/4-inch.*

Main timing belt

Refer to illustrations 8.39 and 8.40

2.0L DOHC engine

39   Align the timing marks located on the camshaft, crankshaft and oil pump sprockets **(see illustration)**. When aligning the oil pump sprocket marks, it is critical that the balance

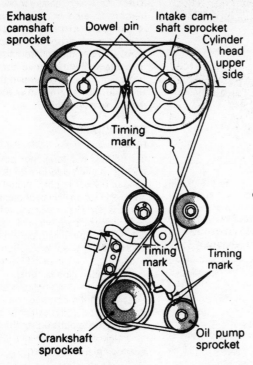

Exhaust camshaft sprocket
Dowel pin
Intake camshaft sprocket
Cylinder head upper side
Timing mark
Timing mark
Timing mark
Crankshaft sprocket
Oil pump sprocket

8.39 Align the timing marks located on the camshaft, crankshaft and oil pump sprockets (2.0L DOHC engine)

8.40 Once the tensioner is compressed, place a small allen wrench, or something similar, through the hole to keep the rod retracted for reassembly on the engine

2A

46 Install the timing belt in the following sequence:

a) *Install the timing belt around the tensioner pulley and crankshaft sprocket and hold the timing belt to the tensioner pulley with your left hand.*

b) *Pulling the belt with your right hand, install it around the oil pump sprocket.*

c) *Install the belt around the idler pulley.*

d) *Install the belt around the intake camshaft sprocket.*

e) *Turn the exhaust camshaft sprocket one tooth to align it's timing mark with the upper surface of the cylinder head. Pull the belt with both hands and install it around the exhaust camshaft.*

f) *Gently raise the tensioner pulley so the belt does not sag, then temporarily tighten the center bolt.*

47 Adjust the timing belt tension in the following sequence:

a) *Turn the crankshaft 1/4 turn counterclockwise, then clockwise to move the number 1 cylinder to TDC.*

b) *Loosen the tensioner center bolt and attach Mitsubishi special tool no. MD998752 (or equivalent) to a torque wrench.* **Note:** *The torque wrench must be capable of measuring small increments between 0 and 30 in-lbs. Apply between 23 and 25 in-lbs. to the tensioner.*

c) *While holding tension on the timing belt tensioner, tighten the center bolt to the torque listed in this Chapter's Specifications.*

d) *Screw Mitsubishi special tool no. MD998738 (or equivalent) into the engine left support bracket until its end makes contact with the tensioner arm. Continue to screw the tool into the pulley and when tension is relieved from the automatic tensioner, remove the allen wrench, or whatever was used to keep the tensioner retracted, that was inserted into the tensioner. An alternate method would be to pry the tensioner pulley towards the front of the vehicle (don't pry against the belt) until the auto-*

shaft has the weighted portion at the bottom of the shaft (it is possible to align the marks with the balance shaft weight at the top; if you do this accidentally, severe engine vibration will result). Before installing the timing belt, slightly rock the oil pump sprocket by hand and watch carefully that the sprocket has the tendency to remain stationary (return to approximately the marks-aligned position) when the sprocket is rotated. This means the sprocket is CORRECTLY timed. If the sprocket has the tendency to rotate clockwise when spun lightly, the shaft is INCORRECTLY timed. If there is any doubt about whether or not the silent shaft is in the correct position, insert a screwdriver through the hole in the left side of the cylinder block **(see illustration 8.17a)**. Make sure the screwdriver extends approximately 2-1/2 inches into the hole and also make sure the sprocket cannot be rotated with the screwdriver in place; now you can be sure the timing is correct.

40 Prepare the automatic tensioner for installation. Place the tensioner in a vise that is equipped with soft jaws (or put a shop rag over the jaws to prevent damage to the tensioner). If the rod is easily retracted, replace it with a new unit. The tensioner should have a fair amount of strength or resistance. **Caution:** *Be sure the tensioner is in a level position when it is in the vise. Also, place a washer over the plug on the bottom of the tensioner to prevent the vise from contacting the plug. Once the tensioner is compressed place a small allen wrench, or something similar, through the hole to keep the rod retracted for reassembly on the engine* **(see illustration)**.

41 Install the automatic tensioner onto the engine, keeping it in the compressed position.

42 Install the tensioner pulley onto the tensioner arm. Position the two small holes in the tensioner pulley hub just to the left of the center bolt. Tighten the center bolt finger tight. Don't remove the allen wrench from the tensioner yet.

43 Turn the two camshaft sprockets until the dowel pins are located at the top **(see illustration 8.39)**. Then align the timing marks facing each other with the upper surface of the cylinder head. **Note:** *When the exhaust camshaft is released, it will tend to rotate one tooth in the counterclockwise direction. This shift must be taken into account when installing the timing belt onto the sprockets. Also, the camshaft sprockets are identical and are provided with two timing marks. When the sprocket is mounted on the exhaust camshaft, use the timing mark on the right with the dowel pin hole on the top. On the intake camshaft sprocket, use the one on the left with the dowel pin hole on the top.*

44 Align the crankshaft sprocket timing mark and the oil pump sprocket timing mark with their pointers **(see illustration 8.39)**.

45 Remove the plug on the side of the block and insert a Phillips screwdriver or a long punch through the hole **(see illustration 8.17a)**. If the tool CAN be inserted into the hole as deep as 2 1/2-inches or more, the timing marks are aligned correctly. If the tool CANNOT be inserted more than 1-inch, the oil pump sprocket must be reset. When it's positioned properly, reinstall the screwdriver and keep it there until the timing belt is installed.

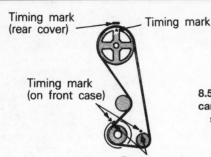

Timing mark (rear cover)

Timing mark

Timing mark (on front case)

Timing mark

8.52 Align the timing marks on the camshaft, crankshaft and oil pump sprockets (1.8L SOHC engine)

matic tensioner is compressed, then remove the allen wrench.

e) *Remove the special tool, if used.*

f) *Rotate the crankshaft six complete turns and wait 15 minutes.* **Caution:** *If you feel resistance while turning the crankshaft, the valves may be hitting the pistons from incorrect valve timing. Stop and recheck the valve timing.* **Note:** *The camshaft, crankshaft and front balance shaft sprocket marks will align every two revolutions of the crankshaft; however, since the rear (oil pump) sprocket turns at 2/3 crankshaft speed, it's marks will only align every six crankshaft revolutions. Measure how far the tensioner plunger protrudes from the tensioner body (the distance between the tensioner arm and the automatic tensioner body). It should be between 5/32 and 3/16-inch (3.8 to 4.5 mm). Also check that all timing marks are still aligned.*

48   If the tensioner protrusion is not as specified, repeat the belt adjustment procedure.

49   Install the timing covers.

50   The remaining steps are the reverse of removal.

1.8L SOHC engine

Refer to illustration 8.52

51   Reinstall the timing belt sprockets, if they were removed. Note that the camshaft sprocket is indexed by a dowel or by punch marks. Slip the belt guide flange onto the crankshaft before installing the lower sprocket - the chamfered side of the flange faces out. The crankshaft sprocket has two different size flats which match those on the crankshaft.

52   Align the timing marks located on the camshaft, crankshaft and oil pump sprockets **(see illustration)**. When aligning the oil pump sprocket marks, it's critical that the balance shaft has the weighted portion at the bottom of the shaft (it's possible to align the marks with the balance shaft weight at the top - if you do this accidentally, severe engine vibration will result). Before installing the timing belt, slightly spin the oil pump sprocket by hand and watch carefully that the sprocket has the tendency to remain stationary (return to approximately the marks-aligned position) when the sprocket is rotated. This means the sprocket is COR-RECTLY timed. If the sprocket has the ten-

dency to rotate clockwise when spun, the shaft is INCORRECTLY timed. If there is any doubt about whether or not the balance shafts are in the correct position, insert a screwdriver through the hole in the side of the cylinder block **(see illustration 8.17a)**. Make sure the screwdriver extends approximately 2-1/2 inches into the hole and also make sure the sprocket cannot be rotated with the screwdriver in place; now you can be sure the timing is correct.

53   Slip the timing belt onto the crankshaft sprocket. While maintaining tension on the rear (firewall) side of the belt, slip the belt onto the camshaft sprocket.

54   Loosen the tensioner hold-down bolt and nut to apply spring tension against the belt. Retighten the bolt.

55   Install the crankshaft pulley, taking care to align the locating pin with the small hole in the pulley. Install the crankshaft pulley bolts (both the pulley securing bolts and the center bolt) and tighten them to the torques listed in this Chapter's Specifications. When tightening the bolts, hold the crankshaft in place using one of the methods discussed in Steps 26 and 27.

56   Using the bolt in the center of the crankshaft pulley, turn the crankshaft clockwise through six complete revolutions. **Caution:** *If you feel resistance while turning the crankshaft, the valves may be hitting the pistons from incorrect valve timing. Stop and recheck the valve timing.* **Note:** *The camshaft, crankshaft and front balance shaft sprocket*

marks will align every two revolutions of the crankshaft; however, since the rear (oil pump) sprocket turns at 2/3 crankshaft speed, it's marks will only align every six crankshaft revolutions. Recheck the alignment of the timing marks **(see illustration 8.52)**. *If the marks do not align properly, loosen the tensioner, slip the belt off the camshaft sprocket, align the marks, reinstall the belt, and check the alignment again.*

57   Tighten the tensioner bolts to the torque listed in this Chapter's Specifications, starting with the adjustment bolt; then tighten the bolt which goes through the tension spring.

58   Reinstall the remaining parts in the reverse order of removal. Note that the timing belt cover bolts come in different lengths **(see illustration 8.23)**.

59   Start the engine, set the ignition timing (see Chapter 1) and road test the vehicle.

9   Crankshaft front oil seal - replacement

Refer to illustrations 9.2 and 9.4

1   Remove the timing belt and the crankshaft sprockets (see Sec-tion 8).

2   Wrap the tip of a small screwdriver with tape. Working from below the left inner fender, use the screwdriver to pry the seal out of its bore **(see illustration)**. Take care to prevent damaging the crankshaft and the seal bore.

3   Thoroughly clean and inspect the seal bore and sealing surface on the crankshaft. Minor imperfections can be removed with emery cloth. If there is a groove worn in the crankshaft sealing surface (from contact with the seal), installing a new seal will probably not stop the leak. Such wear normally indicates the internal engine components are also worn. Consider overhauling the engine.

4   Lubricate the new seal with engine oil and drive the seal into place with a hammer and socket **(see illustration)**.

5   Another method of replacement is used if the front cover has been removed (see Sec-

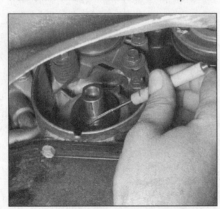

9.2 Wrap the tip of a small screwdriver with tape. Working from below the left inner fender, use the screwdriver to pry the seal out of its bore

9.4 Lubricate the new seal with engine oil and drive the seal into place with a hammer and socket

10.3 If the bearing caps are difficult to remove, use the bolts as levers to help break the caps free

tion 15) and you can drive the seal out from the back side of the cover. If the cover is removed, it's a good idea to replace all the front cover seals at this time (crankshaft, oil pump and balance shaft).

6   Position the seal and front cover assembly on a couple of wood blocks on a workbench and drive the old seal out from the back side with a punch and hammer.

7   Drive the new seal into the retainer with a block of wood or a section of pipe slightly smaller in diameter than the outside diameter of the seal.

8   Lubricate the lip of the new seal with clean engine oil. Position a new gasket on the engine block.

9   Slowly and carefully push the seal onto the crankshaft. The seal lip is stiff, so work it onto the crankshaft with a smooth object such as the end of an extension as you push the retainer against the block.

10   Install and tighten the front cover bolts to the torque listed in this Chapter's Specifi-

cations. The bottom sealing flange of the front cover must not extend below the bottom sealing flange (oil pan rail) of the block.

11   The remaining steps are the reverse of removal.

12   Reinstall the timing belt and related components as described in Section 8.

13   Run the engine and check for oil leaks.

---

10 Camshaft(s) - removal, inspection and installation

Removal

Refer to illustration 10.3

1.8L SOHC engine

1   Once the rocker shaft assembly has been removed (see Section 5), the camshaft can be lifted up and out of the cylinder head **(see illustration 5.7a).**

2.0L DOHC engine

2   Remove the camshaft/crankshaft angle sensor (see Chapter 6).

3   Remove the timing belt and camshaft sprocket(s), then remove the camshaft bearing caps, loosening the bolts a little at a time to prevent distorting the camshaft(s) by loosening the caps from the ends of the shaft towards the center. Once the bearing caps have all been loosened enough for removal, they may still be difficult to remove. Using the bearing cap bolts for extra leverage, move the cap back and forth to loosen the cap from the cylinder head **(see illustration).** If they are still difficult to remove you can tap them gently with a soft face hammer so they can be lifted off. **Caution:** *Store them in order so they can be returned to their original locations, with the same side facing forward. It's a good idea to mark the caps so there's no possibility of making a mistake.* Carefully lift the camshaft(s) out of the cylinder head.

Inspection

Refer to illustrations 10.5 and 10.6

4   Remove the seal(s) from the camshaft(s) and thoroughly clean the camshaft(s) and the gasket surface. Visually inspect the camshaft for wear and/or damage to the distributor drive gear, lobe surfaces, bearing journals and seal contact surfaces. Visually inspect the camshaft bearing surfaces in the cylinder head for scoring and other damage.

5   Measure the camshaft lobe heights **(see illustration)** and compare them to this Chapter's Specifications.

6   Measure the camshaft bearing journal diameters **(see illustration)**, then temporarily install the bearing caps and measure the inside diameter of the camshaft bearing surfaces in the cylinder head, using a telescoping gauge. Subtract the journal measurement from the bearing measurement to obtain the camshaft bearing oil clearance. Compare this clearance with this Chapter's Specifications.

7   Replace the camshaft if it fails any of the above inspections. **Note:** *If the distributor drive gear is faulty, replace the driven gear also. If the lobes are worn, replace the rocker arms along with the camshaft. Cylinder head replacement may be necessary if the camshaft bearing surfaces in the head are damaged or excessively worn.*

Installation

Refer to illustration 10.11a, 10.11b and 10.12

8   Very carefully clean the camshaft and bearing journals/caps. Liberally coat the journals, lobes and thrust portions of the camshaft with assembly lube or engine oil.

9   Carefully install the camshaft(s) in the cylinder head.

10   On SOHC models, install the camshaft and rocker shaft assembly back onto the cylinder head (see Section 5).

11   On DOHC models, install the lash adjusters and rocker arms if they haven't

2A

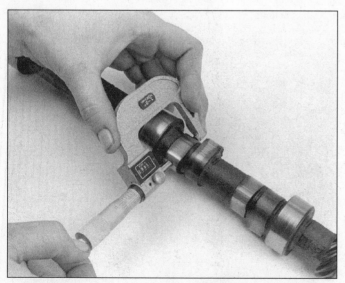

10.5 Measure the camshaft lobe heights with a micrometer

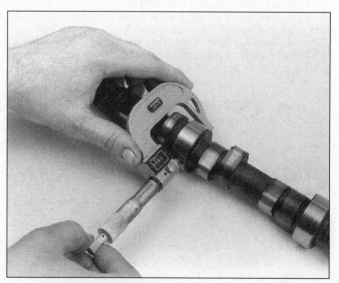

10.6 Measure the camshaft bearing journal diameters

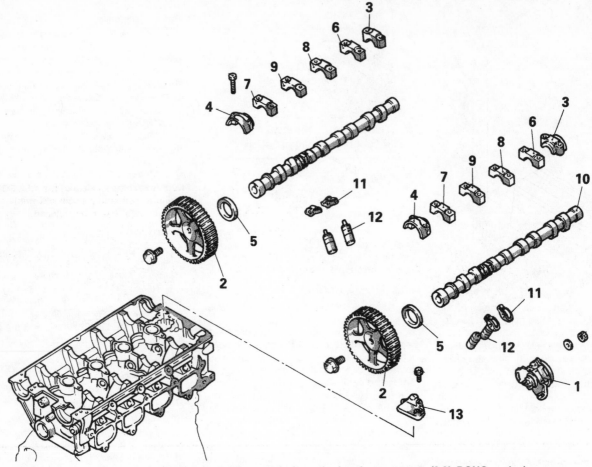

10.11a An exploded view of the camshafts and related components (2.0L DOHC engine)

1	Camshaft position sensor	5	Oil seals	8	No. 4 bearing caps	11	Rocker arms
2	Camshaft sprockets	6	No. 5 bearing caps	9	No. 3 bearing caps	12	Valve lash adjusters
3	No. 6 bearing caps	7	No. 2 bearing caps	10	Camshafts	13	Oil delivery body
4	No. 1 bearing caps						

been reinstalled yet. Next install the camshaft and camshaft bearing caps **(see illustration)**. Make sure the camshaft with the slit to drive the cam angle sensor at the rear of the shaft **(see illustration)** is placed on the intake side of the head. Tighten them a little at a time,

working from the center journals on out, doing one camshaft at a time, until the torque listed in this Chapter's Specifications is reached. **Note:** *On DOHC engines, bearing cap numbers 2 through 5 are the same shape. Check the markings on the caps to*

identify the correct journal number and intake/exhaust position.

12 Coat a new camshaft oil seal with engine oil and press it into place with a hammer and deep socket **(see illustration)**.

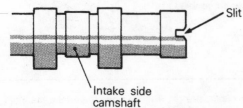

Front of engine (Timing belt side)

Slit

Intake side camshaft

10.11b The intake (rear) camshaft has a slit to drive the camshaft/crankshaft sensor

10.12 Coat a new camshaft oil seal with engine oil and tap it into place with a hammer and deep socket

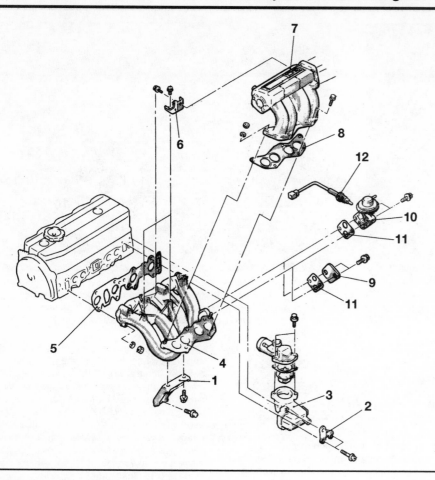

11.9a An exploded view of the 1.8L SOHC intake manifold and plenum assembly, with attached components

1   Intake manifold stay
2   Engine hanger
3   Thermostat housing and cover assembly
4   Intake manifold
5   Intake manifold gasket
6   Air intake plenum stay
7   Air intake plenum
8   Air intake plenum gasket
9   Cover
10 EGR valve
11 EGR gasket
12 EGR temperature sensor (vehicles for California)

2A

13   Install the camshaft sprocket(s) and tighten the bolts to the torque listed in this Chapter's Specifications.
14   Install the timing belt (see Section 8).
15   Reinstall the camshaft/crankshaft angle sensor (see Chapter 6).
16   Reinstall the remaining parts in the reverse order of removal.
17   Start the engine and allow it to warm up (176 to 203 degrees F) while you adjust the ignition timing.
18   Reinstall the valve cover and run the engine while checking for oil leaks.

11   Intake manifold - removal and installation

Removal

Refer to illustrations 11.9a, 11.9b, 11.9c and 11.19

1   Relieve the fuel system pressure (see Chapter 4), then disconnect the cable from the negative battery terminal.
2   Drain the cooling system (see Chapter 1).
3   Remove the air intake hose (see Chapter 4).
4   Clearly label and disconnect all hoses, wires, brackets and emission lines which run to the fuel injection system and intake manifold.

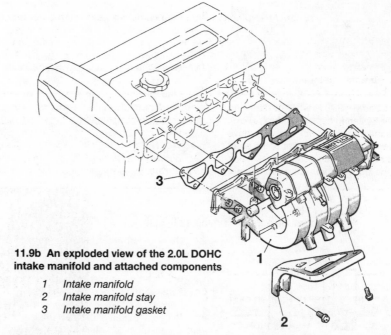

11.9b An exploded view of the 2.0L DOHC intake manifold and attached components

1   Intake manifold
2   Intake manifold stay
3   Intake manifold gasket

5   Disconnect the accelerator cable (see Chapter 4).
6   Disconnect the radiator upper hose (see Chapter 3).
7   Disconnect the overflow tube.
8   Disconnect the water by-pass hose.

9   Remove the Intake manifold stay **(see illustrations)**. Be sure to disconnect any electrical connections that a fastened to the support stay before trying to move the parts out of the way.

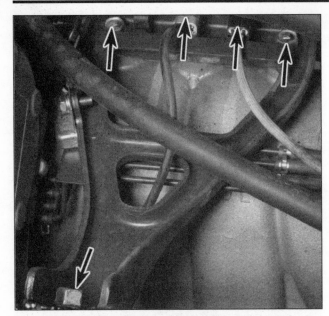

11.9c Remove the two electrical connections and three bolts (arrows), then detach the intake manifold stay (typical 2.0L DOHC engine)

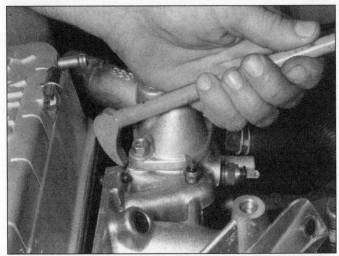

11.19 Unbolt the intake manifold and remove it from the engine. If it sticks, tap the manifold with a soft-face hammer or carefully pry it from the head at a protrusion, as shown (DO NOT pry between the gasket surfaces!)

11.25a Remove the intake manifold gasket by CAREFULLY scraping all traces of gasket material off both the cylinder head and the intake manifold

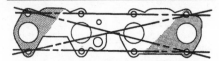

11.25b Lay a precision straightedge across the intake manifold (and plenum on 1.8L engines) gasket mating surface, then try to slip feeler gauges between the straightedge and gasket surface - if a feeler gauge as thick as the limit listed in this Chapter's Specifications fits, have the manifold or plenum re-surfaced by an automotive machine shop. Check the surface four ways, as indicated by the dashed lines in the illustration (1.8L shown, 2.0L similar)

10   Disconnect the control harness **(see Chapter 4)**.
11   Remove the fuel rail, fuel injector and pressure regulator **(see Chapter 4)**.
12   Disconnect the water hose from the throttle body end of the manifold.

1.8L SOHC engine

13   Disconnect the heater hose.
14   Disconnect the brake booster vacuum hose from the manifold (see Chapter 9).
15   Disconnect the PCV hose.
16   Remove the engine hanger bracket that's bolted to the manifold.
17   Thermostat housing **(see illustration 11.9a)**.
18   Unbolt the intake plenum **(see illustration 11.9a)** from the intake manifold (see Chapter 4).
19   Unbolt the intake manifold and remove it from the engine. If it sticks, tap the manifold with a soft-face hammer or carefully pry it from the head **(see illustration)**. **Caution:** *Do*

not pry between gasket sealing surfaces or tap on the fuel injectors.

2.0L DOHC engine

20   Remove the ground plate installation screw.
21   Remove the throttle body stay and ground plate.
22   On non-turbo models, disconnect the brake booster vacuum hose from the manifold.
23   Remove the ignition coil and the ignition power transistor unit (see Chapter 5).
24   Unbolt the intake manifold and remove it from the engine. If it sticks, tap the manifold with a soft-face hammer or carefully pry it from the head **(see illustration 11.19)**. **Caution:** *Do not pry between gasket sealing surfaces or tap on the fuel injectors.*

Installation

Refer to illustrations 11.25a and 11.25b
25   Remove intake manifold gasket by care-

fully scraping all traces of gasket material off both the cylinder head and the intake manifold **(see illustration)**. **Caution:** *The cylinder head and intake manifold are made of aluminum and are easily nicked or gouged. Don't damage the gasket surfaces or a leak may result after the work is complete. Gasket removal solvents are available from auto parts stores and may prove helpful.* After cleaning, check the intake manifold mating surface for warpage **(see illustration)**.
26   Install the manifold, using a new gasket. Tighten the nuts in several stages, working from the center out, until the torque listed in this Chapter's Specifications is reached.
27   Reinstall the remaining parts in the reverse order of removal.
28   Adjust the accelerator cable (see Chapter 4).
29   Add coolant, run the engine and check for leaks and proper operation.

12   Exhaust manifold - removal and installation

Refer to illustrations 12.3a, 12.3b, 12.3c, 12.3d, 12.5a, 12.5b and 12.7
Warning: *Allow the engine to cool completely before beginning this procedure.*

Removal

1   Disconnect the battery cable from the negative terminal of the battery.
2   Set the parking brake and block the rear wheels. Raise the vehicle and support it securely on jackstands.
3   Working from under the vehicle, remove the nuts that secure the exhaust system to the bottom of the exhaust manifold **(see illustrations)**. Apply penetrating oil to the threads to make removal easier.
4   Unplug the oxygen sensor wire (see chapter 6).

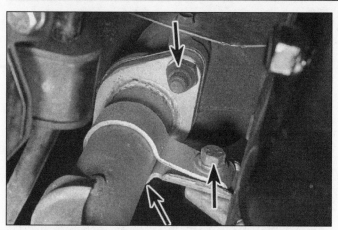

12.3a Working from under the vehicle, remove the nuts that secure the exhaust system to the bottom of the exhaust manifold - it may be necessary to apply penetrating oil to the threads to make removal easier

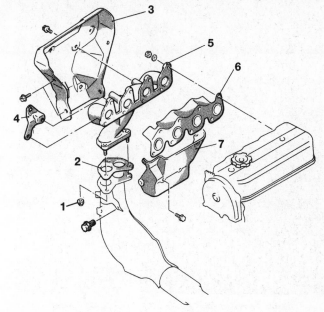

12.3b An exploded view of the 1.8L SOHC exhaust manifold

1   Self-locking nut
2   Gasket
3   Exhaust manifold heat shield (outer)
4   Engine hanger

5   Exhaust manifold
6   Exhaust manifold gasket
7   Exhaust manifold heat shield (inner)

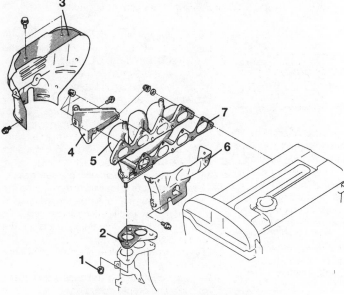

12.3c An exploded view of the 2.0L DOHC (non-turbo model) exhaust manifold

1   Self locking nut
2   Gasket
3   Exhaust manifold heat shield (outer)
4   Engine hanger

5   Exhaust manifold
6   Exhaust manifold gasket
7   Exhaust manifold heat shield (inner)

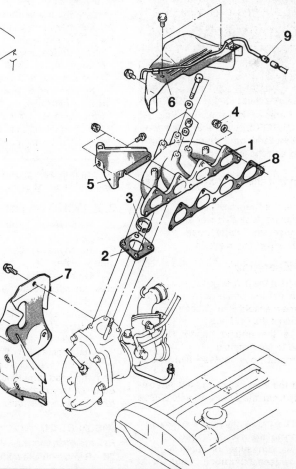

12.3d An exploded view of the 2.0L DOHC (turbo model) exhaust manifold

1   Exhaust manifold
2   Gasket
3   Exhaust gasket ring
4   Self-locking nut
5   Engine hanger
6   Upper exhaust manifold heat shield

7   Lower exhaust manifold heat shield
8   Exhaust manifold gasket
9   Oxygen sensor connector

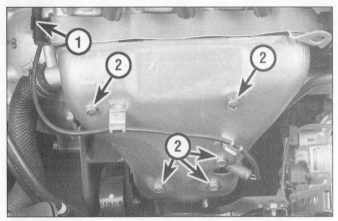

12.5a On the 1.8L SOHC engine, disconnect the oxygen sensor wire (1), detach it from the two clips, then remove the bolts (2) and lift off the heat shield (1.8L SOHC engine)

12.5b On the 2.0L DOHC engine, remove the three bolts (arrows), detach the oxygen sensor wire from the three clips, then slide out the heat shield

12.7 Apply penetrating oil to the threads before removing the exhaust manifold mounting nuts (arrows)

13.9a Using an 8 mm Allen-head socket, loosen the cylinder head bolts, 1/4-turn at a time

5   Remove the bolts that secure the heat shield **(see illustrations)** to the exhaust manifold. Lift the heat shield off.

6   Remove any brackets that may bolted to the exhaust manifold.

7   Apply penetrating oil to the threads and remove the exhaust manifold mounting nuts **(see illustration)**, brackets and emission components.

8   Slip the manifold off the studs and remove it from the engine compartment.

Installation

9   Clean and inspect the exhaust manifold studs, replacing any that show thread damage.

10   Using a scraper, remove all traces of gasket material from the mating surfaces and inspect them for wear and cracks. **Caution:** *When removing gasket material from any surface, especially aluminum, be very careful not to scratch or gouge the gasket surface. Any damage to the surface may a leak after reassembly. Gasket removal solvents are available from auto parts stores and may prove helpful.*

11   Place a new gasket over the studs, install the manifold and tighten the nuts in several stages, working from the center out, to the torque listed in this Chapter's Specifications.

12   Reinstall the remaining parts in the reverse order of removal.

13   Run the engine and check for exhaust leaks.

13   Cylinder head - removal and installation

Caution: *Allow the engine to cool completely before following this procedure.*

Removal

Refer to illustrations 13.9a, 13.9b, 13.9c and 13.10

1   Position the number one piston at Top Dead Center (see Chapter 2B).

2   Disconnect the battery cable from the negative battery terminal.

3   Drain the cooling system and remove the spark plugs (see Chapter 1).

4   Remove the intake manifold (see Section 11).

5   Remove the exhaust manifold (see Section 12).

6   Remove the ignition system components (see Chapter 5).

7   Remove the timing belt (see Section 8).

8   Remove the valve cover (see Section 4).

9   Using an 8 mm Allen-head socket,

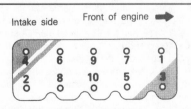

13.9b Loosen the bolts in the sequence shown until they can be removed by hand (1.8L engine)

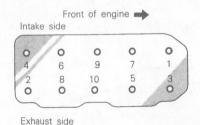

13.9c Cylinder head bolt loosening sequence for the 2.0L DOHC engine

13.10 Carefully lift the cylinder head straight up and place the head on wood blocks to prevent damage to the sealing surfaces. If the head sticks to the engine block, dislodge it by placing a block of wood against the head casting and tapping the wood with a hammer or by prying the head with a prybar placed carefully on a casting protrusion

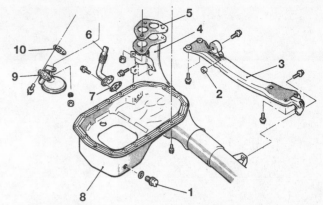

14.6a An exploded view of the oil pan and related components on 2.0L models without All-Wheel Drive (AWD)

1	Drain plug	6	Connection for oil return
2	Self-locking nut		pipe (turbo)
3	Center member	7	Gasket (turbo)
4	Connection for exhaust	8	Oil pan
	pipe	9	Oil screen and pick-up
5	Gasket		tube
		10	Gasket

2A

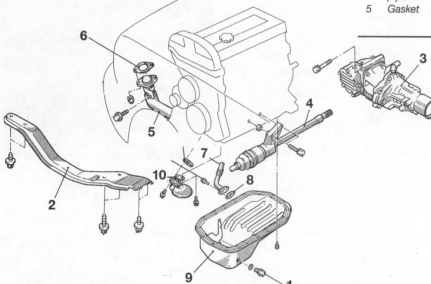

14.6b An exploded view of the oil pan and related components on 2.0L models with All Wheel Drive (AWD)

1	Drain plug	5	Exhaust pipe	8	Gasket
2	Left member		connection	9	Oil pan
3	Transfer assembly	6	Gasket	10	Oil screen and pick-
4	Drive shaft	7	Oil return pipe		up tube
			connection	11	Gasket

loosen the cylinder head bolts, 1/4-turn at a time, in the sequence shown for your engine **(see illustrations)** until they can be removed by hand.

10   Carefully lift the cylinder head **(see illustration)** straight up and place the head on wood blocks to prevent damage to the sealing surfaces. If the head sticks to the engine block, dislodge it by placing a block of wood against the head casting and tapping the wood with a hammer or by prying the head with a prybar placed carefully on a casting protrusion or in an exhaust port. **Note:** *Cylinder head disassembly and inspection procedures are covered in Chapter 2, Part B. It's a good idea to have the*

head checked for warpage, even if you're just replacing the gasket.

11   Remove all traces of old gasket material from the block and head. Do not allow anything to fall into the engine. Clean and inspect all threaded fasteners and be sure the threaded holes in the block are clean and dry.

Installation

12   Place a new gasket and the cylinder head in position on the engine block.

13   The cylinder head bolts should be tightened in several stages in the opposite order of removal **(see illustrations 13.9b and 13.9c)** to the torque listed in this Chap-

ter's Specifications.

14   Reinstall the timing belt (see Section 8).

15   Reinstall the remaining parts in the reverse order of removal.

16   Be sure to refill the cooling system and check all fluid levels. Rotate the crankshaft clockwise slowly by hand through six complete revolutions. Recheck the camshaft timing marks (see Section 8).

17   Start the engine and set the ignition timing (see Chapter 5). Run the engine until normal operating temperature is reached. Check for leaks and proper operation. Shut off the engine. Remove the valve cover and retorque the cylinder head bolts, unless the gasket manufacturer states otherwise.

14   Oil pan - removal and installation

Refer to illustrations 14.6a, 14.6b, 14.7, 14.8 and 14.10

Removal

1   Disconnect the battery cable from the negative battery cable.

2   Raise the vehicle and support it securely on jackstands.

3   Drain the engine oil (see Chapter 1).

4   Remove the splash pan under the drive-belt end of the engine, then remove the dipstick and drain the engine oil (see Chapter 1). On turbo models, unbolt the oil return pipe from the side of the oil pan.

5   Disconnect the exhaust pipe from the manifold and let the exhaust hang loosely under the car.

6   On 2.0L engines, remove the subframe center member **(see illustration)** and, on All Wheel Drive (AWD) models, remove the left member, transfer assembly and driveshaft, as described in Chapters 7C and 8 **(see illustration)**.

14.7 If the pan is stuck, tap it with a soft-face hammer or place a block of wood against the pan and tap the wood with a hammer

14.8 Remove two bolts and one nut (arrows) and remove the oil pump pick-up tube and screen assembly - clean both the tube and screen thoroughly before reassembly

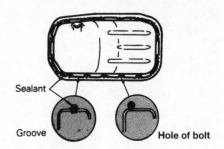

14.10 Apply a 4 mm bead of RTV sealant to the oil pan flange - be sure to apply the sealant on the inside edge of the bolt holes

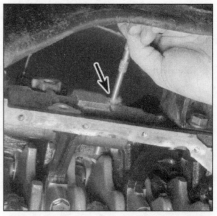

15.4 Remove the plug from the side of the block (arrow) and insert a Phillips screwdriver to keep the balance shaft from turning

7   Remove the bolts and lower the oil pan from the vehicle. If the pan is stuck, tap it with a soft-face hammer **(see illustration)** or place a block of wood against the pan and tap the wood with a hammer. **Caution:** *If you're wedging something between the oil pan and the engine block to separate the two, be extremely careful not to gouge or nick the gasket surface of either part; an oil leak could result.*

8   Remove the oil pump pickup tube and screen assembly **(see illustration)** and clean both the tube and screen thoroughly. Install the pick-up tube and screen with a new gasket.

9   Thoroughly clean the oil pan and sealing surfaces on the block and pan. Use a scraper to remove all traces of old gasket material. Gasket removal solvents are available at auto parts stores and may prove helpful. Check the oil pan sealing surface for distortion. Straighten or replace as necessary. After cleaning and straightening (if necessary), wipe the gasket surfaces of the pan and block clean with a rag soaked in lacquer thinner or acetone.

Installation

10   Apply a 4 mm bead of RTV sealant to the oil pan flange **(see illustration)**. **Note:** *When applying the sealant, lay the bead in the center of the oil pan rail, except for the bolt holes, where you'll need to go around the inside edge of the bolt holes, as shown in the inset to the illustration. If you apply the RTV to the outside of the bolt holes, an oil leak at the bolt-hole area will result.*

11   Place the oil pan into position and install the bolts finger tight. Working side-to-side from the center out, tighten the bolts to the torque listed in this Chapter's Specifications.

12   Reinstall the remaining parts in the reverse order of removal.

13   Refill the crankcase with the proper quantity and grade of oil and run the engine, checking for leaks. Road test the vehicle and check for leaks again.

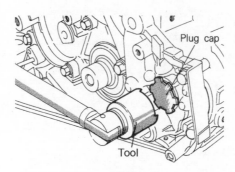

15.3 On 2.0L DOHC engines, remove the plug cap with either the special tool shown or a large pair of locking pliers

15   Front case - removal and installation

Removal

Refer to illustrations 15.3, 15.4, 15.5a, 15.5b, 15.5c, 15.5d, 15.6a, 15.6b and 15.6c

1   Remove the timing belt, sprockets and all tensioner assemblies (see Section 8).

2   Remove the oil pan and oil pump pick-up tube and screen (see Section 14).

3   On DOHC engines, unscrew the plug cap with either a special tool **(see illustration)**, available at most auto parts stores, or strike it squarely on the face of the plug with a hammer two or three times to break it loose, and the plug can be removed with a standard wrench or pliers.

4   Remove the bolt from the side of the block and insert a Phillips screwdriver or a small punch to keep the balance shaft from turning **(see illustration)**.

5   On 1.8L SOHC models, unbolt and remove the oil pump cover, then remove the

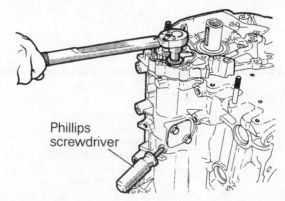

15.5a With the screwdriver in place, remove the nut that attaches the balance shaft to the oil pump driven gear (1.8L SOHC engine)

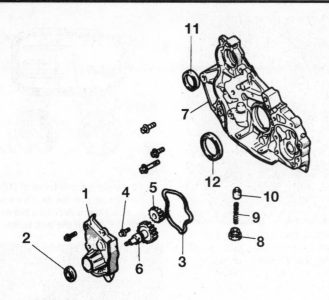

15.5b An exploded view of the 1.8L SOHC engine front case and oil pump assembly

1	Oil pump cover	7	Front case
2	Oil pump cover seal	8	Plug
3	Oil pump housing gasket	9	Relief spring
4	Housing bolt	10	Relief plunger
5	Oil pump driven gear	11	Balance shaft oil seal
6	Oil pump drive gear	12	Crankshaft oil seal

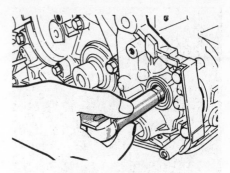

15.5c On 2.0L DOHC engines, unscrew and remove the oil pump driven gear bolt

bolt that attaches the balance shaft to the oil pump driven gear **(see illustrations)**. On 2.0L DOHC models, remove the bolt securing the oil pump driven gear to the balance shaft **(see illustrations)**.

6   Remove the bolts and the front case from the engine block **(see illustrations)**. If the case is difficult to remove use a screwdriver or prybar of some type placed at the location indicated **(see illustration) Caution:** *The bolts are of different lengths, so be sure to mark the bolts to show there original location so they can be placed back in the same locations.*

2A

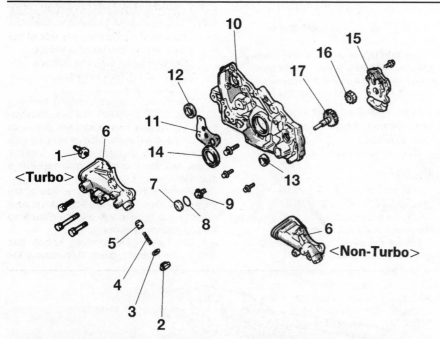

15.5d An exploded view of the 2.0L DOHC engine front case and oil pump assembly

1	Oil pressure switch	10	Front case
2	Oil pressure relief valve plug	11	Gasket
3	Gasket	12	Balance-shaft oil seal
4	Spring	13	Oil pump seal
5	Relief plunger	14	Crankshaft front oil seal
6	Oil filter bracket	15	Oil pump housing cover
7	Plug cap	16	Oil pump driven gear
8	O-ring	17	Oil pump drive gear
9	Driven gear front bolt		

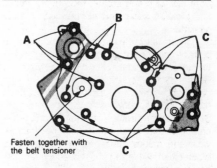

15.6a Front case bolt locations and lengths (1.8L SOHC engine)

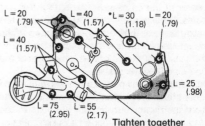

15.6b Front case bolt locations and lengths (2.0L DOHC engine)

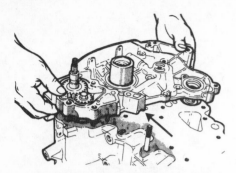

15.6c If the case is difficult to remove, use a screwdriver or prybar of some type placed at the location indicated (arrow)

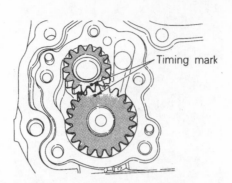

16.12a Install the oil pump gears so the marks line up as shown - if they don't line up, the balance shaft will be out of phase and severe engine vibration will result

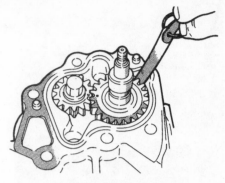

16.12b Use a feeler gauge of the correct thickness and check the tip clearance of the drive gear and . . .

Installation

7   Make sure all gasket surfaces are clean and free of all old gasket material.

8   Be sure to replace the crankshaft, balance shaft and oil pump seals, located in the front case, before reassembly (see Section 9). Lubricate all seal lips before reassembly.

9   Place the new gasket in position.

10   When placing the front case back on the engine be **VERY** careful not to damage the new seals, since you're lining up more than one seal at a time - try to keep the case parallel to the front of the engine at all times.

11   Reassembly of the remaining parts is the reverse procedure of removal.

16   Oil pump - removal, inspection and installation

Note: *Both the 1.8L SOHC and the 2.0L DOHC engines have gear-type oil pumps located in the front case. The 1.8L SOHC engine oil pump may be disassembled without removal of the front case while the disassembly of the 2.0L DOHC engine oil pump requires the removal of the case from the engine block. But it's recommended that the front case be removed on either engine for ease of servicing.*

Removal

1   Remove the timing belt, balance shaft belt and crankshaft sprocket (see Section 8).

2   Unbolt the oil pickup tube and screen from the bottom of the pump housing **(see illustration 14.8).**

1.8L SOHC engine

3   Remove the oil pump-to-front-case bolts **(see illustration 15.6a)** and separate the oil pump cover from the case.

4   Remove the pressure relief plug, spring and plunger **(see illustration 15.5b).**

2.0L DOHC engine

5   Remove the oil pan (see Section 14).

6   Remove the front case (see Section 15).

7   Remove the screws that attach the oil pump cover to the back side of the case **(see illustration 15.5d).**

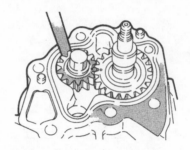

16.12c . . . the driven gear with the specifications in this Chapter - on both measurements, be sure to check the clearances at the points shown in the illustrations (these are the minimum clearance points)

8   Remove the pressure relief plug, spring and plunger.

Inspection

Refer to illustrations 16.12a, 16.12b, 16.12c and 16.12d

9   The inspection and clearance checks are the same for both the 1.8L SOHC and 2.0L DOHC engines. The specifications should be checked for your specific engine model.

10   Clean all parts thoroughly and remove all traces of old gasket material from the sealing surfaces. Visually inspect the gears for chips, score marks or possible overheating conditions (a bluish discoloration of the gears). If any of these conditions are found replace the gears.

11   Also inspect the front case housing where the gears ride to look for similar wear indications, scoring, galling or evidence of an overheat condition. If any of these are found in the pump housing area the front case will have to be replaced.

12   Install the oil pump outer and inner gears so the marks line up as shown **(see illustration)** and measure the clearances **(see illustrations)**. Compare the clearances

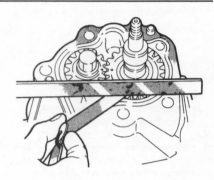

16.12d Using a precision straightedge and a feeler gauge, check the clearance of the gears to the top of the pump housing (side clearance)

to the values listed in this Chapter's Specifications. Measure the free length of the pressure regulator spring and compare the measurement to this Chapter's Specifications. Replace parts as necessary. Pack the pump cavity with petroleum jelly and install the cover. Tighten the bolts to the torque listed in this Chapter's Specifications. **Caution:** *You must line up the oil pump gear marks on reassembly. If you don't, the balance shaft will be out of phase and severe engine vibration will result.*

Installation

13   Install the pressure regulator valve components and tighten the plug securely.

14   Install a new oil pump cover gasket (1.8L SOHC engine only), then install the cover, making sure to install the bolts in their proper locations, according to length **(see illustration 15.6a and 15.6c).** Tighten the bolts to the torque listed in this Chapter's Specifications.

15   Reinstall the remaining parts in the reverse order of removal.

16   Add oil, start the engine and check for oil pressure and leaks.

17.3a On some models, the flywheel/driveplate bolts are staggered so they line up only one way, but . . .

17.3b . . . on other flywheels/driveplates, the bolts are symmetrical, so you'll need to mark the relationship of the flywheel/driveplate to the crankshaft hub to ensure correct alignment during installation

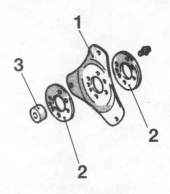

17.5 Remove the flywheel/driveplate from the crankshaft. If you have an automatic transmission, there will be one or two adapter plate(s)

   1   Driveplate
   2   Adapter plate(s)
   3   Crankshaft bushing

17   Flywheel/driveplate - removal and installation

Refer to illustrations 17.3a, 17.3b and 17.5

Removal

1   Raise the vehicle and support it securely on jackstands, then refer to Chapter 7 and remove the transaxle and All Wheel Drive (AWD) components (if equipped). If it's leaking, now would be a very good time to replace the transaxle front seal (the torque converter must be removed to gain access to this seal).

2   Remove the pressure plate and clutch disc (manual transaxle equipped vehicles) (see Chapter 8). Now is a good time to check/replace the clutch components and the pilot bearing.

3   The bolt holes are either staggered or symmetrical on the flywheel/driveplate bolt pattern. To ensure correct alignment during reinstallation, mark the position of the flywheel/driveplate to the crankshaft before removal **(see illustrations)**.

4   Remove the bolts that secure the flywheel/driveplate to the crankshaft. If the crankshaft turns, wedge a screwdriver in the ring gear teeth to jam the flywheel.

5   Remove the flywheel/driveplate from the crankshaft. **Note:** *If you have an automatic transaxle, there will be a reinforcement plate* **(see illustration)** *on each side of the 1.8L engine driveplate, and, on the 2.0L engine, there will be a single reinforcement plate only on the transaxle side of the driveplate. Since the flywheel is fairly heavy, be sure to support it while removing the last bolt.*

6   Clean the flywheel to remove grease and oil. Inspect the surface for cracks, rivet grooves, burned areas and score marks. Light scoring can be removed with emery cloth. Check for cracked and broken ring gear teeth. Lay the flywheel on a flat surface and use a straightedge to check for warpage. **Note:** *Flywheels can be re-surfaced by a machine shop. Also, starter ring gears are available separately and can be installed by*

an automotive machine shop.

7   Clean and inspect the mating surfaces of the flywheel/driveplate and the crankshaft. If the crankshaft rear seal is leaking, replace it before reinstalling the flywheel/driveplate (see Section 18).

Installation

8   Position the flywheel/driveplate against the crankshaft. If the bolt holes aren't staggered, align the previously applied match marks. Before installing the bolts, apply thread locking compound to the threads.

9   Wedge a screwdriver in the ring gear teeth to keep the flywheel/driveplate from turning as you tighten the bolts to the torque listed in this Chapter's Specifications.

10   The remainder of installation is the reverse of the removal procedure.

18   Rear main oil seal - replacement

Refer to illustrations 18.2a, 18.2b, 18.5, 18.6 and 18.7

1   The transaxle must be removed from the vehicle for this procedure (see Chapter 7).

2   The seal can be replaced without removing the oil pan or seal retainer. However, this method is not recommended because the lip of the seal is quite stiff and it's possible to cock the seal in the retainer bore or damage it during installation. If you want to take the chance, pry out the old seal **(see illustration)**. Apply a film of clean oil to the crankshaft seal journal and the lip of the new seal and carefully tap the new seal into place **(see illustration)**. The lip is stiff, so carefully work it onto the seal journal of the crankshaft with a smooth object like the rounded end of a socket extension as you tap the seal into place. Don't rush it or you may damage the seal.

3   The following method is recommended but requires removal of the oil pan (see Sec-

18.2a The quick (but not recommended) way to replace the rear main oil seal is to simply pry the old one out

18.2b Lubricate the crankshaft journal and the lip of the new seal with engine oil and tap the new seal into place - the seal lip is stiff and can be easily damaged during installation if you're not careful

2A

18.5 If the seal housing is removed, support the housing on two wood blocks and drive out the old seal with a punch or screwdriver and hammer

18.6 Drive the new seal into the housing with a block of wood or a section of pipe, if you don't have one large enough - make sure you don't cock the seal in the bore

tion 14) and the seal retainer.

4   After the oil pan has been removed, remove the bolts, detach the seal retainer and peel off all the old gasket material.

5   Position the seal and retainer assembly on a couple of wood blocks on a workbench and drive the old seal out from the back side with a punch and hammer **(see illustration)**.

6   Drive the new seal into the retainer with a block of wood **(see illustration)** or a section of pipe slightly smaller in diameter than the outside diameter of the seal.

7   On the 2.0L DOHC engine, there will be an oil separator **(see illustration)**. Be sure the oil hole is on the bottom as shown in the illustration.

8   Lubricate the crankshaft seal journal and the lip of the new seal with clean engine oil. Position a new gasket on the engine block.

9   Slowly and carefully push the seal onto the crankshaft. The seal lip is stiff, so work it onto the crankshaft with a smooth object such as the rounded end of a socket extension as you push the retainer against the block.

10   Install and tighten the retainer bolts to the torque listed in this Chapter's Specifications. The bottom sealing flange of the

retainer must not extend below the bottom sealing flange (oil pan rail) of the block.

11   The remaining steps are the reverse of removal.

12   Run the engine and check for oil leaks.

19   Engine mounts - check and replacement

1   Engine mounts seldom require attention, but broken or deteriorated mounts should be replaced immediately or the added strain placed on the driveline components may cause damage or wear.

Check

2   During the check, the engine must be raised slightly to remove the weight from the mounts.

3   Raise the vehicle and support it securely on jackstands, then position a jack under the engine oil pan. Place a large block of wood between the jack head and the oil pan to prevent oil pan damage, then carefully raise the engine just enough to take the weight off the mounts. **Warning:** *DO NOT place any part of your body under the engine when it's supported only by a jack!*

4   Check the mounts to see if the rubber is cracked, hardened or separated from the

Oil seal case   **Oil separator**

Oil hole

18.7 On 2.0L DOHC engines, be sure to install the oil separator with the oil hole down

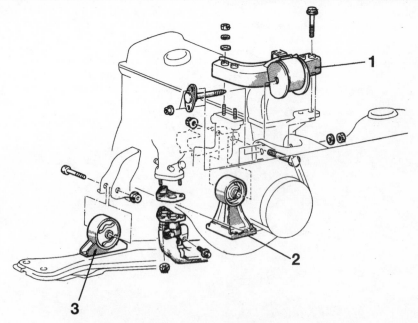

19.8a An exploded view of the engine mounts and brackets on both the 1.8L and 2.0L engines

1   *Engine mount bracket*   3   *Front roll stopper bracket*
2   *Rear roll stopper bracket*

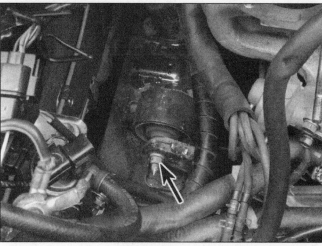

19.8b After supporting the engine, remove the fasteners and detach the mount bracket from the frame and engine

19.8c The rear . . .

metal backing. Sometimes the rubber will split right down the center.

5　Check for relative movement between the mount plates and the engine or frame (use a large screwdriver or pry bar to attempt to move the mounts). If movement is noted, lower the engine and tighten the mount fasteners.

6　Rubber preservative may be applied to the mounts to slow deterioration.

Replacement

Refer to illustrations 19.8a, 19.8b, 19.8c and 19.8d

7　Disconnect the battery cable from the negative battery terminal, then raise the vehicle and support it securely on jackstands (if not already done).

8　Remove the fasteners and detach the mount from the frame and engine **(see illustrations)**. **Caution:** *Do not disconnect more than one mount at a time, except during engine removal.*

9　The rubber portion of the mounts are normally available separately from the bracket that attaches it to the frame or block. Obtain new inserts and take them to an automotive machine shop or dealer service department to be pressed into the existing bracket, if necessary.

10　Installation is the reverse of removal. Use thread locking compound on the mount bolts and be sure to tighten them securely.

19.8d . . . and front roll stoppers are connected to the brackets by through-bolts (arrows)

Notes

Chapter 2 Part B
General engine overhaul procedures

Contents

2B

Specifications

General

Cylinder compression pressure (at 250 to 400 rpm)

1.8L engine

Standard	185 psi
Service limit	131 psi
Difference between cylinders	14 psi maximum

2.0L engine

Turbo

Standard	164 psi
Service limit	121
Difference between cylinders	14 psi maximum

Non-turbo

Standard	192 psi
Service limit	145 psi
Difference between cylinders	14 psi maximum

Oil pressure (engine warm)	11 psi minimum at idle *Check 2B-5*

Intake manifold vacuum at idle (measured in inches of Mercury)

1.8L engine	20 in. Hg

2.0L engine

Turbo

Manual transmission	18.9 in. Hg
Automatic transmission	20.5 in. Hg
Non-turbo	18.3 in. Hg

Cylinder head warpage

Head gasket surface
    Standard .... 0.002 inch
    Service limit .... 0.008 inch
Intake and exhaust manifold mounting surfaces
    Standard.. 0.006 inch
    Service limit .... 0.012 inch

Valves and related components

Face angle .... 45.0 to 45.5 degrees
Seat angle... 44.0 to 44.5-degrees
Seat width... 0.0354 to 0.0512 inch
Valve length
    1.8L engine
        1990 through 1992
            Intake
                Standard .... 4.323 inches
                Service limit...................................... not available
            Exhaust
                Standard 4.280
                Service limit...................................... not available
        1993 and later
            Intake
                Standard .... 3.866 inches
                Service limit...................................... not available
            Exhaust
                Standard .... 3.760 inches
                Service limit...................................... not available
    2.0L (turbo and non-turbo models)
        Intake .... 4.311 inches
        Exhaust.. 4.319 inches
Valve margin width
    1.8L
        1990 through 1992
            Intake
                Standard .... 0.039 inch
                Service limit...................................... 0.028 inch
            Exhaust
                Standard .... 0.028 inch
                Service limit...................................... 0.020 inch
        1993 and later
            Intake
                Standard .... 0.047 inch
                Service limit...................................... 0.028 inch
            Exhaust
                Standard .... 0.059 inch
                Service limit...................................... 0.039 inch
    2.0L (turbo and non-turbo models)
        Intake
             Standard.. 0.040 inch
            Service limit .... 0.028 inch
        Exhaust
             Standard.. 0.059 inch
             Service limit .... 0.040 inch
Valve stem diameter
    1.8L engine
        Intake .... 0.31 inch
        Exhaust.. 0.31 inch
    2.0L engine (turbo and non-turbo models)
        Intake .... 0.2585 to 0.2591 inch
        Exhaust.. 0.2571 to 0.2579 inch
Valve stem-to-guide clearance
    1.8L engine
        Intake
            Standard.. 0.0012 to 0.0024 inch
            Service limit .... 0.004 inch
        Exhaust
            Standard.. 0.0020 to 0.0035 inch
            Service limit .... 0.006 inch

2.0L engine (turbo and non-turbo models)
   Intake
      Standard .... 0.0008 to 0.0019 inch
      Service limit .... 0.004 inch
   Exhaust
      Standard .... 0.002 to 0.0033 inch
      Service limit .... 0.006 inch
Valve spring
   Out-of-square limit 4.0-degrees
   Free length (intake and exhaust)
      1.8L engine
         Standard .... 1.937 inches
         Service limit .... 1.898 inches
      2.0L engine (turbo and non-turbo models)
         Standard .... 1.902 inches
         Service limit .... 1.862 inches
   Installed height
      1.8L engine
         Standard .... 1.469 inches
         Service limit .... 1.516 inches
      2.0L engine .... Not available
   Load
      1.8L engine .... 64 lbs at installed height
      2.0L engine .... 66 lbs at installed height

Crankshaft and connecting rods (all engines)

Connecting rod journal
   Diameter .... 1.771 inches
   Out-of-round limit .... 0.0006 inch
   Taper limit .... 0.0002 inch
   Connecting rod bearing oil clearance
      Standard .... 0.0008 to 0.0020 inch
      Service limit .... 0.004 inch
Connecting rod endplay (side clearance)
   Standard .... 0.0039 to 0.0098 inch
   Service limit .... 0.016 inch
Crankshaft main bearing journal
   Diameter .... 2.243 inches
   Out-of-round limits .... 0.0006 inch
   Taper limit .... 0.0002 inch
Crankshaft endplay .... 0.0020 to 0.0070 inch
Crankshaft main bearing oil clearance
   Standard .... 0.0008 to 0.0020 inch
   Service limit .... 0.0098 inch

Balance shafts

1.8L engine
   Front balance shaft
      Front journal diameter .... 1.5338 to 1.5344 inches
      Rear journal diameter .... 1.4154 to 1.4160 inches
   Rear balance shaft
      Front journal diameter .... 0.7270 to 0.7276 inch
      Rear journal diameter .... 1.4154 to 1.4160 inch
   Oil clearance
      Front journal .... 0.0008 to 0.0024 inch
      Rear journal .... 0.0020 to 0.0036 inch
2.0L engine
   Front balance shaft
      Front journal diameter .... 1.6519 to 1.6526 inches
      Rear journal diameter .... 1.6122 to 1.61219 inches
      Oil clearance
         Front journal
            1990 through 1992 .... 0.0008 to 0.0024 inch
            1993 and 1994 .... 0.0012 to 0.0024 inch
         Rear journal .... 0.0020 to 0.0036 inch
   Rear balance shaft
      Front journal diameter .... 0.7270 to 0.7276
      Rear journal diameter .... 1.6126 to 1.6132

2B

Balance shafts (continued)

Oil clearance
    Front journal .... 0.0008 to 0.0021
    Rear journal .... 0.0017 to 0.0033

Engine block

Cylinder bore diameter
    1.8L engine.. 3.173 inches
    2.0L engine.. 3.3465 inches
Stroke
    1.8L engine.. 3.39 inches
    2.0L engine.. 3.46 inches
Out-of-round and cylinder taper limits (all engines) .... 0.0004 inch
Block deck surface flatness (gasket surface)
    Standard.. 0.0020 inch
    Service limit .... 0.0040 inch

Pistons and rings

Piston diameter (nominal)*
    1.8L engine.. 3.173 inches
    2.0L engine.. 3.3465 inches
    *Measured 5/64-inch up from the bottom of the piston skirt.
Piston-to-bore clearance
    1.8L engine
        1990 through 1992.. 0.0004 to 0.0012 inch
        1993 and later... 0.0008 to 0.0016 inch
    2.0L engine
        Turbo.. 0.0012 to 0.0020 inch
        Non-turbo... 0.0008 to 0.0016 inch
Piston ring side clearance
    1.8L engine
        Number 1 (top) compression ring
            Standard.. 0.0018 to 0.0033 inch
            Service limit .... 0.005 inch
        Number 2 compression ring
            Standard.. 0.0008 to 0.0024 inch
            Service limit .... 0.004 inch
    2.0L engine
        Number 1 (top) compression ring
            Standard.. 0.0012 to 0.0028 inch
            Service limit .... 0.004 inch
        Number 2 compression ring
            Standard.. 0.0012 to 0.0028 inch
            Service limit .... 0.004 inch
Piston ring end gap
    1.8L engine
        Number 1 (top) compression ring
            Standard .... 0.0118 to 0.0177
            Service limit .... 0.031 inch
        Number 2 compression ring
            Standard .... 0.0079 to 0.0138 inch
            Service limit .... 0.031 inch
        Oil ring
            Standard .... 0.079 to 0.0276 inch
            Service limit .... 0.039 inch
    2.0L engine
        Number 1 compression ring
            Standard
                1990 through 1992................................... 0.0098 to 0.0177 inch
                1993 and later... 0.0098 to 0.0157 inch
            Service limit .... 0.031 inch
        Number 2 compression ring
            Standard
                1990 through 1992................................... 0.0138 to 0.0197 inch
                1993 and later... 0.0177 to 0.0236 inch
            Service limit .... 0.031 inch
        Oil ring
            Standard .... 0.0079 to 0.0276 inch
            Service limit 0.040

Torque specifications*

	Ft-lbs
Main bearing cap bolts	
1.8L engine	37 to 39
2.0L engine (turbo and non-turbo models)	18 plus an additional 90 degrees rotation
Connecting rod cap nuts	
1.8L engine	24 to 25
2.0L engine	14.5 plus an additional 90 degrees rotation
Oil jet bolt (turbo models only)	22 to 25

Refer to Part A for additional torque specifications.

1   General information

Included in this portion of Chapter 2 are the general overhaul procedures for the cylinder head and internal engine components. The information ranges from advice concerning preparation for an overhaul and the purchase of replacement parts to detailed, step-by-step procedures covering removal and installation of internal engine components and the inspection of parts.

The following Sections have been written based on the assumption that the engine has been removed from the vehicle. For information concerning in-vehicle engine repair, as well as removal and installation of the external components necessary for the overhaul, see Part A of this Chapter. For information on determining models and engine numbers, refer to the *Vehicle Identification Numbers* at the front of this manual.

The Specifications included in this Part are only those necessary for the inspection and overhaul procedures which follow. Refer to Part A for additional Specifications.

2   Engine overhaul - general information

Refer to illustration 2.4

It's not always easy to determine when, or if, an engine should be completely overhauled, as a number of factors must be considered.

2.4 The oil pressure can be checked by removing the sending unit and installing a pressure gauge in the threaded hole - the oil pressure sending units (arrows) are located on the front of the engine block near the oil filter (either one will work)

High mileage is not necessarily an indication that an overhaul is needed, while low mileage doesn't preclude the need for an overhaul. Frequency of servicing is probably the most important consideration. An engine that's had regular and frequent oil and filter changes, as well as other required maintenance, will most likely give many thousands of miles of reliable service. Conversely, a neglected engine may require an overhaul very early in its life.

Excessive oil consumption is an indication that piston rings, valve seals and/or valve guides are in need of attention. Make sure that oil leaks aren't responsible before deciding that the rings and/or guides are bad. Perform a compression check to determine the extent of the work required (see Section 3).

Check the oil pressure with a gauge installed in place of the oil pressure sending unit **(see illustration)** and compare it to the Specifications in this Chapter. If it's extremely low, the bearings and/or oil pump are probably worn out.

Loss of power, rough running, knocking or metallic engine noises, excessive valve train noise and high fuel consumption rates may also point to the need for an overhaul, especially if they're all present at the same time. If a complete tune-up doesn't remedy the situation, major mechanical work is the only solution.

An engine overhaul involves restoring the internal parts to the specifications of a new engine. During an overhaul, the piston rings are replaced and the cylinder walls are reconditioned (rebored and/or honed). If a rebore is done by an automotive machine shop, new oversize pistons will also be installed. The main bearings, connecting rod bearings and camshaft bearings are generally replaced with new ones and, if necessary, the crankshaft may be reground to restore the journals. Generally, the valves are serviced as well, since they're usually in less-than-perfect condition at this point. While the engine is being overhauled, other components, such as the distributor, starter and alternator, can be rebuilt as well. The end result should be a like-new engine that will give many trouble free miles. **Note:** *Critical cooling system components such as the hoses, drivebelts, thermostat and water pump MUST be replaced with new parts when an engine is overhauled. The radiator should be checked carefully to ensure that it isn't clogged or leaking (see Chapter 3). Also, we don't recommend overhauling the oil pump - always install a new one when an engine is rebuilt.*

Before beginning the engine overhaul, read through the entire procedure to familiarize yourself with the scope and requirements of the job. Overhauling an engine isn't difficult, but it is time consuming. Plan on the vehicle being tied up for a minimum of two weeks, especially if parts must be taken to an automotive machine shop for repair or reconditioning. Check on availability of parts and make sure that any necessary special tools and equipment are obtained in advance. Most work can be done with typical hand tools, although a number of precision measuring tools are required for inspecting parts to determine if they must be replaced. Often an automotive machine shop will handle the inspection of parts and offer advice concerning reconditioning and replacement. **Note:** *Always wait until the engine has been completely disassembled and all components, especially the engine block, have been inspected before deciding what service and repair operations must be performed by an automotive machine shop. Since the block's condition will be the major factor to consider when determining whether to overhaul the original engine or buy a rebuilt one, never purchase parts or have machine work done on other components until the block has been thoroughly inspected. As a general rule, time is the primary cost of an overhaul, so it doesn't pay to install worn or substandard parts.*

As a final note, to ensure maximum life and minimum trouble from a rebuilt engine, everything must be assembled with care in a spotlessly clean environment.

3   Cylinder compression check

Refer to illustration 3.6

1   A compression check will tell you what mechanical condition the upper end (pistons, rings, valves, head gaskets) of your engine is in. Specifically, it can tell you if the compression is down due to leakage caused by worn piston rings, defective valves and seats or a blown head gasket. **Note:** *The engine must be at normal operating temperature and the battery must be fully charged for this check. Also, the choke valve must be all the way open to get an accurate compression reading (if the engine's warm, the choke should be open).*

2   Begin by cleaning the area around the spark plugs before you remove them (compressed air should be used, if available, otherwise a small brush or even a bicycle tire pump will work). The idea is to prevent dirt

3.6 A compression gauge with a threaded fitting for the spark plug hole is preferred over the type that requires hand pressure to maintain the seal - be sure to open the throttle valve as far as possible and disable the ignition system during the compression check!

from getting into the cylinders as the compression check is being done.

3   Remove all of the spark plugs from the engine (Chapter 1).

4   Block the throttle wide open.

5   Disconnect the primary (low voltage) wires from the distributor (1.8L engine) or the ignition power transistor (2.0L engines) (see Chapter 5).

6   Install the compression gauge in the number one spark plug hole **(see illustration)**.

7   Crank the engine over at least seven compression strokes and watch the gauge. The compression should build up quickly in a healthy engine. Low compression on the first stroke, followed by gradually increasing pressure on successive strokes, indicates worn piston rings. A low compression reading on the first stroke, which doesn't build up during successive strokes, indicates leaking valves or a blown head gasket (a cracked head could also be the cause). Deposits on the undersides of the valve heads can also cause low compression. Record the highest gauge reading obtained.

8   Repeat the procedure for the remaining cylinders and compare the results to the Specifications in this Chapter.

9   Add some engine oil (about three squirts from a plunger-type oil can) to each cylinder, through the spark plug hole, and repeat the test.

10   If the compression increases after the oil is added, the piston rings are definitely worn. If the compression doesn't increase significantly, the leakage is occurring at the valves or head gasket. Leakage past the valves may be caused by burned valve seats and/or faces or warped, cracked or bent valves.

11   If two adjacent cylinders have equally low compression, there's a strong possibility that the head gasket between them is blown. The appearance of coolant in the combustion chambers or the crankcase would verify this condition.

12   If one cylinder is 20 percent lower than the others, and the engine has a slightly rough idle, a worn exhaust lobe on the camshaft could be the cause.

13   If the compression is unusually high, the combustion chambers are probably coated with carbon deposits. If that's the case, the cylinder head should be removed and de-carbonized.

14   If compression is way down or varies greatly between cylinders, it would be a good idea to have a leak-down test performed by an automotive repair shop. This test will pinpoint exactly where the leakage is occurring and how severe it is.

---

4   Vacuum gauge diagnostic checks

A vacuum gauge provides valuable information about what is going on in the engine at a low-cost. You can check for worn rings or cylinder walls, leaking head or intake manifold gaskets, incorrect carburetor adjustments, restricted exhaust, stuck or burned valves, weak valve springs, improper ignition or valve timing and ignition problems.

Unfortunately, vacuum gauge readings are easy to misinterpret, so they should be used in conjunction with other tests to confirm the diagnosis.

Both the absolute readings and the rate of needle movement are important for accurate interpretation. Most gauges measure vacuum in inches of mercury (in-Hg). The following references to vacuum assume the diagnosis is being performed at sea level. As elevation increases (or atmospheric pressure decreases), the reading will decrease. For every 1,000 foot increase in elevation above approximately 2000 feet, the gauge readings will decrease about one inch of mercury.

Connect the vacuum gauge directly to intake manifold vacuum, not to ported (throttle-body) vacuum. Be sure no hoses are left disconnected during the test or false readings will result.

Before you begin the test, allow the engine to warm up completely. Block the wheels and set the parking brake. With the transmission in neutral (or Park, on automatics), start the engine and allow it to run at normal idle speed. **Warning:** *Carefully inspect the fan blades for cracks or damage before starting the engine. Keep your hands and the vacuum tester clear of the fan and do not stand in front of the vehicle or in line with the fan when the engine is running.*

Read the vacuum gauge; an average, healthy engine should normally produce about 17 to 22 inches of vacuum with a fairly steady needle. Refer to the following vacuum gauge readings and what they indicate about the engines condition:

1   A low steady reading usually indicates a leaking gasket between the intake manifold and throttle body, a leaky vacuum hose, late ignition timing or incorrect camshaft timing.

Check ignition timing with a timing light and eliminate all other possible causes, utilizing the tests provided in this Chapter before you remove the timing belt cover to check the timing marks.

2   If the reading is three to eight inches below normal and it fluctuates at that low reading, suspect an intake manifold gasket leak at an intake port or a faulty injector.

3   If the needle has regular drops of about two to four inches at a steady rate the valves are probably leaking. Perform a compression or leak-down test to confirm this.

4   An irregular drop or down-flick of the needle can be caused by a sticking valve or an ignition misfire. Perform a compression or leak-down test and read the spark plugs.

5   A rapid vibration of about four in-Hg vibration at idle combined with exhaust smoke indicates worn valve guides. Perform a leak-down test to confirm this. If the rapid vibration occurs with an increase in engine speed, check for a leaking intake manifold gasket or head gasket, weak valve springs, burned valves or ignition misfire.

6   A slight fluctuation, say one inch up and down, may mean ignition problems. Check all the usual tune-up items and, if necessary, run the engine on an ignition analyzer.

7   If there is a large fluctuation, perform a compression or leak-down test to look for a weak or dead cylinder or a blown head gasket.

8   If the needle moves slowly through a wide range, check for a clogged PCV system, incorrect idle fuel mixture, carburetor/throttle body or intake manifold gasket leaks.

9   Check for a slow return after revving the engine by quickly snapping the throttle open until the engine reaches about 2,500 rpm and let it shut. Normally the reading should drop to near zero, rise above normal idle reading (about 5 in-Hg over) and then return to the previous idle reading. If the vacuum returns slowly and doesn't peak when the throttle is snapped shut, the rings may be worn. If there is a long delay, look for a restricted exhaust system (often the muffler or cataLytic converter). An easy way to check this is to temporarily disconnect the exhaust ahead of the suspected part and repeat the test.

---

5   Engine removal - methods and precautions

If you've decided that an engine must be removed for overhaul or major repair work, several preliminary steps should be taken.

Locating a suitable place to work is extremely important. Adequate work space, along with storage space for the vehicle, will be needed. If a shop or garage isn't available, at the very least a flat, level, clean work surface made of concrete or asphalt is required.

Cleaning the engine compartment and engine before beginning the removal procedure will help keep tools clean and organized.

An engine hoist or A-frame will also be necessary. Make sure the equipment is rated in excess of the combined weight of the engine and accessories. Safety is of primary importance, considering the potential hazards involved in lifting the engine out of the vehicle.

If the engine is being removed by a novice, a helper should be available. Advice and aid from someone more experienced would also be helpful. There are many instances when one person cannot simultaneously perform all of the operations required when lifting the engine out of the vehicle.

Plan the operation ahead of time. Arrange for or obtain all of the tools and equipment you'll need prior to beginning the job. Some of the equipment necessary to perform engine removal and installation safely and with relative ease are (in addition to an engine hoist) a heavy duty floor jack, complete sets of wrenches and sockets as described in the front of this manual, wooden blocks and plenty of rags and cleaning solvent for mopping up spilled oil, coolant and gasoline. If the hoist must be rented, make sure that you arrange for it in advance and perform all of the operations possible without it beforehand. This will save you money and time.

Plan for the vehicle to be out of use for quite a while. A machine shop will be required to perform some of the work which the do-it-yourselfer can't accomplish without special equipment. These shops often have a busy schedule, so it would be a good idea to consult them before removing the engine in order to accurately estimate the amount of time required to rebuild or repair components that may need work.

Always be extremely careful when removing and installing the engine. Serious injury can result from careless actions. Plan ahead, take your time and a job of this nature, although major, can be accomplished successfully.

6   Engine - removal and installation

Refer to illustrations 6.7, 6.24 and 6.26
Note: *Read through the entire Section before beginning this procedure. The engine and transaxle are removed as a unit and then separated outside the vehicle.*

Removal

1   If the vehicle is equipped with air conditioning, have the system discharged by a dealer service department or a service station.
2   Place protective covers on the front fenders.
3   Remove the hood (see Chapter 11). Relieve the fuel system pressure (see Chapter 4).
4   Disconnect and remove the battery (see Chapter 5).
5   Remove the air cleaner assembly (see

Chapter 4). On vehicles equipped with a turbocharger, remove the turbocharger intake hose (see Chapter 4).
6   Drain and remove the radiator (see Chapter 3). **Note:** *On vehicles equipped with an automatic transaxle, remove the cooler hoses from the radiator.*
7   Carefully label, then disconnect all vacuum lines, coolant and emissions hoses and wire harness connectors. Masking tape and felt-tip pens work well for marking items **(see illustration)**. If necessary, take instant photos or sketch the locations to ensure correct reinstallation.
8   Disconnect the fuel lines from the fuel injection system (see Chapter 4) and cap them to prevent leakage.
9   Detach the throttle cable (see Chapter 4).
10   Raise the vehicle and support it securely on jackstands.
11   On manual transaxle-equipped models, refer to Chapter 7 and detach the shift cables. Also, unbolt the slave cylinder without disconnecting the hydraulic line (see Chapter 8).
12   On automatic transaxle-equipped vehicles, detach the shift control cable from the transaxle, then remove the bellhousing cover and the driveplate-to-torque converter bolts (see Chapter 7).
13   Detach the speedometer cable from the transaxle.
14   If equipped, remove the air conditioning compressor (see Chapter 3).
15   Remove the power steering pump and reservoir (if equipped) from the brackets without disconnecting the hoses and set them aside.
16   Remove the splash shield (if not already done) located at the drivebelt end of the engine.
17   Drain the engine oil and transaxle fluid and remove the oil filter (see Chapter 1).
18   Disconnect the exhaust pipe from the exhaust manifold.
19   Remove the driveaxles from the transaxle (see Chapter 8). Stuff clean rags into the openings to prevent the entry of foreign material.
20   Attach a chain or an engine lifting fixture

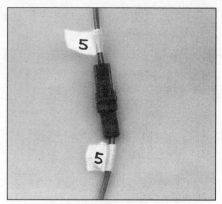

6.7 Label both ends of each wire or vacuum connection before disconnecting them

to the engine lifting brackets (or to bolts which are securely mounted in the cast iron block or accessory mounting bracket) and hook up the hoist. **Warning:** *Attaching the engine lifting chain to a bolt or stud located in an aluminum component (such as the cylinder head) may not provide the necessary strength to support the weight of the engine/transmission assembly during removal.* Take up the slack until there is tension on the chain to support the engine/transaxle assembly.
21   Support the transaxle with a floor jack. Place a block of wood on the jack pad to protect the transaxle. **Warning:** *Do not place any part of your body under the engine/transaxle when it's supported only by a hoist or other lifting device.*
22   Remove the plugs from the right front inner fender.
23   Check for clearance and, if necessary, remove the transaxle mount bracket (see Chapter 7).
24   Remove the mount through-bolts on all of the engine or transaxle mounts **(see illustration)**.
25   Confirm that all of the cables, hoses, wires and other items are disconnected from the engine.
26   Carefully push the transaxle down, or adjust the chain to position the engine slightly higher than the transaxle, while lifting the

6.24 Unscrew the nuts and remove the through-bolts (arrow) from the engine and transaxle mounts (typical mount through-bolt and nut shown)

2B

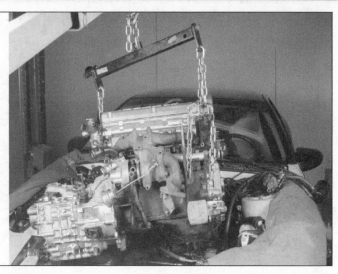

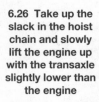

6.26 Take up the slack in the hoist chain and slowly lift the engine up with the transaxle slightly lower than the engine

engine up to clear obstructions **(see illustration)**.

27 Lift the engine and transaxle high enough to clear the front of the vehicle and slowly move the hoist away.

28 Lower the hoist and set the transaxle on blocks - leave the hoist hooked up.

29 With the transaxle securely supported, remove the driveplate-to-torque converter bolts (automatic transaxle only) and transaxle-to-engine bolts and separate the engine from the transaxle. Refer to Chapter 7 if necessary.

30 Remove the clutch components, if equipped (see Chapter 8) and flywheel (or driveplate) (see Chapter 2, Part A) and the engine rear plate. Mount the engine on a stand.

Installation

31 Check the engine/transaxle mounts. If they're worn or damaged, replace them.

32 On manual transaxle equipped models, inspect the clutch components (see Chapter 8) and apply a very small amount of high temperature grease to the transaxle input shaft splines.

33 On automatic transaxle equipped vehicles, inspect the converter seal and bushing.

34 Carefully rejoin the transaxle and engine following the procedure outlined in Chapter 7. **Caution:** *Do not use the bolts to force the engine and transaxle into alignment. It may crack or damage major components.*

35 Install the transaxle-to-engine bolts and tighten them securely.

36 Attach the hoist to the engine and carefully lower the engine/transaxle assembly into the vehicle.

37 Install the mount bolts and tighten them securely.

38 Reinstall the remaining components and fasteners in the reverse order of removal.

39 Add coolant, oil, power steering and transmission fluid/lubricant as needed (see Chapter 1).

40 Run the engine and check for proper operation and leaks. Shut off the engine and recheck the fluid levels.

7   Engine rebuilding alternatives

The do-it-yourselfer is faced with a number of options when performing an engine overhaul. The decision to replace the engine block, piston/connecting rod assemblies and crankshaft depends on a number of factors, with the number one consideration being the condition of the block. Other considerations are cost, access to machine shop facilities, parts availability, time required to complete the project and the extent of prior mechanical experience on the part of the do-it-yourselfer. Some of the rebuilding alternatives include:

Individual parts - If the inspection procedures reveal that the engine block and most engine components are in reusable condition, purchasing individual parts may be the most economical alternative. The block, crankshaft and piston/connecting rod assemblies should all be inspected carefully. Even if the block shows little wear, the cylinder bores should be surface honed.

Short block - A short block consists of an engine block with a crankshaft and piston/connecting rod assemblies already installed. All new bearings are incorporated and all clearances will be correct. The existing camshaft, valve train components, cylinder head(s) and external parts can be bolted to the short block with little or no machine shop work necessary.

Long block - A long block consists of a short block plus an oil pump, oil pan, cylinder head(s), rocker arm cover(s), camshaft and valve train components, timing sprockets and chain or gears and timing cover. All components are installed with new bearings, seals and gaskets incorporated throughout. The installation of manifolds and external parts is all that's necessary.

Give careful thought to which alternative is best for you and discuss the situation with local automotive machine shops, auto parts dealers and experienced rebuilders before ordering or purchasing replacement parts.

8   Engine overhaul - disassembly sequence

1   It's much easier to disassemble and work on the engine if it's mounted on a portable engine stand. A stand can often be rented quite cheaply from an equipment rental yard. Before the engine is mounted on a stand, the flywheel/driveplate should be removed from the engine.

2   If a stand isn't available, it's possible to disassemble the engine with it blocked up on the floor. Be extra careful not to tip or drop the engine when working without a stand.

3   If you're going to obtain a rebuilt engine, all external components must come off first, to be transferred to the replacement engine, just as they will if you're doing a complete engine overhaul yourself. These include:

Alternator and brackets
Emissions control components
Distributor (1.8L engine) or coil pack and
    power transistor (2.0L engine), spark
    plug wires and spark plugs
Thermostat cover, thermostat and
    housing
Water pump
Fuel injection components
Intake/exhaust manifolds
Oil filter
Engine mounts
Clutch and flywheel/driveplate
Engine rear plate

Note: *When removing the external components from the engine, pay close attention to details that may be helpful or important during installation. Note the installed position of gaskets, seals, spacers, pins, brackets, washers, bolts and other small items.*

4   If you're obtaining a short block, which consists of the engine block, crankshaft, pistons and connecting rods all assembled, then the cylinder head, oil pan and oil pump will have to be removed as well. See *Engine rebuilding alternatives* for additional information regarding the different possibilities to be considered.

5   If you're planning a complete overhaul, the engine must be disassembled and the internal components removed in the general following order:

Valve cover
Intake and exhaust manifolds
Rocker arms and shafts (1.8L engine)
Timing belt cover
Timing belt and sprockets
Camshaft
Rocker arms and lash adjusters (2.0L
    engine)
Cylinder head
Oil pan
Oil pump
Rear main oil seal housing
Piston/connecting rod assemblies
Balance shafts
Crankshaft and main bearings

6   Before beginning the disassembly and overhaul procedures, make sure the following

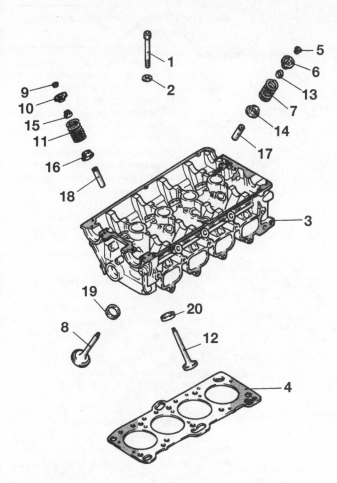

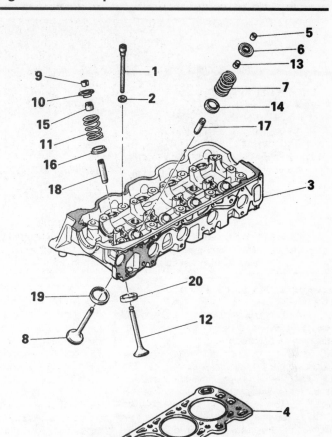

9.1a Exploded view of the 2.0L DOHC cylinder head, valve and spring assembly

1	Cylinder head bolt	11	Valve spring
2	Washer	12	Exhaust valve
3	Cylinder head	13	Valve stem seal
4	Gasket	14	Valve spring seat
5	Keepers	15	Valve stem seal
6	Valve spring retainer	16	Valve spring seat
7	Valve spring	17	Intake valve guide
8	Intake valve	18	Exhaust valve guide
9	Keepers	19	Intake valve seat
10	Valve spring retainer	20	Exhaust valve seat

9.1b Exploded view of the 1.8L SOHC cylinder head, valve and spring assembly

1	Cylinder head bolts	11	Valve spring
2	Washer	12	Exhaust valve
3	Cylinder head	13	Valve stem seal
4	Gasket	14	Valve spring seat
5	Keepers	15	Valve stem seal
6	Valve spring retainer	16	Valve spring seat
7	Valve spring	17	Intake valve guide
8	Intake valve	18	Exhaust valve guide
9	Keepers	19	Intake valve seat
10	Valve spring retainer	20	Exhaust valve seat

2B

items are available. Also, refer to *Engine overhaul - reassembly* sequence for a list of tools and materials needed for engine reassembly.

Common hand tools
Small cardboard boxes or plastic bags for storing parts
Gasket scraper
Ridge reamer
Micrometers
Telescoping gauges
Dial indicator set
Valve spring compressor
Cylinder surfacing hone
Piston ring groove cleaning tool
Electric drill motor
Tap and die set

Wire brushes
Oil gallery brushes
Cleaning solvent

9 Cylinder head - disassembly

Refer to illustrations 9.1a, 9.1b, 9.2, 9.3a, 9.3b and 9.4
Note: *New and rebuilt cylinder heads are commonly available for most engines at dealerships and auto parts stores. Due to the fact that some specialized tools are necessary for the disassembly and inspection procedures, and replacement parts may not be readily available, it may be more practical and economical for the home mechanic to purchase a*

replacement head rather than taking the time to disassemble, inspect and recondition the original.

1 Cylinder head disassembly involves removal of the intake and exhaust valves and related components **(see illustrations)**. If they're still in place, remove the rocker arm shafts and camshaft, on the 1.8L engine (see Chapter 2A) or the bearing caps, camshafts and lash adjusters, on the 2.0L engine (see Chapter 2A). Label the parts or store them separately so they can be reinstalled in their original locations.

2 Before the valves are removed, arrange to label and store them, along with their related components, so they can be kept separate and reinstalled in the same valve

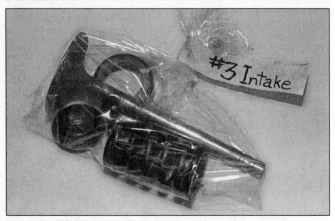

9.2 A small plastic bag, with an appropriate label, can be used to store the valvetrain components so they can be kept together and reinstalled in the correct guide location

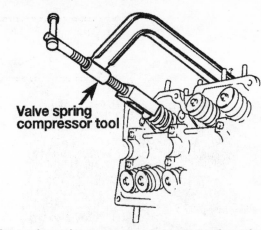

9.3a Use a valve spring compressor to compress the springs . . .

9.3b . . . then remove the keepers from the valve stem with a magnet or small needle-nose pliers

9.4 If the valve won't pull through the guide, deburr the edge of the stem end and the area around the top of the keeper groove with a file or whetstone

guides they are removed from **(see illustration)**.

3   Compress the springs on the first valve with a spring compressor and remove the keepers **(see illustrations)**. Carefully release the valve spring compressor and remove the retainer, the spring and the spring seat (if used).

4   Pull the valve out of the head, then remove the oil seal from the guide. If the valve binds in the guide (won't pull through), push it back into the head and deburr the area around the keeper groove with a fine file or whetstone **(see illustration)**.

5   Repeat the procedure for the remaining valves. Remember to keep all the parts for each valve together so they can be reinstalled in the same locations.

6   Pull off the valve stem seals with pliers and discard them.

7   Once the valves and related components have been removed and stored in an organized manner, the head should be thoroughly cleaned and inspected. If a complete engine overhaul is being done, finish the engine disassembly procedures before beginning the cylinder head cleaning and inspection process.

10   Cylinder head - cleaning and inspection

Refer to illustrations 10.12, 10.15, 10.16, 10.17 and 10.18

1   Thorough cleaning of the cylinder head and related valvetrain components, followed by a detailed inspection, will enable you to decide how much valve service work must be done during the engine overhaul. **Note:** *If the engine was severely overheated, the cylinder head is probably warped* (see Step 12).

Cleaning

2   Scrape all traces of old gasket material and sealing compound off the head gasket, intake manifold and exhaust manifold sealing surfaces. Be very careful not to gouge the cylinder head. Special gasket removal solvents that soften gaskets and make removal much easier are available at auto parts stores.

3   Remove all built-up scale from the coolant passages.

4   Run a stiff wire brush through the various holes to remove deposits that may have formed in them.

5   Run an appropriate size tap into each of the threaded holes to remove corrosion and thread sealant that may be present. If compressed air is available, use it to clear the holes of debris produced by this operation. **Warning:** *Wear eye protection when using compressed air!*

6   Clean the valve adjuster threads in each rocker arm with a wire brush.

7   Clean the cylinder head with solvent and dry it thoroughly. Compressed air will speed the drying process and ensure that all holes and recessed areas are clean. **Note:** *Decarbonizing chemicals are available and may prove very useful when cleaning cylinder heads and valve train components. They are very caustic and should be used with caution. Be sure to follow the instructions on the container.*

8   Clean the rocker arms, springs, wave washers and shafts with solvent and dry them thoroughly (don't mix them up during the cleaning process). Compressed air will speed the drying process and can be used to clean out the oil passages.

9   Clean all the valve springs, spring seats, keepers and retainers with solvent and dry them thoroughly. Do the components from

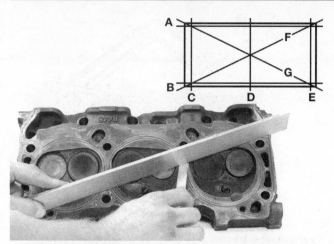

10.12 Check the cylinder head gasket surfaces for warpage by trying to slip a feeler gauge under a precision straightedge (see this Chapter's Specifications for the maximum warpage allowed and use a feeler gauge of that thickness)

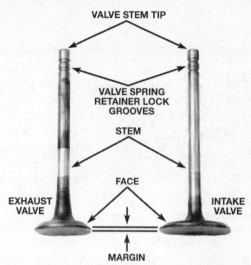

10.15 Check for valve wear at the points shown here

2B

one valve at a time to avoid mixing up the parts.

10   Scrape off any heavy deposits that may have formed on the valves, then use a motorized wire brush to remove deposits from the valve heads and stems. **Warning:** *Wear eye protection!* Again, make sure the valves don't get mixed up.

Inspection

Note: *Be sure to perform all of the following inspection procedures before concluding that machine shop work is required. Make a list of the items that need attention.*

Cylinder head

11   Inspect the head very carefully for cracks, evidence of coolant leakage and other damage. If cracks are found, check with an automotive machine shop concerning repair. If repair isn't possible, a new cylinder head should be obtained.

12   Using a straightedge and feeler gauge, check the head gasket mating surface **(see illustration)**. Check the intake and exhaust manifold surfaces on the cylinder head also. If the warpage on any of the surfaces

exceeds the limits listed in this Chapter's Specifications, they can be resurfaced at an automotive machine shop.

13   Examine the valve seats in each of the combustion chambers. If they're pitted, cracked or burned, the head will require valve service that's beyond the scope of the home mechanic.

14   Check the valve stem-to-guide clearance, using a clamping dial indicator base attached securely to the head, by measuring the lateral movement of the valve stem inside the valve guide. **Note:** *If you only have a magnetic dial indicator base and a steel bench or vise, you can clamp or bolt the head down to the bench and mount the indicator next to the head and extend the dial indicator to the valve stem and measure the side play. The valve must be in the guide and approximately 1/16-inch off the seat. The total valve stem movement indicated by the gauge needle must be divided by two to obtain the actual clearance.* After this is done, if there's still some doubt regarding the condition of the valve guides they should be checked by an automotive machine shop (the cost should be minimal).

Valves

15   Carefully inspect each valve face for uneven wear, deformation, cracks, pits and burned areas **(see illustration)**. Check the valve stem for scuffing and galling and the neck for cracks. Rotate the valve and check for any obvious indication that it's bent. Look for pits and excessive wear on the end of the stem. The presence of any of these conditions indicates the need for valve service by an automotive machine shop.

16   Measure the margin width on each valve **(see illustration)**. Any valve with a margin narrower than listed in this Chapter's Specifications will have to be replaced with a new one.

Valve components

17   Check each valve spring for wear (on the ends) and pits. Measure the free length **(see illustration)** and compare it to the Specifications listed in this Chapter. Any springs that are shorter than specified have sagged and should not be reused. The tension of all springs should be checked with a special fixture before deciding that they're suitable for use in a rebuilt engine (take the springs to an

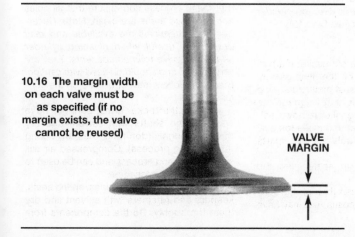

10.16 The margin width on each valve must be as specified (if no margin exists, the valve cannot be reused)

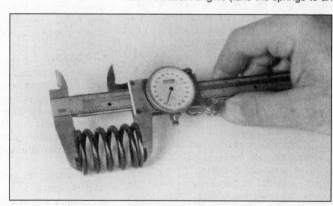

10.17 Measure the free length of each valve spring with a dial or vernier caliper

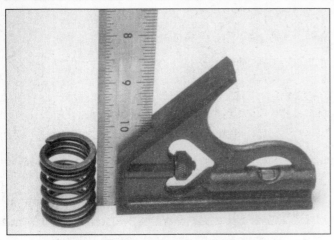

10.18 Check each valve spring for squareness

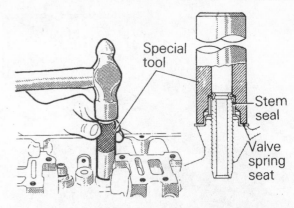

12.3 Valve seals require a special tool for installation (although a deep socket can be used if the tool isn't available) - don't hammer on the seals once they're seated

automotive machine shop for this check).

18   Stand each spring on a flat surface and check it for squareness **(see illustration)**. If any of the springs are distorted or sagged, replace all of them with new parts.

19   Check the spring retainers and keepers for obvious wear and cracks. Any questionable parts should be replaced with new ones, as extensive damage will occur if they fail during engine operation.

Rocker arm components

20   Refer to Chapter 2, Part A, for the rocker arm and shaft inspection procedures.

21   Any damaged or excessively worn parts must be replaced with new ones.

22   If the inspection process indicates that the valve components are in generally poor condition and worn beyond the limits specified, which is usually the case in an engine that's being overhauled, reassemble the valves in the cylinder head and refer to Section 11 for valve servicing recommendations.

11   Valves - servicing

1   Because of the complex nature of the job and the special tools and equipment needed, servicing of the valves, the valve seats and the valve guides, commonly known as a valve job, should be done by a professional.

2   The home mechanic can remove and disassemble the head, do the initial cleaning and inspection, then reassemble and deliver it to a dealer service department or an automotive machine shop for the actual service work. Doing the inspection will enable you to see what condition the head and valvetrain components are in and will ensure that you know what work and new parts are required when dealing with an automotive machine shop.

3   The dealer service department, or automotive machine shop, will remove the valves and springs, recondition or replace the valves and valve seats, recondition the valve guides, check and replace the valve springs, spring retainers and keepers (as necessary), replace

the valve seals with new ones, reassemble the valve components and make sure the installed spring height is correct. The cylinder head gasket surface will also be resurfaced if it's warped.

4   After the valve job has been performed by a professional, the head will be in like-new condition. When the head is returned, be sure to clean it again before installation on the engine to remove any metal particles and abrasive grit that may still be present from the valve service or head resurfacing operations. Use compressed air, if available, to blow out all the oil holes and passages.

12   Cylinder head - reassembly

Refer to illustrations 12.3, 12.6 and 12.8

1   Regardless of whether or not the head was sent to an automotive repair shop for valve servicing, make sure it's clean before beginning reassembly.

2   If the head was sent out for valve servicing, the valves and related components will already be in place. Begin the reassembly procedure with Step 8.

3   Install new seals on each of the intake valve guides. Using a hammer and a deep

socket or seal installation tool, gently tap each seal into place until it's completely seated on the guide **(see illustration)**. Don't twist or cock the seals during installation or they won't seal properly on the valve stems.

4   Beginning at one end of the head, lubricate and install the first valve. Apply molybase grease or clean engine oil to the valve stem.

5   Drop the spring seat over the valve guide and set the valve spring and retainer in place.

6   Compress the spring with a valve spring compressor and carefully install the keepers in the upper groove, then slowly release the compressor and make sure the keepers seat properly. Apply a small dab of grease to each keeper to hold it in place if necessary **(see illustration)**.

7   Repeat the procedure for the remaining valves. Be sure to return the components to their original locations - don't mix them up!

8   Check the installed valve spring height with a vernier or dial caliper. If the head was sent out for service work, the installed height should be correct (but don't automatically assume that it is). The measurement is taken from the spring seat to the top of the valve

12.6 Apply a small dab of grease to each keeper as shown here before installation - it'll hold them in place on the valve stem as the spring is released

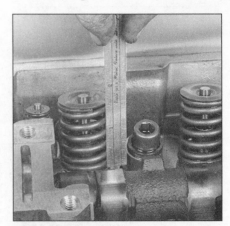

12.8 Be sure to check the valve spring installed height (the distance from the top of the seat/shim to the top of the spring)

13.1 A ridge reamer is required to remove the ridge from the top of each cylinder - do this BEFORE removing the pistons!

13.3 Check the connecting rod side clearance (endplay) with a feeler gauge

stem **(see illustration)**. If the height is greater than listed in this Chapter's Specifications, shims can be added under the springs to correct it. **Caution:** *Do not shim the springs to the point where the installed height is less than specified.*

9   Apply moly-base grease to the rocker arm faces, the camshaft and the rocker shafts, then install the camshaft, rocker arms and shafts (1.8L engine) or the lash adjusters, rocker arms and camshafts (2.0L engine) (refer to Part A).

13 Pistons and connecting rods - removal

Refer to illustrations 13.1, 13.3, 13.4 and 13.6
Note: *Prior to removing the piston/connecting rod assemblies, remove the cylinder head and the oil pan by referring to the appropriate Sections in Chapter 2, Part A.*
1   Use your fingernail to feel if a ridge has formed at the upper limit of ring travel (about 1/4-inch down from the top of each cylinder). If carbon deposits or cylinder wear have produced ridges, they must be completely

removed with a special tool **(see illustration)**. Follow the manufacturer's instructions provided with the tool. Failure to remove the ridges before attempting to remove the piston/connecting rod assemblies may result in piston breakage.
2   After the cylinder ridges have been removed, turn the engine upside-down so the crankshaft is facing up.
3   Before the connecting rods are removed, check the endplay with feeler gauges. Slide them between the first connecting rod and the crankshaft throw until the play is removed **(see illustration)**. The endplay is equal to the thickness of the feeler gauge(s). If the endplay exceeds the service limit, new connecting rods will be required. If new rods (or a new crankshaft) are installed, the endplay may fall under the minimum listed in this Chapter's Specifications (if it does, the rods will have to be machined to restore it - consult an automotive machine shop for advice if necessary). Repeat the procedure for the remaining connecting rods.
4   Check the connecting rods and caps for identification marks **(see illustration)**. If they aren't plainly marked, use a small center-punch to make the appropriate number of

indentations on each rod and cap (1, 2, 3, etc., depending on the cylinder they're associated with).
5   Loosen each of the connecting rod cap nuts 1/2-turn at a time until they can be removed by hand. Remove the number one connecting rod cap and bearing insert. Don't drop the bearing insert out of the cap.
6   Slip a short length of plastic or rubber hose over each connecting rod cap bolt to protect the crankshaft journal and cylinder wall as the piston is removed **(see illustration)**.
7   Remove the bearing insert and push the connecting rod/piston assembly out through the top of the engine. Use a wooden or plastic hammer handle to push on the upper bearing surface in the connecting rod. If resistance is felt, double-check to make sure that all of the ridge was removed from the cylinder.
8   Repeat the procedure for the remaining cylinders.
9   After removal, reassemble the connecting rod caps and bearing inserts in their respective connecting rods and install the cap nuts finger tight. Leaving the old bearing inserts in place until reassembly will help prevent the connecting rod bearing surfaces

13.4 The connecting rods and caps should be marked to indicate which cylinder they're installed in - if they aren't, mark them with a center-punch to avoid confusion during reassembly

13.6 To prevent damage to the crankshaft journals and cylinder walls, slip sections of hose over the rod bolts before removing the pistons

14.1 Checking crankshaft endplay with a dial indicator

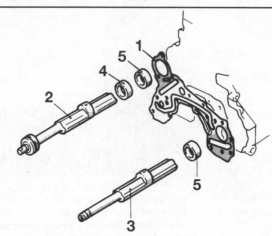

14.4 Check the main bearing caps for an arrow and number cast into the cap indicating direction and location of each main cap - if no marks are found you can number your own with a hammer and a punch using the same method as shown in illustration 13.4

from being accidentally nicked or gouged.

10   Don't separate the pistons from the connecting rods (see Sec-tion 18 for additional information).

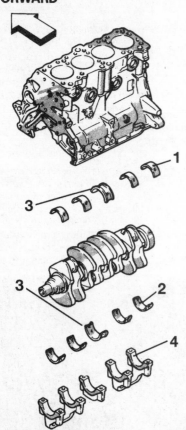

FORWARD

14.5 Exploded view of the "bottom end" consisting of the crankshaft, bearings and main bearing caps

1   *Upper main bearing cap*
2   *Lower main bearing cap*
3   *Thrust bearings (in number 3 position)*
4   *Main caps*

---

14   Crankshaft and balance shafts - removal

Refer to illustrations 14.1, 14.4, 14.5 and 14.7

Crankshaft

Note: *The crankshaft can be removed only after the engine has been removed from the vehicle. It's assumed that the flywheel or driveplate, crankshaft pulley, timing belt, oil pan, oil pump and piston/connecting rod assemblies have already been removed. The rear main oil seal housing must be unbolted and separated from the block before proceeding with crankshaft removal.*

1   Before the crankshaft is removed, check the endplay. Mount a dial indicator with the stem in line with the crankshaft and just touching one of the crank throws **(see illustration)**.

2   Push the crankshaft all the way to the rear and zero the dial indicator. Next, pry the crankshaft to the front as far as possible and check the reading on the dial indicator. The distance that it moves is the endplay. If it's greater than listed in this Chapter's Specifications, check the crankshaft thrust surfaces for wear. If no wear is evident, new main bearings should correct the endplay.

3   If a dial indicator isn't available, feeler gauges can be used. Gently pry or push the crankshaft all the way to the front of the engine. Slip feeler gauges between the crankshaft and the front face of the thrust main bearing to determine the clearance.

4   Check the main bearing caps to see if they're marked to indicate their locations. They should be numbered consecutively from the front of the engine to the rear. If they aren't, mark them with number stamping dies or a center-punch. Main bearing caps generally have a cast-in arrow, which points to the front of the engine **(see illustration)**. Loosen the main bearing cap bolts 1/4-turn at a time each, until they can be removed by hand.

5   Gently tap the caps with a soft-face hammer, then separate them from the engine block. If necessary, use the bolts as levers to remove the caps. Try not to drop the bearing inserts if they come out with the caps **(see illustration)**.

6   Carefully lift the crankshaft out of the engine. It may be a good idea to have an assistant available, since the crankshaft is quite heavy. With the bearing inserts in place in the engine block and main bearing caps, return the caps to their respective locations on the engine block and tighten the bolts finger tight.

14.7 Exploded view of the balance shaft assemblies

1   *Front case gasket*
2   *Balance shaft - front*
3   *Balance shaft - rear*
4   *Balance shaft front bearing*
5   *Balance shaft rear bearing*

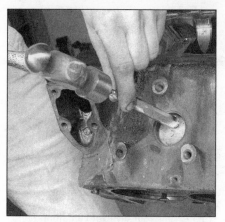

15.1a Use a hammer and a large punch to knock the core plugs sideways in their bores

15.1b Pull the core plugs from the block with pliers

Balance shafts

7   Before the balance shafts can be removed (see illustration), the front case and gasket must be removed (see Chapter 2A).

8   With the front case removed, the shafts will slide right out of the block. **Caution:** *Support the weight of the shaft as you pull it out so there is no damage done to either the front or rear bushings in the block or to the balance shaft.*

Inspection

9   Check the oil holes for clogging.

10   Check the journals of the balance shaft for signs of wear, scuffing and overheating (blue spots). Check the bushings in the cylinder block for the same conditions. If any undesirable conditions exist, the balance shaft and bushings must be replaced. Due to the special tools required to remove the bal-

ance shaft bushings and install the new ones, this job must be left to an automotive machine shop.

15 Engine block - cleaning

Refer to illustrations 15.1a, 15.1b, 15.5, 15.9 and 15.11

1   Remove the core plugs from the engine block. To do this, knock one side of the plugs into the block with a hammer and a punch, then grasp them with large pliers and pull them out **(see illustrations)**.

2   Using a gasket scraper, remove all traces of gasket material from the engine block. Be very careful not to nick or gouge the gasket sealing surfaces.

3   Remove the main bearing caps and separate the bearing inserts from the caps and the engine block. Tag the bearings, indicating which cylinder they were removed from and whether they were in the cap or the block, then set them aside.

4   Remove all of the threaded oil gallery plugs from the block. The plugs are usually very tight - they may have to be drilled out

and the holes retapped. Use new plugs when the engine is reassembled.

5   Remove the oil jets located at the bottom of each cylinder **(see illustration)** and check them for clogged passages.

6   If the engine is extremely dirty it should be taken to an automotive machine shop for cleaning.

7   After the block is returned, clean all oil holes and oil galleries one more time. Brushes specifically designed for this purpose are available at most auto parts stores. Flush the passages with warm water until the water runs clear, dry the block thoroughly and wipe all machined surfaces with a light, rust preventive oil. If you have access to compressed air, use it to speed the drying process and to blow out all the oil holes and galleries. **Warning:** *Wear eye protection when using compressed air!*

8   If the block isn't extremely dirty or sludged up, you can do an adequate cleaning job with hot soapy water and a stiff brush. Take plenty of time and do a thorough job. Regardless of the cleaning method used, be sure to clean all oil holes and galleries very thoroughly, dry the block completely and coat all machined surfaces with light oil.

9   The threaded holes in the block must be clean to ensure accurate torque readings during reassembly. Run the proper size tap into each of the holes to remove rust, corrosion, thread sealant and sludge and restore damaged threads **(see illustration)**. If possible, use compressed air to clear the holes of debris produced by this operation. Now is a good time to clean the threads on the head bolts and the main bearing cap bolts as well.

10   Reinstall the main bearing caps and tighten the bolts finger tight.

11   After coating the sealing surfaces of the new core plugs with Permatex no. 2 sealant (or equivalent), install them in the engine block **(see illustration)**. Make sure they're driven in straight and seated properly or leakage could result. Special tools are available for this purpose, but a large socket, with an outside diameter that will just slip into the

2B

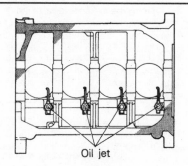

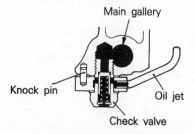

15.5 Remove the oil jets prior to cleaning the engine block

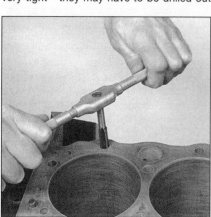

15.9 All bolt holes in the block - particularly the main bearing cap and head bolt holes - should be cleaned and restored with a tap (be sure to remove debris from the holes after this is done)

15.11 A large socket on an extension can be used to drive the new core plugs into the bores

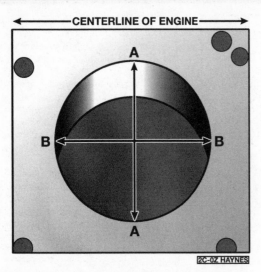

16.4a Measure the diameter of each cylinder just under the wear ridge (A), at the center (B) and at the bottom

16.4b The ability to "feel" when the telescoping gauge is at the correct point will be developed over time, so work slowly and repeat the check until you're satisfied that the bore measurement is accurate

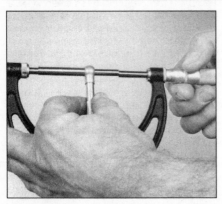

16.4c The gauge is then measured with a micrometer to determine the bore size

core plug, a 1/2-inch drive extension and a hammer will work just as well.

12   Apply non-hardening sealant (such as Permatex no. 2 or Teflon pipe sealant) to the new oil gallery plugs and thread them into the holes in the block. Make sure they're tightened securely.

13   If the engine isn't going to be reassembled right away, cover it with a large plastic trash bag to keep it clean.

16 Engine block - inspection

Refer to illustrations 16.4a, 16.4b, 16.4c and 16.13

1   Before the block is inspected, it should be cleaned as described in Section 15.

2   Visually check the block for cracks, rust and corrosion. Look for stripped threads in the threaded holes. It's also a good idea to have the block checked for hidden cracks by an automotive machine shop that has the special equipment to do this type of work. If defects are found, have the block repaired, if possible, or replaced.

3   Check the cylinder bores for scuffing and scoring.

4   Measure the diameter of each cylinder at the top (just under the ridge area), center and bottom of the cylinder bore, parallel to the crankshaft axis **(see illustrations)**.

5   Next, measure each cylinder's diameter at the same three locations across the crankshaft axis. Compare the results to the Specifications.

6   If the required precision measuring tools aren't available, the piston-to-cylinder clearances can be obtained, though not quite as accurately, using feeler gauge stock. Feeler gauge stock comes in 12-inch lengths and various thicknesses and is generally available at auto parts stores.

7   To check the clearance, select a feeler gauge and slip it into the cylinder along with the matching piston. The piston must be positioned exactly as it normally would be. The feeler gauge must be between the piston and cylinder on one of the thrust faces (90-degrees to the piston pin bore).

8   The piston should slip through the cylinder (with the feeler gauge in place) with moderate pressure.

9   If it falls through or slides through easily, the clearance is excessive and a new piston will be required. If the piston binds at the lower end of the cylinder and is loose toward the top, the cylinder is tapered. If tight spots are encountered as the piston/feeler gauge is rotated in the cylinder, the cylinder is out-of-round.

10   Repeat the procedure for the remaining pistons and cylinders.

11   If the cylinder walls are badly scuffed or scored, or if they're out-of-round or tapered beyond the limits given in the Specifications, have the engine block rebored and honed at an automotive machine shop. If a rebore is done, oversize pistons and rings will be required.

12   If the cylinders are in reasonably good

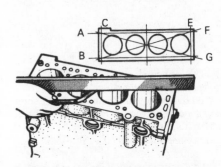

16.13 Check the cylinder block gasket surface for warpage by trying to slip a feeler gauge under a precision straightedge in the different directions shown (see the Specifications for the maximum warpage allowed and use a feeler gauge of that thickness)

condition and not worn to the outside of the limits, and if the piston-to-cylinder clearances can be maintained properly, then they don't have to be rebored. Honing is all that's necessary (see Section 17).

13   Using a precision straightedge and a feeler gauge, check the block deck (the surface that mates with the cylinder head) for distortion **(see illustration)**. If it's distorted beyond the specified limit, it can be resurfaced by an automotive machine shop.

17 Cylinder honing

Refer to illustrations 17.3a and 17.3b

1   Prior to engine reassembly, the cylinder bores must be honed so the new piston rings will seat correctly and provide the best possible combustion chamber seal. **Note:** *If you don't have the tools or don't want to tackle the honing operation, most automotive machine shops will do it for a reasonable fee.*

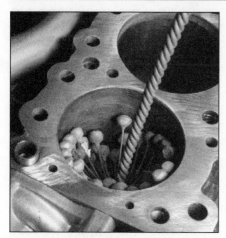

17.3a A "bottle brush" hone will produce better results if you have never honed cylinders before

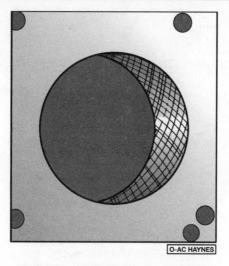

17.3b The cylinder hone should leave a smooth, crosshatch pattern with the lines intersecting at approximately a 60-degree angle

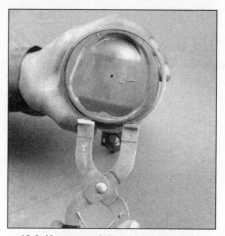

18.2 Use a special tool to remove the piston rings from the piston

2   Before honing the cylinders, install the main bearing caps and tighten the bolts to the torque listed in this Chapter's Specifications.

3   Two types of cylinder hones are commonly available - the flex hone or "bottle brush" type and the more traditional surfacing hone with spring-loaded stones. Both will do the job, but for the less experienced mechanic the "bottle brush" hone will probably be easier to use. You'll also need some kerosene or honing oil, rags and an electric drill motor. Proceed as follows:

a) *Mount the hone in the drill motor, compress the stones and slip it into the first cylinder* (see illustration). *Be sure to wear safety goggles or a face shield!*

b) *Lubricate the cylinder with plenty of honing oil, turn on the drill and move the hone up-and-down in the cylinder at a pace that will produce a fine crosshatch pattern on the cylinder walls. Ideally, the crosshatch lines should intersect at approximately a 60-degree angle* (see illustration). *Be sure to use plenty of lubricant and don't take off any more material than is absolutely necessary to produce the desired finish.* **Note:** *Piston*

ring manufacturers may specify a smaller crosshatch angle than the traditional 60-degrees - read and follow any instructions included with the new rings.

c) *Don't withdraw the hone from the cylinder while it's running. Instead, shut off the drill and continue moving the hone up-and-down in the cylinder until it comes to a complete stop, then compress the stones and withdraw the hone. If you're using a "bottle brush" type hone, stop the drill motor, then turn the chuck in the normal direction of rotation while withdrawing the hone from the cylinder.*

d) *Wipe the oil out of the cylinder and repeat the procedure for the remaining cylinders.*

4   After the honing job is complete, chamfer the top edges of the cylinder bores with a small file so the rings won't catch when the pistons are installed. Be very careful not to nick the cylinder walls with the end of the file.

5   The entire engine block must be washed again very thoroughly with warm, soapy

water to remove all traces of the abrasive grit produced during the honing operation. **Note:** *The bores can be considered clean when a lint-free white cloth - dampened with clean engine oil - used to wipe them out doesn't pick up any more honing residue, which will show up as gray areas on the cloth. Be sure to run a brush through all oil holes and galleries and flush them with running water.*

6   After rinsing, dry the block and apply a coat of light rust preventive oil to all machined surfaces. Wrap the block in a plastic trash bag to keep it clean and set it aside until reassembly.

18   Pistons/connecting rods - inspection

Refer to illustrations 18.2, 18.4a, 18.4b, 18.10 and 18.11

1   Before the inspection process can be carried out, the piston/connecting rod assemblies must be cleaned and the original piston rings removed from the pistons. **Note:** *Always use new piston rings when the engine is reassembled.*

2   Using a piston ring removal tool (see illustration), carefully remove the rings from the pistons. Be careful not to nick or gouge the pistons in the process.

3   Scrape all traces of carbon from the top of the piston. A hand-held wire brush or a piece of fine emery cloth can be used once the majority of the deposits have been scraped away. Do not, under any circumstances, use a wire brush mounted in a drill motor to remove deposits from the pistons. The piston material is soft and may be eroded away by the wire brush.

4   Use a piston ring groove cleaning tool to remove carbon deposits from the ring grooves. If a tool isn't available, a piece broken off the old ring will do the job. Be very careful to remove only the carbon deposits - don't remove any metal and do not nick or scratch the sides of the ring grooves (see illustrations).

18.4a The piston ring grooves can be cleaned with a special tool like this one , .

18.4b . . . or a section of a broken ring

2B

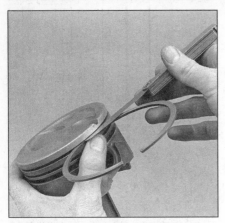

18.10 Check the ring side clearance with a feeler gauge at several points around the groove

18.11 Measure the piston diameter at a 90-degree angle to the piston pin and in line with it. Check for evidence of seizure such as scratches or dark streaks in the piston or cracks in the piston, replace it if any of these indications are found

5   Once the deposits have been removed, clean the piston/rod assemblies with solvent and dry them with compressed air (if available). Make sure the oil return holes in the back sides of the ring grooves are clear.

6   If the pistons and cylinder walls aren't damaged or worn excessively,
and if the engine block is not rebored, new pistons won't be necessary.
Normal piston wear appears as even, vertical wear on the piston thrust surfaces and slight looseness of the top ring in its groove. New piston rings, however, should always be used when an engine is rebuilt.

7   Carefully inspect each piston for cracks around the skirt, at the pin bosses and at the ring lands.

8   Look for scoring and scuffing on the thrust faces of the skirt, holes in the piston crown and burned areas at the edge of the crown. If the skirt is scored or scuffed, the engine may have been suffering from overheating and/or abnormal combustion, which caused excessively high operating temperatures. The cooling and lubrication systems should be checked thoroughly. A hole in the piston crown is an indication that abnormal

combustion (preignition) was occurring. Burned areas at the edge of the piston crown are usually evidence of spark knock (detonation). If any of the above problems exist, the causes must be corrected or the damage will occur again. The causes may include intake air leaks, incorrect fuel/air mixture, incorrect ignition timing and EGR system malfunctions.

9   Corrosion of the piston, in the form of small pits, indicates that coolant is leaking into the combustion chamber and/or the crankcase. Again, the cause must be corrected or the problem may persist in the rebuilt engine.

10   Measure the piston ring side clearance by laying a new piston ring in each ring groove and slipping a feeler gauge in beside it **(see illustration)**. Check the clearance at three or four locations around each groove. Be sure to use the correct ring for each groove - they are different. If the side clearance is greater than specified, new pistons will have to be used.

11   Check the piston-to-bore clearance by

measuring the bore (see Section 16) and the piston diameter. Make sure the pistons and bores are correctly matched. Measure the piston across the skirt 5/64-inch above the bottom of the piston, at a 90-degree angle to and in line with the piston pin **(see illustration)**. Subtract the piston diameter from the bore diameter to obtain the clearance. If it's greater than specified, the block will have to be rebored and new pistons and rings installed.

12   Check the piston-to-rod clearance by twisting the piston and rod in opposite directions. Any noticeable play indicates excessive wear, which must be corrected. The piston/connecting rod assemblies should be taken to an automotive machine shop to have the pistons and rods resized and new pins installed.

13   If the pistons must be removed from the connecting rods for any reason, they should be taken to an automotive machine shop. While they are there have the connecting rods checked for bend and twist, since automotive machine shops have special equipment for this purpose. **Note:** *Unless new pistons and/or connecting rods must be installed, do not disassemble the pistons and connecting rods.*

14   Check the connecting rods for cracks and other damage. Temporarily remove the rod caps, lift out the old bearing inserts, wipe the rod and cap bearing surfaces clean and inspect them for nicks, gouges and scratches. After checking the rods, replace the old bearings, slip the caps into place and tighten the nuts finger tight. **Note:** *If the engine is being rebuilt because of a connecting rod knock, be sure to install new rods.*

19   Crankshaft and balance shafts - inspection

Refer to illustration 19.1, 19.2, 19.4 and 19.7

1   Remove all burrs from the crankshaft oil holes with a stone, file or scraper **(see illustration)**.

19.1 The oil holes should be chamfered so sharp edges don't gouge or scratch the new bearings

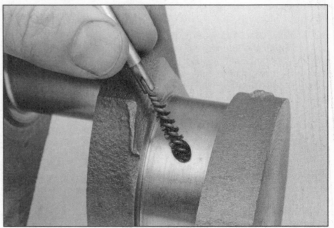

19.2 Use a wire or stiff bristle brush to clean the oil passages in the crankshaft

19.4 Rubbing a penny lengthwise on each journal will reveal its condition - if copper rubs off and is embedded in the crankshaft, the journals should be reground

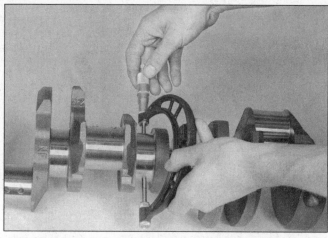

19.7 Measure the diameter of each crankshaft journal at several points to detect taper and out-of-round conditions

2   Clean the crankshaft with solvent and dry it with compressed air (if available). Be sure to clean the oil holes with a stiff brush and flush them with solvent **(see illustration)**. **Warning:** *If compressed air is used always wear eye protection to prevent solvents or debris from causing and injury to your eyes.*

3   Check the main and connecting rod bearing journals for uneven wear, scoring, pits and cracks.

4   Rub a penny across each journal several times. If a journal picks up copper from the penny, it's too rough and must be reground **(see illustration)**.

5   Remove all burrs from the crankshaft oil holes with a stone, file or scraper.

6   Check the rest of the crankshaft for cracks and other damage. It should be magnafluxed to reveal hidden cracks - an automotive machine shop will handle the procedure.

7   Using a micrometer, measure the diameter of the main and connecting rod journals and compare the results to the Specifications **(see illustration)** listed in this Chapter. By measuring the diameter at a number of points around each journal's circumference, you'll be able to determine whether or not the journal is out-of-round. Take the measurement at each end of the journal, near the crank throws, to determine if the journal is tapered.

8   If the crankshaft journals are damaged, tapered, out-of-round or worn beyond the limits given in the Specifications, have the crankshaft reground by an automotive machine shop. Be sure to use the correct size bearing inserts if the crankshaft is reconditioned.

9   Check the oil seal journals at each end of the crankshaft for wear and damage. If the seal has worn a groove in the journal, or if it's nicked or scratched, the new seal may leak when the engine is reassembled. In some cases, an automotive machine shop may be able to repair the journal by pressing on a thin sleeve. If repair isn't feasible, a new or different crankshaft should be installed.

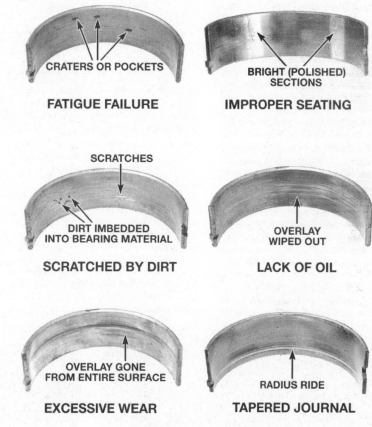

CRATERS OR POCKETS

FATIGUE FAILURE

BRIGHT (POLISHED) SECTIONS

IMPROPER SEATING

SCRATCHES

DIRT IMBEDDED INTO BEARING MATERIAL

SCRATCHED BY DIRT

OVERLAY WIPED OUT

LACK OF OIL

OVERLAY GONE FROM ENTIRE SURFACE

EXCESSIVE WEAR

RADIUS RIDE

TAPERED JOURNAL

20.1 Typical bearing failures

10   Refer to Section 20 and examine the main and rod bearing inserts.

20   Main and connecting rod bearings - inspection

Refer to illustration 20.1

1   Even though the main and connecting rod bearings should be replaced with new ones during the engine overhaul, the old bearings should be retained for close examination, as they may reveal valuable information about the condition of the engine **(see illustration)**.

2   Bearing failure occurs because of lack of lubrication, the presence of dirt or other foreign particles, overloading the engine and corrosion. Regardless of the cause of bearing

2B

failure, it must be corrected before the engine is reassembled to prevent it from happening again.

3   When examining the bearings, remove them from the engine block, the main bearing caps, the connecting rods and the rod caps and lay them out on a clean surface in the same general position as their location in the engine. This will enable you to match any bearing problems with the corresponding crankshaft journal.

4   Dirt and other foreign particles get into the engine in a variety of ways. It may be left in the engine during assembly, or it may pass through filters or the PCV system. It may get into the oil, and from there into the bearings. Metal chips from machining operations and normal engine wear are often present. Abrasives are sometimes left in engine components after reconditioning, especially when parts are not thoroughly cleaned using the proper cleaning methods. Whatever the source, these foreign objects often end up embedded in the soft bearing material and are easily recognized. Large particles will not embed in the bearing and will score or gouge the bearing and journal. The best prevention for this cause of bearing failure is to clean all parts thoroughly and keep everything spotlessly clean during engine assembly. Frequent and regular engine oil and filter changes are also recommended.

5   Lack of lubrication (or lubrication breakdown) has a number of interrelated causes. Excessive heat (which thins the oil), overloading (which squeezes the oil from the bearing face) and oil leakage or throw off (from excessive bearing clearances, worn oil pump or high engine speeds) all contribute to lubrication breakdown. Blocked oil passages, which usually are the result of misaligned oil holes in a bearing shell, will also oil starve a bearing and destroy it. When lack of lubrication is the cause of bearing failure, the bearing material is wiped or extruded from the steel backing of the bearing. Temperatures may increase to the point where the steel backing turns blue from overheating.

6   Driving habits can have a definite effect on bearing life. Full throttle, low speed operation (lugging the engine) puts very high loads on bearings, which tends to squeeze out the oil film. These loads cause the bearings to flex, which produces fine cracks in the bearing face (fatigue failure). Eventually the bearing material will loosen in pieces and tear away from the steel backing. Short trip driving leads to corrosion of bearings because insufficient engine heat is produced to drive off the condensed water and corrosive gases. These products collect in the engine oil, forming acid and sludge. As the oil is carried to the engine bearings, the acid attacks and corrodes the bearing material.

7   Incorrect bearing installation during engine assembly will lead to bearing failure as well. Tight fitting bearings leave insufficient bearing oil clearance and will result in oil starvation. Dirt or foreign particles trapped behind a bearing insert result in high spots on the bearing which lead to failure.

21 Engine overhaul - reassembly sequence

1   Before beginning engine reassembly, make sure you have all the necessary new parts, gaskets and seals as well as the following items on hand:

Common hand tools
A 1/2-inch drive torque wrench
Piston ring installation tool
Piston ring compressor
Short lengths of rubber or plastic hose to fit over connecting rod bolts
Plastigage
Feeler gauges
A fine-tooth file
New engine oil
Engine assembly lube or moly-base grease
Gasket sealant
Thread locking compound

2   In order to save time and avoid problems, engine reassembly must be done in the following general order:

Piston rings
Oil jet valves
Crankshaft and main bearings
Balance shafts
Piston/connecting rod assemblies
Rear main oil seal housing
Front case and oil pump assembly
Oil pan
Cylinder head assembly
Water pump
Timing belt and sprockets
Timing belt cover
Intake and exhaust manifolds
Rocker arm cover
Engine rear plate
Flywheel/driveplate

22 Piston rings - installation

Refer to illustrations 22.3, 22.4, 22.5, 22.9a, 22.9b and 22.12

1   Before installing the new piston rings, the ring end gaps must be checked. It's assumed that the piston ring side clearance has been checked and verified correct (see Section 18).

2   Lay out the piston/connecting rod assemblies and the new ring sets so the ring sets will be matched with the same piston and cylinder during the end gap measurement and engine assembly.

3   Insert the top (number one) ring into the first cylinder and square it up with the cylinder walls by pushing it in with the top of the piston **(see illustration)**. The ring should be near the bottom of the cylinder, at the lower limit of ring travel.

4   To measure the end gap, slip feeler gauges between the ends of the ring until a gauge equal to the gap width is found **(see illustration)**. The feeler gauge should slide between the ring ends with a slight amount of drag. Compare the measurement to the

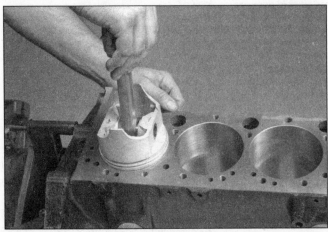

22.3 When checking piston ring end gap, the ring must be square in the cylinder bore (this is done by pushing the ring down with the top of a piston as shown)

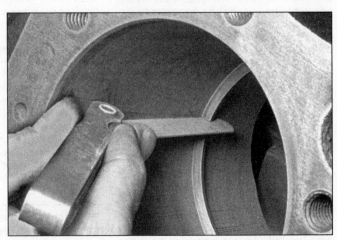

22.4 With the ring square in the cylinder, measure the end gap with a feeler gauge

22.5 If the end gap is too small, clamp a file in a vise and file the ring ends (from the outside end of the file in towards the vise only) to enlarge the gap slightly

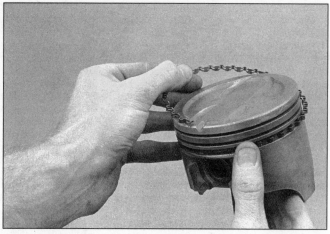

22.9a Installing the spacer/expander in the oil control ring groove

2B

Specifications listed in this Chapter. If the gap is larger or smaller than specified, double-check to make sure you have the correct rings before proceeding.

5   If the gap is too small, it must be enlarged or the ring ends may come in contact with each other during engine operation, which can cause serious damage to the engine. The end gap can be increased by filing the ring ends very carefully with a fine file. Mount the file in a vise equipped with soft jaws, slip the ring over the file with the ends contacting the file face and slowly move the ring to remove material from the ends. When performing this operation, file only by pushing the ring from the outside end of the file towards the vise **(see illustration)**.

6   Excess end gap isn't critical unless it's greater than 0.039-inch. Again, double-check to make sure you have the correct rings for your engine.

7   Repeat the procedure for each ring that will be installed in the first cylinder and for each ring in the remaining cylinders. Remember to keep rings, pistons and cylinders matched up.

8   Once the ring end gaps have been checked/corrected, the rings can be installed on the pistons.

9   The oil control ring (lowest one on the piston) is usually installed first. It's composed of three separate components. Slip the spacer/expander into the groove **(see illustration)**. If an anti-rotation tang is used, make sure it's inserted into the drilled hole in the ring groove. Next, install the lower side rail. Don't use a piston ring installation tool on the oil ring side rails, as they may be damaged. Instead, place one end of the side rail into the groove between the spacer/expander and the ring land, hold it firmly in place and slide a finger around the piston while pushing the rail into the groove **(see illustration)**. Next, install the upper side rail in the same manner.

10   After the three oil ring components have been installed, checκ to make sure that both the upper and lower side rails can be turned smoothly in the ring groove.

11   The number two (middle) ring is installed

22.9b DO NOT use a piston ring installation tool when installing the oil ring side rails

next. It's usually stamped with a mark which must face up, toward the top of the piston. **Note:** *Always follow the instructions printed on the ring package or box - different manufacturers may require different approaches. Do not mix up the top and middle rings, as they have different cross-sections.*

12   Use a piston ring installation tool and make sure the identification mark is facing the top of the piston, then slip the ring into the middle groove on the piston **(see illustration)**. Don't expand the ring any more than necessary to slide it over the piston.

13   Install the number one (top) ring in the same manner. Make sure the mark is facing up. Be careful not to confuse the number one and number two rings.

14   Repeat the procedure for the remaining pistons and rings.

---

23   Crankshaft and balance shafts - installation and main bearing oil clearance check

---

1   Crankshaft installation is the first step in

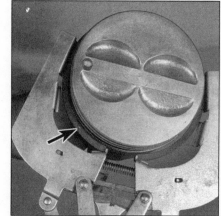

22.12 Install the compression rings with a ring expander - the mark on the ring must face up

engine reassembly. It's assumed at this point that the engine block and crankshaft have been cleaned, inspected and repaired or reconditioned.

2   Position the engine with the bottom facing up.

3   Remove the main bearing cap bolts and lift out the caps. Lay them out in the proper order to ensure correct installation.

4   If they're still in place, remove the original bearing inserts from the block and the main bearing caps. Wipe the bearing surfaces of the block and caps with a clean, lint-free cloth. They must be kept spotlessly clean.

Main bearing oil clearance check

Refer to illustrations 23.11 and 23.15

5   Clean the back sides of the new main bearing inserts and lay one in each main bearing saddle in the block. If one of the bearing inserts from each set has a large groove in it, make sure the grooved insert is installed in the block. Lay the other bearing from each set in the corresponding main bearing cap. Make sure the tab on the bear-

ing insert fits into the recess in the block or cap. **Caution:** *The oil holes in the block must line up with the oil holes in the bearing insert. Do not hammer the bearing into place and don't nick or gouge the bearing faces.* No lubrication should be used at this time.

6   The flanged thrust bearing must be installed in the #3 (center) main cap and saddle **(see illustration 14.5)**.

7   Clean the faces of the bearings in the block and the crankshaft main bearing journals with a clean, lint-free cloth.

8   Check or clean the oil holes in the crankshaft, as any dirt here can go only one way - straight through the new bearings.

9   Once you're certain the crankshaft is clean, carefully lay it in position in the main bearings.

10   Before the crankshaft can be permanently installed, the main bearing oil clearance must be checked.

11   Cut several pieces of the appropriate size Plastigage (they must be slightly shorter than the width of the main bearings) and place one piece on each crankshaft main bearing journal, parallel with the journal axis **(see illustration)**.

12   Clean the faces of the bearings in the caps and install the caps in their respective positions (don't mix them up) with the arrows pointing toward the front of the engine. Don't disturb the Plastigage.

13   Starting with the center main and working out toward the ends, tighten the main bearing cap bolts, in three steps, to the torque listed in this Chapter's Specifications. Don't rotate the crankshaft at any time during this operation.

14   Remove the bolts and carefully lift off the main bearing caps. Keep them in order. Don't disturb the Plastigage or rotate the crankshaft. If any of the main bearing caps are difficult to remove, tap them gently from side-to-side with a soft-face hammer to loosen them.

15   Compare the width of the crushed Plastigage on each journal to the scale printed on the Plastigage envelope to obtain the main bearing oil clearance **(see illustration)**. Check the Specifications listed in this Chapter to make sure it's correct.

16   If the clearance is not as specified, the bearing inserts may be the wrong size (which means different ones will be required). Before deciding that different inserts are needed, make sure that no dirt or oil was between the bearing inserts and the caps or block when the clearance was measured. If the Plastigage was wider at one end than the other, the journal may be tapered (refer to Section 19). If the clearance still exceeds the limit specified, the bearing will have to be replaced with an undersize bearing. **Caution:** *When installing a new crankshaft always use a standard bearing.*

17   Carefully scrape all traces of the Plastigage material off the main bearing journals and/or the bearing faces. Use your fingernail or the edge of a credit card - don't nick or scratch the bearing faces.

23.11 Lay the Plastigage strips (arrow) on the main bearing journals, parallel to the crankshaft centerline

Final crankshaft installation

18   Carefully lift the crankshaft out of the engine.

19   Clean the bearing faces in the block, then apply a thin, uniform layer of moly-base grease or engine assembly lube to each of the bearing surfaces. Be sure to coat the thrust faces as well as the journal face of the thrust bearing.

20   Make sure the crankshaft journals are clean, then lay the crankshaft back in place in the block. **Caution:** *Be sure to install the thrust washers in the Number 3 journal* **(see illustration 14.5)**.

21   Clean the faces of the bearings in the caps, then apply lubricant to them.

22   Install the caps in their respective positions with the arrows pointing toward the front of the engine.

23   Install the bolts.

24   Tighten all except the thrust bearing cap bolts to the torque listed in this Chapter's Specifications (work from the center out and approach the final torque in three steps).

25   Tighten the thrust bearing cap bolts to 10-to-12 ft-lbs.

26   Tap the ends of the crankshaft forward and backward with a lead or brass hammer to line up the main bearing and crankshaft thrust surfaces.

27   Retighten all main bearing cap bolts to the torque listed in this Chapter's Specifications, starting with the center main and working out toward the ends.

28   On manual transmission equipped models, install a new pilot bearing in the end of the crankshaft (see Chapter 8).

29   Rotate the crankshaft a number of times by hand to check for any obvious binding.

30   Recheck the crankshaft endplay with a feeler gauge or a dial indicator as described in Section 14. The endplay should be correct if the crankshaft thrust faces aren't worn or damaged and new bearings have been installed.

31   Refer to Chapter 2A and install the new rear main oil seal, then bolt the housing to the block.

23.15 Compare the width of the crushed Plastigage to the scale on the envelope to determine the main bearing oil clearance (always take the measurement at the widest point of the Plastigage) - be sure to use the correct scale; standard and metric scales are included

Balance shaft oil clearance check

32   Using a micrometer, measure the diameter of the balance shaft journals and record these figures. Then measure the Inside diameter of the corresponding bushings using a telescoping gauge and micrometer (similar to the technique shown In illustrations 16.4b and 16.4c). Subtract the diameter of each balance shaft journal from the inside diameter of its corresponding bushing to calculate the oil clearance. Compare your findings with the values listed in this Chapter's Specifications. If any of the oil clearances are excessive, compare the measurement of the balance shaft journals with the values listed in this Chapter's Specifications. If the journal diameters are within the specified range, have new balance shaft bushings installed. **Note:** *Because of the complex nature of the job and the special tools and equipment needed, replacement of the bushings should be done by an automotive machine shop.*

Balance shaft installation

33   Clean the bushings in the block, then apply a thin, uniform layer of moly-base grease or engine assembly lube to all of the bushing surfaces.

34   Make sure the balance shaft journals are clean, then apply a thin coat of moly-base grease or engine assembly lube to the journals. Carefully slide each balance shaft into its bore.

35   Install the front case (see Chapter 2, Part A).

---

24   Pistons and connecting rods - installation and rod bearing oil clearance check

---

Refer to illustrations 24.5, 24.9, 24.11, 24.13, 24.14 and 24.17

1   Before installing the piston/connecting

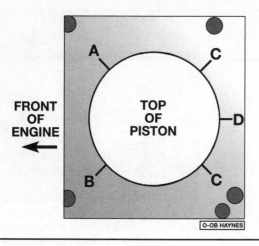

24.5 Ring end gap positions - Align the oil ring spacer gap A, the oil ring side rails at D (one inch either side of the pin centerline), and the compression rings at B and C, one inch either side of the pin centerline

24.9 Check to be sure both the mark on the piston and the mark on the connecting rod are aligned and are facing the timing belt end of the engine

rod assemblies, the cylinder walls must be perfectly clean, the top edge of each cylinder must be chamfered, and the crankshaft must be in place.

2   Remove the cap from the end of the number one connecting rod (refer to the marks made during removal). Remove the original bearing inserts and wipe the bearing surfaces of the connecting rod and cap with a clean, lint-free cloth. They must be kept spotlessly clean.

Connecting rod bearing oil clearance check

3   Clean the back side of the new upper bearing insert, then lay it in place in the connecting rod. Make sure the tab on the bearing fits into the recess in the rod. Don't hammer the bearing insert into place and be very careful not to nick or gouge the bearing face. Don't lubricate the bearing at this time.

4   Clean the back side of the other bearing insert and install it in the rod cap. Again, make sure the tab on the bearing fits into the recess in the cap, and don't apply any lubricant. It's critically important that the mating surfaces of the bearing and connecting rod are perfectly clean and oil free when they're

assembled.

5   Position the piston ring gaps at 90-degree intervals around the piston **(see illustration)**.

6   Slip a section of plastic or rubber hose over each connecting rod cap bolt.

7   Lubricate the piston and rings with clean engine oil and attach a piston ring compressor to the piston. Leave the skirt protruding about 1/4-inch to guide the piston into the cylinder. The rings must be compressed until they're flush with the piston.

8   Rotate the crankshaft until the number one connecting rod journal is at BDC (bottom dead center) and apply a coat of engine oil to the cylinder walls.

9   With the mark on top of the piston **(see illustration)** facing the front (timing belt end) of the engine, gently insert the piston/connecting rod assembly into the number one cylinder bore and rest the bottom edge of the ring compressor on the engine block. **Note:** *The connecting rod also has a mark on it that must face the front of the engine (if it faces the opposite direction, the piston and connecting rod have been assembled improperly.*

10   Tap the top edge of the ring compressor to make sure it's contacting the block around

its entire circumference.

11   Gently tap on the top of the piston with the end of a wooden or plastic hammer handle **(see illustration)** while guiding the end of the connecting rod into place on the crankshaft journal. The piston rings may try to pop out of the ring compressor just before entering the cylinder bore, so keep some downward pressure on the ring compressor. Work slowly, and if any resistance is felt as the piston enters the cylinder, stop immediately. Find out what's hanging up and fix it before proceeding. Do not, for any reason, force the piston into the cylinder - you might break a ring and/or the piston.

12   Once the piston/connecting rod assembly is installed, the connecting rod bearing oil clearance must be checked before the rod cap is permanently bolted in place.

13   Cut a piece of the appropriate size Plastigage slightly shorter than the width of the connecting rod bearing and lay it in place on the number one connecting rod journal, parallel with the journal axis **(see illustration)**.

14   Clean the connecting rod cap bearing face, remove the protective hoses from the

24.11 The piston can be driven gently into the cylinder bore with the end of a wooden or plastic hammer handle

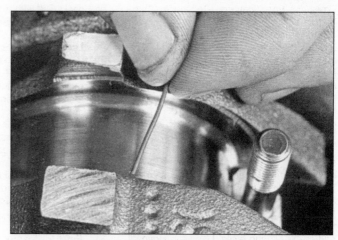

24.13 Lay the Plastigage strips on each rod bearing journal, parallel to the crankshaft centerline

connecting rod bolts and install the rod cap. Make sure the mating mark on the cap is on the same side as the mark on the connecting rod **(see illustration)**. **Note:** *Check to make sure the identification mark on the connecting rod faces toward the front (timing belt) end of the engine.*

15   Install the nuts and tighten them to the torque listed in this Chapter's Specifications, working up to it in three steps. **Note:** *Use a thin-wall socket to avoid erroneous torque readings that can result if the socket is wedged between the rod cap and nut. If the socket tends to wedge itself between the nut and the cap, lift up on it slightly until it no longer contacts the cap. Do not rotate the crankshaft at any time during this operation.*

16   Remove the nuts and detach the rod cap, being very careful not to disturb the Plastigage.

17   Compare the width of the crushed Plastigage to the scale printed on the Plastigage envelope to obtain the oil clearance **(see illustration)**. Compare it to the Specifications (listed in this Chapter) to make sure the clearance is correct.

18   If the clearance is not as specified, the bearing inserts may be the wrong size (which means different ones will be required). Before deciding that different inserts are needed, make sure that no dirt or oil was between the bearing inserts and the connecting rod or cap when the clearance was measured. Also, recheck the journal diameter. If the Plastigage was wider at one end than the other, the journal may be tapered (refer to Section 19). If the clearance still exceeds the limit specified, the bearing will have to be replaced with an undersize bearing. **Caution:** *When installing a new crankshaft always use a standard bearing.*

Final connecting rod installation

19   Carefully scrape all traces of the Plastigage material off the rod journal and/or bearing face. Be very careful not to scratch the bearing - use your fingernail or the edge of a credit card.

20   Make sure the bearing faces are perfectly clean, then apply a uniform layer of clean moly-base grease or engine assembly lube to both of them. You'll have to push the piston into the cylinder to expose the face of the bearing insert in the connecting rod - be sure to slip the protective hoses over the rod bolts first.

21   Slide the connecting rod back into place on the journal, remove the protective hoses from the rod cap bolts, install the rod cap and tighten the nuts to the torque listed in this Chapter's Specifications. Again, work up to the torque in three steps.

22   Repeat the entire procedure for the remaining pistons/connecting rods.

23   The important points to remember are:

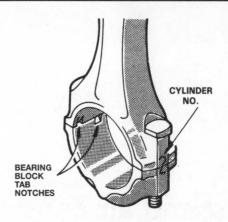

24.14 Install the connecting rod caps with the cylinder numbers and tab notches as shown

a)   *Keep the back sides of the bearing inserts and the insides of the connecting rods and caps perfectly clean when assembling them.*

b)   *Make sure you have the correct piston/rod assembly for each cylinder.*

c)   *The mark on the piston must face the front of the engine.*

d)   *Lubricate the cylinder walls with clean oil.*

e)   *Lubricate the bearing faces when installing the rod caps after the oil clearance has been checked.*

24   After all the piston/connecting rod assemblies have been properly installed, rotate the crankshaft a number of times by hand to check for any obvious binding.

25   As a final step, the connecting rod endplay must be checked. Refer to Section 13 for this procedure.

26   Compare the measured endplay to the Specifications to make sure it's correct. If it was correct before disassembly and the original crankshaft and rods were reinstalled, it should still be right. If new rods or a new crankshaft were installed, the endplay may be inadequate. If so, the rods will have to be removed and taken to an automotive machine shop for resizing.

25   Initial start-up and break-in after overhaul

Warning: *Have a fire extinguisher handy when starting the engine for the first time.*

1   Once the engine has been installed in the vehicle, double-check the engine oil and coolant levels. Add transaxle fluid as needed.

2   With the spark plugs out of the engine and the ignition system disabled (disconnect the primary [low voltage] wires from the distributor [1.8L engine] or the power transistor [2.0L engine]), crank the engine until the oil

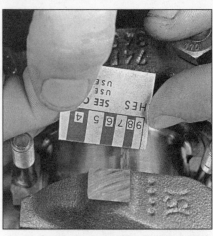

24.17 Compare the width of the crushed Plastigage to the scale on the envelope to determine the rod bearing oil clearance (always take the measurement at the widest point of the Plastigage) - be sure to use the correct scale; standard and metric scales are included

pressure light goes out.

3   Install the spark plugs, hook up the plug wires and restore the ignition system functions.

4   Start the engine. It may take a few moments for the fuel system to build up pressure, but the engine should start without a great deal of effort. **Note:** *If backfiring occurs through the throttle body, recheck the valve timing and ignition timing.*

5   After the engine starts, it should be allowed to warm up to normal operating temperature. Try to keep the engine speed at approximately 2000 rpm. While the engine is warming up, make a thorough check for fuel, oil and coolant leaks. Check the automatic transaxle fluid level (if so equipped).

6   Shut the engine off and recheck the engine oil and coolant levels.

7   Drive the vehicle to an area with minimum traffic, accelerate at full throttle from 30 to 50 mph, then allow the vehicle to slow to 30 mph with the throttle closed. Repeat the procedure 10 or 12 times. This will load the piston rings and cause them to seat properly against the cylinder walls. Check again for oil and coolant leaks.

8   Drive the vehicle gently for the first 500 miles (no sustained high speeds) and keep a constant check on the oil level. It is not unusual for an engine to use oil during the break-in period.

9   At approximately 500 to 600 miles, change the oil and filter.

10   For the next few hundred miles, drive the vehicle normally. Do not pamper it or abuse it.

11   After 2000 miles, change the oil and filter again and consider the engine broken in.

Chapter 3
Cooling, heating and air conditioning systems

Contents

Specifications

General

Radiator cap pressure rating	11 to 15 psi
Thermostat rating (opening temperature)	190-degrees F
Cooling system capacity	See Chapter 1
Cooling system testing pressure	13 psi
Refrigerant capacity	2.06 lbs
Refrigerant oil capacity (complete system)	5.0 ounces

Torque specifications

	Ft-lbs (unless otherwise indicated)
Thermostat cover bolts	12 to 14
Water pump-to-engine block bolts	
Short bolts	108 to 132 in-lbs
Long bolt	14 to 20

1 General information

Engine cooling system

All vehicles covered by this manual employ a pressurized engine cooling system with thermostatically controlled coolant circulation. An impeller type water pump mounted on the drivebelt end of the block pumps coolant through the engine. The coolant flows around each cylinder and toward the transaxle end of the engine. Cast-in coolant passages direct coolant around the intake and exhaust ports, near the spark plug areas and in close proximity to the exhaust valve guides.

A wax pellet type thermostat is located in a housing on the other end of the engine. During warm up, the closed thermostat prevents coolant from circulating through the radiator. As the engine nears normal operating temperature, the thermostat opens and allows hot coolant to travel through the radiator, where it's cooled before returning to the engine.

The cooling system is sealed by a pressure type radiator cap, which raises the boiling point of the coolant and increases the cooling efficiency of the radiator. If the system pressure exceeds the cap pressure relief value, the excess pressure in the system forces the spring-loaded valve inside the cap off its seat and allows the coolant to escape through the overflow tube into a coolant reservoir. When the system cools, the excess coolant is automatically drawn from the reservoir back into the radiator.

The coolant reservoir serves as both the

point at which fresh coolant is added to the cooling system to maintain the proper fluid level and as a holding tank for overheated coolant.

This type of cooling system is known as a closed design because coolant that escapes past the pressure cap is saved and reused.

Heating system

The heating system consists of a blower fan and heater core located in the heater box, the hoses connecting the heater core to the engine cooling system and the heater/air conditioning control head on the dashboard. Hot engine coolant is circulated through the heater core. When the heater mode is activated, a flap opens to expose the heater box to the passenger compartment. A fan switch on the control head activates the blower motor, which forces air through the core, heating the air.

Air conditioning system

The air conditioning system consists of a condenser mounted in front of the radiator, an evaporator mounted adjacent to the heater core, a compressor mounted on the engine, a receiver-drier which contains a high pressure relief valve and the plumbing connecting all of the above components.

A blower fan forces the warmer air of the passenger compartment through the evaporator core (sort of a radiator-in-reverse), transferring the heat from the air to the refrigerant. The liquid refrigerant boils off into low pressure vapor, taking the heat with it when it leaves the evaporator.

2   Antifreeze - general information

Warning: *Do not allow antifreeze to come in contact with your skin or painted surfaces of the vehicle. Rinse off spills immediately with plenty of water. Antifreeze is highly toxic if ingested. Never leave antifreeze lying around in an open container or in puddles on the floor; children and pets are attracted by it's sweet smell and may drink it. Check with local authorities about disposing of used antifreeze. Many communities have collection centers which will see that antifreeze is disposed of safely.*

The cooling system should be filled with a water/ethylene glycol based antifreeze solution, which will prevent freezing down to at least -20-degrees F, or lower if local climate requires it. It also provides protection against corrosion and increases the coolant boiling point.

The cooling system should be drained, flushed and refilled at the specified intervals (see Chapter 1). Old or contaminated antifreeze solutions are likely to cause damage and encourage the formation of corrosion and scale in the system. Use distilled water with the antifreeze.

Before adding antifreeze, check all hose

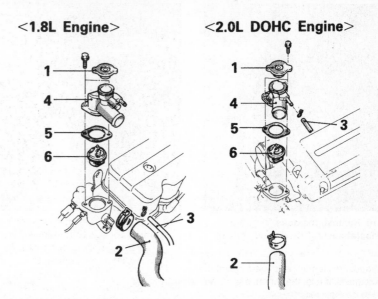

<1.8L Engine>   **<2.0L DOHC Engine>**

3.7 Exploded views of the thermostat housing on 1.8L and 2.0L engines

1	Radiator cap	4	Thermostat cover
2	Upper radiator hose	5	Gasket
3	Overflow tube	6	Thermostat

connections, because antifreeze tends to leak through very minute openings. Engines don't normally consume coolant, so if the level goes down, find the cause and correct it.

The exact mixture of antifreeze-to-water which you should use depends on the relative weather conditions. The mixture should contain at least 50-percent antifreeze, but should never contain more than 70-percent antifreeze. Consult the mixture ratio chart on the antifreeze container before adding coolant. Hydrometers are available at most auto parts stores to test the coolant. Use antifreeze which meets the vehicle manufacturer's specifications.

3   Thermostat - check and replacement

Warning: *Do not remove the radiator cap, drain the coolant or replace the thermostat until the engine has cooled completely. Do not allow antifreeze to come in contact with your skin or painted surfaces of the vehicle. Rinse off spills immediately with plenty of water. Antifreeze is highly toxic if ingested. Never leave antifreeze lying around in an open container or in puddles on the floor; children and pets are attracted by it's sweet smell and may drink it. Check with local authorities about disposing of used antifreeze. Many communities have collection centers which will see that antifreeze is disposed of safely.*

Check

1   Before assuming the thermostat is to blame for a cooling system problem, check the coolant level, drivebelt tension (see

Chapter 1) and temperature gauge operation.
2   If the engine seems to be taking a long time to warm up (based on heater output or temperature gauge operation), the thermostat is probably stuck open. Replace the thermostat with a new one.
3   If the engine runs hot, use your hand to check the temperature of the upper radiator hose. If the hose isn't hot, but the engine is, the thermostat is probably stuck closed, preventing the coolant inside the engine from escaping to the radiator. Replace the thermostat. **Caution:** *Don't drive the vehicle without a thermostat. The computer may stay in open loop, causing emissions and fuel economy to suffer.*
4   If the upper radiator hose is hot, it means that the coolant is flowing and the thermostat is open. Consult the *Troubleshooting* section at the front of this manual for cooling system diagnosis.

Replacement
Refer to illustrations 3.7 and 3.10
5   Disconnect the cable from the negative terminal of the battery.
6   Drain the cooling system (see Chapter 1). If the coolant is relatively new or in good condition, save it and reuse it.
7   Follow the upper radiator hose to the engine to locate the thermostat cover **(see illustration)**.
8   Loosen the hose clamp and detach the hose from the fitting. If the hose is stuck, grasp it near the end with a pair of adjustable pliers and twist it to break the seal, then pull it off. If the hose is old or deteriorated, cut it off and install a new one.
9   If the outer surface of the large fitting that mates with the hose is deteriorated (cor-

3.10 Remove the bolts from the thermostat cover (2.0L engine shown)

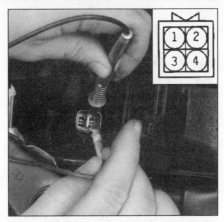

4.3a Using a fused jumper wire, apply battery voltage to terminals 2 and 4 on the electrical connector for the main cooling fan

4.3b Using a fused jumper wire, apply battery voltage to the lower terminals on the electrical connector for the condenser fan

roded, pitted, etc.) it may be damaged further by hose removal. If it is, the thermostat cover will have to be replaced.

10 Remove the bolts and detach the thermostat cover **(see illustration)**. If the cover is stuck, tap it with a soft-face hammer to jar it loose. Be prepared for some coolant to spill as the gasket seal is broken.

11 Note the position of the air bleed valve and how the thermostat is installed, then remove the thermostat and all traces of old gasket material and sealant from the housing and cover with a gasket scraper.

12 Apply a thin, uniform layer of RTV sealant to both sides of the new gasket and position it on the housing.

13 Install the new thermostat in the housing. Make sure the air bleed valve faces up and the spring end is directed into the engine.

14 Install the thermostat cover and bolts. Tighten the bolts to the torque listed in this Chapter's Specifications.

15 Reattach the hose to the fitting and tighten the hose clamp securely.

16 Refill the cooling system (see Chapter 1).

17 Start the engine and allow it to reach

normal operating temperature, then check for leaks and proper thermostat operation (as described in Steps 3 and 4).

---

4 Engine cooling fan(s) and circuit - check and component replacement

Refer to illustrations 4.3a, 4.3b, 4.4, 4.5 and 4.6

Check

1 The engine cooling fan(s) are controlled by a fan motor relay which is mounted on the left engine compartment relay center and a radiator fan thermo switch. The two fans operate separately. When the coolant reaches a predetermined temperature, the switch opens the ground return for the fan motor relay, completing the circuit.

2 First, check the fuses (see Chapter 12).

3 To test the fan motor, unplug the electrical connector and use fused jumper wires **(see illustrations)** to connect the fan directly

to the battery. If the fan still does not work, replace the motor.

4 If the motor tested okay, the fault lies in the radiator fan thermo switch, the relay or the wiring harness (see Chapter 12). Remove the relay and bridge the indicated terminals with a jumper wire **(see illustration)**. If the fan motor now works, replace the relay.

5 Turn on the ignition switch, unplug the electrical connector from the radiator fan thermo switch **(see illustration)** and, using a jumper wire or paper clip, connect the terminals together.

6 If the fan does not operate, check the wiring (see Chapter 12). Remove the radiator fan relay and connect a jumper wire from terminal number 2 to the battery positive (+) terminal and connect terminal number 4 to the negative terminal of the battery (-) **(see illustration)**.

4.4 Install a jumper wire into these two terminals of the cooling fan relay connector to energize the cooling fan

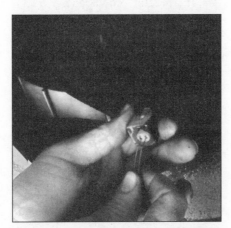

4.5 Unplug the electrical connector from the radiator fan thermo switch and use a paper clip to bridge the terminals of the electrical connector together

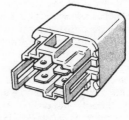

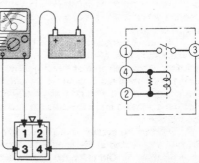

4.6 Apply battery voltage to terminal number 2, ground terminal number 4, and check the resistance across terminals 1 and 3 of the relay

3

4.15 Remove the thermo switch from the radiator (radiator removed for clarity)

7   Using an ohmmeter, check for continuity between terminals 1and 3. There should be continuity.
8   Remove the battery leads (no voltage) and check for continuity between terminals 1 and 3. There should be no continuity.
9   Also, check for continuity between terminals 2 and 4. There should be continuity. If any of the test results are incorrect, replace the relay. If all the test results are correct, check the thermo switch.
10   Unplug the electrical connector from the thermo switch.
11   With the engine cold (under 160-degrees) use an ohmmeter and check for continuity across the terminals of the switch. There should be no continuity. If there is, replace the thermo switch
12   Start the engine and allow it to reach normal operating temperature. Check the continuity of the switch again - it should have continuity. If not, replace the thermo switch.

Replacement

Radiator fan thermo switch

Refer to illustration 4.15
13   Drain the coolant from the radiator (see Chapter 1).
14   Disconnect the electrical connector from the thermo switch.
15   Unscrew the thermo switch from the radiator **(see illustration)**.

Main cooling fan

Refer to illustration 4.18
16   Disconnect the cable from the negative terminal of the battery.
17   Unplug the cooling fan electrical connector.
18   Remove the radiator fan shroud bolts **(see illustration)**.
19   Lift the fan assembly out of the engine compartment, being careful not to damage the radiator. To remove the motor, unscrew the nut from the center of the fan, remove the fan, then remove the four bolts and separate the fan motor from the shroud.
20   Installation is the reverse of removal.

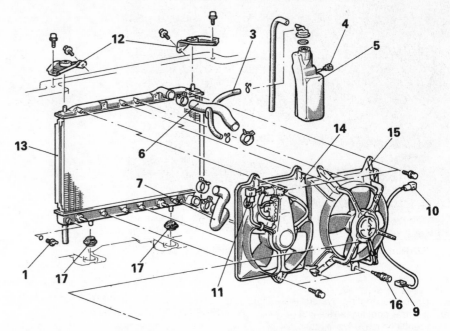

4.18 Radiator fan assembly - exploded view

1	Drain plug	10	Radiator fan motor connector
2	Radiator cap	11	Condenser fan motor connector
3	Overflow tube	12	Upper insulator
4	Coolant level switch	13	Radiator assembly
5	Coolant expansion tank	14	Condenser fan motor assembly
6	Radiator upper hose	15	Radiator fan motor assembly
7	Radiator lower hose	16	Thermo fan switch
9	Thermo switch electrical connector	17	Lower insulator

Air conditioning condenser fan

Refer to illustration 4.24
21   Air conditioned models have an additional fan located in front of the condenser.
22   Disconnect the negative battery cable from the battery.
23   Disconnect the fan motor electrical connector.
24   Remove the three bolts holding the condenser fan to the radiator **(see accompanying illustration and illustration 4.18)**. Remove the assembly, being careful not to damage the radiator. If it's necessary to replace the motor, refer to Step 19.
25   Installation is the reverse of the removal procedure.

5   Radiator - removal and installation

Refer to illustration5.6
Warning: *Do not start this procedure until the engine is completely cool. Do not allow antifreeze to come in contact with your skin or painted surfaces of the vehicle. Rinse off spills immediately with plenty of water. Antifreeze is highly toxic if ingested. Never leave antifreeze lying around in an open container or in puddles on the floor; children and pets are attracted by it's sweet smell and may drink it. Check with local authorities about disposing of used antifreeze. Many communities have collection centers which will see that antifreeze is disposed of safely.*

Removal

1   Disconnect the cable from the negative terminal of the battery.
2   Raise the front of the vehicle and support it securely on jackstands. Remove the lower splash shields.

4.24 Remove the bolts (arrows) from the condenser fan assembly (the lower bolt is not in visible in this photo)

5.6 Remove the bolts (arrows) from the radiator supports

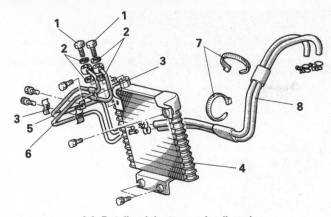

6.6 Details of the transaxle oil cooler

1	Banjo bolt	5	Oil cooler feed line
2	Sealing washers	6	Oil cooler return line
3	Bracket	7	Band
4	Oil cooler	8	Oil cooler hoses

3   Drain the cooling system (see Chapter 1). If the coolant is relatively new or in good condition, save it and reuse it.

4   Disconnect the electrical connector from the radiator fan thermo switch.

5   Disconnect the coolant reservoir hose from the radiator. Loosen the upper and lower radiator hose clamps, then detach the radiator hoses from the fittings. If they're stuck, grasp each hose near the end with a pair of adjustable pliers and twist it to break the seal, then pull it off - be careful not to damage the radiator fittings! If the hoses are old or deteriorated, cut them off and install new ones.

6   Remove the radiator supports **(see illustration)**.

7   Disconnect the electrical connector(s) from the cooling fan(s).

8   If the vehicle is equipped with an automatic transaxle, disconnect the transmission fluid cooler lines and plug the lines and fittings.

9   Carefully lift out the radiator. Don't spill coolant on the vehicle or scratch the paint. Remove the bolts securing the cooling fan to the radiator and pull it free.

10   With the radiator removed, it can be inspected for leaks and damage. If it needs repair, have a radiator shop or dealer service department perform the work, as special techniques are required.

11   Bugs and dirt can be removed from the radiator with a garden hose or a soft brush. Don't bend the cooling fins as this is done.

Installation

12   Installation is the reverse of the removal procedure. Be sure the rubber cushions are seated properly at the base of the radiator.

13   After installation, fill the cooling system with the proper mixture of antifreeze and water (see Chapter 1).

14   Start the engine and check for leaks. Allow the engine to reach normal operating temperature, indicated by the upper radiator

hose becoming hot. Recheck the coolant level and add more if required.

15   If you're working on an automatic transaxle equipped vehicle, check and add fluid as needed (see Chapter 1).

6   Transaxle oil cooler (turbo models) - removal and installation

Refer to illustrations 6.6

1   Remove the radiator from the engine compartment (see Section 5).

2   Drain the automatic transaxle fluid from the transaxle (see Chapter 1).

3   Remove the air cleaner (see Chapter 4).

4   Remove the front bumper (see Chapter 11).

5   Remove the fresh air ducts from the engine compartment.

6   Remove the banjo bolts and disconnect the fluid lines from the transaxle cooler **(see illustration)**.

7   Remove the mounting bolts.

8   Lift the transaxle oil cooler from the engine compartment.

9   Installation is the reverse of removal.

7   Coolant reservoir - removal and installation

Warning: *Do not start this procedure until the engine is completely cool. Do not allow antifreeze to come in contact with your skin or painted surfaces of the vehicle. Rinse off spills immediately with plenty of water. Antifreeze is highly toxic if ingested. Never leave antifreeze lying around in an open container or in puddles on the floor; children and pets are attracted by it's sweet smell and may drink it. Check with local authorities about disposing of used antifreeze. Many communities have collection centers which will see that antifreeze is disposed of safely.*

1   Disconnect the hose from the radiator filler neck and inspect the hose for cracks.

2   Follow the hose from the filler neck to the reservoir cap and lift the cap off the coolant reservoir and withdraw the overflow hose.

3   Remove the hold down bolt.

4   Slide the coolant reservoir straight up from its guides to remove it **(see illustration 4.18)**.

5   Pour the coolant into a container. Wash out and inspect the reservoir for cracks and chafing. Replace it if it's damaged.

6   Installation is the reverse of removal.

8   Water pump - check

1   A failure in the water pump can cause serious engine damage due to overheating.

2   There are two ways to check the operation of the water pump while it's installed on the engine. If the pump is defective, it should be replaced with a new or rebuilt unit.

3   Loosen the tension on the water pump belt (see Chapter 1). Grasp the water pump pulley and try to rock it up-and-down. If any play is felt, the shaft bearings are worn out and the pump should be replaced.

4   Remove the timing belt cover(s) (see Chapter 2A). Water pumps are equipped with weep or vent holes. If a failure occurs in the pump seal, coolant will leak from the hole. In most cases you'll need a flashlight to find the hole on the water pump from underneath to check for leaks. On both the 1.8L and 2.0L engines any water coming from this hole is vented to the outside of the timing belt cover on the back side of the engine in order to prevent damage to the timing belt.

5   If the water pump shaft bearings fail there may be a howling sound at the drive-belt end of the engine while it's running. Don't mistake drivebelt slippage, which causes a squealing sound, for water pump bearing failure.

3

9.6a Exploded view of the water pump and surrounding components on the 1.8L engine

12	Ignition wire set	20	Flange
13	Valve cover	21	Timing belt B tensioner
14	Valve cover gasket	22	Timing belt B
15	Semi-circular seal	23	Alternator brace
16	Upper timing belt cover	24	Water pump
17	Lower timing belt cover	25	Water pump gasket
18	Timing belt	26	O-ring
19	Crankshaft sprocket		

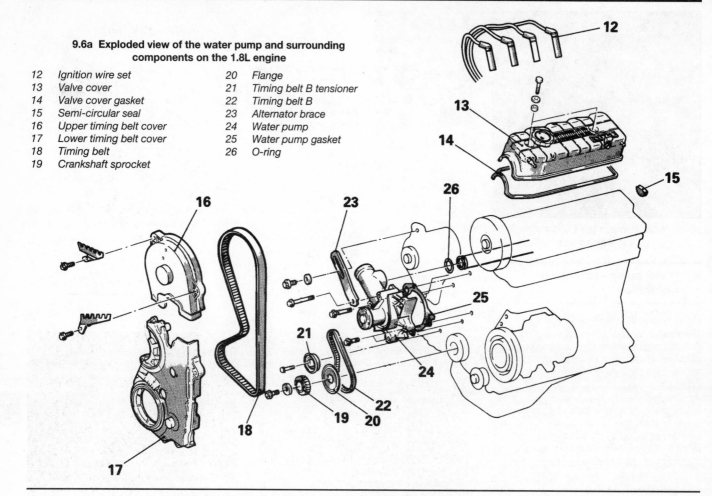

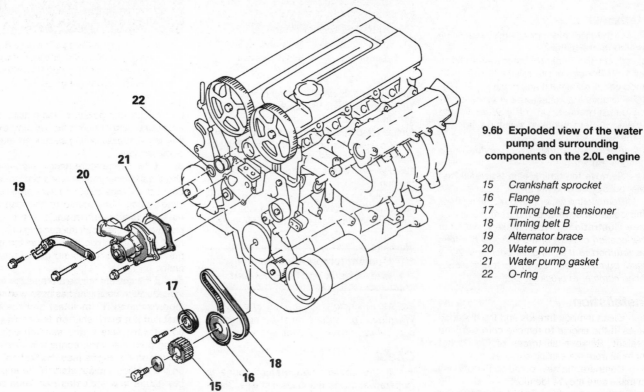

9.6b Exploded view of the water pump and surrounding components on the 2.0L engine

15	Crankshaft sprocket
16	Flange
17	Timing belt B tensioner
18	Timing belt B
19	Alternator brace
20	Water pump
21	Water pump gasket
22	O-ring

9.6c Remove the bolts from the water pump

9 Water pump - removal and installation

Refer to illustration 9.6a, 9.6b and 9.6c
Warning: *Wait until the engine is completely cool before beginning this procedure. Do not allow antifreeze to come in contact with your skin or painted surfaces of the vehicle. Rinse off spills immediately with plenty of water. Antifreeze is highly toxic if ingested. Never leave antifreeze lying around in an open container or in puddles on the floor; children and pets are attracted by it's sweet smell and may drink it. Check with local authorities about disposing of used antifreeze. Many communities have collection centers which will see that antifreeze is disposed of safely.*

Removal

1   Disconnect the cable from the negative terminal of the battery.
2   Drain the cooling system (see Chapter 1). If the coolant is relatively new or in good condition, save it and reuse it.
3   Remove the bolts from the power steering pump bracket. Do not disconnect the fluid lines. Set the power steering pump out of the way.
4   Remove the timing belt cover(s) (see Chapter 2A).
5   Remove the timing belt, tensioner and idler pulley (see Chapter 2A).
6   Remove the water pump mounting bolts and detach the water pump from the engine **(see illustrations). Note:** *Make a sketch of the location of each of the bolts so they can be returned to their original positions. If the water pump is stuck, gently tap it with a soft-faced hammer to break the seal.*

Installation

7   Clean the bolt threads and the threaded holes in the engine to remove corrosion and sealant. Remove all traces of old gasket material from the sealing surfaces.
8   Compare the new pump to the old one to make sure they're identical.
9   Apply a thin film of RTV sealant to the

10.3a Sensor locations on the 1.8L and 2.0L engines

1   *Coolant temperature sending unit*
2   *Coolant temperature sensor (ECM)*
3   *Coolant temperature switch (A/C)*

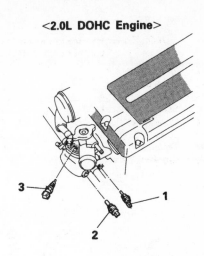

<2.0L DOHC Engine>

<1.8L Engine>

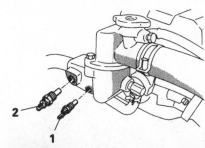

10.3b Location of the temperature sending unit on the 2.0L engine

new gasket and install it on the pump.
10   Carefully mate the pump to the engine.
11   Install the bolts. Tighten them to the torque listed in this Chapter's Specifications. Don't over-tighten them or the pump may be damaged.
12   Reinstall all parts removed for access to the pump.
13   Refill the cooling system (see Chapter 1) and check the timing belt tension (see Chapter 2A). Run the engine and check for leaks.

10 Coolant temperature sending unit - check and replacement

Refer to illustrations 10.3a, 10.3b and 10.4
Warning: *The engine must be completely cool before removing the sending unit.*

Check

1   If the coolant temperature gauge is inoperative, check the fuses first (see Chapter 12).

10.4 Connect a jumper wire to the sending unit wire and touch it to ground - this should make the temperature gauge read hot

2   If the temperature indicator shows excessive temperature after running awhile, see the *Troubleshooting* section in the front of the manual.
3   If the temperature gauge indicates Hot shortly after the engine is started cold, disconnect the wire at the coolant temperature sending unit - it's located on the thermostat housing **(see illustrations)**. If the gauge reading drops, replace the sending unit. If the reading remains high, the wire to the gauge may be shorted to ground or the gauge is faulty.
4   If the coolant temperature gauge fails to indicate after the engine has been warmed up (approximately 10 minutes) and the fuses checked out okay, shut off the engine. Disconnect the wire at the sending unit and, using a jumper wire, connect it to a clean ground on the engine **(see illustration)**. Turn on the ignition without starting the engine. If the gauge now indicates Hot, replace the sending unit.

3

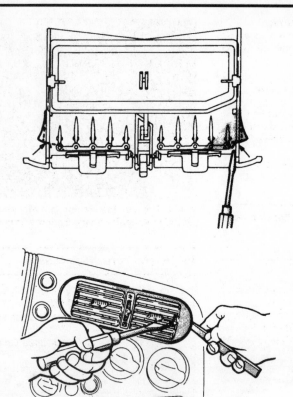

11.1 Use a screwdriver to disengage the tabs of the center air outlet before prying the assembly out

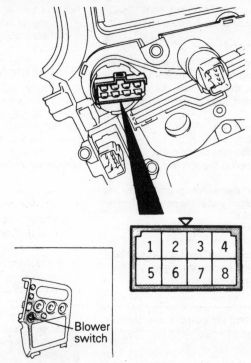

Terminal Switch position	5	3	6	2	7	8	1	4
OFF								
• (Low)	O—	—O				O—	—O	
● (Medium first step)	O—	—	—O			O—	—O	
● (Medium second step)	O—	—	—	—O		O—	—O—	—O
● (High)	O—	—	—	—	—O	O—	—O—	—O

NOTE
O—O indicates that there is continuity between the terminals.

11.2 Terminal guide and continuity table for the blower switch

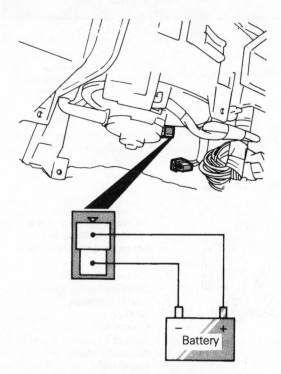

11.4 Working below the dash, apply battery voltage to the blower motor to confirm that the motor runs

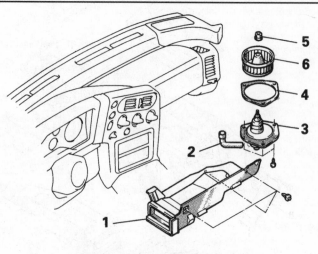

12.2 Exploded view of the blower motor

1	Lower duct panel	4	Seal
2	Motor cooling hose	5	Nut
3	Blower motor	6	Fan

5   If the gauge still does not work, the circuit may be open or the gauge may be faulty.

Replacement

6   With the engine completely cool, remove the cap from the radiator to release any pressure, then reinstall the cap. This reduces coolant loss during sending unit replacement.
7   Disconnect the electrical connector from the sending unit.
8   Prepare the new sending unit for installation by wrapping the threads with Teflon tape.
9   Unscrew the sending unit from the engine and quickly install the new one to prevent coolant loss.
10   Tighten the sending unit securely and connect the electrical connector.
11   Check the coolant level and add, if necessary. Start the engine and check for leaks and proper gauge operation.

11   Heater and air conditioner blower motor and circuit - check and switch replacement

Blower motor switch check

Refer to illustrations 11.1, 11.2 and 11.4
1   Carefully remove the center air outlet assembly from the instrument cluster panel **(see illustration).**
2   Disconnect the electrical connector from the blower motor switch and, using an ohmmeter, check for continuity between the

indicated terminals **(see illustration).**
3   If any of the tests indicate an open circuit where there should be continuity, replace the switch.

Blower motor check

4   Disconnect the electrical connector from the blower motor **(see illustration).**
5   Using jumper wires, apply battery voltage to the blower motor and observe that the motor runs smoothly.
6   If the blower motor does not operate, replace it (see Section 12).

12   Heater and air conditioner blower motor - removal and installation

Refer to illustration 12.2
1   Disconnect the cable from the negative terminal of the battery.
2   Locate the blower motor on passenger side behind the glove compartment. Remove the lower duct panel beneath the glove compartment **(see illustration).**
3   Remove the three blower motor retaining screws and lower the unit from the housing.
4   Disconnect the blower motor electrical connector.
5   Remove the motor cooling hose.
6   If you are replacing the motor, detach the fan and transfer it to the new motor.
7   Installation is the reverse of removal.
8   Run the blower and check for proper operation.

13.3 Remove the clamps (arrows) and detach the heater hoses from the firewall

13   Heater core - replacement

Refer to illustrations 13.3, 13.6, 13.8, 13.9a, 13.9b, 13.10, 13.11a and 13.11b
1   Disconnect the cable from the negative terminal of the battery.
2   Drain the cooling system (see Chapter 1).
3   Working in the engine compartment, disconnect the heater hoses where they enter the firewall **(see illustration).**
4   Remove the panels covering the center reinforcement and the panels under the dash (see Chapter 11).
5   Remove the dash from the vehicle (see Chapter 12).
6   Remove the metal center reinforcement structures from the the passenger compartment **(see illustration).**

3

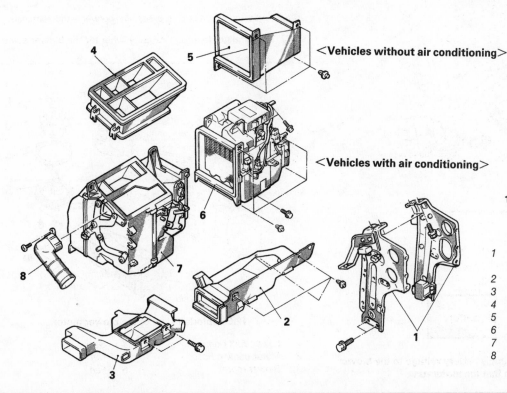

⟨Vehicles without air conditioning⟩

⟨Vehicles with air conditioning⟩

13.6 Exploded view of the heater assembly and surrounding components

1   *Center reinforcement structures*
2   *Lower duct panel*
3   *Air duct*
4   *Center duct*
5   *Air duct*
6   *Evaporator case*
7   *Heater unit*
8   *Lap cooler duct*

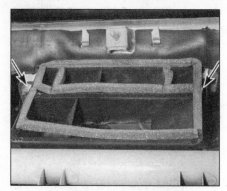

13.8   Remove the nuts (arrows) from the center duct

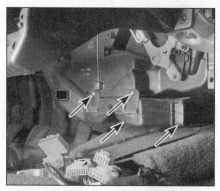

13.9a   First remove the screws and nuts (arrows) from the lower duct . . .

13.9b   . . . then remove the nuts (arrows) from the lower section of the heater unit

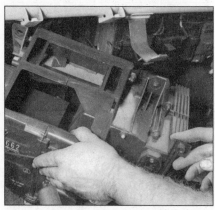

13.10   Remove the heater unit from the passenger compartment

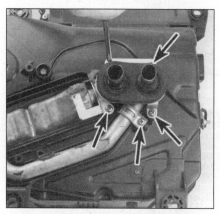

13.11a   Use a Phillips screwdriver to remove the screws (arrows) from the heater core brackets . . .

13.11b   . . . then lift the heater core from the heater assembly

14.4   Carefully pry the cable ends down and off the control knobs

14.5   Remove the screws (arrows) from the control assembly

7   Disconnect the temperature control cable and the mode control cable at the heater case.

8   Remove the nuts at the upper center duct assembly and remove the duct from the vehicle **(see illustration)**.

9   Remove the lower duct from the heater unit **(see illustration)**, then remove the nuts from the lower portion of the heater unit **(see illustration)**.

10   Remove the screws and clips and sepa-rate the heater assembly from the inside of the passenger compartment **(see illustration)**. **Note:** *Some heater units may not have the heat shield attached to the heater core which will cause it to melt the flame resistant material covering the firewall. Be sure to care-fully separate the two and not tear the mate-rial from the firewall.*

11   Take out the old heater core and install the new unit **(see illustrations)**.

12   Reassemble the heater unit and check the operation of the control flaps. If any parts bind, correct the problem before installation.

13   Reinstall the remaining parts in the reverse order of removal.

14   Refill the cooling system (see Chap-ter 1), reconnect the battery and start the engine. Check for leaks and proper system operation.

14   Air conditioner and heater control assembly - removal, installation and adjustment

Refer to illustrations 14.4, 14.5, 14.9a, 14.9b and 14.9c

1   Disconnect the cable from the negative terminal of the battery.

2   Remove the knobs from the levers of the heater control unit.

3   Remove cluster panel assembly which surrounds the radio and heater control assembly (see Chapter 11).

4   Remove the cable ends holding the cables for the temperature, mode control and fresh/recirculated air levers **(see illustration)**.

5   Remove the screws holding the control unit in the dash and pull the assembly from the dash **(see illustration)**.

6   Disconnect the electrical connectors

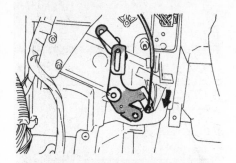

14.9a Make sure the temperature control lever is positioned all the way down (direction of arrow) and turn the knob all the way to the HOT position before connecting the cables

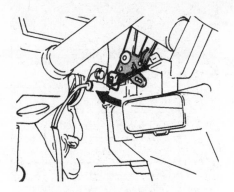

14.9b Move the mode selection lever all the way in (direction of arrow) before connecting the cables

14.9c Set the fresh/recirculating lever to the stopper (arrow) before connecting the cables

from the control assembly.

7   Remove the control assembly.

8   Installation is the reverse of the removal procedure.

9   Adjustment for the temperature, mode control and fresh/recirculated air control cables are as follows:

a) *Place the temperature control lever all the way to the right position (hot)* **(see illustration)**.

b) *Place the mode control selection all the way to the right position (defrost)* **(see illustration)**.

c) *Place the fresh/recirculating lever all the way to the left position (fresh)* **(see illustration)**.

10   Pull all three cables out to full length from their housings.

11   Attach the cables to their respective levers and attach the clips.

12   Check for full travel and proper operation.

---

15 Air conditioning system - check and maintenance

Warning: *The air conditioning system is under high pressure. Do not loosen any fittings or remove any components until after the system has been discharged. Air conditioning refrigerant should be properly discharged into an EPA-approved container at a* dealer service department or an automotive air conditioning repair facility. Always wear eye protection when disconnecting air conditioning system fittings.

General checks

1   The following maintenance checks should be performed on a regular basis to ensure that the air conditioner continues to operate at peak efficiency.

a) *Check the compressor drivebelt. If it's worn or deteriorated, replace it (see Chapter 1).*

b) *Check the drivebelt tension and, if necessary, adjust it (see Chapter 1).*

c) *Check the system hoses. Look for cracks, bubbles, hard spots and deterioration. Inspect the hoses and all fittings for oil bubbles and seepage. If there's any evidence of wear, damage or leaks, replace the hose(s).*

d) *Inspect the condenser fins for leaves, bugs and other debris. Use a "fin comb" or compressed air to clean the condenser.*

e) *Make sure the system has the correct refrigerant charge.*

f) *Check the evaporator housing drain tube for blockage.*

2   It's a good idea to operate the system for about ten minutes, at least once a month, particularly during the winter. Long term non-use can cause hardening, and subsequent failure, of the seals.

3   Because of the complexity of the air conditioning system and the special equipment necessary to service it, in-depth troubleshooting and repairs are not included in this manual. However, simple checks and component replacement procedures are provided in this Chapter. For more complete information on the air conditioning system, refer to the *Haynes Automotive Heating and Air Conditioning Manual.*

4   The most common cause of poor cooling is simply a low system refrigerant charge. If a noticeable drop in cool air output occurs, one of the following quick checks will help you determine if the refrigerant level is low.

5   Warm the engine up to normal operating temperature.

6   Place the air conditioning temperature selector at the coldest setting and put the blower at the highest setting. Open the doors (to make sure the air conditioning system doesn't cycle off as soon as it cools the passenger compartment).

7   With the compressor engaged - the clutch will make an audible click and the center of the clutch will rotate - inspect the sight glass, if equipped (it's usually on top of the receiver/drier). If the refrigerant looks foamy, it's low. Have the system charged by a dealer service department or other qualified repair shop.

8   If there's no sight glass, feel the inlet and outlet pipe sat the compressor. One side should be much colder than the other. If there's no perceptible difference between the two pipes, there's something wrong with the compressor or the system. It might be a low charge - it might be something else. Take the vehicle to a dealer service department or other qualified repair shop.

A/C switch check

Refer to illustrations 15.10 and 15.11

9   Remove the radio (see Chapter 12).

10   Reach inside the access hole and remove the air conditioning switch **(see illustration)**.

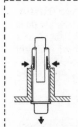

15.10 After removing the radio, reach inside the panel and squeeze the tabs (arrows) on the switch and pull the switch forward to remove it from the dash

3

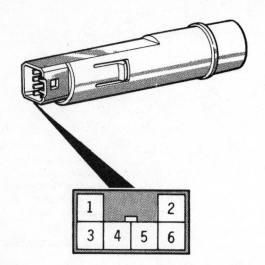

Switch position \ Terminal No.	1	2	4	5	3	6
OFF						
ECONOMY (If pressed 1 step)	○—		—○----	Indicator light	Illumination light	
A/C (If pressed 2 steps)	○—	—○—	—○			

NOTE
(1) The ○—○ symbol indicates continuity.
(2) The broken line (-----) indicates the connection during ECONOMY use.
(3) The chain line (—-—--) indicates the connection during air conditioning use.

15.11 Terminal guide and continuity chart for the air conditioning switch

11   Detach the electrical connector from the switch and, using an ohmmeter, check the continuity across the indicated terminals **(see illustration)**.
12   If the ohmmeter indicates that a circuit is open, replace the switch.

16 Air conditioning receiver/drier - removal and installation

Refer to illustration 16.3
Warning: *The air conditioning system is under high pressure. Do not loosen any fittings or remove any components until after the system has been discharged. Air conditioning refrigerant should be properly discharged into an EPA-approved container at a dealer service department or an automotive air conditioning repair facility. Always wear eye protection when disconnecting air conditioning system fittings.*
1   Have the refrigerant discharged at a dealer service department or an automotive air conditioning repair facility.
2   The receiver/drier, which acts as a reservoir and filter for the refrigerant, is located in front of the air conditioning condenser. The receiver/drier bracket is attached to the right side of the air conditioning condenser.
3   Detach the refrigerant lines and electrical connector from the receiver/drier **(see illustration)**. Immediately cap the open fittings to prevent the entry of dirt and moisture.
4   Remove the receiver/drier mounting bolts and detach it from the condenser.
5   Install new O-rings on the lines and lubricate them with clean refrigerant oil.
6   If a new receiver/drier is being installed, add one fluid ounce of refrigerant oil to the system.

7   Installation is the reverse of removal.
Note: *Do not remove the sealing caps until you are ready to reconnect the lines.*
8   Have the system evacuated, charged and leak tested by the shop that discharged it.

17 Air conditioning compressor - removal and installation

Refer to illustrations 17.5a and 17.5b
Warning: *The air conditioning system is under high pressure. Do not loosen any fittings or remove any components until after the system has been discharged. Air conditioning refrigerant should be properly discharged into an EPA-approved container at a dealer service department or an automotive air conditioning repair facility. Always wear eye protection when disconnecting air conditioning system fittings.*
1   Have the refrigerant discharged at a dealer service department or an automotive air conditioning repair facility.
2   Disconnect the negative cable from the battery and remove the battery (see Chapter 5).
3   Disconnect the electrical connector from the compressor clutch.
4   Remove the air conditioning drivebelt (see Chapter 1) from the engine compartment.
5   Remove the tensioner pulley assembly from the air conditioning bracket assembly **(see illustrations)**.
6   Detach the refrigerant lines from the compressor and immediately cap the open fittings to prevent the entry of dirt and moisture.
7   Raise the vehicle and support it securely on jackstands.
8   Remove the mounting bolts and lower

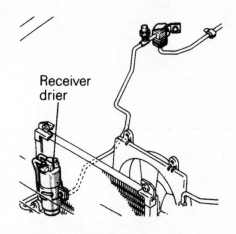

16.3 The receiver/drier is mounted on the right (passenger) side of the condenser

the compressor from the engine compartment. **Note:** *Keep the compressor level during handling and storage. If the compressor seized or you find metal particles in the refrigerant lines, the system must be flushed out by an air conditioning technician and the receiver/drier must be replaced (see Section 14).*
9   Prior to installation, turn the center of the clutch six times to disperse any oil that has collected in the head.
10   Install the compressor in the reverse order of removal.
11   If you are installing a new compressor, refer to the manufacturer's instructions for adding refrigerant oil to the system. **Note:** *Drain out any oil that is present in the compressor, then add 1.7 ounces of new refrigerant oil to the compressor.*
12   Have the system evacuated, charged and leak tested by the shop that discharged it.

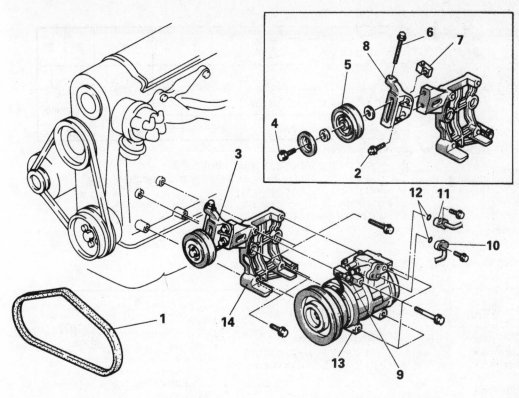

17.5a Exploded view of the air conditioning compressor and mounting hardware on the 1.8L engine

1   Drivebelt
2   Bolt
3   Tensioner pulley assembly
4   Bolt
5   Tensioner pulley
6   Bolt
7   Adjustment plate
8   Pulley bracket
9   Electrical connector for the compressor clutch
10 Suction side (High)
11 Discharge side (Low)
12 O-rings
13 Air conditioning compressor
14 Compressor bracket

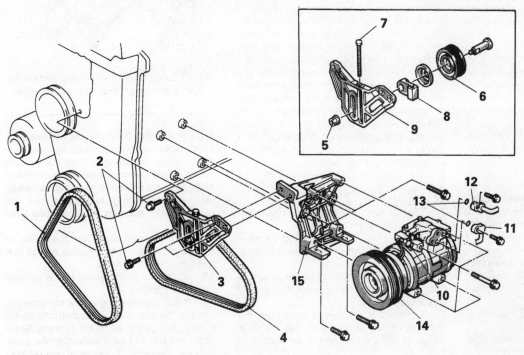

17.5b Exploded view of the air conditioning compressor and mounting hardware on the 2.0L engine

1   Drivebelt
2   Bolt
3   Tensioner pulley assembly
4   Drivebelt
5   Nut
6   Tensioner pulley
7   Bolt
8   Adjustment plate
9   Pulley bracket
10 Harness connector for the clutch
11 Suction side (High)
12 Discharge side (Low)
13 O-rings
14 Air conditioning compressor
15 Compressor bracket

3

18.8 Remove the two bolts from the condenser and lift the assembly from the engine compartment

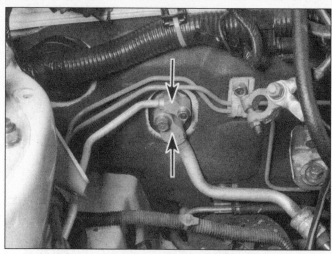

19.3 Disconnect the refrigerant lines from the evaporator from inside the engine compartment

18 Air conditioning condenser - removal and installation

Refer to illustration 18.8

Warning: *The air conditioning system is under high pressure. Do not loosen any fittings or remove any components until after the system has been discharged. Air conditioning refrigerant should be properly discharged into an EPA-approved container at a dealer service department or an automotive air conditioning repair facility. Always wear eye protection when disconnecting air conditioning system fittings.*

1   Have the refrigerant discharged at a dealer service department or an automotive air conditioning repair facility.
2   Remove the radiator supports **(see illustration 5.6)**.
3   Disconnect the condenser fan electrical connector (see Section 4) and the main fan

electrical connector.
4   Remove the radiator (see Section 5).
5   Disconnect the electrical connector from the receiver/drier (see Section 14). Also detach the refrigerant outlet line from the receiver/drier.
6   Disconnect the compressor discharge line from the condenser.
7   Immediately cap the open fittings to prevent the entry of dirt and moisture.
8   Lift out the condenser **(see illustration)** and the receiver/drier. Store the condenser upright to prevent oil loss.
9   If a new condenser is to be installed, add one ounce of new refrigerant oil to the system.
10   Installation is the reverse of removal.
11   Have the system evacuated, charged and leak tested by the shop that discharged it.

19 Air conditioning evaporator - removal and installation

Refer to illustrations 19.3, 19.6 and 19.9

Warning: *The air conditioning system is under high pressure. Do not loosen any fittings or remove any components until after the system has been discharged. Air conditioning refrigerant should be properly discharged into an EPA-approved container at a dealer service department or an automotive air conditioning repair facility. Always wear eye protection when disconnecting air conditioning system fittings.*

1   Have the refrigerant discharged at a dealer service department or an automotive air conditioning repair facility.
2   Disconnect the cable from the negative terminal of the battery.
3   Remove the refrigerant lines from the evaporator **(see illustration)**.
4   Immediately cap the open fittings to prevent the entry of dirt and moisture.
5   Remove the dashboard (see Chapter 11)

and the heater assembly (see Section 13).
6   Remove the evaporator case retaining nuts from the firewall in the engine compartment **(see illustration)**.
7   Disconnect all electrical connectors from the air conditioning thermostatic switch and the blower motor resistor.
8   Remove the evaporator case assembly.
9   Split the evaporator case by removing the clips and lifting the upper case half off **(see illustration)**.
10   Separate the evaporator core from the lower case half.
11   Check the evaporator fins for blockage; if they are dirty clean them with compressed air - never use water for this purpose!
12   Check the fittings for cracks and signs of wear; replace parts as necessary.
13   Installation is the reverse of the removal procedure. Be sure to replace all O-rings removed during disassembly with new ones.
14   If a new evaporator was installed, add 1.7 ounces of new refrigerant oil to the system.
15   Have the system evacuated, charged and leak tested by the shop that discharged it.

20 Air conditioning expansion valve - removal and installation

Warning: *The air conditioning system is under high pressure. Do not loosen any fittings or remove any components until after the system has been discharged. Air conditioning refrigerant should be properly discharged into an EPA-approved container at a dealer service department or an automotive air conditioning repair facility. Always wear eye protection when disconnecting air conditioning system fittings.*

1   Have the refrigerant discharged at a dealer service department or an automotive air conditioning repair facility.
2   Disconnect the cable from the negative

19.6 The dash and the heater assembly must be removed before attempting to remove the evaporator

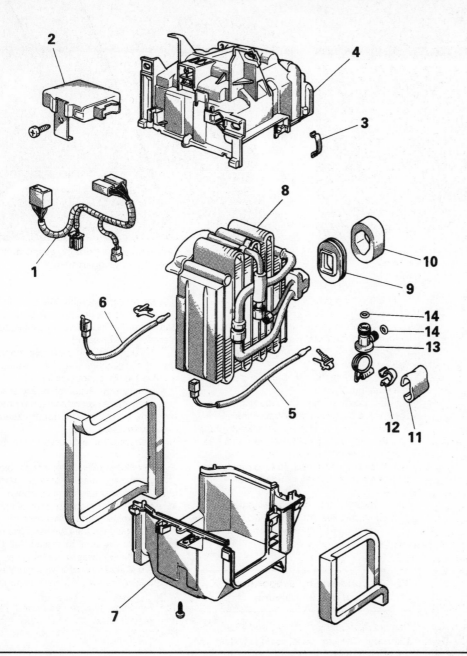

19.9 Exploded view of the evaporator

1   Wiring harness
2   Air conditioning control unit
3   Clips
4   Evaporator case
5   Air inlet sensor
6   Air thermo sensor
7   Evaporator case (lower section)
8   Evaporator assembly
9   Grommet
10   Insulator
11   Rubber insulator
12   Clip
13   Expansion valve
14   O-ring

3

terminal of the battery.
3   Remove the evaporator from the passenger compartment (see Section 19).
4   Remove the clips from the case and separate the two case half-sections.

5   Remove the flare nut that secures the evaporator inlet fitting to the expansion valve **(see illustration 19.9)**, using two back-up wrenches.
6   Remove the expansion valve from the

evaporator inlet.
7   Installation is the reverse of the removal.
Note: *Always use new O-rings when reassembling air conditioning components.*

Notes

Chapter 4
Fuel and exhaust systems

Contents

4

Specifications

Fuel pressure

Fuel system pressure (at idle)
  Non turbocharged engines
    Vacuum hose detached .... 47 to 50 psi
    Vacuum hose attached .... 37 to 39 psi
  Turbocharged engines with manual transmission
    Vacuum hose detached .... 36 to 38 psi
    Vacuum hose attached .... 26 to 28 psi
  Turbocharged engines with automatic transmission
    Vacuum hose detached .... 41 to 46 psi
    Vacuum hose attached .... 32 to 34 psi
Fuel system hold pressure .... 21 psi
Fuel pump pressure (maximum) .... 60 psi
Fuel pump hold pressure .... 50 psi

Idle speed control (ISC) motor

2.0L engines
  Terminals 2 and 1 (or 2 and 3) .... 28 to 33 ohms
  Terminals 5 and 6 (or 5 and 4) .... 28 to 33 ohms
1.8L engines
  Terminals 1 and 2 .... 5 to 35 ohms

Injector resistance

Non-turbo engines .... 13.0 to 16.0 ohms
Turbo engines .... 2.0 to 3.0 ohms

Torque specifications   Ft-lbs

Air intake plenum-to-intake manifold bolts (1.8L engine) 12
Throttle body-to-air intake plenum bolts 14
Turbocharger-to-exhaust manifold bolts 44
Turbocharger-to-exhaust flange nuts 22

1   General information

The fuel system consists of a fuel tank, an electric fuel pump (located in the fuel tank), a fuel pump relay, fuel injectors, an air cleaner assembly and a throttle body unit. The fuel injection components are all equipped with a Multi Point Fuel Injection (MPFI) system.

Multi Point Fuel Injection (MPFI) system

Multi Point Fuel Injection uses timed impulses to inject the fuel directly into the intake port of each cylinder. The injectors are controlled by the Electronic Control Module (ECM). The ECM monitors various engine parameters and delivers the exact amount of fuel required into the intake ports. The throttle body serves only to control the amount of air passing into the system. Because each cylinder is equipped with its own injector, much better control of the fuel/air mixture ratio is possible.

Fuel pump and lines

Fuel is circulated from the fuel tank to the fuel injection system, and back to the fuel tank, through a pair of metal lines running along the underside of the vehicle. An electric fuel pump is located inside the fuel tank.

The fuel pump will operate as long as the engine is cranking or running and the ECM is receiving ignition reference pulses from the electronic ignition system. If there are no reference pulses, the fuel pump will shut off after two or three seconds.

Turbo systems are equipped with a fuel pressure solenoid (VSV) that is directly controlled by the ECM. When intake temperature is high (engine warmed-up), the ECM raises fuel pressure to prevent the generation of fuel vapor at very high temperatures.

Exhaust system

The exhaust system includes an exhaust manifold fitted with an exhaust oxygen sensor, a catalytic converter, an exhaust pipe, and a muffler.

The catalytic converter is an emission control device added to the exhaust system to reduce pollutants. A single-bed converter is used in combination with a three-way (reduction) catalyst. Refer to Chapter 6 for more information regarding the catalytic converter.

2   Fuel pressure relief procedure

Refer to illustration 2.3a and 2.3b

Warning 1: *Gasoline is extremely flammable, so take extra precautions when you work on any part of the fuel system. Don't smoke or allow open flames or bare light bulbs near the work area, and don't work in a garage where a natural gas-type appliance (such as a water heater or clothes dryer) with a pilot light is present. If you spill any fuel on your skin, rinse it off immediately with soap and water. When you perform any kind of work on the fuel system, wear safety glasses and have a Class B type fire extinguisher on hand.*

Warning 2: *After the fuel pressure has been relieved, wrap shop towels around any fuel connection you'll be disconnecting. They'll absorb the residual fuel that may leak out, reducing the risk of fire and preventing contact with your skin.*

1   Before servicing any fuel system component, you must relieve the fuel pressure to minimize the risk of fire or personal injury.

2   Remove the fuel filler cap - this will relieve any pressure built up in the tank.

3   Disconnect the fuel pump electrical connector at the fuel tank **(see illustrations)**.

4   Start the engine and wait for it to stall, then turn off the ignition key.

5   The fuel system is now depressurized.

Note: *Place a rag around the fuel line before removing any hose clamp or fitting to prevent any residual fuel from spilling onto the engine.*

2.3a The fuel pump electrical connector on models with a 1.8L engine is clipped to a bracket on the fuel tank

3   Fuel pump/fuel pressure - check

Warning: *Gasoline is extremely flammable, so take extra precautions when you work on any part of the fuel system. Don't smoke or allow open flames or bare light bulbs near the work area, and don't work in a garage where a natural gas-type appliance (such as a water heater or clothes dryer) with a pilot light is present. If you spill any fuel on your skin, rinse it off immediately with soap and water. When you perform any kind of work on the fuel system, wear safety glasses and have a Class B type fire extinguisher on hand.*

Note 1: *To perform the fuel pressure test, you will need to obtain a fuel pressure gauge and adapter set (compatible with the fuel line fittings on your vehicle).*

Note 2: *The fuel pump will operate as long as the engine is cranking or running and the ECM is receiving ignition reference pulses from the electronic ignition system. If there are no reference pulses, the fuel pump will shut off after two or three seconds.*

Preliminary inspection

Refer to illustrations 3.2 and 3.3

1   Should the fuel system fail to deliver the proper amount of fuel, or any fuel at all, inspect it as follows. Remove the fuel filler

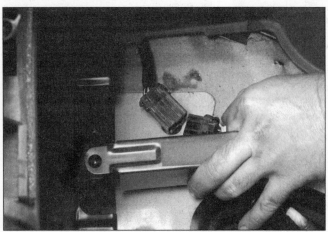

2.3b On models with a 2.0L engine, the fuel pump electrical connector is located in the trunk area, to the left of the spare tire, under the carpet

3.2 Install a jumper wire from the positive (+) terminal of the battery to the fuel pump check terminal (taped to the wiring harness on the firewall, behind the battery) to energize the fuel pump directly

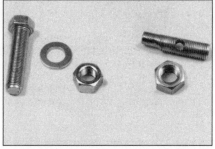

3.3 With the ignition key ON (engine not running), check for battery voltage to the EFI control relay on terminal number 10 (2.0L engine) or terminal number 8 (1.8L engine)

3.8b Install the adapter bolt, the banjo fitting and sealing washers, then install and tighten the nut securely. Attach the pressure gauge hose to the end of the bolt and tighten the hose clamp

3.8a To fabricate a fuel pressure gauge adapter, cut the head off a bolt (12mm diameter/1.25 thread pitch) and drill a hole directly through it lengthwise. Grind one end down, if necessary, so the hose on your pressure gauge fits over it. Drill another hole through it, perpendicular to its length to allow system pressure to flow. It is important that this hole is drilled in the correct location (when installed, it must be completely covered by the banjo fitting).

cap. Have an assistant turn the ignition key to the On position while you listen at the fuel filler opening. You should hear a whirring sound that lasts for a couple of seconds.

2   If you don't hear anything, install a jumper wire from the positive (+) side of the battery onto the fuel pump check terminal **(see illustration)**. Listen at the fuel filler opening again - if you now hear the whirring sound, the fuel pump relay or its control circuit is faulty. If there still is no whirring sound, there is a problem in the fuel pump circuit from the control panel to the fuel pump, or a defective fuel pump.

3   Remove the EFI control relay (see Step 24), unplug it from its electrical connector and check for power to the connector **(see illustration)**. Check the control relay itself (refer to Steps 24 through 39 in this Section).

4   If there is no voltage present, check the fuse(s) and the wiring circuit for the EFI control relay. If the supply voltage reading is correct and the fuel pump only runs with the jumper wire in place, replace the fuel pump relay with a new one.

5   If there is voltage present, check for battery voltage at the fuel pump electrical con-

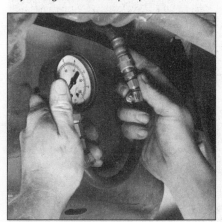

3.16 To check the output pressure of the fuel pump, connect the fuel pressure gauge directly to the fuel feed line by the tank

nector. If there is voltage present at the fuel pump connector, replace the fuel pump.

Operating pressure check

Refer to illustrations 3.8a and 3.8b

6   Relieve the fuel system pressure (see Section 2).

7   Detach the cable from the negative battery terminal.

8   Remove the fitting located on the fuel filter and attach a fuel pressure gauge **(see illustration)**, using a special adapter which can be fabricated from a bolt and nut **(see illustration)** or purchased from a tool dealer. **Note:** *The factory specified tool is mounted between the fuel line and the fuel pressure regulator, not at the fuel filter. The homemade tool is recommended because of the difficulty ordering and installing the factory tool (adapter).*

9   Attach the cable to the negative battery terminal, then start the engine.

10   Note the fuel pressure and compare it with the pressure listed in this Chapter's Specifications.

11   If the system fuel pressure is less than specified:

   a) *Inspect the system for a fuel leak. Repair any leaks and recheck the fuel pressure.*
   b) *If the fuel pressure is still low, replace the fuel filter (it may be clogged) and recheck the pressure.*
   c) *If the pressure is still low, check the fuel pump output pressure (see below) and the fuel pressure regulator (see Section 16).*

12   If the pressure is higher than specified:

   a) *Check the fuel return line for an obstruction.*
   b) *Check the fuel pressure regulator (see Section 16).*

13   Turn the ignition switch to Off, wait five minutes then check the pressure on the gauge. Compare the reading with the hold

pressure listed in this Chapter's Specifications. If the hold pressure is less than specified:

   a) *The fuel lines may be leaking.*
   b) *The fuel pressure regulator may be allowing the fuel pressure to bleed through to the fuel return line (see Section 16).*
   c) *A fuel injector (or injectors) may be leaking.*

Fuel pump output pressure check

Refer to illustration 3.16

Warning: *For this test it is necessary to use a fuel pressure gauge with a bleeder valve in order to relieve the fuel pressure after the test is completed (the normal procedure for pressure relief will not work because the gauge is connected directly to the the fuel pump).*

14   Relieve the system fuel pressure (see Section 2).

15   Detach the cable from the negative battery terminal.

16   Attach a fuel pressure gauge directly to the fuel fuel feed line at the fuel tank **(see illustration)**.

17   Attach the cable to the negative battery terminal.

18   Using a jumper wire from the positive (+) battery terminal, connect it to the terminal of the fuel pump check connector **(see illustration 3.2)**.

19   Note the pressure reading on the gauge and compare the reading to the value listed in this Chapter's Specifications.

20   If the indicated pressure is less than specified, inspect the fuel line for leaks between the pump and gauge. If no leaks are found, replace the fuel pump.

21   Turn the ignition key to Off and wait five minutes. Note the reading on the gauge and compare it to the hold pressure listed in this Chapter's Specifications. If the hold pressure is less than specified, check the fuel line between the pump and gauge for leaks. If no

4

3.24 Remove the center console side panels and remove the relay mounting screws

leaks are found, replace the fuel pump.

22 Remove the jumper wire.

23 Open the bleeder valve on the gauge and allow the pressurized fuel to drain into an approved fuel container. Remove the gauge and reconnect the fuel line.

Fuel injection control relay check

Note: *Failure in the electronic fuel injection control relay will prevent power supply to the fuel pump, fuel injectors and ECM resulting in engine start failure.*

1.8L engine

Refer to illustrations 3.24, 3.25 and 3.26

24 Remove the electronic fuel injection relay from the passenger compartment. It is located near the ECM under the center console panel **(see illustration)**.

25 Inspect the resistance between the relay terminals **(see illustration)**:

a) *Using an ohmmeter first check the resistance between terminals 3 and 5. Next check the resistance between terminals 2 and 5. Both readings should be approximately 95 ohms.*

b) *Next, check the resistance between ter-*

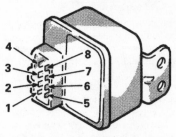

3.25 Check the resistance of the EFI fuel control relay by connecting the probes of an ohmmeter onto the terminals specified in Step 25 (1.8L engine)

minals 6 and 7. It should read approximately 35 ohms.

c) *Also, check the resistance between terminals 6 and 8. There should be continuity in one direction only.*

26 Install jumper leads from terminal number 7 to the battery positive (+) terminal and terminal number 6 to the battery negative terminal (-) **(see illustration)**.

27 With the positive and negative leads connected to the relay, check for continuity between terminals 1 and 4 - there should be continuity. Remove the ground jumper from terminal number 6 on the relay - the ohmmeter should now indicate an open (infinite) circuit.

28 Install jumper leads from terminal number 2 to the battery positive (+) terminal and terminal 5 to the battery negative (-) terminal.

29 With the leads connected to the relay, check for continuity between terminals 1 and 4 - there should be continuity. Remove the ground lead from terminal number 5 on the relay - the ohmmeter should now indicate an open (infinite) circuit.

30 Install jumper leads from terminal number 8 to the battery positive (+) terminal and terminal 6 to the battery negative (-) terminal.

31 With the leads connected to the relay, check for continuity between terminals 2 and 4 - there should be continuity. Remove the ground lead from terminal 6 on the relay - the ohmmeter should now indicate an open (infinite) circuit.

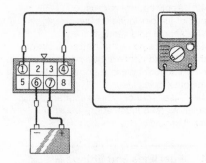

3.26 Connect jumper wires from the negative (-) battery terminal to pin number 6 and the positive (+) battery terminal to number 7 of the EFI relay and check the resistance between terminals 1 and 4 - there should be 35 ohms present (1.8L engine)

2.0L engines

Refer to illustration 3.33

32 Remove the electronic fuel injection relay from the passenger compartment. It's located near the ECM under the center console **(see illustration 3.24)**.

33 Install jumper leads from terminal 10 to the battery positive (+) terminal and terminal 8 to the battery negative (-) terminal **(see illustration)**.

34 With the relay energized, check for voltage across terminals 4 and 5. There should be approximately 12 volts. Remove the ground lead from terminal number 8 on the relay - the voltmeter should indicate zero voltage.

35 Connect the jumper leads from terminal number 9 to the battery positive (+) terminal and terminal 6 to the battery negative (-) terminal.

36 With the leads connected to the relay, check for continuity between terminals 3 and 2 - there should be continuity. Remove the ground lead from terminal 6 on the relay - the ohmmeter should now indicate no continuity (infinity).

37 Install jumper leads from terminal 3 to the battery positive (+) terminal and terminal 7 to the battery negative (-) terminal.

38 With the leads connected to the relay, check for voltage across terminal number 2 and the battery ground terminal - there should be approximately 12 volts. Remove the ground lead from terminal 7 on the relay - the voltmeter should indicate zero voltage.

39 If the test results are incorrect, replace the relay with a new part.

Fuel pressure solenoid vacuum switching valve (VSV) check (turbo models only)

Refer to illustrations 3.41 and 3.44

40 Detach the vacuum hoses from the fuel pressure control vacuum switching valve (VSV).

41 Unplug the electrical connector from the VSV and connect a hand-held vacuum pump to the VSV where the black hose was installed **(see illustration)**.

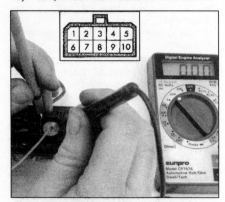

3.33 Check the resistance of the EFI fuel control relay by energizing the relay and connecting the probes of an ohmmeter to the terminals specified in Step 34 (2.0L engine)

3.41 The fuel pressure solenoid (VSV) should hold vacuum when battery voltage is applied and should lose vacuum when battery voltage is removed from the solenoid

42   Apply battery voltage to the VSV using a pair of jumper leads and apply vacuum. The VSV should hold vacuum.

43   Now remove the battery voltage from the VSV and confirm that the valve does not hold vacuum unless a finger is placed over the other port.

44   Also, check the resistance of the solenoid **(see illustration)** using an ohmmeter. It should be 36 to 46 ohms resistance.

---

4   Fuel lines and fittings - inspection and replacement

Warning: *Gasoline is extremely flammable, so take extra precautions when you work on any part of the fuel system. Don't smoke or allow open flames or bare light bulbs near the work area, and don't work in a garage where a natural gas-type appliance (such as a water heater or clothes dryer) with a pilot light is present. If you spill any fuel on your skin, rinse it off immediately with soap and water. When you perform any kind of work on the fuel system, wear safety glasses and have a Class B type fire extinguisher on hand.*

Inspection

1   Once in a while, you will have to raise the vehicle to service or replace some component (an exhaust pipe hanger, for example). Whenever you work under the vehicle, always inspect fuel lines and all fittings and connections for damage or deterioration.

2   Check all hoses and pipes for cracks, kinks, deformation or obstructions.

3   Make sure all hoses and pipe clips attach their associated hoses or pipes securely to the underside of the vehicle.

4   Verify all hose clamps attaching rubber hoses to metal fuel lines or pipes are snug enough to assure a tight fit between the hoses and pipes.

Replacement

5   If you must replace any damaged sections, use original equipment replacement hoses or pipes constructed from exactly the same material as the section you are replacing. Do not install substitutes constructed from inferior or inappropriate material or you could cause a fuel leak or a fire.

6   Always, before detaching or disassembling any part of the fuel system, note the routing of all hoses and pipes and the orientation of all clamps and clips to assure that replacement sections are installed in exactly the same manner.

7   Before detaching any part of the fuel system, be sure to relieve the fuel system pressure (see Section 2). Also cover the fitting being disconnected with a rag to absorb any fuel that may drip or spray out.

---

5   Fuel tank - removal and installation

Refer to illustrations 5.7a, 5.7b and 5.10

Warning: *Gasoline is extremely flammable, so take extra precautions when you work on any part of the fuel system. Don't smoke or allow open flames or bare light bulbs near the work area, and don't work in a garage where a natural gas-type appliance (such as a water heater or clothes dryer) with a pilot light is present. If you spill any fuel on your skin, rinse it off immediately with soap and water. When you perform any kind of work on the fuel system, wear safety glasses and have a Class B type fire extinguisher on hand.*

Note: *Don't begin this procedure until the fuel gauge indicates the tank is empty or nearly empty. If the tank must be removed when it's full (for example, if the fuel pump malfunctions), drain any remaining fuel from the tank prior to removal.*

3.44 Check the resistance of the VSV - it should be 36 to 46 ohms

1   Unless the vehicle has been driven far enough to completely empty the tank, it's a good idea to drain the residual fuel into an approved gasoline container before removing the tank from the vehicle. A drain plug in the bottom of the fuel tank is provided for this purpose.

2   Relieve the fuel pressure (see Section 2).

3   Detach the cable from the negative terminal of the battery.

4   If you're working on a four-wheel drive model, locate the fuel pump electrical connector in the trunk and unplug it **(see illustration 2.3b)**. Remove the screws from the access panel and pass it through the hole in the floor.

5   Raise the vehicle and place it securely on jackstands.

6   If you're working on a two-wheel drive model, locate the electrical connectors for the electric fuel pump and fuel gauge sending unit at the rear of the tank **(see illustration 2.3a)** and unplug them.

7   Disconnect the fuel feed and return lines, the vapor return line and the filler neck and vent tubes **(see illustrations)**.

4

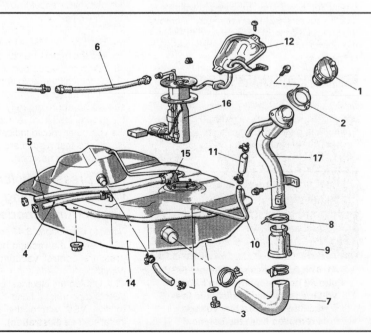

5.7a Exploded view of the fuel tank on a four-wheel drive (4WD) model

1   *Fuel tank cap*
2   *Sealing ring*
3   *Drain plug*
4   *Return hose*
5   *Vapor hose*
6   *High pressure fuel hose*
7   *Fuel filler hose hose*
8   *Cable band*
9   *Protector*
10   *Vapor hose*
11   *Vapor hose*
12   *Access plate*
13   *Self-locking nut*
14   *Fuel tank*
15   *Two-way valve*
16   *Fuel pump/gauge assembly*
17   *Fuel filler neck*

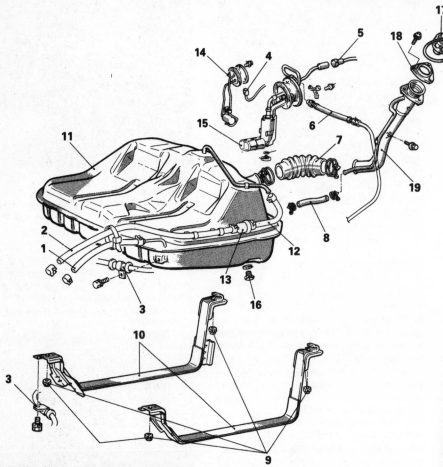

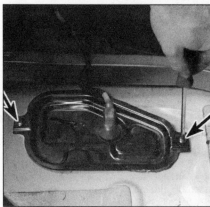

**7.3 Remove the two screws (arrows) from
the fuel pump access cover**

**5.10 Remove the bolts (arrows) from the
perimeter of the tank on 4WD models**

8   Support the fuel tank with a piece of wood and a floor jack.

9   If you're working on a two-wheel drive model, remove the fuel tank straps from the chassis.

10   If you're working on a four-wheel drive model, remove the retaining bolts from the perimeter of the tank **(see illustration)**.

11   Carefully lower the tank from the vehicle.

12   Installation is the reverse of removal.

---

6   Fuel tank cleaning and repair - general information

1   All repairs to the fuel tank or filler neck should be carried out by a professional who has experience in this critical and potentially dangerous work. Even after cleaning and flushing of the fuel system, explosive fumes can remain and ignite during repair of the tank.

2   If the fuel tank is removed from the vehicle, it should not be placed in an area where sparks or open flames could ignite the fumes coming out of the tank. Be especially careful inside garages where a natural gas-type appliance is located, because the pilot light could cause an explosion.

---

7   Fuel pump – removal and installation

*Refer to illustrations 7.4
and 7.6*

Warning: *Gasoline is extremely flammable, so take extra precautions when you work on any part of the fuel system. Don't smoke or allow open flames or bare light bulbs near the work area, and don't work in a garage where a natural gas-type appliance (such as a water*

heater or clothes dryer) with a pilot light is present. If you spill any fuel on your skin, rinse it off immediately with soap and water. When you perform any kind of work on the fuel system, wear safety glasses and have a Class B type fire extinguisher on hand.

Four-wheel drive (4WD) models

Removal

Refer to illustrations 7.3, 7.4, 7.5, 7.6, 7.7a, 7.7b, 7.7c and 7.8

1   Relieve the fuel pressure (see Section 2).

2   Remove the cable from the negative battery terminal.

3   Remove the screws from the access panel **(see illustration)** in the luggage compartment. Lift the panel away.

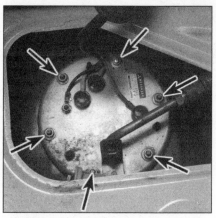

7.4 Remove the nuts (arrows) from the fuel pump cover plate

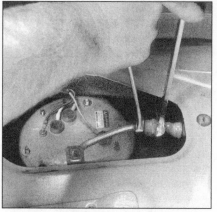

7.5 Use a back-up wrench and a flare-nut wrench to disconnect the fuel line from the fuel pump assembly

7.6 Lift the fuel pump from the fuel tank

4   Remove the nuts from the top of the fuel pump cover **(see illustration)**.

5   Using a back-up wrench and a flare-nut wrench, disconnect the fuel line **(see illustration)**.

6   Pull the fuel pump assembly out of the tank **(see illustration)**.

7   Inspect the filter on the lower end of the fuel pump **(see illustrations)**. If it's dirty, remove it, clean it with solvent and blow it out with compressed air. If it's too dirty to be cleaned, replace it.

8   If you have to separate the fuel pump from the bracket, detach the electrical connectors **(see illustration)** and slide the pump away from the bottom support. Care should be taken to prevent damage to the rubber insulator and fuel strainer during removal. After the pump is clear of the bottom support, pull it out of the rubber washer.

Installation

9   Position a new gasket around the opening of the fuel tank and guide the fuel pump assembly into the tank.

10   Install the screws and tighten them securely.

11   Install the fuel tank (see Section 5).

Two-wheel drive (2WD) models

12   Relieve the fuel pressure (see Section 2).

13   Detach the cable from the negative battery terminal.

14   Using a back-up wrench and a flare-nut wrench, disconnect the fuel lines from the fuel pump assembly on the rear of the tank **(see illustration 5.7b)**.

15   Loosen the self-locking nuts on the fuel tank retaining straps but do not remove them. Stop near the end of the studs so the fuel tank hangs down slightly.

16   Remove the lateral rod attaching bolt and lower the rod on one side to make clearance for the fuel pump removal (see Chapter 10).

17   Remove the screws from the top of the fuel pump.

18   Pull the fuel pump out of the tank.

19   Inspect the filter on the lower end of the fuel pump. If it's dirty, remove it, clean it with solvent and blow it out with compressed air. If it's too dirty to be cleaned, replace it **(see illustration 7.7c)**.

20   If you have to separate the fuel pump from the bracket, remove the retaining screw and slide the pump away from the bottom support. Care should be taken to prevent

damage to the rubber insulator and fuel strainer during removal. After the pump is clear of the bottom support, pull it out of the rubber connector.

21   Installation is the reverse of removal.

7.7a Remove the set screw from the lower bracket

7.7b Lift the rubber grommet from the base of the pump

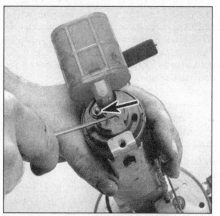

7.7c Remove the clip (arrow) from the retaining stud and lift the filter from the assembly

7.8 Remove the two nuts from the fuel pump electrical connectors. Be sure to note the location of each wire so you don't reverse them on reassembly.

4

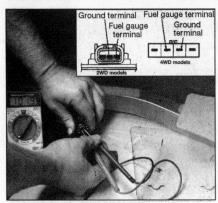

8.3 Working inside the trunk area, probe the correct terminals with an ohmmeter to determine the resistance of the fuel level sending unit with the tank full and empty. If the readings are incorrect, replace the sending unit

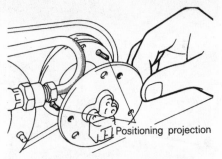

8.9 Be sure to align the positioning projections into the holes on the cover plate on 2WD models

8.6 The fuel level sending unit (arrow) is a separate unit located next to the fuel pump on 2WD models

7   Lift the sending unit from the tank. Carefully angle the sending unit out of the opening without damaging the fuel level float located at the bottom of the assembly.

8   Remove the screws that secure the fuel level sending unit to the bracket.

9   Installation is the reverse of removal. Be sure to install a new gasket, and tighten the screws securely. **Note**: *Be sure to align the positioning projection into the correct holes of the sending unit cover on 2WD vehicles* **(see illustration)**.

9.2a Remove the three nuts (arrows) from the cruise control unit and lift it off the bracket

9   Air cleaner housing - removal and installation

Refer to illustration 9.2a, 9.2b, 9.3a, 9.3b and 9.5

1   Detach the cable from the negative terminal of the battery.

2   If the vehicle is equipped with cruise control, remove the cruise control unit **(see illustration)** and its mounting bracket **(see illustration)**.

3   Loosen the clamp(s) from the air intake duct on the throttle body and the air cleaner

9.2b Remove the bolts (arrows) from the cruise control mounting bracket

Replacement

6   Remove the fuel pump assembly (see Section 7) on four-wheel drive models or just the fuel level sending unit assembly on two-wheel drive models. **Note:** *The fuel level sending unit (the smaller diameter flange) is located next to the fuel pump on 2WD models* **(see illustration)**.

8   Fuel level sending unit – check and replacement

Refer to illustrations 8.3, 8.6 and 8.9

Check

1   Raise the vehicle and support it securely on jackstands.

2   Disconnect the electrical connector for the fuel level sending unit **(see illustrations 5.7a and 5.7b)**.

3   Working inside the trunk area, position the ohmmeter probes into the electrical connector and check the resistance **(see illustration)**. Use the 200-ohm scale on the ohmmeter.

4   With the fuel tank completely full, the resistance should be about 2.0 to 3.0 ohms. With the fuel tank nearly empty, the resistance of the sending unit should be about 115 to 120 ohms. **Note:** *A more accurate check of the sending unit can be made by removing it from the fuel tank and checking its resistance while manually operating the float arm.*

5   If the readings are incorrect, replace the sending unit.

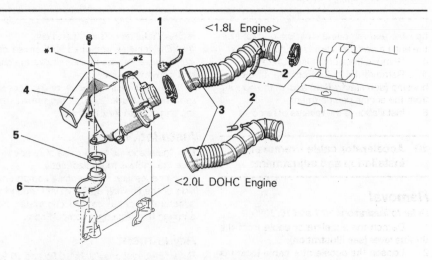

9.3a Exploded view of the air cleaner assembly on non-turbo models

1	*Airflow meter electrical connector*	*4*	*Air cleaner housing*
2	*Breather hose*	*5*	*Gasket*
3	*Air intake hose*	*6*	*Metal pipe*

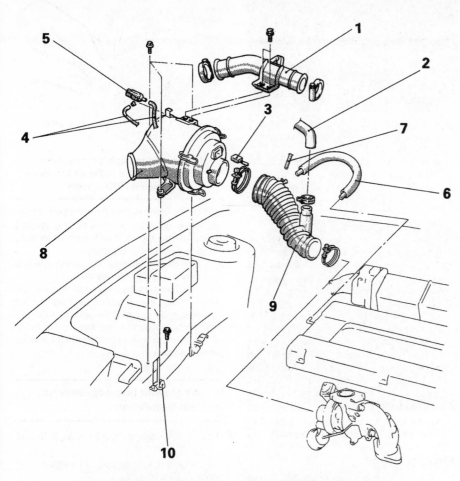

9.5 Remove the bolts (arrows) that retain the air cleaner housing

9.3b Exploded view of the air cleaner assembly on turbo models

1	Air pipe	6	Breather hose
2	By-pass air hose	7	Purge hose for EVAP system
3	Airflow meter electrical connector	8	Air cleaner housing
4	Vacuum hose	9	Air intake hose
5	Turbocharger wastegate solenoid	10	Air cleaner bracket

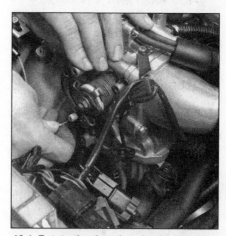

10.1 Rotate the throttle valve and remove the cable end from the slotted portion of the throttle valve

housing and remove the air intake duct from the engine compartment **(see illustrations)**.

4   Remove the air filter (see Chapter 1).

5   Remove the bolts from the air cleaner housing **(see illustration)** and lift the housing from the engine compartment.

6   Installation is the reverse of removal.

10 Accelerator cable - removal, installation and adjustment

Removal

Refer to illustrations 10.1 and 10.2

1   Detach the accelerator cable from the throttle lever **(see illustration)**.

2   Loosen the accelerator cable locknuts and remove the bracket **(see illustration)** from the plenum/intake manifold.

3   On vehicles without cruise control, pull the cable end out from the accelerator pedal

recess in the driver's compartment.

4   On vehicles equipped with cruise control, remove the cover and remove the cable end from the bellcrank.

5   On vehicles without cruise control, remove the cable through the firewall from the engine compartment.

Installation

6   Installation is the reverse of removal. Be sure the cable is routed correctly.

7   If necessary, at the engine compartment side of the firewall, apply sealant around the accelerator cable to prevent water from entering the passenger compartment.

Adjustment

Refer to illustrations 10.9a, 10.9b and 10.9c

8   On vehicles without cruise control, loosen the bolts on the plenum/intake manifold and tighten the bolts when the freeplay on the accelerator cable is 3/64 to 3/32-inch

10.2 Remove the two bolts from the plenum/intake manifold and lift the cable assembly from the engine

on manual transmission models or 3/32 to 1/8-inch on automatic transmission models. The freeplay is measured by the distance (slack) on the cable when the finger is depressed near the midpoint.

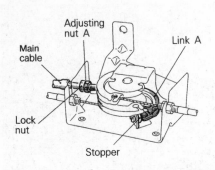

10.9a Use adjusting nut A to increase or decrease tension on the main cable

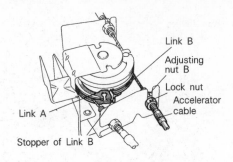

10.9b Use adjusting nut B to increase or decrease cable tension on the accelerator cable

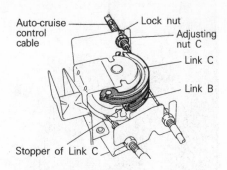

10.9c Use adjusting nut C to increase or decrease cable tension on the cruise control cable

9   On vehicles with cruise control, it is necessary to adjust three cables; the accelerator cable, the cruise control cable and the main cable. All three are adjusted at the bellcrank.

a) *Adjust the main cable with adjusting nut A. Working at the bellcrank. use your finger and press the cable between the link and the adjusting nut. The freeplay on the main cable should be 0.0 to 3/64-inch on manual transmission models or 3/32 to 1/8-inch on automatic transmission models* **(see illustration)**.

b) *Adjust the accelerator cable with adjusting nut B. With the link stop B seated against link A, use your finger and press the cable between link B and the adjusting nut. It should be 3/64 to 3/32-inch* **(see illustration)**.

c) *Adjust the cruise cable with adjusting nut C. With the link stop C seated against link B, use your finger and press the cable between link C and the adjusting nut. It should be 3/64 to 3/32-inch* **(see illustration)**.

10   Have an assistant operate the accelerator pedal and make sure the throttle opens and closes completely without binding.

11 Electronic Fuel Injection (EFI) system - general information

Electronic fuel injection provides optimum fuel/air mixture ratios at all stages of combustion and offers immediate throttle response characteristics. It also enables the engine to run at the leanest possible fuel/air mixture ratio, reducing exhaust gas emissions.

These models are equipped with a Multi Port Fuel Injection (MPFI) system. The MPFI systems are controlled by an Electronic Control Module (ECM) or computer located under the center console (see Chapter 6). The ECM monitors engine performance and adjusts the air/fuel mixture according to the information it receives from the information sensors (oxygen sensor, Intake Air Temperature (IAT) sensor, Throttle Position Sensor (TPS) etc. See Chapter 6 for additional information and descriptions of the information sensors and

the ECM control system.

An electric fuel pump located in the fuel tank, pumps fuel to the fuel injection system through the fuel feed line and an in-line fuel filter. The fuel pump will operate as long as the engine is cranking or running and the ECM is receiving ignition reference pulses from the electronic ignition system. If there are no reference pulses, the fuel pump will shut off after 2 or 3 seconds.

The throttle body has a throttle valve to control the amount of air delivered to the engine. The Throttle Position Sensor (TPS) and Idle Air Control (IAC) valves are located on the throttle body.

The fuel rail is mounted on the top of the intake manifold. It distributes fuel to the individual injectors. Fuel is delivered to the input end of the rail by the fuel feed line. At the other end of the fuel rail is the fuel pressure regulator, which keeps the pressure to the injectors at the required level. The excess fuel is bled off through the pressure regulator and is returned to the fuel tank via a separate line.

12 Fuel injection system - check

Refer to illustrations 12.6, 12.7, 12.8 and 12.9
Warning: *Gasoline is extremely flammable, so take extra precautions when you work on any part of the fuel system. Don't smoke or allow open flames or bare light bulbs near the work area, and don't work in a garage where a natural gas-type appliance (such as a water heater or clothes dryer) with a pilot light is present. If you spill any fuel on your skin, rinse it off immediately with soap and water. When you perform any kind of work on the fuel system, wear safety glasses and have a Class B type fire extinguisher on hand.*
Note: *The following procedure is based on the assumption that the fuel pump is working and the fuel pressure is adequate (see Section 3).*

1   Check all electrical connectors that are related to the system. Loose electrical connectors and poor grounds can cause many problems that resemble more serious malfunctions.

2   Check to see that the battery is fully

charged, as the control unit and sensors depend on an accurate supply voltage in order to properly meter the fuel.

3   Check the air filter element - a dirty or partially blocked filter will severely impede performance and economy (see Chapter 1).

4   If a blown fuse is found, replace it and see if it blows again. If it does, search for a grounded wire in the harness to the fuel pump.

5   Check the air intake duct to the intake plenum for leaks, which will result in an excessively lean mixture. Also check the condition of the vacuum hoses connected to the intake manifold.

6   Remove the air intake duct from the throttle body and check for dirt, carbon or other residue build-up in the throttle body, particularly around the throttle plate. If it's dirty, clean it with carburetor cleaner and a toothbrush **(see illustration)**.

7   With the engine running, place a stethoscope against each injector, one at a time, and listen for a clicking sound, indicating operation **(see illustration)**. If you don't have a stethoscope, place the tip of a screwdriver against the injector and press your ear against the handle.

8   If an injector isn't functioning (not clicking), purchase a special injector test light

12.6 Clean the throttle body with carburetor cleaner to remove sludge deposits

12.7 Use a stethoscope to determine if the injectors are working properly - they should make a steady clicking sound that rises and falls with engine speed changes

12.8 Install the "noid" light into the fuel injector harness and confirm that it blinks when the engine is running

(sometimes called a "noid" light) and plug it into the injector electrical connector **(see illustration)**. Start the engine and make sure the noid light flashes. This will test for the proper voltage signal to the injector. If the light doesn't flash, the ECM, the injector resistor or the circuit is faulty.

9   With the engine turned Off and the fuel injector electrical connectors disconnected, measure the resistance of each injector **(see illustration)**. Compare your findings with the resistance values listed in this Chapter's Specifications. If the resistance of an injector is not as specified, replace it.

10   Check the fuel pressure (see Section 3) and the fuel pressure regulator (see Section 16).

11   All other checks to the system should be left to a dealer service department or other qualified repair shop, as there is a chance that the control unit may be damaged if the tests are not performed properly.

13   Throttle body - check, removal and installation

Check

1   Detach the air intake duct from the throttle body (see Section 9) and move the duct out of the way.

2   Have an assistant depress the throttle pedal while you watch the throttle valve. Check that the throttle valve moves smoothly when the throttle is moved from closed (idle position) to fully open (wide open throttle). **Note:** *Spray carburetor cleaner into the throttle body, especially around the shaft area, to free-up any binding caused by the accumulation of carbon deposits or sludge buildup* **(see illustration 12.6).**

3   Wiggle the throttle lever while watching the throttle shaft inside the bore. If it appears worn (loose), replace the throttle body unit.

Removal and installation

Refer to illustrations 13.6a, 13.6b and 13.10

4   Disconnect the cable from the negative terminal of the battery.

5   Unplug all electrical connectors from the throttle body.

6   Mark and disconnect any vacuum hoses or coolant lines **(see illustrations)** connected to the throttle body. Plug the coolant lines to prevent leakage.

12.9 Measure the resistance of each injector - it should be between 2.0 and 3.0 ohms on turbo models and 13.0 to 16.0 ohms on non-turbo models

4

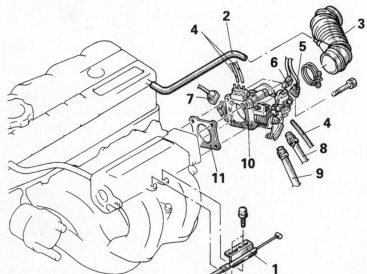

13.6a Exploded view of the throttle body on the 1.8L engine

1   Bracket
2   Breather hose
3   Air intake hose
4   Vacuum hose
5   ISC motor electrical connector
6   ISC motor position sensor electrical connector
7   TPS electrical connector
8   Coolant hose
9   Coolant hose
10   Throttle body
11   Gasket

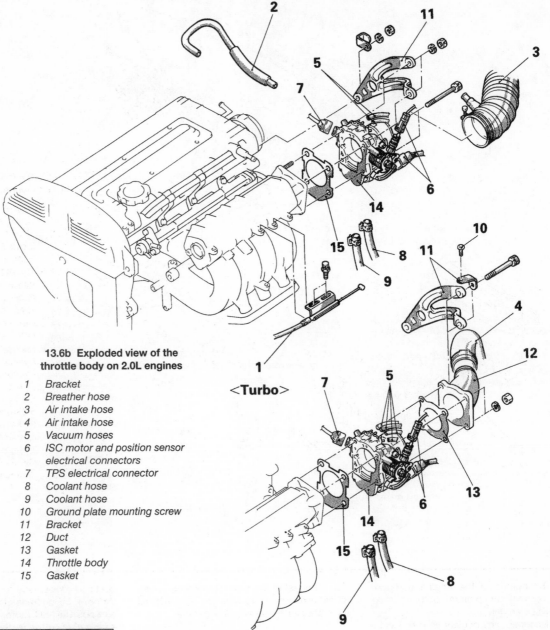

13.6b Exploded view of the throttle body on 2.0L engines

1   Bracket
2   Breather hose
3   Air intake hose
4   Air intake hose
5   Vacuum hoses
6   ISC motor and position sensor
    electrical connectors
7   TPS electrical connector
8   Coolant hose
9   Coolant hose
10 Ground plate mounting screw
11 Bracket
12 Duct
13 Gasket
14 Throttle body
15 Gasket

\<Turbo\>

13.10 Remove the throttle body mounting nuts (arrows) (lower right nut not visible in this photo)

7   Disconnect the accelerator cable from the throttle lever, then detach the cable housing from its bracket (see Section 10).

8   Remove the breather hose.

9   Detach the air intake duct (see Section 9).

10   Remove the throttle body bolts and detach the throttle body **(see illustration)**. Clean off all traces of old gasket material

11   Install the throttle body and a new gasket and tighten the bolts to the torque listed in this Chapter's Specifications.

12   The rest of the procedure is the reverse of removal. Be sure to check the coolant level (see Chapter 1) and add, if necessary.

14   Air intake plenum (1.8L engine) - removal and installation

Refer to illustration 14.9

1   Disconnect the cable from the negative terminal of the battery.

2   Detach the accelerator cable from the throttle body and remove the accelerator cable bracket (see Section 10).

3   Remove the throttle body (see Section 13).

4   Remove the EGR valve (see Chapter 6).

5   Raise the vehicle and support it securely on jackstands.

6   Working under the engine, remove the bolts from the lower section of the air intake plenum. Lower the vehicle.

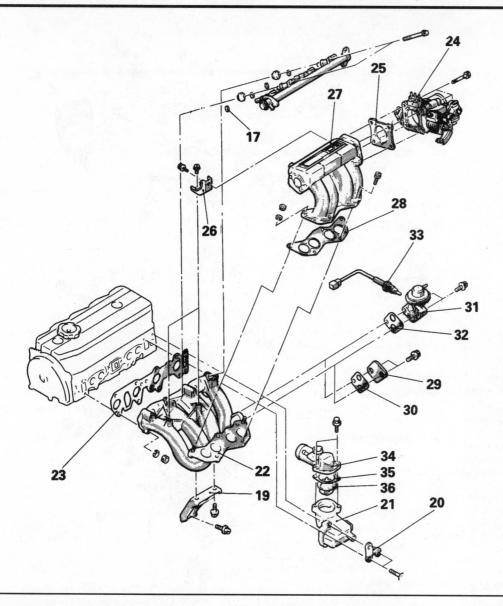

14.9 Exploded view of the air intake plenum on the 1.8L engine

16	Fuel rail
17	Grommet
18	Grommet
19	Intake manifold brace
20	Engine hanger
21	Thermostat housing
22	Intake manifold
23	Intake manifold gasket
24	Throttle body assembly
25	Gasket
26	Intake manifold brace
27	Intake plenum
28	Plenum gasket
29	Manifold cover
30	Gasket
31	EGR valve
32	EGR gasket
33	EGR gas temperature sensor (California only)
34	Thermostat housing
35	Gasket
36	Thermostat

4

7   Working inside the engine compartment, remove the plenum bolts that are accessible from the top.

8   Disconnect any coolant lines or electrical connectors from the air intake plenum and throttle body. Plug the coolant lines to prevent leakage. Also mark and detach all vacuum lines that may interfere with removal.

9   Remove the air intake plenum **(see illustration)** and gaskets. If the plenum sticks, use a block of wood and a hammer to dislodge it. Do not pry between the sealing flanges, as this will damage the machined surfaces and vacuum leaks may develop.

10   Remove all traces of old gasket material from the plenum and intake manifold mating surfaces. It's a good idea to stuff rags into the intake manifold openings to prevent debris and old gasket material from falling in.

11   Install the new gaskets and set the plenum into position.

12   Install the plenum bolts and tighten them to the torque listed in this Chapter's Specifications.

13   The rest of the procedure is the reverse of removal. Be sure to check the coolant level (see Chapter 1) and add, if necessary.

15   Idle speed Control (ISC) motor and idle speed adjustment - check, removal and installation

Refer to illustrations 15.3, 15.4, 15.6, 15.7 and 15.8

Check

1   The idle speed control motor (ISC) controls the engine idle speed. This output actuator is mounted on the throttle body and is controlled by voltage pulses sent from the ECM (computer). The ISC valve pintle moves in or out allowing more or less intake air into the system according to the engine conditions. To increase idle speed, the ECM retracts the ISC valve pintle away from the seat and allows more air to bypass the throttle bore. To decrease idle speed, the ECM extends the ISC motor pintle towards the seat, reducing the air flow. 1.8L engines are equipped with a servo type motor while 2.0L engines are equipped with stepper motor. **Note:** *1.8L engines (1991 and later) are equipped with an ISC position sensor. This sensor relays information to the ECM on the operating position of the ISC motor pintle. 1990 1.8L and all 2.0L engines are equipped with a separate idle position switch. Refer to Chapter 6, Section 4 for the check and replacement procedures.*

2   To check the system, first check for the voltage signal from the ECM. Turn the ignition key On (engine not running) and with a voltmeter, probe the terminals of the ISC motor electrical connector **(see illustration 15.4 and 15.7)**. It should read battery voltage on one terminal while the others read less than battery voltage. This indicates that the ISC motor is receiving the proper signal from the ECM.

15.3 Spray carburetor cleaner into the ISC motor housing on the throttle body (throttle body removed for clarity)

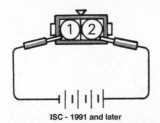

ISC - 1991 and later

ISC - 1990

15.4 Apply 6 volts to terminals 1 and 2 of the ISC motor connector and observe that the pintle retracts and extends - interchange the leads to reverse the motion of the pintle (1.8L engine)

15.6 Connect the probes of the ohmmeter to terminals 2 and 3 of the ISC motor position sensor - the resistance should be 4K to 6K ohms. The ISC motor position sensor is located on the throttle body

3   Next, remove the motor (see Step 4) and inspect it. Check the pintle for excessive carbon deposits. If necessary, clean it with carburetor cleaner spray. Also clean the IAC valve housing to remove any deposits **(see illustration)**.

1.8L engines

ISC motor

4   Apply 6 volts to terminals number 1 and 2 of the ISC valve and observe that the valve pintle retracts with the voltage signal **(see illustration)**. If there is no movement from the valve, replace it with a new one. **Note**: *Using a 12-volt battery will destroy the motor!* The IAC valve should retract when the positive (+) is applied to terminal number 1 or extend when the positive (+) is applied to terminal number 2.

5   Also check the continuity of the ISC motor coil. Position the probes of an ohmmeter onto terminals number 1 and 2. It should read 5 to 35 ohms at approximately 68-degrees F.

ISC motor position sensor

6   Disconnect the ISC motor position sensor connector and check the continuity between terminals 2 and 3 **(see illustration)**. It should be between 4K and 6K ohms.

2.0L engines

7   Check the resistance of the ISC motor

a) *Using an ohmmeter, check the resistance between terminal 2 and either terminal 1 or 3. It should be 28 to 33 ohms* **(see illustration)**.

b) *Using an ohmmeter, check the resistance between terminal number 5 and either terminal 6 or 4. It should be 28 to 33 ohms.*

8   Use a 6-volt battery and apply 6 volts to the ISC motor. Connect the positive (+) lead of the jumper wire to terminals 2 and 5 and the negative jumper leads to 3 and 6 **(see illustration)**. If there is no movement or vibration from the motor, replace it with a new one. **Note**: *Using a 12-volt battery will destroy the motor!*

Removal

9   Unplug the electrical connector from the ISC motor.

10   Remove the throttle body (see Section 13).

11   Remove the two ISC motor attaching screws and withdraw the assembly.

12   Check the condition of the rubber O-ring. If it's hardened or deteriorated, replace it.

13   Clean the sealing surface and the bore of the idle air/vacuum signal housing assembly to ensure a good seal. **Caution:** *The ISC valve itself is an electrical component and must not be soaked in any liquid cleaner, as damage may result.*

14   Before installing the ISC valve, the position of the pintle must be checked. If the pintle is extended too far, damage to the assembly may occur.

Installation

15   Position the new O-ring on the ISC motor. Lubricate the O-ring with a light film of engine oil.

16   Install the ISC motor and tighten the screws securely.

15.7 Check the resistance of the ISC motor coil on terminals 1 and 2 - it should read between 28 to 33 ohms (2.0L engine)

15.8 In order to apply voltage to both terminals, install a paper clip or a small jumper wire between terminals 2 and 5 and then another clip between terminals 3 and 6. Apply 6 volts to the appropriate jumper leads.

15.22 Install a paper clip into the CRC test connector and hook up a tachometer to the clip (1.8L engine shown)

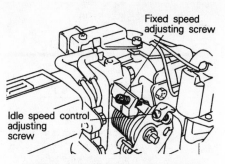

15.24 Turn the fixed speed adjusting screw to adjust the idle speed

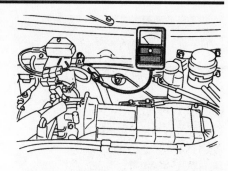

15.32 Hook up a tachometer to the test connector on the firewall

17   Plug in the electrical connector to the ISC motor. **Note:** *No adjustment is made to the ISC assembly. The ISC resetting is controlled by the ECM when the engine is started.*

Idle speed adjustment

1.8L engines

Refer to illustrations 15.22 and 15.24

18   Warm the engine until it reaches operating temperature (185 to 205-degrees F).
19   All accessories, lights and the cooling fan(s) must be OFF.
20   Set the transaxle in Park on automatic transaxles or if the engine is equipped with power steering, select Neutral.
21   Check the adjustment of the accelerator cable (see Chapter 4). Adjust if necessary.
22   Install a paper clip into the CRC test connector near the distributor **(see illustration)** and connect a tachometer to the clip.
23   Disconnect all the electrical connectors from the ISC motor. **Note:** *It is very important that the ISC plunger is left completely retracted when the connector is removed. This can be achieved by allowing the ignition key turned ON for 15 seconds or more. Initially the ISC goes to a high idle (extended pintle) when the key is first turned ON but will retract after 15 seconds.*
24   Back out the fixed speed adjusting screw **(see illustration)** and start the engine

and let it run at idle.
25   Check the idle speed. It should be 700 ± 50 rpm.
26   If necessary, adjust the idle speed as follows;

   a) *Turn in the adjusting screw until the idle speed rises. Then back it out until it reaches the touch point. The touch point is when the idle speed does not continue to fall (just barely touching the throttle lever).*
   b) *Now back it out an additional 1/2-turn*
   c) *Stop the engine*
   d) *Check the TPS output voltage (see Chapter 6, Section 4) and adjust if necessary. It should be 0.48 to 0.52 volts.*
   e) *Reconnect the electrical connectors onto the ISC motor.*
   f) *Start the engine and check the curb idle speed. It should be 700 + 50 rpm.*
   g) *Turn the ignition key OFF and disconnect the negative battery cable. Wait 10 seconds (clear diagnosis data) and reconnect the battery cable.*

27   Restart the engine and run it for approximately 5 minutes and check for a smooth idle.

2.0L engines

Refer to illustrations 15.32, 15.33, 15.34 and 15.36

28   Warm the engine until it reaches operating temperature (185 to 205-degrees F).
29   All accessories, lights and the cooling fan(s) must be OFF.

30   Set the transaxle in Park (automatic transaxle) or Neutral (manual transaxle).
31   Check the adjustment of the accelerator cable (see Section 10). Adjust it if necessary.
32   Install a paper clip into the test connector near the firewall **(see illustration)** and connect a tachometer to the clip.
33   Install a jumper wire into the ignition timing adjustment terminal and ground it to the firewall **(see illustration)**.
34   Connect terminal number 10 of the self diagnosis connector to ground with a jumper wire **(see illustration)**.
35   Start the engine and check the idle speed. It should be 700 ± 50 rpm.
36   If necessary, adjust the idle speed as follows:

   a) *Turn in the speed adjusting screw until the idle speed lowers or turn it out to raise the rpm's* **(see illustration)**.
   b) *If the idle speed is higher than the specified range even after the screw is turned all the way in, check the idle position switch and the TPS adjustment (see Chapter 6, Section 4).*
   c) *Stop the engine*
   d) *Adjust the TPS output voltage (see Chapter 6, Section 4) if necessary.*
   e) *Reconnect the electrical connectors onto the ISC motor.*
   f) *Start the engine and check the curb idle speed. It should be 700 + 50 rpm.*

37   Restart the engine and run it for approximately 5 minutes and check for a smooth idle.

4

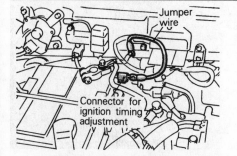

15.33 Ground the ignition timing adjustment connector

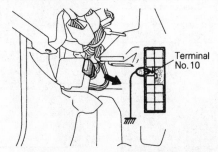

15.34 Ground terminal number 10 on the diagnostic connector under the driver's side of the dash

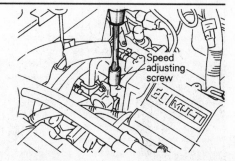

15.36 Turn the speed adjusting screw in (to lower engine rpm) or out (to raise engine rpm)

16.5 Carefully watch the fuel pressure gauge as vacuum is applied - fuel pressure should decrease as vacuum increases

16.10 Make sure there is vacuum to the fuel pressure regulator at idle

16.15 The fuel pressure regulator is retained to the fuel rail by two bolts

16   Fuel pressure regulator - check and replacement

Warning: *Gasoline is extremely flammable, so take extra precautions when you work on any part of the fuel system. Don't smoke or allow open flames or bare light bulbs near the work area, and don't work in a garage where a natural gas-type appliance (such as a water heater or clothes dryer) with a pilot light is present. If you spill any fuel on your skin, rinse it off immediately with soap and water. When you perform any kind of work on the fuel system, wear safety glasses and have a Class B type fire extinguisher on hand.*

Check

Refer to illustrations 16.5 and 16.10
Note: *This procedure assumes the fuel filter is in good condition.*

1   Relieve the fuel system pressure (see Section 2).
2   Detach the cable from the negative battery terminal.
3   Disconnect the fuel line and install a fuel pressure gauge (see Section 3). Reconnect the battery cable.
4   Start the engine and check for leakage around the gauge connections.
5   Disconnect the vacuum hose from the fuel pressure regulator and hook up a hand-held vacuum pump to the port on the fuel pressure regulator **(see illustration)**.
6   Read the fuel pressure gauge with vacuum applied to the pressure regulator and also with no vacuum applied. The fuel pressure should decrease as vacuum increases (and increase as vacuum decreases).
7   Reconnect the vacuum hose to the regulator and check the fuel pressure at idle, comparing your reading with the value listed in this Chapter's Specifications. Disconnect the vacuum hose and watch the gauge – the pressure should jump up considerably as soon as the hose is disconnected. If it doesn't, proceed to Step 10.
8   If the fuel pressure is low, pinch the fuel

return line shut and watch the gauge. If the pressure doesn't rise, the fuel pump is defective or there is a restriction in the fuel feed line. If the pressure rises sharply, replace the pressure regulator.
9   If the fuel pressure is too high, turn the engine off. Disconnect the fuel return line and blow through it to check for a blockage. If there is no blockage, replace the fuel pressure regulator.
10   Connect a vacuum gauge to the vacuum hose to the pressure regulator. Start the engine and check for vacuum **(see illustration)**. If there isn't vacuum present, check for a clogged hose or vacuum port. If the amount of vacuum is adequate, replace the fuel pressure regulator.

Replacement

Refer to illustration 16.15

11   Relieve the fuel pressure from the system (see Section 2). Disconnect the cable from the negative terminal of the battery.
12   Clean any dirt from around the fuel pressure regulator.
13   Detach the vacuum hose from the fuel pressure regulator.
14   Detach the fuel return line from the pressure regulator.
15   Remove the bolts that retain the fuel pressure regulator **(see illustration)**.
16   Install new O-rings and lubricate them with a light coat of clean engine oil.
17   Installation is the reverse of removal. Tighten the pressure regulator mounting bolts securely.

17   Fuel rail and injectors - removal and installation

Warning: *Gasoline is extremely flammable, so take extra precautions when you work on any part of the fuel system. Don't smoke or allow open flames or bare light bulbs near the work area, and don't work in a garage where a natural gas-type appliance (such as a water heater or clothes dryer) with a pilot light is present. If you spill any fuel on your skin, rinse it off immediately with soap and water. When*

you perform any kind of work on the fuel system, wear safety glasses and have a Class B type fire extinguisher on hand.

Fuel rail and related components

Refer to illustrations 17.3, 17.6 and 17.7
Caution: *To prevent dirt from entering the combustion chambers, the area around the injectors should be cleaned before servicing.*
Note: *An identification number is stamped on the side of the fuel rail assembly. Refer to this number if servicing or parts replacement is required.*

1   Relieve the fuel system pressure (see Section 2).
2   Detach the cable from the negative terminal of the battery.
3   Disconnect the fuel return line from the fuel pressure regulator and the fuel feed line on the opposite end of the fuel rail assembly **(see illustration)**.
4   Detach the vacuum line from the regulator.
5   Label and unplug the injector electrical connectors.
6   Remove the fuel rail retaining bolts **(see illustration)**.

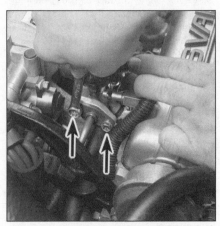

17.3 Remove the bolts (arrows) that hold the fuel line to the fuel rail (2.0L engine shown)

17.6 Remove the fuel rail mounting bolts and separate the fuel rail from the intake manifold (2.0L engine shown)

17.7 Lift the fuel rail assembly from the engine - if it sticks, carefully pry on the fuel rail mounting bosses

7   Carefully remove the fuel rail with the injectors **(see illustration)**. **Caution:** *Use care when handling the fuel rail assembly to avoid damaging the injectors.*

Fuel injectors

Refer to illustrations 17.8 and 17.9

8   To remove the fuel injectors, carefully wiggle the end of the injector from the housing **(see illustration)** and remove it from the fuel rail.

9   Inspect the injector O-ring seal(s). These should be replaced whenever the fuel rail is removed **(see illustration)**.

10   Install the new O-ring(s) on the in-jec-tor(s) and lubricate them with engine oil.

11   Install the injectors on the fuel rail.

12   Secure the injectors with the retaining clips.

13   Installation is the reverse of removal.

18 Turbocharger - general information

The turbocharger increases power by using an exhaust gas-driven turbine to pressurize the fuel/air mixture before it enters the combustion chambers. The amount of boost (intake manifold pressure) is controlled by the wastegate (exhaust bypass valve). The wastegate is operated by a spring-loaded actuator assembly which controls the maximum boost level by allowing some of the exhaust gas to bypass the turbine. The wastegate is controlled by the computer.

Only the 2.0L engine is equipped with the turbocharger option. All turbocharger systems are equipped with an intercooler, which cools the compressed air and makes it even more dense.

The computerized fuel injection and emission control system is equipped with self-diagnosis capabilities that can access certain turbocharging system components. Refer to Chapter 6 for information pertaining to trouble codes and diagnosis.

19 Turbocharger - check

General checks

1   While it is a relatively simple device, the turbocharger is also a precision component which can be severely damaged by an interrupted oil or coolant supply or loose or damaged ducts.

2   Due to the special techniques and equipment required, checking and diagnosis of suspected problems dealing with the turbocharger should be left to a dealer service department. The home mechanic can, however, check the connections and linkages for security, damage and other obvious problems. Also, the home mechanic can check components that govern the turbocharger such as the wastegate solenoid, bypass valve and wastegate actuator. Refer to the checks later in this section.

3   Because each turbocharger has its own distinctive sound, a change in the noise level can be a sign of potential problems.

4   A high-pitched or whistling sound is a symptom of an inlet air or exhaust gas leak.

5   If an unusual sound comes from the vicinity of the turbine, the turbocharger can be removed and the turbine wheel inspected. **Caution:** *All checks must be made with the*

engine off and cool to the touch and the turbocharger stopped or personal injury could result. Operating the engine without all the turbocharger ducts and filters installed is also dangerous and can result in damage to the turbine wheel blades.

6   With the engine turned off and completely cool, reach inside the housing and turn the turbine wheel to make sure it spins freely. If it doesn't, it's possible the cooling oil has sludged or cooked from overheating. Push in on the turbine wheel and check for binding. The turbine should rotate freely with no binding or rubbing on the housing. If it does, the turbine bearing is worn out.

7   Check the exhaust manifold for cracks and loose connections.

8   Because the turbine wheel rotates at speeds up to 140,000 rpm, severe damage can result from the interruption of coolant or contamination of the oil supply to the turbine bearings. Check for leaks in the coolant and oil inlet lines and obstructions in the oil drain-back line, as this can cause severe oil loss through the turbocharger seals. Burned oil on the turbine housing is a sign of this. **Caution:** *Whenever a major engine bearing such as a main or connecting rod bearing is replaced, the turbocharger should be flushed with clean engine oil.*

4

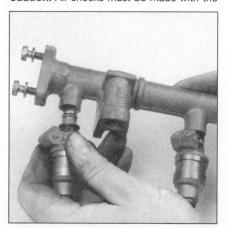

17.8 Separate the injectors from the rail

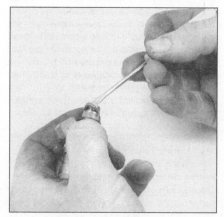

17.9 Be sure to replace the O-rings with new ones

19.9 The wastegate solenoid (arrow) is mounted on top of the air cleaner housing

19.13 Remove the vacuum line (arrow) from the bypass valve and attach a hand-held vacuum pump

Component checks

Refer to illustrations 19.9 and 19.13

Wastegate solenoid

9   Remove the vacuum hoses and electrical connector from the wastegate solenoid **(see illustration)**.

10   Install a hand held vacuum pump onto the valve port on which the white striped vacuum hose was attached and apply vacuum. Using jumper wires installed onto the battery terminals, connect them to the wastegate solenoid.

11   With the voltage applied, the vacuum gauge should indicate a leak. Now release the voltage from the solenoid and the vacuum gauge should indicate no leaks.

12   If the test results are incorrect, replace the wastegate solenoid.

Bypass valve

13   Connect a hand held vacuum pump to the port on the bypass valve **(see illustration)**. Apply vacuum.

14   At approximately 15.0 in-Hg, the valve should start opening and allowing air to flow.

15   If the test results are incorrect, replace the bypass valve with a new part.

Wastegate actuator

16   Using a hand-held vacuum/pressure pump (with the hose attached to the output side), apply pressure to the wastegate actuator **(see illustration 20.7)** and make sure the rod moves. **Note**: *Do not apply more than 12.4psi. or the diaphragm may be damaged.*

17   The rod should move at 11.1 psi on manual transmission models and 10.4 psi on automatic transmission models.

18   If the test results are incorrect, replace the wastegate actuator.

20 Turbocharger - removal and installation

Refer to illustrations 20.4, 20.6, 20.7, 20.8, 20.10, 20.13, 20.14a and 20.14b

Removal

1   Disconnect the cable from the negative

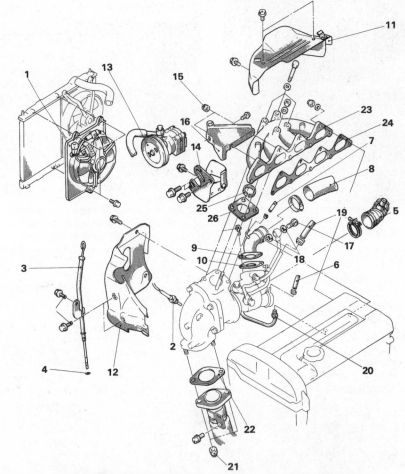

20.4 Exploded view of the turbocharger and related components

1	Condenser fan motor assembly	9	Air outlet	18	Gasket
2	Oxygen sensor	10	Gasket	19	Coolant hose
3	Dipstick tube	11	Heat shield	20	Coolant line
4	O-ring	12	Heat shield	21	Nut
5	Air intake hose	13	Power steering oil pump	22	Gasket
6	Vacuum hose	14	Oil pump bracket	23	Exhaust manifold
7	Vacuum hose	15	Nut	24	Gasket
8	Intercooler intake duct	16	Engine hanger	25	Ring
		17	Banjo bolt	26	Gasket

20.6 Remove the banjo fitting from the oil feed line on the cylinder head

20.7 Remove the banjo fitting on the turbocharger and detach the coolant line

1 Coolant line fitting
2 Wastegate actuator
3 Wastegate actuator rod

20.8 Remove the two flange nuts (arrows) and separate the oil return tube from the turbocharger

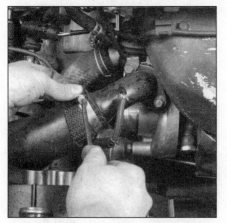

20.10 Remove the intercooler duct from the turbocharger

20.13 Lift off the exhaust manifold along with the turbocharger as a complete assembly

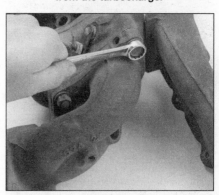

20.14a Separate the exhaust flange from the turbocharger on the bench

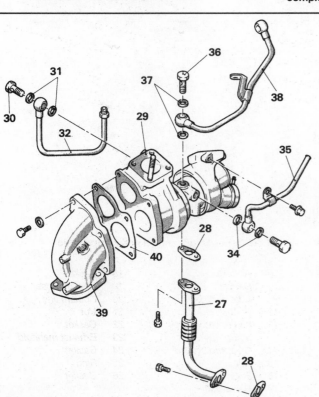

20.14b Exploded view of the turbocharger

27 Oil return pipe
28 Gasket
29 Turbocharger
30 Banjo bolt
31 Gasket
32 Coolant line
33 Banjo bolt
34 Gasket
35 Coolant line
36 Banjo bolt
37 Gasket
38 Oil pipe
39 Exhaust flange
40 Gasket

terminal of the battery.
2 Drain the cooling system (see Chapter 1).
3 On vehicles equipped with air conditioning, remove the condenser fan assembly from the radiator (see Chapter 3).
4 Remove the oil dipstick tube **(see illustration).**
5 Remove the air intake hose (see Section 9).
6 Remove the banjo fitting from oil feed line located on the cylinder head **(see illustration).**
7 Remove the coolant line from the turbocharger housing **(see illustration).**
8 Separate the oil return line from the turbocharger housing **(see illustration).**
9 Remove the wastegate rod-to-gate retaining clip.
10 Remove the intercooler hose from the turbocharger **(see illustration).** 11 Remove the exhaust manifold heat shield and the retaining bolts from the cylinder head (see Chapter 2A). *Note: Follow the procedure in Chapter 2A but do not disconnect the turbocharger from the exhaust manifold.*
12 Disconnect the oxygen sensor wire (see Chapter 6) and any vacuum lines that might be in the way.
13 Lift the turbocharger and the exhaust manifold as a complete assembly from the engine compartment **(see illustration).**
14 Separate the turbocharger from the exhaust manifold **(see illustrations).**

4

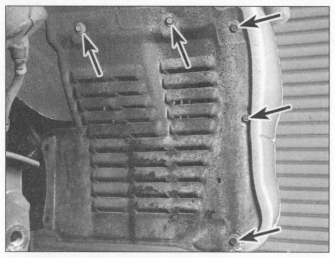

21.3 Remove the mounting screws (arrows) and lower the splash shield from the inner fenderwell

21.5a Remove the mounting bolts (arrows) from the intercooler

Installation

15   Carefully clean the mating surfaces of the turbocharger and exhaust manifold.

16   Place the turbocharger in position on the manifold studs.

17   Apply anti-seize compound to the studs and install the nuts. Tighten the nuts to the torque listed in this Chapter's Specifications.

18   Apply thread sealant into the lower inlet coolant line fitting and install the fitting into the turbocharger housing.

19   Install the upper coolant line.

20   Install the oil drain-back tube and fitting, along with a new gasket, to the turbocharger housing.

21   Reposition the exhaust pipe and tighten the bolts to the torque listed in this Chapter's Specifications.

22   Reconnect the oxygen sensor electrical connector and any vacuum lines that were disconnected.

23   Install the wastegate rod-to-gate retaining clip.

24   Attach the oil feed line to the cylinder head. Tighten the fitting securely.

25   Check the coolant level and add some, if necessary (see Chapter 1).

26   Change the engine oil (see Chapter 1).

21 Intercooler - removal and installation

Refer to illustrations 21.3, 21.5a and 21.5b

1   The intercooler lowers the temperature of the intake air on turbo engines, which make the air more dense.

2   Raise the vehicle and support it securely on jackstands.

3   Remove the right side inner splash shield **(see illustration)**.

4   Loosen the hose clamps, then disconnect the air hoses from the intercooler.

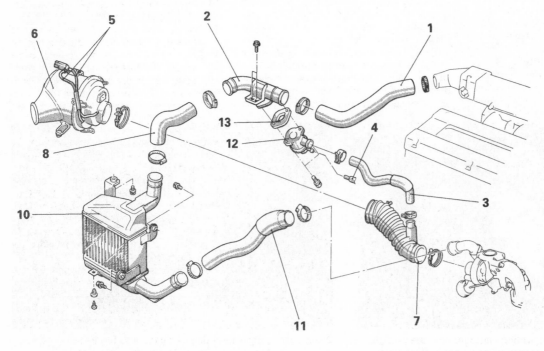

21.5b Exploded view of the intercooler and related components

1   Air intake hose
2   Air intake pipe
3   Air bypass hose
4   Vacuum line
5   Vacuum line
6   Air cleaner
7   Air intake hose
8   Air intake hose
9   Splash shield
10 Intercooler
11 Air intake hose
12 Turbocharger bypass
    valve
13 Gasket

22.1 Exploded view of a typical exhaust system

1	Protector	14	Hanger
2	Gasket	15	Protector
3	Hanger	16	Hanger bracket
4	Main muffler	17	Center exhaust pipe
5	Moulding	18	Gasket
6	Hanger bracket	19	Catalytic converter
7	Rear heat protector panel	20	Gasket
8	Self locking nut	21	Self locking nut
9	O-ring	22	Hanger
10	Hook	23	Front exhaust pipe
11	Bracket	24	Gasket
12	Stopper	25	Floor heat shield
13	Hanger bracket		

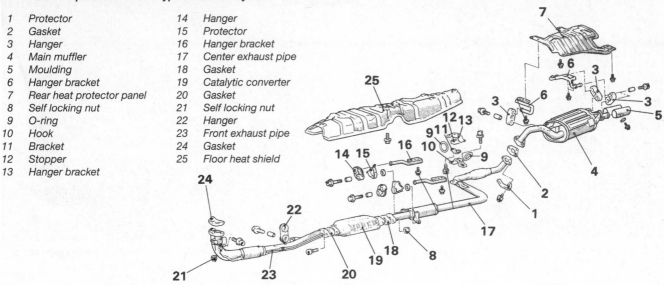

5   Remove the mounting bolts **(see illus-trations)** and lower the intercooler from the fenderwell.

6   Inspect the intercooler for cracks and damage to the flanges, tubes and fins. Replace it or have it repaired if necessary.

7   Installation is the reverse of removal.

22   Exhaust system servicing – general information

Refer to illustrations 22.1, 22.4a and 22.4b

Warning: *Inspection and repair of exhaust system components should be done only after enough time has elapsed after driving the vehicle to allow the system components to cool completely. Also, when working under the vehicle, make sure it is securely supported on jackstands.*

1   The exhaust system consists of the exhaust manifold(s), the catalytic converter, the muffler, the tailpipe and all connecting pipes, brackets, hangers and clamps **(see illustration)**. The exhaust system is attached to the body with mounting brackets and rubber hangers. If any of the parts are improperly installed, excessive noise and vibration will be transmitted to the body.

2   Conduct regular inspections of the exhaust system to keep it safe and quiet. Look for any damaged or bent parts, open seams, holes, loose connections, excessive corrosion or other defects which could allow exhaust fumes to enter the vehicle. Deteriorated exhaust system components should not be repaired; they should be replaced with new parts.

3   If the exhaust system components are extremely corroded or rusted together, welding equipment will probably be required to remove them. The convenient way to accomplish this is to have a muffler repair shop remove the corroded sections with a cutting torch. If, however, you want to save money by doing it yourself (and you don't have a welding outfit with a cutting torch), simply cut off the old components with a hacksaw. If you have compressed air, special pneumatic cutting chisels can also be used. If you do decide to tackle the job at home, be sure to wear safety goggles to protect your eyes from metal chips and work gloves to protect your hands.

4   Here are some simple guidelines to follow when repairing the exhaust system:

a) *Work from the back to the front when removing exhaust system components.*

b) *Apply penetrating oil to the exhaust system component fasteners to make them easier to remove (see illustrations).*

c) *Use new gaskets, hangers and clamps when installing exhaust systems components.*

d) *Apply anti-seize compound to the threads of all exhaust system fasteners during reassembly.*

e) *Be sure to allow sufficient clearance between newly installed parts and all points on the underbody to avoid overheating the floor pan and possibly damaging the interior carpet and insulation. Pay particularly close attention to the catalytic converter and heat shield.*

4

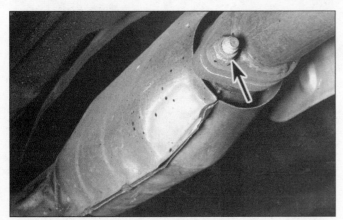

22.4a Be sure to spray penetrating lubricant onto the catalytic converter mounting nuts before trying to break them loose

22.4b Also apply penetrating lubricant onto the threads and nuts on the exhaust flange at the exhaust manifold

Notes

Chapter 5
Engine electrical systems

Contents

Specifications

Ignition coil

1.8L engines
Primary resistance .... 0.9 to 1.2 ohms
Secondary resistance .... 19,000 to 27,000 ohms
Insulation resistance .... More than 10M ohms

2.0L engines
1990
Primary resistance .... 0.77 to 0.95 ohms
Secondary resistance .... 10,300 to 13,900 ohms
1991
Primary resistance .... 0.77 to 0.95 ohms
Secondary resistance .... 10,300 to 13,900 ohms
1992 and later
Primary resistance .... 0.7 to 0.86 ohms
Secondary resistance .... 11,300 to 15,300 ohms
Insulation resistance .... More than 10M ohms
Ignition timing .... 5-degrees BTDC at 700 rpm (refer to VECI label)

1   General information

Ignition system

The ignition system is composed of the battery, distributor, coil, ignition switch, spark plugs and the primary (low tension) and secondary (high tension) wiring circuits.

The engines covered by this manual are equipped with either a solid state ignition system (1.8L engine) or a distributorless ignition system (DIS) (2.0L engines). The solid state ignition (1.8L engine) is only available as a single, replaceable unit. The ignition coil and the pick-up coil are integral components contained within the distributor. If replacement is necessary, exchange the old distributor at a dealer parts department or other auto parts store. The ignition system (DIS) on 2.0L engines consists of the crankshaft position sensor, camshaft position sensor, ignition power transistor and the ignition coil. Additional tests for the DIS system camshaft and crankshaft sensors can be found in Chapter 6, Section 4.

Charging system

The charging system consists of a belt-driven alternator with an integral voltage regulator and the battery. These components work together to supply electrical power for the ignition system, the lights and all accessories.

These vehicles are equipped with only one type of alternator but there are three different ratings available for each model depending upon what accessories the engine is equipped with. The alternator comes in a

2.3 To remove the battery, detach the negative (first) and positive (last) cables, then remove the hold-down strap bolts (arrows) and remove the hold-down strap from the engine compartment

60, 75 or 90 amp output rating. All types use a conventional pulley and fan.

Starting system

The starting circuit consists of the battery, starter motor, ignition switch and other related electrical wiring. The starter motor is equipped with a solenoid mounted directly to the assembly. Parts are available for repair of the motor and solenoid as separate units.

2 Battery – removal and installation

Refer to illustration 2.3
1   Disconnect both cables from the battery terminals. **Caution:** *Always disconnect the negative cable first and hook it up last or the battery may be shorted by the tool being used to loosen the cable clamps.*
2   The battery is located at the front of the engine compartment. It is held in place by a hold-down clamp.
3   Remove the battery hold-down clamp bolts **(see illustration)**.
4   Lift out the battery. Be careful - it's heavy.
5   While the battery is out, inspect the carrier (tray) for corrosion.
6   If you are replacing the battery, make sure that you get one that's identical, with the same dimensions, amperage rating, cold cranking rating, etc.
7   Installation is the reverse of removal.

3 Battery – emergency jump starting

Refer to the *Booster battery (jump) starting* procedure at the front of this manual.

4 Battery cables – check and replacement

1   Periodically inspect the entire length of each battery cable for damage, cracked or burned insulation and corrosion. Poor battery cable connections can cause starting problems and decreased engine performance.
2   Check the cable-to-terminal connections at the ends of the cables for cracks, loose wire strands and corrosion. The presence of white, fluffy deposits under the insulation at the cable terminal connection is a sign that the cable is corroded and should be replaced. Check the terminals for distortion, missing mounting bolts and corrosion.
3   When removing the cables, always disconnect the negative cable first and hook it up last or the battery may be shorted by the tool used to loosen the cable clamps. Even if only the positive cable is being replaced, be sure to disconnect the negative cable from the battery first (see Chapter 1 for further information regarding battery cable removal).
4   Disconnect the old cables from the battery, then trace each of them to their opposite ends and detach them from the starter solenoid and ground terminals. Note the routing of each cable to ensure correct installation.
5   If you are replacing either or both of the old cables, take them with you when buying new cables. It is vitally important that you replace the cables with identical parts. Cables have characteristics that make them easy to identify: positive cables are usually red, larger in cross-section and have a larger diameter battery post clamp; ground cables are usually black, smaller in cross-section and have a slightly smaller diameter clamp for the negative post.
6   Clean the threads of the solenoid or ground connection with a wire brush to remove rust and corrosion. Apply a light coat of battery terminal corrosion inhibitor, or petroleum jelly, to the threads to prevent future corrosion.
7   Attach the cable to the solenoid or ground connection and tighten the mounting nut/bolt securely.
8   Before connecting a new cable to the battery, make sure that it reaches the battery post without having to be stretched.
9   Connect the positive cable first, followed by the negative cable.

5 Ignition system – general information and precautions

Warning: *Because of the very high voltage generated by the electronic ignition system, extreme care should be taken whenever an operation involving ignition components is performed. This not only includes the distributor, coil, ignition power transistor and spark plug wires, but related wires that are connected to the system as well (such as plug connections, tachometer and testing equipment). Consequently, before any work is performed, the ignition should be turned OFF and the negative battery cable disconnected.*

1   Engines covered by this manual are equipped with either a solid state ignition system (1.8L engine) or a distributorless ignition system (DIS) (2.0L engines).
2   Solid state systems incorporate the coil and ignition power transistor into the distributor. Models with DIS are equipped with a separate ignition coil (coil pack), ignition power transistor, cam and crankshaft position sensors and the Electronic Control Module (ECM), which monitors data from various engine sensors, computes the desired spark timing and signals the distributor to change the timing accordingly. No vacuum or mechanical advance is used.
3   When working on the ignition system, take the following precautions:
a)   *Don't keep the ignition switch on for more than ten seconds if the engine won't start.*
b)   *Always connect a tachometer in accordance with the tool manufacturer's instructions. Some tachometers may be incompatible with this ignition system. Consult a dealer service department before buying a tachometer for use with this vehicle.*
c)   *Never allow the ignition coil terminals to touch ground. Grounding the coil could result in damage to the module or the ignition coil.*
d)   *Don't disconnect the battery when the engine is running.*

6 Ignition system – check

Refer to illustration 6.1
Warning: *Because of the high voltage generated by the ignition system, extreme care should be taken whenever an operation is performed involving ignition components. This not only includes the power transistor, coil, distributor and spark plug wires, but related*

6.1 To use a calibrated ignition tester (available at most auto parts stores), simply disconnect a spark plug wire, attach the wire to the tester and clip the tester to a good ground -if there is enough power to fire the plug, sparks will be clearly visible between the electrode tip and the tester body as the engine is cranked

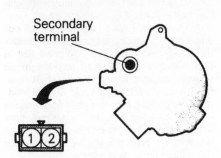

7.4 Disconnect the electrical connector for the coil and measure the resistance between terminals 1 and 2 to measure the primary resistance (1.8L engines)

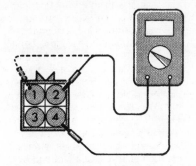

7.8a On 1990 models, first check the primary resistance across terminals 4 and 2 (it should read the same as terminals 4 and 1)

7.8b On 1991 and later models, first check the primary resistance across terminals 3 and 2 (it should read the same as terminals 3 and 1)

components such as plug connectors, tachometer and and other test equipment also.

1   If the engine turns over but won't start, disconnect the spark plug wire from any spark plug and attach it to a calibrated tester (available at most auto parts stores). Connect the clip on the tester to a bolt or metal bracket on the engine **(see illustration)**. If you're unable to obtain a calibrated ignition tester, remove the wire from one of the spark plugs and using an insulated tool, pull back the boot and hold the end of the wire about 1/4-inch from a good ground.

2   Crank the engine and watch the end of the tester or spark plug wire to see if bright blue, well-defined sparks occur. If you're not using a calibrated tester, have an assistant crank the engine for you.

3   If sparks occur, sufficient voltage is reaching the plug to fire it (repeat the check at the remaining plug wires to verify that the distributor cap and rotor are OK). However, the plugs themselves may be fouled, so remove and check them as described in Chapter 1.

1.8L engine

4   If no sparks or intermittent sparks occur, remove the distributor cap and check the cap and rotor as described in Chapter 1. If moisture is present, dry out the cap and rotor, then reinstall the cap and repeat the spark test.

5   If no sparks occur, check the primary wire connections at the distributor to make sure they're clean and tight. Check for voltage to the coil. Check the coil (see Section 7). Make any necessary repairs, then repeat the check again.

6   If there's still no spark, the coil-to-cap wire may be bad (check the resistance with an ohmmeter and compare it to this Chapter's Specifications). If a known good wire doesn't make any difference in the test results, the distributor assembly, which houses the power transistor, crank angle sensor and ignition coil and is not serviceable, may be defective. **Note:** Before replacing the distributor assembly, check on the availability of a solid state

ignition unit (which consists of the internal workings of the distributor) or a rebuilt distributor on an exchange basis. Either of these options will cost considerably less than a new distributor.

2.0L engines

7   If no sparks, or intermittent sparks occur, proceed to Section 7 and check the coil pack.

7   Ignition coil - check, removal and installation

1   Disconnect the cable from the negative terminal of the battery.

Check

1.8L engines

Refer to illustration 7.4

2   Check the coil for opens and grounds by performing the following three tests with an ohmmeter.

3   Unplug the primary (low voltage) electrical connector (two-terminal) from the coil, which is part of the distributor. Using the ohmmeter's high scale, hook up the ohmmeter leads to the coil body (negative probe) and to the number 1 terminal on the coil connector (positive probe). The ohmmeter should indicate a very high, or infinite, resistance value (this checks the coil body insulation resistance). If it doesn't, the coil is defective and the entire distributor must be replaced.

4   Next, check the coil primary resistance. Using the low scale, connect the probes to terminals 1 and 2 **(see illustration)** on the coil electrical connector. The ohmmeter should indicate a very low resistance value. Refer to the Specifications listed in this Chapter for the actual value. If it doesn't, replace the distributor assembly.

5   Next, check the coil secondary resistance. Using the high scale, hook up the leads between the secondary terminal (coil tower) and terminal number 1 or 2 **(see illustration 7.4)**. The ohmmeter should not indicate an infinite resistance. Refer to the Specifications

listed in this Chapter for the actual value. If it does, replace the distributor assembly. **Note:** Before replacing the distributor assembly, check on the availability of a solid state ignition unit (which consists of the internal workings of the distributor) or a rebuilt distributor on an exchange basis. Either of these options will cost considerably less than a new distributor.

2.0L engines

Refer to illustrations 7.8a, 7.8b and 7.9

6   Check the coil for opens and grounds by performing the following three tests with an ohmmeter.

7   Using the ohmmeter's high scale, hook up the ohmmeter leads to the coil pack body (negative probe) and to the number 1 terminal on the coil primary connector (positive probe). The ohmmeter should indicate a very high, or infinite, resistance value. If it doesn't, replace the coil. This checks the coil body insulation resistance.

8   Next check the coil primary resistance.

a)   On 1990 models, using the low scale, connect the probes to terminals 4 and 2 (Number 1 and 4 cylinders) of the electrical connector **(see illustration)**. The ohmmeter should indicate a very low resistance value. Refer to the Specifications listed in this Chapter. If it doesn't, replace the coil. Also check coil resistance on terminals 4 and 1 (number 2 and 3 cylinders).

b)   On 1991 and later models, using the low scale, connect the probes to terminals 3 and 2 (number 1 and 4 cylinders) of the electrical connector **(see illustration)**. The ohmmeter should indicate a very low resistance value. Refer to the Specifications listed in this Chapter. If it doesn't, replace the coil. Also check coil resistance across terminals 3 and 1 (number 2 and 3 cylinders).

5

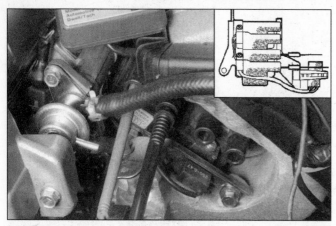

7.9 Check the secondary resistance on the coil pack by probing the first two posts of the coil pack with an ohmmeter. Next, check the last two posts. The resistance should be the same on each pair.

7.12 Remove the three bolts (arrows) from the coil and lift the coil assembly from the intake manifold (the third bolt is hidden from view)

9   Next, check the coil secondary resistance. Using the high scale, hook up the leads to the first two posts on the coil (number 2 and 3 cylinders) **(see illustration)**. The ohmmeter should not indicate an infinite resistance. Refer to the Specifications listed in this Chapter. If it does, replace the coil. Also, check the resistance on the last two posts of the coil pack (number 1 and 4 cylinders).

Removal and installation

1.8L engine

10   The coil is not replaceable separately. Refer to Section 8 for the distributor removal and installation procedure. **Note:** *Before replacing the distributor assembly, check on the availability of a solid state ignition unit (which consists of the internal workings of the distributor) or a rebuilt distributor on an exchange basis. Either of these options will cost considerably less than a new distributor.*

2.0L engines

Refer to illustration 7.12

11   Clearly label and disconnect all wires from the coil pack.
12   Remove the mounting bolts **(see illustration)** and detach the coil pack from the intake manifold, sliding it out toward the left (driver's) side of the engine compartment.
13   Installation is the reverse of removal.

---

8   Distributor (1.8L engine) - removal and installation

Refer to illustrations 8.3 and 8.5

Removal

1   Detach the cable from the negative terminal of the battery.
2   Unplug the electrical connectors from the side of the distributor base.
3   Remove the distributor cap **(see illus-**

tration) and move it out of the way (leave the spark plug wires connected).
4   Mark the position of the distributor housing in relation to the engine.
5   Mark the position of the rotor in relation to the distributor housing **(see illustration)**.
6   Remove the distributor hold-down bolt and clamp.
7   Remove the distributor. **Caution:** *Avoid turning the crankshaft while the distributor is removed. Turning the crankshaft while the distributor is removed will necessitate retiming the engine.*

Installation (crankshaft not turned after distributor removal)

8   Position the rotor in the exact location it was in when the distributor was removed.
9   Insert the distributor into its hole in the cylinder head. To mesh the tangs at the bottom of the distributor with the slot in the end of the camshaft it may be necessary to turn the rotor slightly.
10   With the base of the distributor seated

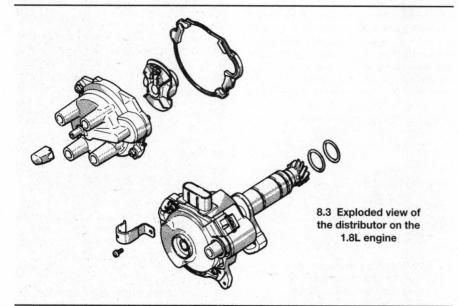

8.3 Exploded view of the distributor on the 1.8L engine

8.5 Before removing the distributor, make an alignment mark on the edge of the distributor base directly beneath the rotor tip - DO NOT use a pencil

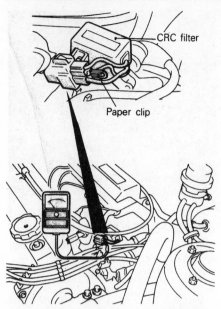

9.3 Install a paper clip into the CRC filter located near the distributor and connect the tachometer lead to the paper clip

against the cylinder head, turn the distributor housing to align the marks made on the distributor base and the hold-down bolt.

11   Tighten the hold-down bolt securely.
12   Reconnect the ignition wiring harness.
13   Install the distributor cap.
14   Reconnect the electrical connectors.
15   Check the ignition timing (see Section 9).

Installation (crankshaft turned after distributor removal)

16   Remove the number one spark plug.
17   Place your finger over the spark plug hole while turning the crankshaft with a wrench on the pulley bolt at the front of the engine.
18   When you feel compression, continue turning the crankshaft slowly until the timing mark on the vibration damper is aligned with the "0" on the engine timing indicator.
19   Position the rotor pointing toward the number one spark plug wire terminal on the distributor cap.
20   Perform Steps 9 through 15.

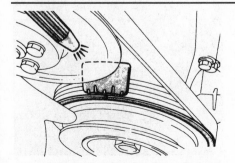

9.9 Check the position of the TDC (white) mark against the degree scale on the timing cover

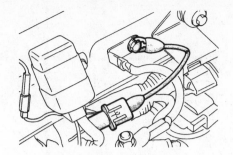

9.5 Ground the ignition test connecter with a jumper wire

9   Ignition timing - check and adjustment

Note: *It is imperative that the procedures included on the Vehicle Emissions Control Information label be followed when adjusting the ignition timing. The label will include all information concerning preliminary steps to be performed before adjusting the timing, as well as the timing specifications.*

1   Locate the VECI label under the hood and read through and perform all preliminary instructions concerning ignition timing.

1.8L engine

Refer to illustrations 9.3, 9.5, 9.8, 9.9 and 9.10

2   Apply the parking brake and block the wheels. Run the engine until the coolant reaches normal operating temperature. If the vehicle is equipped with an automatic transaxle, place the gear selector into Neutral or Park.
3   Install a paper clip into the CRC filter connector **(see illustration)** and attach a tachometer lead to the paper clip.
4   Check and adjust if necessary, the curb idle speed (refer to Section 15 in Chapter 4). It should be between 600 and 800 rpm.
5   Turn the engine off and connect a jumper lead between the terminal for ignition timing adjustment and a good ground **(see illustration)**. This will bypass the computer.
6   Locate the timing mark pointer plate located beside the crankshaft pulley. The 0 mark represents Top Dead Center (TDC). The

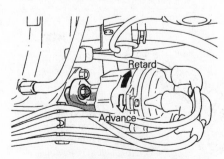

9.10 Turn the distributor one way or the other to advance or retard the ignition timing

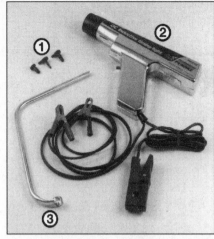

9.8 Tools needed to check and adjust the ignition timing

1   *Vacuum plugs* - Vacuum hoses will, in most cases, have to be disconnected and plugged. Molded plugs in various shapes and sizes are available for this.
2   *Inductive pick-up timing light* - Flashes a bright, concentrated beam of light when the number one spark plug fires. Connect the leads according to the instructions supplied with the light.
3   *Distributor wrench* - On some models, the hold-down bolt for the distributor is difficult to reach and turn with conventional wrenches or sockets. A special wrench like this must be used.

pointer plate will be marked in either one or two-degree increments and should have the proper timing mark for your particular engine noted. If not, count from the 0 mark the correct number of degrees BTDC, as noted on the VECI label, and mark the plate.
7   Locate the notch on the crankshaft pulley and mark it with chalk or a dab of paint so it will be visible under the timing light.
8   With the ignition off, connect the pick-up lead of the timing light to the number one spark plug wire. Use an inductive-type pick-up **(see illustration)**. Do not pierce the wire or attempt to insert a wire between the boot and the spark plug wire. Connect the timing light power leads according to the manufacturer's instructions.
9   Start the engine, aim the timing light at the timing mark by the crankshaft pulley and note which timing mark the notch on the pulley is lining up with **(see illustration)**.
10   If the notch is not lining up with the correct mark, loosen the distributor hold-down bolt and rotate the distributor **(see illustration)** until the notch is lined up with the correct timing mark. Refer to this Chapter's Specifications for the proper timing specification.
11   Retighten the hold-down bolt and recheck the timing.
12   Turn off the engine and disconnect the

5

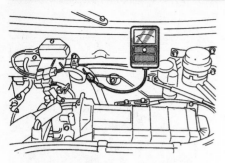

9.14 Install a paper clip into the tachometer connector on the firewall

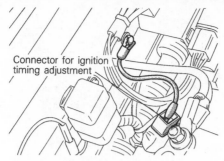

Connector for ignition timing adjustment

9.16 Ground the test connector for the ignition timing adjustment

9.21 Loosen the hold-down nuts and turn the camshaft sensor one way or the other to advance or retard the ignition timing

timing light. Reconnect the number one spark plug wire, if removed. Remove the jumper wires from the diagnostic terminals.

2.0L engines

Refer to illustrations 9.14, 9.16 and 9.21

13   Apply the parking brake and block the wheels. Run the engine until the coolant reaches normal operating temperature. Place the gear selector into Neutral.

14   Connect a tachometer to the tachometer connector, which is taped to the wiring harness on the firewall **(see illustration)**.

15   Check and adjust if necessary, the curb idle speed (refer to Section 15 in Chapter 4). It should be between 700 and 800 rpm.

16   Turn the engine off and ground the terminal for ignition timing adjustment with a jumper wire **(see illustration)**. This will bypass the computer.

17   Find the timing mark pointer plate located beside the crankshaft pulley. The 0 mark represents Top Dead Center (TDC). The pointer plate will be marked in either one or two-degree increments and should have the proper timing mark for your particular engine noted. If not, count from the 0 mark the correct number of degrees BTDC, as noted on the VECI label, and mark the plate.

18   Locate the notch on the crankshaft pulley and mark it with chalk or a dab of paint so it will be visible under the timing light.

19   With the ignition off, connect the pick-up lead of the timing light to the number one spark plug wire. Use an inductive-type pick-up. Do not pierce the wire or attempt to insert a wire between the boot and the spark plug wire. Connect the timing light power leads according to the manufacturer's instructions.

20   Start the engine, aim the timing light at the timing mark by the crankshaft pulley and note which timing mark the notch on the pulley is lining up with.

21   If the notch is not lining up with the correct mark, loosen the camshaft sensor hold-down nuts and rotate the sensor **(see illustration)** until the notch is lined up with the correct timing mark.

22   Tighten the hold-down nuts and recheck the timing.

23   Turn off the engine and disconnect the timing light. Reconnect the number one spark plug wire, if removed. Remove the jumper wires from the diagnostic terminals.

10   Ignition power transistor - check and replacement

Refer to illustrations 10.2, 10.3, 10.7, 10.9, 10.13, 10.15, 10.19 and 10.21

Check

1.8L engine

1   Check for a spark at the coil and spark plug wires (see Section 6).

2   If there is no spark, disconnect the distributor electrical connector. Connect two

jumper wires to a 1.5-volt battery **(see illustration)** and connect the negative (-) lead to terminal 5 and the positive (+) jumper lead to terminal 6.

3   Using an ohmmeter, measure the resistance of the power transistor across terminals 5 and 8 when the positive lead (+) is attached and then removed from terminal number 6 **(see illustration)**. There should be continuity when voltage is present and no continuity when the voltage is removed.

4   If the test results are incorrect, the distributor assembly must be replaced, as the power transistor is not available separately. **Note:** *Before replacing the distributor assembly, check on the availability of a solid state ignition unit (which consists of the internal workings of the distributor) or a rebuilt distributor on an exchange basis. Either of these options will cost considerably less than a new distributor.*

1990 2.0L engines

5   Check for a spark from the spark plug wires (see Section 6).

6   If there is no spark, disconnect the distributor electrical connector from the power transistor, which is mounted on the left (driver's) side of the intake manifold. Connect two jumper wires to a 1.5-volt battery **(see illustration 10.2)** and connect the negative (-) wire to terminal number 3 and the positive (+) jumper lead to terminal number 2.

7   First test the power transistor on the

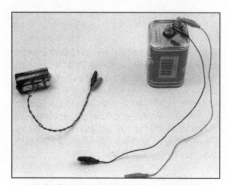

10.2 Certain electrical components require a small amount of voltage to test for continuity, open circuits or operation. The 1.5 volt is a D cell battery with jumper leads taped on while the 9 volt battery uses alligator clips to attach the jumper leads

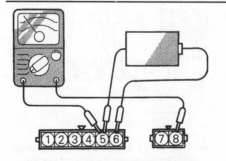

10.3 Terminal designations for checking the power transistor on the 1.8L engine

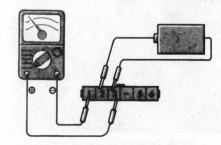

10.7 Terminal designations for checking cylinder numbers 1 and 4 of the the power transistor on the 1990 2.0L engine

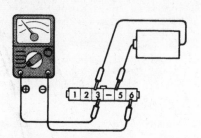

10.9 Terminal designations for checking cylinder numbers 2 and 3 of the the power transistor on the 1990 2.0L engine

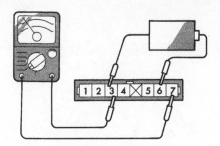

10.13 Terminal designations for checking cylinder numbers 1 and 4 of the the power transistor (1991 2.0L engine)

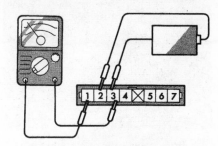

10.15 Terminal designations for checking cylinder numbers 2 and 3 of the the power transistor (1991 2.0L engine)

number 1 and 4 cylinders. Using an ohmmeter, measure the resistance of the power transistor on terminals number 1 and number 3 when the positive lead (+) is attached and then removed from terminal number 2 **(see illustration)**. There should be continuity when voltage is present and no continuity when the voltage is removed.

8   Next test the power transistor on the number 2 and 3 cylinders. Working with the 1.5 volt battery, position the negative (-) lead on terminal number 3 and the positive (+) jumper lead on terminal number 5.

9   Using an ohmmeter, measure the resistance of the power transistor on terminals 6 and 3 when the positive lead (+) is attached and then removed from terminal number 5 **(see illustration)**. There should be continuity when voltage is present and no continuity when the voltage is removed.

10   If the test results are incorrect, replace the ignition power transistor with a new part.

1991 2.0L engines

11   Check for a spark from the spark plug wires (see Section 6).

12   If there is no spark, disconnect the electrical connector from the power transistor, which is mounted on the left (driver's) side of the intake manifold. Connect two jumper wires to a 1.5-volt battery **(see illustration**

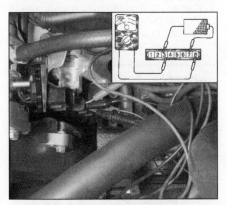

10.19 Terminal designations for checking cylinder numbers 1 and 4 of the the power transistor (1992 and later 2.0L engines)

10.2) and attach the negative (-) lead to terminal number 3 and the positive (+) jumper lead to terminal number 6.

13   First test the power transistor on the number 1 and 4 cylinders. Using an ohmmeter, measure the resistance of the power transistor across terminals 7 and 3 when the positive lead (+) is attached and then removed from terminal number 6 **(see illustration)**. There should be continuity when voltage is present and no continuity when the voltage is removed.

14   Next test the power transistor on the number 2 and 3 cylinders. Working with the 1.5 volt battery, connect the negative (-) jumper wire to terminal 3 and the positive (+) jumper wire to terminal number 2.

15   Using an ohmmeter, measure the resistance of the power transistor across terminals 1 and 3 when the positive lead (+) is attached and then removed from terminal number 2 **(see illustration)**. There should be continuity when voltage is present and no continuity when the voltage is removed.

16   If the test results are incorrect, replace the ignition power transistor with a new part.

1992 and later 2.0L engines

17   Check for a spark from the spark plug wires (see Section 6).

18   If there is no spark, disconnect the elec-

10.21 Terminal designations for checking cylinder numbers 2 and 3 of the the power transistor (1992 and later 2.0L engine)

trical connector from the power transistor, which is mounted on the left (driver's) side of the intake manifold. Connect two jumper wires to a 1.5-volt battery **(see illustration 10.2)** and attach the negative (-) jumper wire to terminal number 3 and the positive (+) jumper wire to terminal number 7.

19   First test the power transistor on the number 1 and 4 cylinders. Using an ohmmeter, measure the resistance of the power transistor across terminals 8 and 3 when the positive lead (+) is attached and then removed from terminal number 7 **(see illustration)**. There should be continuity when voltage is present and no continuity when the voltage is removed.

20   Next test the power transistor on the number 2 and 3 cylinders. Working with the 1.5 volt battery, connect the negative (-) jumper wire to terminal number 3 and the positive (+) jumper wire to terminal number 2.

21   Using an ohmmeter, measure the resistance of the power transistor across terminals 1 and 3 when the positive lead (+) is attached and then removed from terminal number 2 **(see illustration)**. There should be continuity when voltage is present and no continuity when the voltage is removed.

22   If the test results are incorrect, replace the ignition power transistor with a new part.

Replacement

1.8L engine

Note: *On 1.8L engines, the power transistor is not available separately - it's an integral part of the distributor. Before replacing the distributor assembly, check on the availability of a solid state ignition unit (which consists of the internal workings of the distributor) or a rebuilt distributor on an exchange basis. Either of these options will cost considerably less than a new distributor.*

2.0L engines

Refer to illustration 10.26

23   Detach the cable from the negative terminal of the battery.

24   Mark and detach the wires from the coil pack.

25   Disconnect the electrical connector from the power transistor.

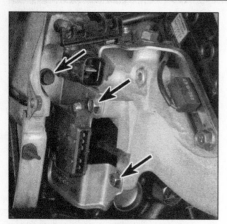

10.26 Remove the bolts (arrows) from the power transistor bracket and lift it off the intake manifold

26   Remove the attaching bolts **(see illustration)** and lift the power transistor from the engine.
27   Install the new power transistor and attach the electrical connectors.
28   Install the ignition wire set (see Chapter 1).
29   Attach the cable to the negative terminal of the battery.

11   Charging system - general information and precautions

General information

The charging systems used on the vehicles covered in this manual are equipped with internal regulation systems. This system incorporates a rectifier/voltage regulator/brush holder assembly that is mounted inside the alternator housing to the rear of the unit.

These models are equipped with either a 65, 75 or 90 amp alternator depending upon the engine size and if it is turbocharged. Perform the charging system checks (see Section 12) to diagnose any problems with the alternator.

The purpose of the voltage regulator is to limit the alternator's voltage to a preset value. This prevents power surges, circuit overloads, etc., during peak voltage output.

The rectifier/voltage regulator and the alternator brushes are mounted as a single assembly. This unit can be disassembled (see Section 15) and the components serviced individually.

The alternator on all models is mounted on the left end (driver's side) of the engine and utilizes a belt and pulley drive system. Drivebelt tension and battery service are the two primary maintenance requirements for these systems. See Chapter 1 for the procedures regarding engine drivebelt checking and battery servicing.

The charging system doesn't ordinarily require periodic maintenance. However, the drivebelt, battery and wires and connections

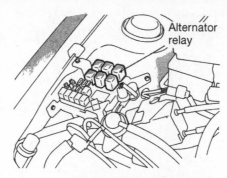

12.1 Location of the alternator relay in the engine compartment

should be inspected at the intervals outlined in Chapter 1.

The charging indicator light on the dash lights up when the ignition switch is turned on and goes out when the engine starts. If the lamp stays on or comes on once the engine is running, a charging system problem has occurred. See Section 12 for charging system diagnosis.

Precautions

Be very careful when making electrical circuit connections to a vehicle equipped with an alternator and note the following:

a)   *When reconnecting wires to the alternator from the battery, be sure to note the polarity.*
b)   *Before using arc welding equipment to repair any part of the vehicle, disconnect the wires from the alternator and the battery terminals.*
c)   *Never start the engine with a battery charger connected.*
d)   *Always disconnect both battery leads before using a battery charger.*
e)   *The alternator is turned by an engine drivebelt which could cause serious injury if your hands, hair or clothes become entangled in it with the engine running.*
f)   *Because the alternator is connected directly to the battery, it could arc or cause a fire if overloaded or shorted out.*
g)   *Wrap a plastic bag over the alternator and secure it with rubber bands before steam cleaning the engine.*

12   Charging system - check

Refer to illustration 12.1

1   If a malfunction occurs in the charging circuit, don't automatically assume that the alternator is causing the problem. First check the following items:

a)   *Check the drivebelt tension and condition (see Chapter 1). Replace it if it's worn or deteriorated.*
b)   *Make sure the alternator mounting and adjustment bolts are tight.*
c)   *Inspect the alternator wiring harness and the connectors at the alternator and*

voltage regulator. They must be in good condition and tight. **Note:** *Be sure to check the B+ terminal connector. Sometimes the connector will crimp and cause a voltage drop. This in turn will cause dim lights and inoperative accessories. This problem prevents the alternator's full output from reaching the entire electrical system.*
d)   *Check the fusible link (if equipped) located between the starter solenoid and the alternator. If it's burned, determine the cause, repair the circuit and replace the link (the vehicle won't start and/or the accessories won't work if the fusible link blows). Sometimes a fusible link may look good, but still be bad. If in doubt, remove it and check for continuity.*
e)   *Start the engine and check the alternator for abnormal noises (a shrieking or squealing sound indicates a bad bearing).*
f)   *Check the specific gravity of the battery electrolyte. If it's low, charge the battery (doesn't apply to maintenance free batteries).*
g)   *Make sure the battery is fully charged (one bad cell in a battery can cause overcharging by the alternator).*
h)   *Disconnect the battery cables (negative first, then positive). Inspect the battery posts and the cable clamps for corrosion. Clean them thoroughly if necessary (see Chapter 1) Reconnect the cable to the positive terminal.*
i)   *With the key off, connect a test light between the negative battery post and the disconnected negative cable clamp.*
    1)   *If the test light does not come on, reattach the clamp and proceed to Step 3.*
    2)   *If the test light comes on, there is a short (drain) in the electrical system of the vehicle. The short must be repaired before the charging system can be checked.*
j)   *If the charging light on the dash does not go ON when the ignition key is turned on before the engine is started, check the bulb.*
    1)   *If the light stays ON after the engine is started, check the voltage regulator.*
    2)   *If the light stays lit dimly, check the diode within the combination meter for a short circuit.*
    3)   *Also check the alternator relay. If there is a disconnected or damaged wire to the relay* **(see illustration)** *the system will experience charging problems and/or charging light problems. Check the relay as well as the wiring.*

2   Using a voltmeter, check the battery voltage with the engine off. If should be approximately 12-volts.
3   Start the engine and check the battery voltage again. It should now be approximately 14-to-15 volts.

13.6 Disconnect the alternator electrical connectors and the B+ terminal from the backside of the alternator (the B+ terminal is covered by the plastic cap)

4   Turn on the headlights. The voltage should drop, and then come back up, if the charging system is working properly.
5   If the voltage reading is more than the specified charging voltage, replace the voltage regulator (refer to Section 13). If the voltage is less, the alternator diode(s), stator or rectifier may be bad or the voltage regulator may be malfunctioning.

13.7 Remove the alternator pivot bolt

6   If the battery is constantly discharging, the alternator drivebelt is loose (see Chapter 1), the alternator brushes are worn, dirty or disconnected (see Section 14), the voltage regulator is malfunctioning (see Section 13) or the rectifier, stator coil or rotor coil is defective. Repairing or replacing the rectifier, stator coil or rotor coil is beyond the scope of the home mechanic. Replace the alternator.

13   Alternator - removal and installation

Refer to illustrations 13.6, 13.7 and 13.8
1   Detach the cable from the negative terminal of the battery.
2   On vehicles equipped with air conditioning, remove the condenser fan motor (see Chapter 3).
3   If you're working on a model with a 1.8L engine, remove the drivebelt from the air conditioning compressor (see Chapter 1).
4   Remove the alternator drivebelt.
5   Raise the vehicle and support it securely on jackstands. Remove the splash shield from the inner fender panel on the driver's side of the vehicle (see Chapter 11).
6   Detach the electrical connectors from the back of the alternator **(see illustration)**. Also remove the nut and detach the battery positive cable from the back of the alternator.
7   Working under the vehicle, remove the alternator pivot bolt **(see illustration)**.
8   Working inside the engine compartment, remove the upper mounting bolt and the alternator brace **(see illustration)**, if equipped.
9   Detach any wiring harness clips and remove the alternator from the vehicle.

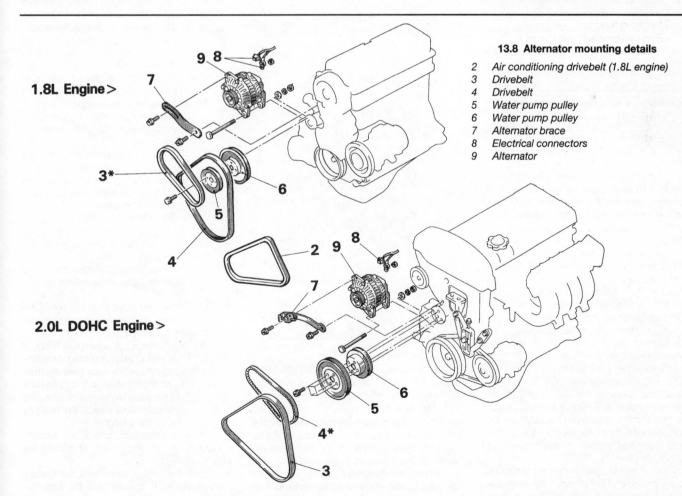

1.8L Engine >

2.0L DOHC Engine >

13.8 Alternator mounting details

2   *Air conditioning drivebelt (1.8L engine)*
3   *Drivebelt*
4   *Drivebelt*
5   *Water pump pulley*
6   *Water pump pulley*
7   *Alternator brace*
8   *Electrical connectors*
9   *Alternator*

14.2a Exploded view of the alternator

1	Alternator pulley	10	Plate
2	Seal	11	Regulator and
3	Rotor assembly		brush holder
4	Rear bearing	12	Brush
5	Bearing retainer	13	Brush spring
6	Front bearing	14	Slinger (if equipped)
7	Front case	15	Rectifier
8	Stator	16	Rear case
9	Terminal		

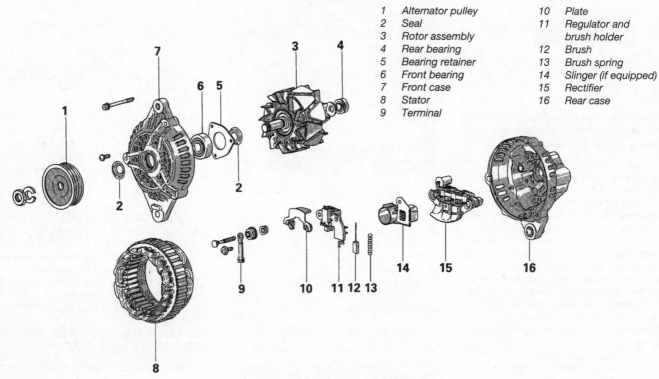

10   Installation is the reverse of the removal procedure.

14 Voltage regulator and alternator brushes - replacement

Refer to illustrations 14.2a, 14.2b, 14.5a, 14.5b, 14.6, 14.7a, 14.7b, 14.8 and 14.9

1   Remove the alternator from the vehicle (see Section 13).
2   Remove the nuts and separate the end cover from the alternator body **(see illustrations)**.

14.5b Remove the rotor assembly if it does not get removed with the front cover

14.2b Remove the bolts (arrows) from the alternator body

3   Mount the front of the alternator face down in a vise. Using rags as a cushion, clamp the front case portion of the alternator in the jaws of the vise.
4   Remove all the nuts from the back of the alternator.
5   Insert two standard screwdrivers into the two halves of the alternator (not too deep or you will damage the stator) and pry the rear case off the alternator **(see illustrations)**. **Caution:** *Pry gently or you will break the aluminum case.*
6   Unsolder the regulator/brush holder assembly **(see illustration)**. **Note:** *While applying heat to electrical components, it's a*

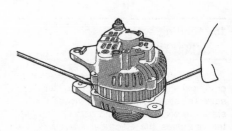

14.5a Use two screwdrivers to pry apart the alternator halves

14.6 To separate the brush holder from the regulator assembly, unsolder the two connectors (arrows)

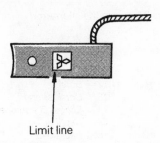

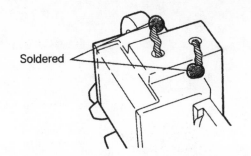

14.7a If the brushes are worn past the wear limit line, they should be replaced

good idea to use a pair of needle-nose pliers as a heat sink. Don't apply heat for more than about five seconds.

7   Measure the length of the brushes **(see illustration)**. Replace them if necessary by unsoldering them from the holder **(see illustration)**.

8   When installing new brushes, solder the pigtails so the brush limit line will be about 5/64 to 1/8-inch above the end of the brush holder **(see illustration)**.

9   To reassemble, compress the brushes into their holder and retain them with a straightened paper clip that can be pulled from the back of the alternator when reassembled **(see illustration)**.

10   The remainder of installation is the reverse of removal.

15   Starting system - general information

The function of the starting system is to crank the engine rapidly enough to allow it to start. The starting system is composed of the starter motor, solenoid and battery. The battery supplies the electrical energy to the solenoid, which then completes the circuit to the starter motor, which does the actual work of cranking the engine.

The solenoid and starter motor are mounted together at the rear side of the engine, bolted to the transaxle bellhousing. No periodic lubrication or maintenance is required.

The electrical circuitry of the vehicle is arranged so that the starter motor can only be operated when the clutch pedal is depressed (manual transaxle) or the transmission selector lever is in Park or Neutral (automatic transaxle).

Never operate the starter motor for more than 10 seconds at a time without pausing to allow it to cool for at least two minutes. Excessive cranking can cause overheating, which can seriously damage the starter.

16   Starter motor - testing in vehicle

Refer to illustration 16.6

1   If the starter motor does not turn at all when the ignition switch is operated, make

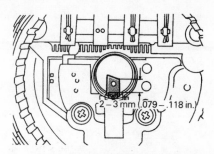

14.7b If the brushes are being replaced, unsolder and solder the pigtails at the area shown

sure the shift lever is in Neutral or Park (automatic transmission) or that the clutch pedal is depressed (manual transmission).

2   Make sure the battery is charged and that all cables, both at the battery and starter solenoid terminals, are secure.

3   If the starter motor spins but the engine is not cranking, the overrunning clutch in the starter motor is slipping and the motor must be removed from the engine for replacement.

4   If, when the switch is actuated, the starter motor does not operate at all but the solenoid clicks, then the problem lies with either the battery, the main solenoid contacts or the starter motor itself. **Note:** *Before diagnosing starter problems, make sure the battery is fully charged.*

5   If the solenoid plunger cannot be heard when the switch is actuated, the solenoid itself is defective or the solenoid circuit is open.

6   To check the solenoid, connect a jumper wire between the battery (+) and the "S" terminal on the solenoid. If the starter motor now operates, the solenoid is OK and the problem is in the ignition switch, neutral start switch, starter relay **(see illustration)** or in the wiring.

7   If the starter motor still does not operate, remove the starter/solenoid for disassembly, testing and repair.

8   If the starter motor cranks the engine at an abnormally slow speed, first make sure that the battery is charged and that all terminal connections are tight. If the engine is partially seized, or has the wrong viscosity oil in it, it will crank slowly.

9   Run the engine until normal operating temperature is reached, then disconnect the primary (low voltage) wires from the distributor (1.8L engine) or the coil pack (2.0L engines).

10   Connect a voltmeter positive lead to the starter motor terminal of the solenoid and connect the negative lead to ground.

11   Crank the engine and take the voltmeter readings as soon as a steady figure is indicated. Do not allow the starter motor to turn for more than 10 seconds at a time. A reading of 9-volts or more, with the starter motor turning at normal cranking speed, is normal.

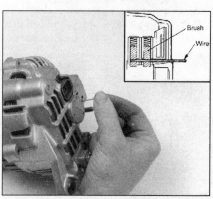

14.8 When installing new brushes, they should extend out of the holder the proper amount

14.9 When reassembling the two halves of the alternator, use a piece of wire inserted through the rear case and into the brush holder to retain the brushes in the holder

5

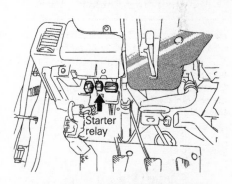

16.6 The starter relay is located under the dash on the driver's side. Remove the relay and check for battery voltage with the ignition key ON (engine not running). If the vehicle has a manual transmission, depress the clutch. If battery voltage is present, have the relay checked at an auto repair shop or dealer service department

If the reading is 9-volts or more but the cranking speed is slow, the motor is faulty. If the reading is less than 9-volts and the cranking speed is slow, the solenoid contacts are probably burned.

17.2 Remove the two bolts (arrows) that hold the battery tray to the inner fender panel

17.3 Working under the vehicle, remove the lower battery tray bolts

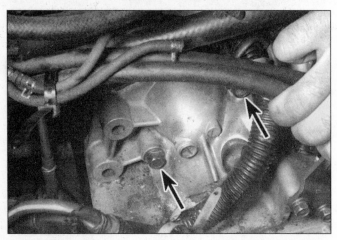

17.5 Remove the two starter motor mounting bolts (arrows)

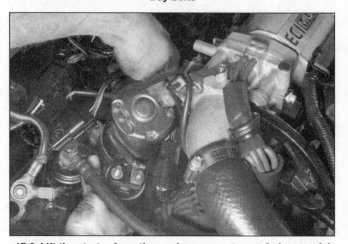

17.6 Lift the starter from the engine compartment, being careful not to damage any of the hoses or wiring harnesses

18.4a Exploded view of a direct drive starter motor

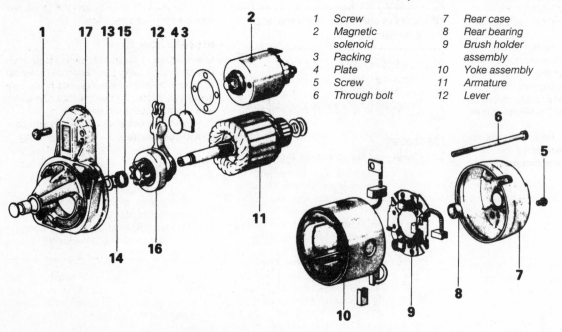

1	Screw	7	Rear case	13	Washer
2	Magnetic	8	Rear bearing	14	Snap-ring
	solenoid	9	Brush holder	15	Stop-ring
3	Packing		assembly	16	Overrunning
4	Plate	10	Yoke assembly		clutch
5	Screw	11	Armature	17	Front case
6	Through bolt	12	Lever		

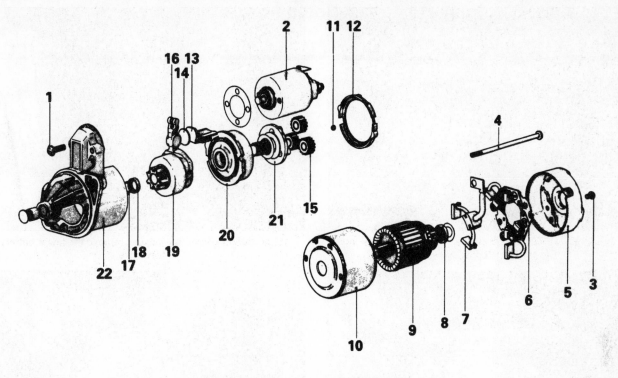

18.4b Exploded view of a gear reduction starter motor

1	Screw	7	Brush	13	Packing B	18	Stop-ring
2	Solenoid	8	Rear bearing	14	Plate	19	Overrunning clutch
3	Screw	9	Armature	15	Planetary gear	20	Internal gear
4	Screw	10	Yoke assembly	16	Lever	21	Planetary gear holder
5	Rear case	11	Ball	17	Snap-ring	22	Front case
6	Brush holder	12	Packing A				

17   Starter motor - removal and installation

Refer to illustration 17.2, 17.3, 17.5 and 17.6

1   Detach the cable from the negative terminal of the battery.

2   Remove the battery and the battery tray bolts that are accessible from the engine compartment **(see illustration)**.

3   Raise the vehicle and support it securely on jackstands. Remove the remaining bolts from the underside of the battery tray **(see illustration)**.

4   Detach the wires from the starter solenoid, then lower the vehicle.

5   Remove the two starter mounting bolts **(see illustration)**.

6   Remove the starter **(see illustration)**.

7   Installation is the reverse of removal.

18   Starter solenoid - removal and installation

Refer to illustrations 18.4a and 18.4b

1   Disconnect the cable from the negative terminal of the battery.

2   Remove the starter motor (see Section 17).

Removal

3   Disconnect the strap from the solenoid to the starter motor terminal.

4   Remove the two screws which secure the solenoid to the starter motor **(see illustrations)**.

5   Pull and lift slightly to disengage the flange from the starter body.

Installation

6   Make sure the return spring is in position on the solenoid, then insert the solenoid body into the starter housing and make sure the slotted portion of the solenoid arm aligns with the lever of the starter motor.

7   Install the two solenoid screws and connect the motor strap.

5

Notes

Chapter 6
Emissions and engine control systems

Contents

Specifications

EGR gas temperature sensor resistance
122-degrees F .... 60 to 83K ohms
212-degrees F .... 11 to 14K ohms

1   General information

Refer to illustrations 1.1a through 1.1l and 1.6

To minimize pollution of the atmosphere from incompletely burned and evaporating gases and to maintain good driveability and fuel economy, a number of emission control systems are used on these vehicles **(see illustrations)**. They include the:

Positive Crankcase Ventilation (PCV) system
Evaporative Emission Control (EVAP) system
Exhaust Gas Recirculation (EGR) system
Three way catalytic converter (TWC) system
Electronic Fuel Injection (EFI) system

The sections in this chapter include general descriptions, checking procedures within the scope of the home mechanic and component replacement procedures (when possible) for each of the systems listed above.

Before assuming an emissions control system is malfunctioning, check the fuel and ignition systems carefully (see Chapters 4 and 5). The diagnosis of some emission control devices requires specialized tools, equipment and training. If checking and servicing become too difficult or if a procedure is beyond the scope of your skills, consult your dealer service department or other repair shop.

This doesn't mean, however, that emission control systems are particularly difficult to maintain and repair. You can quickly and easily perform many checks and do most of the regular maintenance at home with common tune-up and hand tools. **Note:** *The most frequent cause of emissions problems is simply a loose or broken electrical connector or vacuum hose, so always check the electrical connectors and vacuum hoses first.*

Pay close attention to any special precautions outlined in this chapter. It should be noted that the illustrations of the various systems may not exactly match the system installed on your vehicle because of changes

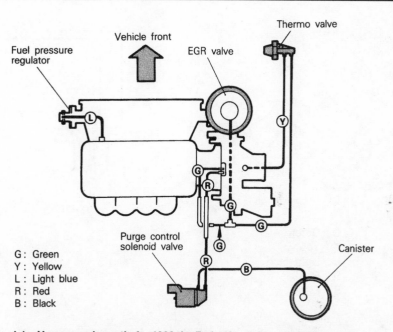

G : Green
Y : Yellow
L : Light blue
R : Red
B : Black

1.1a Vacuum schematic for 1990 the Federal and Canada 1.8L engine

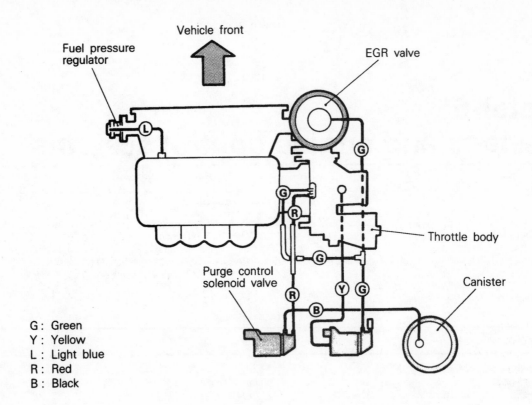

G : Green
Y : Yellow
L : Light blue
R : Red
B : Black

1.1b Vacuum schematic for the 1990 California 1.8L engine

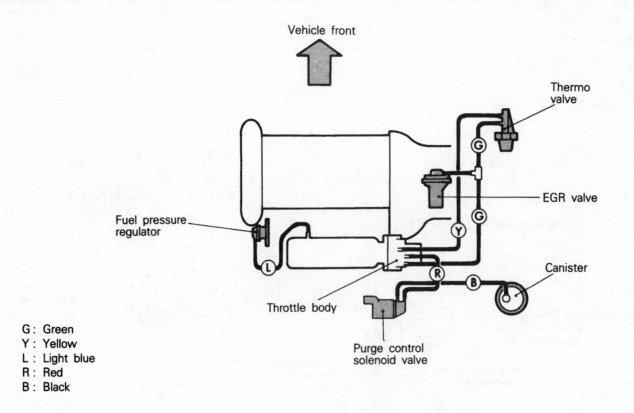

G : Green
Y : Yellow
L : Light blue
R : Red
B : Black

1.1c Vacuum schematic for the 1990 Federal and Canada 2.0L non-turbo engine

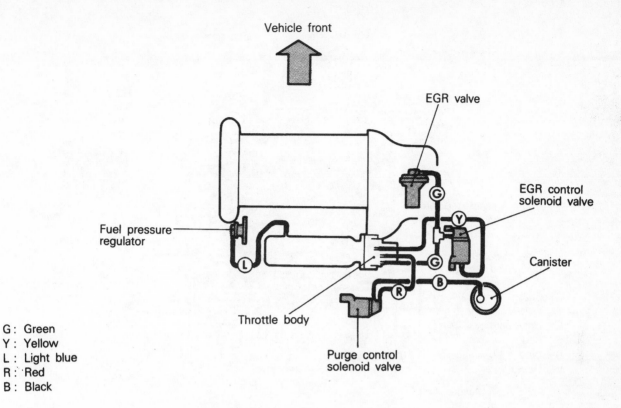

G : Green
Y : Yellow
L : Light blue
R : Red
B : Black

1.1d Vacuum schematic for the 1990 California 2.0L non-turbo engine

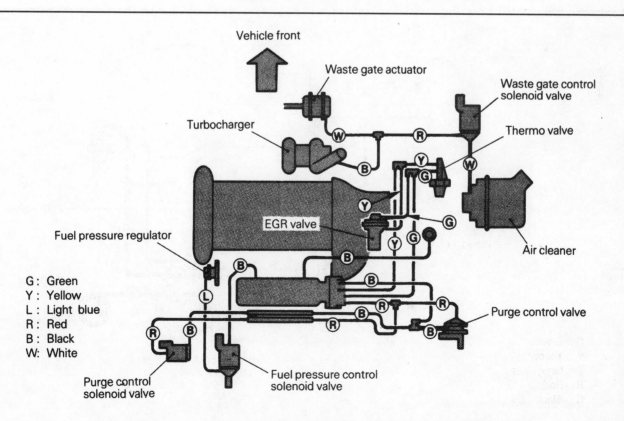

G : Green
Y : Yellow
L : Light blue
R : Red
B : Black
W : White

1.1e Vacuum schematic for the 1990 Federal and Canada 2.0L turbo engine

6

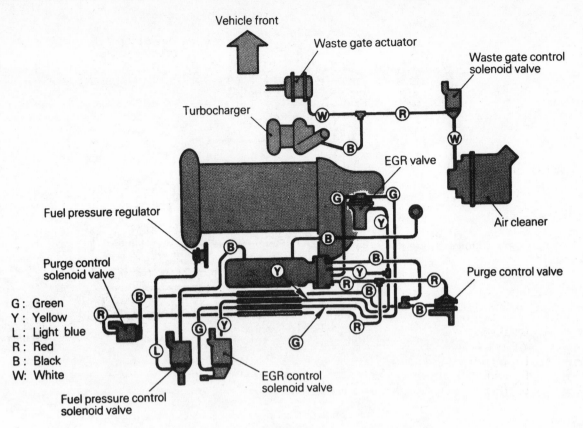

G : Green
Y : Yellow
L : Light blue
R : Red
B : Black
W: White

1.1f Vacuum schematic for the 1990 California 2.0L turbo engine

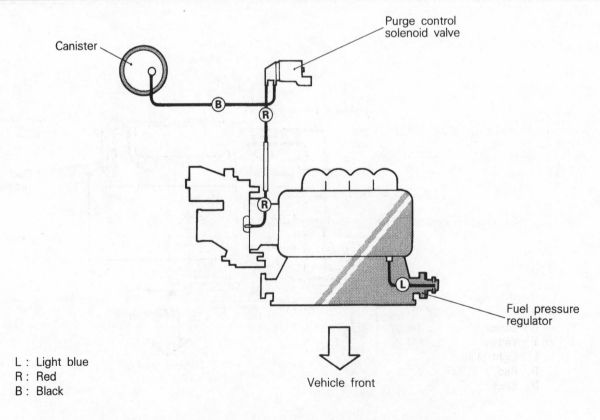

L : Light blue
R : Red
B : Black

1.1g Vacuum schematic for the 1991 and later Federal and Canada 1.8L engine

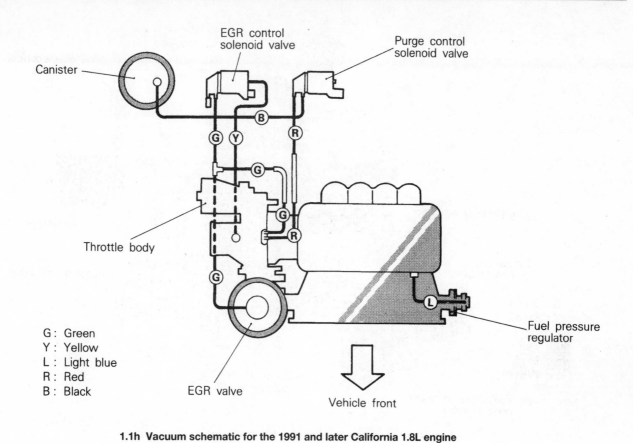

G : Green
Y : Yellow
L : Light blue
R : Red
B : Black

1.1h Vacuum schematic for the 1991 and later California 1.8L engine

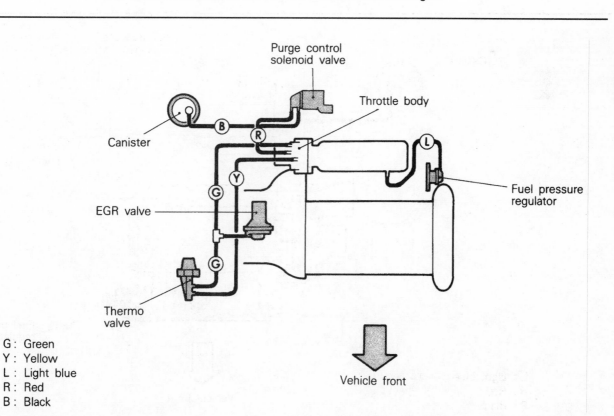

G : Green
Y : Yellow
L : Light blue
R : Red
B : Black

1.1i Vacuum schematic for the 1991 and later Federal and Canada 2.0L non-turbo engine

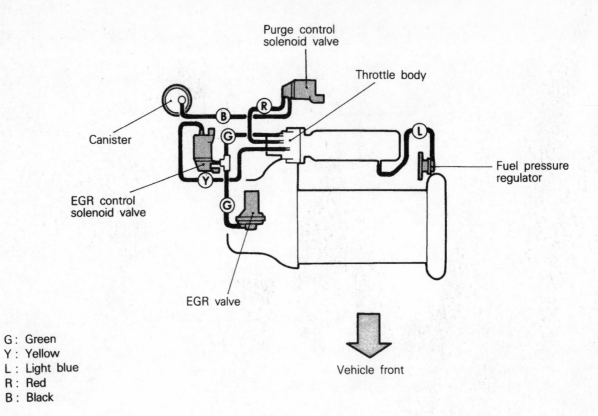

Purge control solenoid valve

Throttle body

Canister

Fuel pressure regulator

EGR control solenoid valve

EGR valve

G : Green
Y : Yellow
L : Light blue
R : Red
B : Black

Vehicle front

1.1j Vacuum schematic for the 1991 and later California 2.0L non-turbo engine

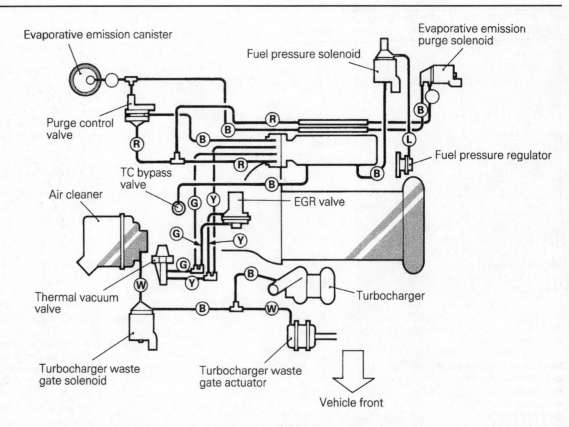

Evaporative emission canister

Fuel pressure solenoid

Evaporative emission purge solenoid

Purge control valve

Fuel pressure regulator

TC bypass valve

Air cleaner

EGR valve

Thermal vacuum valve

Turbocharger

G : Green
Y : Yellow
L : Light blue
R : Red
B : Black
W : White

Turbocharger waste gate solenoid

Turbocharger waste gate actuator

Vehicle front

1.1k Vacuum schematic for the 1991 and later Federal and Canada 2.0L turbo engine

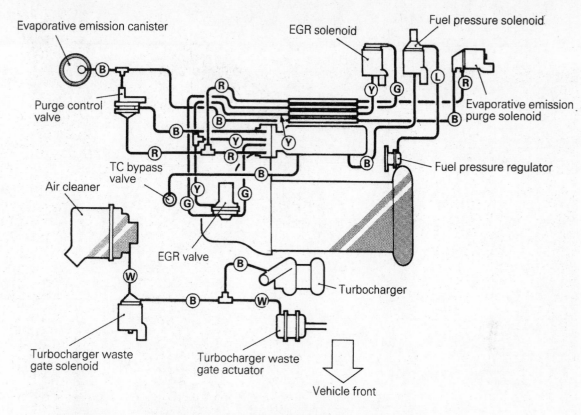

G : Green
Y : Yellow
L : Light blue
R : Red
B : Black
W : White

1.1l Vacuum schematic for the 1991 and later California 2.0L turbo engine

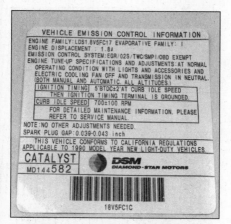

1.6 The Vehicle Emissions Control Information (VECI) label contains such essential information as the types of emission control systems installed on the engine and the idle speed and ignition timing specifications (1.8L engine shown)

made by the manufacturer during production or from year-to-year.

The Vehicle Emissions Control Information (VECI) label **(see illustration)** and a vacuum hose diagram are located on the underside of the hood. These contain important emissions specifications and setting procedures, and a vacuum hose schematic with emissions components identified. When servicing the engine or emissions systems, the VECI label in your particular vehicle should always be checked for up-to-date information.

2   Electronic control system

General description

Refer to illustrations 2.1a and 2.1b

The electronic control system controls the Multi Port Fuel Injection system and some emissions control devices by means of a microcomputer known as the Electronic Control Module (ECM).

The ECM receives signals from various sensors which monitor changing engine operating conditions such as intake air volume, intake air temperature, coolant temperature, engine rpm, acceleration/deceleration, exhaust oxygen content, etc. These signals are utilized by the ECM to determine the correct injection duration **(see illustrations)**.

The system is analogous to the central nervous system in the human body: The sensors (nerve endings) constantly relay signals to the ECM (brain), which processes the data and, if necessary, sends out a command to change the operating parameters of the engine (body).

Here's a specific example of how one portion of this system operates: An oxygen sensor, located in the exhaust manifold, constantly monitors the oxygen content of the exhaust gas. If the percentage of oxygen in the exhaust gas is incorrect, an electrical signal is sent to the ECM. The ECM takes this information, processes it and then sends a command to the fuel injection system telling it to change the air/fuel mixture. This happens in a fraction of a second and it goes on continuously when the engine is running. The end result is an air/fuel mixture ratio which is constantly maintained at a predetermined ratio, regardless of driving conditions.

In the event of a sensor malfunction, a backup circuit will take over to provide driveability until the problem is identified and fixed.

Precautions

a) *Always disconnect the power by either turning off the ignition switch or disconnecting the battery terminals before removing electrical connectors.*

b) *When installing a battery, be particularly careful to avoid reversing the positive and negative battery cables.*

c) *Do not subject EFI, emissions related components or the ECM to severe impact during removal or installation.*

d) *Do not be careless during troubleshooting. Even slight terminal contact can invalidate a testing procedure and damage one of the numerous transistor circuits.*

e) *Never attempt to work on the ECM or open the ECM cover. The ECM is pro-*

6

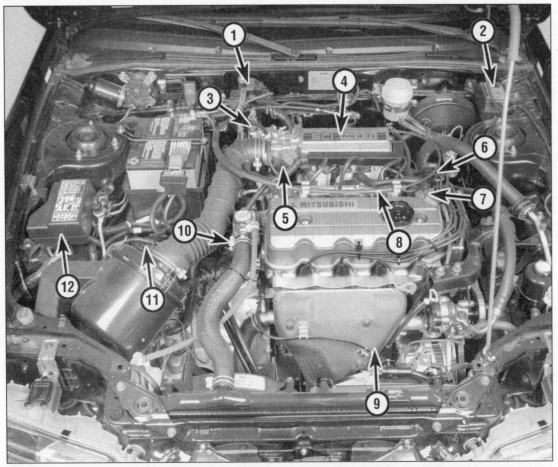

2.1a Emission and engine control components on the 1.8L SOHC engine

1   Purge control solenoid
2   Fuse box
3   Idle Speed Control (ISC) motor
4   Air intake plenum
5   Throttle Position Sensor (TPS)
6   Crankshaft position sensor (contained within distributor)
7   PCV valve
8   Fuel injector
9   Oxygen sensor (in exhaust manifold but not visible in photo)
10 Coolant temperature sensor (under thermostat housing)
11 Airflow meter assembly (contained within air cleaner housing)
12 Relay and fuse center

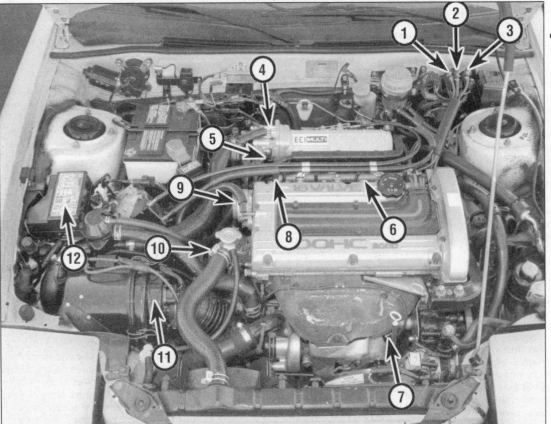

2.1b Emission and engine control components on the 2.0L DOHC engine (turbo model shown, non-turbo similar)

1   Purge control solenoid
2   Fuel pressure solenoid (turbo engines only)
3   EGR solenoid
4   Idle speed control (ISC) motor
5   Throttle Position Sensor (TPS)
6   Fuel injector
7   Oxygen sensor
8   PCV valve
9   Crankshaft position sensor
10 Coolant temperature sensor (under thermostat housing)
11 Airflow meter assembly (contained within air cleaner housing)
12 Relay and fuse center

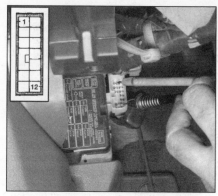

3.4 To output any stored trouble codes, locate the test terminal under the driver's side of the dash and, using an analog type voltmeter, connect the probes to terminals 1 and 12

4.2 To check the coolant temperature sensor, use an ohmmeter to measure the resistance between the two sensor terminals

tected by a government mandated extended warranty that will be nullified if you tamper with or damage the ECM.

f) If you are inspecting electronic control system components during rainy weather, make sure that water does not enter any part. When washing the engine compartment, do not spray these parts or their electrical connectors with water.

3   Diagnosis system - general information and obtaining code output

General description

1   The ECM contains a built-in self-diagnosis system which detects and identifies malfunctions occurring in the network. When the ECM detects a problem, three things happen: the CHECK ENGINE light comes on, the trouble is identified and a diagnostic code is stored in the computer's memory. The ECM stores the failure code assigned to the specific problem area until the diagnosis system is canceled by removing the STOP fuse with the ignition switch off.

2   The CHECK ENGINE warning light, which is located on the instrument panel, comes on when the ignition switch is turned to On and the engine is not running. When the engine is started, the warning light should go out. If the light remains on, the diagnosis system has detected a malfunction in the system.

Obtaining diagnostic code output

Refer to illustration 3.4

3   To obtain an output of diagnostic codes, verify first that the battery voltage is above 11 volts, the throttle is fully closed, the transaxle is in Neutral, the accessory switches are off and the engine is at normal operating temperature.

4   Connect an analog voltmeter between terminal numbers 12 and 1 of the data link connector located under the driver's side under the dash **(see illustration)**. **Note:** *Use only an analog type voltmeter because it will be necessary to observe the sweeps of the needle to determine the trouble codes.*

5   Turn the ignition switch to On, but don't start the engine.

6   Read the diagnosis code as indicated by the number of sweeps from the needle on the voltmeter. Normal system operation is indicated by Code No. 1 (On, Off, pause, next trouble code, if any) on all models. The voltmeter displays a Code No. 1 by a single sweep of the needle through a 0 to 12-volt range, repeating constantly. This is exactly the opposite of NO CODE when the ECM is faulty and the needle on the voltmeter will remain on 12 volts and not move at all.

7   If there are any malfunctions in the system, their corresponding trouble codes are stored in computer memory and the voltmeter needle will sweep the requisite number of times for the indicated trouble codes. Single digit codes will sweep the designated number of times with a short pause between each count (sweep). All double digit numbers will count (sweep) the first digit first, with a longer pause between digits. The second digit of the number will be counted with a normal pause between counts (sweeps). For example: Code 24, vehicle speed sensor (VSS) will be indicated on the voltmeter with two slow sweeps of the needle, pause, then four quick sweeps of the needle. If there's more than one trouble code in the memory, they'll be displayed in numerical order (from lowest to highest) with a pause interval between each one. After the code with the largest number of sweeps (counts) has been displayed, there will be another pause and then the sequence will begin all over again.

8   To ensure correct interpretation of the sweeps on the voltmeter, watch carefully for the interval between the end of one code and the beginning of the next (otherwise, you will become confused by the apparent number of sweeps and misinterpret the display).

Canceling a diagnostic code

9   After the malfunctioning component has been repaired/replaced, the trouble code(s) stored in computer memory must be canceled. To accomplish this, simply remove the negative battery cable from the battery for at least 10 seconds with the ignition switch off.

10   Cancellation by removing the cable from the battery negative terminal will effect other systems (such as the clock will also be canceled).

11   If the diagnosis code is not canceled, it will be stored by the ECM and appear with any new codes in the event of future trouble.

12   Should it become necessary to work on engine components requiring removal of the battery terminal, first check to see if a diagnostic code has been recorded.

4   Information sensors

Note: *Most of the components described in this section are protected by a Federally-mandated extended warranty. See your dealer for the details regarding your vehicle. It therefore makes little sense to either check or replace any of these parts yourself as long as they are still under warranty. However, once the warranty has expired, you may wish to perform some of the component checks and/or replacement procedures in this Chapter to save money.*

Note: *Refer to Chapters 4 and 5 for additional information on the location and the diagnostics of the information sensors that are not directly covered in this section.*

Coolant temperature sensor

Refer to illustrations 4.2 and 4.3

General description

1   The coolant temperature sensor is a thermistor (a resistor which varies the value of its resistance in accordance with temperature changes). The change in the resistance values will directly affect the voltage signal from the coolant temperature sensor. As the sensor temperature DECREASES, the resistance values will INCREASE. As the sensor temperature INCREASES, the resistance values will DECREASE. A failure in this sensor circuit should set a Code 21. This code indicates a failure in the coolant temperature sensor circuit, so in most cases the appropriate solution to the problem will be either repair of a wire or replacement of the sensor.

Check

2   To check the sensor, check the resistance value **(see illustration)** of the coolant temperature sensor while it is completely cold (50 to 80-degrees F = 2,200 to 2,700 ohms). Next, start the engine and warm it up until it reaches operating temperature. The resistance should be lower (180 to 200-degrees F = 280 to 350 ohms). **Note:** *Access to the coolant temperature sensor makes it difficult to position test probes on the termi-*

6

Diagnostic trouble code		Diagnostic item	Check item (Remedy)	Memory
No.	Output signal pattern			
–	H L ⎍‾‾‾‾‾‾	Engine control module (see Section 3)	(Replace engine control module)	–
11	H L ⎍⎍‾	Oxygen sensor (see Section 4)	• Harness and connector • Oxygen sensor • Fuel pressure • Injectors (Replace if defective.) • Intake air leaks	Retained
12	H L ⎍⎍⎍	Volume air flow sensor (see Section 4)	• Harness and connector (If harness and connector are normal, replace volume air flow sensor assembly.)	Retained
13	H L ⎍⎍⎍⎍	Intake air temperature sensor (see Section 4)	• Harness and connector • Intake air temperature sensor	Retained
14	H L ⎍⎍⎍⎍⎍	Throttle position sensor (see Section 4)	• Harness and connector • Throttle position sensor • Closed throttle position switch	Retained
15	H L ⎍⎍⎍⎍⎍⎍	Idle speed control motor position sensor (see Section 4)	• Harness and connector • Idle speed control motor position sensor • Throttle position sensor	Retained
21	H L ⎍⎍⎍⎍	Engine coolant temperature sensor (see Section 4)	• Harness and connector • Engine coolant temperature sensor	Retained
22	H L ⎍⎍⎍⎍⎍	Crankshaft position sensor (see Section 4)	• Harness and connector (If harness and connector are normal, replace distributor assembly.)	Retained

Self-diagnosis code chart for 1.8L engines

Diagnostic trouble code		Diagnostic item	Check item (Remedy)	Memory
No.	Output signal pattern			
23	H ⎍ L pattern	Camshaft position sensor (see Section 4)	• Harness and connector (If harness and connector are normal, replace distributor assembly.)	Retained
24	H ⎍ L pattern	Vehicle speed sensor (reed switch) (see Section 4)	• Harness and connector • Vehicle speed sensor (reed switch)	Retained
25	H ⎍ L pattern	Barometric pressure sensor (see Section 4)	• Harness and connector (If harness and connector are normal, replace barometric pressure sensor assembly.)	Retained
36	H ⎍ L pattern	Ignition timing adjustment signal (1991 on) (see Section 6)	• Harness and connector	–
41	H ⎍ L pattern	Injector (see Section 4)	• Harness and connector • Injector coil resistance	Retained
42	H ⎍ L pattern	Fuel pump (see Section 4)	• Harness and connector • MFI relay	Retained
43	H ⎍ L pattern	EGR <California> (see Section 6)	• Harness and connector • EGR temperature sensor • EGR valve • EGR solenoid • EGR valve control vacuum	Retained
–	H ⎍ L pattern	Normal state	–	–

Self-diagnosis code chart for 1.8L engines

6

Diagnostic trouble code		Diagnostic item	Check item (Remedy)	Memory
No.	Output signal pattern			
–	H ⎍ L	Engine control module (see Section 3)	(Replace engine control module)	–
11	H L	Heated oxygen sensor (see Section 4)	• Harness and connector • Heated oxygen sensor • Fuel pressure • Injectors (Replace if defective.) • Intake air leaks	Retained
12	H L	Volume air flow sensor (see Section 4)	• Harness and connector (If harness and connector are normal, replace volume air flow sensor assembly.)	Retained
13	H L	Intake air temperature sensor (see Section 4)	• Harness and connector • Intake air temperature sensor	Retained
14	H L	Throttle position sensor (see Section 4)	• Harness and connector • Throttle position sensor • Closed throttle position switch	Retained
21	H L	Engine coolant temperature sensor (see Section 4)	• Harness and connector • Engine coolant temperature sensor	Retained
22	H L	Crankshaft position sensor (see Section 4)	• Harness and connector (If harness and connector are normal, replace crankshaft position assembly.)	Retained
23	H L	Camshaft position sensor (see Section 4)	• Harness and connector (If harness and connector are normal, replace crankshaft position assembly.)	Retained

Self-diagnosis code chart for 2.0L engines

Diagnostic trouble code		Diagnostic item	Check item (Remedy)	Memory
No.	Output signal pattern			
24	H ___ L ___	Vehicle speed sensor (reed switch) (see Section 4)	• Harness and connector • Vehicle speed sensor (reed switch)	Retained
25	H ___ L ___	Barometric pressure sensor (see Section 4)	• Harness and connector (If harness and connector are normal, replace barometric pressure sensor assembly.)	Retained
31	H ___ L ___	Knock sensor <Turbo> (see Section 4)	• Harness and connector (If harness and connector are normal, replace knock sensor.)	Retained
41	H ___ L ___	Injector (see Section 4)	• Harness and connector • Injector coil resistance	Retained
42	H ___ L ___	Fuel pump (see Section 4)	• Harness and connector • MFI relay	Retained
43	H ___ L ___	EGR <California> (see Section 6)	• Harness and connector • EGR temperature sensor • EGR valve • EGR solenoid • EGR valve control vacuum	Retained
44	H ___ L ___	Ignition coil, Ignition power transistor unit (see Section 5)	• Harness and connector • Ignition coil • Ignition power transistor	Retained
–	H ___ L ___	Normal state	–	–

Self-diagnosis code chart for 2.0L engines

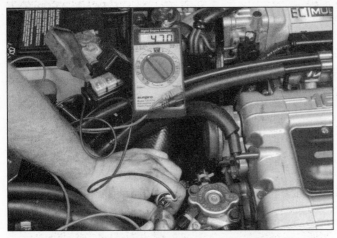

4.3 Use a voltmeter to check the signal voltage at the coolant temperature sensor connector (ignition key On, engine not running) - it should read between 4.5 to 4.9 volts

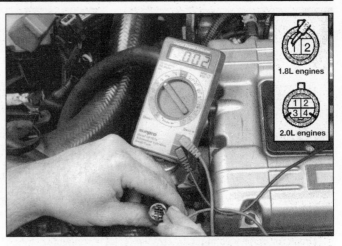

4.13 Working on the oxygen sensor side of the electrical connector, check for voltage output on the number 2 terminal on 2.0L engines or number 1 terminal on 1.8L engines. There should be 0 to 0.4 volts at idle and 0.5 to 1.0 volts at high rpm

nals. *If necessary, remove the sensor and perform the tests in a pan of heated water to simulate the conditions.*

3   If the resistance values of the coolant temperature sensor are correct, check the circuit for the proper signal voltage. Turn the ignition key ON (engine not running) and check for signal voltage **(see illustration)**. It should be approximately 4.5 to 4.9 volts.

Replacement

4   To remove the sensor, depress the locking tabs, unplug the electrical connector, then carefully unscrew the sensor.

5   Before installing the new sensor, wrap the threads with Teflon sealing tape to prevent leakage and thread corrosion. **Caution:** *Handle the coolant sensor with care. Damage to this sensor will affect the operation of the entire fuel injection system.*

6   Installation is the reverse of removal.

Oxygen sensor

General description

7   The oxygen sensor, which is located in the exhaust manifold, monitors the oxygen content in the exhaust gas stream. The oxygen content in the exhaust reacts with the oxygen sensor to produce a voltage output which varies from 0.1-volt (high oxygen, lean mixture) to 0.9-volts (low oxygen, rich mixture). The ECM constantly monitors this variable voltage output to determine the ratio of oxygen to fuel in the mixture. The ECM alters the air/fuel mixture ratio by controlling the pulse width (open time) of the fuel injectors. A mixture ratio of 14.7 parts air to 1 part fuel is the ideal mixture ratio for minimizing exhaust emissions, thus allowing the catalytic converter to operate at maximum efficiency. It is this ratio of 14.7 to 1 which the ECM and the oxygen sensor attempt to maintain at all times.

8   The oxygen sensor produces no voltage

when it is below its normal operating temperature of about 600-degrees F. During this initial period before warm-up, the ECM operates in open loop mode.

9   If the engine reaches normal operating temperature and/or has been running for two or more minutes, and if the oxygen sensor is producing a steady signal voltage below 0.45-volts at 1,500 rpms or greater, the ECM will set a Code 11. Code 11 will also set if there is a problem with the oxygen sensor heater circuit (2.0L engines only).

10   When there is a problem with the oxygen sensor or its circuit, the ECM operates in the open loop mode - that is, it controls fuel delivery in accordance with a programmed default value instead of feedback information from the oxygen sensor.

11   The proper operation of the oxygen sensor depends on four conditions:

a) *Electrical - The low voltages generated by the sensor depend upon good, clean connections which should be checked whenever a malfunction of the sensor is suspected or indicated.*

b) *Outside air supply - The sensor is designed to allow air circulation to the internal portion of the sensor. Whenever the sensor is removed and installed or replaced, make sure the air passages are not restricted.*

c) *Proper operating temperature - The ECM will not react to the sensor signal until the sensor reaches approximately 600-degrees F. This factor must be taken into consideration when evaluating the performance of the sensor.*

d) *Unleaded fuel - The use of unleaded fuel is essential for proper operation of the sensor. Make sure the fuel you are using is of this type.*

12   In addition to observing the above conditions, special care must be taken whenever the sensor is serviced.

a) *The oxygen sensor has a permanently attached pigtail and electrical connector which should not be removed from the sensor. Damage or removal of the pigtail or electrical connector can adversely affect operation of the sensor.*

b) *Grease, dirt and other contaminants should be kept away from the electrical connector and the louvered end of the sensor.*

c) *Do not use cleaning solvents of any kind on the oxygen sensor.*

d) *Do not drop or roughly handle the sensor.*

e) *The silicone boot must be installed in the correct position to prevent the boot from being melted and to allow the sensor to operate properly.*

Check

Refer to illustrations 4.13, 4.16, 4.17 and 4.18

13   Warm up the engine and let it run at idle. Disconnect the oxygen sensor electrical connector and connect the positive probe of a voltmeter to the oxygen sensor connector terminal **(see illustration)** and the negative probe to ground.

14   Increase and then decrease the engine speed and monitor the voltage.

15   When the speed is increased, the voltage should increase to 0.5 to 1.0 volts. When the speed is decreased, the voltage should decrease to about 0 to 0.4 volts.

16   Check for supply voltage to the oxygen sensor with the ignition key ON (engine not running). Working on the harness side, check for battery voltage **(see illustration)**.

17   Also inspect the oxygen sensor heater on 2.0L engines. Disconnect the oxygen sensor electrical connector and connect an ohmmeter between terminal numbers 3 and 4 **(see illustration)**. There should be approximately 12 ohms at 68-degrees F.

18   Also inspect the oxygen sensor heater ground circuit on 2.0L engines. Disconnect

4.16 Working on the harness side of the oxygen sensor electrical connector, check for battery voltage on terminal number 3 on 2.0L engines

4.17 On 2.0L engines, working on the oxygen sensor side of the harness connector, check the resistance across terminals number 3 and number 4 - it should be approximately 12 ohms at 68-degrees F

4.18 On 2.0L engines, check the oxygen sensor circuit ground on terminal number 2, then number 4 (there should be continuity)

the oxygen sensor electrical connector and connect the leads of an ohmmeter between terminal numbers 2 and 4, in turn, and ground **(see illustration)**. There should be continuity.

19   Also, check the output voltage of the oxygen sensor at different rpm ranges.

Replacement

Refer to illustration 4.23

Note: *Because it is installed in the exhaust manifold or pipe, which contracts when cool, the oxygen sensor may be very difficult to loosen when the engine is cold. Rather than risk damage to the sensor (assuming you are planning to reuse it in another manifold or pipe), start and run the engine for a minute or two, then shut it off. Be careful not to burn yourself during the following procedure.*

20   Disconnect the cable from the negative terminal of the battery.

21   Raise the vehicle and place it securely on jackstands.

22   Carefully disconnect the electrical connector from the sensor.

23   Unscrew the oxygen sensor **(see illustration)**. **Caution:** *Excessive force may damage the threads.*

24   Anti-seize compound must be used on the threads of the sensor to facilitate future

removal. The threads of new sensors will already be coated with this compound, but if an old sensor is removed and reinstalled, recoat the threads.

25   Install the sensor and tighten it securely.

26   Reconnect the electrical connector of the pigtail lead to the main engine wiring harness.

27   Lower the vehicle and reconnect the cable to the negative terminal of the battery.

Throttle Position Sensor (TPS)

General description

28   The Throttle Position Sensor (TPS) is located on the end of the throttle shaft on the throttle body (see Section 13 in Chapter 4). By monitoring the output voltage from the TPS, the ECM can determine fuel delivery based on throttle valve angle (driver demand). A broken or loose TPS can cause intermittent bursts of fuel from the injector and an unstable idle because the ECM thinks the throttle is moving.

Check

Refer to illustrations 4.29, 4.31 and 4.32

Note: *The ISC motor and idle speed adjust-*

ment is performed in conjunction with the TPS adjustment procedure. Refer to Chapter 4, Section 15 for the ISC motor adjustment.

29   To check the TPS, first check the resistance with the throttle closed. Connect the probes of an ohmmeter to the designated terminals of the TPS electrical connector, sensor side **(see illustration)**.

   a) 1990 1.8L engines - terminals 2 and 1
   b) 1990 2.0L engines - terminals 2 and 3
   c) 1991 and later (all engines) - terminals 4 and 1

30   The sensor should read 3.5 to 6.5K ohms.

31   Also, check the TPS resistance through its complete range of motion from closed to open. First unplug the electrical connector and connect the probes **(see illustration)** to the proper terminals.

   a) 1990 1.8L engines terminals 2 and 3
   b) 1990 2.0L engines terminals 2 and 4
   c) 1991 and later (all engines) terminals 4 and 2

Slowly move the throttle valve and observe a distinct change in the resistance values as the sensor travels from idle to full throttle. The resistance should range from 1,100 to

6

4.23 Special slotted sockets are available to ease removal of the oxygen sensor

4.29 Connect the probes of the ohmmeter to the designated terminals and, with the throttle fully closed, check the resistance

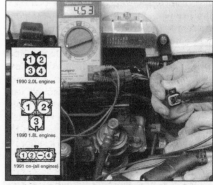

4.31 Connect the probes of the ohmmeter to the designated terminals, and while moving the throttle valve from closed to open, observe that the resistance fluctuates evenly

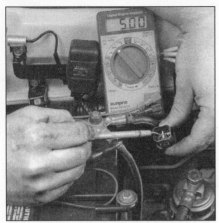

4.32 With the ignition key ON (engine not running), probe the harness for the signal voltage terminal - the meter should read approximately 5.0 volts

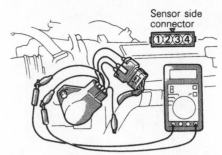

1990 2.0L engines

1990 1.8L engines

4.33 Unplug the connector from the TPS, connect jumper wires between the corresponding terminals and check the TPS output voltage with the throttle fully closed. On 1990 1.8L engines, probe terminals 2 and 3. On all other engines, probe terminals 2 and 4. It should read 0.48 to 0.52 volts. Note: *Be sure the negative probe of the voltmeter is attached to the green/black wire.*

4.40a With the ignition key ON, check the signal voltage to the airflow meter by probing terminal 1 (non-turbo engines) or terminal 2 (turbo engine). It should be between 4.8 and 5.2 volts

4.40b With the ignition key ON, check the battery voltage to the airflow meter by probing terminal number 2 on non-turbo engines or terminal number 3 on turbo engines. It should read approximately 12 volts if the battery is fully charged

5,600 ohms. If the TPS does not perform as indicated, replace it with a new one.

32   Working on the harness side of the electrical connector, probe each terminal and check for signal voltage with the ignition key ON (engine not running) **(see illustration)**. It should be approximately 5.0 volts. If the TPS circuit is faulty, refer to the *wiring diagrams* in Chapter 12. A problem in any of the TPS circuits will set a Code 14. Once a trouble code is set, the ECM will use an artificial default value for the TPS and some vehicle performance will return.

Adjustment

Refer to illustration 4.33

33   The TPS must be adjusted in the event it is replaced or if there is a problem with the idle speed control. Unplug the electrical connector from the TPS, attach jumper wires between the corresponding terminals and probe the indicated wires on the TPS using a voltmeter to determine the output voltage **(see illustration)**. The voltmeter should read 0.48 to 0.52 volts. If it is out of adjustment, turn the ignition key ON (engine not running), loosen the throttle position sensor mounting screws and rotate the sensor clockwise (increase output voltage) or counterclockwise (decrease output voltage). Should the TPS require replacement, the complete procedure is contained in Chapter 4, Section 13. **Note:** *If the TPS adjustment is performed in conjunction with the ISC motor adjustment, be sure to detach the negative battery cable for more than 10 seconds to clear any diagnostic data accumulated during testing.*

Closed throttle position switch

General description and check

34   The closed throttle position switch or idle position switch senses accelerator operation. The switch is located at the tip of the ISC motor on some models or on the throttle body as a separate switch on other models. If the switch is integrated within the ISC motor,

refer to Chapter 4, Section 15 for the diagnostic procedure. If it is a separate switch (identified with a single electrical connector) follow this simple test.

35   Connect the terminals of an ohmmeter to the terminal of the switch and ground and check for continuity. With the throttle fully closed, there should be continuity. With the throttle open, there should be no continuity. If the test results are incorrect, replace the switch with a new part.

36   If the switch is integrated within the ISC motor, replace the ISC motor.

Airflow meter

General description

37   The airflow meter is located in the air cleaner housing. The airflow meter measures the amount of air entering the engine. The ECM uses this information to control fuel delivery. A large volume of air indicates acceleration, while a small volume of air indicates deceleration or idle. The airflow meter is equipped with an intake air temperature (IAT) sensor as well as a barometric pressure sensor as a single integral unit. Any malfunctions with the airflow meter will be recorded as Code 12.

Check

Refer to illustrations 4.40a and 4.40b

38   Remove the airflow meter (see Steps 42 through 47).

39   Check the airflow meter for cracks or any obvious damage.

40   Disconnect the harness connector, turn

the ignition key ON (engine not running) and working on the harness side, check for signal voltage and battery voltage(**see illustrations**)

41   If the supply (battery) voltage is correct but the signal voltage reading is incorrect, the airflow meter may be faulty. **Note:** *A special scan tool is required to test the airflow meter. If you suspect the airflow meter is defective, have it meter tested at a dealer service department or other qualified repair shop.*

Removal and installation

Refer to illustration 4.45

42   Remove the air filter (see Chapter 1).

43   Disconnect the electrical connector from the meter.

44   Loosen the hose clamp.

45   Remove the screws that retain the airflow meter to the housing **(see illustration)**.

46   Separate the airflow meter from the air cleaner housing.

47   Installation is the reverse of removal.

4.45 Working outside the airflow meter housing, remove the screws (arrows) that retain the airflow meter to the housing

Intake Air Temperature (IAT) sensor

General description

48   The Intake Air Temperature (IAT) sensor is located in the airflow meter assembly. This sensor acts as a resistor which changes values according to the temperature of the air entering the engine. Low temperatures produce a high resistance value (for example, at 77-degrees F the resistance is about 3,000 ohms) while high temperatures produce low resistance values (at 185-degrees F the resistance is 400 ohms). The voltage will change according to the temperature of the incoming air. The IAT sensor is incorporated into the airflow meter assembly. If the IAT resistance values are incorrect, replace the airflow meter with a new part to repair the IAT sensor malfunction.

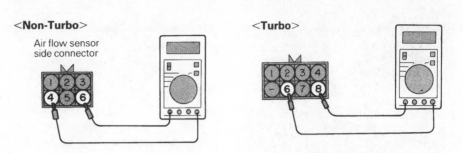

Temperature °C (°F)	Resistance kΩ
0 (32)	6.0
20 (68)	2.7
80 (176)	0.4

4.52 Probe the terminals with an ohmmeter and check the resistance readings at the temperatures shown

Check

Refer to illustration 4.52

49   Remove the airflow meter (see Steps 42 through 47).
50   Check the airflow meter for cracks or any obvious damage.
51   Disconnect the electrical connector, turn the ignition key ON (engine not running) and working on the harness side, check for battery voltage. **Note:** *The battery voltage check for the IAT sensor is the same test performed in step 40* **(refer to illustration 4.40b)**.
52   Using an ohmmeter, probe terminals 4

and 6 (non-turbo models) or 6 and 8 (turbo models) of the sensor side of the electrical connector **(see illustration)**. Replace the airflow meter if the resistance readings are incorrect.

Barometric pressure sensor

General description

53   The barometric pressure sensor is located in the airflow meter assembly. This sensor detects the altitude of the vehicle by converting barometric pressure. The barometric pressure sensor is incorporated into the airflow meter assembly. If the test results are incorrect, replace the airflow meter assembly with a new part. Any problems with the barometric pressure sensor or sensor circuit will set a code 25.

Check

Refer to illustrations 4.56a and 4.56b

54   Remove the airflow meter (see Steps 42 through 47).
55   Check the airflow meter for cracks or any obvious damage.
56   Disconnect the harness connector, turn the ignition key ON (engine not running) and working on the harness side, check for signal voltage, battery voltage and continuity of the ground circuit **(see illustrations)**. **Note:** *The battery voltage check for the barometric pressure sensor is the same test performed in step 40* **(see illustration 4.40b)**.
57   If the voltage readings are incorrect, replace the airflow meter. **Note:** *There are no specific tests for the airflow meter itself. If in doubt, have the airflow meter tested at a dealer service department.*

4.56a With the ignition key ON, check the signal voltage to the barometric pressure sensor by probing terminal number 3 on non-turbo engines or terminal number 4 on turbo engines. It should be between 4.8 and 5.2 volts

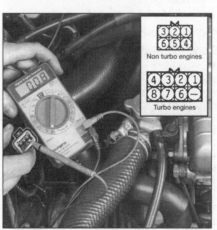

4.56b Check the continuity of the ground circuit for the barometric pressure sensor by probing terminal number 4 on non-turbo engines or terminal number 6 on turbo engines (there should be continuity)

4.59 Check that the resistance of the EGR gas temperature sensor varies with a change in temperature - you'll need to use two long jumper wires for this test, since the connector for the sensor is difficult to reach (arrow)

4.60 Working on the harness side, check that the signal voltage for the EGR gas temperature sensor is 4.3 to 4.7 volts with the ignition key On

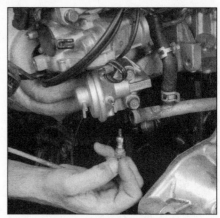

4.63 The EGR gas temperature sensor is located under the EGR valves (engine removed for clarity)

EGR gas temperature sensor (California models only)

General Description

58   All California models are equipped with an EGR gas temperature sensor mounted near the EGR valve. This sensor detects the temperature of the exhaust as it moves through the EGR valve. The information is sent to the ECM and, in turn, the EGR on/off time is regulated precisely and more efficiently.

Check

Refer to illustrations 4.59 and 4.60

59   Disconnect the electrical connector for the EGR gas temperature sensor, located behind and almost underneath the intake plenum. There are two sensors in this location - the EGR gas temperature sensor is the one on the right (passenger's) side **(see illustration)**. Measure the resistance of the sensor at the various temperatures. Refer to the

Specifications listed in this Chapter for a list of the temperatures and the corresponding resistance values.
60   Turn the ignition key ON (engine not running) and check terminal number 1 on the harness side for supply voltage. It should be 4.3 to 4.7 volts **(see illustration)**.
61   Check the ground circuit for continuity using terminal number 2.
62   If the resistance of the EGR gas temperature sensor fails to fluctuate with temperature changes, replace it with a new one.

Replacement

Refer to illustration 4.63

63   Disconnect the electrical connector for the EGR gas temperature sensor and unscrew the sensor from the EGR valve **(see illustration)**.
64   Installation is the reverse of removal.

Knock sensor (turbo models only)

65   Irregular octane levels in modern gasoline can cause detonation in an engine. Deto-

nation is sometimes referred to as "spark knock". The knock sensor sends a voltage signal to the ECM when no spark knock is occurring and the ECM provides normal advance. When the knock sensor detects abnormal vibration (spark knock), the ECM turns off the circuit to the ECM and consequently the distributor timing is retarded until the knock is eliminated. Any problems with the knock sensor or sensor circuit will set a code 31.

Check

Refer to illustration 4.66

66   Turn the ignition key ON (engine not running) and check terminal number 1 on the harness side for power supply. It should be 8.0 to 11.0 volts **(see illustration)**.
67   Check the ground circuit for continuity using terminal number 2.
68   The operation of the sensor can be checked with the engine running. Reconnect the electrical connector and connect a timing light in accordance with the tool manufacturer's instructions. Start the engine and point the timing light at the timing marks on the crankshaft pulley. Have an assistant sharply tap the backside of the air intake plenum with a hammer. The ignition timing should momentarily retard a few degrees. If it does, the system is working properly.
69   If the harness tests are correct but the system is not working properly, the sensor is probably faulty. Replace the knock sensor with a new part.

Replacement

Refer to illustration 4.70

70   Disconnect the electrical connector from the knock sensor and, using and open-end wrench, unscrew the sensor from the engine block **(see illustration)**. Installation is the reverse of removal.

Vehicle speed sensor

General description

71   The Vehicle Speed Sensor (VSS) is

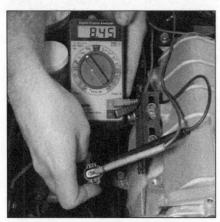

4.66 Working on the harness side, check that the signal voltage for the knock sensor is 8.0 to 11.0 volts with the ignition key On

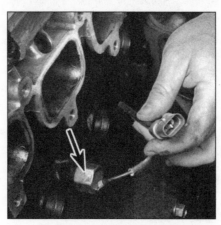

4.70 The knock sensor (arrow) is located in the engine block directly below the intake manifold

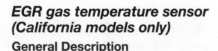

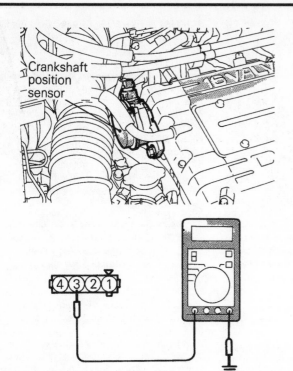

4.75 Check for battery voltage on terminal number 3 on the harness side of the electrical connector for the camshaft/crankshaft position sensor

5.2 The ECM is located under the center console. It is retained by bolts (arrow) located on each side of the console frame

83 Check the ground circuit for continuity using terminal number 4.
84 If the crankshaft position sensor circuit tests are correct, replace the sensor with a new part (see Chapter 5, Section 9).

---

5 Electronic Control Module (ECM) - removal and installation

Refer to illustrations 5.2 and 5.4

1 Disconnect the negative cable from the battery (see Chapter 5).
2 Remove the center console from the dash (see Chapter 11). The ECM is located under the center of the dash **(see illustration)**.
3 Remove the bolts from the ECM brackets.
4 Lift the ECM from the vehicle **(see illustration)**.
5 Installation is the reverse of removal.

5.4 Lift the ECM up and out of the locking tab and slide the unit out on the passenger side of the console

---

located in the speedometer head. The sensor converts the rpm of the cable to a pulsing voltage signal to the ECM, which the ECM converts to miles per hour.
72 Any problem with the VSS and its circuit will set a code 24. Have the vehicle speed sensor, circuit and the ECM diagnosed by a dealer service department or other qualified repair shop, as special tools are required.

Camshaft position sensor (2.0L engines)

Note 1: *The camshaft and crankshaft position sensors on the 1.8L engine are contained as a single unit within the distributor. In the event of failure, the distributor must be replaced as a complete unit.*
Note 2: *The camshaft and crankshaft position sensors on the 2.0L engine are combined into one unit.*

73 The camshaft position sensor **(see illustration 9.21** in Chapter 5) detects the dead point in the number 1 and number 4 cylinder compression stroke, converts the pulse signal and sends the information to the ECM. From here the ECM determines the firing order.
74 Any problem with the camshaft position sensor will set a code 23.

Check

Refer to illustration 4.75
75 Disconnect the electrical connector for the camshaft position sensor, turn the ignition key ON (engine not running) and measure the supply voltage on terminal number 3 **(see illustration)**. It should be approximately 12 volts.
76 Turn the ignition key ON (engine not run-

ning) and check terminal number 1 on the harness side for signal voltage. It should be 4.8 to 5.2 volts.
77 Check the ground circuit for continuity using terminal number 4.
78 If the camshaft position sensor circuit tests check out OK, replace the sensor with a new part (see Chapter 5, Section 9).

Crankshaft position sensor (2.0L engines)

Note 1: *The camshaft and crankshaft position sensors on the 1.8L engine are contained as a single unit within the distributor. In the event of failure, the distributor must be replaced as a complete unit.*
Note 2: *The camshaft and crankshaft position sensors on the 2.0L engine are combined into one unit.*

79 The crankshaft position sensor **(see illustration 9.21** in Chapter 5) detects the piston position of each cylinder, converts the pulse signal and sends the information to the ECM. From here the ECM determines the fuel injection firing order.
80 Any problem with the crankshaft position sensor will set a code 22.

Check

81 Disconnect the harness connector for the camshaft position sensor, turn the ignition key ON (engine not running) **(see illustration 4.75)** and measure the supply voltage on terminal number 3. It should be approximately 12 volts (B+).
82 Turn the ignition key ON (engine not running) and check terminal number 2 on the harness side for signal voltage. It should be 4.8 to 5.2 volts.

6

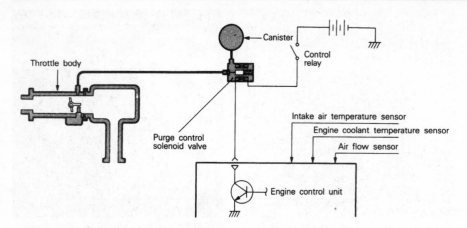

6.2a Schematic of the EVAP system on non-turbo engines

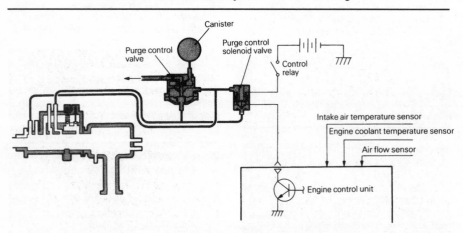

6.2b Schematic of the EVAP system on turbo engines

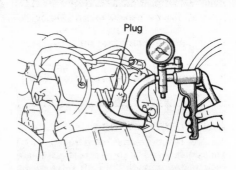

6.11a To check the purge control system, first detach the vacuum line (the one with the red stripes) from the throttle body and hook up a hand-held vacuum pump (1.8L engine) . . .

6.11b . . . then apply vacuum and confirm that the vacuum level remains steady at idle and at 3,000 rpm when the engine is cold (2.0L engine shown)

6   Evaporative Emission Control (EVAP) system

General description

Refer to illustrations 6.2a and 6.2b

1   This system is designed to trap and store fuel that evaporates from the fuel tank, throttle body and intake manifold that would normally enter the atmosphere in the form of hydrocarbon (HC) emissions.

2   The Evaporative Emission Control (EVAP) system consists of a charcoal-filled canister, the lines connecting the canister to the fuel tank and a purge control solenoid valve **(see illustrations)**.

3   Fuel vapors are transferred from the fuel tank and throttle body to a canister where they're stored when the engine isn't running. When the engine is running, the fuel vapors are purged from the canister by intake air flow and consumed in the normal combustion process.

4   The charcoal canister is equipped with a purge control valve on turbo models. Depending upon the running conditions (coolant temperature, volume of airflow, intake air temperature and barometric pressure) and the pressure in the fuel tank, the ECM opens or closes the passageways to the throttle body.

Check

5   Rough idle, stalling and poor driveability can be caused by an inoperative purge control solenoid valve, a damaged canister, split or cracked hoses or hoses connected to the wrong fittings. Check the fuel filler cap for a damaged or deformed gasket (see Chapter 1).

6   Evidence of fuel loss or fuel odor can be caused by liquid fuel leaking from fuel lines, a cracked or damaged canister, an inoperative check valve, disconnected, misrouted, kinked, deteriorated or damaged vapor or control hoses.

7   Inspect each hose attached to the canister for kinks, leaks and cracks along its entire length. Repair or replace as necessary.

8   Inspect the canister. If it's cracked or damaged, replace it.

9   Look for fuel leaking from the bottom of the canister. If fuel is leaking, replace the canister and check the hoses and hose routing.

10   Further testing should be left to a dealer service department or other qualified repair shop.

Purge control system test

Refer to illustrations 6.11a and 6.11b

11   Disconnect the vacuum hose (the one with a red stripe) from the throttle body and connect a hand-held vacuum pump to the vacuum hose. Plug the open port on the throttle body **(see illustrations)**.

12   Apply vacuum and run the engine at idle, then at 3,000 rpm. The EVAP system should maintain vacuum under both conditions when the engine is cold (140-degrees F or less).

13   Warm up the engine (150-degrees F or more), apply vacuum and confirm that at idle the vacuum remains steady but at 3,000 rpm the vacuum bleeds down. This indicates the system is working (purging the vapors) properly.

Purge solenoid

Refer to illustrations 6.16a, 6.16b and 6.18

14   Disconnect the vacuum hoses from the purge solenoid.

15   Disconnect the electrical connector from the purge solenoid.

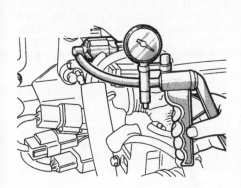

6.16a To check the purge solenoid, detach the vacuum hose, remove the connector and apply battery voltage (1.8L engine shown)

6.16b Confirm that when battery voltage is applied, the solenoid leaks down (purges) and when the voltage is removed, the solenoid holds vacuum (2.0L engine shown)

6.18 Check the resistance of the purge solenoid - it should be 36 to 44 ohms

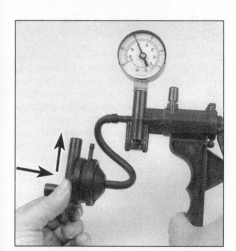

6.21 Apply vacuum and blow air through the purge control valve - it should pass air

6.25 Flip up the clamp (arrow) on the charcoal canister bracket and remove the canister

6.27 Pry the clip down and back to release the purge solenoid from the bracket

16 Connect a hand held vacuum pump to the port with the red-striped vacuum hose **(see illustrations)** and apply vacuum.

17 Use jumper wires and apply battery voltage to the solenoid. When the solenoid is energized, the vacuum should leak down. When no voltage is applied, the vacuum should hold steady.

18 Also, measure the resistance of the purge solenoid **(see illustration)**. It should be 36 to 44 ohms.

19 If the test results are incorrect, replace the purge solenoid with a new part.

Purge control valve (turbo engines only)

Refer to illustration 6.21

20 Remove the vacuum hoses from the valve and install a hand held vacuum pump to the vacuum port (bottom).

21 Apply vacuum and confirm that air can pass through the purge ports **(see illustration)**.

22 Remove the vacuum and observe that no air is allowed to pass through the purge control valve.

23 If the test results are incorrect, replace the purge control valve with a new part.

Replacement

Charcoal canister

Refer to illustration 6.25

24 Clearly label, then detach the vacuum hoses from the canister.

25 Loosen the mounting clamp **(see illustration)**, disconnect the hoses and remove the canister from the vehicle.

26 Installation is the reverse of removal.

Purge solenoid

Refer to illustration 6.27

27 Remove the vacuum hoses and electrical connector and use a small screwdriver to press down the retaining clip on the backside **(see illustration)**.

28 Installation is the reverse of removal

7   Exhaust Gas Recirculation (EGR) system

General description

1 To reduce oxides of nitrogen (NOx) emissions, some of the exhaust gases are recirculated through the EGR valve to the intake manifold to lower combustion chamber temperatures.

2 The EGR system consists of the EGR valve, the EGR solenoid (California models only), thermal vacuum valve (Federal and Canada models only), Electronic Control Module (ECM) and the EGR gas temperature sensor (California models only). **Note:** *Refer to Section 4 for the testing procedure for the EGR gas temperature sensor.*

Check

EGR valve

Refer to illustration 7.4

3 Start the engine and allow it to idle.

6

7.4 Apply vacuum to the EGR valve - the engine should run poorly (it might even stall)

7.6a Confirm that when voltage is applied to the EGR solenoid, the solenoid holds vacuum and when the voltage is removed, the solenoid does not hold vacuum (2.0L engine shown)

4   Detach the vacuum hose from the EGR valve and attach a hand-held vacuum pump in its place **(see illustration)**.

5   Apply vacuum to the EGR valve. Vacuum should remain steady and the engine should run poorly.

   a) *If the vacuum doesn't remain steady and the engine doesn't run poorly, replace the EGR valve and recheck it.*

   b) *If the vacuum remains steady but the engine doesn't run poorly, remove the EGR valve and check the valve and the intake manifold for blockage. Clean or replace parts as necessary and recheck.*

EGR solenoid (California models only)

Refer to illustrations 7.6a, 7.6b and 7.11

6   Remove the vacuum hose with the yellow and green stripe from the solenoid valve **(see illustrations)** and install a hand-held vacuum pump to the port.

7   Disconnect the electrical connector from the solenoid.

8   Use a pair of jumper leads and apply battery voltage to the EGR solenoid.

9   With battery voltage and vacuum applied, the solenoid should maintain steady vacuum. When the voltage is removed from the solenoid, the vacuum should leak down.

10   If the test results are incorrect, replace the solenoid with a new part.

11   Also, measure the resistance of the EGR solenoid **(see illustration)**. It should be 36 to 44 ohms.

Thermo vacuum valve (TVV) (Federal and Canadian models only)

Refer to illustrations 7.12a and 7.12b

12   Disconnect the hoses from the thermo vacuum valve and attach a hand held vacuum pump **(see illustrations)** to one of the ports.

13   Apply vacuum and observe the thermo vacuum valve operation:

   a) With the coolant temperature below 122-degrees F (cold), check that the vacuum leaks through the valve.

   b) With the engine warm (176-degrees F or more), check that the valve holds vacuum.

   c) If the tests are incorrect, replace the valve with a new part.

Component replacement

EGR valve

Refer to illustration 7.14

14   Detach the vacuum hose, remove the two EGR valve mounting bolts **(see illustration)**, remove the EGR valve from the intake manifold and check it for sticking and heavy carbon deposits. If the valve is sticking or clogged with deposits, clean or replace it.

15   Installation is the reverse of removal.

EGR solenoid

16   Remove the vacuum hoses and electrical connector and use a small screwdriver to press down the retaining clip on the backside.

17   Installation is the reverse of removal.

---

8   Positive Crankcase Ventilation (PCV) system

Refer to illustration 8.5

General description

1   The Positive Crankcase Ventilation (PCV) system reduces hydrocarbon emis-

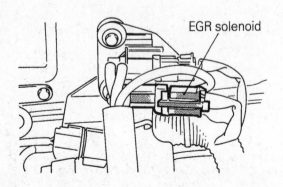

7.6b This is what the EGR solenoid on models with a 1.8L engine looks like

7.11 Check the resistance of the EGR solenoid - it should be 36 to 44 ohms

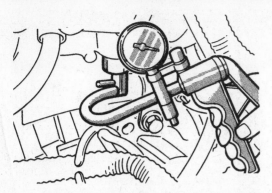

7.12a On the 1.8L engine, the thermo vacuum valve is located on the underside of the thermostat housing

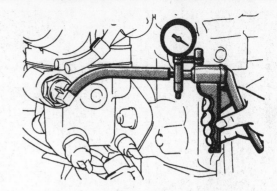

7.12b On 2.0L engines, the thermo vacuum valve is located on the side of the thermostat housing

sions by scavenging crankcase vapors. It does this by circulating fresh air from the air cleaner through the crankcase, where it mixes with blow-by gases and is then rerouted through a PCV valve to the intake manifold.

2 The main components of the PCV system are the PCV valve, a fresh air intake and the vacuum hoses connecting these components with the engine (valve cover).

3 To maintain idle quality, the PCV valve restricts the flow when the intake manifold vacuum is high. If abnormal operating conditions (such as piston ring problems) arise, the system is designed to allow excessive amounts of blow-by gases to flow back through the crankcase vent tube into the air cleaner to be consumed by normal combustion.

4 This system directs the blow-by into the throttle body which over time can cause an oily residue build-up in that area of the throttle plate. Consequently, it's a good idea to periodically clean this residue from the throttle body. Refer to Chapter 4 for this cleaning procedure.

Check

5 To check the valve, first unscrew it from the valve cover **(see illustration)** and shake the valve. It should rattle, indicating that it is not clogged with deposits. If the valve does not rattle, try cleaning the valve with carburetor cleaner. If it does rattle, reconnect the hose to the valve but don't install it in the valve cover.

6 Start the engine and allow it to idle, then place your finger over the end of the valve. You should feel vacuum, and you should hear the plunger inside the valve move back and forth as you cover and uncover the valve with your finger.

7 If the valve doesn't operate as described, replace it with a new one.

8 Check the hose for damage, wear and deterioration. Make sure it fits snugly on the fittings. If it doesn't, replace it with a new one. **Note:** *Don't use fuel line as a substitute - use only a molded vacuum hose intended for this purpose.*

---

9 Catalytic converter

Note: *Because of a federally mandated extended warranty which covers emissions-related components such as the catalytic converter, check with a dealer service department before replacing the converter at your own expense.*

General description

1 To reduce hydrocarbon, carbon monoxide and oxides of nitrogen emissions, all vehicles covered by this manual are equipped with a three-way catalyst system which oxidizes and reduces these chemicals, converting them into harmless nitrogen, carbon dioxide and water.

2 The catalytic converter is mounted in the exhaust system much like a muffler **(see illustration 22.4a** in Chapter 4).

Check

3 Periodically inspect the catalytic converter-to-exhaust pipe mating flanges and bolts. Make sure that there are no loose bolts and no leaks between the flanges.

4 Look for dents in or damage to the catalytic converter protector. If any part of the protector is damaged or dented enough to touch the converter, repair or replace it.

5 Inspect the heat insulator for damage. Make sure there is adequate clearance between the heat insulator and the catalytic converter.

Replacement

6 To replace the catalytic converter, refer to Chapter 4.

6

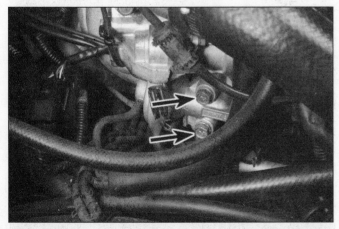

7.14 Remove the two mounting bolts (arrows) and separate the EGR valve from the intake manifold (2.0L engine shown)

8.5 The PCV valve (arrow) is threaded into the corner of the valve cover (1.8L engine shown - on the 2.0L engine, it's located at the other end of the valve cover)

Notes

Chapter 7 Part A
Manual transaxle

Contents

Specifications

Torque specifications

	Ft-lbs
Backup light switch	22 to 25
Transaxle-to-engine bolts	
12 mm bolts	32 to 39
10 mm bolts	22 to 25

1   General information

The vehicles covered by this manual are equipped with either a 5-speed manual or a 4-speed automatic transaxle. Information on the manual transaxle is included in this part of Chapter 7. Service procedures for the automatic transaxle are contained in Chapter 7, Part B.

Both the manual transaxle and the differential are house in a compact, lightweight, two-piece aluminum alloy housing.

The procedures in this Chapter tell you how to replace and adjust those parts of the transaxle that can be serviced at home, as well as how to remove and install the transaxle itself. Because of the complexity of the transaxle internals, the difficulty of obtaining replacement parts and the special tools needed to service those parts, we don't recommend repairing the transaxle at home. Nevertheless, we've included exploded views and a brief information section on transaxle overhaul for those readers who wish to tackle a transaxle rebuild.

One final note: The transfer case (4WD models only) is bolted to, but is not an integral part of, the transaxle. If you're looking for service information regarding the transfer case, refer to Chapter 7, Part C.

2   Oil seal replacement

1   Oil leaks frequently occur at the driveaxle seals and at the speedometer drive-

2.4 Using a large screwdriver or prybar, carefully pry the oil seal out of the transaxle (if you can't remove the oil seal with a screwdriver or prybar, you may need to obtain a special seal removal tool - available at most auto parts stores - to do the job)

gear oil seal or O-ring. Replacing these seals is relatively easy, since you don't have to remove the transaxle to get to them.

Driveaxle seals

Refer to illustrations 2.4 and 2.6

2   The driveaxle seals are located in the sides of the transaxle, where the splined inner ends of the driveaxles mate with the differential side gears. If you suspect that one of these seals is leaking, raise the vehicle and support it securely on jackstands. If these seal is in fact leaking, you'll see lubricant running down the side of the transaxle below the seal.

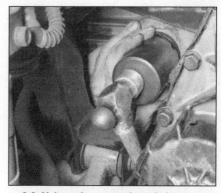

2.6 Using a large section of pipe or a large deep socket as a drift, drive the new seal squarely into the bore and make sure that it's completely seated; lubricate the tip of the new seal with multi-purpose grease

3   Remove the driveaxle (see Chapter 8).
4   Using a large screwdriver or prybar, carefully pry the oil seal out of the transaxle **(see illustration)**.
5   If you can't remove the oil seal with a screwdriver or pry bar, you may need to obtain a special seal removal tool (available at most auto parts stores) to do the job.
6   Using a large section of pipe or a large deep socket as a drift, install the new oil seal **(see illustration)**. Drive it into the bore squarely and make sure that it's completely seated. Lubricate the lip of the new seal with multi-purpose grease.
7   Install the driveaxle (see Chapter 8). Be careful not to damage the lip of the new seal.

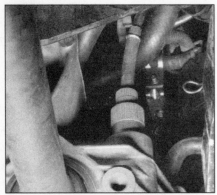

2.9 The speedometer driven-gear assembly is located on the upper rear area of the transaxle, just behind the differential housing; to remove it, simply unscrew and disconnect the speedometer cable, remove the driven-gear hold-down bolt and pull the driven-gear assembly straight up

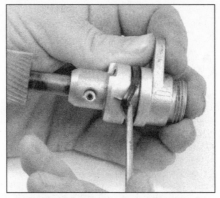

2.11 If the speedometer driven-gear O-ring is damaged, remove it from the sleeve, coat the new O-ring with clean engine oil or transmission lubricant, slide it onto the sleeve and into its groove and install the driven gear assembly

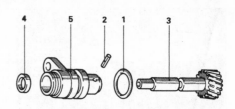

2.12 An exploded view of the speedometer driven-gear assembly:

1   O-ring
2   Spring pin
3   Speedometer driven-gear
4   Oil seal
5   Speedometer driven-gear sleeve

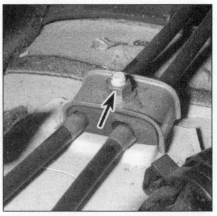

3.4 Remove the rear cable retainer nut (arrow) and detach the retainer from the floor

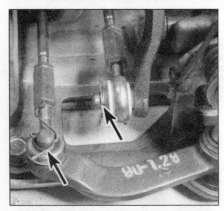

3.2 Remove the cotter pin(s) (arrows) from the select and/or shift cable(s) and slide the cable end(s) off the pin(s)

3.3 Pry out the cable retainer clip(s) with a screwdriver

Speedometer driven-gear seal and O-ring

Refer to illustrations 2.9, 2.11 and 2.12

8   The speedometer driven-gear housing is located on top of the differential housing, immediately above and behind the left (driver's side) side-gear seal. If you suspect that the driven-gear seal or O-ring is leaking, look for telltale streaks of lubricant on the sides of the housing below the driven-gear assembly.

9   Unscrew and disconnect the speedometer cable **(see illustration)**.

10   If the seal or the O-ring is leaking, clean the area around the driven-gear assembly to prevent dirt from falling into the differential assembly, remove the driven-gear hold-down bolt and pull the driven-gear straight up and out of the differential.

11   If the O-ring is damaged, remove it from the sleeve **(see illustration)**, coat the new O-ring with clean engine oil or transmission lubricant, slide it onto the sleeve and into its groove, and install the driven gear assembly.

12   If the seal is leaking, knock out the

spring pin with a pin punch and disassemble the driven-gear assembly **(see illustration)**. You can remove the old seal with a small hooked seal removal tool or a small screwdriver. Coat the new seal with clean engine oil or transaxle lubricant and use a small socket of the appropriate diameter as a drift to install it. Reassemble the driven gear assembly and install it in the transaxle. **Caution:** *Do NOT try to replace the seal without disassembling the driven-gear assembly - you may get the old seal out but it's very difficult to install a new seal without damaging it because the seal bore is deeply recessed into the sleeve assembly and a socket small enough to drive it into this recess will not clear the driven-gear shaft.*

3   Select and shift cables - replacement and adjustment

Replacement

Refer to illustrations 3.2, 3.3, 3.4, 3.5 and 3.6

1   Remove the center console assembly (see Chapter 11).

2   Remove the cotter pin(s) from the select

and/or shift cable(s) **(see illustration)**.

3   Pry out the cable retainer clip(s) with a screwdriver **(see illustration)**.

4   Remove the rear cable retainer nut and detach the retainer from the floor **(see illustration)**.

5   Remove the forward retainer bolts and the retainer **(see illustration)**.

3.5 Remove the forward retainer bolts (arrows), detach the retainer from the firewall and pull the cable grommet through the firewall

3.6 At the transaxle, remove the cotter pin(s) (arrows) from the select (upper cable in this photo) and/or shift (lower) cable(s), then pry off the cable retainer clip(s) with a screwdriver

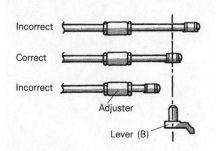

3.11 Turn the adjuster so that the end of the select cable is positioned in relation to lever B like this

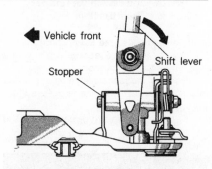

3.14 Move the shift lever inside the vehicle downward, in the direction of fourth gear, until it touches the stopper

6   At the transaxle, remove the cotter pin(s) from the select and/or shift cables **(see illustration)** and pry off the cable retaining clip(s) from the cable bracket(s) with a screwdriver.

7   Pry the cable grommet out of the firewall and pull the cable(s) out through the firewall from the engine compartment side.

8   Installation is the reverse of removal. Be sure to adjust the cable(s) when you're done.

Adjustment
Select cable

Refer to illustrations 3.9, 3.10, 3.11 and 3.12

9   Move the *transaxle* shift lever (not the

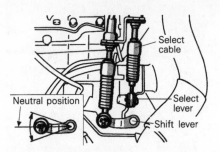

3.9 Move the transaxle shift lever (not the shift lever inside the car) to the Neutral position; this also sets the select lever to the Neutral position

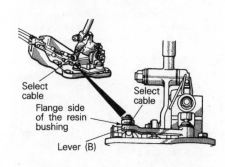

3.12 When you're done, the flange side of the resin bushing at the select cable should be at the lever B end surface

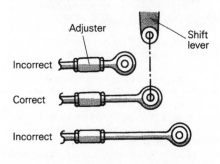

3.15 Turn the adjuster so that the end of the shift cable is positioned like this in relation to the shift lever inside the vehicle.

shift lever inside the car) to the Neutral position; this also sets the select lever to the Neutral position **(see illustration)**.

10   Move lever B to the Neutral position **(see illustration)**.

11   Turn the adjuster so that the end of the select cable is positioned in relation to lever B as shown **(see illustration)**.

12   When you're done, the flange side of the resin bushing at the select cable should be at the lever B end surface **(see illustration)**.

Shift cable

Refer to illustrations 3.13, 3.14, 3.15, 3.16 and 3.17

13   With the select lever in Neutral, move

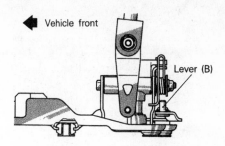

3.10 Move lever B to the Neutral position

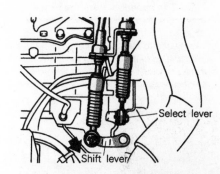

3.13 With the select lever in Neutral, move the transaxle shift lever as shown to put it into fourth gear (if the shift lever is difficult to move, depress and hold the clutch pedal down)

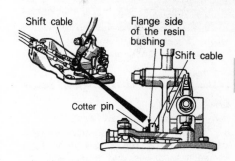

3.16 The flange side of the resin bushing at the shift cable end should be at the cotter pin side

the *transaxle* shift lever as shown to put it into fourth gear **(see illustration)**. If the shift lever is difficult to move, depress and hold the clutch pedal down.

14   Move the shift lever inside the vehicle downward, in the direction of fourth gear, until it touches the stopper **(see illustration)**.

15   Turn the adjuster so the end of the shift cable is positioned as shown **(see illustration)** in relation to the shift lever inside the vehicle.

16   The flange side of the resin bushing at the shift cable end should be at the cotter pin side **(see illustration)**.

7A

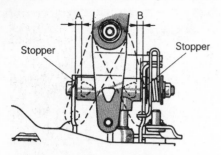

3.17 Turn the adjuster until dimensions A and B between the shift lever and the two stoppers are equal when the shift lever is shifted to 3rd and 4th gear

4.3 To remove the shift lever assembly, unbolt the four shift lever bracket bolts (arrows)

5.1 The backup light switch (arrow) is located at the right front corner of the transaxle assembly

17   Adjust the length of the shift cable by turning the adjuster until dimensions A and B between the shift lever and the two stoppers are equal when the shift lever is shifted to 3rd and 4th gear **(see illustration)**.
18   Move the shift lever to each position and verify that it shifts smoothly.

4   Shift lever - removal and installation

Refer to illustration 4.3
1   Remove the center console assembly (see Chapter 11).
2   Disconnect the select and shift cables (see Section 3).
3   Unbolt the shift lever bracket bolts **(see illustration)** and remove the shift lever.
4   Installation is the reverse of removal. Be sure to adjust the select and shift cables when you're done (see Section 3).

5   Backup light switch - check and replacement

Check

Refer to illustration 5.1
1   The backup light switch **(see illustration)** is located on top of the transaxle, near the right (passenger's side) front corner of the housing.
2   Turn the ignition key to the On position and move the shift lever to the Reverse position. The backup light switch should turn on the backup lights.
3   If it doesn't, check the 10A backup light fuse (fuse number 12) in the fuse box under the instrument panel on the driver's side (see Chapter 12).
4   If the fuse is okay, verify that there's voltage available on the battery side of the switch (with the ignition turned to On, of course).
5   If there's no voltage on the battery side of the switch, check the wire between the fuse and the switch; if there is voltage, put the shift lever in Reverse and see if there's voltage on the ground side of the switch.
6   If there's no voltage on the ground side of the switch, replace the switch (see below);

6.1 To check the transaxle mount for excessive wear, insert a large screwdriver or prybar between the mount and the transaxle bracket and try to pry it back and forth; the transaxle should not move excessively - if it does, replace the mount

if there is voltage, note whether only one or both back-up light bulbs are out.
7   If only one bulb is out, replace it; if they're both out, it could be the bulbs but it's more likely that the wire between the switch and the bulbs has an open somewhere.

Replacement

8   Unplug the electrical connector from the backup light switch.
9   Unscrew the switch.
10   Screw in the new switch and tighten it to the torque listed in this Chapter's Specifications.
11   Plug in the connector.
12   Check the operation of the backup lights to be sure the switch is working correctly.

6   Transaxle mount - check and replacement

Refer to illustrations 6.1, 6.3a and 6.3b
1   Insert a large screwdriver or prybar between the mount and the transaxle and pry up **(see illustration)**.
2   The transaxle should not move excessively away from the mount. If it does, replace the mount.

6.3a To replace the transaxle mount, support the transaxle with a jack, remove the nut (arrow) and through-bolt (the two bolts indicated by the other two arrows only need to be removed if you're removing the mount <u>bracket</u> in order to remove the transaxle) . . .

3   To replace a mount, support the transaxle with a jack, remove the nuts and bolts and remove the mount **(see illustrations)**. It may be necessary to raise the transaxle slightly to provide enough clearance to remove the mount.
4   Installation is the reverse of removal.

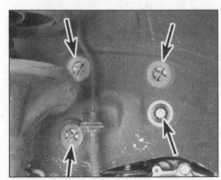

6.3b . . . and remove the four mounting bolts (arrows) from inside the right wheel well (protective plug already removed from hole for lower right bolt, other three bolt holes still plugged in this photo); you may have to raise the transaxle slightly to provide enough clearance to remove the through-bolt and the four wheel well-to-mount bolts

7.4 Remove the bracket bolts (arrows) and the bracket for the select and shift cables (if you disconnect the cables themselves, you'll have to readjust them after reassembly)

7.5 Disconnect this ground strap (arrow) - it's located next to the backup light switch

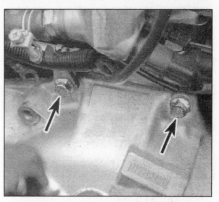

7.7 Remove the upper transaxle-to-engine bolts (arrows)

7.10a Remove the clutch release cylinder bolts (two lower arrows) and detach the release cylinder assembly from the transaxle (upper arrow points to the lower transaxle-to-engine bolt) . . .

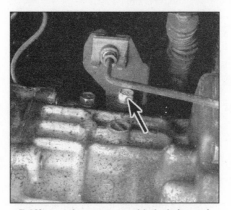

7.10b . . . then remove this bolt (arrow) and detach the bracket that attaches the clutch fluid line to the transaxle and set the release cylinder, line, bracket and hose aside (don't disconnect the fittings at either end of metal line or you'll have to bleed the clutch hydraulic system when you reassemble everything)

7.15 Remove the flywheel inspection cover bolts (arrows) and the cover (on 4WD models, you can't get at that upper rear bolt until the transfer case is removed)

7 Manual transaxle - removal and installation

Refer to illustrations 7.4, 7.5, 7.7, 7.10a, 7.10b, 7.15, 7.19a and 7.19b

1   Detach both battery cables (negative cable first) and remove the battery (see Chapter 5).
2   Disconnect the speedometer cable (see Section 2).
3   Remove the air cleaner assembly and the intake duct (see Chapter 4).
4   Disconnect the bracket for the select and shift cables **(see illustration)**.
5   Unplug the electrical connector for the backup light switch (see Section 5) and disconnect the ground strap from the transaxle **(see illustration)**.
6   Remove the starter (see Chapter 5).
7   Remove the upper transaxle-to-engine bolts **(see illustration)**.
8   Remove the transaxle mounting bracket (see Section 6).
9   Loosen the front wheel lug nuts. Raise the vehicle and place it securely on jackstands. Remove the front wheels.

10   Disconnect the clutch release cylinder from the transaxle **(see illustration)**, but don't disconnect the clutch fluid line fitting from the release cylinder. Instead, disconnect the bracket that attaches the clutch fluid line to the transaxle **(see illustration)** and set the release cylinder, line, bracket and hose aside. (If you disconnect the line either at the hose-to-line bracket or at the release cylinder, you'll have to bleed the clutch hydraulic system when you reassemble everything.)
11   Remove any exhaust components which will interfere with transaxle removal (see Chapter 4).
12   Remove the under cover.
13   Drain the transaxle fluid (see Chapter 1).
14   Remove both driveaxle assemblies and, if equipped, the center driveaxle assembly (see Chapter 8). If the vehicle is a 4WD model, disconnect the driveshaft from the transfer case (see Chapter 8). On 4WD models, remove the transfer case (see Chapter 7, Part C).
15   Remove the flywheel inspection cover **(see illustration)**.
16   Support the engine from above with a hoist (see Chapter 2), or place a jack and a

block of wood under the oil pan to spread the load.
17   Support the transaxle with a transmission jack, if available, or with a floor jack. Safety chains will help steady the transaxle on the jack.
18   Remove any remaining chassis or suspension components which will interfere with transaxle removal.
19   Remove the lower transaxle-to-engine bolt **(see illustration 7.10a)** and the two lower engine-to-transaxle bolts **(see illustrations)**.
20   Make a final check that all wires and

7.19a Remove this engine-to-transaxle bolt . . .

7.19b . . . and this engine-to-transaxle bolt (arrow)

hoses have been disconnected from the transaxle, then move the transaxle and jack toward the side of the vehicle until the transaxle is clear of the engine. Make sure you keep the transaxle level as you do this.

21   Once the input shaft is clear, lower the transaxle and remove it from under the vehicle. **Caution:** *Do not depress the clutch pedal while the transaxle is removed from the vehicle.*

22   Inspect the clutch components (see Chapter 8). In most cases, the clutch components should be replaced with new ones whenever the transaxle is removed.

Installation

23   Install the clutch components if you removed them (see Chapter 8).

24   With the transaxle secured to the jack, raise it into position and carefully slide it for-ward, engaging the input shaft with the clutch splines. Do not use excessive force to install the transaxle - if the input shaft doesn't slide into place, readjust the angle of the transaxle so it's level. You may also need to turn the input shaft so the splines are properly engaged with the clutch.

25   Install the two lower engine-to-transaxle bolts and the lower transaxle to engine bolt and tighten them to the torque listed in this Chapter's Specifications.

26   Install the flywheel inspection cover and tighten the bolts securely.

27   If the vehicle is a 4WD model, install the transfer case (see Chapter 7, Part C). Install all drivetrain components that were removed (see Chapter 8).

28   Install the under cover.

29   Install any exhaust components you removed (see Chapter 4).

30   Install the wheels and lug nuts. Lower the vehicle, and tighten the lug nuts to the torque listed in the Chapter 1 Specifications.

31   Install the transaxle mounting bracket (see Section 6) and tighten the bolts and nuts securely.

32   Install the two upper transaxle-to-engine bolts and tighten them to the torque listed in this Chapter's Specifications.

33   Install the starter (see Chapter 5).

34   Plug in the electrical connector for the backup light switch (see Section 5) and reattach the ground wire to the transaxle.

35   Attach the clutch fluid hose bracket and the clutch release cylinder to the transaxle (see Chapter 8).

36   Attach the select and shift cable bracket and tighten the two bolts securely.

37   Connect the speedometer cable (see Section 2).

38   Install the air cleaner assembly and the intake duct (see Chapter 4).

39   Install the battery and attach the battery cables (see Chapter 5).

40   Fill the transaxle with lubricant (see Chapter 1).

41   Fill the clutch hydraulic system and bleed it (see Chapter 8).

8   Manual transaxle overhaul - general information

Refer to illustrations 8.4a through 8.4g

1   Overhauling a manual transaxle is a difficult job for the do-it-yourselfer. It involves the disassembly and reassembly of many small parts. Numerous clearances must be precisely measured and, if necessary, changed with select fit spacers and snap-rings. As a result, if transaxle problems arise, it can be removed and installed by a competent do-it-yourselfer, but overhaul should be left to a transmission repair shop. Rebuilt transaxles may be available - check with your dealer parts department and auto parts stores. At any rate, the time and money involved in an overhaul is almost sure to exceed the cost of a rebuilt unit.

2   Nevertheless, it's not impossible for an inexperienced mechanic to rebuild a transaxle if the special tools are available and the job is done in a deliberate step-by-step

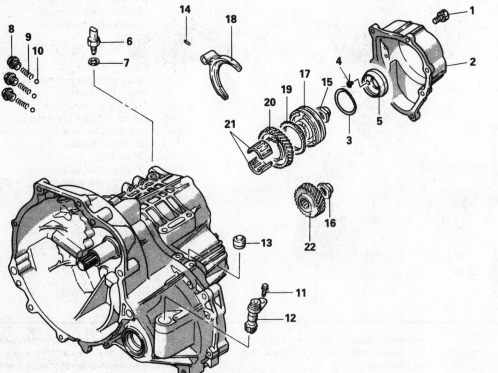

8.4a An exploded view of a typical 2WD transaxle assembly (F5M33, used on non-turbo and turbo DOHC engines, shown; F5M22, used on SOHC engines, similar)

1   Bolt
2   Rear cover
3   Wave spring
4   Screw bolts
5   Reverse brake cone
6   Backup light switch
7   Gasket
8   Poppet plug
9   Poppet spring
10 Poppet ball
11 Bolt
12 Speedometer driven gear assembly
13 Air breather
14 Spring pin
15 Locknut
16 Locknut
17 Fifth-gear synchronizer assembly
18 Fifth-gear shift fork
19 Synchronizer ring
20 Fifth-speed gear
21 Needle bearing
22 Fifth-gear intermediate gear

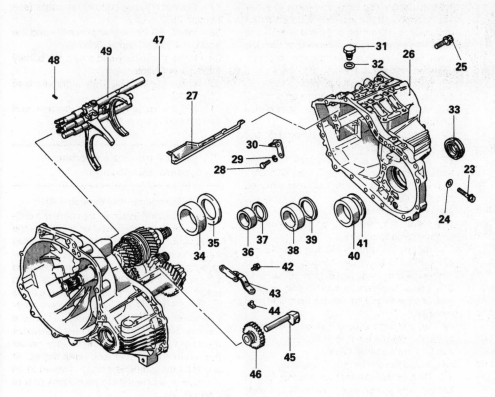

8.4b An exploded view of a typical (F5M33) 2WD transaxle assembly (continued)

23	Reverse idler gear shaft bolt
24	Gasket
25	Bolt
26	Transaxle case
27	Oil guide
28	Bolt
29	Spring washer
30	Stopper bracket
31	Restrict ball assembly
32	Gasket
33	Oil seal
34	Bearing outer race (not used on F5M22 units)
35	Spacer (not used on F5M22 units)
36	Bearing outer race
37	Spacer
38	Bearing outer race
39	Spacer
40	Bearing outer race
41	Spacer
42	Bolt
43	Reverse shift-lever assembly
44	Reverse shift-lever shoe
45	Reverse idler-gear shaft
46	Reverse idler gear
47	Spring pin
48	Spring pin
49	Shift rail assembly

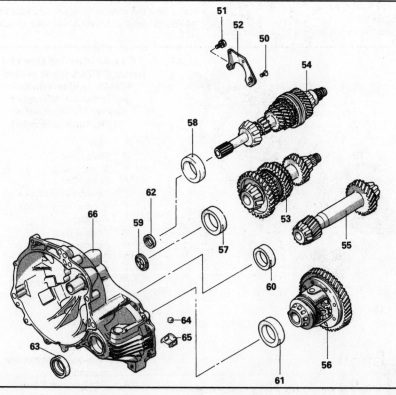

8.4c An exploded view of a typical (F5M33) 2WD transaxle assembly (continued)

50	Screw
51	Bolt
52	Bearing retainer
53	Intermediate gear assembly
54	Input shaft assembly
55	Output shaft assembly
56	Differential gear assembly
57	Bearing outer race
58	Bearing outer race
59	Oil guide
60	Bearing outer race
61	Bearing outer race
62	Oil seal
63	Oil seal
64	Magnet
65	Magnet holder
66	Clutch housing assembly

manner so nothing is overlooked.

3   The tools necessary for an overhaul include internal and external snap-ring pliers, a bearing puller, a slide hammer, a set of pin punches, a dial indicator and possibly a hydraulic press. In addition, a large, sturdy workbench and a vise or transaxle stand will be required.

4   During disassembly of the transaxle, make careful notes of how each piece comes off, where it fits in relation to other pieces and what holds it in place. Exploded views are included **(see illustrations)** to show where the parts go - but actually noting how they are installed when you remove the parts will

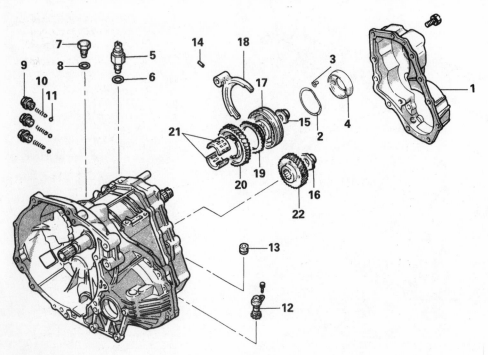

8.4d An exploded view of the 4WD transaxle assembly

1 Rear cover
2 Wave spring
3 Screw bolts
4 Reverse brake cone
5 Backup light switch
6 Gasket
7 Restrict ball assembly
8 Gasket
9 Poppet plug
10 Poppet spring
11 Poppet ball
12 Speedometer driven gear assembly
13 Air breather
14 Spring pin
15 Locknut
16 Locknut
17 Fifth-gear synchronizer assembly
18 Shift fork
19 Synchronizer ring
20 Fifth gear
21 Needle bearing
22 Fifth-gear intermediate gear

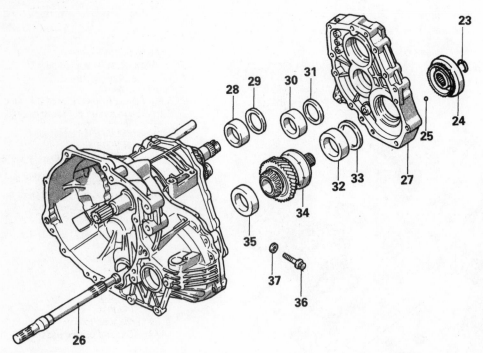

8.4e An exploded view of the 4WD transaxle assembly (continued)

23 Snap-ring
24 Viscous coupling
25 Steel ball
26 Center shaft
27 Transaxle case adapter
28 Outer race
29 Spacer
30 Outer race
31 Spacer
32 Outer race
33 Spacer
34 Center differential
35 Outer race
36 Reverse idler gear shaft bolt
37 Gasket

make it much easier to get the transaxle back together.

5   Before taking the transaxle apart for repair, it will help if you have some idea what area of the transaxle is malfunctioning. Certain problems can be closely tied to specific areas in the transaxle, which can make component examination and replacement easier.

Refer to the *Troubleshooting* section at the front of this manual for information regarding possible sources of trouble.

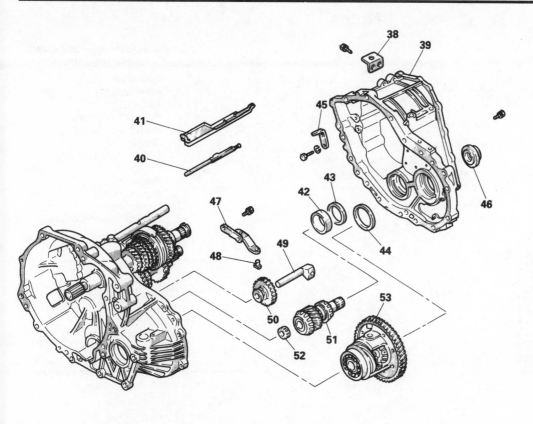

8.4f An exploded view of the 4WD transaxle assembly (continued)

38 Clutch oil line bracket
39 Transaxle case
40 Oil guide
41 Oil guide
42 Outer race
43 Spacer
44 Spacer
45 Stopper bracket
46 Oil seal
47 Reverse shift-lever assembly
48 Reverse shift-lever shoe
49 Reverse idler-gear shaft
50 Reverse idler gear
51 Front output shaft assembly
52 Needle bearing
53 Front differential

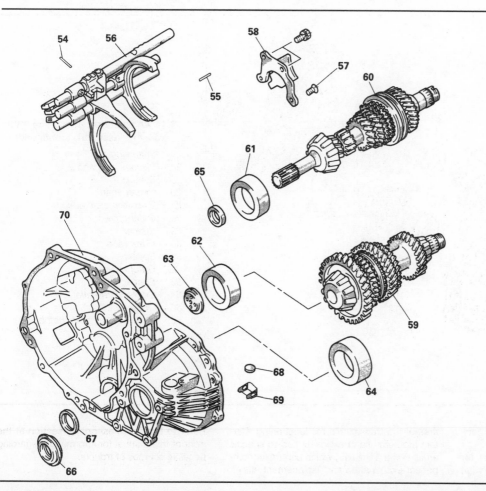

8.4g An exploded view of the 4WD transaxle assembly (continued)

54 Spring pin
55 Spring pin
56 Shift rail assembly
57 Bolt
58 Bearing retainer
59 Intermediate gear assembly
60 Input shaft assembly
61 Outer race
62 Outer race
63 Oil guide
64 Outer race
65 Oil seal
66 Oil seal
67 Oil seal
68 Magnet
69 Magnet holder
70 Clutch housing assembly

7A

Notes

Chapter 7 Part B
Automatic transaxle

Contents

Specifications

General

Fluid type and capacity	See Chapter 1
Shift lock cable dimension A	3/64 to 5/32-inch

Torque specifications

Ft-lbs (unless otherwise indicated)

Neutral start switch mounting bolts	84 to 108 in-lbs
Shift cable-to-manual control lever adjusting nut	84 to 120 in-lbs
Kickdown servo	
Inner socket (MD998916)	
Initial	86 in-lbs
Final	43 in-lbs
Locknut	18 to 23
Lower engine-to-transaxle bolt	22 to 25
Upper and lower transaxle-to-engine bolts	32 to 39
Torque converter-to-driveplate bolts	33 to 38

1 General information

All vehicles covered in this manual come equipped with either a 5-speed manual or a 4-speed automatic transaxle. All information on the automatic transaxle is included in this Part of Chapter 7. Information for the manual transaxle can be found in Part A of this Chapter, and information on the transfer case can be found in Part C.

Due to the complexity of the automatic transaxles covered in this manual and to the specialized equipment necessary to perform most service operations, this Chapter contains only those procedures related to general diagnosis, routine maintenance, adjustment and removal and installation.

If the transaxle requires major repair work, it should be left to a dealer service department or an automotive or transmission repair shop. You can, however, remove and install the transaxle yourself and save the expense, even if the repair work is done by a transmission shop.

2 Diagnosis - general

Note: *Automatic transaxle malfunctions may be caused by five general conditions: poor engine performance, improper adjustments, hydraulic malfunctions, mechanical malfunctions or malfunctions in the computer or its signal network. Diagnosis of these problems should always begin with a check of the easily repaired items: fluid level and condition (see Chapter 1), shift cable adjustment and shift lever installation. Next, perform a road test to determine if the problem has been corrected or if more diagnosis is necessary. If the problem persists after the preliminary tests and corrections are completed, additional diagnosis should be done by a dealer service department or transmission repair shop. Refer to the Troubleshooting section at the front of this manual for information on symptoms of transaxle problems.*

Preliminary checks

1 Drive the vehicle to warm the transaxle to normal operating temperature.
2 Check the fluid level as described in Chapter 1:

a) If the fluid level is unusually low, add enough fluid to bring the level within the designated area of the dipstick, then check for external leaks (see below).

b) If the fluid level is abnormally high, drain off the excess, then check the drained fluid for contamination by coolant. The presence of engine coolant in the automatic transmission fluid indicates that a failure has occurred in the internal radiator walls that separate the coolant from the transmission fluid (see Chapter 3).

c) If the fluid is foaming, drain it and refill the transaxle, then check for coolant in the fluid, or a high fluid level.

3   Check the engine idle speed. **Note:** *If the engine is malfunctioning, do not proceed with the preliminary checks until it has been repaired and runs normally.*

4   Check and adjust the shift cable, if necessary (see Section 5).

5   Inspect the shift lever linkage under the console (see Section 7) and the manual lever on the transaxle (see Section 5). Make sure that both are operating properly and smoothly.

Fluid leak diagnosis

6   Most fluid leaks are easy to locate visually. Repair usually consists of replacing a seal or gasket. If a leak is difficult to find, the following procedure may help.

7   Identify the fluid. Make sure it's transmission fluid and not engine oil or brake fluid (automatic transmission fluid is a deep red color).

8   Try to pinpoint the source of the leak. Drive the vehicle several miles, then park it over a large sheet of cardboard. After a minute or two, you should be able to locate the leak by determining the source of the fluid dripping onto the cardboard.

9   Make a careful visual inspection of the suspected component and the area immediately around it. Pay particular attention to gasket mating surfaces. A mirror is often helpful for finding leaks in areas that are hard to see.

10   If the leak still cannot be found, clean the suspected area thoroughly with a degreaser or solvent, then dry it.

11   Drive the vehicle for several miles at normal operating temperature and varying speeds. After driving the vehicle, visually inspect the suspected component again.

12   Once the leak has been located, the cause must be determined before it can be properly repaired. If a gasket is replaced but the sealing flange is bent, the new gasket will not stop the leak. The bent flange must be straightened.

13   Before attempting to repair a leak, check to make sure that the following conditions are corrected or they may cause another leak. **Note:** *Some of the following conditions cannot be fixed without highly specialized tools and expertise. Such problems must be referred to a transmission shop or a dealer service department.*

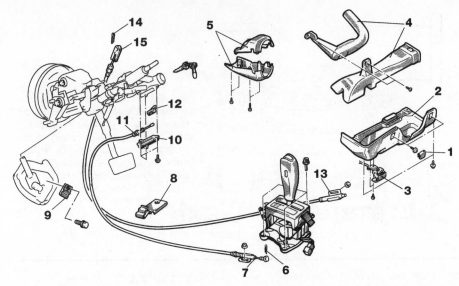

3.6 An exploded view of the key interlock cable and the shift lock cable assembly

1	Plug	9	Clip
2	Knee protector assembly	10	Cover
3	Hook lock release handle	11	Key interlock cable (steering lock end)
4	Lap cooler duct and shower duct	12	Slide lever
5	Steering column covers	13	Shift lock cable (shift lever end)
6	Cotter pin	14	Cotter pin
7	Key interlock cable (shift lever end)	15	Shift lock cable (brake pedal end)
8	Clamp		

Gasket leaks

14   Check the pan periodically. Make sure the bolts are tight, no bolts are missing, the gasket is in good condition and the pan is flat (dents in the pan may indicate damage to the valve body inside).

15   If the pan gasket is leaking, the fluid level or the fluid pressure may be too high, the vent may be plugged, the pan bolts may be too tight, the pan sealing flange may be warped, the sealing surface of the transaxle housing may be damaged, the gasket may be damaged or the transaxle casting may be cracked or porous. If sealant instead of gasket material has been used to form a seal between the pan and the transaxle housing, it may be the wrong sealant.

Seal leaks

16   If a transaxle seal is leaking, the fluid level or pressure may be too high, the vent may be plugged, the seal bore may be damaged, the seal itself may be damaged or improperly installed, the surface of the shaft protruding through the seal may be damaged or a loose bearing may be causing excessive shaft movement.

17   Make sure the dipstick tube seal is in good condition and the tube is properly seated. Periodically check the area around the speedometer gear or sensor for leakage. If transmission fluid is evident, check the O-ring for damage.

Case leaks

18   If the case itself appears to be leaking, the casting is porous and will have to be repaired or replaced.

19   Make sure the oil cooler hose fittings are tight and in good condition.

Fluid comes out vent pipe or fill tube

20   If this condition occurs, the transaxle is overfilled, there is coolant in the fluid, the case is porous, the dipstick is incorrect, the vent is plugged or the drain-back holes are plugged.

---

3   Key interlock cable - check and replacement

Note: *Some early models aren't equipped with this system.*

Check

Note: *The vehicle must the stopped and the engine turned off for the following test.*

1   Turn the ignition key to the Lock (Off) position and depress the brake pedal. You should not be able to move the shift lever from the Park position to any other position, and you should not be able to depress the shift lever push button.

2   Now turn the ignition key to the Accessory position, depress the brake pedal and depress the shift lever push button. You should be able to move the shift lever from the Park position to any other position. Press the button a few times and verify that the shift lever moves smoothly.

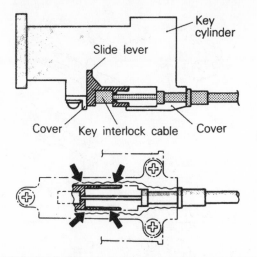

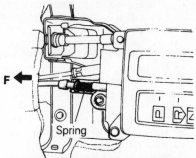

3.10 With the ignition key either in the Lock position or removed, install the slide lever in the key cylinder, insert the key interlock cable into the slide lever and the key cylinder as shown and apply a light coating of multi-purpose grease to the areas indicated by the arrows

3.14 Move the shift lever to the Park position, attach the key interlock cable to the shift lever assembly's lock cam (make sure the spring is installed as shown), gently press the lock cam forward and tighten the nut to secure the key interlock cable

3   Verify that, at all other positions of the shift lever besides Park, the ignition key can't be turned to the Lock position, and that the key turns smoothly to the Lock position when the shift lever is placed in the Park position and the button is released.

4   If the key interlock mechanism doesn't operate as described, the cable may need to be adjusted or replaced (see below).

Replacement

Refer to illustrations 3.6, 3.10 and 3.14

5   Remove the center console (see Chapter 11).

6   Remove the knee protector assembly, the hood lock release handle, the lap cooler duct and shower duct (the two ducts right above the knee protector) and the steering column cover **(see illustration)**.

7   Remove the cotter pin that attaches the key interlock cable to the shift lever and disconnect the cable from the shift lever.

8   Trace the cable to the clamp on the firewall and remove the clamp.

9   Trace the cable up to the steering lock assembly, remove the cover screw and cover, remove the slide lever and disconnect the cable from the steering lock. Pay close attention to how the key interlock cable and the slide lever fit together.

10   With the ignition key either in the Lock position or removed, install the slide lever in the key cylinder **(see illustration)**.

11   Insert the key interlock cable into the slide lever and the key cylinder as shown in **(see illustration 3.10)**.

12   Apply a light coating of multipurpose grease to the areas indicated by the arrows in illustration 3.10.

13   Move the shift lever to the Park position.

14   Attach the key interlock cable to the shift lever assembly's lock cam. Make sure the spring is installed as shown **(see illustration)**.

15   Gently press the lock cam forward **(see illustration 3.14)** and tighten the nut to secure the key interlock cable.

16   Before completing reassembly, check the operation of the key interlock mechanism (see above).

17   The remainder of installation is otherwise the reverse of removal.

4   Shift lock cable - check, replacement and adjustment

Note: *Some early models aren't equipped with this system.*

Check

1   Place the shift lever in the Park position. Turn the ignition key to the Accessory position. With your foot off the brake, depress the shift lever push button and try to move the shift lever. You should not be able to move the lever from the Park position.

2   Now, with the key still in the Accessory position, step on the brake pedal and again press the shift lever button. You should be able to move the shift lever smoothly from the Park position to any other position.

3   Finally, move the shift lever to the Reverse position. With the key still in the Accessory position, release the brake pedal, press the shift lever button and verify that the shift lever can be moved from Reverse to the Park position.

4   If the shift lock mechanism doesn't operate as described, you'll have to adjust and maybe even replace the shift lock cable mechanism (see below).

Replacement and adjustment

Refer to illustration 4.13

5   Remove the center console (see Chapter 11).

6   Remove the knee protector assembly, the hood lock release handle, the lap cooler duct and shower duct (the two ducts right above the knee protector) and the steering column cover **(see illustration 3.6)**.

7   Remove the nut that attaches the shift lock cable to the shift lever and disconnect the cable from the lever.

8   Trace the cable to the clamp on the firewall and remove the clamp.

9   Trace the cable up to the top of the

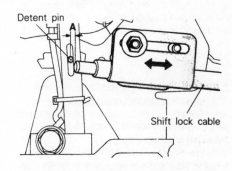

4.13 When installing a new shift lock cable, slide the cable so that dimension A (the distance between the shift lever assembly detent pin and the end of the shift lock cable) is within the limits listed in this Chapter's Specifications

brake pedal, remove the cotter pin and disconnect the cable from the brake pedal.

10   Move the shift lever to the Reverse position.

11   Start by clamping the new cable to the firewall.

12   Connect the new cable to the shift lever and temporarily tighten the nut.

13   Slide the cable so that the distance between the shift lever assembly detent pin and the end of the shift lock cable **(see illustration)** is within the limits listed in this Chapter's Specifications.

14   The remainder of installation is the reverse of removal.

5   Shift cable - replacement

Refer to illustrations 5.3, 5.9 and 5.10

1   Remove the center console (see Chapter 11).

2   Remove the knee protector assembly, the hood lock release handle, the lap cooler duct and shower duct (the two ducts right above the knee protector) and the steering column cover **(see illustration 3.6)**.

7B

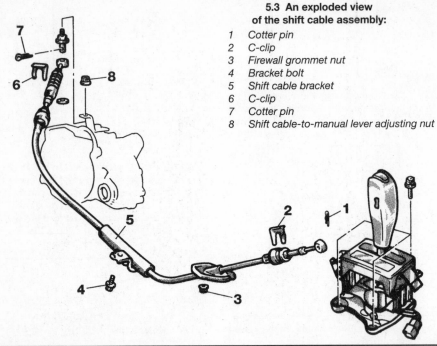

**5.3 An exploded view
of the shift cable assembly:**

1   *Cotter pin*
2   *C-clip*
3   *Firewall grommet nut*
4   *Bracket bolt*
5   *Shift cable bracket*
6   *C-clip*
7   *Cotter pin*
8   *Shift cable-to-manual lever adjusting nut*

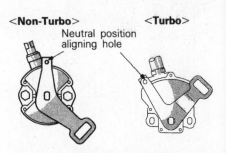

**5.9 Place the shift lever and the neutral-
start switch in the Neutral position before
you attach the new shift cable**

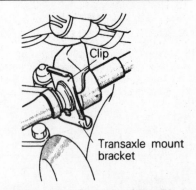

**5.10 When you connect the shift cable to
the transaxle mounting bracket with the
C-clip, make sure you push the clip all the
way down until it contacts the
bracket as shown**

3   Remove the cotter pin **(see illustration)** that attaches the shift cable to the shift lever.
4   Remove the C-clip that attaches the large cable grommet to the shift lever bracket.
5   Remove the nut that attaches the cable grommet at the firewall (this nut can be reached from inside the engine compartment).
6   Remove the shift cable bracket bolt.
7   Remove the C-clip that attaches the forward end of the cable to the transaxle bracket.
8   Remove the cotter pin and disconnect the forward end of the shift cable from the lever arm of the neutral start switch.
9   Place the shift lever and the neutral-start switch in the Neutral position **(see illustration)** and attach the new shift cable.
10   When you connect the shift cable to the transaxle mounting bracket with the C-clip, make sure the clip contacts the cable as shown **(see illustration)**.
11   To adjust the shift cable, refer to the neutral start switch adjustment procedure in Section 6.
12   Installation is otherwise the reverse of removal. Be sure to tighten the cable adjuster nut at the neutral start switch to the torque listed in this Chapter's Specifications.

6   Neutral start switch - replacement and adjustment

Replacement

Refer to illustration 6.3
1   Place the shift lever in the Neutral position.
2   Disconnect the shift cable (see Section 5).

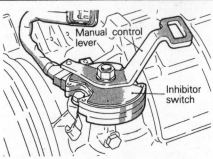

**6.3 To remove the neutral start switch
(inhibitor switch), unplug the electrical
connector, disconnect the shift cable,
remove the manual control lever and
remove the two switch mounting bolts**

3   Remove the manual control lever **(see illustration)**, the neutral start switch bolts and remove the switch.
4   Installation is the reverse of removal. Be sure to adjust the switch when you're done (see below).

Adjustment

Refer to illustrations 6.7 and 6.9
5   Place the shift lever in the Neutral Position.
6   Place the manual control lever in the Neutral position.
7   Rotate the switch body so that the manual control lever hole and the switch body are aligned **(see illustration)**. A small drill bit of the appropriate diameter can be helpful for aligning the holes precisely. Note that 1990 models have larger alignment holes (0.47-inch) than the alignment hole dimensions shown in the accompanying illustration.
8   Tighten the switch body mounting bolts to the torque listed in this Chapter's Specifications.

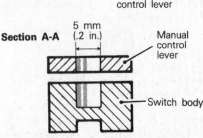

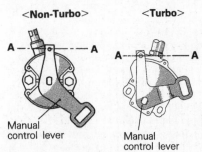

**6.7 To adjust the neutral start switch,
rotate the switch body so that the
holes in the manual control lever and
the switch body are aligned; a small
drill bit of the appropriate diameter
can be helpful for aligning the holes.**
Note: *1990 models have larger (0.47 inch)
alignment holes than those
shown in this illustration*

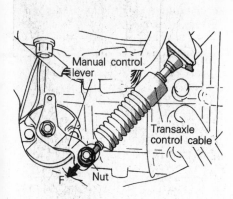

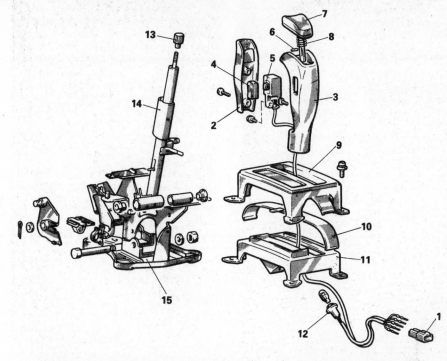

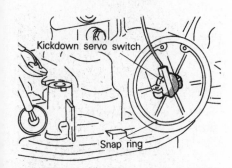

6.9 Loosen the adjusting nut that attaches the shift cable to the manual control lever, pull forward lightly on the end of the cable and tighten the nut to the torque listed in this Chapter's Specifications

7.5 An exploded view of the shift lever assembly:

1	Overdrive control switch connector	9	Upper indicator panel
2	Cover	10	Slider
3	Shift lever knob	11	Lower indicator panel
4	Overdrive control switch button	12	Indicator panel light socket
5	Overdrive control switch	13	Sleeve
6	Drift pin	14	Shift lever assembly
7	Push button	15	Shift lever assembly base
8	Spring		

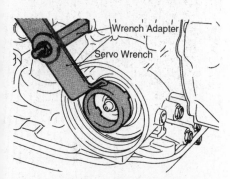

8.2 Before you can adjust the kickdown servo, you'll need to remove this large snap ring and the kickdown servo switch

8.4 To immobilize the servo piston, engage the pawl of the kickdown servo wrench with the notch in the piston. Install the wrench adapter and hand-tighten the adapter nut (applying more torque could damage the piston). If you obtain the special kickdown servo wrench, be aware that there is a difference between the tool for 1990 models and the tool for later models

9   Loosen the adjusting nut **(see illustration)** that attaches the shift cable to the manual control lever, pull forward lightly on the end of the cable and tighten the nut to the torque listed in this Chapter Specifications.
10   Verify that the shift lever is in the Neutral position.
11   Verify that it operates securely and that the transaxle end of the shift cable functions in the range which corresponds to each position of the shift lever.

7   Shift lever - removal and installation

Refer to illustration 7.5
1   Remove the center console (see Chapter 11).
2   Disconnect the key interlock cable (see Section 3).
3   Disconnect the shift lock cable (see Section 4).
4   Disconnect the shift cable (see Section 5).
5   Remove the shift lever base mounting bolts **(see illustration)**. Unplug the electrical connector for the overdrive control switch and the shift position indicator panel light and

remove the shift lever assembly.
6   Installation is the reverse of removal.

8   Kickdown servo - check and adjustment

Refer to illustrations 8.2, 8.4, 8.5, 8.6 and 8.8
Note: You'll need some special tools - available at most auto parts stores that carry special tools - to adjust the kickdown servo.
1   Raise the vehicle and place it securely on jackstands. Locate the kickdown servo switch, on the lower right side of the transaxle. Remove any dirt from the area around the switch.
2   Remove the snap-ring **(see illustration)**.
3   Remove the kickdown servo switch.
4   The piston must not rotate during the following procedure. To immobilize it, engage the pawl of the kickdown servo wrench with the notch in the piston, install the wrench adapter as shown **(see illustration)** and tighten the adapter nut hand tight (don't apply more torque or you could damage the piston). This locks the piston in place. **Caution:** *Don't press the piston in during installation of the kickdown servo wrench.*
5   Loosen the locknut with a deep socket,

7B

but don't back it out far enough to cover the V-groove in the adjusting rod. Now insert the inner socket of the socket wrench set as shown **(see illustration)** and tighten it until it contacts the lock nut.

6   Engage the outer socket of the socket wrench set on the locknut. Rotate the outer socket counterclockwise and the inner socket clockwise, locking the locknut and the inner socket **(see illustration)**.

7   Using a torque wrench, tighten the inner socket to the initial torque figure listed in this Chapter's Specifications. Then loosen it and torque it to this initial figure a second time. Finally, loosen it one more time and tighten it to the final torque listed in this Chapter's Specifications. Back off the inner socket 2

to 2-1/4 turns.

8   Engage the outer socket with the locknut again. Rotating the outer socket clockwise and the inner socket counterclockwise, unlock the locknut and the inner socket **(see illustration)**. As you unlock the locknut, apply equal force to both sockets.

9   Tighten the locknut by hand until it contacts the piston. Then use a torque wrench to tighten the locknut to the torque listed in this Chapter's Specifications. **Note:** *If you try to turn the locknut too quickly, the adjusting rod may rotate with it.*

10   Remove the kickdown servo wrench and the adapter and install the servo switch and the snap-ring.

9   Automatic transaxle - removal and installation

Removal

Refer to illustrations 9.3, 9.12 and 9.16

1   Detach the cable from the negative battery terminal.

2   Remove the air cleaner and air intake duct assembly (see Chapter 4). If the vehicle is equipped with cruise control, remove the cruise control actuator.

3   Clearly label, then unplug, all electrical connectors **(see illustration)**.

4   Disconnect the shift cable from the manual lever (see Section 5).

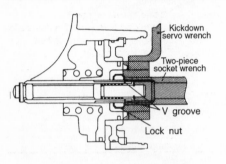

8.5 Loosen the locknut with a deep socket (but don't back it out far enough to cover the V-groove in the adjusting rod), insert the inner socket of the socket wrench set as shown and tighten it until it contacts the lock nut

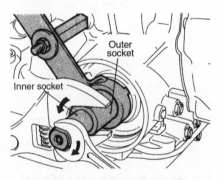

8.6 Engage the outer socket of the socket wrench set on the locknut. Rotate the outer socket counterclockwise and the inner socket clockwise, locking the locknut and the inner socket

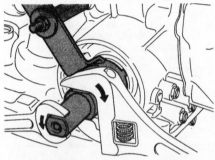

8.8 Engage the outer socket with the locknut again. Rotating the outer socket clockwise and the inner socket counterclockwise, unlock the locknut and the inner socket; make sure you apply equal force to both sockets as you unlock the locknut

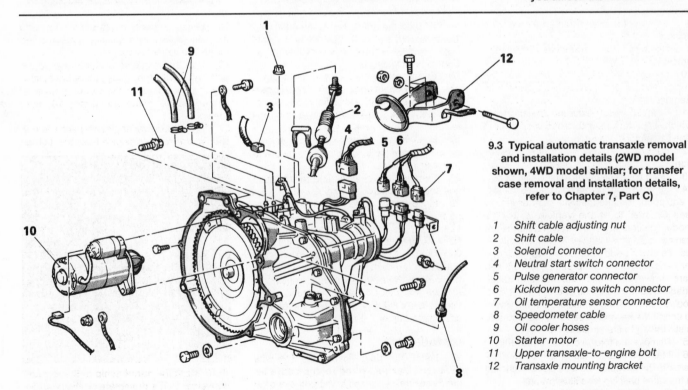

9.3 Typical automatic transaxle removal and installation details (2WD model shown, 4WD model similar; for transfer case removal and installation details, refer to Chapter 7, Part C)

1   Shift cable adjusting nut
2   Shift cable
3   Solenoid connector
4   Neutral start switch connector
5   Pulse generator connector
6   Kickdown servo switch connector
7   Oil temperature sensor connector
8   Speedometer cable
9   Oil cooler hoses
10   Starter motor
11   Upper transaxle-to-engine bolt
12   Transaxle mounting bracket

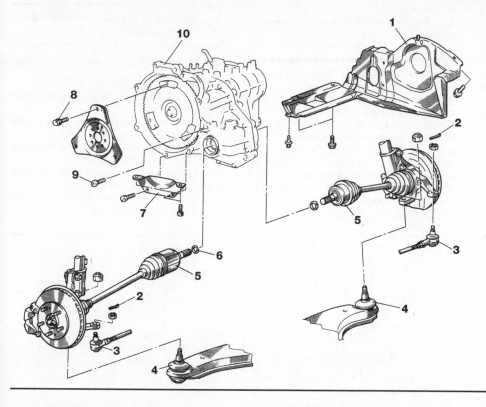

9.12 Automatic transaxle removal and installation details (continued from illustration 9.3) (2WD model shown, 4WD model similar; for transfer case removal and installation details, refer to Chapter 7, Part C)

1   Under guard
2   Cotter pins
3   Tie-rod ends
4   Lower arm balljoints
5   Inner CV joints
6   Circlips
7   Torque converter cover
8   Torque converter-to-driveplate bolt
9   Lower engine-to-transaxle bolt
10 Transaxle assembly

5   Disconnect the speedometer cable from the speedometer driven gear (see "Oil seal - replacement" in Chapter 7, Part A).

6   Loosen the hose clamps and disconnect the oil cooler hoses. Plug the hoses to prevent contamination and leaks.

7   Remove the starter motor (see Chapter 5).

8   Remove the upper transaxle-to-engine bolts.

9   Remove the transaxle mounting bracket.

10 Loosen the wheel lug nuts, raise the vehicle and support it securely on jackstands. Remove the wheels.

11 Remove any exhaust components which will interfere with transaxle removal (see Chapter 4).

12 Remove the under guard **(see illustration)**.

13 Drain the transaxle fluid (see Chapter 1).

14 Remove both driveaxle assemblies and, if equipped, the intermediate shaft assembly (see Chapter 8). If the vehicle is a 4WD model, disconnect the driveshaft from the transfer case (see Chapter 8). On 4WD models, it's also a good idea to remove the transfer case now (see Chapter 7, Part C). You can, however, leave the transfer case attached to the transaxle and remove it after you've removed the transaxle, but it's easier to unbolt the transfer case while the transaxle is still bolted to the engine.

15 Remove the torque converter cover.

16 Mark the relationship of the torque converter to the driveplate so they can be installed in the same position **(see illustration)**.

17 Remove all three torque converter-to-

driveplate bolts. Turn the crankshaft 120-degrees at a time for access to each bolt. After all three bolts are removed, push the torque converter into the bellhousing so it doesn't stay with the engine when the transaxle is removed.

18 Support the engine from above with a hoist or a 4x4 wood post across the engine compartment, or place a jack and a block of wood under the oil pan to spread the load (see "Transaxle - removal and installation" in Chapter 7, Part A).

19 Support the transaxle with a transmission jack (a special jack made for this purpose), if available, or with a floor jack. Safety chains will help steady the transaxle on the jack.

20 Remove any remaining chassis or suspension components which will interfere with transaxle removal.

21 Remove the lower engine-to-transaxle bolt and the transaxle-to-engine bolts.

22 Move the transaxle to the side to disengage it from the engine block dowel pins. Make sure the torque converter is detached from the driveplate. Secure the torque converter to the transaxle so that it will not fall out during removal. Lower the transaxle from the vehicle. If you're swapping transaxles, remove the transaxle fluid filler tube. If the vehicle is a 4WD model, remove the transfer case (see Chapter 7, Part C).

Installation

23 Install the fluid filler tube, if it was removed. Make sure the torque converter hub is securely engaged in the pump prior to installation. This can be confirmed by push-

ing on the torque converter and turning it (if it isn't seated completely, it will drop into place as this is done, evidenced by one or more "clunks").

24 With the transaxle secured to the jack, raise it into position. Be sure to keep it level so the torque converter does not slide forward.

25 Move the transaxle carefully into place until the dowel pins are engaged and the torque converter is engaged.

26 Turn the torque converter to line up the bolt holes with the holes in the driveplate. The match marks on the torque converter and driveplate, made during step 16, must line up.

27 Install the lower engine-to-transaxle bolt and the transaxle-to-engine bolts and tighten

7B

9.16 Mark the relationship of the torque converter to the driveplate so they can be installed in the same position

them to the torque listed in this Chapter's Specifications.

28   Install the torque converter-to-driveplate bolts and tighten them to the torque listed in this Chapter's Specifications. **Note:** *Install all of the bolts before tightening any of them.* Install the torque converter cover and tighten the bolts securely.

29   If the vehicle is a 4WD model, and you removed the transfer case, install it now (see Chapter 7, Part C). Install all drivetrain components that were removed (see Chapter 8). Tighten all drivetrain components to the torque listed in the Chapter 8 Specifications.

30   Install all suspension components that were removed. Tighten all suspension fasteners to the torque listed in the Chapter 10

Specifications.

31   Remove the jacks supporting the transaxle and the engine. Install the under guard. Install any exhaust system components that were removed (see Chapter 4).

32   Install the wheels, remove the jack stands and lower the vehicle.

33   Install the upper transaxle-to-engine bolts and tighten them to the torque listed in this Chapter's Specifications.

34   Install the transaxle mounting bracket and tighten the bolts securely.

35   Install the starter motor (see Chapter 5).

36   Unplug the oil cooler hoses and reattach them to the transaxle. This is a good time to inspect and if necessary, replace the hoses (see Chapter 3). Use new hose clamps - once

they've been removed, the original wire-type clamps can cause leaks.

37   Reconnect the speedometer cable to the speedometer driven gear.

38   Reconnect the shift cable to the manual lever (see Section 5).

39   Plug in all electrical connectors.

40   If the vehicle is equipped with cruise control, reattach the cruise control actuator.

41   Install the air cleaner assembly and the intake duct (see Chapter 4).

42   Attach the cable to the negative battery terminal.

43   Fill the transaxle (see Chapter 1). Run the vehicle and check for fluid leaks.

Chapter 7 Part C
Transfer case

Contents

Specifications

Lubricant type.. See Chapter 1

Torque specifications **Ft-lbs**
Transfer case mounting bolts
    Manual.. 40 to 43
    Automatic .... 43 to 58

1   General information

Some models are equipped with an optional full-time four-wheel-drive (4WD) system (sometimes referred to as All-Wheel Drive). On 1990 vehicles, this system is available only on models with a manual transaxle; on 1991 and later vehicles, it's available on both manual and automatic models.

Models with the 4WD option are equipped with a transfer case, a driveshaft connecting it to a rear differential, and a pair of rear driveaxles. The transfer case is covered in this Part of Chapter 7; the driveshaft, differential and driveaxles are covered in Chapter 8.

Because of the complexity of the transfer case and the need for specialized equipment to perform most service operations, this Chapter only includes procedures for seal replacement, transfer case removal and installation, and general information regarding overhaul.

If the transfer case requires major repair work, take it to a dealer service department or an automotive or transmission repair shop.

You can, however, save money by removing and installing the transfer case yourself.

2   Transfer case driveshaft seal - replacement

Removal
Refer to illustration 2.4

1   Raise the vehicle and place it securely on jackstands.
2   Drain the transfer case lubricant (see Chapter 1).

2.4 Using a large screwdriver or a seal removal tool, carefully pry the oil seal out

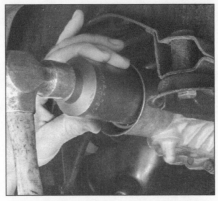

2.7 Carefully drive the seal into the bore with a hammer and a large socket or piece of pipe of the appropriate size

3.5 To detach the transfer case from the transaxle, remove the four mounting bolts (arrows; upper rear bolt not visible in this photo), pull the transfer case to the left (toward the front wheel move it down and forward and carefully slide it off the front end of the driveshaft

3   Remove the driveshaft (see Chapter 8).
4   Using a large screwdriver or a seal removal tool, carefully pry and pull on the outer curved lip of the driveshaft seal **(see illustration)** and remove it from the transfer case.

Installation

Refer to illustration 2.7
5   Inspect the surface on the seal bore and the oil seal surface on the driveshaft for scoring or burrs that may damage the new oil seal. If any minor scratches are evident, remove them with fine emery cloth or wet-or-dry sandpaper. Use a clean cloth dipped in solvent and remove any sanding residue from the counterbore.
6   Apply multi-purpose grease to the new seal. Position the seal into the bore and make sure the seal isn't cocked in the bore.

7   Carefully drive the seal into the bore with a hammer and a large socket or piece of pipe of the appropriate size **(see illustration)**.
8   Install the driveshaft (see Chapter 8).
9   Fill the transfer case with the specified amount and type of lubricant (see Chapter 1).
10   Remove the jackstands and lower the vehicle.

3   Transfer case - removal and installation

Refer to illustration 3.5
1   Loosen the left front wheel lug nuts, raise the vehicle and place it securely on jackstands. Remove the left front wheel.
2   Remove the front exhaust pipe (see Chapter 4).
3   Remove the under cover (see *Transaxle*

- *removal and installation* in Part A (manual) or Part B (automatic) of this Chapter).
4   Drain the transfer case lubricant (see Chapter 1).
5   Remove the four transfer case mounting bolts **(see illustration)**, pull the transfer case to the left (toward the front wheel), then move it down and forward and carefully slide it off the front end of the driveshaft. Be extremely careful when sliding the transfer case off the driveshaft or you could damage the oil seal lip (unless, of course, you're planning to replace the seal anyway). Support the forward end of the driveshaft with a piece of wire.
6   Be sure to inspect the condition of the driveshaft seal while the transfer is removed.

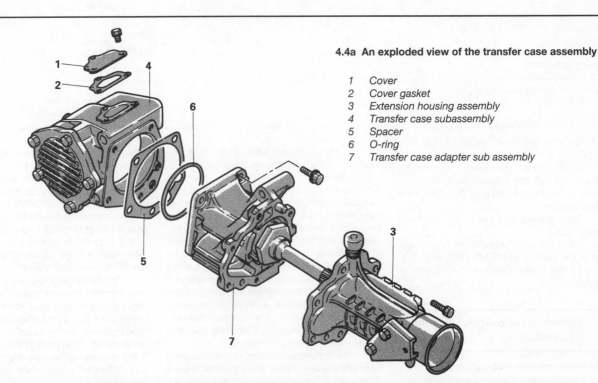

4.4a An exploded view of the transfer case assembly

1   Cover
2   Cover gasket
3   Extension housing assembly
4   Transfer case subassembly
5   Spacer
6   O-ring
7   Transfer case adapter sub assembly

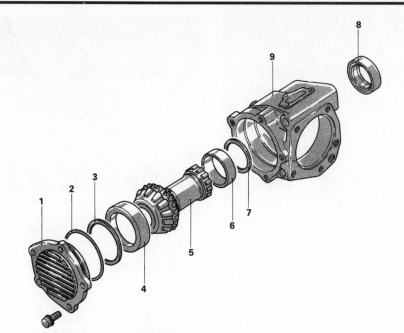

4.4b An exploded view of the transfer case subassembly

1   Transfer cover
2   O-ring
3   Spacer
4   Outer race
5   Drive bevel gear assembly
6   Outer race
7   Spacer
8   Oil seal
9   Transfer case

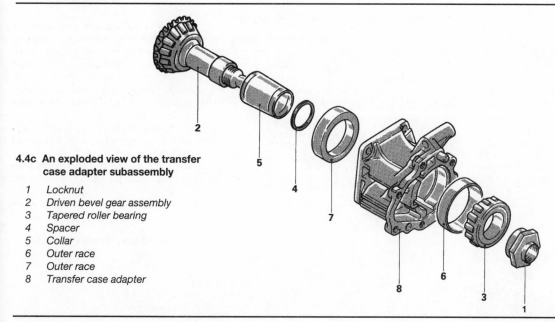

4.4c An exploded view of the transfer case adapter subassembly

1   Locknut
2   Driven bevel gear assembly
3   Tapered roller bearing
4   Spacer
5   Collar
6   Outer race
7   Outer race
8   Transfer case adapter

If it's worn or damaged, replace it (see Section 2).

7   Installation is the reverse of removal. Be sure to tighten the transfer case mounting bolts to the torque listed in this Chapter's Specifications.

8   Refill the transfer case with lubricant (see Chapter 1).

9   Install the wheel, remove the jackstands, lower the vehicle and tighten the wheel lug nuts to the torque listed in the Chapter 1 Specifications.

4   Transfer case overhaul - general information

Refer to illustrations 4.4a, 4.4b and 4.4c

Overhauling a transfer case is a difficult job for the do-it-yourselfer, involving disassembly and reassembly of many small parts. Numerous clearances must be precisely measured and, if necessary, changed with select fit spacers. The time and money involved in an overhaul will likely exceed the cost of a rebuilt unit. If transfer case problems arise, you can remove and install it yourself, but try to exchange your core for a rebuilt unit at your dealer parts department or local auto parts store. If rebuilt units aren't available, have the transfer case overhauled by a transmission repair shop. If that's not possible, of course, you'll have to either purchase a used transfer at a local salvage yard or buy a new unit from a dealer.

Nevertheless, it's not impossible for a home mechanic to rebuild a transfer case, if the special tools are available and the job is done in a methodical, step-by-step manner so that nothing is overlooked.

The tools needed for an overhaul include a dial indicator, an inch-pound torque wrench, a special tool (MB991013) for removing and installing the driven bevel gear locknut, a hydraulic press and bearing puller and installer tools. In addition, of course, you'll also need a large, sturdy workbench and a vise or transmission stand.

During disassembly of the transfer case, make careful notes of how each piece comes off, where it fits in relation to other pieces and what holds it in place. Exploded views **(see illustrations)** are included to show you the relationship of the parts in each subassembly - but actually noting how they fit together as you take them apart will further simplify reassembly.

7C

Notes

Chapter 8
Clutch and driveline

Contents

Specifications

Clutch

Fluid type	See Chapter 1
Type	Single dry plate, diaphragm spring
Actuation	Hydraulic

CV joint boot dimensions

1990
  Front driveaxles (following specs refer to boot for *inner* joint only)
    1.8L engine
      Left driveaxle

Vehicles built up to April 1989	3-5/32 $\pm$ 1/8 inches
Vehicles built from May 1989	2-61/64 $\pm$ 1/8 inches

      Right driveaxle

Vehicles built up to April 1989	3-5/32 $\pm$ 1/8 inches
Vehicles built from May 1989	3-23/64 $\pm$ 1/8 inches

    2.0L engine (2WD models)
      Left driveaxle

Vehicles built up to April 1989	2-61/64 $\pm$ 1/8 inches
Vehicles built from May 1989	3-5/32 $\pm$ 1/8 inches
Right driveaxle	3-5/32 $\pm$ 1/8 inches
2.0L engine (4WD models)	3-23/64 $\pm$ 1/8 inches

  Rear driveaxles (4WD only; refers to boot for *outer* joint only)

1990 and 1991	3 $\pm$ 1/4 inches
1992 and later	3-23/64 $\pm$ 1/8 inches

Rear differential pinion preload (4WD models)

4 to 5 in-lbs

Universal joint (4WD models)

Clearance between snap-ring and spider bearing cap (standard)	0.0008 to 0.0024 inch

Torque specifications

	Ft-lbs
Pressure plate-to-flywheel bolts	11 to 16
Intermediate shaft bearing bracket bolts	26 to 33
Rear axleshaft-to-CV joint bolts (4WD models)	40 to 47
Rear axleshaft/wheel bearing companion flange nut (4WD models)	116 to 159
Driveshaft (4WD models)	
Support bearing assembly mounting nuts	22 to 29
Differential companion flange-to-rear U-joint yoke nuts and bolts	22 to 25
Center yoke-to-center driveshaft nut	116 to 159
Companion flange-to-rear driveshaft nut	116 to 159
Rear differential (4WD models)	
Crossmember-to-differential bolts	72 to 87
Support member-to-differential bolts	58 to 72
Differential support member nuts	80 to 94
Companion flange nut	116 to 159

1 General information

The information in this Chapter deals with the components that transmit power to the wheels, except for the transaxle and transfer case, which are in Chapter 7. The components covered in this Chapter are grouped into three categories - clutch, driveaxles and driveshaft. You'll find general descriptions, inspection and overhaul procedures for all of these components in this Chapter (those Sections covering the driveshaft, the rear differential and the rear driveaxles apply only to 4WD models).

Warning: *Since nearly all the procedures covered in this Chapter involve working under the vehicle, make sure it's securely supported on sturdy jackstands or on a hoist where the vehicle can be easily raised and lowered.*

2 Clutch - description and check

Refer to illustration 2.1

1   All vehicles with a manual transaxle use a single dry plate, diaphragm spring type clutch **(see illustration)**. The clutch disc has a splined hub which allows it to slide along the splines of the transaxle input shaft. The clutch and pressure plate are held in contact by spring pressure exerted by the diaphragm in the pressure plate.

2   The clutch release system is operated by hydraulic pressure. The hydraulic release system consists of the clutch pedal, a master cylinder and fluid reservoir, the hydraulic line, a slave cylinder which actuates the clutch release lever and the clutch release (or throwout) bearing.

3   When pressure is applied to the clutch pedal to release the clutch, hydraulic pressure is exerted against the outer end of the clutch release lever. As the lever pivots, the shaft fingers push against the release bearing. The bearing pushes against the fingers of the diaphragm spring of the pressure plate assembly, which in turn releases the clutch plate.

4   Terminology can be a problem regarding the clutch components because common names have in some cases changed from that used by the manufacturer. For example, the driven plate is also called the clutch plate or disc, the pressure plate assembly is sometimes referred to as the clutch cover, the clutch release bearing is sometimes called a throwout bearing, and the release cylinder is sometimes called the operating or slave cylinder.

5   Other than replacing components that have obvious damage, some preliminary checks should be performed to diagnose a clutch system failure.

a) *The first check should be of the fluid level in the clutch master cylinder (see Chapter 1). If the fluid level is low, add fluid as necessary and inspect the hydraulic clutch system for leaks. If the master cylinder reservoir has run dry, bleed the system (see Section 7) and retest the clutch operation.*

b) *To check "clutch spin down time," run the engine at normal idle speed with the transaxle in Neutral (clutch pedal up - engaged). Disengage the clutch (pedal down), wait several seconds and shift the transaxle into Reverse. No grinding noise should be heard. A grinding noise would most likely indicate a problem in the pressure plate or the clutch disc.*

c) *To check for complete clutch release, run the engine (with the parking brake applied to prevent movement) and hold the clutch pedal approximately 1/2-inch from the floor. Shift the transaxle between 1st gear and Reverse several times. If the shift is not smooth, component failure is indicated. Check the release cylinder pushrod travel. With the clutch pedal depressed completely the release cylinder pushrod should extend substantially. If it doesn't, check the fluid level in the clutch master cylinder.*

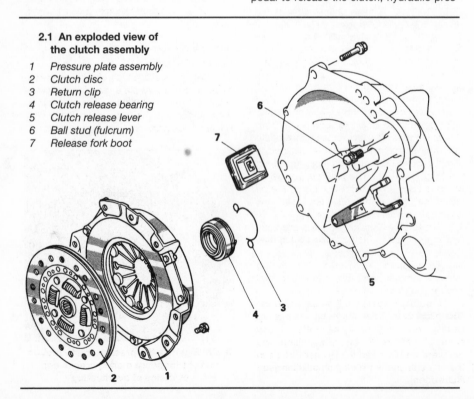

2.1 An exploded view of the clutch assembly

1   *Pressure plate assembly*
2   *Clutch disc*
3   *Return clip*
4   *Clutch release bearing*
5   *Clutch release lever*
6   *Ball stud (fulcrum)*
7   *Release fork boot*

3.6 If you're going to re-use the same pressure plate, mark the relationship of the pressure plate to the flywheel

d) *Visually inspect the clutch pedal bushing at the top of the clutch pedal to make sure there is no sticking or excessive wear.*

e) *Under the vehicle, check that the clutch release lever is solidly mounted on the ball stud.*

---

3 Clutch components - removal, inspection and installation

Warning: *Dust produced by clutch wear and deposited on clutch components may contain asbestos, which is hazardous to your health. DO NOT blow it out with compressed air and DO NOT inhale it. DO NOT use gasoline or petroleum based solvents to remove the dust. Brake system cleaner should be used to flush the dust into a drain pan. After*

NORMAL FINGER WEAR

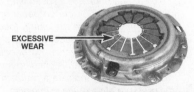

EXCESSIVE WEAR

EXCESSIVE FINGER WEAR

BROKEN OR BENT FINGERS

3.12a Replace the pressure plate if excessive wear or damaged fingers are noted

3.10 Inspect the clutch disc for signs of excessive wear such as smeared friction material, chewed-up rivets, worn hub splines and distorted damper cushions or springs

the clutch components are wiped clean with a rag, dispose of the contaminated rags and cleaner in a labeled, covered container.

Removal

Refer to illustration 3.6

1   Access to the clutch components is normally accomplished by removing the transaxle, leaving the engine in the vehicle. If, of course, the engine is being removed for major overhaul, then the opportunity should always be taken to check the clutch for wear and replace worn components as necessary. However, the relatively low cost of the clutch components compared to the time and labor involved in gaining access to them warrants their replacement any time the engine or transaxle is removed, unless they are new or in near-perfect condition. The following procedures assume that the engine will stay in place.

2   Remove the release cylinder (see Section 6). Hang it out of the way with a piece of wire - it's not necessary to disconnect the hose.

3   Remove the transaxle from the vehicle (see Chapter 7A). Support the engine while the transaxle is out. Preferably, an engine hoist should be used to support it from above. However, if a jack is used underneath the engine, make sure a piece of wood is used between the jack and oil pan to spread the load. **Caution:** *The pick-up for the oil pump is very close to the bottom of the oil pan. If the pan is bent or distorted in any way, engine oil starvation could occur.*

4   The release fork and release bearing can remain attached to the transaxle for the time being.

5   To support the clutch disc during removal, install a clutch alignment tool through the clutch disc hub.

6   Carefully inspect the flywheel and pressure plate for indexing marks. The marks are usually an X, an O or a white letter. If they cannot be found, scribe marks yourself so the pressure plate and the flywheel will be in the same alignment during installation **(see illustration).**

7   Slowly loosen the pressure plate-to-flywheel bolts. Work in a diagonal pattern and loosen each bolt a little at a time until all spring pressure is relieved. Then hold the pressure plate securely and completely remove the bolts, followed by the pressure plate and clutch disc.

Inspection

Refer to illustrations 3.10, 3.12a and 3.12b

8   Ordinarily, when a problem occurs in the clutch, it can be attributed to wear of the clutch driven plate assembly (clutch disc). However, all components should be inspected at this time.

9   Inspect the flywheel for cracks, heat checking, score marks and other damage. If the imperfections are slight, a machine shop can resurface it to make it flat and smooth. Refer to Chapter 2 for the flywheel removal procedure.

10   Inspect the lining оｕn the clutch disc. There should be at least 1/16-inch of lining above the rivet heads. Check for loose rivets, distortion, cracks, broken springs and other obvious damage **(see illustration)**. As mentioned above, ordinarily the clutch disc is replaced as a matter of course, so if in doubt about the condition, replace it with a new one.

11   The release bearing should be replaced along with the clutch disc (see Section 4).

12   Check the machined surface and the diaphragm spring fingers of the pressure plate **(see illustrations)**. If the surface is grooved or otherwise damaged, replace the pressure plate assembly. Also check for obvious damage, distortion, cracking, etc. Light glazing can be removed with emery cloth or sandpaper. If a new pressure plate is indicated, new or factory rebuilt units are available.

Installation

Refer to illustration 3.14

13   Before installation, carefully wipe the flywheel and pressure plate machined surfaces clean. It's important that no oil or grease is on these surfaces or the lining of the clutch disc. Handle these parts only with clean hands.

3.12b Examine the pressure plate friction surface for score marks, cracks and evidence of overheating

8

3.14 Center the clutch disc in the pressure plate with a clutch alignment tool or a wooden dowel of the appropriate diameter

4.4 To check the operation of the release bearing, hold it by the outer race and rotate the inner race while applying pressure - the bearing should turn smoothly - if it doesn't replace it

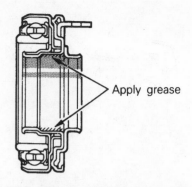

Apply grease

4.5 Fill the groove of the release bearing with high-temperature grease in the indicated area; also apply a light coat of the same grease to the transaxle input shaft splines and bearing retainer sleeve

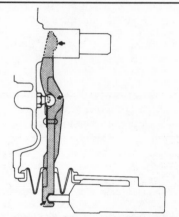

4.6 Using high-temperature grease, lubricate the release lever ball socket (where the ball stud seats into the underside of the lever), the ball stud itself, the contact surfaces on the lever tips that push against the release bearing and the release cylinder pushrod socket

14   Position the clutch disc and pressure plate with the clutch held in place with an alignment tool **(see illustration)**. Make sure it's installed properly (most replacement clutch plates will be marked "flywheel side" or something similar - if not marked, install the clutch disc with the damper springs or cushion toward the transaxle).

15   Install the pressure plate-to-flywheel bolts only finger tight, working around the pressure plate.

16   Center the clutch disc by ensuring the alignment tool is through the splined hub and into the recess in the crankshaft. Wiggle the tool up, down or side-to-side as needed to bottom the tool. Tighten the pressure plate-to-flywheel bolts a little at a time, working in a criss-cross pattern to prevent distortion of the cover. After all of the bolts are snug, tighten them to the torque listed in this Chapter's Specifications. Remove the alignment tool.

17   Using high-temperature grease, lubricate the inner groove of the release bearing (see Section 4). Also place grease on the release lever contact areas and the transaxle input shaft bearing retainer.

18   Install the clutch release bearing (see Section 4).

19   Install the transaxle, release cylinder and all components removed previously, tightening all fasteners to the proper torque specifications.

4   Clutch release bearing and lever - removal, inspection and installation

Warning: *Dust produced by clutch wear and deposited on clutch components may contain asbestos, which is hazardous to your health. DO NOT blow it out with compressed air and DO NOT inhale it. DO NOT use gasoline or petroleum-based solvents to remove the dust. Brake system cleaner should be used to flush it into a drain pan. After the*

clutch components are wiped clean with a rag, dispose of the contaminated rags and cleaner in a labeled, covered container.

Removal

1   Disconnect the negative cable from the battery.

2   Remove the transaxle (see Chapter 7).

3   Remove the clutch release lever from the ball stud, then remove the bearing from the lever.

Inspection

Refer to illustration 4.4

4   Hold the bearing by the outer race and rotate the inner race while applying pressure **(see illustration)**. If the bearing doesn't turn smoothly or if it's noisy, replace the bearing with a new one. Wipe the bearing with a clean rag and inspect it for damage, wear and cracks. Don't immerse the bearing in solvent - it's sealed for life and to do so would ruin it. Also check the release lever for cracks and bends.

Installation

Refer to illustrations 4.5 and 4.6

5   Fill the inner groove of the release bearing with high-temperature grease. Also apply a light coat of the same grease to the transaxle input shaft splines and the front bearing retainer **(see illustration)**.

6   Lubricate the release lever ball socket, lever ends and release cylinder pushrod socket with high-temperature grease **(see illustration)**.

7   Attach the release bearing to the release lever.

8   Slide the release bearing onto the transaxle input shaft front bearing retainer while passing the end of the release lever through the opening in the clutch housing. Push the clutch release lever onto the ball stud until it's firmly seated.

9   Apply a light coat of high-temperature grease to the face of the release bearing

where it contacts the pressure plate diaphragm fingers.

10   The remainder of installation is the reverse of the removal procedure.

5   Clutch master cylinder - removal, overhaul and installation

Note: *Before beginning this procedure, contact local parts stores and dealer service departments concerning the purchase of a rebuild kit or a new master cylinder. Availability and cost of the necessary parts may dictate whether the cylinder is rebuilt or replaced with a new one. If it's decided to rebuild the cylinder, inspect the bore as described in Step 9 before purchasing parts.*

Removal

Refer to illustration 5.2

1   Disconnect the negative cable from the battery.

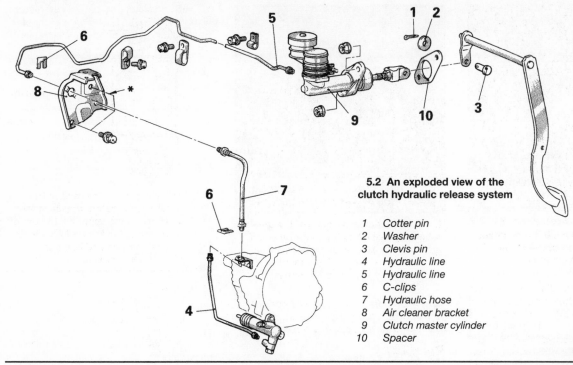

5.2 An exploded view of the clutch hydraulic release system

1 Cotter pin
2 Washer
3 Clevis pin
4 Hydraulic line
5 Hydraulic line
6 C-clips
7 Hydraulic hose
8 Air cleaner bracket
9 Clutch master cylinder
10 Spacer

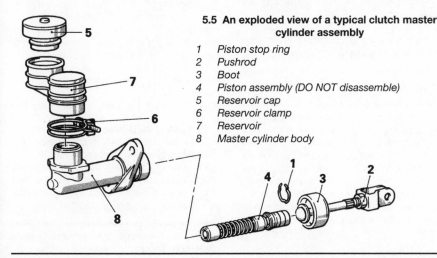

5.5 An exploded view of a typical clutch master cylinder assembly

1 Piston stop ring
2 Pushrod
3 Boot
4 Piston assembly (DO NOT disassemble)
5 Reservoir cap
6 Reservoir clamp
7 Reservoir
8 Master cylinder body

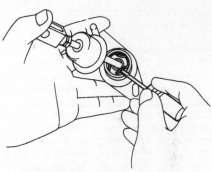

5.6 Pull back the dust cover on the pushrod and pry the snap-ring from its groove

5.8 To remove the piston assembly from the clutch master cylinder, grasp the cylinder with its open end facing down and tap it against a block of wood

2   Under the dashboard, remove the cotter pin and clevis pin and disconnect the pushrod clevis from the clutch pedal lever **(see illustration)**.

3   Disconnect the hydraulic line at the clutch master cylinder. If available, use a flare-nut wrench on the fitting to prevent the fitting from being rounded off. Have some rags handy to absorb any fluid lost as the line is removed. **Caution:** *Don't allow brake fluid to come into contact with paint, as it will damage the finish.*

4   Working in the engine compartment, remove the nuts which secure the master cylinder to the firewall. Remove the master cylinder, again being careful not to spill any of the fluid.

Overhaul

Refer to illustrations 5.5, 5.6, 5.8 and 5.13
Caution: *Do not attempt to disassemble the*
piston/spring/seal assembly. If any part is defective, you must replace the entire assembly; separate pieces aren't available.

5   Remove the reservoir cap and drain all fluid from the master cylinder. Loosen the clamp that secures the reservoir to the master cylinder body **(see illustration)** and separate the reservoir from the body.

6   Pull back the dust cover on the pushrod and remove the snap-ring **(see illustration)**.

7   Remove the pushrod and boot from the cylinder.

8   Tap the master cylinder on a block of wood to eject the piston assembly from inside the bore **(see illustration)**.

9   Inspect the bore of the master cylinder for deep scratches, score marks and ridges. The surface must be smooth to the touch. If the bore isn't perfectly smooth, the master cylinder must be replaced with a new or factory rebuilt unit.

10   If you're rebuilding the master cylinder, use the new parts contained in the rebuild kit and follow any specific instructions which

8

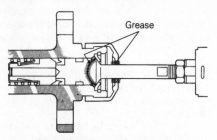

5.13 Apply a liberal amount of rubber grease to the contact surfaces between the pushrod and the piston assembly, and between the pushrod and the boot as shown

may have accompanied the rebuild kit. Wash all parts to be re-used with brake cleaner, denatured alcohol or clean brake fluid. DO NOT use petroleum-based solvents.
11   Lubricate the bore of the cylinder and the seals with plenty of fresh brake fluid.
12   Carefully guide the new piston assembly into the bore, being careful not to damage the seals. Make sure the spring end is installed first, with the pushrod end of the piston closest to the opening.
13   Apply a liberal amount of rubber grease to the contact surfaces between the pushrod and the piston and between the pushrod and the boot **(see illustration)**. Position the pushrod in the bore, compress the spring and install a new snap-ring.
14   Install the fluid reservoir and tighten the reservoir clamp (the clamp screw should be

6.3 Remove the banjo fitting bolt (upper arrow) from the release cylinder (catch any spilled fluid with a small can and a rag); to remove the release cylinder, remove the two mounting bolts (lower arrows)

positioned across the master cylinder body, not parallel with it).

Installation

15   Position the master cylinder on the firewall and install the mounting nuts finger-tight.
16   Connect the hydraulic line to the master cylinder, moving the cylinder slightly as necessary to thread the fitting properly into the bore. Don't cross-thread the fitting.
17   Tighten the mounting nuts and the hydraulic line fitting securely.
18   Apply a light film of grease to the clevis pin and washer, then connect the pushrod to the clutch pedal lever with the clevis pin, washer and a new cotter pin.

19   Fill the clutch master cylinder reservoir with the brake fluid listed in the Chapter 1 Specifications and bleed the clutch system (see Section 7).
20   Check and, if necessary, adjust the clutch pedal height and freeplay (see Chapter 1). Connect the negative battery cable.

6   Clutch release cylinder - removal, overhaul and installation

Note: *Before beginning this procedure, contact local parts stores and dealer service departments concerning the purchase of a rebuild kit or a new release cylinder. Availability and cost of the necessary parts may dictate whether the cylinder is rebuilt or replaced with a new one. If it's decided to rebuild the cylinder, inspect the bore as described in Step 8 before purchasing parts.*

Removal
Refer to illustration 6.3
1   Disconnect the negative cable from the battery.
2   Raise the vehicle and support it securely on jackstands.
3   Disconnect the hydraulic line banjo fitting **(see illustration)** from the release cylinder. Plug the open fitting to prevent fluid loss and contamination. Have a small can and rags handy, as some fluid will be spilled as the line is removed. Discard the sealing washers and be sure to use new ones upon installation.
4   Remove the release cylinder mounting bolts.
5   Remove the release cylinder.

Overhaul
Refer to illustration 6.6
6   Remove the pushrod and the boot **(see illustration)**.
7   Tap the cylinder on a block of wood to eject the piston and seal. Remove the spring from inside the cylinder. If the piston is stuck in the bore, you may have to use compressed air to pop it out. If you do so, wear goggles to protect your eyes and place a rag over the end of the release cylinder to prevent the piston from shooting out of the cylinder. Use only enough compressed air to ease the piston out of the bore.
8   Carefully inspect the bore of the cylinder. Check for deep scratches, score marks and ridges. The bore must be smooth to the touch. If any imperfections are found, the release cylinder must be replaced with a new one.
9   Using the new parts in the rebuild kit, assemble the components using plenty of fresh brake fluid for lubrication. Note the installed direction of the spring and the seal.

Installation
10   Install the release cylinder on the clutch housing. Make sure the pushrod is seated in the release fork pocket.

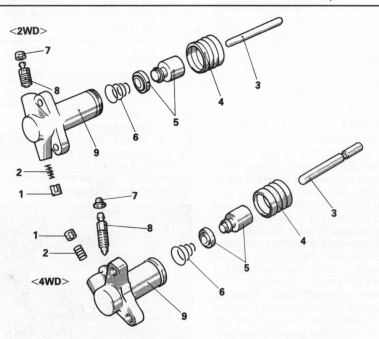

6.6 An exploded view of the clutch release cylinder assembly

1	*Valve plate*	6	*Conical spring*
2	*Spring*	7	*Cap*
3	*Pushrod*	8	*Bleeder plug*
4	*Boots*	9	*Release cylinder*
5	*Piston and cup*		

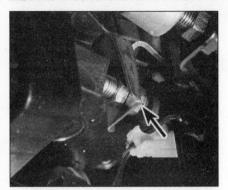

8.5 To remove the clutch start switch, remove the nut nearest the plunger end of the switch (arrow), unscrew the switch, pull it down and unplug the electrical connector

11   Using new sealing washers, connect the hydraulic line to the release cylinder. Tighten the banjo bolt securely.

12   Fill the clutch master cylinder with brake fluid (conforming to DOT 3 specifications).

13   Bleed the system (see Section 7).

14   Lower the vehicle and connect the negative battery cable.

7   Clutch hydraulic system - bleeding

1   The hydraulic system should be bled of all air whenever any part of the system has been removed or if the fluid level has been allowed to fall so low that air has been drawn into the master cylinder. The procedure is very similar to bleeding a brake system.

2   Fill the master cylinder with new brake fluid conforming to DOT 3 specifications. **Caution:** *Do not re-use any of the fluid coming from the system during the bleeding operation or use fluid which has been inside an open container for an extended period of time.*

3   Raise the vehicle and place it securely on jackstands to gain access to the release cylinder, which is located on the left side of the clutch housing.

4   Remove the dust cap which fits over the bleeder valve and push a length of plastic hose over the valve. Place the other end of the hose into a clear container with about two inches of brake fluid in it. The hose end must be submerged in the fluid.

5   Have an assistant depress the clutch pedal and hold it. Open the bleeder valve on the release cylinder, allowing fluid to flow through the hose. Close the bleeder valve when fluid stops flowing from the hose. Once closed, have your assistant release the pedal slowly.

6   Continue this process until all air is evacuated from the system, indicated by a full, solid stream of fluid being ejected from the bleeder valve each time and no air bubbles in the hose or container. Keep a close watch on the fluid level inside the clutch master cylinder reservoir; if the level drops too

low, air will be sucked back into the system and the process will have to be started all over again.

7   Install the dust cap and lower the vehicle. Check carefully for proper operation before placing the vehicle in normal service.

8   Clutch switch - check and adjustment

Refer to illustration 8.5
Note: *This procedure applies only to vehicles with cruise control.*

1   Check the clutch pedal height (distance between the clutch pedal and the firewall when the clutch is disengaged), pedal freeplay and clutch start switch pushrod play (see *Clutch pedal freeplay check and adjustment* in Chapter 1). If the clutch pedal freeplay and the clutch pedal height don't match the specified values, either there's air in the system or the master cylinder or clutch is faulty. Bleed the air from the system (see Section 7) and, if that doesn't do it, disassemble and inspect the clutch master cylinder or clutch.

2   Verify that the cruise control deactivates when the clutch pedal is depressed.

3   Using an ohmmeter, verify that there is continuity between the clutch start switch terminals when the switch is On.

4   Verify that no continuity exists between the switch terminals when the switch is Off.

5   If the switch fails either test, replace it. Remove the nut nearest the plunger end of the switch **(see illustration)**, unscrew the switch, pull it down and unplug the electrical connector. Installation is the reverse of removal.

6   To adjust the clutch start switch, turn the switch in or out to achieve the distance shown in Chapter 1.

9   Driveaxles - general information and inspection

1   Power is transmitted from the transaxle to the front wheels and also (on 4WD models only) from the rear differential to the rear wheels through a pair of driveaxles. The inner end of each driveaxle is splined to the (front or rear) differential side gears. The outer ends of the front driveaxles are splined to the axle hubs and locked in place by a large nut; the outer ends of the rear driveaxles are bolted to the flanges of the rear axleshafts.

2   The inner ends of the front driveaxles are equipped with sliding constant velocity joints which are capable of both angular and axial motion. Each inner joint assembly consists of a tripod-type bearing and a joint tulip (housing). On rear driveaxles, the outer joints are a "ball-and-cage" design, which consists of ball bearings running between an inner race and an outer cage. Both types allow the joint to slide in-and-out as the driveaxle moves up-and-down with the wheel. Front

driveaxle inner joints and rear driveaxle outer joints can be disassembled and cleaned in the event of a boot failure, but if any parts are damaged, the joints must be replaced as a unit (see Section 14).

3   The outer joints on front driveaxles and the inner joints on rear driveaxles are the ball-and-cage type capable of angular but not axial movement.

4   The boots should be inspected periodically for damage and leaking lubricant. Torn CV joint boots must be replaced immediately or the joints can be damaged. Boot replacement involves removal of the driveaxle (front driveaxle, see Section 10; rear driveaxle, see Section 12).

Note: *Some auto parts stores carry "split" type replacement boots, which can be installed without removing the driveaxle from the vehicle. This may seem like a convenient alternative, but the CV joint(s) should be disassembled and cleaned to ensure the joint is free from contaminants such as moisture and dirt which will accelerate CV joint wear. The most common symptom of worn or damaged CV joints, besides lubricant leaks, is a clicking noise in turns, a clunk when accelerating after coasting and vibration at highway speeds. To check for wear in the CV joints and driveaxle shafts, grasp each axle (one at a time) and rotate it in both directions while holding the CV joint housings, feeling for play indicating worn splines or sloppy CV joints. Also check the driveaxle shafts for cracks, dents and distortion.*

10   Front driveaxle - removal and installation

Removal

Refer to illustrations 10.4, 10.5, 10.6, 10.9, 10.10 and 10.11

1   Disconnect the cable from the negative terminal of the battery.

2   Set the parking brake.

3   Loosen the front wheel lug nuts, raise the vehicle and support it securely on jackstands. Remove the wheel.

4   Remove the cotter pin from the driveaxle/hub nut **(see illustration)**.

10.4   Remove the cotter pin from the driveaxle/hub nut

8

10.5 To prevent the hub from turning when you're breaking loose the driveaxle/hub nut, wedge a prybar between two of the wheel studs and allow the prybar to rest against the ground or the floorpan of the vehicle

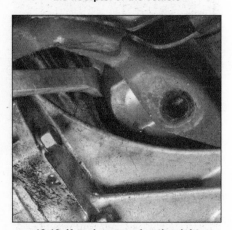

10.10 If you're removing the right driveaxle from any model, or the left driveaxle from a 2WD model, carefully pry the inner CV joint out of the transaxle (if you're removing the left driveaxle on a 4WD model, refer to Section 11)

5   Remove the driveaxle/hub nut and washer. To prevent the hub from turning, wedge a prybar between two of the wheel studs and allow the prybar to rest against the ground or the floor pan of the vehicle **(see illustration).**

6   To loosen the driveaxle from the hub splines, tap the end of the driveaxle with a soft-faced hammer or a hammer and a soft metal drift **(see illustration).** If the driveaxle is stuck in the hub splines and won't move, it may be necessary to remove the brake disc (see Chapter 9) and push it from the hub with a two-jaw puller.

7   Place a drain pan underneath the transaxle to catch any lubricant that leaks out when the driveaxle is removed.

8   Separate the control arm from the steering knuckle (see Chapter 10).

9   Pull out on the steering knuckle and detach the driveaxle from the hub **(see illustration).**

10.6 To loosen the driveaxle from the hub splines, tap the end of the driveaxle with a soft-faced hammer or a hammer and a soft metal punch; if the driveaxle is stuck in the hub splines and won't move, it may be necessary to remove the brake disc (see Chapter 9) and push it from the hub with a two-jaw puller

10   If you're removing the right driveaxle on any model, or the left driveaxle on a 2WD model, carefully pry the inner CV joint out of the transaxle **(see illustration).** If you're removing the left driveaxle on a 4WD model, refer to the next Section; the driveaxle and the intermediate shaft must be removed as a single assembly, then separated.

11   Should it become necessary to move the vehicle while the driveaxle is out, place a large bolt with two large washers (one on each side of the hub) through the hub and tighten the nut securely **(see illustration).**

12   Refer to Chapter 7 for the differential seal replacement procedure for 2WD models.

Installation

13   Installation is the reverse of the removal procedure, but with the following additional points:

a) *When installing the splined inner end of the driveaxle, push the driveaxle sharply inward to seat the retaining ring on the splined inner end of the CV joint into the groove in the bore of the differential side gear.*

b) *Tighten the driveaxle hub nut to the torque listed in this Chapter's Specifications, then install a new cotter pin.*

c) *Install the wheel and lug nuts, lower the vehicle and tighten the lug nuts to the torque listed in the Chapter 1 Specifications.*

d) *Check the transaxle lubricant and add, if necessary, to bring it to the proper level (see Chapter 1).*

11   Intermediate shaft - removal and installation

Refer to illustrations 11.2 and 11.4

1   Set the parking brake. Loosen the left

10.9 Pull out on the steering knuckle and detach the driveaxle from the hub

front wheel lug nuts, raise the vehicle, place it securely on jackstands and remove the left front wheel. Detach the outer end of the driveaxle from the hub following the Steps 9 through 12 of Section 10.

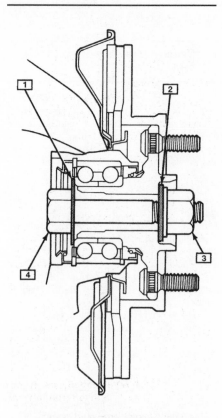

10.11 It's not a good idea to move the vehicle with a driveaxle removed; the bearings in the hub could be damaged. If you must do so, first install a bolt and a pair of washers as shown here, and tighten them securely

1   *2-inch (OD) washer*
2   *1-3/4 inch (OD) washer*
3   *9/16-inch nut*
4   *9/16-inch bolt*

11.2 The intermediate shaft bearing bracket is fastened to the engine block with two bolts (arrows)

2   Remove the intermediate shaft bearing bracket bolts **(see illustration)**.

3   Before removing the shaft, position a drain pan underneath the transaxle and inspect the differential seal for evidence of leakage. Refer to Chapter 7A for the seal replacement procedure. Lightly tap the bearing bracket with a plastic hammer to free the intermediate shaft splines from the differential side gear and pull the shaft straight out of the side gear.

4   Check the intermediate shaft bearing for smooth operation. If it feels rough or sticky it should be replaced **(see illustration)**. Special tools are needed for disassembling the intermediate shaft/bearing bracket/CV joint housing assembly. Take it to a dealer service department or an automotive machine shop to have the bearing bracket, axleshaft and the left inner CV joint housing separated. You can, however, overhaul the inner CV joint or replace a CV joint boot without removing the CV joint housing from the bearing bracket (see Section 14).

5   Installation is the reverse of removal. Make sure you tighten the bearing bracket bolts to the torque listed in this Chapter's Specifications.

12   Rear driveaxle - removal and installation

Refer to illustrations 12.2 and 12.4

1   Block the front wheels, loosen the rear wheel lug nuts, raise the vehicle and support it securely on jackstands. Remove the rear wheel.

2   Remove the nuts and bolts that attach the rear axleshaft flange to the outer CV joint **(see illustration)**.

3   Place a drain pan under the rear differential to catch any lubricant that might spill over the seal lip when the driveaxle is removed. Inspect the seal for evidence of lubricant leaking past the side gear seal. If you see any signs of leakage, replace the seal (see Section 17) after removing the driveaxle.

4   Using a large screwdriver or prybar, pry the inner CV joint out of the differential side gear **(see illustration)**.

5   While the driveaxle is out, inspect both CV joint boots; if either boot is damaged,

12.2 Before you separate the rear driveaxle outer CV joint housing from the axleshaft flange, mark both of them to preserve dynamic balance when they're reassembled, then remove the three nuts (third nut not visible in this photo)

12.4 Carefully pry the inner CV joint from the rear differential side gear with a large screwdriver or prybar

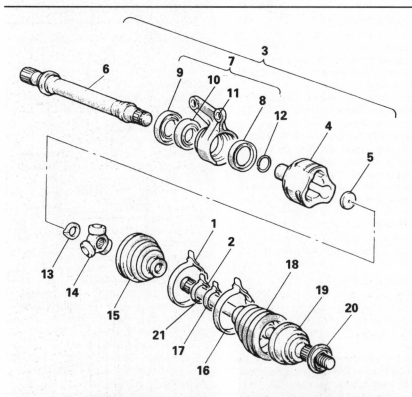

11.4 An exploded view of the intermediate shaft, bearing bracket and left front driveaxle assembly (4WD models)

1	Inner CV joint large boot clamp	12	Circlip
2	Inner CV joint small boot clamp	13	Snap-ring
3	Inner CV joint, bearing bracket and intermediate shaft assembly	14	Spider (tripod) assembly
4	Inner CV joint housing	15	Inner CV joint boot
5	Seal plate	16	Outer CV joint large boot clamp
6	Intermediate shaft	17	Outer CV joint small boot clamp
7	Bearing bracket assembly	18	Outer CV joint boot
8	Outer dust seal	19	Outer CV joint assembly
9	Inner dust seal	20	Dust cover
10	Support bearing	21	Axleshaft (available only as an integral part of outer CV joint assembly)
11	Bearing bracket		

8

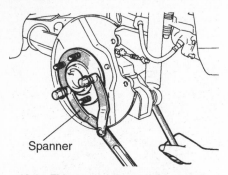

13.4a This special flange holder tool is designed to immobilize the rear axleshaft/wheel bearing assembly . . .

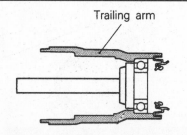

13.6 Drive the inner bearing and seal out of the trailing arm

remove it, clean the joint, repack it and install a new boot (see Section 14). Also check the circlip on the splined inner end of the driveaxle assembly and replace it if necessary.

6   Installation is the reverse of removal. Be sure to tighten the axleshaft flange-to-CV joint nuts/bolts to the torque listed in this Chapter's Specifications.

13 Rear axleshaft/wheel bearing (4WD models) - replacement

Refer to illustrations 13.4a, 13.4b, 13.5 and 13.6

1   Block the front wheels and loosen the rear wheel lug nuts. Raise the vehicle and place it securely on jackstands. Remove the rear wheel.

14.3 Lift the tabs on all the boot clamps with a screwdriver, then open the clamps

13.4b . . . so you can break loose this nut (arrow), but you can also hold it with a large prybar (see illustration 10.5) or even apply the parking brake

2   Remove the rear brake caliper and disc and, on vehicles equipped with an ABS braking system, remove the rear wheel speed sensor (see Chapter 9).
3   Remove the rear driveaxle (see Section 12).
4   Using a special spanner, available at most auto parts stores, or a large screwdriver or prybar, immobilize the axleshaft flange **(see illustration)** and remove the companion flange nut **(see illustration)**. If you don't have the special factory tool or a big enough screwdriver, you can also use the parking brake to hold the axleshaft while you break the nut loose.
5   Using a slide hammer and puller attachment **(see illustration)**, remove the axleshaft from the trailing arm.
6   Using a hammer and a bearing driver (or a long punch), drive the inner bearing out of the trailing arm **(see illustration)**. Coat the outer circumference of the new inner bearing with grease, then drive it into place in the control arm using a bearing driver. If a bearing driver isn't available, a large socket or a piece of pipe, with an outside diameter slightly smaller then that of the bearing, can be used. Use the same method to install the new seal, and make sure the lips of the seal are facing the bearing. Lubricate the lips of the seal with grease, as well.
6   A number of expensive special tools are

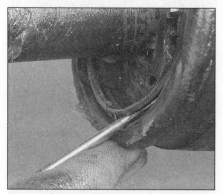

14.4 Pry the retaining ring out of the outer race, then slide the outer race (housing) off the bearing assembly

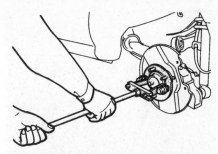

13.5 To remove the rear axleshaft/wheel bearing assembly from the trailing arm, you'll need a slide hammer/puller setup

needed to remove the old outer bearing from the axleshaft and install the new one. Buying all these tools to do a one-time job just isn't cost effective. So, at this point, we recommend that you take the axleshaft assembly to an automotive machine shop or to a dealer service department to have the old bearing and seals removed and the new bearing and seals installed.

7   Installation is the reverse of removal. Be sure to use a new companion flange nut and tighten it to the torque listed in this Chapter's Specifications.

14 Driveaxle boot replacement and CV joint overhaul

Note: *If the CV joints must be overhauled (usually due to torn boots), explore all options before beginning the job. Complete rebuilt driveaxles are available on an exchange basis, which eliminates much time and work. Whichever route you choose to take, check on the cost and availability of parts before disassembling the vehicle.*
1   Remove the driveaxle from the vehicle, referring to the appropriate Section.
2   Mount the driveaxle in a vise with wood lined jaws (to prevent damage to the axleshaft). Check for smooth operation throughout the full range of motion for each CV joint. If a boot is torn, the recommended procedure is to disassemble the joint, clean the components and inspect for damage due to loss of lubrication and possible contamination by foreign matter. **Note:** *The inner CV joint on rear driveaxles (4WD models) and the outer joint on front driveaxles can't be disassembled, but they can be cleaned, checked and packed with new grease).*

Outer rear CV joint (4WD models)

Disassembly
Refer to illustrations 14.3, 14.4, 14.5a, 14.5b, 14.6, 14.7, 14.9, 14.10a and 14.10b
3   Pry the retaining tabs of the boot clamps up and slide the clamp off the boot **(see illustration)**.
4   Slide the boot back on the axleshaft and pry the retaining ring from the outer race **(see illustration)**.

14.5a Mark the relationship of the outer race to the axleshaft

14.6 Apply marks to the inner race, cage and axleshaft . . .

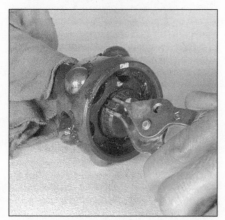

14.7 . . . then remove the outer snap-ring

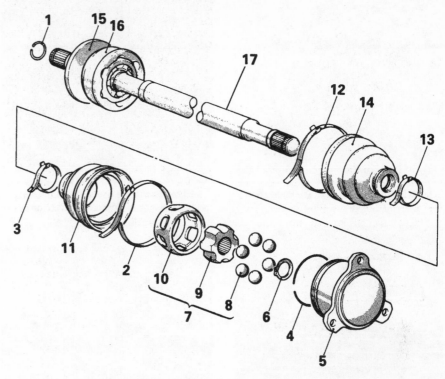

14.5b An exploded view of the rear driveaxle assembly

1	Circlip	11	Outer CV joint boot
2	Boot clamp	12	Boot clamp
3	Boot clamp	13	Boot clamp
4	Retaining ring	14	Inner CV joint boot
5	Outer CV joint housing	15	Inner CV joint dust cover
6	Snap-ring	16	Inner CV joint assembly (do NOT disassemble)
7	Outer CV joint assembly (balls, inner race and cage)	17	Axleshaft (available only as an integral part of inner CV joint assembly)
8	Balls		
9	Inner race		
10	Cage		

5   Mark the relationship of the outer race to the axleshaft and pull the outer race off the inner bearing assembly **(see illustrations)**.

6   Mark the inner race, cage and axleshaft end to ensure that they are reassembled in the same position **(see illustration)**.

7   Remove the snap-ring from the groove in the axleshaft with a pair of snap-ring pliers **(see illustration)**.

8   Slide the inner bearing assembly off the axleshaft.

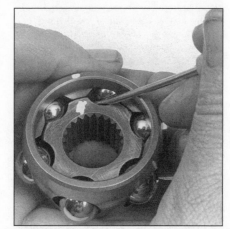

14.9 Pry the balls out of the cage, but be careful not to nick or scratch them

9   Using a small screwdriver or a piece of wood, pry the balls from the cage **(see illustration)**. Be careful not to scratch the inner race, the balls or the cage.

14.10a Align the lands of the inner race with the window of the cage . . .

10   Align the inner race lands with the cage windows and pull the race out of the cage **(see illustrations)**.

8

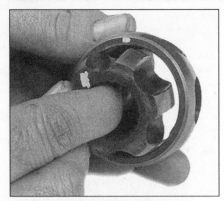

14.10b . . . then remove the inner race from the cage

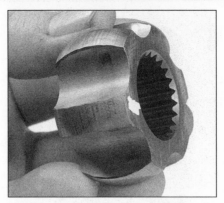

14.11a Check the inner race lands and grooves for pitting and score marks

14.11b Check the cage for cracks, pitting and score marks (shiny spots are normal and don't affect operation)

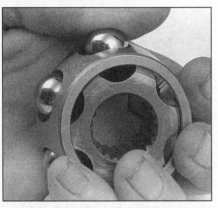

14.13 Press the balls into the cage through the windows using thumb pressure only

14.14 Wrap the splined area of the axle with tape to prevent damage to the boot when installing it

14.17 Pack the inner race and cage assembly full of CV joint grease (also note that the larger diameter side, or bulge, is facing the axleshaft end)

14.20 Remove the boot from the inner CV joint and slide the tripod from the joint housing

14.21 Use a center-punch to place marks (arrows) on the tripod and the driveaxle to ensure that they are reassembled properly

Check

Refer to illustrations 14.11a and 14.11b

11   Clean all components with solvent to remove grease. Inspect the cage and races for pitting, score marks, cracks and other signs of wear and damage. Shiny, polished spots are normal and will not affect CV joint operation **(see illustrations)**.

Reassembly

Refer to illustrations 14.13, 14.14 and 14.17

12   Insert the inner race into the cage and

align the match marks.

13   Press the balls into the cage windows with your thumbs **(see illustration)**.

14   Wrap the axleshaft splines with tape to avoid damaging the boot **(see illustration)**. Slide the small boot clamp and boot onto the axleshaft, then remove the tape.

15   Install the inner race and cage assembly on the axleshaft with the larger diameter side, or "bulge" of the cage (and the previously applied marks) facing the axleshaft end.

16   Install the snap-ring in the groove. Make

sure it's completely seated by pushing on the inner race and cage assembly.

17   Fill the outer race and boot with the specified type and quantity of CV joint grease (normally included with the new boot kit). Pack the inner race and cage assembly with grease, by hand, until grease is worked completely into the assembly **(see illustration)**.

18   Slide the outer race down onto the inner race, aligning the match marks and install the wire ring retainer.

19   Wipe any excess grease from the boot groove in the outer race. Seat the small diameter of the boot in the recessed area on the axleshaft. Push the other end of the boot onto the outer race, making sure it seats in the groove. Install the boot clamp, but before tightening the clamps proceed to Step 26.

Inner front CV joint

Disassembly

Refer to illustrations 14.20, 14.21, 14.22 and 14.23

20   After removing the boot clamps **(see illustration 14.3)**, pull the boot back from the inner joint and slide the tulip from the tripod **(see illustration)**.

21   Use a center punch to mark the tripod and driveaxle to ensure that they are reassembled properly **(see illustration)**.

14.22 Remove the snap-ring with a pair of snap-ring pliers

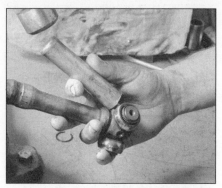

14.23 Drive the tripod joint from the driveaxle with a brass punch and hammer (be careful not to damage the bearing surfaces or the splines on the shaft)

22   Remove the tripod joint snap-ring with a pair of snap-ring pliers **(see illustration)**.
23   Use a hammer and a brass punch to drive the tripod joint from the driveaxle **(see illustration)**.

Check

24   Clean all components with solvent to remove the grease, and check for cracks, pitting, scoring and other signs of wear.

Reassembly

Refer to illustrations 14.25a, 14.25b, 14.25c, 14.25d, 14.26, 14.27a, 14.27b and 14.27c
25   Wrap the splines on the axleshaft with tape to prevent damaging the boot **(see illustration 14.14)**. Slide the clamps and boot onto the axleshaft, then place the tripod on the shaft **(see illustrations)**. Apply grease to the tripod assembly and inside the tulip **(see illustrations)**.
26   Slide the boot into place, making sure both ends seat in their grooves. Adjust the length of the CV joint **(see illustration)** to the dimension listed in this Chapter's Specifications.

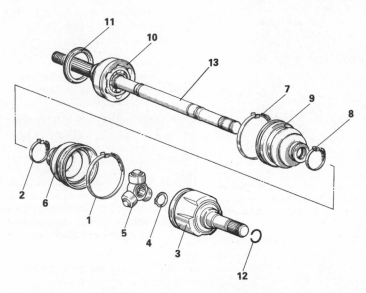

14.25a An exploded view of the front driveaxle assembly (left and right driveaxles on 2WD models; right driveaxle only on 4WD models)

1 Boot clamp	9 Outer CV joint boot
2 Boot clamp	10 Outer CV joint assembly
3 Inner CV joint housing	11 Dust cover
4 Snap-ring	12 Circlip
5 Spider (tripod) assembly	13 Axleshaft (available only as
6 Inner CV joint boot	an integral part of outer
7 Boot clamp	CV joint)
8 Boot clamp	

14.25b Install the tripod with the recessed portion of the splines facing the axleshaft

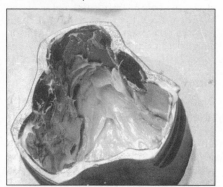

14.25c Place grease at the bottom of the CV joint housing

14.25d Insert the tripod into the tulip, followed by the rest of the grease

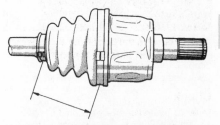

14.26 Before tightening down the boot clamps, make sure you adjust the inner front or outer rear driveaxle boot dimension as shown in accordance with the dimensions listed in this Chapter's Specifications (this dimension is critical for maintaining the correct *pressure* inside sliding CV joints)

8

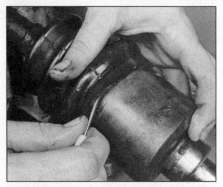

14.27a Equalize the pressure inside the boot by inserting a small, dull screwdriver between the boot and the outer race

14.31 After the old grease has been rinsed away and the solvent blown out with compressed air, rotate the joint housing through its full range of motion and inspect the bearing surfaces for wear and damage - if any of the balls, the race or the cage look damaged, replace the driveaxle and joint assembly

27   Equalize the pressure in the boot, then tighten and secure the boot clamps **(see illustrations)**.

Inner rear (4WD models) outer front CV joints

Disassembly

28   If you're working on the outer CV joint of a front driveaxle, remove the inner CV joint following Steps 20 through 23. If you're removing the inner CV joint of a rear driveaxle, remove the outer CV joint following Steps 3 through 8.
29   Remove the CV joint boot clamps, using the technique described in Step 3. Slide the boot off the axleshaft.

Inspection

Refer to illustration 14.31
30   Thoroughly wash the inner and outer CV joints in clean solvent and blow them dry with compressed air, if available. **Warning:** *Wear eye protection.* **Note:** *Because the outer joint (front driveaxle) or inner joint (rear driveaxle) can't be disassembled, it is difficult to wash away all the old grease and to rid the bearing of solvent once it's clean. But it's imperative*

14.27b To install the new boot clamps, bend the tang down . . .

the job be done thoroughly, so take your time and do it right.
31   Bend the CV joint housing at an angle to the driveaxle to expose the bearings, inner race and cage **(see illustration)**. Inspect the bearing surfaces for signs of wear. If the bearings are damaged or worn, replace the driveaxle/CV joint assembly.

Reassembly

32   Slide the new outer boot (front driveaxle) or inner boot (rear driveaxle) and boot clamps. Be sure to wrap the splines on the axleshaft with tape so the boot isn't damaged **(see illustration 14.14)**. Fill the joint with the specified amount of CV joint grease (usually included with the boot kit), then slide the boot into position. **Note:** *Pack the joint with as mush grease as it will hold and put the rest into the boot.*
33   Install the boot clamps and tighten them

14.27c . . . then bend the tabs over to hold it in place

(see illustrations 14.27a, 14.27b and 14.27c).
34   Install the inner CV joint and boot (front driveaxle) following Steps 25 through 27, or the outer CV joint and boot (rear driveaxle) following Steps 12 through 19.

15   Driveshaft (4WD models) - removal and installation

Refer to illustrations 15.2, 15.3, 15.4 and 15.5
Caution: *It would be a good idea to have a helper for this procedure. Trying to support the driveshaft and remove the support bearing bolts and yoke-to-flange bolts by yourself could result in damage to the driveshaft components.*
1   Raise the rear of the vehicle and support it securely on jackstands. Block the front tires to keep the vehicle from rolling.

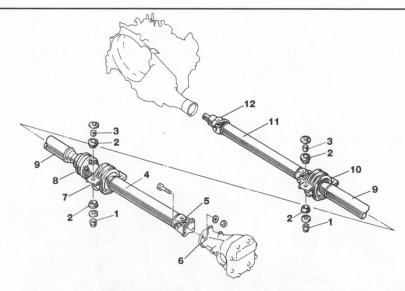

15.2 An exploded view of the driveshaft assembly

1	Self-locking nut	7	Rear support bearing assembly
2	Insulator	8	Löbro joint and boot
3	Spacer	9	Center part of driveshaft
4	Rear part of driveshaft	10	Forward support bearing assembly
5	Rear U-joint and companion flange yoke	11	Front part of driveshaft
6	Rear differential companion flange	12	Forward U-joint and slip-yoke

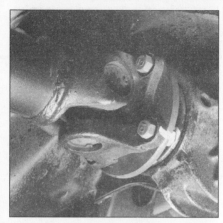

15.3 Start driveshaft removal by marking the U-joint companion flange yoke (at the rear end of the driveshaft) to the differential companion flange, then remove the nuts and bolts

15.4 With an assistant supporting the driveshaft, remove the mounting nuts (arrows) from the forward support bearing assemblies

2   The driveshaft is composed of three pieces: A front shaft from the transmission to the forward support bearing, a middle section from the forward support bearing to the rear support bearing; and a rear shaft from the support bearing to the rear differential **(see illustration)**.

3   Start by marking the relationship of the flange yoke (at the rear end of the driveshaft) to the differential companion flange with paint or a center punch **(see illustration)**, then remove the nuts and bolts from the flanges.

4   Next, with an assistant supporting the driveshaft, remove the mounting nuts, insulators and spacers from the support bearing assemblies **(see illustration)**. The number of spacers used with each nut varies, so draw a sketch of each support bearing assembly and write down the number of spacers used at each location for reference during reassembly. The spacers must be returned to their original locations when the support bearings are installed.

5   Lower the rear end of the driveshaft assembly and carefully withdraw the front

end of the driveshaft from the transfer extension housing. Try to keep the three driveshaft sections straight as you lower the driveshaft to the ground. **Caution:** *Allowing rear end of the driveshaft to droop in relation to the center section could pinch and possibly tear the boot protecting the "Löbro" joint at the rear support bearing assembly* **(see illustration)**. Plug the extension housing to prevent fluid loss (as long as the rear end of the vehicle is level with, or higher than, the front end, fluid shouldn't leak from the transfer case).

6   Check the support bearing assemblies, the Löbro joint and boot, and the U-joints for wear (see Section 16) and repair as necessary.

7   Installation of the driveshaft is basically the reverse of removal. However the following points should be noted: Return all spacers to their original locations at each support bearing. Hand tighten the support bearing nuts initially, then, after the flange yoke joint-to-companion flange bolts and nuts are installed, verify that the support bearing brackets are at a right angle to the driveshaft. Once they're correctly aligned, tighten the

support bearing mounting nuts to the torque listed in this Chapter's Specifications. Check the transfer case oil level and add oil if necessary (see Chapter 1).

---

16 Driveshaft (4WD models) - check and overhaul

Universal joints

Check

Refer to illustration 16.2

1   Wear in the universal joints is characterized by vibration in the transmission, noise during acceleration, and in extreme cases of lack of lubrication, metallic squeaking and grating sounds as the bearings disintegrate.

2   It's unnecessary to remove the driveshaft to determine whether the needle bearings are worn: Try to turn each section of the driveshaft with one hand while holding the U-joint yoke with the other hand **(see illustration)**. Any relative play or movement between any of the three sections of the driveshaft assembly and their respective U-joints is evidence of considerable wear. If you find signs of wear, you'll have to remove the driveshaft (see Section 15) to rebuild or replace the U-joint(s).

3   With the driveshaft assembly removed, you can check the U-joints by holding each part of the driveshaft in one hand and turning the yoke or flange with the other. If there's axial freeplay at any U-joint, rebuild or replace it.

Replacement

Refer to illustrations 16.6a, 16.6b, 16.8a and 16.8b

4   Remove the driveshaft, if you haven't already done so (see Section 15). Mark the relationship of the corresponding yokes of each U-joint you're planning to disassemble.

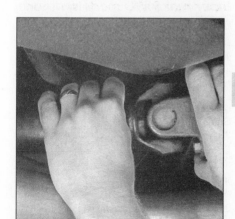

16.2 To check a U-joint for excessive freeplay, hold the yoke with one hand and try to turn the driveshaft with the other like this; there shouldn't be any play in the joint - if there is, you need to rebuild or replace it

8

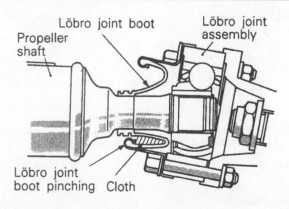

15.5 When removing the driveshaft, keep it straight! If the driveshaft sections hinge at the "Löbro" joint (in front of the rear support bearing assembly), the joint boot could be torn

Löbro joint boot

Propeller shaft

Löbro joint assembly

Löbro joint boot pinching

Cloth

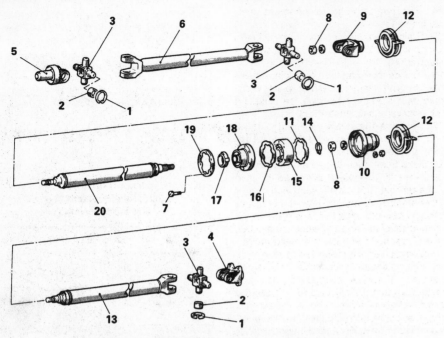

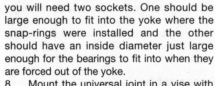

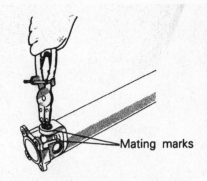

16.6b   Remove the snap-rings from their grooves with snap-ring pliers

16.6a   An exploded view of the driveshaft assembly

1	U-joint spider snap-ring	11	Löbro joint rubber gasket
2	U-joint spider bearing	12	Support bearing assembly
3	U-joint spider	13	Rear driveshaft
4	Flange yoke	14	Löbro joint-to-center driveshaft snap-
5	Sleeve yoke		ring 15 Löbro joint assembly
6	Front driveshaft	16	Löbro joint rubber gasket
7	Boot-to-Löbro joint bolt	17	Löbro joint boot clamp
8	Companion flange-to-rear driveshaft	18	Löbro joint boot
	nut	19	Löbro joint washer
9	Center yoke	20	Center driveshaft
10	Companion flange		

5   Using a socket extension or similar tool and hammer, tap lightly on the bearing outer races of the universal joint to relieve pressure on the snap-rings.

6   Using snap-ring pliers, remove the snap-rings from their grooves **(see illustrations)**.

7   To remove the bearings from the yokes,

you will need two sockets. One should be large enough to fit into the yoke where the snap-rings were installed and the other should have an inside diameter just large enough for the bearings to fit into when they are forced out of the yoke.

8   Mount the universal joint in a vise with the large socket on one side of the yoke and

the small socket on the other side, pushing against the bearing. Carefully tighten the vise until the bearing is pushed out of the yoke and into the large socket **(see illustration)**. If it cannot be pushed all the way out, remove the universal joint from the vise and use pliers to finish removing the bearing **(see illustration)**.

9   Reverse the sockets and push out the bearing on the other side of the yoke. This time, the small socket will be pushing against the cross-shaped universal joint spider end.

10   Before pressing out the two remaining bearings, make sure the yokes are marked so they can be installed in the same relative position during reassembly.

11   The remaining universal joints can be disassembled following the same procedure. Be sure to mark all components for each universal joint so they can be kept together and reassembled in the proper position. It's a good idea to replace one U-joint at a time so you don't mix up any parts.

12   Check the spider journals for scoring, needle roller impressions, rust and pitting. Replace it if any of the above conditions exist.

13   Check the sleeve yoke, center yoke and flange yoke for wear, damage and cracks; if damage or wear are evident, replace that yoke. Check the yokes on both ends of the front driveshaft and on the rear end of the rear driveshaft for wear, damage and cracks; if any of them are damaged or worn, replace that part of the driveshaft.

14   When reassembling the universal joints, use a new spider, new needle bearings, new dust seals and new snap-rings (the U-joint kit includes these parts).

15   Before reassembly, pack each grease cavity in the spiders with a small amount of grease. Also, apply a thin coat of grease to the new needle bearing rollers and the roller contact areas on the spiders.

16   Apply a thin coat of grease to the dust seal lips and install the bearings and spider into the yoke using the vise and sockets that were used to remove the old bearings. Work slowly and be very careful not to damage the bearings as they are being pressed into the yokes.

16.8a   Use a vise, a large socket (left) and a small socket (right) to press the bearing out of the U-joint

16.8b   You may need to use pliers to finish removing the bearing

16.22 Put alignment marks on the Löbro joint and the companion flange, remove the bolts (arrows) attaching the joint and the flange, then separate the joint from the flange

17   Press in the new bearings until they're flush with or below the snap-ring grooves in the bore of the yoke. Install snap-rings of the same thickness on each side and, using a feeler gauge of the appropriate thickness, verify that the clearance between the snap-rings and the spider/bearing assembly is within the standard dimension listed in this Chapter's Specifications. If the clearance exceeds the standard limit, use thicker snap-rings.

18   Make sure that the spider moves freely in the bearings, then check the axial play. If it's excessive, thicker snap-rings must be used to reduce the play.

19   Assemble any other U-joints disassembled as described above.

20   Install the driveshaft (see Section 15).

Löbro joint

Disassembly and inspection

Refer to illustrations 16.22, 16.25, 16.26 and 16.28

21   Remove the driveshaft, if you haven't already done so (see Section 15).

22   Put mating marks on the Löbro joint and the companion flange **(see illustration)**.

23   Remove the bolts and nuts that attach the Löbro joint boot to the companion flange **(see illustration 16.22)**

24   Separate the Löbro joint from the companion flange.

25   Using a screwdriver, pry apart the Löbro joint boot and the Löbro joint assembly **(see illustration)**.

26   Before removing the Löbro joint assembly from the center driveshaft, place alignment marks on the outer race, the cage and the inner race **(see illustration)**.

27   Remove the outer race and balls. If you're planning to reuse the same Löbro joint, the balls must be returned to the same locations from which they're removed during disassembly. The easiest way to do this is to put each ball in a plastic sandwich bag or other small container and label it. For example, you could number the bags one through six and label the first ball removed as "Ball No. 1, first ball to right of alignment mark," then simply remove the balls in a clockwise fashion, putting the second ball in the No. 2 bag, etc. Whatever method you use, just make sure that the balls are returned to the same locations; failure to do so will accelerate wear on the balls and their grooved bearing surfaces in the inner and outer races.

28   Remove the inner race from the center driveshaft with a puller **(see illustration)**.

29   Inspect the boot for tears and cracks. Replace it if it's damaged (a boot kit is available): Cut the boot band and slide off the old boot. If you're planning to re-use the boot - but need to remove it to switch it to another center driveshaft - make sure you don't damage the boot when removing the old boot clamp (you'll have to use a new boot clamp when you install the old boot on the new driveshaft section).

30   Inspect the splines on the driveshaft for wear or damage. Inspect the ball grooves in the inner and outer races, the cage and the balls themselves, for uneven wear, damage and rust. If anything is worn or damaged, replace the Löbro joint (a joint kit, which includes the boot kit mentioned above, is available).

Reassembly

Refer to illustrations 16.31, 16.34, 16.37, 16.41 and 16.43

31   Slide the washer and new boot band

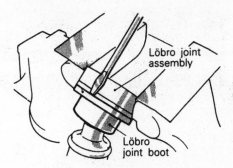

16.25 Using a screwdriver, pry apart the Löbro joint boot and the Löbro joint assembly

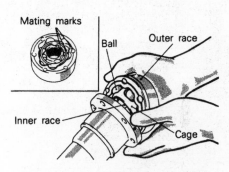

16.26 Before removing the Löbro joint assembly from the center driveshaft, put alignment marks on the outer race, the cage and the inner race (if you're planning to reuse the same joint)

onto the center driveshaft and wrap the splined end of the shaft with tape to protect the new boot from damage during installation **(see illustration)**.

32   Slide the Löbro joint boot onto the end of the shaft and remove the adhesive tape.

33   Apply a thin coat of the grease included with the repair kit to the grooves of the inner and outer races.

34   Put the inner race inside the cage and align the mating marks you made prior to disassembly **(see illustration)**. Insert two of the

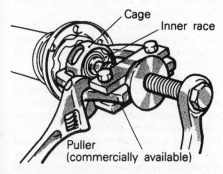

16.28 You'll probably need a small puller to remove the inner race from the center driveshaft splines

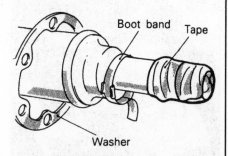

16.31 Slide the washer and new boot band onto the center driveshaft and wrap the splined end of the shaft with tape to protect the new boot from damage during installation

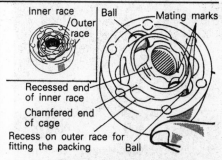

16.34 Put the inner race inside the cage and align the mating marks you made prior to disassembly, then insert two of the balls into the grooves at 12 o'clock and 6 o'clock

8

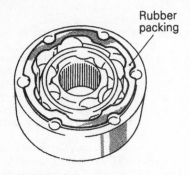

16.37   Apply a thin coating of repair kit grease to the new rubber gasket and install the gasket as shown

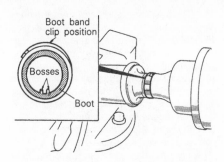

16.41   Position the boot clamp so that the clip is opposite the bosses in the boot provided for ventilation; if there's any excess grease on the bosses, be sure to wipe it off - grease obstructs the vent passages

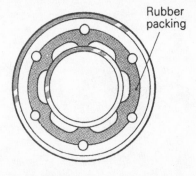

16.43   Apply a thin coat of repair kit grease and install the other rubber gasket to the other face of the outer race

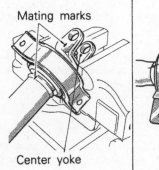

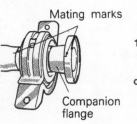

16.50   Put match marks on the center yoke and center driveshaft (left) and/or the companion flange and the rear driveshaft (right)

balls into the grooves at 12 o'clock and 6 o'clock (grooves directly opposite each other) to hold this alignment. Make sure the balls are returned to the same grooves from which they were removed in Step 27.

35   Install the inner race, cage and two balls into the outer race. Make sure the recessed end of the inner race (where the snap-ring fits), the recessed end of the outer race (where the rubber gasket fits) and the chamfered end of the cage are all on the same side. Now install the rest of the balls in the same positions from which they were removed. Verify that the outer race rotates smoothly on the inner race.

36   Apply about two ounces of the grease from the repair kit to the Löbro joint assembly. Make sure you work the grease down into the joint so that it coats all the bearing surfaces.

37   Apply a thin coating of repair kit grease to the new rubber gasket and install the gasket as shown **(see illustration)**.

38   Make sure that the concave side of the outer race is facing toward the boot and the holes in the outer race are aligned with the holes in the boot flange, then drive the Löbro assembly onto the center shaft splines with a hammer and a socket about the same size as the inner race.

39   Secure the inner race with a new snap-ring.

40   Insert the bolts through the boot flange and rotate the boot until the bolts are aligned with the holes in the outer race. Install the

bolts but don't install the nuts yet.

41   Install a new boot clamp. Position the clamp so that the clip is opposite the bosses in the boot provided for ventilation **(see illustration)**. If there's any excess grease on the bosses, be sure to wipe it off - grease obstructs the vent passages.

42   Verify that the Löbro joint operates smoothly.

43   Apply a thin coat of repair kit grease and install the other rubber gasket to the other face of the outer race **(see illustration)**.

44   Align the mating marks you made on the outer race and the companion flange, install the nuts and tighten them securely.

Support bearing assemblies

Refer to illustrations 16.50, 16.52, 16.53 and 16.54

45   Raise the vehicle and support it on jackstands.

46   To check either support bearing, rotate the driveshaft and listen carefully to the bearing. It should rotate smoothly and silently. If you hear a grating, grinding metallic sound from either support bearing, replace it. Also inspect the rubber bushing around each bearing for cracks or other deterioration. If the bushing is damaged or worn, replace the bearing.

47   Remove the driveshaft, if you haven't already done so (see Section 15).

48   If you're replacing the forward support bearing assembly, you'll need to disconnect the front and center parts of the driveshaft by

disassembling the U-joint that connects them (see Steps 4 through 9); if you're replacing the rear support bearing assembly, disconnect the center and rear parts of the driveshaft by disassembling the Löbro joint that connects them (see above).

49   To remove the forward support bearing, place the center yoke in a vise and break the nut loose; to remove the rear support bearing, place the rear driveshaft in a vise and break the nut loose (don't vise up the companion flange - tightening the vise enough to hold the shaft will damage the flange). **Caution:** *Tightening the vise too much will damage the driveshaft tube.*

50   Before pulling the center yoke or the companion flange off the driveshaft, be sure to put alignment marks on the yoke and shaft or on the companion flange and shaft **(see illustration)**.

51   Pull off the yoke or flange. If the yoke/flange sticks, use a small puller to get it off.

52   Put alignment marks on the forward support bearing assembly and the center driveshaft, or on the rear support bearing assembly and the rear driveshaft, then remove the support bearing bracket assembly **(see illustration)**.

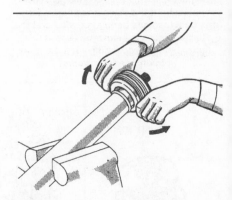

16.52   Put alignment marks on the forward support bearing assembly and the center driveshaft, or on the rear support bearing assembly and the rear driveshaft, then remove the support bearing bracket assembly

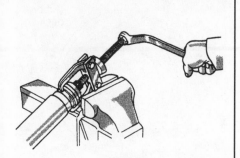

16.53 Remove either support bearing with a small puller

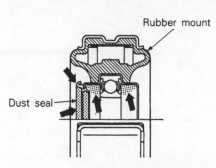

16.54 Apply multi-purpose grease to the front and rear grease grooves in the support bearing and to the dust seal lip

17.1 An exploded view of the pinion seal and related components and the side-gear seal

1   Companion flange nut
2   Washer
3   Companion flange
4   Pinion seal
5   Pinion bearing
6   Rear differential
7   Side-gear seal

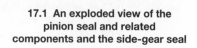

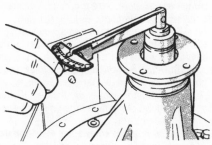

17.5 Using an inch-pound torque wrench, see how much torque is required to turn the pinion shaft within the range of gear backlash - if the axles and wheels turn, the backlash has been exceeded and the torque figure is incorrect; record this figure before proceeding - it's the drive pinion bearing preload

17.6 To break the companion flange nut loose, place a punch or screwdriver through one of the bolt holes in the flange and rotate the flange until the punch/screwdriver is up against the left (driver's) side of the differential housing

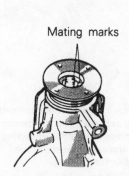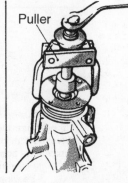

17.7 Make match marks on the companion flange and the pinion shaft, then pull off the companion flange with a two-jaw puller

53   Remove either support bearing with a small puller **(see illustration)**.
54   Apply multi-purpose grease to the front and rear grease grooves in the support bearing and to the dust seal lip **(see illustration)**.
55   Install the bearing into the rubber mounting groove on the support bearing bracket. The bearing dust seal should face toward the side of the support bearing bracket mating mark you made before removing the bearing bracket.
56   Press the bearing onto the center and/or rear driveshaft(s). If you're using the old bearing bracket, make sure it's oriented the same it was when you took it off, *i.e. the mating mark on the bracket faces toward the mating mark on the shaft.*
57   Reassemble the driveshaft by reattaching the U-joint (center driveshaft) or the companion flange (rear driveshaft).
58   Install the driveshaft (see Section 15).
59   Remove the jackstands and lower the vehicle.

---

17   Rear differential oil seal replacement (4WD models)

Pinion seal

Refer to illustrations 17.1, 17.5, 17.6 and 17.7

1   The pinion oil seal can be replaced without removing or disassembling the differential **(see illustration)**.
2   Raise the vehicle and set it on jackstands.
3   Remove the drain and fill plugs from the rear axle housing and allow the differential lubricant to drain into a container (see Chapter 1). When the draining is complete, loosely install the drain plug.
4   Separate the driveshaft from the differential (see Section 15). Be sure to tie the end of the driveshaft up, out of the way.
5   Using an inch-pound torque wrench, see how much torque is required to turn the pinion shaft within the range of gear backlash **(see illustration)**. If the axles and wheels turn, the backlash has been exceeded and the torque figure is incorrect). This figure is the drive pinion bearing preload. Record it before proceeding.
6   Remove the nut and washer from the companion flange. To prevent the flange from turning, place a long punch through one of the bolt holes and brace it against a casting projection on the differential housing **(see illustration)**.
7   Mark the companion flange and pinion shaft before separating them, then remove the companion flange with a puller **(see illustration)**.
8   After noting what the visible side of the oil seal looks like, carefully pry it out of the differential with a screwdriver or a prybar. Be careful not to damage the splines on the pinion shaft.
9   Clean the seal mounting area, the outside diameter of the seal and the pinion shaft with a clean rag.

8

17.24 Pry the side-gear seal out of the rear differential . . .

17.25 . . . and use a large socket or section of pipe and a hammer to install the new side-gear seal into the rear differential

18.5 Working on the upper side of the crossmember, remove the two bolts (arrow) that attach the forward part of the rear differential to the crossmember (the rear bolt isn't visible in this photo, but it's right behind the one that is)

10   Lubricate the new seal lip with multi-purpose grease and carefully install it in position in the differential. Tap the seal into place with a hammer and a block of wood or short section of pipe. Work around the entire circumference of the seal, a little at a time, until the face of the seal is flush with the end of the differential. Work slowly and do not damage the rubber lip of the seal. DO NOT drive the seal beyond the depth listed in this Chapter's Specifications.

11   Clean the sealing lip contact surface of the companion flange. Apply a thin coat of multi-purpose grease to the seal contact surface and the shaft splines and carefully install the flange onto the end of the pinion shaft. You may have to rotate the flange slightly to line up the splines.

12   Lubricate the companion flange washer with grease. Install the washer and a new self-locking companion flange nut.

13   Disengage the parking brake and snug-up the companion flange nut as you let the flange rotate. This will help to seat the pinion shaft bearings properly as the nut is tightened.

14   Tighten the companion flange nut to the torque listed in this Chapter's Specifications, while holding the flange to keep the pinion shaft from turning.

15   Turn the flange and pinion shaft several times in each direction to make sure that the bearings are seated, then check the preload as described in Step 5. If the torque required to start the shaft turning is excessive, the shim(s) on the pinion shaft must be replaced with a thicker one. **Caution:** *If the torque on the nut is exceeded, a new preload adjusting sleeve will have to be installed. This procedure should be done by a dealer service department or other repair shop to avoid damage to the internal parts of the differential.*

16   If the preload is less than the figure recorded before disassembly, a thinner shim must be installed.

17   Fasten the rear of the driveshaft to the differential (see Section 15).

18   Tighten the drain plug in the rear axle housing and fill the housing to the proper level with the recommended gear lubricant (see Chapter 1). Install the filler plug and tighten it securely.

19   Remove the jackstands and lower the vehicle to the ground.

20   Test drive the vehicle and check around the differential companion flange for leaks.

Differential side gear seals

Refer to illustrations 17.24 and 17.25

21   Raise the rear of the vehicle and support it on jackstands.

22   Remove the driveaxle (see Section 12) and suspend it out of the way **(see illustration)**.

23   Use a large screwdriver or prybar to pry the seal out **(see illustration)**.

24   Use a seal driver, a large socket or section of pipe and a hammer to install the new seal **(see illustration)**.

25   The rest of installation is the reverse of removal. Be sure to apply grease to the lip of the seal before installing the driveaxle.

---

18   Differential carrier (4WD models) - removal and installation

---

Refer to illustrations 18.5 and 18.6

1   Loosen the rear wheel lug nuts. Raise the rear of the vehicle and support it securely on jackstands. Remove the rear wheels.

2   Drain the differential lubricant (see Chapter 1).

3   Remove the rear driveaxles (see Section 12).

3   Disconnect the rear end of the drive-shaft from the differential carrier (see Section 15) and hang the driveshaft from the exhaust pipe with a piece of wire to prevent it from bending.

4   Place a transaxle jack or a large floor jack directly underneath the differential carrier and raise the jack head until it's support-

ing the carrier.

5   Working on the upper side of the cross-member, remove the two bolts that attach the forward part of the differential carrier to the crossmember **(see illustration)**.

6   Remove the nuts and washers from the two large bolts that attach the differential support member to the underside of the vehicle **(see illustration)**.

7   Carefully lower the differential carrier and support member as a single assembly and slide them out from underneath the vehicle.

8   Remove the two bolts that attach the differential support member to the rear differential.

9   Installation is the reverse of removal. Be sure to tighten the two support member-to-carrier bolts, the two large support member self-locking nuts and the two crossmember-to-carrier bolts to the torque listed in this Chapter's Specifications.

18.6 Remove the nuts and washers from the two large bolts (arrows) that attach the differential support member to the underside of the vehicle

Chapter 9 Brakes

Contents

Specifications

General

Brake fluid type	See Chapter 1
Brake pedal	
Height (between pedal and floorboard)	6-29/32 to 7-7/64 inches
Freeplay (amount of pedal movement before resistance is met)	7/64 to 19/64 inch
Reserve distance (between depressed pedal and floorboard)	3-7/64 inches
Brake light switch-to-brake pedal stopper	1/64 to 3/64 inch
Power brake booster pushrod-to-master cylinder piston clearance	
9-inch brake booster	1/32 to 3/64 inch
7 and 8-inch brake boosters	1/64 to 1/32-inch

Brakes

Minimum brake pad thickness	See Chapter 1
Disc thickness limit	
Front discs	0.882 inch
Rear discs	0.331 inch
Disc runout limit	0.0031 inch
Disc thickness variation	0.0006 inch

Torque specifications

Ft lbs (unless otherwise indicated)

Front brake caliper	
Caliper mounting bolts	58 to 72
Guide pin bolt	
Single-piston caliper	
Up to April 1989	16 to 23
May 1989 on	46 to 62
Double-piston caliper	54
Lock pin bolt	
Single-piston caliper	
Up to April 1989	16 to 23
May 1989 on	46 to 62
Double-piston caliper	54
Rear brake caliper	
Caliper mounting bolts	36 to 43
Guide pin and lock pin bolts	16 to 23
Brake hose-to-rear caliper banjo fitting bolt	18 to 25
Master cylinder-to-brake booster nuts	72 to 108 in-lbs
Power brake booster mounting nuts	96 to 144 in-lbs
Wheel lug nuts	See Chapter 1

9

1   General information

The vehicles covered by this manual are equipped with hydraulically operated front and rear disc brake systems. Except for a two-piston caliper available as an option on some 1993 models, all calipers are a single-piston design. Both the front and rear brakes automatically compensate for disc and pad wear: As the pads wear down, the pistons gradually protrude farther from the calipers, but don't retract as far, automatically compensating for the thinner pads.

Hydraulic system

The hydraulic system consists of two separate circuits that are diagonally split (one circuit operates the left front and right rear brakes, while the other circuit operates the right front and left rear brakes). The master cylinder has separate reservoirs for the two circuits, and, in the event of a leak or failure in one hydraulic circuit, the other circuit will remain operative. A dual proportioning valve on the firewall provides brake balance between the front and rear brakes.

Power brake booster

The power brake booster, which is mounted on the firewall, utilizes engine manifold vacuum and atmospheric pressure to provide assistance to the hydraulically operated brakes.

Parking brake

The parking brake operates the rear brakes only, through cable actuation. It's activated by a lever mounted in the center console.

Service

After completing any operation involving disassembly of any part of the brake system, always test drive the vehicle to check for proper braking performance before resuming normal driving. When testing the brakes, perform the tests on a clean, dry, flat surface. Conditions other than these can lead to inac-

curate test results.

Test the brakes at various speeds with both light and heavy pedal pressure. The vehicle should stop evenly without pulling to one side or the other. Avoid locking the brakes, because this slides the tires and diminishes braking efficiency and control of the vehicle.

Tires, vehicle load and wheel alignment are factors which also affect braking performance.

2   Anti-lock Brake System (ABS) - general information

The anti-lock brake system is designed to maintain vehicle steerability, directional stability and optimum deceleration under severe braking conditions on most road surfaces. It does so by monitoring the rotational speed of each wheel and controlling the brake line pressure to each wheel during braking. This prevents the wheels from locking up.

The ABS system has three main components - the wheel speed sensors, the electronic control unit (ECU) and the hydraulic unit. Four wheel speed sensors - one at each wheel - send a variable voltage signal to the control unit, which monitors these signals, compares them to its program and determines whether a wheel is about to lock up. When a wheel is about to lock up, the control unit signals the hydraulic unit to reduce hydraulic pressure (or not increase it further) at that wheel's brake caliper. Pressure modulation is handled by electrically-operated solenoid valves.

If a problem develops within the system, an "ABS" warning light will glow on the dashboard. Sometimes, a visual inspection of the ABS system can help you locate the problem. Carefully inspect the ABS wiring harness. Pay particularly close attention to the harness and connections near each wheel. Look for signs of chafing and other damage caused by incorrectly routed wires. If a wheel sensor harness is damaged, the sensor must be replaced. **Warning:** *Do NOT try to repair an ABS wiring harness. The ABS system is sensitive to even the smallest changes in resistance. Repairing the harness could alter resistance values and cause the system to malfunction. If the ABS wiring harness is damaged in any way, it must be replaced.* **Caution:** *Make sure the ignition is turned off before unplugging or reattaching any electrical connections.*

Diagnosis and repair

If a dashboard warning light comes on and stays on while the vehicle is in operation, the ABS system requires attention. Although special electronic ABS diagnostic testing tools are necessary to properly diagnose the system, you can perform a few preliminary checks before taking the vehicle to a dealer service department.

a) Check the brake fluid level in the reservoir.
b) Verify that the computer master cylinder connectors are securely connected.
c) Check the electrical connectors at the hydraulic control unit.
d) Check the fuses.
e) Follow the wiring harness to each wheel and verify that all connections are secure and that the wiring is undamaged.

If the above preliminary checks do not rectify the problem, the vehicle should be diagnosed by a dealer service department. Due to the complex nature of this system, all actual repair work must be done by a dealer service department.

3   Front disc brake pads - replacement

Refer to illustrations 3.5 and 3.6a through 3.6o

Warning: *Disc brake pads must be replaced on both front or rear wheels at the same time - never replace the pads on only one wheel. Also, the dust created by the brake system may contain asbestos, which is harmful to your health. Never blow it out with compressed air and don't inhale any of it. An approved filtering mask should be worn when working on the brakes. Do not, under any circumstances, use petroleum-based solvents to clean brake parts. Use brake system cleaner only! When servicing the disc brakes, use only high-quality, nationally recognized brand-name pads.*

1   Remove the cap from the brake fluid reservoir.

2   Loosen the front wheel lug nuts, raise the front of the vehicle and support it securely on jackstands. Block the rear wheels.

3   Remove the front wheels. Work on one brake assembly at a time, using the assembled brake for reference if necessary.

4   Inspect the brake disc carefully as outlined in Section 7. If machining is necessary, follow the information in that Section to remove the disc, at which time the pads can be removed as well.

5   Push the piston back into its bore to provide room for the new brake pads. A C-clamp can be used to accomplish this **(see illustration)**. As the piston is depressed to the bottom of the caliper bore, the fluid in the master cylinder will rise. Make sure that it doesn't overflow. If necessary, siphon off some of the fluid.

6   Follow the accompanying photos, beginning with **illustration 3.6a,** for the actual pad replacement procedure. Be sure to stay in order and read the caption under each illustration.

7   When reinstalling the caliper, be sure to tighten the guide pin to the torque listed in this Chapter's Specifications. After the job has been completed, firmly depress the

3.5 Push the piston back into the caliper bore with a large C-clamp

3.6a Remove the caliper guide pin (lower arrow) - it's only necessary to remove the lock pin (upper arrow) if you're removing the caliper from the vehicle

3.6b Swing the caliper up like this . . .

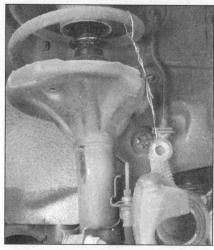

3.6c . . . and support it in this position with a piece of wire

3.6d Remove the inner pad and shim(s)

3.6e Remove the outer pad . . .

3.6f . . . and pull off the anti-squeal shim(s)

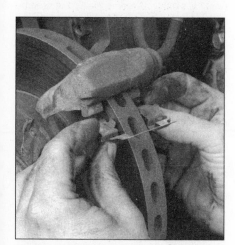

3.6g Remove the upper anti-rattle clip . .

3.6h . . . and the lower anti-rattle clip, paying close attention to how they're installed in the torque plate

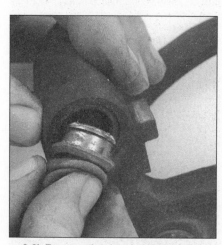

3.6i Remove the dust boots from the torque plate (removed for clarity), inspect them for cracks and tears, and replace as necessary

9

3.6j Install the upper anti-rattle clip . . .

3.6k . . . and the lower anti-rattle clip in the torque plate - make sure both fully seated

3.6l Apply anti-squeal compound (available at auto parts stores - follow label instructions) to the back of the brake pad and install the anti-squeal shim(s)

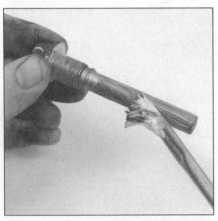

3.6m Lubricate the guide pin with multi-purpose grease before installing it

3.6n Install the inner pad . . .

3.6o . . . and the outer pad into the torque plate - make sure both pads are fully seated, then swing the caliper down into place, install the guide pin and tighten it to the torque listed in this Chapter's Specifications

brake pedal a few times to bring the pads into contact with the disc. Check the level of the brake fluid, adding some if necessary. Check the operation of the brakes carefully before placing the vehicle into normal service.

4 Front disc brake caliper - removal, overhaul and installation

Warning: *Dust created by the brake system may contain asbestos, which is harmful to your health. Never blow it out with compressed air and don't inhale any of it. An approved filtering mask should be worn when working on the brakes. Do not, under any circumstances, use petroleum-based solvents to clean brake parts. Use brake system cleaner only!*
Note: *If an overhaul is indicated (usually because of fluid leakage), explore all options before beginning the job. New and factory rebuilt calipers are available on an exchange basis, which makes this job quite easy. If it's decided to rebuild the calipers, make sure a*

rebuild kit is available before proceeding. Always rebuild the calipers in pairs - never rebuild just one of them.

Removal
Refer to illustration 4.1
1   Loosen the brake hose fitting at the strut bracket **(see illustration 9.3)**, then remove the U-clip. Unscrew the brake hose from the caliper **(see illustration)**. **Note:** *If you're removing the caliper to replace the brake pads or to remove the brake disc, go to Section 3 - it isn't necessary to disconnect the brake hose from the caliper unless you're completely removing the caliper from the vehicle.*
2   Plug the brake hose to keep contaminants out of the brake system and to prevent losing any more brake fluid than is necessary.
3   Remove the caliper (see Section 3 - it's part of the brake pad replacement procedure).

Overhaul
Refer to illustrations 4.4a, 4.4b, 4.4c, 4.5 and 4.7
4   Remove the boot retaining ring and the boot **(see illustrations)**.

4.1 After the fitting at the other end of the hose has been disconnected, unscrew the brake hose from the caliper (use a flare-nut wrench to protect the fitting)

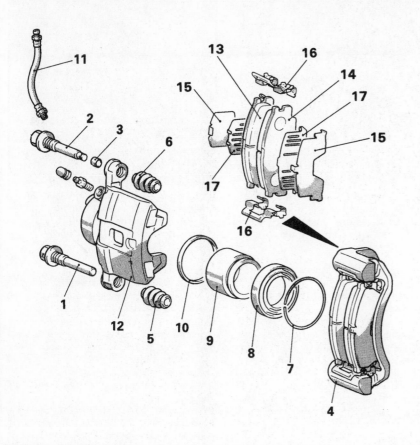

4.4a An exploded view of the single-piston brake caliper assembly

1   Guide pin
2   Lock pin
3   Bushing
4   Torque plate (caliper mounting bracket)
5   Guide pin boot
6   Lock pin boot
7   Boot ring
8   Piston boot
9   Piston
10 Piston seal
11 Brake hose
12 Caliper body
13 Inner brake pad
14 Outer brake pad
15 Outer brake pad shim
16 Anti-rattle clip
17 Inner brake pad shim (1992 and 1993 only)

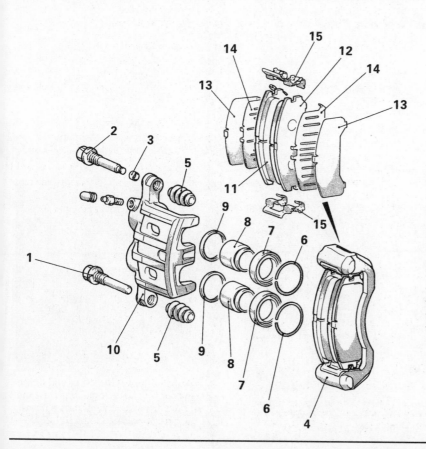

4.4b An exploded view of the dual-piston brake caliper assembly

1   Guide pin
2   Lock pin
3   Bushing
4   Torque plate (caliper mounting bracket)
5   Guide pin boot (below); lock pin boot (above)
6   Boot ring
7   Piston boot
8   Piston
9   Piston seal
10 Caliper body
11 Inner brake pad
12 Outer brake pad
13 Outer brake pad shim
14 Inner brake pad shim
15 Anti-rattle clip

9

4.4c Remove the boot retaining ring with a small screwdriver - be extremely careful not to gouge or scratch the piston or the piston bore

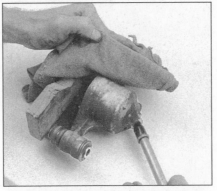

4.5 With the caliper padded to catch the piston, use compressed air to force the piston out of its bore - make sure your fingers aren't between the piston and the caliper

4.7 Remove the piston seal from the caliper bore with a plastic or wood tool - a pencil will do the job (metal tools may damage the cylinder bore)

5   Place a wood block between the piston and caliper to prevent damage as it is removed. Apply compressed air to the brake fluid hose connection on the caliper body **(see illustration)**. Use only enough pressure to ease the piston out of its bore. **Warning:** *Be careful not to place your fingers between the piston and the caliper, as the piston may come out with some force.* **Note:** *On models with dual-piston calipers, only one piston will be ejected. Block it back in place, against its seal and apply air pressure again to eject the other piston.*

6   Inspect the mating surfaces of the piston and caliper bore wall. If there is any scoring, rust, pitting or bright areas, replace the complete caliper unit with a new one.

7   If these components are in good condition, remove the piston seal from the caliper bore using a wooden or plastic tool **(see illustration)**. Metal tools may damage the cylinder bore.

8   Remove the dust boots from the caliper ears **(see illustration 3.6i)**.

9   Wash all the components with brake system cleaner.

10   Submerge the new piston seal and the piston in brake fluid and install them into the caliper bore. Do not force the piston into the bore, but make sure that it is squarely in

place, then apply firm pressure to bottom it in the bore.

11   Install the new piston dust boot and the retaining ring.

12   Lubricate the guide pin, lock pin and sleeves with the special grease supplied with the rebuild kit, then push them into the caliper ears and install the dust boots.

Installation

13   Install the caliper by reversing the removal procedure. Tighten the guide pin and the lock pin to the torque listed in this Chapter's Specifications.

14   Bleed the brake system (see Section 10). Make sure there are no leaks from the hose connections. Test the brakes carefully before returning the vehicle to normal service.

5   Rear disc brake pads - replacement

Refer to illustrations 5.5a through 5.5r

Warning: *Disc brake pads must be replaced on both front or rear wheels at the same time - never replace the pads on only one wheel. Also, the dust created by the brake system*

may contain asbestos, which is harmful to your health. Never blow it out with compressed air and don't inhale any of it. An approved filtering mask should be worn when working on the brakes. Do not, under any circumstances, use petroleum-based solvents to clean brake parts. Use brake system cleaner only! When servicing the disc brakes, use only high-quality, nationally recognized brand-name pads.

1   Remove the cap from the brake fluid reservoir.

2   Loosen the wheel lug nuts, raise the front or rear of the vehicle and support it securely on jackstands. Block the wheels at the opposite end.

3   Remove the wheels. Work on one brake assembly at a time, using the assembled brake for reference if necessary.

4   Inspect the brake disc carefully as outlined in Section 7. If machining is necessary, follow the information in that Section to remove the disc, at which time the pads can be removed as well.

5   Follow the accompanying photos, beginning with **illustration 5.5a,** for the actual pad replacement procedure. Be sure to stay in order and read the caption under each illustration.

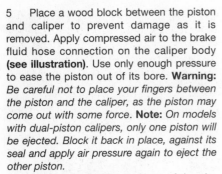

5.5a To disconnect the parking brake cable from the rear caliper, remove this retaining clip from the spindle lever . . .

5.5b . . . pull the spring clip from the cable-to-caliper bracket with a pair of pliers . . .

5.5c . . . pull on the cable end plug and lift the cable straight up out of its groove in the caliper bracket (diagonal cutting pliers are being used here because they grip the cable end well - *not* for cutting purposes)

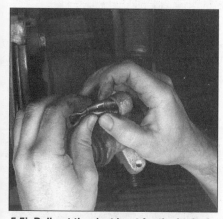

5.5d Remove the caliper lock pin (arrow)

5.5e . . . swivel the caliper up off the brake pads and support it with a piece of wire (see illustration 3.6c)

5.5f Remove the outer pad from the torque plate . . .

5.5g . . . and separate the shim(s) from the pad

5.5h Remove the inner pad from the torque plate and separate the shim(s) from the pad

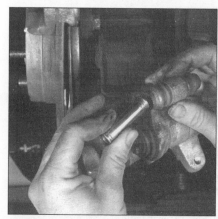

5.5i Remove the lock pin sleeve from the caliper ear, clean it thoroughly and inspect it for wear or damage; if it's scored, inspect the lock pin closely for damage - you'll probably want to replace both parts; if the sleeve is okay, coat it with multi-purpose grease and set it aside for a moment

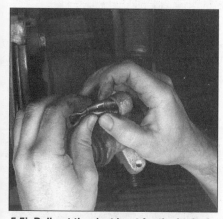

5.5j Pull out the dust boot for the lock pin and sleeve, clean it, inspect it for cracks and tears and replace it if necessary; lubricate the boot with multi-purpose grease, fold it as shown and shove it back through its bore in the caliper ear, then slide the sleeve into the caliper ear

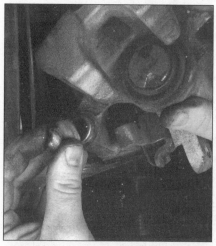

5.5k Pull off the other dust boot for the guide pin, clean it, inspect it for cracks and tears and replace as necessary; be sure to lubricate the inside edges before installing the caliper

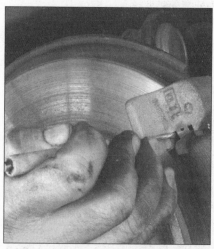

5.5l Pry out the upper anti-rattle clip with a small screwdriver and inspect it; if it's bent or broken, replace it

9

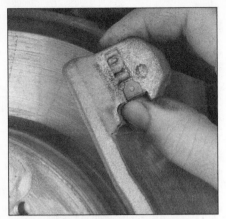

5.5m When you install the upper anti-rattle clip in the torque plate, make sure it's fully seated

5.5n Remove the lower anti-rattle clip and, again, replace it if it's bent or broken

5.5o Make sure the lower anti-rattle clip is fully seated in its notch in the torque plate

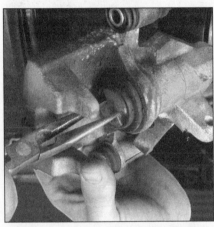

5.5p If you're installing new rear brake pads, do NOT try to fit the caliper onto the torque plate and over the new pads until you have retracted the piston; to retract the piston into the rear caliper, engage the tips of a pair of needle-nose pliers into the notches in the face of the piston as shown and turn the piston clockwise (turn the piston slowly and make sure you don't allow the pliers to slip, or you could gouge the piston dust boot!)

6   When reinstalling the caliper, be sure to tighten the mounting bolts to the torque listed in this Chapter's Specifications. After the job has been completed, firmly depress the brake pedal a few times to bring the pads into contact with the disc. Check the level of the brake fluid, adding some if necessary. Check the operation of the brakes carefully before placing the vehicle into normal service.

---

6   Rear disc brake caliper - removal and installation

Warning: *Dust created by the brake system may contain asbestos, which is harmful to your health. Never blow it out with com-*

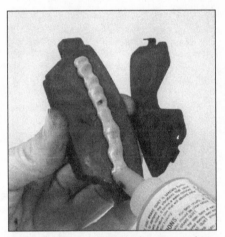

5.5q Apply an anti-squeal compound to the back of each new outer brake pad . . .

pressed air and don't inhale any of it. An approved filtering mask should be worn when working on the brakes. Do not, under any circumstances, use petroleum-based solvents to clean brake parts. Use brake cleaner or denatured alcohol only!

Note: *Due to the complex nature of the rear disc brake caliper and the special tools required to disassemble it, overhaul of the caliper should be left to a dealer service department or other repair shop. It may be more cost effective to simply replace the caliper with a new or factory rebuilt unit. Always replace the calipers in pairs - never replace just one of them.*

Removal

Refer to illustration 6.1

1   Loosen the brake hose fitting at the strut bracket **(see illustration 9.3)**, then remove the U-clip. Unscrew the brake hose from the caliper **(see illustration)**. **Note:** *If you're removing the caliper to replace the brake pads or to remove the brake disc, go to Section 5 - it isn't necessary to disconnect the brake hose from the caliper unless you're completely removing the caliper from the vehicle.*

5.5r . . . then install the shim(s) on the pad

2   Plug the brake hose to keep contaminants out of the brake system and to prevent losing any more brake fluid than is necessary.

3   Detach the parking brake cable from the caliper.

6.1 After the fitting on the other end of the hose has been loosened, unscrew the brake hose from the caliper (use a flare-nut wrench to protect the fitting)

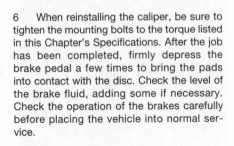
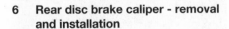

7.2a The torque plate (mounting bracket) for the front caliper is attached to the steering knuckle by two bolts (arrows)

7.4a Use a dial indicator to measure disc runout - if the reading exceeds the maximum allowable runout limit, the disc will have to be machined or replaced

4   Remove the caliper (see Section 5 - it's part of the brake pad replacement procedure).

Installation

5   Install the caliper by reversing the removal procedure.
6   Bleed the brake circuit (see Section 10). Make sure there are no leaks from the hose connections. Test the brakes carefully before returning the vehicle to normal service.

7   Brake disc - inspection, removal and installation

Note: *This procedure applies to both front and rear brake discs.*

Inspection

Refer to illustrations 7.2a, 7.2b, 7.3, 7.4a, 7.4b, 7.5a and 7.5b

1   Loosen the wheel lug nuts, raise the vehicle and support it securely on jackstands. Remove the wheel and install three lug nuts to hold the disc in place. If the rear brake disc is being worked on, release the parking brake.
2   If you're working on the front brake, remove the brake caliper (see Section 3) but don't disconnect the brake hose from the caliper, or you'll have to bleed the brakes when everything is reassembled. After

7.2b The torque plate (or mounting bracket) for the rear caliper is attached to the trailing arm by two bolts (arrows); to avoid the necessity of disconnecting the parking brake cable from the caliper, simply swing the caliper up out of the way as shown to get at the torque plate bolts

removing the caliper bolts, suspend the caliper out of the way with a piece of wire **(see illustration 3.6c)**. If you're working on the rear brake, remove the lower caliper bolt (see Section 5) and swing the caliper up out of the way so you can get at the torque plate bolts. Again, it isn't necessary to disconnect the brake hose. Remove the two torque plate-to-steering knuckle bolts (front) or the torque plate-to-trailing arm bolts (rear) **(see illustrations)** and detach the torque plate.
3   Visually inspect the disc surface for score marks and other damage. Light scratches and shallow grooves are normal after use and may not always be detrimental to brake operation, but deep scoring - over 0.039-inch (1.0 mm) - requires disc removal and refinishing by an automotive machine shop. Be sure to check both sides of the disc **(see illustration)**. If pulsating has been noticed during application of the brakes, suspect disc runout.
4   To check disc runout, place a dial indicator at a point about 1/2-inch from the outer edge of the disc **(see illustration)**. Set the indicator to zero and turn the disc. The indicator reading should not exceed the specified allowable runout limit. If it does, the disc should be refinished by an automotive machine shop. **Note:** *The discs should be resurfaced regardless of the dial indicator*

7.5a The minimum wear dimension is cast into the back side of the disc

7.3 The brake pads on this vehicle were obviously neglected - they wore down to the rivets and cut deep grooves into the disc (wear this severe means the disc must be replaced)

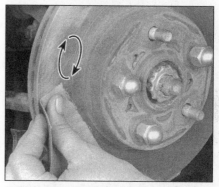

7.4b Using a swirling motion, remove the glaze from the disc surface with sandpaper or emery cloth

reading, as this will impart a smooth finish and ensure a perfectly flat surface, eliminating any brake pedal pulsation or other undesirable symptoms related to questionable discs. At the very least, if you elect not to have the discs resurfaced, remove the glaze from the surface with emery cloth using a swirling motion **(see illustration)**.
5   It's absolutely critical that the disc not be machined to a thickness under the specified minimum allowable disc refinish thickness. The minimum wear (or discard) thickness is cast into the inside of the disc **(see illustration)**. The disc thickness can be checked with a micrometer **(see illustration)**.

9

7.5b Use a micrometer to measure disc thickness

Removal

Refer to illustration 7.6

6   Remove the lug nuts which were put on to hold the disc in place and remove the disc from the hub. If the disc is stuck to the hub and won't come off, thread bolts into the holes provided and tighten them. Alternate between the bolts, turning them 1/4-turn at a time, until the disc is free **(see illustration)**.

Installation

7   Place the disc in position over the threaded studs.

8   Install the torque plate and caliper assembly over the disc and position it on the steering knuckle. Tighten the torque plate bolts to the torque listed in this Chapter's Specifications.

9   Install the wheel, then lower the vehicle to the ground. Tighten the lug nuts to the torque listed in the Chapter 1 Specifications. Depress the brake pedal a few times to bring the brake pads into contact with the disc. Bleeding won't be necessary unless the brake hose was disconnected from the caliper. Check the operation of the brakes carefully before driving the vehicle.

8   Master cylinder - removal, overhaul and installation

Note: *Before deciding to overhaul the master cylinder, check on the availability and cost of a new or factory rebuilt unit and also the availability of a rebuild kit.*

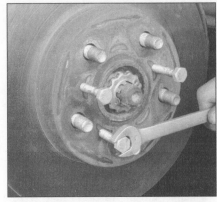

7.6 To help free a stuck disc, thread bolts of the appropriate size into the holes provided in the disc. Alternate between the bolts, turning them a little at a time until the disc is free

Removal

Refer to illustrations 8.4 and 8.7

1   The master cylinder, which is located in the engine compartment, is mounted on the power brake booster. The remote reservoir is mounted on the firewall, next to the booster.

2   Remove as much fluid as possible from the reservoir with a syringe.

3   Place rags under the fittings and prepare caps or plastic bags to cover the ends of the lines once they're disconnected. **Caution:** *Brake fluid will damage paint. Cover all body parts and be careful not to spill fluid during this procedure.*

4   Loosen the fittings that attach the brake

8.4 Completely loosen the brake line fittings (arrows) - use a flare nut wrench so you don't round off the fittings

lines to the master cylinder **(see illustration)**. To prevent rounding off the flats, use a flare-nut wrench, which wraps around the fitting hex.

5   Pull the brake lines away from the master cylinder and plug the ends to prevent contamination.

6   Loosen the hose clamps and detach the two reservoir hoses from the master cylinder. Plug the ends of the hoses to prevent fluid spills and contamination.

7   Remove the nuts attaching the master cylinder to the power booster **(see illustration)** and pull the master cylinder off the studs. Again, be careful not to spill the fluid as this is done.

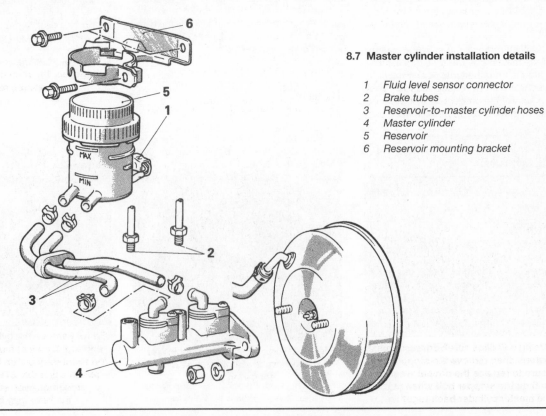

8.7 Master cylinder installation details

1   *Fluid level sensor connector*
2   *Brake tubes*
3   *Reservoir-to-master cylinder hoses*
4   *Master cylinder*
5   *Reservoir*
6   *Reservoir mounting bracket*

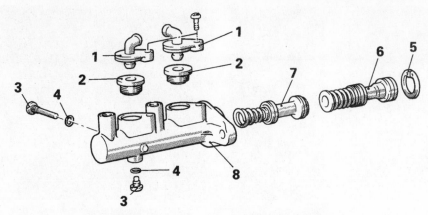

8.9a An exploded view of the master cylinder assembly

1	Inlet fitting	5	Snap-ring
2	Grommet	6	Primary piston assembly
3	Piston stopper bolt	7	Secondary piston assembly
4	Gasket	8	Master cylinder body

8.9b After the reservoir, hoses and inlet fittings have been removed, pull out the grommets from the cylinder body

Overhaul

Refer to illustrations 8.9a, 8.9b, 8.10, 8.11a, 8.11b and 8.11c

8   Before attempting the overhaul of the master cylinder, obtain the proper rebuild kit, which will contain the necessary replacement parts and also any instructions which may be specific to your model.

9   Place the cylinder in a vise and remove the inlet fittings and grommets from the master cylinder (see illustrations).

10   Use a punch or Phillips screwdriver to depress the pistons until they bottom against the other end of the master cylinder. Hold the pistons in this position and remove the stopper bolt from the master cylinder (see illustration).

11   Carefully remove the snap-ring at the end of the master cylinder (see illustration). The internal components can now be removed from the bore (see illustrations). Make a note of the proper order of the components so they can be returned to their orig-

inal locations. Note: *The two springs are different, so pay particular attention to their installed order.*

12   Carefully inspect the bore of the master cylinder. Any deep score marks or other damage will mean a new master cylinder is required. DO NOT attempt to hone the bore.

13   Replace all parts included in the rebuild kit, following any instructions in the kit. Clean all reused parts with new brake fluid, brake system cleaner. **Warning:** *Do not use any petroleum-based solvents. During reassembly, lubricate all parts liberally with clean brake fluid.*

14   Push the assembled components into the bore, bottoming them against the end of the master cylinder, then install the stopper bolt.

15   Install the new snap-ring, making sure it's seated properly in the groove.

16   Install the reservoir grommets and inlet fittings.

17   Before installing the master cylinder, it

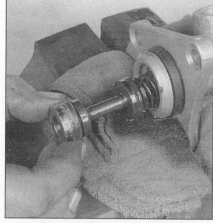

8.11b After the snap-ring has been removed, the primary piston assembly can be removed

8.10 Using a Phillips screwdriver, depress the pistons, then remove the stopper bolt; be sure to replace the copper washer (gasket) on the stopper bolt when putting the master cylinder back together

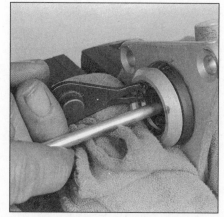

8.11a Depress the pistons again and remove the snap-ring with snap-ring pliers

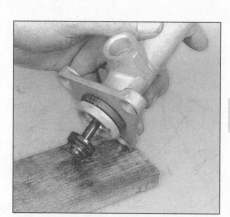

8.11c Remove the cylinder from the vise and tap it against a block of wood until the secondary piston is exposed; pull the piston assembly STRAIGHT OUT - if it becomes even slightly cocked, the bore may be damaged

9

9.3 To disconnect a brake hose from a metal line, locate the bracket on the strut where they're connected, hold the hose fitting with an open-end wrench and unscrew the brake line fitting from the hose with a flare-nut wrench to prevent rounding off the corners

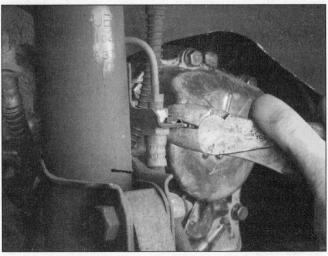

9.4 Remove the U-clip from the female fitting at the bracket with pliers, then pass the hose through the bracket

should be bench bled. Since you'll have to apply pressure to the master cylinder piston and, at the same time, control flow from the brake line outlets, the master cylinder should be mounted in a vise, with the jaws of the vise clamping on the mounting flange.

18   Insert threaded plugs into the brake line outlet holes and snug them down so no air will leak past them, but not so tight that they can't be easily loosened.

19   Fill the reservoir with brake fluid of the recommended type (see Chapter 1).

20   Remove one plug and push the piston assembly into the bore to expel the air from the master cylinder. A large Phillips screwdriver can be used to push on the piston assembly.

21   To prevent air from being drawn back into the master cylinder, the plug must be replaced and snuggled down before releasing the pressure on the piston.

22   Repeat the procedure until only brake fluid is expelled from the brake line outlet hole. When only brake fluid is expelled, repeat the procedure at the other outlet hole and plug. Be sure to keep the master cylinder reservoir filled with brake fluid to prevent the introduction of air into the system.

23   Since high pressure isn't involved in the bench bleeding procedure, an alternative to the removal and replacement of the plugs with each stroke of the piston assembly is available. Before pushing in on the piston assembly, remove the plug as described in Step 20. Before releasing the piston, however, instead of replacing the plug, simply put your finger tightly over the hole to keep air from being drawn back into the master cylinder. Wait several seconds for brake fluid to be drawn from the reservoir into the bore, then depress the piston again, removing your finger as brake fluid is expelled. Be sure to put your finger back over the hole each time before releasing the piston, and when the bleeding procedure is complete for that outlet, replace the plug and tighten it before going on to the other port.

Installation

24   Install the master cylinder over the studs on the power brake booster and tighten the nuts only finger-tight at this time. Connect the reservoir hoses to the inlet fittings and install the clamps.

25   Thread the brake line fittings into the master cylinder. Since the master cylinder is still a bit loose, it can be moved slightly so the fittings thread in easily. Don't strip the threads as the fittings are tightened.

26   Tighten the mounting nuts and the brake line fittings.

27   Fill the master cylinder reservoir with fluid, then bleed the master cylinder and the brake system (see Section 10). To bleed the master cylinder on the vehicle, have an assistant depress the brake pedal and hold it down. Loosen the fitting to allow air and fluid to escape. Tighten the fitting, then allow your assistant to return the pedal to its rest position. Repeat this procedure on both fittings until the fluid is free of air bubbles. Check the operation of the brake system carefully before driving the vehicle.

**9   Brake hoses and lines -
inspection and replacement**

Inspection

1   About every six months, with the vehicle raised and supported securely on jackstands, the rubber hoses which connect the steel brake lines with the front and rear brake assemblies should be inspected for cracks, chafing of the outer cover, leaks, blisters and other damage. These are important and vulnerable parts of the brake system and inspection should be complete. A light and mirror will be helpful for a thorough check. If a hose exhibits any of the above conditions, replace it with a new one.

Replacement

Front brake hose

Refer to illustrations 9.3 and 9.4

2   Loosen the wheel lug nuts, raise the vehicle and support it securely on jackstands. Remove the wheel.

3   At the strut or frame bracket, hold the hose fitting with an open-end wrench and unscrew the brake line fitting from the hose **(see illustration)**. Use a flare-nut wrench to prevent rounding off the corners.

4   Remove the U-clip from the female fitting at the bracket with a pair of pliers, then pass the hose through the bracket **(see illustration)**.

5   Unscrew the hose from the caliper (if you're replacing the hose between the strut and the metal line on the frame, ignore this step).

6   To install the hose, thread the hose into the caliper and tighten it securely (if you're replacing the hose between the strut and the metal line on the frame, ignore this step).

7   Insert the female end of the hose into the strut bracket and install the U-clip. Make sure the hose isn't twisted. If you're replacing the hose between the strut and the frame, do this at the other end too.

8   Connect the brake line fitting, starting the threads by hand. Tighten the fitting securely.

9   Bleed the caliper (see Section 10).

10   Install the wheel and lug nuts, lower the vehicle and tighten the lug nuts to the torque listed in the Chapter 1 Specifications.

Rear brake hose

11   Perform Steps 2, 3 and 4, then repeat Steps 3 and 4 at the other end of the hose. Be sure to bleed the caliper (see Section 10).

Metal brake lines

12   When replacing brake lines, be sure to use the correct parts. Don't use copper tubing for any brake system components. Pur-

chase steel brake lines from a dealer or auto parts store.

13 Prefabricated brake line, with the tube ends already flared and fittings installed, is available at auto parts stores and dealer parts departments. These lines are also bent to the proper shapes.

14 When installing the new line, make sure it's securely supported in the brackets and has plenty of clearance between moving or hot components.

15 After installation, check the master cylinder fluid level and add fluid as necessary. Bleed the brake system (see Section 10) and test the brakes carefully before driving the vehicle in traffic.

10 Brake hydraulic system - bleeding

Refer to illustration 10.8

Warning: *Wear eye protection when bleeding the brake system. If the fluid comes in contact with your eyes, immediately rinse them with water and seek medical attention.*

Note: *Bleeding the hydraulic system is necessary to remove any air that manages to find its way into the system when it's been opened during removal and installation of a hose, line, caliper or master cylinder.*

1 You'll probably have to bleed the system at all four brakes if air has entered it due to low fluid level, or if the brake lines have been disconnected at the master cylinder.

2 If a brake line was disconnected only at a wheel, then only that caliper or wheel cylinder must be bled.

3 If a brake line is disconnected at a fitting located between the master cylinder and any of the brakes, that part of the system served by the disconnected line must be bled.

4 Remove any residual vacuum from the brake power booster by applying the brake several times with the engine off.

5 Remove the master cylinder reservoir cover and fill the reservoir with brake fluid. Reinstall the cover. **Note:** *Check the fluid level often during the bleeding operation and add fluid as necessary to prevent the fluid level from falling low enough to allow air bubbles into the master cylinder.*

6 Have an assistant on hand, as well as a supply of new brake fluid, a clear plastic container partially filled with clean brake fluid, a length of 3/16-inch plastic, rubber or vinyl tubing to fit over the bleeder valve and a wrench to open and close the bleeder valve.

7 Beginning at the right rear wheel, loosen the bleeder valve slightly, then tighten it to a point where it's snug but can still be loosened quickly and easily.

8 Place one end of the tubing over the bleeder valve and submerge the other end in brake fluid in the container **(see illustration)**.

9 Have the assistant pump the brakes slowly a few times to get pressure in the system, then hold the pedal down firmly.

10 While the pedal is held down, open the bleeder valve just enough to allow a flow of fluid to leave the valve. Watch for air bubbles to exit the submerged end of the tube. When the fluid flow slows after a couple of seconds, close the valve and have your assistant release the pedal.

11 Repeat Steps 9 and 10 until no more air is seen leaving the tube, then tighten the bleeder valve and proceed to the left front wheel, the left rear wheel and the right front wheel, in that order, and perform the same procedure. Be sure to check the fluid in the master cylinder reservoir frequently.

12 Never use old brake fluid. It contains moisture which can boil, rendering the brakes useless.

13 Refill the master cylinder with fluid at the end of the operation.

14 Check the operation of the brakes. The pedal should feel solid when depressed, with no sponginess. If necessary, repeat the entire process. **Warning:** *Do not operate the vehicle*

if you're in doubt about the effectiveness of the brake system.

11 Power brake booster - check, removal and installation

Operating check

1 Depress the brake pedal several times with the engine off and make sure there's no change in the pedal reserve distance.

2 Depress the pedal and start the engine. If the pedal goes down slightly, operation is normal.

Airtightness check

3 Start the engine and turn it off after one or two minutes. Depress the brake pedal slowly several times. If the pedal depresses less each time, the booster is airtight.

4 Depress the brake pedal while the engine is running, then stop the engine with the pedal depressed. If there's no change in the pedal reserve travel after holding the pedal for 30 seconds, the booster is airtight.

Removal

Refer to illustrations 11.7 and 11.11

5 Power brake booster units shouldn't be disassembled. They require special tools not normally found in most automotive repair stations or shops. They're fairly complex and, because of their critical relationship to brake performance, should be replaced with a new or rebuilt one.

6 To remove the booster, first remove the brake master cylinder (see Section 8).

7 Remove the left side under-dash panel. Locate the pushrod clevis connecting the booster to the brake pedal **(see illustration)**. It's accessible from inside the vehicle, under the dash on the driver's side.

8 Remove the clevis pin retaining clip with pliers and pull out the pin.

10.8 When bleeding the brakes, a hose is connected to the bleed screw at the caliper or wheel cylinder and then submerged in brake fluid - air will be seen as bubbles in the tube and container (all air must be expelled before moving to the next wheel)

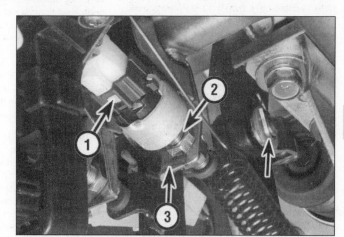

11.7 To disconnect the brake booster pushrod from the brake pedal, remove the cotter pin (arrow), pull out the clevis pin and detach the clevis from the brake pedal; to replace the brake light switch, unplug the electrical connector (1) from the switch, loosen the locknut (2) and unscrew the switch from the pedal bracket (3)

9

11.11 Remove the four nuts (arrows) and washers holding the brake booster to the firewall (you may need a light to see them)

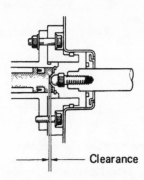

11.14a The clearance between the booster pushrod and the master cylinder pushrod must be within the specified range. If there's clearance between the two pushrods, brake pedal travel will be excessive; if there's interference between the two, the brakes may drag

9   Holding the clevis with pliers, unscrew the locknut with a wrench. The clevis is now loose.

10   Disconnect the hose leading from the engine to the booster. Be careful not to damage the hose when removing it from the booster fitting.

11   Remove the four nuts and washers holding the brake booster to the firewall **(see illustration).** You may need a light to see them.

12   Slide the booster straight out from the firewall until the studs clear the holes.

Installation

Refer to illustrations 11.14a and 11.14b

13   Installation procedures are basically the reverse of removal. Tighten the clevis locknut securely and the booster mounting nuts to the torque listed in this Chapter's Specifications.

14   If the power booster unit is being replaced, the clearance between the master cylinder piston and the pushrod in the vacuum booster must be measured and, if necessary, adjusted. Using a depth micrometer

or vernier calipers, measure the distance from the seat (recessed area) in the master cylinder to the master cylinder mounting flange. Next, measure the distance from the end of the vacuum booster pushrod to the mounting face of the booster (including gasket) where the master cylinder mounting flange seats. The measurements should be the same **(see illustration).** If not, turn the adjusting screw on the end of the power booster pushrod until the clearance is within the specified limit **(see illustration).**

15   After the final installation of the master cylinder and brake hoses and lines, the brake pedal height and freeplay must be adjusted and the system must be bled. See the appropriate Sections of this Chapter for the procedures.

12   Parking brake - adjustment

Refer to illustration 12.3

1   The parking brake lever, when properly adjusted, should travel five to seven clicks when a moderate pulling force is applied. If it

travels less than four clicks, there's a chance the parking brake might not be releasing completely and might be dragging on the drum or disc. If the lever can be pulled up more than eight clicks, the parking brake may not hold adequately on an incline, allowing the car to roll.

2   To gain access to the parking brake cable adjuster, remove the center console (see Chapter 11).

3   Loosen the or tighten the adjusting nut **(see illustration)** until the desired travel is attained. Tighten the nut.

4   Install the console.

13   Parking brake cables - replacement

Equalizer-to-caliper cable

Refer to illustration 13.4

1   Loosen the rear wheel lug nuts, raise the rear of the vehicle and support it securely on

11.14b To adjust the length of the booster pushrod, hold the serrated portion of the rod with a pair of pliers and turn the adjusting screw in or out, as necessary, to achieve the desired setting

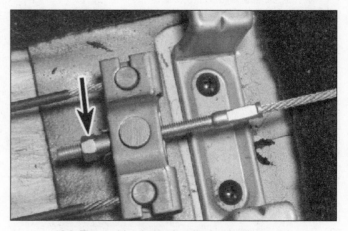

12.3 The parking brake is adjusted by tightening this nut (arrow) at the parking brake equalizer

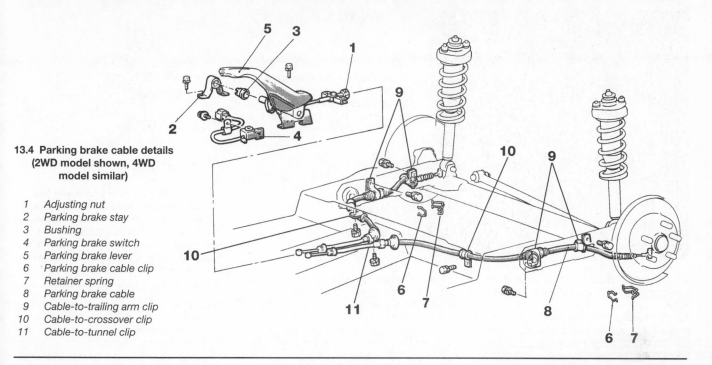

13.4 Parking brake cable details (2WD model shown, 4WD model similar)

1   Adjusting nut
2   Parking brake stay
3   Bushing
4   Parking brake switch
5   Parking brake lever
6   Parking brake cable clip
7   Retainer spring
8   Parking brake cable
9   Cable-to-trailing arm clip
10 Cable-to-crossover clip
11 Cable-to-tunnel clip

jackstands. Block the front wheels. Remove the rear wheel.

2   Make sure the parking brake is completely released.

3   Disconnect the cable from the parking brake lever on the caliper (see Section 6).

4   Unbolt the cable clip(s) from the trailing arm **(see illustration)**. On 2WD models, there are two cable clips on the trailing arms; on 4WD models, there's only one.

5   Follow the cable towards the front of the vehicle and detach the cable clip from the crossover.

6   Locate the cable clip(s) in the vicinity of the driveshaft/exhaust pipe tunnel and detach them from the vehicle. There is one clip in the tunnel on 2WD models; 4WD models have two clips in the tunnel area.

7   Pry the cable and grommet out of the guide just to the rear of the equalizer.

8   Remove the adjusting nut (see Section 12) and disconnect the front end of the cable end from the equalizer. Slide the cable end out of the hole.

9   To install the cable, reverse the removal procedure. Adjust the parking brake as outlined previously (see Section 12).

Brake lever-to-equalizer cable

Refer to illustration 13.12

10 Remove the center console (see Chapter 11).

11 With the lever in the down (off) position, remove the adjusting nut from the equalizer (see Section 12) and detach the cable from the equalizer.

12 Remove the cotter pin from the clevis pin that attaches the forward end of the cable to the parking brake lever shaft **(see illustration)**, remove the clevis pin and disconnect the cable.

13 Installation is the reverse of the removal procedure. Apply a light coat of grease to the portion of the cable end that contacts the equalizer. Adjust the parking brake lever as outlined previously (see Section 12).

---

14   Brake light switch - removal, installation and adjustment

Removal and installation

1   The brake light switch is located on a bracket at the top of the brake pedal **(see illustration 11.7)**.

2   Disconnect the negative battery cable from the battery.

3   Disconnect the wiring harness at the brake light switch.

4   Loosen the locknut and unscrew the switch from the pedal bracket.

5   Installation is the reverse of removal.

Adjustment

6   Loosen the locknut, adjust the switch so the threaded portion lightly contacts the pedal stop, then tighten the locknut.

7   Connect the wires at the switch and the battery. Make sure the brake lights are functioning properly.

13.12 To disconnect the forward end of the cable between the equalizer and the parking brake lever, remove this cotter pin (arrow) and pull out the clevis pin

9

Notes

Chapter 10
Suspension and steering systems

Contents

Specifications

Torque specifications

Ft-lbs (unless otherwise indicated)

Front suspension

Strut

Upper mounting nuts	29 to 36
Damper rod-to-insulator nut	43 to 51
Strut-to-steering knuckle bolts/nuts	80 to 101

Stabilizer bar

Bracket bolts	22 to 30
Link nuts (balljoint-type links)	25 to 33

Balljoint-to-steering knuckle nut ... 43 to 52

Control arm

U-bracket-to-body bolts/nuts

Long bolt	72 to 87
Short bolt	58 to 72
Nuts	25 to 34
Pivot bolt nuts	72 to 87

Rear suspension

Shock absorber

Upper mounting nuts	29 to 36
Shock-to-rear axle assembly nut (2WD models)	58 to 72
Shock-to-trailing arm bolt (4WD models)	65 to 80

Lateral rod (2WD models)

Rear axle-to-lateral rod bolt/nut	72 to 82
Body-to-lateral rod bolt/nut	58 to 72
Rear axle trailing arm pivot bolts (2WD models)	72 to 87

10

Torque specifications (continued)

Ft-lbs (unless otherwise indicated)

Rear suspension

Rear stabilizer bar (4WD models)	
Bar-to-link stud nut	25 to 33
Bracket bolt...	84 to 120 in-lbs
Rear suspension arms (4WD models)	
Lower arm	
Lower arm-to-crossmember pivot bolt nut...........................	65 to 80
Lower arm-to-trailing arm balljoint stud nut	43 to 52
Upper arm	
Upper arm-to-crossmember pivot bolt nut	101 to 116
Upper arm-to-trailing arm balljoint stud nut	43 to 52
Rear wheel bearing nut torque	
2WD models	144 to 188
4Wd models...	116 to 159
Trailing arm-to-crossmember pivot bolt/nut (4WD models)............	101 to 116
Rear axleshaft-to-companion flange nut (4WD models)	116 to 159

Steering system

Steering wheel nut...	25
Steering gear mounting bracket bolts	43 to 58
Intermediate shaft pinch bolt..	132 to 188 in-lbs
Tie-rod end-to-steering knuckle	17 to 25
Power steering pressure line banjo fitting nut	120 to 180 in-lbs
Wheel lug nuts...	See Chapter 1

1 General information

Refer to illustrations 1.1a, 1.1b, 1.2a and 1.2b

The front suspension is a Macpherson strut design. The upper end of each strut is attached to the vehicle body. The lower end of the strut is connected to the upper end of the steering knuckle. The steering knuckle is attached to a balljoint in the outer end of the control arm. A stabilizer bar is attached to both control arms to minimize body roll during cornering **(see illustration)**.

The rear suspension utilizes shock absorber/coil spring assemblies. The upper end of each shock is attached to the vehicle body. The lower end of the shock is attached to the rear axle assembly on 2WD models and to the trailing arms on 4WD models. The rear axle assembly is located by a lateral rod on 2WD models; the trailing arms are located by upper and lower suspension arms on 4WD models. 4WD models also use a rear stabilizer bar, attached to the trailing arms **(see illustration)**.

The rack-and-pinion steering gear is located below and behind the engine/transaxle assembly on the crossmember and actuates the tie-rods, which are attached to the steering knuckles. The steering column is designed to collapse in the event of an accident.

Frequently, when working on the sus-

1.1a An underside view of the front suspension components (2WD models)

1 *Strut/coil spring assembly*
2 *Stabilizer bar link*
3 *Stabilizer bar*
4 *Control arm*
5 *Control arm clamp*
6 *Gusset*
7 *Center member*

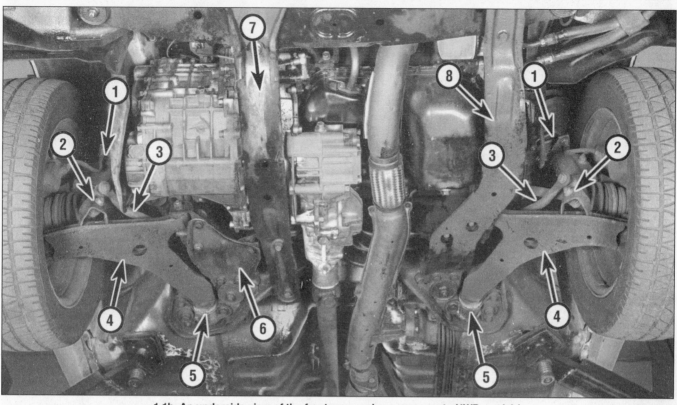

1.1b An underside view of the front suspension components (4WD models)

1	Strut/coil spring assembly	5	Control arm clamp
2	Stabilizer bar link	6	Gusset
3	Stabilizer bar	7	Right center member
4	Control arm	8	Left center member

1.2a An underside view of the rear suspension components (2WD models)

1	Shock absorber/coil spring assembly	3	Trailing arm
2	Lateral rod	4	Rear axle beam

10

1.2b An underside view of the rear suspension components (4WD models)

1 Shock absorber/coil spring assembly
2 Stabilizer bar
3 Trailing arm

4 Lower suspension arm
5 Driveaxle assembly
6 Rear crossmember

pension or steering system components, you may come across fasteners which seem impossible to loosen. These fasteners on the underside of the vehicle are continually subjected to water, road grime, mud, etc., and can become rusted or "frozen," making them extremely difficult to remove. In order to unscrew these stubborn fasteners without damaging them (or other components), be sure to use lots of penetrating oil and allow it to soak in for a while. Using a wire brush to clean exposed threads will also ease removal of the nut or bolt and prevent damage to the threads. Sometimes a sharp blow with a hammer and punch will break the bond between a nut and bolt threads, but care must be taken to prevent the punch from slipping off the fastener and ruining the threads. Heating the stuck fastener and surrounding area with a torch sometimes helps too, but isn't recommended because of the obvious dangers associated with fire. Long breaker bars and extension, or "cheater," pipes will increase leverage, but never use an extension pipe on a ratchet - the ratcheting mechanism could be damaged. Sometimes tightening the nut or bolt first will help to break it loose. Fasteners that require drastic measures to remove should always be replaced with new ones.

Since most of the procedures dealt with

in this Chapter involve jacking up the vehicle and working underneath it, a good pair of jackstands will be needed. A hydraulic floor jack is the preferred type of jack to lift the vehicle, and it can also be used to support certain components during various operations. **Warning**: *Never, under any circumstances, rely on a jack to support the vehicle while working on it. Whenever any of the suspension or steering fasteners are loosened or removed they must be inspected and, if necessary, replaced with new ones of the same part number or of original equipment quality and design. Torque specifications must be followed for proper reassembly and component retention. Never attempt to heat or straighten any suspension or steering components. Instead, replace any bent or damaged part with a new one.*

---

2   Front stabilizer bar and bushings - removal and installation

Removal

Refer to illustrations 2.3a, 2.3b, 2.5a, 2.5b and 2.6
1   Raise the front of the vehicle and support it securely on jackstands. Apply the parking brake and block the rear wheels to

keep the vehicle from rolling off the stands.
2   Remove the front exhaust pipe (see Chapter 4).
3   On 2WD models, remove the center member **(see illustration)**. On 4WD models, there are two center members - remove the right (passenger's side) member **(see illustration)**.
4   On 4WD models, remove the transfer case (see Chapter 7, Part C).
5   Detach the stabilizer bar links from the control arms **(see illustrations)**.
6   Detach both stabilizer bar brackets from the crossmember **(see illustration)**.
7   Remove the stabilizer bar.
8   While the stabilizer bar is off the vehicle, slide the bracket bushings off and inspect them. If they're cracked, worn or deteriorated, replace them.
9   Clean the bushing area of the stabilizer bar with a stiff wire brush to remove any rust or dirt.

Installation

10   Lubricate the inside and outside of the new bushing with vegetable oil (used in cooking) to simplify reassembly. **Caution:** *Don't use petroleum or mineral-based lubricants or brake fluid - they will lead to deterioration of the bushings.*
11   Installation is the reverse of removal.

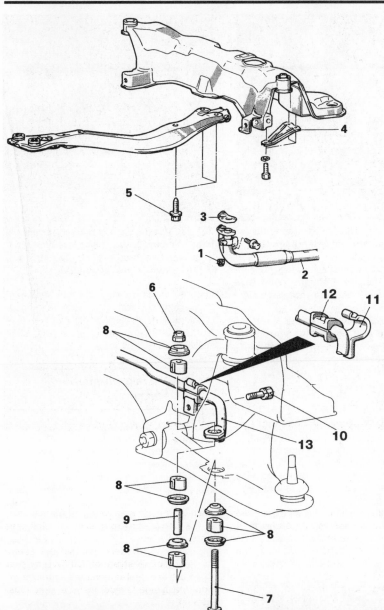

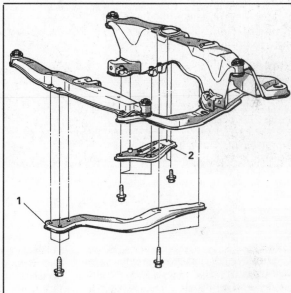

2.3a An exploded view of a stabilizer bar assembly with a rubber-bushing type link; this setup is used only on 2WD models, which use a single center member underneath the engine/transaxle assembly, as shown:

1 Exhaust pipe-to-exhaust manifold flange nut
2 Front exhaust pipe
3 Gasket
4 Stay
5 Center member rear bolt
6 Stabilizer bar link bolt nut
7 Stabilizer bar link bolt
8 Bushings and joint cups
9 Collar
10 Stabilizer bar bracket bolt
11 Stabilizer bar bracket
12 Bushing
13 Stabilizer bar

2.3b An exploded view of the center members and crossmember assembly used on 4WD models

1 Right center member   2 Gusset

2.5a On models with a bushing-type stabilizer bar link, remove the upper nut (arrow) to detach the stabilizer bar from the control arm or the link bolt (arrow) to remove the link itself

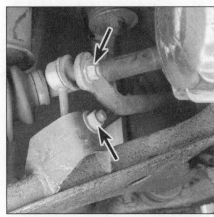

2.5b On models using a balljoint-type link, remove the upper nut (arrow) to detach the stabilizer bar from the control arms or the lower nut (arrow) to remove the link itself

2.6 Remove the stabilizer bar bracket bolt (arrow) from each stabilizer bar bracket (right bracket shown, left bracket similar) and detach the stabilizer bar and the brackets from the crossmember; before installing the stabilizer bar, inspect the rubber bushings and replace them if they're cracked or torn

10

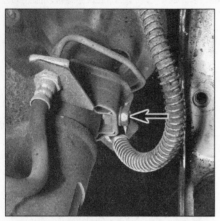

3.2 To remove the brake hose bracket from the strut, remove this bolt (arrow)

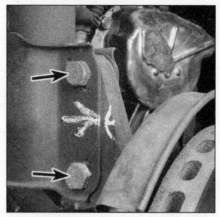

3.3 Remove the strut-to-steering knuckle bolts (arrows) and nuts

3.5 Support the strut and spring assembly with one hand (or have an assistant hold it for you) and remove the three strut-to-shock tower nuts (arrows)

3   Front strut assembly - removal, inspection and installation

Removal

Refer to illustrations 3.2, 3.3 and 3.5

1   Loosen the wheel lug nuts, raise the vehicle and support it securely on jackstands. Remove the wheel.

2   Unbolt the brake hose bracket from the strut **(see illustration)**. If the vehicle is equipped with ABS, detach the speed sensor wiring harness from the strut by removing the clamp bracket bolt. Remove the brake caliper (see Chapter 9) and hang it safely out of the way with a piece of wire. **Warning:** *If the caliper is allowed to hang unsupported, it could damage the brake hose or line, causing brake failure.*

3   Remove the strut-to-knuckle nuts and knock the bolts out with a hammer and punch **(see illustration)**.

4   Separate the strut from the steering knuckle. Be careful not to overextend the inner CV joint. And make sure you don't push down too far on the control arm or you could

overextend - and damage - the ABS speed sensor wiring harness. **Caution:** *Don't allow the steering knuckle and hub assembly swing outward.*

5   Support the strut and spring assembly with one hand and remove the three strut upper mounting nuts **(see illustration)**. Remove the assembly out from the fender-well.

Inspection

6   Check the strut body for leaking fluid, dents, cracks and other obvious damage which would warrant repair or replacement.

7   Check the coil spring for chips or cracks in the spring coating (this will cause premature spring failure due to corrosion). Inspect the spring seat for cuts, hardness and general deterioration.

8   If any undesirable conditions exist, proceed to the strut disassembly procedure (see Section 4).

Installation

9   Guide the strut assembly up into the fenderwell and insert the three mounting studs through the holes in the strut tower. Once the three studs protrude from the shock tower, install the nuts so the strut won't fall back through. This is most easily accomplished with the help of an assistant, as the strut is quite heavy and awkward.

10   Slide the steering knuckle into the strut flange and insert the two bolts. Install the nuts and tighten them to the torque listed in this Chapter's Specifications.

11   Install the brake caliper (see Chapter 9) and attach the brake hose bracket to the strut. If the vehicle is equipped with ABS, attach the speed sensor wiring harness bracket.

12   Install the wheel and lug nuts, then lower the vehicle and tighten the lug nuts to the torque listed in the Chapter 1 Specifications.

13   Tighten the three upper mounting nuts to the torque listed in this Chapter's Specifications.

14   If a new strut assembly has been

installed, drive the vehicle to an alignment shop to have the front end alignment checked, and if necessary, adjusted (this isn't necessary if the same strut has been installed).

4   Strut/spring assembly - replacement

1   If the struts or coil springs exhibit the telltale signs of wear (leaking fluid, loss of damping capability, chipped, sagging or cracked coil springs) explore all options before beginning any work. The strut/shock absorber assemblies are not serviceable and must be replaced if a problem develops. However, strut assemblies complete with springs may be available on an exchange basis, which eliminates much time and work. Whichever route you choose to take, check on the cost and availability of parts before disassembling your vehicle. **Warning:** *Disassembling a strut assembly is a potentially dangerous undertaking and utmost attention must be directed to the job, or serious injury may result. Use only a high quality spring compressor and carefully follow the manufacturer's instructions furnished with the tool. After removing the coil spring from the strut assembly, set it aside in a safe, isolated area.*

Disassembly

Refer to illustrations 4.3, 4.4, 4.5, 4.6 and 4.7

2   Remove the strut and spring assembly following the procedure described in the previous Section. Mount the strut assembly in a vise. Line the vise jaws with wood or rags to prevent damage to the unit and don't tighten the vise excessively.

3   Following the tool manufacturer's instructions, install the spring compressor (which can be obtained at most auto parts stores or equipment yards on a daily rental basis) on the spring and compress it sufficiently to relieve all pressure from the strut insulator **(see illustration)**. This can be verified by wiggling the spring.

4.3 Install the spring compressor in accordance with the tool manufacturer's instructions and compress the spring until all pressure is relieved from the upper spring seat (you can verify the spring is loose by wiggling it)

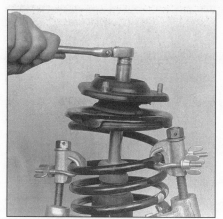

4.4 Remove the damper shaft nut

4.5 Lift the strut insulator off the shaft

4.6 Remove the upper spring seat and the upper pad from the damper shaft

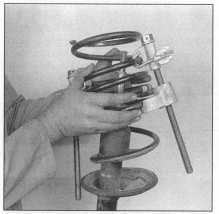

4.7 Remove the compressed spring from the strut assembly - keep the ends of the spring pointed away from your body

4.10 When installing the spring, make sure the end fits into the recessed portion of the lower seat

4.11a The flat on the damper shaft (arrow)

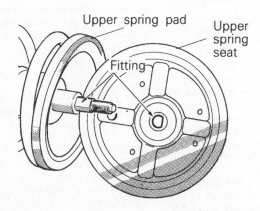

Upper spring pad

Upper spring seat

Fitting

4.11b . . . must match up with the flat in the upper spring seat

from the assembly (see illustration) and set it in a safe place. Warning: *Never place your head near the end of the spring!*

8   Slide the rubber bumper and dust cover off the damper shaft.

Reassembly

Refer to illustrations 4.10, 4.11a and 4.11b

9   If the lower insulator is being replaced, set it into position with the dropped portion seated in the lowest part of the seat. Extend the damper rod to its full length and install the rubber bumper and dust cover.

10   Carefully place the coil spring onto the lower insulator, with the end of the spring resting in the lowest part of the insulator (see illustration).

11   Install the upper pad and upper spring seat, making sure that the flats in the hole in the seat match up with the flats on the damper shaft (see illustrations).

12   Install the strut insulator onto the damper shaft.

13   Install the nut and tighten it to the torque listed in this Chapter's Specifications.

14   Install the strut/shock absorber and coil spring assembly following the procedure outlined previously (see Section 3).

4   Loosen the damper shaft nut with a socket wrench (see illustration).

5   Remove the nut and the strut insulator (see illustration). Inspect the bearing in the insulator for smooth operation. If it doesn't turn smoothly, replace the insulator. Inspect the rubber portion of the insulator for crack-

ing and general deterioration. If there is any separation of the rubber, replace it.

6   Lift the upper spring seat and upper pad from the damper shaft (see illustration). Check the spring seat for cracking and hardness, replacing it if necessary.

7   Carefully lift the compressed spring

10

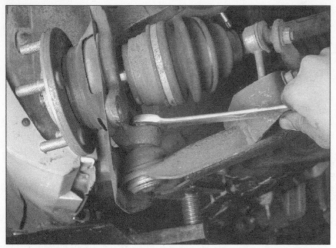

5.3a Remove the nut from the balljoint stud, give the knuckle a few firm hits with a large ball peen hammer in the vicinity of the ball stud . . .

5.3b . . . then use a prybar to separate the control arm f rom the steering knuckle

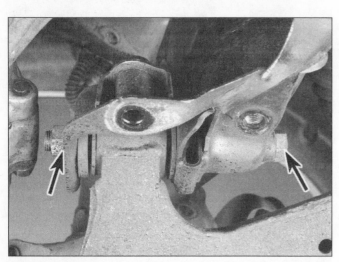

5.4 Remove the nut (arrow) from the control arm pivot bolt and pull out the bolt (arrow) (gusset removed for clarity - but it's not necessary to remove it to get at the pivot bolt and nut)

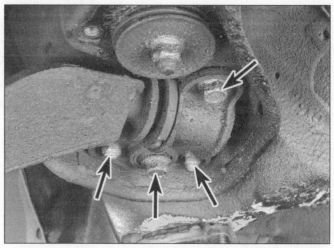

5.5 Remove the two nuts and two bolts (arrows) from the clamp for the rear control arm bushing and remove the control arm

5 Control arm - removal, inspection and installation

Removal

Refer to illustrations 5.3a, 5.3b, 5.4 and 5.5

1   Loosen the wheel lug nuts on the side to be disassembled, raise the front of the vehicle, support it securely on jackstands and remove the wheel.

2   Disconnect the stabilizer bar from the control arm (see Section 2).

3   Remove the nut from the balljoint stud that's connected to the steering knuckle **(see illustration)**. Using a large ball peen hammer (and wearing goggles to protect your eyes), give the steering knuckle a few good whacks in the vicinity of the balljoint stud to break the stud loose from the knuckle. Use a prybar to disconnect the control arm from the steering knuckle **(see illustration)**.

4   Remove the nut and washer from the control arm pivot bolt **(see illustration)**. Pull out the pivot bolt.

5   Remove the two nuts and two bolts from the clamp for the rear control arm bushing **(see illustration)**.

6   Remove the control arm.

Inspection

7   Check the control arm for distortion and the bushings for wear. If the arm is bent or any of the bushings are cracked, torn or worn out, replace the control arm. These parts are not replaceable and you can't straighten a bent control arm. Also check the balljoint (see Section 6). If a balljoint is worn out, you'll have to replace the control arm; the balljoint is not available separately.

Installation

8   Installation is the reverse of removal. Do NOT reuse self-locking nuts. Replace them with new ones. Tighten all of the fasteners to the torque values listed in this Chapter's Specifications.

9   Install the wheel and lug nuts, lower the vehicle and tighten the lug nuts to the torque listed in the Chapter 1 Specifications.

10   It's a good idea to have the front wheel alignment checked, and if necessary, adjusted after this job has been performed.

6 Balljoints - check and replacement

Refer to illustration 6.2

1   Raise the vehicle and support it securely on jackstands.

6.2 If there is any play apparent in the balljoint when prying on the control arm, the entire control arm must be replaced

2   Place a large block of wood under the tire, block the wheel with chocks and lower the jack until there's about half a load on the coil spring. Now move the control arm up and down with a prybar **(see illustration)** and verify that there's no freeplay in the balljoint. If there is, replace the control arm (see Section 5). The balljoint is not available separately nor is it removable.
3   Remove the chocks, the block of wood and the jackstands and lower the vehicle.

7   Steering knuckle and hub - removal and installation

Warning: *Dust created by the brake system may contain asbestos, which is harmful to your health. Never blow it out with compressed air and don't inhale any of it. Do not, under any circumstances, use petroleum-based solvents to clean brake parts. Use brake system cleaner only.*

Removal

1   Loosen the wheel lug nuts, raise the vehicle and support it securely on jackstands. Remove the wheel.
2   Remove the brake caliper and support it with a piece of wire as described in Chapter

9.2 On 4WD models, remove this bolt (arrow) and detach the brake hose clip from the shock absorber

9. Remove the caliper torque plate, separate the brake disc from the hub, then loosen the driveaxle/hub nut (see Chapter 8).
3   Loosen, but do not remove the strut-to-steering knuckle bolts **(see illustration 3.3)**.
4   Separate the tie-rod end from the steering knuckle arm (see Section 18).
5   Remove the balljoint-to-steering knuckle nut and separate the control arm from the steering knuckle **(see illustrations 5.3a and 5.3b)**.
6   Push the driveaxle from the hub as described in Chapter 8. Support the end of the driveaxle with a piece of wire.
7   Remove the bolts and carefully separate the steering knuckle from the strut and lower arm.

Installation

8   Guide the knuckle and hub assembly into position, inserting the driveaxle into the hub.
9   Push the knuckle into the strut flange and install the bolts and nuts, but don't tighten them yet.
10   Connect the balljoint to the control arm and install the bolt and nuts (don't tighten them yet).
11   Attach the tie-rod end to the steering knuckle arm (see Section 18). Tighten the

strut bolt nuts, the balljoint-to-control arm bolt and nuts and the tie-rod end nut to the torque values listed in this Chapter's Specifications.
12   Place the brake disc on the hub and install the caliper as outlined in Chapter 9.
13   Install the driveaxle/hub nut and tighten it to the torque listed in the Chapter 8 Specifications.
14   Install the wheel and lug nuts.
15   Lower the vehicle and tighten the lug nuts to the torque listed in the Chapter 1 Specifications.

8   Front hub and bearing assembly - removal and installation

Due to the special tools and expertise required to press the hub and bearing from the steering knuckle, this job should be left to a professional mechanic. However, the steering knuckle and hub may be removed and the assembly taken to a dealer service department or other repair shop. See Section 7 for the steering knuckle and hub removal procedure.

9   Rear shock absorber assembly - removal, inspection and installation

Removal

Refer to illustrations 9.2, 9.3a, 9.3b, 9.5a and 9.5b
1   Loosen the wheel lug nuts, raise the vehicle and support it securely on jackstands. Remove the wheel.
2   On 4WD models, detach the brake hose clip from the shock absorber **(see illustration)**.
3   Raise the hatch and remove the small plastic access cover from the rear side trim panel **(see illustration)**. Inside, you'll find a small protective cap over the shock damper nut. Remove this cap **(see illustration)**.
4   Support the axle beam (2WD models) or

10

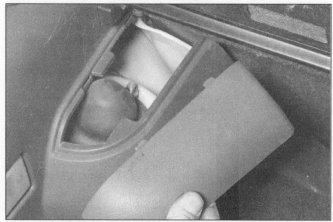

9.3a Remove this small plastic access cover from the rear side trim panel

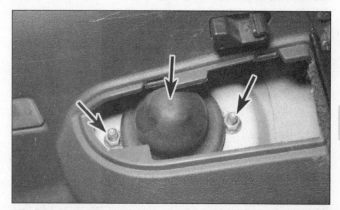

9.3b Pry off the cap (upper arrow) that covers the shock absorber damper nut, but don't remove the nut. Then, with the trailing arm (4WD models) or the axle beam (2WD models) supported by a jack, remove the two upper mounting nuts (arrows)

9.5a Shock absorber lower mounting bolt (arrow) (2WD models)

9.5b Shock absorber lower mounting bolt (arrow) (4WD models)

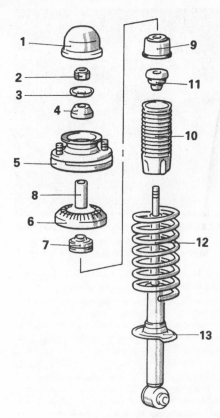

9.6 An exploded view of a typical rear shock absorber

1   Cap
2   Damper shaft nut
3   Washer
4   Upper bushing
5   Bracket assembly
6   Spring pad
7   Lower bushing
8   Collar
9   Cup assembly
10 Dust cover
11 Bump stop
12 Coil spring
13 Shock absorber assembly

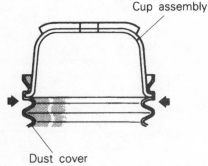

9.8 Make sure the dust cover and cup assembly fit together like this

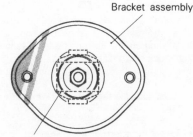

9.9 Before tightening the damper shaft nut, make sure the bracket and lower bushing are aligned like this

the trailing arm (4WD models) with a floor jack. Raise the jack just enough to take the load off the shock absorber, then remove the two upper shock absorber mounting nuts **(see illustration 9.3b)**.
5   Remove the shock absorber lower mounting bolt **(see illustrations)** and remove the shock.

Inspection

Refer to illustrations 9.6, 9.8 and 9.9
6   Follow the inspection procedures described in Section 3. If the shock absorber assembly must be disassembled for replacement of the shock or the coil spring, refer to Section 4 **(see illustration)**.
7   When reassembling the shock, make sure the lower end of the coil spring is correctly seated **(see illustration 4.10)** and the upper end is seated in the spring pad groove.
8   Make sure the dust cover and cup assembly fit together as shown **(see illustration)**.
9   Before tightening the damper shaft nut, make sure the bracket and lower bushing are aligned as shown **(see illustration)**.

Installation

10   Maneuver the shock absorber assembly up into the fenderwell and insert the mounting studs through the holes in the body.

Install the nuts, but don't tighten them yet.
11   Push the lower end of the shock into its bracket on the axle assembly (2WD models) or the trailing arm (4WD models), install the bolt and nut, and tighten them to the torque listed in this Chapter's Specifications.
12   Reattach the brake hose bracket to the shock absorber.
13   Install the wheel and lug nuts, lower the vehicle and tighten the lug nuts to the torque listed in the Chapter 1 Specifications.
14   Tighten the two upper mounting nuts to the torque listed in this Chapter's Specifications.

10   Lateral rod (2WD models) - removal and installation

Refer to illustrations 10.3, 10.4 and 10.5
1   Loosen the wheel lug nuts, raise the vehicle and support it securely on jackstands placed under the frame (not under the rear axle assembly). Remove the wheels.
2   Place a floor jack underneath the center of the rear axle assembly. Make sure the jack doesn't contact the lateral rod. Raise the jack just enough to support the axle assembly.
3   Remove the nut, washer and bolt that attach the upper end of the lateral rod to the body **(see illustration)**.

10.3 Remove the nut (arrow), washer and bolt that attach the upper end of the lateral rod to the body

10.4 Remove the nut (arrow), washer and bolt that attach the lower end of the lateral rod to the rear axle assembly

4   Remove the nut, washer and bolt that attach the lower end of the lateral rod to the rear axle assembly **(see illustration)**, and remove the lateral rod.

5   Inspect the bushings in each lateral rod "eye" **(see illustration)** for cracks and deterioration. If either bushing is worn, replace it.

6   Installation is the reverse of removal. Make sure you install the bolts with the heads facing forward. Be sure to tighten the bolts/nuts to the torque listed in this Chapter's Specifications.

11 Rear hub and bearing assembly (2WD models) - removal and installation

Refer to illustration 11.2
Warning: *Dust created by the brake system may contain asbestos, which is harmful to your health. Never blow it out with compressed air and don't inhale any of it. Do not, under any circumstances, use petroleum-based solvents to clean brake parts. Use brake system cleaner only.*
Note: *The rear hub and bearing assembly cannot be disassembled. If the bearing is damaged or defective, the hub unit must be replaced.*

1   Loosen the wheel lug nuts, raise the vehicle and support it securely on jackstands. Remove the wheel.

2   On vehicles with an Anti-lock Brake System (ABS), detach the rear wheel speed sensor **(see illustration)** and carefully set it aside.

3   Disconnect parking brake cable, remove the brake caliper and remove the brake disc (see Chapter 9).

4   Remove the grease cap, wheel bearing nut and washer. To immobilize the hub unit while you're breaking the nut loose, place a large prybar or screwdriver between the wheel studs **(see illustration 10.5** in Chapter 8).

5   Remove the hub and bearing assembly. Inspect the oil seal for cracks or other damage. Hold the hub in one hand and turn the

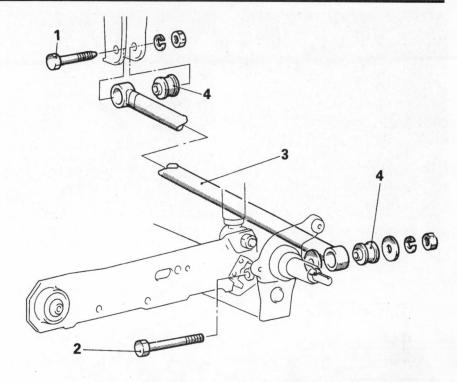

10.5 Lateral rod mounting details

1	*Upper mounting bolt*	3	*Lateral rod*
2	*Lower mounting bolt*	4	*Bushing*

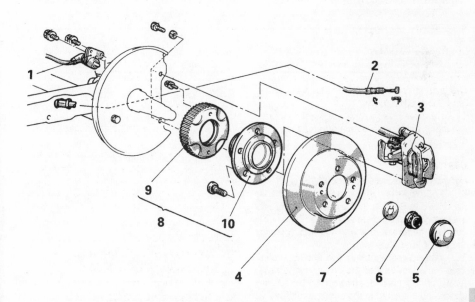

11.2 An exploded view of the rear hub and bearing assembly (2WD models)

1	*Rear wheel speed sensor (vehicles with ABS)*	7	*Washer*
2	*Parking brake cable*	8	*Rear hub and bearing and ABS rotor assembly*
3	*Brake caliper assembly*	9	*Pulse wheel (or rotor) (vehicles with ABS)*
4	*Brake disc*	10	*Rear hub and bearing assembly*
5	*Grease cap*		
6	*Wheel bearing nut*		

10

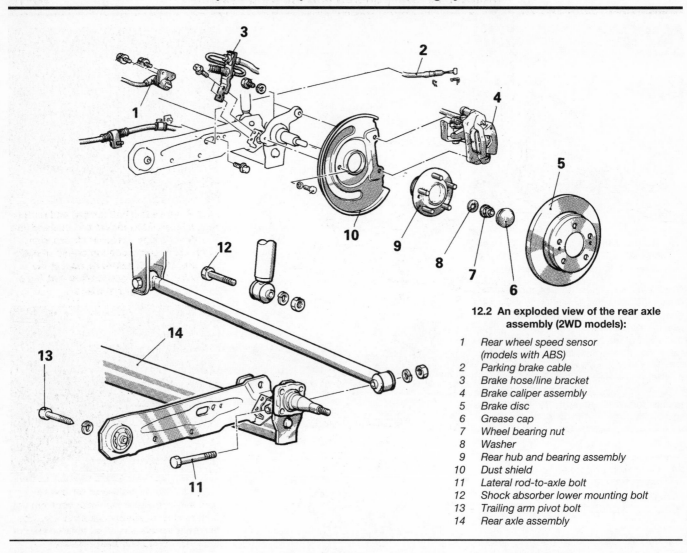

12.2 An exploded view of the rear axle assembly (2WD models):

1   Rear wheel speed sensor (models with ABS)
2   Parking brake cable
3   Brake hose/line bracket
4   Brake caliper assembly
5   Brake disc
6   Grease cap
7   Wheel bearing nut
8   Washer
9   Rear hub and bearing assembly
10 Dust shield
11 Lateral rod-to-axle bolt
12 Shock absorber lower mounting bolt
13 Trailing arm pivot bolt
14 Rear axle assembly

bearing with your other hand. If the bearing doesn't turn smoothly and quietly, replace the hub and bearing assembly.

6   If you're replacing the hub and bearing assembly on a vehicle with an Anti-lock Brake System (ABS), have the ABS pulse

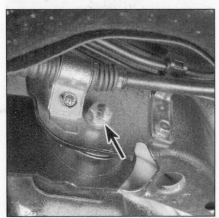

12.9 To disconnect the rear axle assembly from the vehicle, remove both trailing arm pivot bolts (arrow, left side bolt shown, right similar)

wheel (sometimes referred to as a rotor) pressed off the old hub and pressed onto the new unit by an automotive machine shop or a dealer service department.

7   Clean off the spindle and install the new hub and bearing assembly. Push it onto the spindle until the inner race is seated against the spindle shoulder. Using a new wheel bearing nut, tighten it to the torque listed in this Chapter's Specifications. After tightening the new bearing nut, stake it at the point aligned with the groove in the top of the spindle.

8   The remainder of installation is the reverse of removal.

12   Rear axle assembly (2WD models) - removal and installation

Refer to illustrations 12.2 and 12.9

1   Loosen the wheel lug nuts, raise the vehicle and support it securely on jackstands. Remove the wheels.

2   On vehicles with an Anti-lock Brake System (ABS), remove the rear wheel speed sen-

sors **(see illustration)**.

3   Disconnect the parking brake cables and remove the brake calipers and brake discs (see Chapter 9).

4   Remove the rear hub and wheel bearing assemblies (see Section 11).

5   Remove the dust shield retaining screws and remove the dust shields.

6   Place a floor jack underneath the center of the rear axle assembly. Make sure the jack doesn't contact the lateral rod. Raise the jack just enough to support the axle assembly. **Note:** *If two floor jacks are available, place one at each end of the axle beam.*

7   Disconnect the lower end of the lateral rod from the axle assembly (see Section 10).

8   Disconnect the lower ends of both shock absorbers (see Section 9).

9   Remove the pivot bolts **(see illustration)** for the trailing arms and, with an assistant helping to balance the axle assembly, carefully lower the axle on the jack.

10   Installation is the reverse of removal. Make sure you tighten all fasteners to the torque listed in this Chapter's Specifications. cause the tires to wear improperly by making them scrub against the road surface.

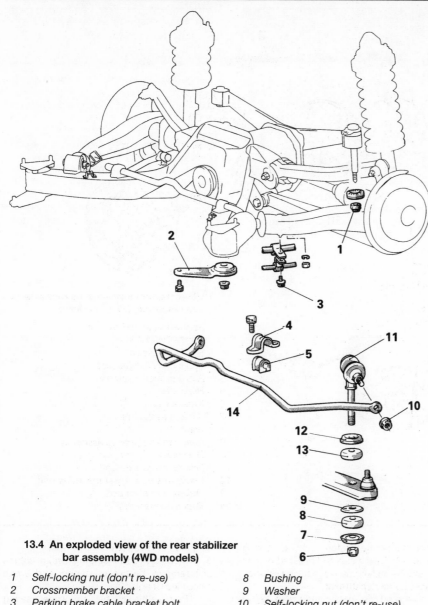

13.6 Remove this bolt (arrow) and remove the stabilizer bar bracket and bushing (left - driver's side - bracket shown, right bracket in same location on top of right end of crossmember); inspect the bushing for cracks and tears and, if it's damaged, replace it

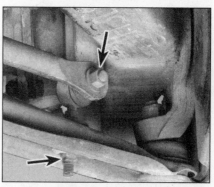

13.7 Remove this nut (arrow) to disconnect the rear stabilizer bar from the link; to disconnect the link assembly from the lower suspension arm, remove the nut (arrow) underneath the arm

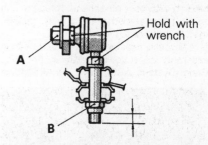

13.10 If you ever have to replace a link balljoint, make sure the distance between the locknut (B) and the end of the link is between 23/64 and 7/16-inch

13.4 An exploded view of the rear stabilizer bar assembly (4WD models)

1	Self-locking nut (don't re-use)	8	Bushing
2	Crossmember bracket	9	Washer
3	Parking brake cable bracket bolt	10	Self-locking nut (don't re-use)
4	Stabilizer bar bracket	11	Stabilizer link assembly
5	Bushing	12	Washer
6	Self-locking nut (don't re-use)	13	Bushing
7	Washer	14	Stabilizer bar

13 Rear stabilizer bar and bushings (4WD models) - removal and installation

Refer to illustrations 13.4, 13.6, 13.7 and 13.10
1   Loosen the wheel lug nuts, raise the vehicle and support it securely on jackstands. Remove the wheels.
2   Place a transmission jack or a floor jack underneath the rear differential. Put a block of wood between the jack head and the differential to protect the differential housing. Raise the jack just enough to support the differential and take the load off the rear suspension crossmember.
3   Remove the left (driver's side) retaining nut from the rear differential support member **(see illustration 18.6 in Chapter 8)**.
4   Remove the crossmember bracket **(see illustration)**.
5   Detach the parking brake cable bracket from the trailing arm.
6   Unbolt the stabilizer bar bushing brackets from the body **(see illustration)**.
7   Remove the stabilizer bar link-to-stabilizer bar nuts **(see illustration)**.
8   To remove the stabilizer bar, lower the jack slightly, just enough to provide a gap between the underside of the vehicle body and the suspension assembly, then pull the stabilizer bar out the left (driver's) side.
9   Pull the brackets off the stabilizer bar (if they haven't fallen off already) and check the bushings for wear, hardness, distortion, cracking and other signs of deterioration. Replace them if necessary. Check the link balljoint by grasping the ballstud and trying to twist it. If it feels loose or sloppy, replace the link balljoint (see next step). Also check the link bushings for the same kinds of damage and wear.
10   To replace a link balljoint, place the link in a bench vise, loosen the locknut, unscrew the old balljoint, install a new balljoint and tighten the locknut securely. Make sure that

10

14.3a If you're removing the upper suspension arm, loosen, but don't remove, the balljoint stud nut (arrow) from the outer end of the upper arm

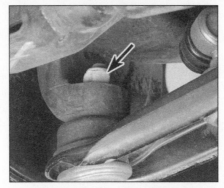

14.3b If you're removing the lower suspension arm, loosen, but don't remove, the balljoint stud nut (arrow) from the outer end of the lower arm

the distance between the locknut and the end of the link is between 23/64 and 7/16-inch **(see illustration)**.

11   Using a wire brush, clean the areas of the bar where the bushings ride.

12   Installation is the reverse of the removal

procedure. If necessary, use a light coat of vegetable oil to ease bushing and bracket installation (don't use petroleum based products or brake fluid, as these will damage the rubber).

14   Rear suspension arms (4WD models) - removal and installation

Refer to illustrations 14.3a, 14.3b, 14.3c, 14.4 and 14.5

1   Raise the rear of the vehicle and support it securely on jackstands. Block the front wheels. Support the trailing arm with a floor jack.

2   If you're removing the lower arm, disconnect the rear stabilizer bar (see Section 13).

3   Loosen, but don't remove, the self-locking balljoint stud nut from the outer end of the upper and/or lower arm(s) **(see illustrations)**.

4   Using a special balljoint splitter tool or a similar tool, disconnect the upper and/or lower arm balljoint(s) from the knuckle(s) **(see illustration)**. **Note:** *A picklefork-type balljoint separator will work, but may damage the balljoint boot.*

5   Remove the nut and pivot bolt from the inner end(s) of the upper and/or lower arm(s) **(see illustration)**.

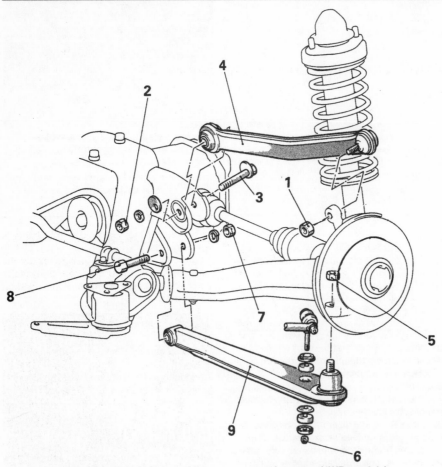

14.3c An exploded view of the rear suspension arms (4WD models)

1	*Upper arm balljoint nut (don't reuse)*	6	*Rear stabilizer bar link nut*
2	*Upper arm pivot bolt nut*	7	*Lower arm pivot bolt nut*
3	*Upper arm pivot bolt*	8	*Lower arm pivot bolt*
4	*Upper arm*	9	*Lower arm*
5	*Lower arm balljoint nut (don't reuse)*		

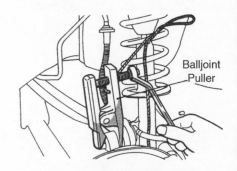

14.4 Using a balljoint splitter tool or a similar tool, break the balljoint loose from the knuckle, remove the nut and disconnect the outer end of the arm from the knuckle

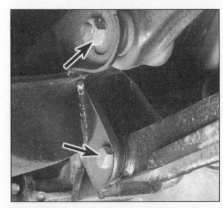

14.5 To disconnect the inner end of the upper suspension arm, remove the nut (upper arrow) and pivot bolt from the crossmember bracket; to disconnect the inner end of the lower arm, remove the nut (not visible in this photo) and pivot bolt (arrow) from the crossmember bracket

15.4 An exploded view of the trailing arm assembly (4WD models)

1	Parking brake cable end	10	Dust shield
2	Rear brake caliper assembly	11	Upper arm balljoint stud nut
3	Rear brake disc	12	Lower arm balljoint stud nut
4	Driveaxle-to-companion flange bolt and nut	13	Parking brake cable/rear wheel speed sensor bracket bolt
5	Companion flange-to-axleshaft nut	14	Trailing arm-to-crossmember nut and pivot bolt
6	Companion flange	15	Rear shock absorber-to-trailing arm bolt
7	Rear wheel speed sensor (vehicles with ABS)	16	Trailing arm
8	O-ring (vehicles with ABS)	17	Connecting rod
9	Rear axleshaft		

6   Remove the suspension arm(s) from the vehicle.

7   Inspect the balljoint(s) for wear by immobilizing the arm(s) in a bench vise and trying to wiggle the ball stud(s). If a balljoint is loose, replace the suspension arm.

8   Installation is the reverse of removal. Be sure to tighten all fasteners to the torque listed in this Chapter's Specifications.

9   After you're finished, be sure to have the rear wheel alignment checked by a dealer service department or a wheel alignment shop.

15 Trailing arm (4WD models) - removal and installation

Refer to illustrations 15.4 and 15.8

1   Raise the rear of the vehicle and support it securely on jackstands. Block the front wheels.

2   Disconnect the parking brake cable, remove the rear brake caliper and remove the rear brake disc (see Chapter 9).

3   Disconnect the outer end of the driveaxle from the axleshaft companion flange (see Chapter 8).

4   On vehicles equipped with an Anti-Lock Brake System (ABS), disconnect the rear wheel speed sensor **(see illustration)**.

5   Disconnect the upper and lower arms from the knuckle (see Section 14).

6   Disconnect the parking brake cable/rear wheel speed sensor bracket from the trailing arm.

7   Disconnect the shock absorber from the trailing arm (see Section 9).

8   Remove the trailing arm-to-crossmember nut and bolt **(see illustration)** and remove the trailing arm.

9   Inspect the trailing arm bushing for cracks, tears and deformation. If it's damaged, take the trailing arm to an automotive machine shop and have the bushing replaced. This procedure requires special tools.

10   Installation is the reverse of removal. Be sure to tighten the drivetrain fasteners to the torque listed in the Chapter 8 Specifications, the brake fasteners to the torque listed in the Chapter 9 Specifications and the suspension fasteners to the torque listed in this Chapter's Specifications.

11   After you're finished, be sure to have the rear wheel alignment checked by a dealer service department or wheel alignment shop (see Section 24).

10

15.8 Remove the trailing arm-to-body nut and bolt (arrows) and remove the trailing arm

17.2 Remove the screw from the bottom of the steering wheel hub, pull the horn pad from the steering wheel and unplug the horn wire from the spade connector on the backside of the horn pad

17.3 Remove the steering wheel retaining nut, then mark the relationship of the steering shaft to the hub (arrows) to simplify installation and ensure proper steering wheel alignment

17.4 Use a puller to disconnect the steering wheel from the shaft18.2b . . . and mark the relationship of the tie-rod end to the tie-rod (arrow)

16 Steering system - general information

All models are equipped with rack-and-pinion steering. The steering gear is bolted to the crossmember and operates the steering arms via tie-rods. The inner ends of the tie-rods are protected by rubber boots which should be inspected periodically for secure attachment, tears and leaking lubricant.

The power assist system consists of a belt-driven pump and associated lines and hoses. The fluid level in the power steering pump reservoir should be checked periodically (see Chapter 1).

The steering wheel operates the steering shaft, which actuates the steering gear through universal joints. Looseness in the steering can be caused by wear in the steering shaft universal joints, the steering gear, the tie-rod ends and loose retaining bolts.

17 Steering wheel - removal and installation

Removal

Refer to illustrations 17.2, 17.3 and 17.4
1   Disconnect the cable from the negative terminal of the battery.
2   Remove the horn pad retaining screw from the bottom of the steering wheel and pull the horn pad from the steering wheel **(see illustration)**. Unplug the horn wire from the spade connector on the backside of the horn pad.
3   Remove the steering wheel retaining nut, then mark the relationship of the steering shaft to the hub (if marks don't already exist or don't line up) to simplify installation and ensure steering wheel alignment **(see illustration)**.
4   Use a puller to disconnect the steering wheel from the shaft **(see illustration)**. Do

18.2a Loosen the tie-rod end jam nut . . .

NOT beat on the shaft in an attempt to remove the wheel.

Installation

5   To install the wheel, align the mark on the steering wheel hub with the mark on the shaft and slip the wheel onto the shaft. Install the nut and tighten it to the torque listed in this Chapter's Specifications.
6   Connect the horn wire and install the horn pad. Install the pad retaining screw and tighten it securely.
7   Connect the negative battery cable.

18 Tie-rod ends - removal and installation

Removal

Refer to illustrations 18.2a, 18.2b and 18.4
1   Loosen the wheel lug nuts. Raise the front of the vehicle, support it securely on jackstands, block the rear wheels and set the parking brake. Remove the front wheel.
2   Hold the tie-rod with a pair of locking pliers or wrench and loosen the jam nut enough to mark the position of the tie-rod end in relation to the threads **(see illustrations)**.

18.2b . . . and mark the relationship of the tie-rod end to the tie-rod (arrow)

3   Remove the cotter pin and loosen the nut on the tie-rod end stud.
4   Disconnect the tie-rod from the steering knuckle arm with a puller **(see illustration)**. Remove the nut and separate the tie-rod end.
5   Unscrew the tie-rod end from the tie-rod.

18.4 A tie-rod end separator is being used here to detach the tie-rod end from the steering knuckle - if you don't have one of these tools, a two-jaw puller will work

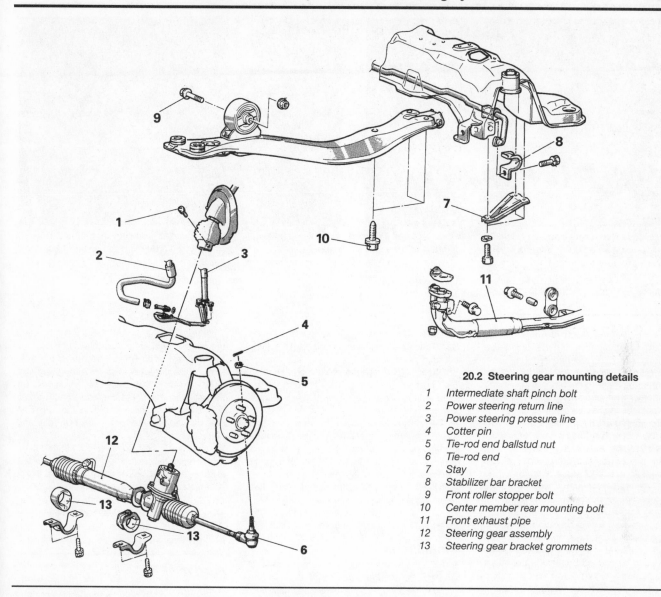

20.2 Steering gear mounting details

1 Intermediate shaft pinch bolt
2 Power steering return line
3 Power steering pressure line
4 Cotter pin
5 Tie-rod end ballstud nut
6 Tie-rod end
7 Stay
8 Stabilizer bar bracket
9 Front roller stopper bolt
10 Center member rear mounting bolt
11 Front exhaust pipe
12 Steering gear assembly
13 Steering gear bracket grommets

Installation

6   Thread the tie-rod end on to the marked position and insert the tie-rod stud into the steering knuckle arm. Tighten the jam nut securely.

7   Install the castle nut on the stud and tighten it to the torque listed in this Chapter's Specifications. Install a new cotter pin.

8   Install the wheel and lug nuts. Lower the vehicle and tighten the lug nuts to the torque listed in the Chapter 1 Specifications.

9   Have the alignment checked by a dealer service department or an alignment shop.

19 Steering gear boots - replacement

1   Loosen the lug nuts, raise the vehicle and support it securely on jackstands. Remove the wheel.

2   Remove the tie-rod end and jam nut (see Section 18).

3   Remove the steering gear boot clamps and slide the boot off.

4   Before installing the new boot, wrap the threads and serrations on the end of the steering rod with a layer of tape so the small end of the new boot isn't damaged.

5   Slide the new boot into position on the steering gear until it seats in the grooves, then install new clamps.

6   Remove the tape and install the tie-rod end (see Section 18).

7   Install the wheel and lug nuts. Lower the vehicle and tighten the lug nuts to the torque listed in the Chapter 1 Specifications.

20 Steering gear - removal and installation

Removal

Refer to illustrations 20.2, 20.7a and 20.7b

1   Loosen the front wheel lug nuts, raise the front of the vehicle and support it securely on jackstands. Apply the parking brake and remove the wheels.

2   Mark the relationship of the lower universal joint to the steering gear input shaft. Remove the lower intermediate shaft pinch bolt **(see illustration)**.

3   Place a drain pan under the steering gear. Detach the power steering pressure and return lines and cap the ends to prevent excessive fluid loss and contamination.

4   Separate the tie-rod ends from the steering knuckle arms (see Section 18).

5   Detach the stay **(see illustration 20.2)** and the left stabilizer bar bracket (see Section 2) from the crossmember.

6   On 2WD models, remove the front exhaust pipe (see Chapter 4). Remove the front roll stopper mounting bolt and the center member rear mounting bolts **(see illustration 20.2)** and lower the rear end of the center member.

7   Support the steering gear and remove the steering gear bracket-to-crossmember

10

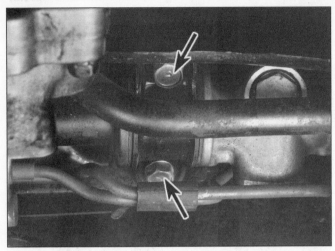

20.7a To detach the steering gear from the crossmember, support the steering gear and remove the left (driver's side) steering gear bracket-to-crossmember mounting bolts (arrows) . .

20.7b . . . and the right (passenger's side) bracket-to-crossmember bolts (arrows)

mounting bolts **(see illustrations)**. Separate the intermediate shaft from the steering gear input shaft, move the steering gear unit to the right as far as it will go, then lower the left end down and pull it out to the left.

8   Check the steering gear mounting grommets for excessive wear or deterioration, replacing them if necessary.

Installation

9   Raise the steering gear into position and connect the U-joint, aligning the marks.

10   Install the mounting brackets and bolts and tighten them to the torque listed in this Chapter's Specifications.

11   Connect the tie-rod ends to the steering knuckle arms (see Section 18).

12   Install the U-joint pinch bolt and tighten it to the torque listed in this Chapter's Specifications.

13   Connect the power steering pressure and return hoses to the steering gear and fill the power steering pump reservoir with the recommended fluid (see Chapter 1).

14   Install the center member rear mounting bolts and tighten them securely. Install the front roll stopper mounting bolt and tighten it securely. On 2WD models, install the front exhaust pipe (see Chapter 4).

15   Lower the vehicle and bleed the steering system (see Section 21).

21   Power steering pump - removal and installation

Removal

1   Disconnect the cable from the negative battery terminal.

2   Using a large syringe or suction gun, suck as much fluid out of the power steering fluid reservoir as possible. Place a drain pan under the vehicle to catch any fluid that spills

out when the hoses are disconnected.

3   Raise the vehicle and support it securely on jackstands.

4   Unplug the pressure switch connector.

5   Loosen the clamp and disconnect the fluid suction hose from the power steering pump.

6   Remove the pressure line-to-pump banjo nut and separate the line from the pump. Remove the copper sealing washers on each side of the fitting - these should be replaced when installing the pump.

7   Loosen the pivot and adjuster bolt and remove the drivebelt.

8   Remove the pivot, adjuster and mounting bolts and lower the pump from the vehicle.

Installation

9   To install the pump, reverse the removal procedure. Tighten the banjo bolt to the torque listed in this Chapter's Specifications. Adjust the drivebelt tension following the procedure described in Chapter 1.

10   Top up the fluid level in the reservoir (see Chapter 1) and bleed the system (see Section 21).

22   Power steering system - bleeding

1   Following any operation in which the power steering fluid lines have been disconnected, the power steering system must be bled to remove all air and obtain proper steering performance.

2   With the front wheels in the straight ahead position, check the power steering fluid level and, if low, add fluid until it reaches the Cold mark on the dipstick.

3   Start the engine and allow it to run at fast idle. Recheck the fluid level and add more if necessary to reach the Cold mark on the dipstick.

4   Bleed the system by turning the wheels from side to side, without hitting the stops.

This will work the air out of the system. Keep the reservoir full of fluid as this is done.

5   When the air is worked out of the system, return the wheels to the straight ahead position and leave the vehicle running for several more minutes before shutting it off.

6   Road test the vehicle to be sure the steering system is functioning normally and noise free.

7   Recheck the fluid level to be sure it is up to the Hot mark on the dipstick while the engine is at normal operating temperature. Add fluid if necessary (see Chapter 1).

23   Wheels and tires - general information

Refer to illustration 23.1

1   Vehicles covered by this manual are equipped with metric-sized fiberglass or steel belted radial tires **(see illustration)**. Use of other size or type of tires may affect the ride and handling of the vehicle. Don't mix different types of tires, such as radials and bias belted, on the same vehicle as handling may be seriously affected. It's recommended that tires be replaced in pairs on the same axle, but if only one tire is being replaced, be sure it's the same size, structure and tread design as the other.

2   Because tire pressure has a substantial effect on handling and wear, the pressure on all tires should be checked at least once a month or before any extended trips (see Chapter 1).

3   Wheels must be replaced if they are bent, dented, leak air, have elongated bolt holes, are heavily rusted, out of vertical symmetry or if the lug nuts won't stay tight. Wheel repairs that use welding or peening are not recommended.

4   Tire and wheel balance is important in the overall handling, braking and performance of the vehicle. Unbalanced wheels

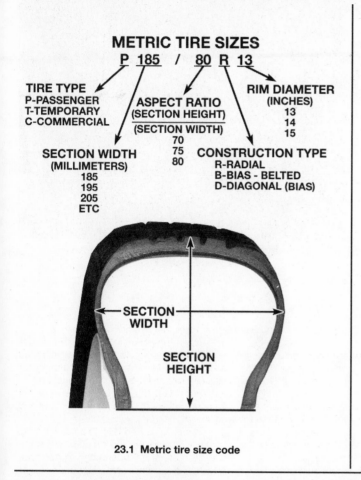

METRIC TIRE SIZES

P 185 / 80 R 13

TIRE TYPE
P-PASSENGER
T-TEMPORARY
C-COMMERCIAL

ASPECT RATIO
(SECTION HEIGHT)
(SECTION WIDTH)
70
75
80

RIM DIAMETER
(INCHES)
13
14
15

SECTION WIDTH
(MILLIMETERS)
185
195
205
ETC

CONSTRUCTION TYPE
R-RADIAL
B-BIAS - BELTED
D-DIAGONAL (BIAS)

SECTION WIDTH

SECTION HEIGHT

23.1 Metric tire size code

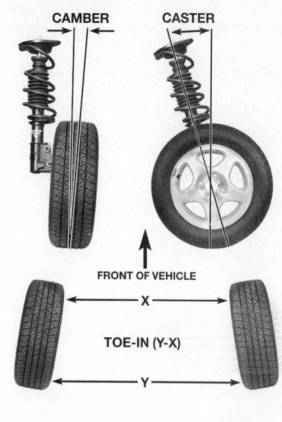

CAMBER   CASTER

FRONT OF VEHICLE

X

TOE-IN (Y-X)

Y

24.1 Camber, caster and toe-in angles

can adversely affect handling and ride characteristics as well as tire life. Whenever a tire is installed on a wheel, the tire and wheel should be balanced by a shop with the proper equipment.

24 Wheel alignment - general information

Refer to illustration 24.1

1   A wheel alignment refers to the adjustments made to the wheels so they are in proper angular relationship to the suspension and the ground. Wheels that are out of proper alignment not only affect vehicle control, but also increase tire wear. The front end should be measured for camber, caster and toe-in **(see illustration)**; toe-in can be adjusted by turning the tie-rods in or out but camber and caster are pre-set at the factory and cannot be adjusted. If camber and caster aren't within the specified dimensions, suspension

parts are bent or worn and must be replaced. The rear should be measured for camber and toe-in, but neither is adjustable. It's set at the factory. If it is not within the standard dimensions, suspension parts are bent or worn and must be replaced.

Getting the proper wheel alignment is a very exacting process, one in which complicated and expensive machines are necessary to perform the job properly. Because of this, you should have a technician with the proper equipment perform these tasks. We will, however, use this space to give you a basic idea of what is involved with a wheel alignment so you can better understand the process and deal intelligently with the shop that does the work.

Toe-in is the turning in of the wheels. The purpose of a toe specification is to ensure parallel rolling of the wheels. In a vehicle with zero toe-in, the distance between the front edges of the wheels will be the same as the distance between the rear edges of the

wheels. The actual amount of toe-in is normally only a fraction of an inch. On the front end, toe-in is controlled by the tie-rod end position on the tie-rod. Incorrect toe-in will cause the tires to wear improperly by making them scrub against the road surface.

Camber is the tilting of the wheels from vertical when viewed from one end of the vehicle. When the wheels tilt out at the top, the camber is said to be positive (+). When the wheels tilt in at the top the camber is negative (-). The amount of tilt is measured in degrees from vertical and this measurement is called the camber angle. This angle affects the amount of tire tread which contacts the road and compensates for changes in the suspension geometry when the vehicle is cornering or traveling over an undulating surface.

Caster is the tilting of the front steering axis from the vertical. A tilt toward the rear is positive caster and a tilt toward the front is negative caster.

10

Notes

Chapter 11 Body

Contents

1 General information

These models feature a "unibody" layout, using a floor pan with front and rear frame side rails which support the body components, front and rear suspension systems and other mechanical components. Certain components are particularly vulnerable to accident damage and can be unbolted and repaired or replaced. Among these parts are the body moldings, bumpers, hood, liftgate and some glass.

Only general body maintenance practices and body panel repair procedures within the scope of the do-it-yourselfer are included in this Chapter.

2 Body – maintenance

1   The condition of your vehicle's body is very important, because the resale value depends a great deal on it. It's much more difficult to repair a neglected or damaged body than it is to repair mechanical components. The hidden areas of the body, such as the wheel wells, the frame and the engine compartment, are equally important, although they don't require as frequent attention as the rest of the body.
2   Once a year, or every 12,000 miles, it's a good idea to have the underside of the body steam cleaned. All traces of dirt and oil will be removed and the area can then be inspected

carefully for rust, damaged brake lines, frayed electrical wires, damaged cables and other problems. The front suspension components should be greased after completion of this job.
3   At the same time, clean the engine and the engine compartment with a steam cleaner or water soluble degreaser.
4   The wheel wells should be given close attention, since undercoating can peel away and stones and dirt thrown up by the tires can cause the paint to chip and flake, allowing rust to set in. If rust is found, clean down to the bare metal and apply an anti-rust paint.
5   The body should be washed about once a week. Wet the vehicle thoroughly to soften the dirt, then wash it down with a soft sponge and plenty of clean soapy water. If the surplus dirt is not washed off very carefully, it can wear down the paint.
6   Spots of tar or asphalt thrown up from the road should be removed with a cloth soaked in solvent.
7   Once every six months, wax the body and chrome trim. If a chrome cleaner is used to remove rust from any of the vehicle's plated parts, remember that the cleaner also removes part of the chrome, so use it sparingly.

3 Vinyl trim – maintenance

Don't clean vinyl trim with detergents, caustic soap or petroleum-based cleaners.

Plain soap and water works just fine, with a soft brush to clean dirt that may be ingrained. Wash the vinyl as frequently as the rest of the vehicle.

After cleaning, application of a high quality rubber and vinyl protectant will help prevent oxidation and cracks. The protectant can also be applied to weatherstripping, vacuum lines and rubber hoses, which often fail as a result of chemical degradation, and to the tires.

4 Upholstery and carpets – maintenance

1   Every three months remove the carpets or mats and clean the interior of the vehicle (more frequently if necessary). Vacuum the upholstery and carpets to remove loose dirt and dust.
2   Leather upholstery requires special care. Stains should be removed with warm water and a very mild soap solution. Use a clean, damp cloth to remove the soap, then wipe again with a dry cloth. Never use alcohol, gasoline, nail polish remover or thinner to clean leather upholstery.
3   After cleaning, regularly treat leather upholstery with a leather wax. Never use car wax on leather upholstery.
4   In areas where the interior of the vehicle is subject to bright sunlight, cover leather seats with a sheet if the vehicle is to be left out for any length of time.

11

5   Body repair – minor damage

See photo sequence

Repair of minor scratches

1   If the scratch is superficial and does not penetrate to the metal of the body, repair is very simple. Lightly rub the scratched area with a fine rubbing compound to remove loose paint and built-up wax. Rinse the area with clean water.

2   Apply touch-up paint to the scratch, using a small brush. Continue to apply thin layers of paint until the surface of the paint in the scratch is level with the surrounding paint. Allow the new paint at least two weeks to harden, then blend it into the surrounding paint by rubbing with a very fine rubbing compound. Finally, apply a coat of wax to the scratch area.

3   If the scratch has penetrated the paint and exposed the metal of the body, causing the metal to rust, a different repair technique is required. Remove all loose rust from the bottom of the scratch with a pocket knife, then apply rust inhibiting paint to prevent the formation of rust in the future. Using a rubber or nylon applicator, coat the scratched area with glaze-type filler. If required, the filler can be mixed with thinner to provide a very thin paste, which is ideal for filling narrow scratches. Before the glaze filler in the scratch hardens, wrap a piece of smooth cotton cloth around the tip of a finger. Dip the cloth in thinner and then quickly wipe it along the surface of the scratch. This will ensure that the surface of the filler is slightly hollow. The scratch can now be painted over as described earlier in this section.

Repair of dents

4   When repairing dents, the first job is to pull the dent out until the affected area is as close as possible to its original shape. There is no point in trying to restore the original shape completely as the metal in the damaged area will have stretched on impact and cannot be restored to its original contours. It is better to bring the level of the dent up to a point which is about 1/8-inch below the level of the surrounding metal. In cases where the dent is very shallow, it is not worth trying to pull it out at all.

5   If the back side of the dent is accessible, it can be hammered out gently from behind using a soft-face hammer. While doing this, hold a block of wood firmly against the opposite side of the metal to absorb the hammer blows and prevent the metal from being stretched.

6   If the dent is in a section of the body which has double layers, or some other factor makes it inaccessible from behind, a different technique is required. Drill several small holes through the metal inside the damaged area, particularly in the deeper sections. Screw long, self-tapping screws into the holes just enough for them to get a good grip in the metal. Now the dent can be pulled out by pulling on the protruding heads of the screws with locking pliers.

7   The next stage of repair is the removal of paint from the damaged area and from an inch or so of the surrounding metal. This is done with a wire brush or sanding disk in a drill motor, although it can be done just as effectively by hand with sandpaper. To complete the preparation for filling, score the surface of the bare metal with a screwdriver or the tang of a file, or drill small holes in the affected area. This will provide a good grip for the filler material. To complete the repair, see the subsection on filling and painting later in this Section.

Repair of rust holes or gashes

8   Remove all paint from the affected area and from an inch or so of the surrounding metal using a sanding disk or wire brush mounted in a drill motor. If these are not available, a few sheets of sandpaper will do the job just as effectively.

9   With the paint removed, you will be able to determine the severity of the corrosion and decide whether to replace the whole panel, if possible, or repair the affected area. New body panels are not as expensive as most people think and it is often quicker to install a new panel than to repair large areas of rust.

10   Remove all trim pieces from the affected area except those which will act as a guide to the original shape of the damaged body, such as headlight shells, etc. Using metal snips or a hacksaw blade, remove all loose metal and any other metal that is badly affected by rust. Hammer the edges of the hole in to create a slight depression for the filler material.

11   Wire brush the affected area to remove the powdery rust from the surface of the metal. If the back of the rusted area is accessible, treat it with rust inhibiting paint.

12   Before filling is done, block the hole in some way. This can be done with sheet metal riveted or screwed into place, or by stuffing the hole with wire mesh.

13   Once the hole is blocked off, the affected area can be filled and painted. See the following subsection on filling and painting.

Filling and painting

14   Many types of body fillers are available, but generally speaking, body repair kits which contain filler paste and a tube of resin hardener are best for this type of repair work. A wide, flexible plastic or nylon applicator will be necessary for imparting a smooth and contoured finish to the surface of the filler material. Mix up a small amount of filler on a clean piece of wood or cardboard (use the hardener sparingly). Follow the manufacturer's instructions on the package, otherwise the filler will set incorrectly.

15   Using the applicator, apply the filler paste to the prepared area. Draw the applicator across the surface of the filler to achieve the desired contour and to level the filler surface. As soon as a contour that approximates the original one is achieved, stop working the paste. If you continue, the paste will begin to stick to the applicator. Continue to add thin layers of paste at 20-minute intervals until the level of the filler is just above the surrounding metal.

16   Once the filler has hardened, the excess can be removed with a body file. From then on, progressively finer grades of sandpaper should be used, starting with a 180-grit paper and finishing with 600-grit wet-or-dry paper. Always wrap the sandpaper around a flat rubber or wooden block, otherwise the surface of the filler will not be completely flat. During the sanding of the filler surface, the wet-or-dry paper should be periodically rinsed in water. This will ensure that a very smooth finish is produced in the final stage.

17   At this point, the repair area should be surrounded by a ring of bare metal, which in turn should be encircled by the finely feathered edge of good paint. Rinse the repair area with clean water until all of the dust produced by the sanding operation is gone.

18   Spray the entire area with a light coat of primer. This will reveal any imperfections in the surface of the filler. Repair the imperfections with fresh filler paste or glaze filler and once more smooth the surface with sandpaper. Repeat this spray-and-repair procedure until you are satisfied that the surface of the filler and the feathered edge of the paint are perfect. Rinse the area with clean water and allow it to dry completely.

19   The repair area is now ready for painting. Spray painting must be carried out in a warm, dry, windless and dust free atmosphere. These conditions can be created if you have access to a large indoor work area, but if you are forced to work in the open, you will have to pick the day very carefully. If you are working indoors, dousing the floor in the work area with water will help settle the dust which would otherwise be in the air. If the repair area is confined to one body panel, mask off the surrounding panels. This will help minimize the effects of a slight mismatch in paint color. Trim pieces such as chrome strips, door handles, etc., will also need to be masked off or removed. Use masking tape and several thicknesses of newspaper for the masking operations.

20   Before spraying, shake the paint can thoroughly, then spray a test area until the spray painting technique is mastered. Cover the repair area with a thick coat of primer. The thickness should be built up using several thin layers of primer rather than one thick one. Using 600-grit wet-or-dry sandpaper, rub down the surface of the primer until it is very smooth. While doing this, the work area should be thoroughly rinsed with water and the wet-or-dry sandpaper periodically rinsed as well. Allow the primer to dry before spraying additional coats.

21   Spray on the top coat, again building up the thickness by using several thin layers of paint. Begin spraying in the center of the repair area and then, using a circular motion, work out until the whole repair area and

about two inches of the surrounding original paint is covered. Remove all masking material 10 to 15 minutes after spraying on the final coat of paint. Allow the new paint at least two weeks to harden, then use a very fine rubbing compound to blend the edges of the new paint into the existing paint. Finally, apply a coat of wax.

6   Body repair – major damage

1   Major damage must be repaired by an auto body shop specifically equipped to perform unibody repairs. These shops have the specialized equipment required to do the job properly.
2   If the damage is extensive, the body must be checked for proper alignment or the vehicle's handling characteristics may be adversely affected and other components may wear at an accelerated rate.
3   Due to the fact that all of the major body components (hood, fenders, etc.) are separate and replaceable units, any seriously damaged components should be replaced rather than repaired. Sometimes the components can be found in a wrecking yard that specializes in used vehicle components, often at considerable savings over the cost of new parts.

7   Hinges and locks – maintenance

Once every 3000 miles, or every three months, the hinges and latch assemblies on the doors, hood and liftgate should be given a few drops of light oil or lock lubricant. The door latch strikers should also be lubricated with a thin coat of grease to reduce wear and ensure free movement. Lubricate the door and trunk locks with spray-on graphite lubricant.

8   Windshield and fixed glass – replacement

Replacement of the windshield and fixed glass requires the use of special fast-setting adhesive/caulk materials and some specialized tools. It is recommended that these operations be left to a dealer or a shop specializing in glass work.

9   Hood – removal, installation and adjustment

Refer to illustrations 9.8 and 9.10
Note: *The hood is heavy and somewhat awkward to remove and install – at least two people should perform this procedure.*

Removal and installation

1   Make marks around the bolt heads to ensure proper alignment during installation.
2   Use blankets or pads to cover the cowl

9.8 Loosen the bolts (arrows) and move the hood to adjust the position

area of the body and fenders. This will protect the body and paint as the hood is lifted off.
3   Disconnect any cables or wires that will interfere with removal.
4   Have an assistant support the hood. Remove the hinge-to-hood bolts **(see illustration 9.8)**.
5   Lift off the hood.
6   Installation is the reverse of removal.

Adjustment

7   Fore-and-aft and side-to-side adjustment of the hood is done by moving the hinge plate slot after loosening the bolts or nuts.
8   Scribe or draw a line around the bolt heads and the entire hinge plate so you can judge the amount of movement **(see illustration)**.
9   Loosen the bolts or nuts and move the hood into correct alignment. Move it only a little at a time. Tighten the hinge bolts or nuts and carefully lower the hood to check the position.
10   If necessary after installation, the entire

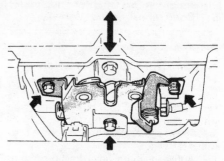

9.10 Loosen the bolts and move the latch to adjust the hood closed position

hood latch assembly can be adjusted up-and-down as well as from side-to-side on the radiator support so the hood closes securely, flush with the fenders. To make the adjustment, scribe a line around the hood latch mounting bolts to provide a reference point, then loosen them and reposition the latch assembly, as necessary **(see illustration)**. Following adjustment, retighten the mounting bolts.
11   Finally, adjust the hood bumpers on the radiator support so the hood, when closed, is flush with the fenders.
12   The hood latch assembly, as well as the hinges, should be periodically lubricated with lithium-base grease to prevent binding and wear.

10   Front fender – removal and installation

Refer to illustrations 10.2, 10.3 and 10.4
1   Remove the headlight, turn signal light and front bumper cover (see Section 18).
2   Remove the screws and detach the splash shield and extension **(see illustration)**.

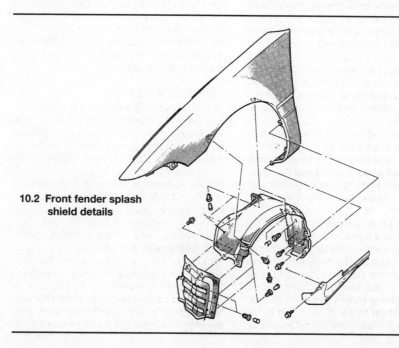

10.2 Front fender splash shield details

These photos illustrate a method of repairing simple dents. They are intended to supplement *Body repair - minor damage* in this Chapter and should not be used as the sole instructions for body repair on these vehicles.

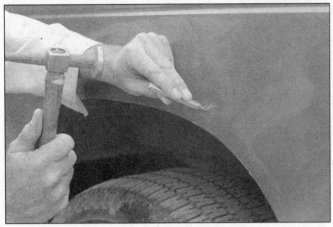

1   If you can't access the backside of the body panel to hammer out the dent, pull it out with a slide-hammer-type dent puller. In the deepest portion of the dent or along the crease line, drill or punch hole(s) at least one inch apart . . .

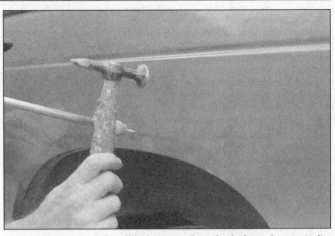

2   . . . then screw the slide-hammer into the hole and operate it. Tap with a hammer near the edge of the dent to help 'pop' the metal back to its original shape. When you're finished, the dent area should be close to its original contour and about 1/8-inch below the surface of the surrounding metal

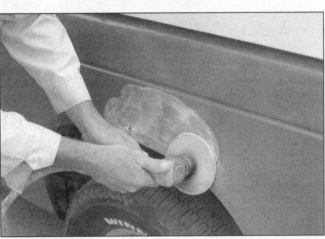

3   Using coarse-grit sandpaper, remove the paint down to the bare metal. Hand sanding works fine, but the disc sander shown here makes the job faster. Use finer (about 320-grit) sandpaper to feather-edge the paint at least one inch around the dent area

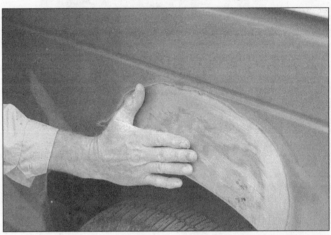

4   When the paint is removed, touch will probably be more helpful than sight for telling if the metal is straight. Hammer down the high spots or raise the low spots as necessary. Clean the repair area with wax/silicone remover

5   Following label instructions, mix up a batch of plastic filler and hardener. The ratio of filler to hardener is critical, and, if you mix it incorrectly, it will either not cure properly or cure too quickly (you won't have time to file and sand it into shape)

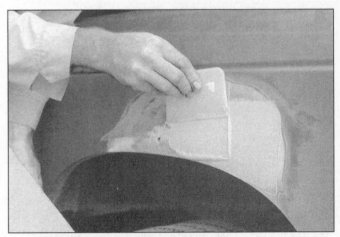

6   Working quickly so the filler doesn't harden, use a plastic applicator to press the body filler firmly into the metal, assuring it bonds completely. Work the filler until it matches the original contour and is slightly above the surrounding metal

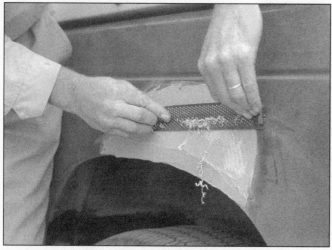

7   Let the filler harden until you can just dent it with your fingernail. Use a body file or Surform tool (shown here) to rough-shape the filler

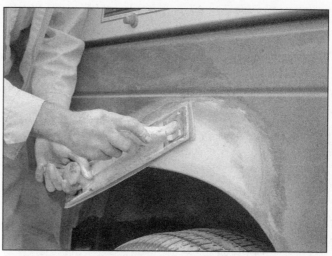

8   Use coarse-grit sandpaper and a sanding board or block to work the filler down until it's smooth and even. Work down to finer grits of sandpaper - always using a board or block - ending up with 360 or 400 grit

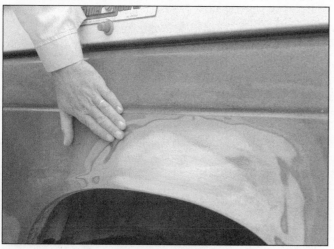

9   You shouldn't be able to feel any ridge at the transition from the filler to the bare metal or from the bare metal to the old paint. As soon as the repair is flat and uniform, remove the dust and mask off the adjacent panels or trim pieces

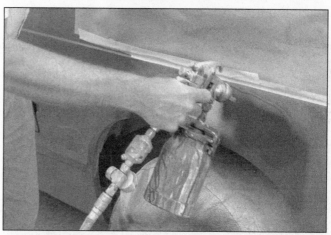

10   Apply several layers of primer to the area. Don't spray the primer on too heavy, so it sags or runs, and make sure each coat is dry before you spray on the next one. A professional-type spray gun is being used here, but aerosol spray primer is available inexpensively from auto parts stores

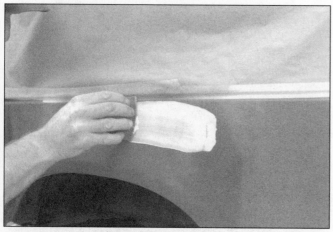

11   The primer will help reveal imperfections or scratches. Fill these with glazing compound. Follow the label instructions and sand it with 360 or 400-grit sandpaper until it's smooth. Repeat the glazing, sanding and respraying until the primer reveals a perfectly smooth surface

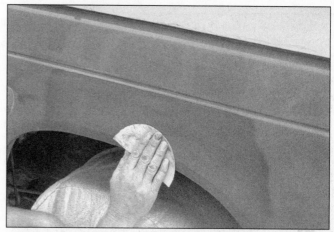

12   Finish sand the primer with very fine sandpaper (400 or 600-grit) to remove the primer overspray. Clean the area with water and allow it to dry. Use a tack rag to remove any dust, then apply the finish coat. Don't attempt to rub out or wax the repair area until the paint has dried completely (at least two weeks)

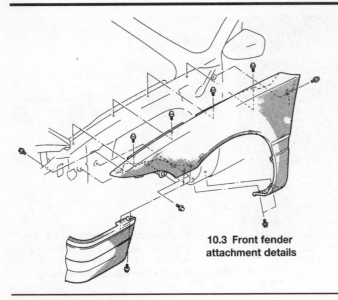

10.3 Front fender attachment details

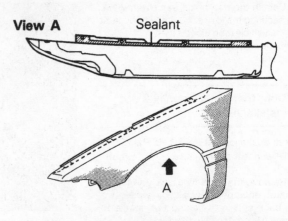

10.4 Apply silicone sealant at the points shown when installing the fender

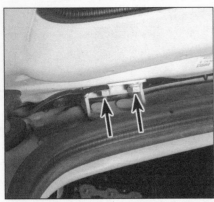

11.3 After marking their position, remove the liftgate attachment bolts (arrows)

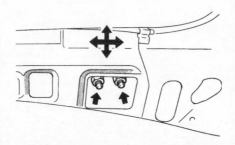

11.8 The liftgate position can be adjusted after loosening the nuts (arrows)

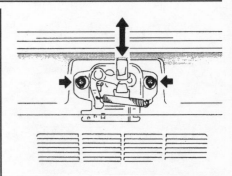

11.9 Loosen the bolts and move the latch to adjust the liftgate closed position

3   Remove the bolts and detach the fender **(see illustration)**.
4   Prior to installation, apply silicone sealant to the contact surfaces of the fender and body **(see illustration)**. Installation is the reverse of removal.

11   Liftgate – removal, installation and adjustment

Refer to illustrations 11.3, 11.8 and 11.9
Note: *The liftgate is heavy and somewhat awkward to remove and install – at least two people should perform this procedure.*
1   Open the liftgate and cover the edges of the rear compartment with pads or cloths to protect the painted surfaces when the lid is removed.
2   Disconnect any cables or electrical connectors attached to the trunk lid that would interfere with removal.
3   Make alignment marks around the hinge bolt mounting flanges **(see illustration)**.
4   Have an assistant support the liftgate and detach the support struts (see Section 12).
5   While an assistant supports the liftgate,

remove the lid-to-hinge bolts on both sides and lift it off.
6   Installation is the reverse of removal.
Note: *When reinstalling the liftgate, align the lid-to-hinge bolts with the marks made during removal.*
7   After installation, close the liftgate and make sure it's in proper alignment with the surrounding body.
8   Forward-or-backward and side-to-side adjustments are made by detaching the headliner, loosening the hinge-to-liftgate nuts and gently moving the liftgate into correct alignment **(see illustration)**.
9   The liftgate latch can be adjusted up-and-down as well as from side-to-side. To make the adjustment, scribe a line around the mounting bolts to provide a reference point, then loosen them and reposition the latch assembly, as necessary **(see illustration)**. Following adjustment, retighten the mounting bolts.

12   Liftgate support struts – replacement

Refer to illustrations 12.1 and 12.2
Warning: *The support strut is filled with pressurized gas – do not disassemble this compo-*

nent (if it is faulty replace it with a new one).
Note: *The trunk lid/rear liftgate is heavy and somewhat awkward to hold securely while replacing the struts – at least two people should perform this procedure.*
1   With the liftgate supported in the open position, use an open end wrench to loosen the nut and a Torx-head screwdriver to unscrew the strut end **(see illustration)**. **Caution:** *Guide the end of the strut away from the liftgate glass, because it will extend suddenly when released.*

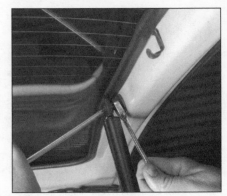

12.1 Loosen the nut with an open end wrench, then use a Torx-head screwdriver to remove the screw

2   Detach the trim panel, remove the two bolts securing the lower end, and lift the strut from the vehicle **(see illustration)**.

3   Installation is the reverse of the removal procedure.

13   Door trim panel – removal and installation

Refer to illustrations 13.2, 13.3, 13.5 and 13.6

1   Disconnect the negative cable from the battery.

2   Remove the window crank on manual regulator equipped models by working a cloth back-and-forth behind the handle to dislodge the clip **(see illustration)**.

3   Remove any door trim panel retaining screws and door pull/armrest assemblies **(see illustration)**.

12.2 After detaching the trim panel for access, remove the two bolts and lift the lower end of the strut out

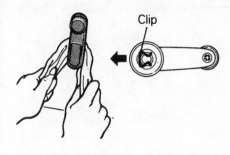

13.2 On models with manual window regulators, work a cloth back and forth behind the window crank until the clip is dislodged

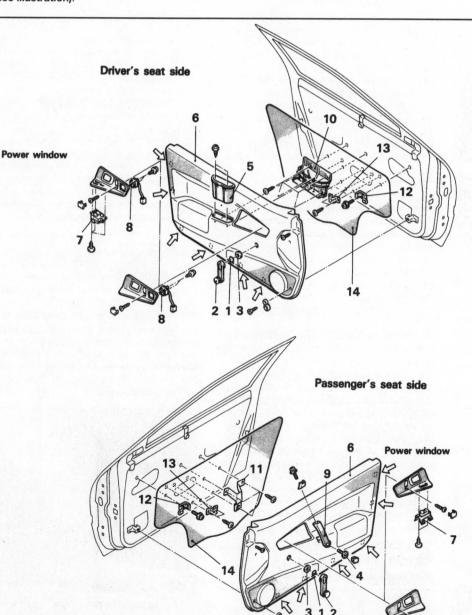

13.3 Door trim panel details

1   Clip
2   Manual window crank
3   Trim piece
4   Screw
5   Pull handle
6   Door trim panel
7   Power window switch
8   Power window switch
9   Door pull
10   Door pull bracket
11   Power window switch
12   Bracket
13   Bracket
14   Water deflector

11

13.5 Unplug the electrical connector from the back side of the door trim panel

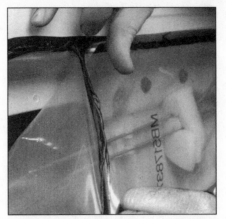

13.6 Peel the water deflector carefully away from the door, taking care not to tear or distort it

14.3 Detach the center pin by tapping it up with a plastic hammer

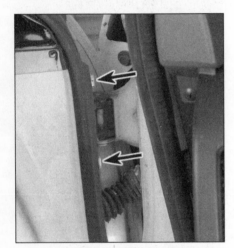

14.5 With the door supported, remove the bolts (arrows)

5   Once all of the clips are disengaged, detach the trim panel, unplug any electrical connectors and remove the trim panel from the vehicle by gently pulling it up and out **(see illustration)**.

6   For access to the inner door, peel back the plastic water deflector, taking care not to tear it **(see illustration)**. To install the trim panel, first press the water deflector into place.

7   Prior to installation of the door panel, be sure to reinstall any clips in the panel which may have come out during the removal procedure and stayed in the door.

8   Plug in any electrical connectors and place the panel in position. Press it into place until the clips are seated and install any retaining screws and armrest/door pulls. Install the manual regulator window crank.

14   Door – removal, installation and adjustment

Removal and installation

Refer to illustrations 14.3, 14.5, 14.6a and 14.6b

1   Remove the door trim panel (see Section 13), disconnect any electrical connectors and push them through the door opening so they won't interfere with removal.

2   Position a floor jack under the door or have an assistant on hand to support the door when the hinge bolts are removed. **Note:** *If a jack is used, place a rag between it and the door to protect the door's paint.*

3   Remove the center pin from the door stop strut **(see illustration)**.

4   Scribe around the door bolts.

5   Remove the hinge-to-door bolts and carefully detach the door **(see illustration)**. Installation is the reverse of removal.

Adjustment

6   Following installation, make sure the door is aligned properly. Adjust it if necessary as follows:

a) *Up-and-down and forward-and-backward adjustments are made by loosening the hinge-to-body bolts and moving the door, as necessary. A special offset tool may be required to reach some of the bolts (see illustration).*

b) *In-and-out and up-and-down adjustments are made by loosening the door side hinge bolts and moving the door, as necessary.*

c) *The door lock striker can also be adjusted both up-and-down and sideways to provide a positive engagement with the locking mechanism (see illustration). This is done by loosening the screws and moving the striker, as necessary.*

15   Door latch, lock cylinder and handle – removal and installation

Refer to illustrations 15.2, 15.3 and 15.10

1   Remove the door trim panel and water deflector (see Section 13).

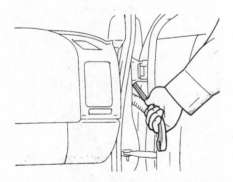

14.6a A cranked wrench such as this one may be required to reach the hinge-to-body bolts when adjusting the doors

4   Insert a wide putty knife or screwdriver between the trim panel and door to disengage the retaining clips. Work around the outer edge until the panel is free.

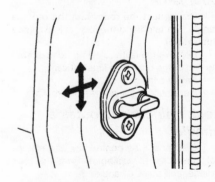

14.6b Adjust the door lock striker by loosening the screws and tapping the striker in the desired direction with a plastic mallet

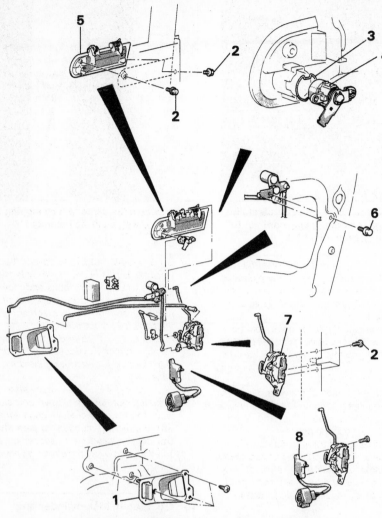

15.2 Door latch, lock cylinder and handle details

1	Inside handle	5	Outside handle
2	Bolt	6	Bellcrank mounting bolt
3	Clip	7	Latch assembly
4	Lock cylinder	8	Latch switch

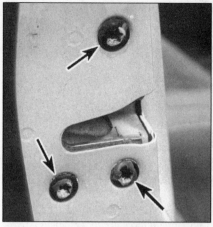

15.3 A Torx head tool will be necessary to remove the door latch screws in the end of the door (arrows)

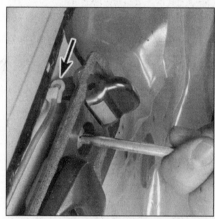

15.10 Detach the lock rod (arrow) and remove the door handle with a Phillips head screwdriver

Door latch

2   Disconnect the rods from the outside handle, the latch and the lock cylinder **(see illustration)**.
3   Remove the latch retaining screws from the end of the door **(see illustration)**.
4   Remove the door latch.
5   Installation is the reverse of removal.

Lock cylinder and outside handle

6   Disconnect the control link and electrical connector (if equipped) from the lock cylinder and outside handle.
7   Remove the outside handle retention screws and detach the handle **(see illustration 15.2)** and lock cylinder from the door.
8   Use a screwdriver to pry the retaining clip off and remove the lock cylinder from the door.
9   Installation is the reverse of removal.

Inside handle

10   Disconnect the control rods, remove the handle-to-door screws and lift the handle off the door **(see illustration)**.
11   Installation is the reverse of removal.

16   Door window glass – removal, installation and adjustment

Refer to illustrations 16.3 and 16.4

1   Remove the door trim panel and water deflector (see Section 13).
2   Raise the window until the retaining bolts are accessible through the access hole.
3   Remove the two bolts and the glass holder, then detach the glass from the regulator and lift it up and out of the door **(see illustration)**.

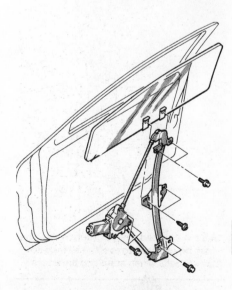

16.3 Details of the door glass and regulator assembly (power shown, manual similar)

11

4   Adjust the glass position by loosening the regulator bolts and move the regulator assembly forward-and-back to achieve the desired angle **(see illustration)**.

5   Installation is the reverse of the removal procedure.

17   Window regulator – removal and installation

1   Remove the door trim panel and water deflector (see Section 13).

2   Remove the door window glass (see Section 16). If the vehicle you are working on has power windows, unplug the electrical connector from the motor.

3   Remove the bolts, then detach the regulator from the door **(see illustration 16.3)**.

4   Pull the regulator through the access hole in the door hole to remove it.

5   Installation is the reverse of removal.

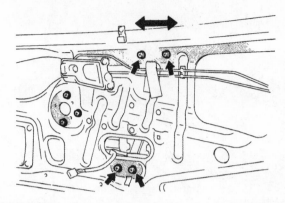

16.4 Loosen the regulator retaining bolts (arrows) and move the assembly back-and-forth to adjust the glass tilt angle

18   Bumpers – removal and installation

Front bumper

Refer to illustration 18.3

1   Apply the parking brake, block the rear wheels, lift the front of the vehicle and support it securely on jackstands.

2   Disconnect the negative battery cable from the battery and disconnect any wiring that would interfere with bumper removal.

3   Remove the splash shield mounting clip **(see illustration)**.

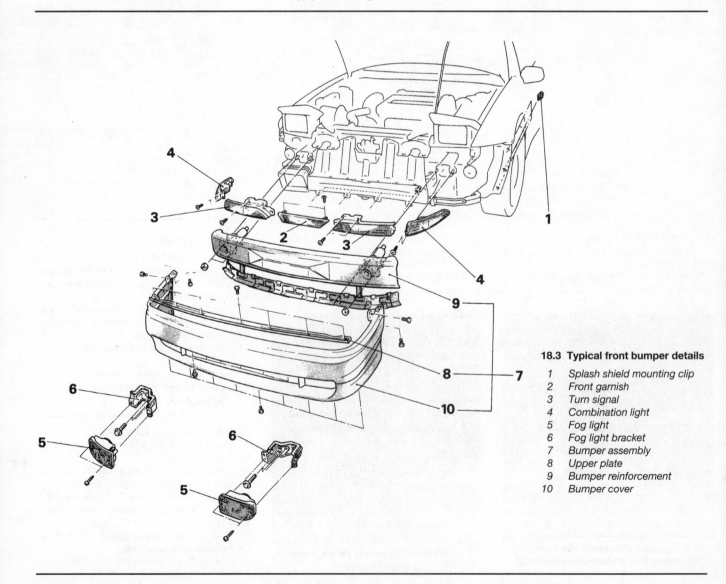

18.3 Typical front bumper details

1   *Splash shield mounting clip*
2   *Front garnish*
3   *Turn signal*
4   *Combination light*
5   *Fog light*
6   *Fog light bracket*
7   *Bumper assembly*
8   *Upper plate*
9   *Bumper reinforcement*
10   *Bumper cover*

18.10 Typical rear bumper details

1	License plate light	5	Energy absorber
2	Backup light	6	Rear bumper reinforcement
3	Rear marker light	7	License plate bracket
4	License plate wiring harness	8	Bumper cover

4   Remove the front garnish (some models).
5   Remove the turn signal fog and parking light assemblies.
6   Remove the bolts and nuts and detach the bumper assembly.

7   Pull the bumper assembly from the vehicle. To remove the bumper cover from the bumper unit remove the upper and lower cover nuts/bolts.
8   Installation is the reverse of removal.

Rear bumper

Refer to illustration 18.10

9   Remove the tail light assemblies and disconnect any wiring that would interfere with bumper removal.
10   Remove the clips, nuts and bolts and detach the rear bumper assembly from the vehicle **(see illustration)**.
11   Installation is the reverse of removal.

19 Outside mirror – removal and installation

Refer to illustrations 19.2 and 19.3

1   Remove the door trim panel (see Section 13).
2   On manually controlled models, remove the screw and detach the control handle.
3   Pry off the trim cover. On power mirrors, detach the electrical connector **(see illustration)**.
4   Remove the retaining nuts and detach the mirror **(see illustration)**.
5   Installation is the reverse of removal.

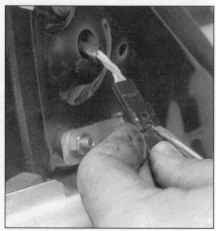

19.3 Use a small screwdriver to detach the power mirror electrical connector

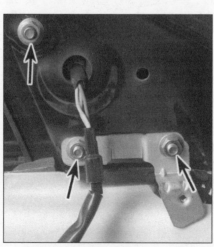

19.4 Remove the nuts (arrows) and detach the mirror

11

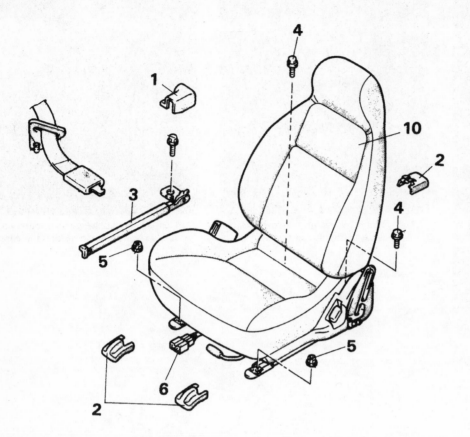

20.1 Front seat mounting details

1   Slider rail cover
2   Seat anchor cover
3   Slider rail
4   Mounting bolts
5   Mounting nuts
6   Seat belt switch connector
7   Seat belt

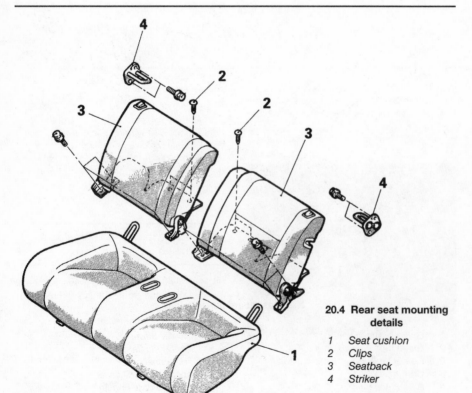

20.4 Rear seat mounting details

1   Seat cushion
2   Clips
3   Seatback
4   Striker

20   Seats – removal and installation

Front seats

Refer to illustration 20.1

1   Remove the retaining nuts and bolts, unplug any electrical connectors and lift the seat from the vehicle **(see illustration)**.

2   Installation is the reverse of removal.

Rear seats

Refer to illustration 20.4

3   Reach under the lower seat cushion, lifting up on the release levers, then pull the cushion out.

4   Remove the mounting bolts and lift the seat back assembly out of the vehicle **(see illustration)**.

5   Installation is the reverse of removal.

21   Instrument cluster bezel – removal and installation

Refer to illustrations 21.3a, 21.3b and 21.4

1   Disconnect the negative cable from the battery.

2   Remove the steering column cover and the knee protector panel.

21.3a Pull the trim panel off for access to

21.3b . . . the two screws (arrows) at the side of the cluster bezel

21.4 Grasp the cluster bezel securely and pull it straight back to detach the clips

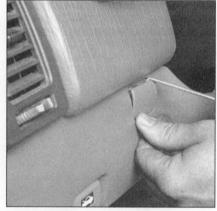

22.1 Pry out the covers for access to the screws

3 Remove the four screws from the bezel, then pull off the trim panel for access and remove the two screws at the edge **(see illustrations)**.

4 Grasp the bezel securely and pull it straight out sharply to detach the clips **(see illustration)**.

5 Rotate the bezel forward, pull it out then unplug the electrical connectors and remove the bezel from the vehicle.

6 Installation is the reverse of the removal procedure.

22 Dashboard trim panels - removal and installation

Refer to illustrations 22.1, 22.2, 22.4a, 22.4b, 22.6, 22.7a, 22.7b and 22.9

Knee protector panel

1 Pry out the two covers and remove the screws **(see illustration)**.

2 Remove the screws, detach the hood release handle and lower the it from the instrument panel **(see illustration)**.

3 Installation is the reverse of the removal procedure.

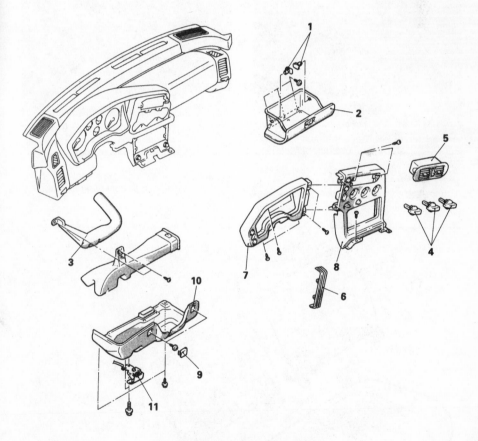

22.2 Dashboard panel details

1	Glove box retainers	7	Cluster bezel
2	Glove box	8	Center cluster panel
3	Heater air duct	9	Trim panel
4	Control knobs	10	Knee protector panel
5	Air outlet vent	11	Hood release handle
6	Trim panel		

11

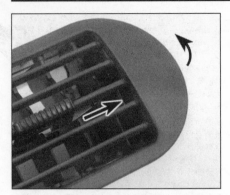

22.4a Use a small screwdriver to press the release lever (arrow) while prying out on the edge of the vent to detach it from the dash . . .

22.4b . . . then remove the screws (arrow)

22.6 Grasp the control knobs securely and pull them off

22.7a Pull off the trim panel at the bottom of the center cluster

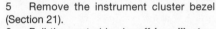

22.7b Remove the two screws (there's one at either side of the cluster lower edge)

Center cluster panel

4   Detach the center air outlet vent assembly by using a screwdriver to press on the release lever while prying the vent free of the dash, then remove the screws **(see illustrations)**.

5   Remove the instrument cluster bezel (Section 21).
6   Pull the control knobs off **(see illustration)**.
7   Detach the trim cover and remove the screws in the center and the bottom of the panel **(see illustrations)**.
8   Pull the panel out, unplug the electrical connectors and remove it from the instrument panel.

Glove box

9   Pull the two plastic retainers back and withdraw them, then remove the screws and lower the glove box from the instrument panel **(see illustration)**.

23   Steering column cover – removal and installation

Refer to illustrations 23.4

1   Remove the knee protector panel (Section 22).
2   Remove the steering wheel (see Chapter 10) and the instrument cluster bezel (see Section 21).
3   Remove the screw and detach the ignition key illumination light.
4   Remove the column cover screws. On models with a tilt column it will be necessary to lower the steering column tilt lever as there is one screw hidden under it **(see illustration)**.

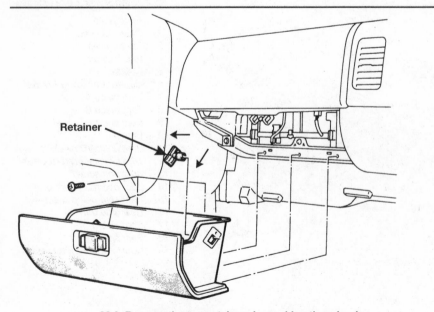

22.9 Remove the two retainers by pushing them back in their slots, then pulling straight out

Retainer

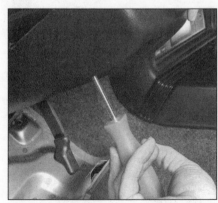

23.4 Lower the tilt lever for access to the column cover screw hidden under it

5   Rotate the upper cover up and off, then remove the lower cover.
6   Installation is the reverse of the removal procedure.

24   Console – removal and installation

Refer to illustration 24.3
1   Disconnect the negative cable from the battery.

24.3 Center console details

1   Screw covers
2   Side panels
3   Power/economy switch
4   Side panel
5   Trim panel
6   Cup holder
7   Cover
8   Wiring harness connector
9   Seat belt guide
10   Shoulder belt
11   Console

2   Remove the shift knob by unscrewing it (manual) or removing the screws and detaching the handle (automatic).
3   Pry out the covers and remove the screws holding the side covers in place and bolts holding the seat belts to the console **(see illustration)**.
4   Remove the screws located in the bottom of the console compartment by lifting out the cup holder (if equipped) and cover to gain access **(see illustration 24.3)**.
5   Remove the trim cover and remove the screws attaching the console to the center cluster panel and rotate the console up and out of the vehicle.

25   Interior trim panels – removal and installation

Refer to illustrations 25.2, 25.5, 25.7 and 25.11
1   Disconnect the cable from the negative terminal of the battery.

Cowl side trim panel

2   Remove the scuff plate, then remove the remove the screws and detach the cowl side trim panel **(see illustration)**.

Quarter trim panel

3   Remove the rear seat (Section 20).
4   Remove the scuff plate.

25.2 Interior trim panel details

1   Scuff plate
2   Cowl side trim
3   Center shelf
4   Shelf holder
5   Quarter trim
6   Quarter trim lower bracket
7   Trim piece A
8   Trim piece B
9   Rear end trim panel
10   Bracket
11   Bracket (2WD models)
12   Trim bracket (4WD models)
13   Seat belt screw
14   Seat belt retractor cover
15   Rear seat belt protector
16   Rear side trim
17   Shelf catch
18   Rear speaker
19   Quarter trim upper bracket

11

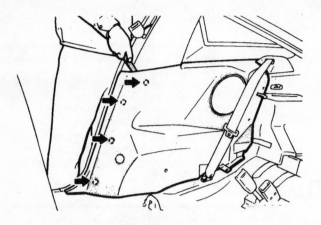

25.5 After removing the screws and clip, pry along the edge of the panel to detach the hidden clips (arrows)

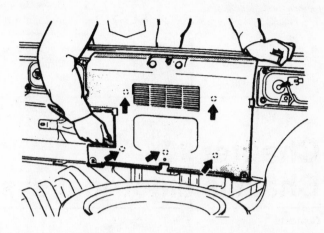

25.7 Remove the mounting screws and clips, then pry to detach the clips and remove the panel

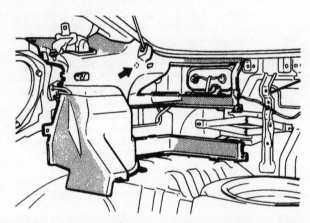

25.11 Once the seat, screws and other components are removed, pull the rear side trim toward the front of the vehicle and detach the hidden clip (arrow)

5   Remove the screws and detach quarter trim panel and bracket **(see illustration)**.

Center shelf

6   Lift out the center shelf, remove the screws and detach the holders **(see illustration 25.2)**.

Rear end trim panel

7   Pry out trim pieces A and B, remove the screws and detach the rear end panel **(see illustration)**.

Rear s de trim

8   Remove the rear seat (Section 20).
9   Remove the scuff plate, center shelf and

shelf holder.
10   Remove the quarter and rear end trim panels.
11   Remove the rear seat belt anchor plate, retractor cover and protector **(see illustration)**.
12   Remove the side trim, shelf catcher, rear speaker bracket and quarter trim upper bracket.
13   Installation is the reverse of the removal procedure.

26 Seat belt check

1   Check the seat belts, buckles, latch plates and guide loops for any obvious damage or signs of wear.
2   Make sure the seat belt reminder light comes on when the key is turned on.
3   The seat belts are designed to lock up during a sudden stop or impact, yet allow free movement during normal driving. The retractors should hold the belt against your chest while driving and rewind the belt when the buckle is unlatched.
4   If any of the above checks reveal problems with the seat-belt system, replace parts as necessary.

Chapter 12
Chassis electrical system

Contents

1   General information

The electrical system is a 12-volt, negative ground type. Power for the lights and all electrical accessories is supplied by a lead/acid-type battery which is charged by the alternator.

This Chapter covers repair and service procedures for the various electrical components not associated with the engine. Information on the battery, alternator, distributor and starter motor can be found in Chapter 5.

It should be noted that when portions of the electrical system are serviced, the cable should be disconnected from the negative battery terminal to prevent electrical shorts and/or fires.

2   Electrical troubleshooting - general information

A typical electrical circuit consists of an electrical component, any switches, relays, motors, fuses, fusible links or circuit breakers related to that component and the wiring and electrical connectors that link the component to both the battery and the chassis. To help you pinpoint an electrical circuit problem, wiring diagrams are included at the end of this book.

Before tackling any troublesome electrical circuit, first study the appropriate wiring diagrams to get a complete understanding of what makes up that individual circuit. Trouble spots, for instance, can often be narrowed down by noting if other components related to the circuit are operating properly. If several components or circuits fail at one time, chances are the problem is in a fuse or ground connection, because several circuits are often routed through the same fuse and ground connections.

Electrical problems usually stem from simple causes, such as loose or corroded connections, a blown fuse, a melted fusible link or a bad relay. Visually inspect the condition of all fuses, wires and connections in a problem circuit before troubleshooting it.

If testing instruments are going to be utilized, use the diagrams to plan ahead of time where you will make the necessary connections in order to accurately pinpoint the trouble spot.

The basic tools needed for electrical troubleshooting include a circuit tester or voltmeter (a 12-volt bulb with a set of test leads can also be used), a continuity tester, which includes a bulb, battery and set of test leads, and a jumper wire, preferably with a circuit breaker incorporated, which can be used to bypass electrical components. Before attempting to locate a problem with test instruments, use the wiring diagram(s) to decide where to make the connections.

Voltage checks

Voltage checks should be performed if a circuit is not functioning properly. Connect one lead of a circuit tester to either the negative battery terminal or a known good ground. Connect the other lead to a electrical connector in the circuit being tested, preferably nearest to the battery or fuse. If the bulb of the tester lights, voltage is present, which means that the part of the circuit between the electrical connector and the battery is problem free. Continue checking the rest of the circuit in the same fashion. When you reach a point at which no voltage is present, the problem lies between that point and the last test point with voltage. Most of the time the problem can be traced to a loose connection. **Note:** *Keep in mind that some circuits receive voltage only when the ignition key is in the Accessory or Run position.*

Finding a short

One method of finding shorts in a circuit is to remove the fuse and connect a test light or voltmeter in its place to the fuse terminals.

**3.1a The main fuse box is located under
the left side of the dash, under a cover**

**3.1b The engine compartment fuse box
is located near the battery**

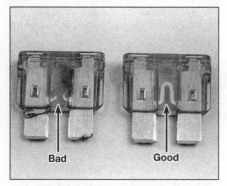

**3.3 The fuses used in these models can
be checked visually to determine if they
are blown, left, or functioning**

Bad   Good

There should be no voltage present in the circuit. Move the wiring harness from side to side while watching the test light. If the bulb goes on, there is a short to ground somewhere in that area, probably where the insulation has rubbed through. The same test can be performed on each component in the circuit, even a switch.

Ground check

Perform a ground test to check whether a component is properly grounded. Disconnect the battery and connect one lead of a self-powered test light, known as a continuity tester, to a known good ground. Connect the other lead to the wire or ground connection being tested. If the bulb goes on, the ground is good. If the bulb does not go on, the ground is not good.

Continuity check

A continuity check is done to determine if there are any breaks in a circuit - if it is passing electricity properly. With the circuit off (no power in the circuit), a self-powered continuity tester can be used to check the circuit. Connect the test leads to both ends of the circuit (or to the "power" end and a good ground), and if the test light comes on the circuit is passing current properly. If the light

doesn't come on, there is a break somewhere in the circuit. The same procedure can be used to test a switch, by connecting the continuity tester to the power in and power out sides of the switch. With the switch turned On, the test light should come on.

Finding an open circuit

When diagnosing for possible open circuits, it is often difficult to locate them by sight because oxidation or terminal misalignment are hidden by the electrical connectors. Merely wiggling an electrical connector on a sensor or in the wiring harness may correct the open circuit condition. Remember this when an open circuit is indicated when troubleshooting a circuit. Intermittent problems may also be caused by oxidized or loose connections.

Electrical troubleshooting is simple if you keep in mind that all electrical circuits are basically electricity running from the battery, through the wires, switches, relays, fuses and fusible links to each electrical component (light bulb, motor, etc.) and to ground, from which it is passed back to the battery.

3   Fuses - general information

Refer to illustrations 3.1a, 3.1b and 3.3

The electrical circuits of the vehicle are protected by a combination of fuses and fusible links. The fuse blocks are located on the kick panel below the left side of the instrument panel under a cover, and in the engine compartment near the battery **(see illustrations)**.

Each of the fuses is designed to protect a specific circuit, and the various circuits are identified on the fuse panel cover.

Miniaturized fuses are employed in the fuse block. These compact fuses, with blade terminal design, allow fingertip removal and replacement. If an electrical component fails, always check the fuse first. A blown fuse is easily identified through the clear plastic body. Visually inspect the element for evi-

dence of damage **(see illustration)**. If a continuity check is called for, the blade terminal tips are exposed in the fuse body.

Be sure to replace blown fuses with the correct type. Fuses of different ratings are physically interchangeable, but only fuses of the proper rating should be used. Replacing a fuse with one of a higher or lower value than specified is not recommended. Each electrical circuit needs a specific amount of protection. The amperage value of each fuse is molded into the fuse body.

If the replacement fuse immediately fails, don't replace it again until the cause of the problem is isolated and corrected. In most cases, this will be a short circuit in the wiring caused by a broken or deteriorated wire.

4   Fusible links - general information

Refer to illustration 4.2

Some circuits are protected by fusible links. The links are used in circuits which are not ordinarily fused, such as the ignition circuit.

The fusible links on these models are located in a housing on the battery negative cable **(see illustration)** and in the

**4.2 Some of the fusible links are located
next to the battery, under a cover**

5.2 The relays for the air conditioning system are located in the rear corner of the engine compartment

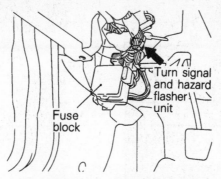

6.1a On 1991 and earlier models, the turn signal/hazard flasher unit is located in the wiring harness above the fuse block

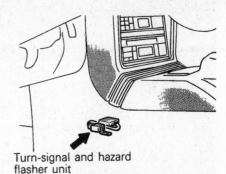

6.1b On 1992 and later models, the turn signal/hazard flasher is located under the front of the center console

fuse/relay/fusible link box on the right (passenger's) side of the engine compartment. They are similar to fuses in that they can be visually checked to determine if they are melted.

To replace a fusible link, first disconnect the negative cable from the battery. Unplug the burned-out link and replace it with a new one (available from your dealer or auto parts store). Always determine the cause for the overload which melted the fusible link before installing a new one.

5   Relays - general information

Refer to illustration 5.2

Several electrical accessories in the vehicle use relays to transmit the electrical signal to the component. If the relay is defective, that component will not operate properly.

The various relays are mounted in several locations throughout the vehicle, although many key relays are located in the engine compartment fuse block **(see illustration 3.1b)** and in the fuse/relay block in the left rear corner of the engine compartment **(see illustration)**.

If a faulty relay is suspected, it can be removed and tested by a dealer or other qualified shop. Defective relays must be replaced as a unit.

6   Turn signal/hazard flasher - check and replacement

Refer to illustrations 6.1a and 6.1b

1   The turn signal/hazard flasher, a square module located in the wiring harness next to the fuse block under the dash (1991 and earlier models) or under the front of the console (1992 and later models) **(see illustrations)**, flashes the turn signals and hazard flashers.

2   When the flasher unit is functioning properly, an audible click can be heard during its operation. If the turn signals fail on one side or the other and the flasher unit does not

make its characteristic clicking sound, a faulty turn signal bulb is indicated.

3   If both turn signals fail to blink, the problem may be due to a blown fuse, a faulty flasher unit, a broken switch or a loose or open connection. If a quick check of the fuse box indicates that the turn signal fuse has blown, check the wiring for a short before installing a new fuse.

4   To replace the flasher, remove it from the wiring harness (early models) or remove the console (see Chapter 11) and detach it (later models).

5   Make sure the replacement unit is identical to the original. Compare the old one to the new one before installing it.

6   Installation is the reverse of removal.

7   Combination switch - removal and installation

Refer to illustration 7.4

1   Disconnect the negative cable at the battery.

2   Remove the steering wheel (see Chapter 10).

3   Remove the knee protector panel and steering column cover (see Chapter 11).

4   Remove the combination switch retaining screws **(see illustration)**.

7.4 Combination switch screw locations (arrows)

5   Trace the wiring harness down the steering column to the connector. Release the wiring retainer clamps, if equipped, unplug the connector and slide the switch off the column.

6   Installation is the reverse of removal.

8   Steering column switches - check and replacement

Refer to illustrations 8.3, 8.4a, 8.4b and 8.4c

1   Disconnect the cable from the negative terminal of the battery.

2   Remove the knee protector panel and steering column cover (see Chapter 11).

Check

3   Trace the wiring harness down the steering column to the connectors of the switch you want to check **(see illustration)**.

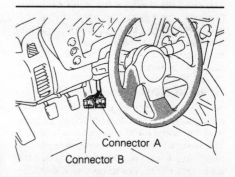

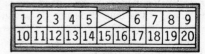

8.3 Terminal location guide for the light switch, turn signal switch and washer switch dimmer/passing switch, wiper switch

12

LIGHTING SWITCH

Switch position \ Terminal	3	4	12	5	6	14
OFF				O—	—O	
≡O O≡	O—	—O		O—	—O	
≡D	O—	—O—	—O	O		O

TURN SIGNAL SWITCH

Switch position \ Terminal	15	16	17
Left	O—	—O	
Neutral			
Right	O—	—	—O

DIMMER/PASSING SWITCH

Switch position \ Terminal		11	21	22	25	26
Dimmer switch	Low		O—	—O		
Dimmer switch	High			O—	—O	
Passing switch	P1	O	O—|—O	O—|—O	
Passing switch	P2	O		O—|—O—|—O	

NOTE
(1) O—O indicates that there is continuity between the terminals.
(2) P1 represents the passing operation when the dimmer switch is in the "Low" position, and P2 represents the operation when it is in the "High" position.

8.4a Use these tables to check continuity between the terminals of the lighting, turn signal and dimmer/passing switches (for the location of the proper terminals, refer to illustration 8.3)

WIPER SWITCH

Switch position \ Terminal		23	24	27	28
Wiper switch	OFF	O—	—	—O	
Wiper switch	INT	O—	—	—O	
Wiper switch	LO	O—	—	—	—O
Wiper switch	HI		O—	—	—O

8.4b Use these tables to check continuity between the terminals of the wiper and washer switches (for the location of the proper terminals, refer to illustration 8.3)

WASHER SWITCH

Switch position \ Terminal	7	28
OFF		
ON	O—	—O

NOTE
O—O indicates that there is continuity between the terminals.

---

4   Unplug the electrical connectors and use an ohmmeter to check for continuity between the terminals with the switch in the indicated position **(see illustrations)**.
5   Replace the switch if continuity is not as specified.

Replacement

Combination switch mounted switches

6   The combination switch will have to be removed and replaced as a unit if any of the switches in it are faulty (see Section 7).

Ignition switch

7   Refer to Section 9 for the ignition switch replacement procedure.

9   Ignition switch - removal and installation

Refer to illustration 9.4
1   Disconnect the cable from the negative terminal of the battery.
2   Remove the knee protector panel and the steering column cover (see Chapter 11).
3   Unplug the electrical connector, remove the screw, then detach the switch from the housing.
4   Installation is basically the reverse of removal, but be sure to align the slot in the ignition switch with the tab on the lock cylinder **(see illustration)**.

10   Ignition lock cylinder - removal and installation

Refer to illustration 10.5
1   Disconnect the cable from the negative terminal of the battery.
2   Remove the steering wheel (see Chapter 10).
3   Remove the knee protector panel and the steering column cover (see Chapter 11).
4   Remove the combination switch (see Section 8).
5   With the key in the Off position, insert a pin in the hole in the casting, pull the lock cylinder straight out and remove it from the steering column **(see illustration)**.
6   Installation is the reverse of removal.

11   Rear window defogger - check and repair

Refer to illustration 11.5
1   The rear window defogger consists of a number of horizontal elements baked onto the glass surface.
2   Small breaks in the element can be repaired without removing the rear window.

Check

3   Turn the ignition switch and defogger system switches On.

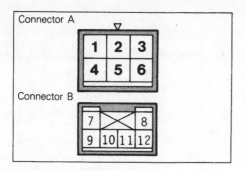

9.4 Be sure to align the slot in the ignition switch with the lock cylinder tab when installing the switch

Terminal		Ignition switch						Key reminder switch				Ignition key illumination light	
Position	Key	6	3	4	2	5	1	7	8	9	12	10	11
LOCK	Removed									O—O		O	
ACC	Inserted	O—O											
ON		O—O—O—O					O—O						
START		O—		—O		O—O							

NOTE
O—O indicates that there is continuity between the terminals.

8.4c Ignition switch terminal number guide and continuity chart

10.5 Turn the key to the ACC position and depress the retaining pin while at the same time pulling out on the lock cylinder

9   Prior to repairing a break, turn off the system and allow it to cool off for a couple of hours.
10   Lightly buff the element area with fine steel wool, then clean it thoroughly with rubbing alcohol.
11   Use masking tape to mask off the area being repaired.
12   Thoroughly mix the epoxy thoroughly, following the instructions provided with the repair kit.
13   Apply the epoxy material to the slit in the masking tape, overlapping the undamaged area about 3/4-inch on either end.
14   Allow the repair to cure for 24 hours before removing the tape and using the system.

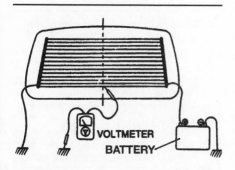

11.5 Check the center of the heating elements - the meter should read 6 volts

12.2 Pry the trim cover off for access to the radio mounting screws

4   When measuring voltage during the next two tests, wind a piece of aluminum foil around the tip of the voltmeter positive probe and press the foil against the wire with your finger. Place the negative lead against the negative (ground) bus bar.
5   Check the voltage at the center of each heat wire **(see illustration)**. If the voltage is 6-volts, the wire is okay (there is no break). If the voltage is 10-volts or more, the wire is broken somewhere between the point being checked and ground.
6   Connect the negative lead to a good body ground. The reading should stay the same.
7   To find the break, place the voltmeter positive lead against the defogger positive terminal. Place the voltmeter negative lead

with the foil strip against the heat wire at the positive terminal end and slide it toward the negative terminal end. The point where the voltmeter deflects from zero to several volts is the point at which the heat element is broken. **Note:** *If the heat element is not broken, the voltmeter will indicate no voltage at the positive end of the heat element but gradually increase to about 12-volts.*

Repair

8   Repair the break in the element using a repair kit specifically recommended for this purpose, such as Dupont paste No. 4817 (or equivalent). Included in this kit is plastic conductive epoxy.

12   Radio and speakers - removal and installation

Refer to illustrations 12.2, 12.3, 12.7a and 12.7b
1   Disconnect the cable from the negative terminal of the battery.

Radio

2   Use a small screwdriver to carefully pry out the trim panel **(see illustration)**.

12

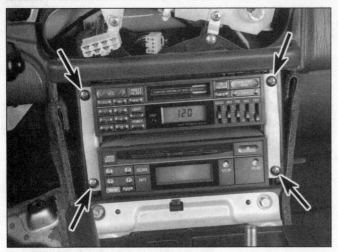

12.3 The radio is held in place by four screws (arrows)

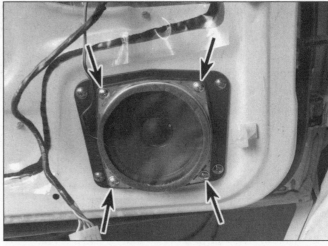

12.7a Remove the mounting screws (arrows), pull the speaker out and unplug it

3   Remove the radio mounting screws **(see illustration)**.

4   Pull the radio out, reach behind it, unplug the electrical connector and the antenna lead and lift the radio from the instrument panel.

5   Installation is the reverse of removal.

Speakers

6   Remove the door trim panel or speaker covers (see Chapter 11).

7   Remove the speaker retaining screws, pull the speaker out, unplug the electrical connector to remove the speaker **(see illustrations)**.

8   Installation is the reverse of removal.

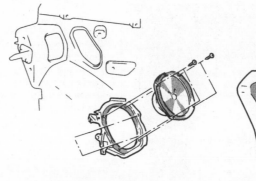

12.7b Rear speaker mounting details

---

13   Radio antenna - removal and installation

Refer to illustrations 13.1, 13.2 and 13.4

1   Use a small wrench to unscrew the antenna mast **(see illustration)**.

2   Use a screwdriver to remove the ring nut **(see illustration)**.

3   Inside the vehicle, remove the trim panel for access (see Chapter 11) to the antenna base.

4   Unplug the antenna lead, remove the mounting nuts and detach the base, guide it out through the access hole and remove it from the vehicle **(see illustration)**.

5   Installation is the reverse of removal.

14   Headlights- replacement

1991 and earlier models

Refer to illustrations 14.2a, 14.2b and 14.3

1   Turn on the headlights to bring them to the raised position, then disconnect the cable from the negative terminal of the battery.

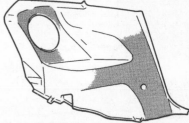

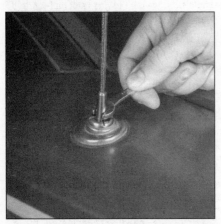

13.1 Use a small wrench to unscrew the antenna mast

13.2 Unscrew the ring nut with a screwdriver

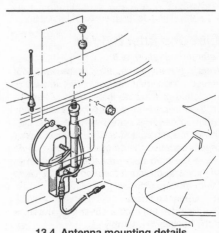

13.4 Antenna mounting details

14.2a Remove the screws and detach the headlight door trim . . .

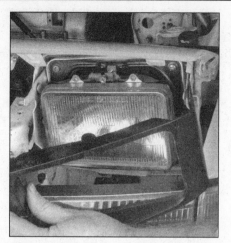

14.2b . . . then remove the headlight bezel

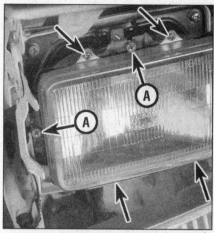

14.3 To remove the headlight, unscrew the four retainer screws (the screws marked (A) are the *adjustment* screws)

15.1 The upper screw (1) adjusts the headlight vertically - the screw on the side (2) controls horizontal adjustment (1991 and earlier models)

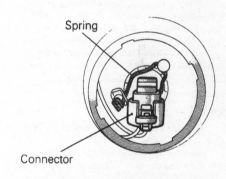

14.8 Remove the rubber cover, then detach the spring and unplug the bulb connector

2   Remove the screws and detach the headlight door trim and the headlight bezel **(see illustrations)**.
3   Remove the headlight retaining screws. Don't disturb the adjustment screws **(see illustration)**.
4   Pull the headlight out, unplug the electrical connector and remove the headlight assembly.
5   Installation is the reverse of removal.

1992 and later models

Refer to illustration 14.8
Warning: *Halogen gas filled bulbs are under pressure and may shatter if the surface is scratched or the bulb is dropped. Wear eye protection and handle the bulbs carefully, grasping only the base whenever possible. Do not touch the surface of the bulb with your fingers because the oil from your skin could cause the bulb to overheat and fail prematurely. If you do touch the bulb surface, clean it with rubbing alcohol.*
6   Open the hood.
7   Remove the rubber cover from the back of the headlight assembly.
8   Detach the spring and withdraw the bulb and holder assembly from the headlight

housing **(see illustration)**.
9   Lift the tab on the electrical connector, unplug the connector from the bulb assembly and withdraw the bulb.
10   Without touching the glass with your bare fingers, plug in the electrical connector, insert the new bulb assembly into the headlight housing, and install the retaining spring.
11   Test headlight operation, then close the hood.

15 Headlights - adjustment

Refer to illustrations 15.1, 15.10 and 15.11

1991 and earlier models

1   On these models, the headlights have adjusting screws on the top controlling up-and-down movement and one on the side controlling left-and-right movement **(see illustration)**.
2   There are several methods of adjusting the headlights. The simplest method requires a blank wall 25 feet in front of the vehicle and a level floor.
3   Position masking tape vertically on the

wall in reference to the vehicle centerline and the centerlines of both headlights.
4   Position a horizontal tape line in reference to the centerline of all the headlights. **Note:** *It may be easier to position the tape on the wall with the vehicle parked only a few inches away.*
5   Adjustment should be made with the vehicle sitting level, the gas tank half-full and no unusually heavy load in the vehicle.
6   Starting with the low beam adjustment, position the high intensity zone so it is two inches below the horizontal line and two inches to the right of the headlight vertical line. Turn the adjustment screws until the desired level has been achieved.
7   With the high beams on, the high intensity zone should be vertically centered with the exact center just below the horizontal line. **Note:** *It may not be possible to position the headlight aim exactly for both high and low beams. If a compromise must be made, keep in mind that the low beams are the most used and have the greatest effect on driver safety.*
8   Have the headlights adjusted by a dealer service department or other repair shop at the earliest opportunity.

12

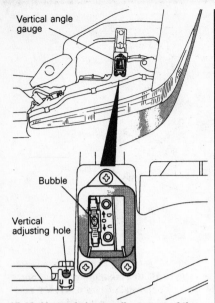

15.10 Up-and-down adjustment of the headlight is made by inserting a screwdriver into the vertical adjusting hole and turning the screw until the bubble is centered in the angle gauge (1992 and later models)

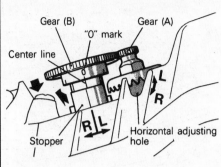

15.11 Side-to-side adjustment is made by pulling out the stopper, pushing in on gear (B) to disengage the gears, then turning gear (A) with a screwdriver - align the "0" mark with the line on the stopper after adjustment (1992 and later models)

1992 and later models

9   Later models also have two adjustment devices, one at the top controlling vertical (up-and-down) movement and one below the light for horizontal (left-and-right) movement. The vertical adjusters incorporate spirit levels that assure that the headlights are always level in relation to the chassis.

10   Vertical headlight movement is simply a matter of inserting a screwdriver into the adjustment hole and turning the adjustment screw until the spirit level bubble is centered **(see illustration)**.

11   Adjust the headlight position horizontally (left-and-right) by pulling out the stopper, and pushing in on gear B to disengage it from gear A. Insert a screwdriver into the adjustment hole and turn it to adjust the headlight position as described in steps 2 through 8 **(see illustration)**. After adjustment, line up the "0" mark on gear B with the centerline, then press the stopper in to lock the adjustment.

16   Headlight housing - removal and installation

Refer to illustrations 16.3 and 16.10

1   Disconnect the negative battery cable from the battery.

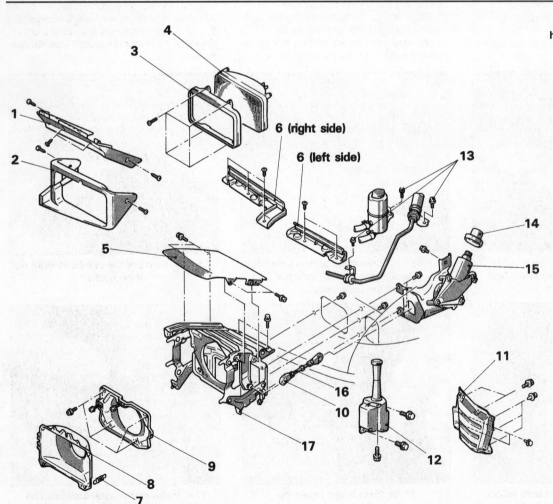

16.3 1991 and earlier headlight housing details

1	Headlight door trim
2	Headlight bezel
3	Retaining ring
4	Headlight
5	Headlight door
6	Door protector
7	Spring
8	Mount
9	Bracket
10	Pop-up link
11	Splash shield
12	Washer reservoir
13	Power steering reservoir and pipes
14	Boot
15	Pop-up motor and bracket
16	Link assembly
17	Housing

1991 and earlier models

2   Remove the headlight (see Section 14).

3   Remove the screws and detach the headlight door and door protector (**see illustration**).

4   Detach the headlight spring and remove the headlight mount and bracket.

5   Use a screwdriver to disconnect the pop-up link from the housing.

6   On the left side housing, remove the splash shield, windshield washer reservoir and power steering pump.

7   Remove the pop-up motor and link assembly for access, then remove the hinge bolts and detach the housing (**see illustration 16.3**).

8   Installation is the reverse of removal.

1992 and later models

9   Remove the headlight bulb (see Section 14).

10   Remove the screws and bolts and detach the turn signal housing followed by the headlight housing (**see illustration**).

11   Installation is the reverse of removal.

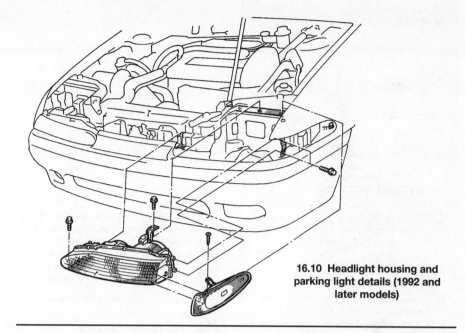

16.10 Headlight housing and parking light details (1992 and later models)

17   Bulb replacement

Refer to illustrations 17.1a, 17.1b, 17.1c, 17.3a, 17.3b, and 17.4

1   The lenses of many lights are held in place by screws. To gain access to the bulbs in these assemblies, simply remove the lenses (**see illustrations**).

2   The lenses or covers of some light assemblies are held in place by clips. You can remove them by unsnapping them or by prying them off with a small screwdriver.

3   Some bulbs can be removed simply by pushing them in and turning them counterclockwise while other can simply be pulled straight out of the socket (**see illustrations**).

4   The instrument cluster bulbs are accessible after removing the cluster (**see illustration**).

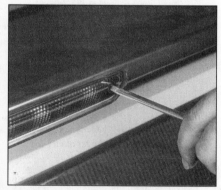

17.1a Use a Phillips screwdriver to remove the high mounted brake light screws and lens . . .

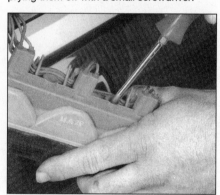

17.1b . . . remove the screws from the back of the housing and pull off the bulb holder . . .

17.1c . . . then pull the bulb(s) straight out of the socket

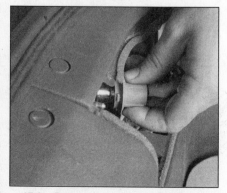

17.3a Rotate the tail light bulb holder counterclockwise and withdraw it

17.3b Push in and rotate the bulb to remove it

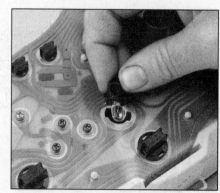

17.4 Instrument cluster bulbs can be replaced after the cluster is removed

12

18.2 Remove the bolts (arrows), unplug the connector and pull the wiper motor out of the firewall

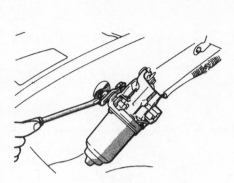

18.3 Detach the wiper link from the motor with a screwdriver

18.6 Lift up the cover and remove the nut and wiper arm assembly

18 Wiper motor - removal and installation

1   Disconnect the cable from the negative terminal of the battery.

18.8 Unplug the electrical connector, remove the bolts (arrows) and detach the wiper motor from the liftgate

Windshield wiper motor

Refer to illustrations 18.2 and 18.3

2   Unplug the electrical connector and remove the mounting bolts **(see illustration)**.
3   Pull the motor out and use a screwdriver to pry the wiper link from the motor crank **(see illustration)**.
4   Lift the motor from the engine compartment.
5   Installation is the reverse of removal.

Rear window wiper motor

Refer to illustrations 18.6 and 18.8

6   Lift up the cap, remove the nut and remove the rear wiper arm **(see illustration)**.
7   Remove the wiper shaft nut and washers, taking care to keep them in order.
8   Open the liftgate and detach liftgate inner trim panel. Unplug the electrical connector, then remove the bolts and detach the wiper motor **(see illustration)**.
9   Installation is the reverse of removal.

19 Instrument cluster - removal and installation

Refer to illustration 19.3

1   Disconnect the cable from the negative battery terminal.
2   Remove the instrument cluster trim panel (see Chapter 11).
3   Remove the four retaining screws, grasp the cluster securely and pull it straight out to detach it **(see illustration)**.
4   Reach behind the cluster, unplug the connectors and remove the cluster from the instrument panel.
5   Installation is the reverse of the removal procedure.

20 Instrument panel switches - check and replacement

Refer to illustrations 20.2a, 20.2b, 20.3a, 20.3b, 20.3c, 20.3d, 20.3e and 20.5

1   Disconnect the cable from the negative battery terminal.
2   Remove the center trim or instrument cluster trim panel (see Chapter 11) **(see illustrations)**.

19.3 The instrument cluster is secured by four screws (arrows)

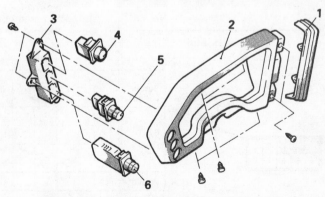

20.2a Instrument cluster panel and switch details

1	Trim panel	4	Headlight pop-up switch
2	Cluster	5	Fog light switch
3	Switch holder	6	Rheostat

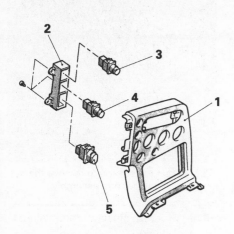

20.2b Center cluster panel
and switch details

1   Cluster panel
2   Switch holder
3   Hazard switch
4   Rear window defogger switch
5   Rear wiper/washer switch

Check

3   Use an ohmmeter to check the continuity between the terminals with the switch in the indicated position **(see illustrations)**.
4   Replace the switch if continuity is not as specified.

Replacement

5   Most of the switches are held in place by screws. Unplug the electrical connectors, detach the clips and push the switch out of the panel **(see illustration)**. Remove the screws, lift the switch holder off, then squeeze the tabs and withdraw the switch.
6   Installation is the reverse of the removal procedure.

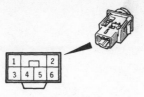

Switch position \ Terminal	1	3	4	2	5
OFF	o———		———o	Illumination	light
ON	o——o			Illumination	light

NOTE
o—o indicates that there is continuity between the terminals.

20.3a Headlight switch terminal number guide and continuity chart

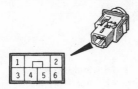

Switch position \ Terminal	1	3	2	6	4	5
OFF					Illumination	light
ON	o——o	o——o			Illumination	light

NOTE
o—o indicates that there is continuity between the terminals.

20.3b Fog light switch terminal number guide and continuity chart

Switch position \ Terminal	1	2	4	5	6	7	9	10
OFF				o——o			Illumination	light
ON	o——o——o			o——o			Illumination	light

NOTE
(1) o—o indicates that there is continuity between the terminals.

20.3c Hazard switch terminal number guide and continuity chart

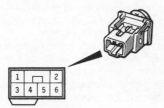

Switch position \ Terminal	3	4	1	5	2	6
OFF			Illumination	light	Indicator	light
ON	o——o		Illumination	light	Indicator	light

NOTE
o—o indicates that there is continuity between the terminals.

20.3d Rear window defogger switch terminal number guide and continuity chart

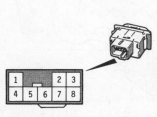

	Switch position \ Terminal	2	4	5	6	7	8	3	1
Wiper switch	OFF		o——o					Illumination	light
	ON			o——o				Illumination	light
	INT	o	o——o					Illumination	light
Washer switch					o——o			Illumination	light

NOTE
o—o indicates that there is continuity between the terminals.

20.3e Rear wiper/washer switch terminal number guide and continuity chart

20.5 Remove the screws (arrows) and
detach the switch holders

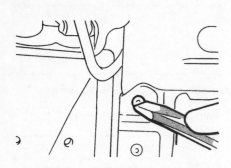

21.4a Use a hammer and chisel to unscrew the horn bolts

21   Horn - check and replacement

Refer to illustrations 21.4a, 21.4b and 21.4c

Check

1   If one of the horns sounds but not the other, that horn is probably faulty.

2   If neither horn sounds, check the 10 amp combination headlight/horn fuse located in the fuse block under the dash **(see illustration 3.1a)**.

3   If the fuse is good and the horns do not sound, unplug the electrical connector at each horn and connect one test light lead to the connector and the other to a good ground. If the lamp lights, the horn unit is faulty.

Replacement

4   The horn units are held in place by special shear-head bolts. To remove these bolts it will be necessary to use a chisel and hammer to unscrew each bolt in a counterclockwise direction **(see illustrations)**.

5   Install the new horn unit and special bolts (available at your dealer). Tighten the bolts until the heads break off.

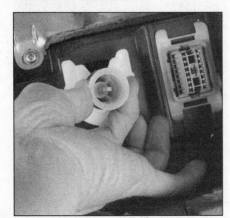

22.2 Lift the speedometer cable adapter off

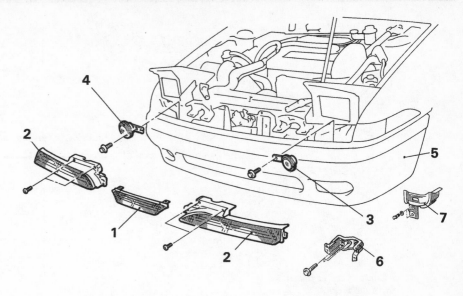

21.4b Horn installation details (1991 and earlier models)

1	Front garnish	5	Front bumper
2	Turn signal	6	Fog light bracket
3	Horn (low sound)	7	Horn mount
4	Horn (high sound)		

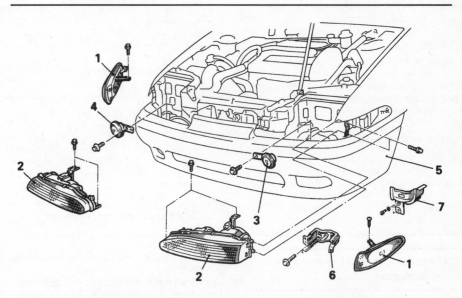

21.4c Horn installation details (1992 and later models)

1	Front marker light	5	Front bumper
2	Headlight	6	Fog light bracket
3	Horn (low sound)	7	Horn mount
4	Horn (high sound)		

22   Speedometer cable - replacement

Refer to illustration 22.2

1   Disconnect the cable from the negative terminal of the battery.

2   Remove the instrument cluster (see Section 19). Lift off the speedometer cable adapter **(see illustration)**.

3   In the engine compartment, detach the cable grommet from the firewall.

4   Raise the vehicle and support it securely on jackstands.

5   Remove the bolt or unscrew the collar and remove the speedometer from the transaxle.

6   Remove the cable assembly from the engine compartment.

7   Installation is the reverse of removal.

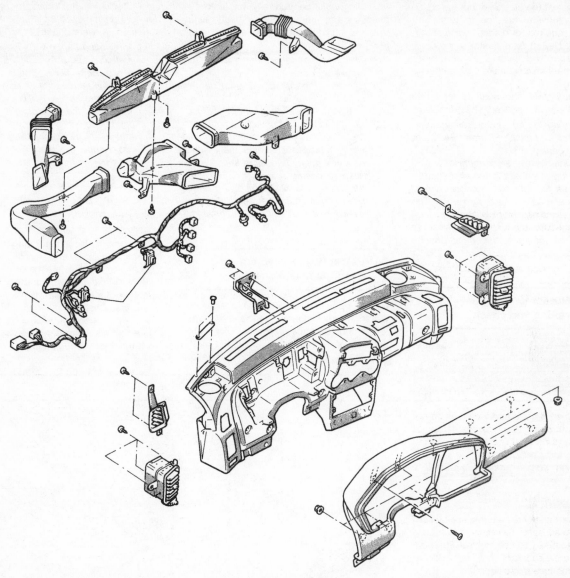

23.9a Instrument panel details

23 Instrument panel - removal and installation

Refer to illustrations 23.9a and 23.9b

1 Disconnect the cable from the negative battery.
2 Remove the steering wheel (see Chapter 10).
3 Remove the combination switch (see Section 7).
4 Remove the hood release handle.
5 Remove the dashboard trim panels (see Chapter 11).
6 Remove the radio and the dashboard mounted speakers (see Section 12).
7 Remove the instrument cluster housing and the cluster (see Section 19).
8 Remove the steering column nuts.
9 Remove the attaching nuts and bolts and carefully lift the instrument panel back for

access to the electrical connectors **(see illustrations)**.
10 Unplug the electrical connectors and disconnect any component which would interfere with removal. Lift the instrument panel from the vehicle.
11 Installation is the reverse of removal. Make sure none of the wiring is crimped when the instrument panel is rotated back into position.

24 Cruise control system - description and check

The cruise control system maintains vehicle speed by means of a vacuum actuated servo motor located in the engine compartment which is connected to the throttle linkage by a cable. The system consists of the servo motor, clutch switch, brake light

23.9b Pull the instrument panel back and remove it through the door opening

12

switch, control switches, a relay and associated vacuum hoses.

Because of the complexity of the cruise control system and the special tools and techniques required for diagnosis and repair, this should be left to a dealer or properly equipped shop. However, it is possible for the home mechanic to make simple checks of the wiring
and vacuum connections for minor faults which can be easily repaired. These include:

a) *Inspecting the cruise control actuating switches and wiring for broken wires or loose connections.*
b) *Checking the cruise control fuse.*
c) *Checking the hoses in the engine compartment for tight connections, cracked hoses and obvious vacuum leaks. The cruise control system is operated by a vacuum so it is critical that all vacuum switches, hoses and connections be secure.*

25 Power door lock system - description and check

The power door lock system operates the door lock actuators mounted in each door. The system consists of the switches, actuators and associated wiring.

Diagnosis can usually be limited to checks of the wiring connections and actuators for minor faults which can be easily repaired. These include:

a) *Checking the system fuse and/or circuit breaker.*
b) *Checking the switch wiring for damage or loose connections.*
c) *Checking the switches for continuity.*
d) *Removing the door panel(s) and checking the actuator wiring connections for looseness or damage. Inspect the actuator rods (if equipped) to make sure they are not bent, damaged or binding. The actuator can be checked by applying battery power momentarily. A solid click indicates the solenoid is operating properly.*

26 Power window system - description and check

The power window system operates the electric motors mounted in the doors which lower and raise the windows. The system consists of the control switches, the motors (regulators), glass mechanisms and associated wiring.

Diagnosis can usually be limited to sim-ple checks of the wiring connections and motors for minor faults which can be easily repaired. These include:

a) *Inspecting the power window actuating switches and wiring for broken wires or loose connections.*
b) *Checking the power window fuse and/or circuit breaker.*
c) *Removing the door panel(s) and checking the power window motor wiring connections for looseness and damage, and inspecting the glass mechanisms for damage which could cause binding.*

27 Wiring diagrams - general information

Prior to troubleshooting any circuits, check the fuse and circuit breakers (if equipped) to make sure they are in good condition. Make sure the battery is properly charged and has clean, tight cable connections (see Chapter 1).

When checking the wiring system, make sure that all electrical connectors are clean, with no broken or loose pins. When unplugging an electrical connector, do not pull on the wires, only on the connector housings themselves.

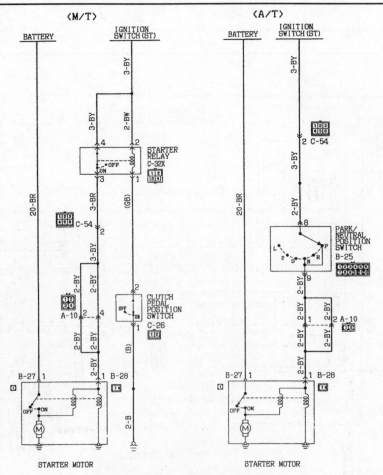

Typical starting system wiring diagram

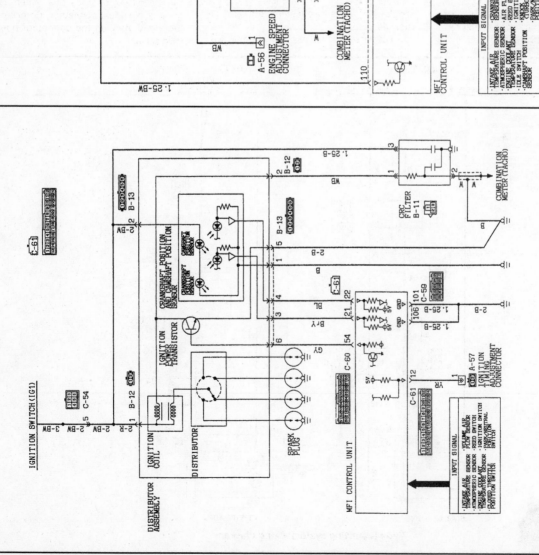

Typical 2.0L engine ignition system wiring diagram

Typical 1.8L engine ignition system wiring diagram

12

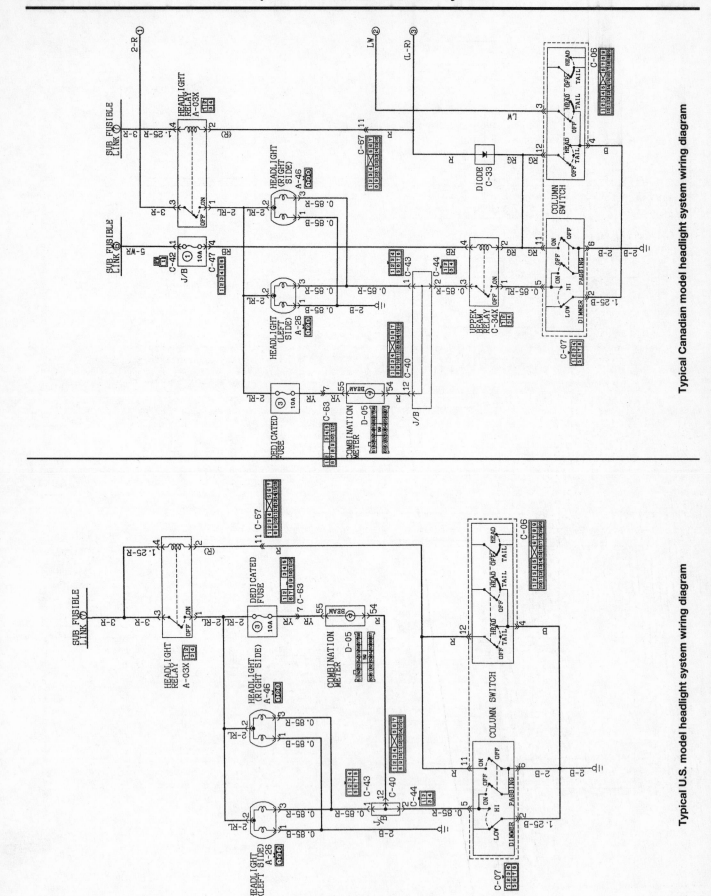

Typical Canadian model headlight system wiring diagram

Typical U.S. model headlight system wiring diagram

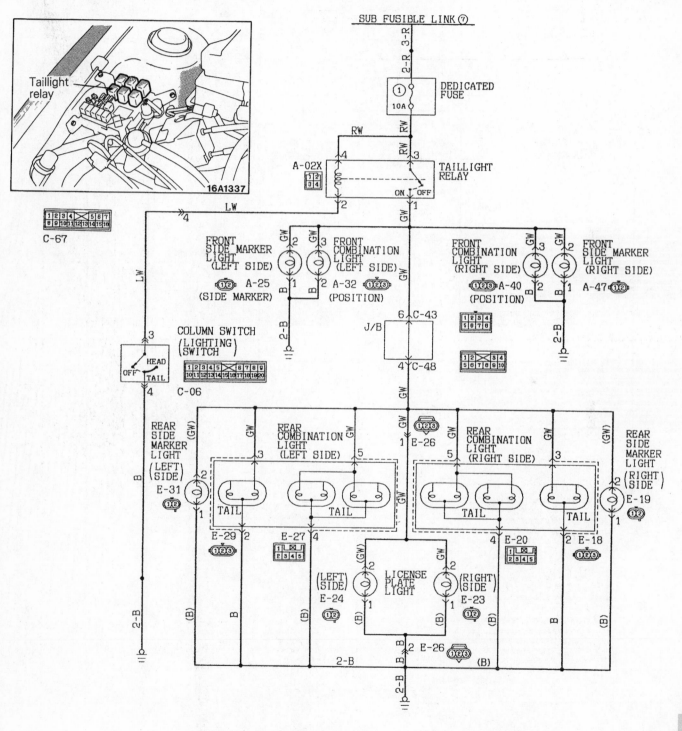

Typical tail, running and license plate light wiring diagram

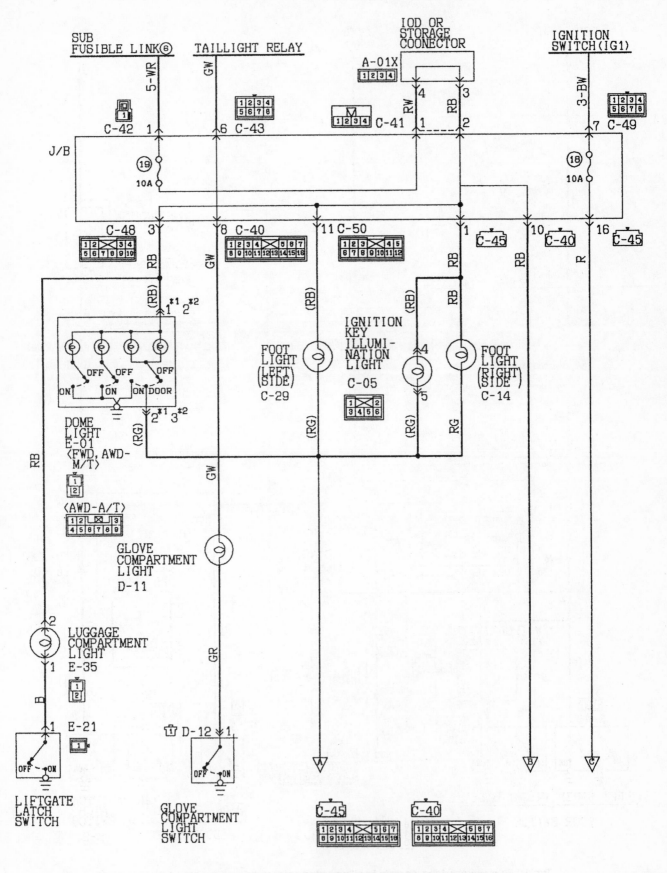

Typical dome, key, glove and luggage compartment light wiring diagram

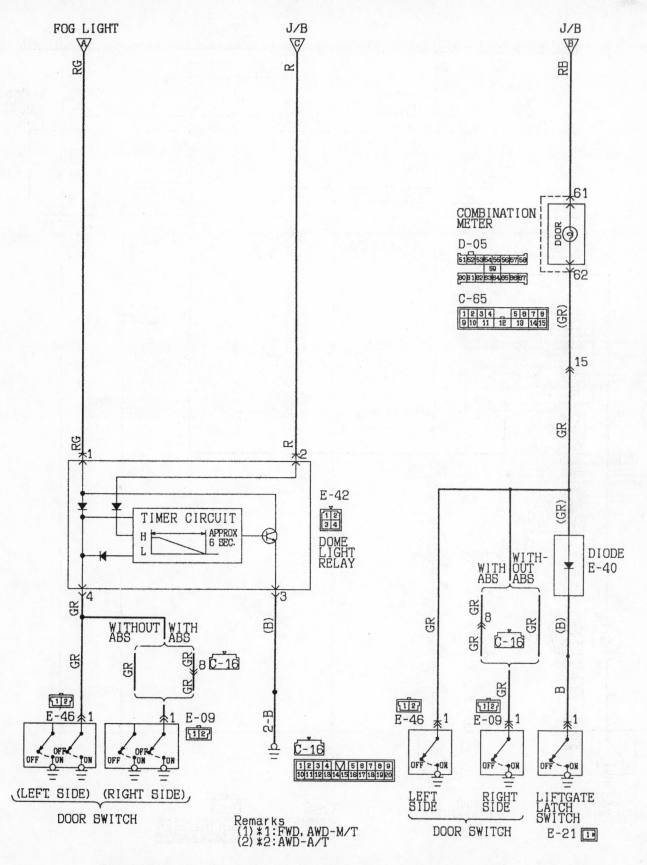

Typical door switch wiring diagram (for illuminated entry and door ajar light on dash)

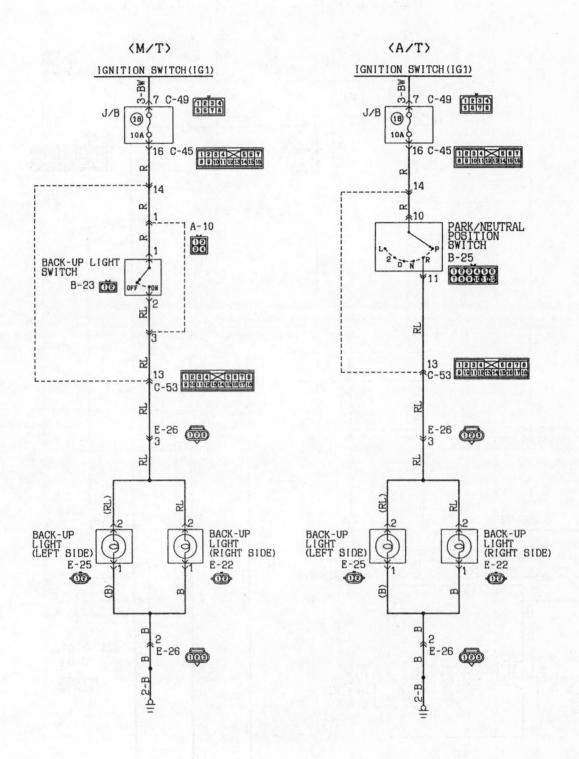

Typical backup light wiring diagram

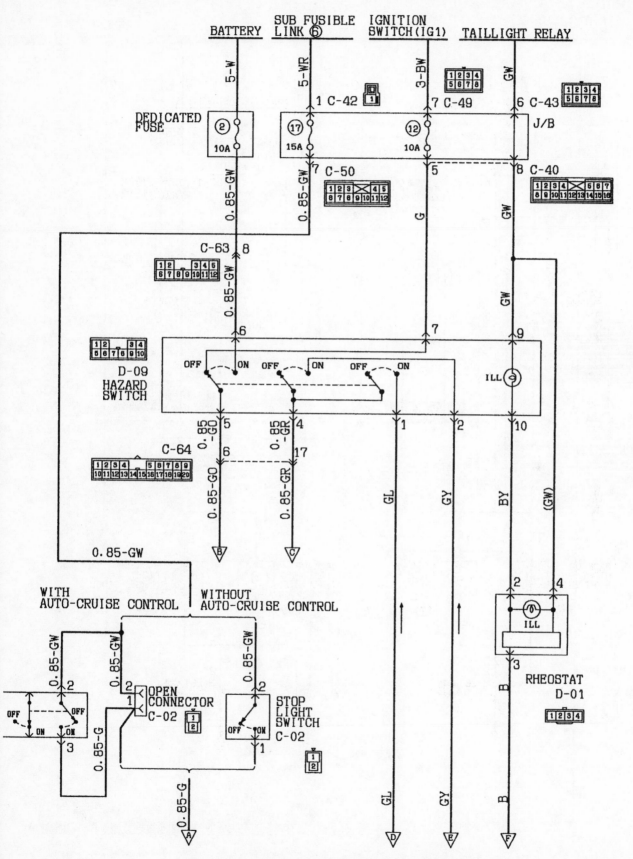

Typical turn signal, hazard and brake light wiring diagram (1 of 3)

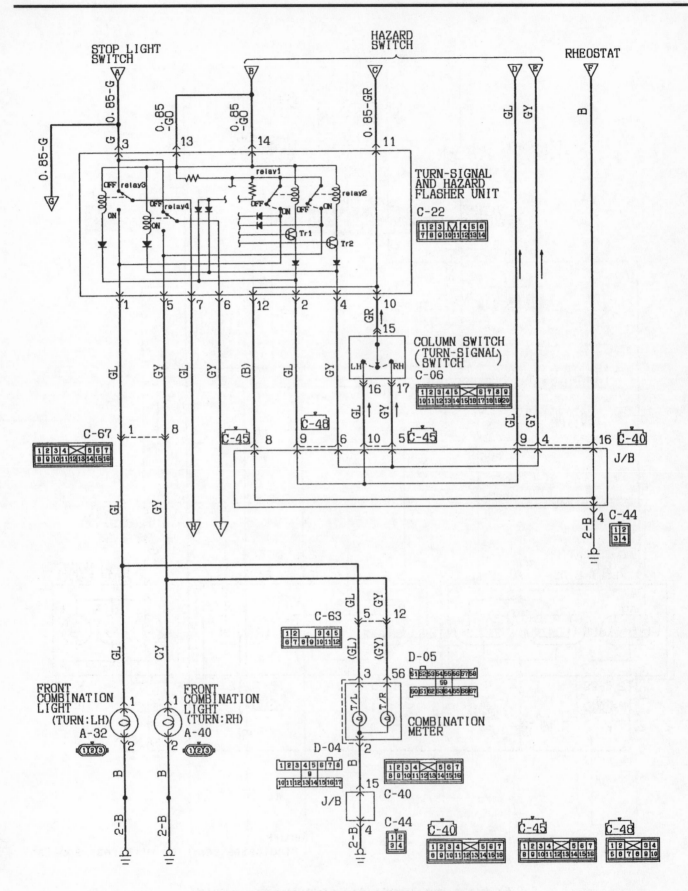

Typical turn signal, hazard and brake light wiring diagram (2 of 3)

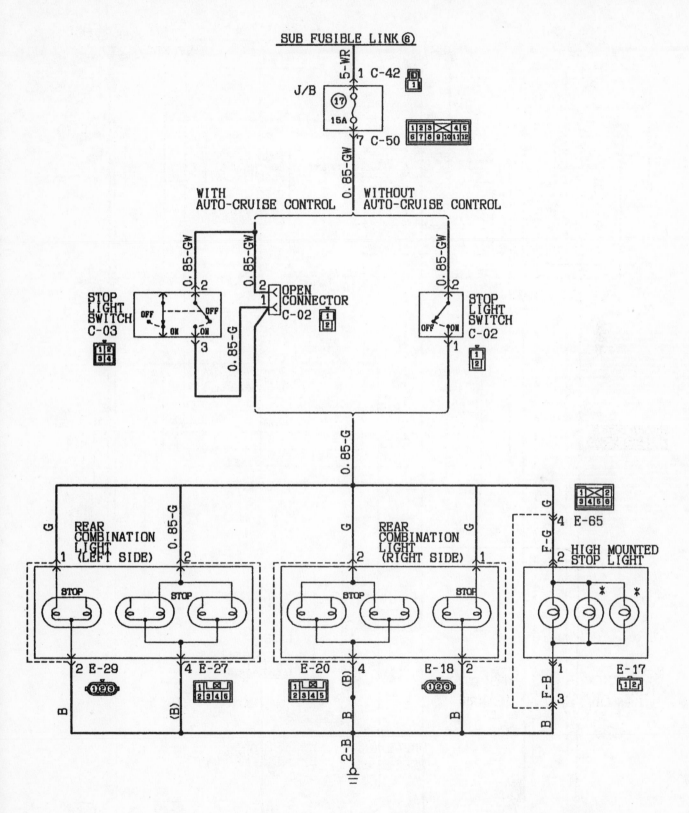

Typical turn signal, hazard and brake light wiring diagram (3 of 3)

Remark
· *Indicates vehicles with rear spoiler

12

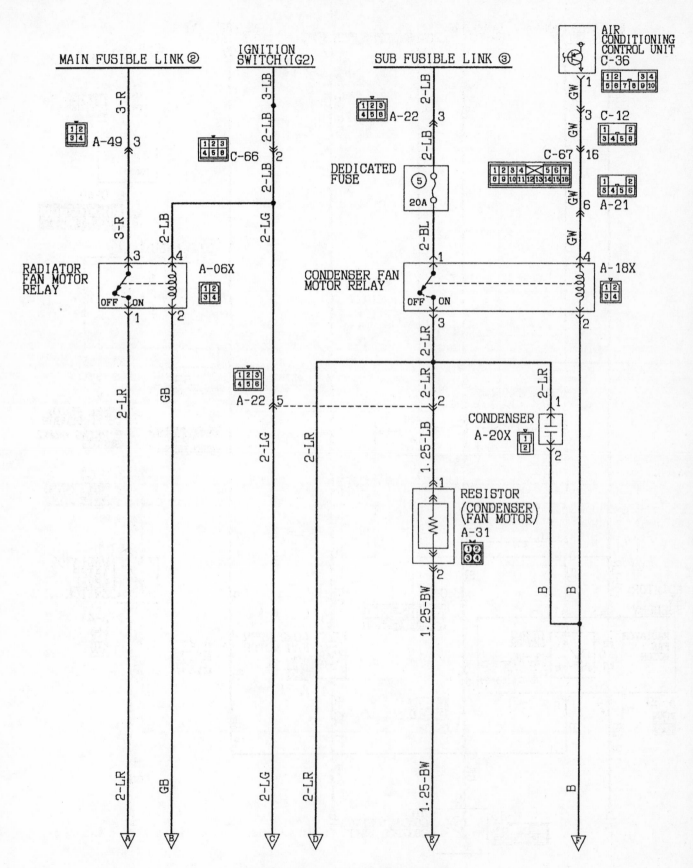

Typical cooling fan wiring diagram (1 of 2)

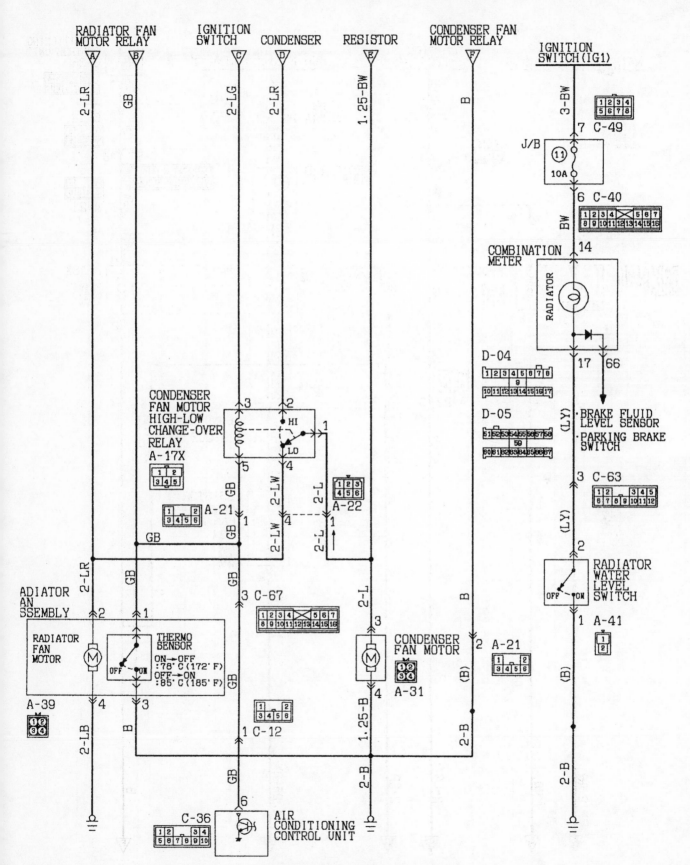

Typical cooling fan wiring diagram (2 of 2)

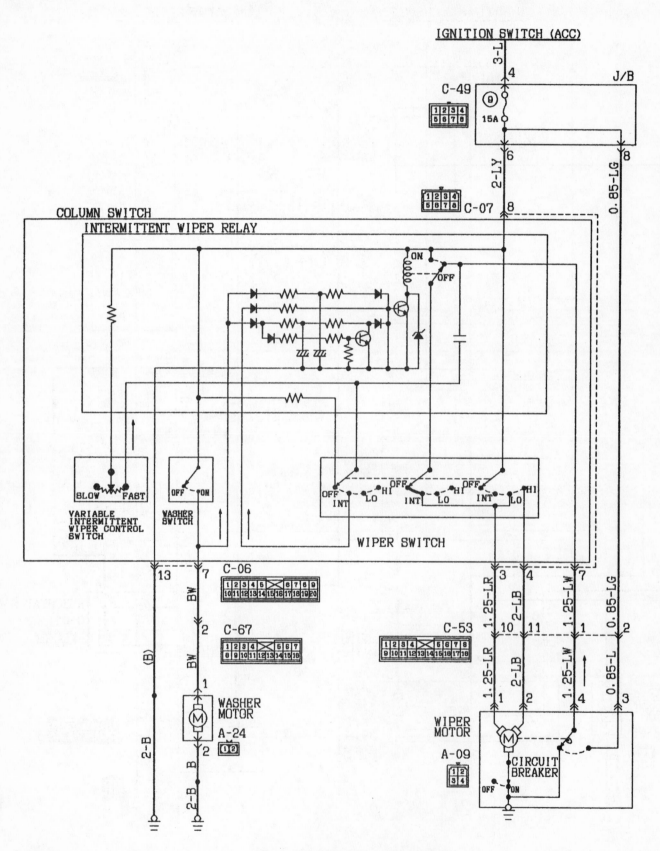

Typical windshield wiper wiring diagram

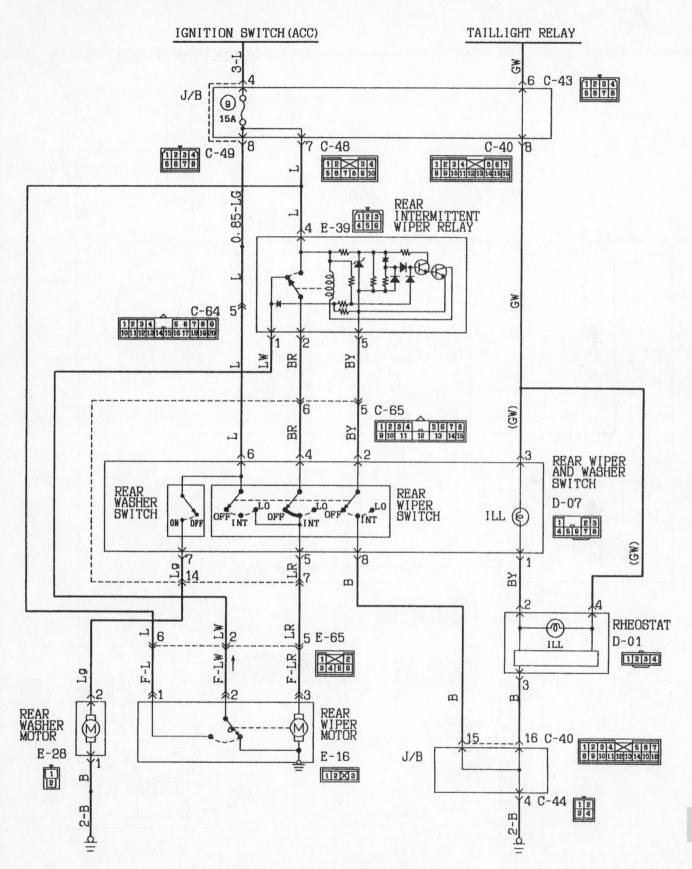

Typical rear window wiper wiring diagram

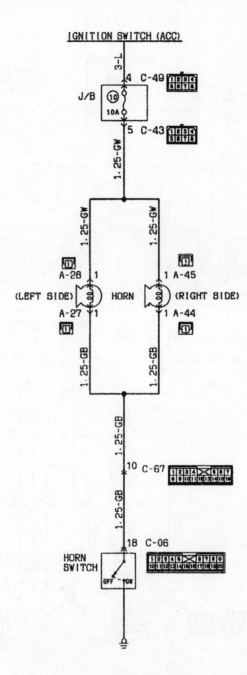

Typical horn wiring diagram

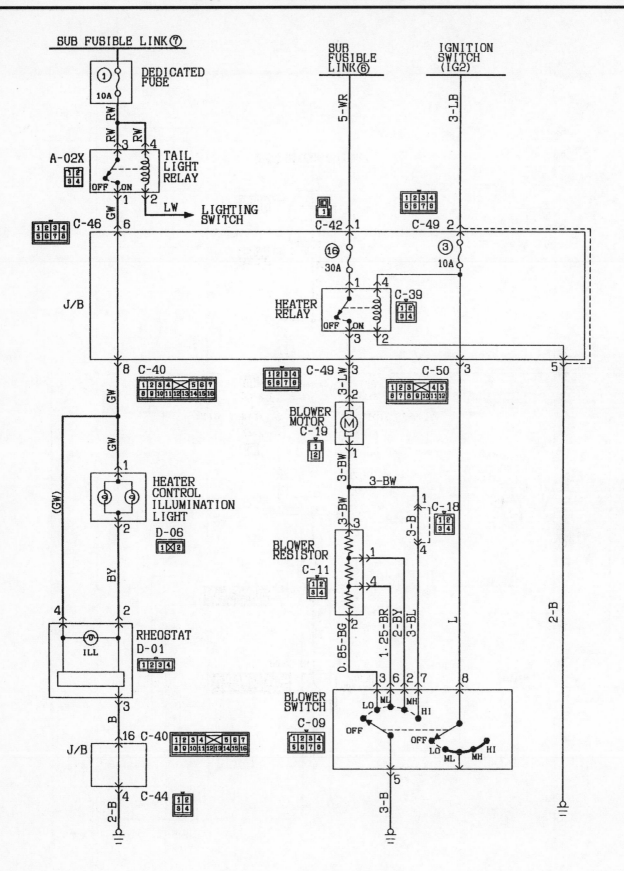

Typical heater system wiring diagram

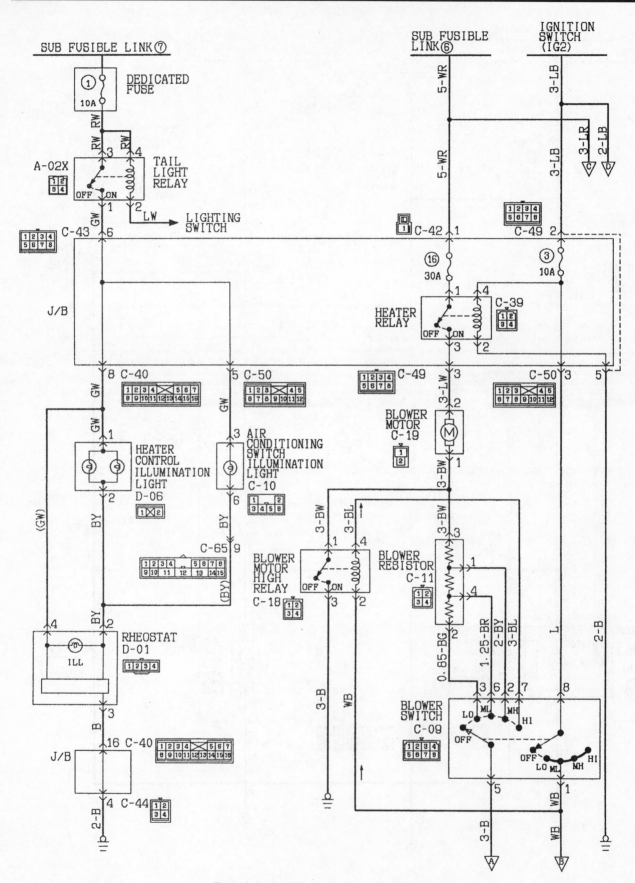

Typical air conditioning system wiring diagram (1 of 3)

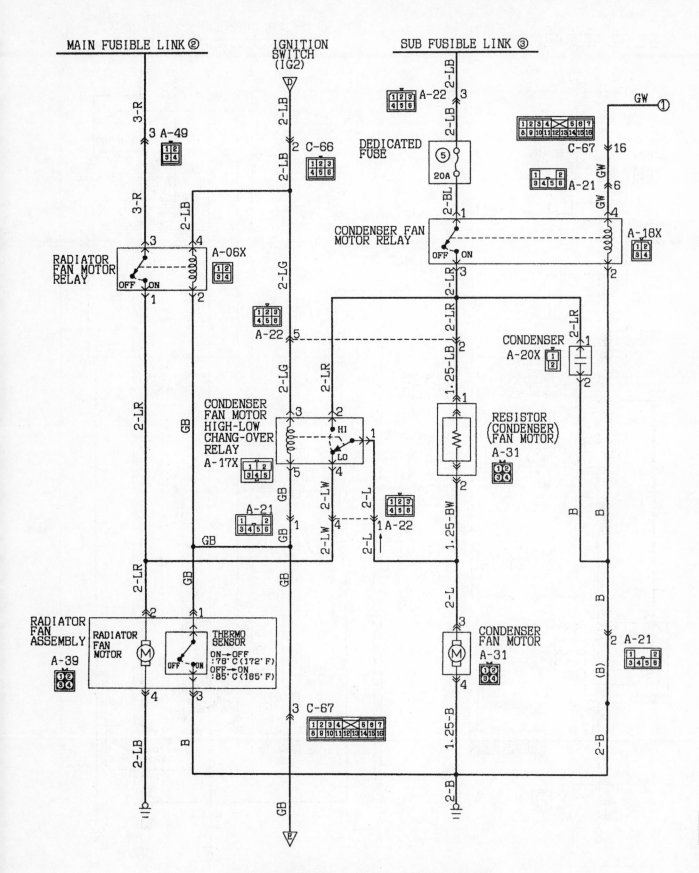

Typical air conditioning system wiring diagram (2 of 3)

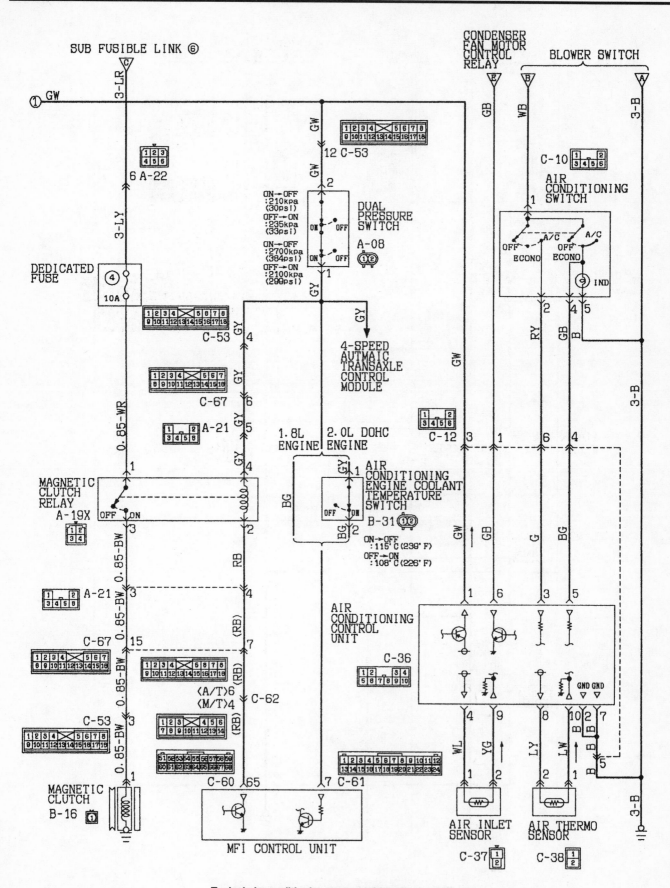

Typical air conditioning system wiring diagram (3 of 3)

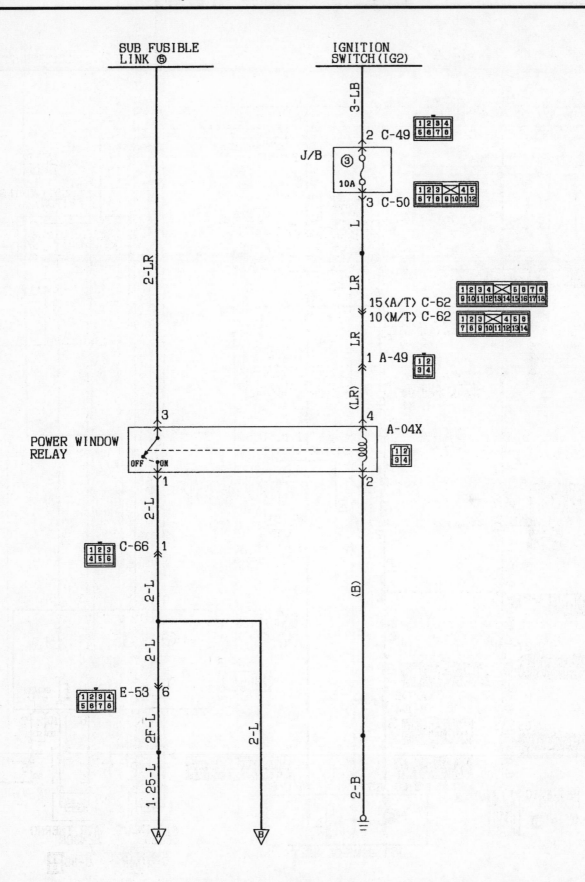

Typical power window wiring diagram (1 of 2)

12

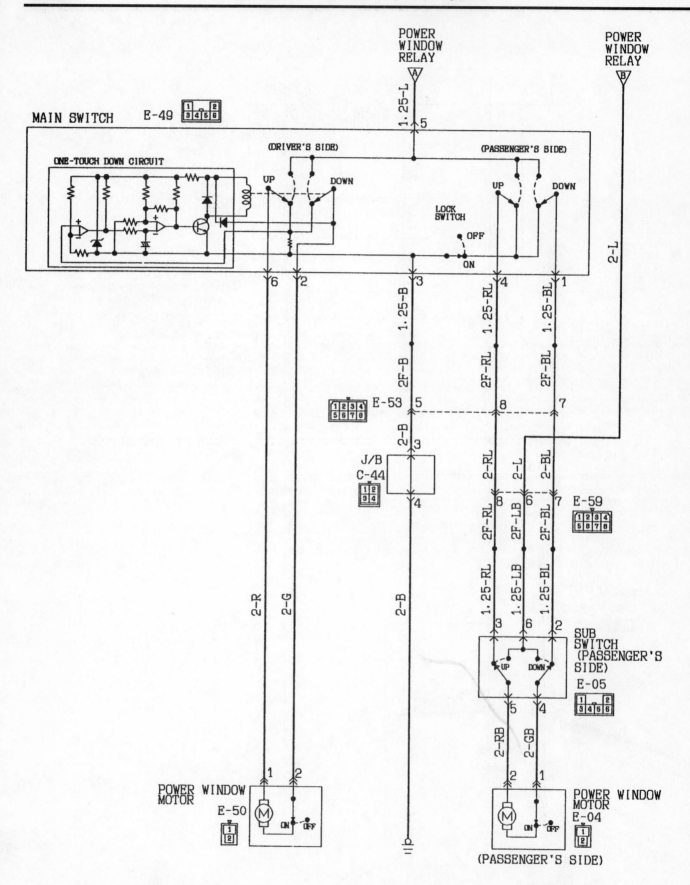

Typical power window wiring diagram (2 of 2)

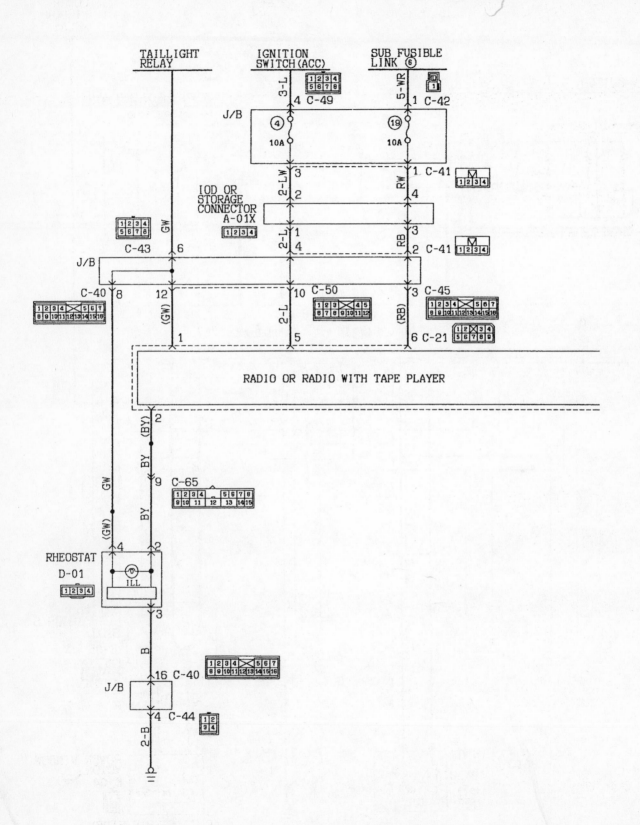

Typical audio system wiring diagram (1 of 2)

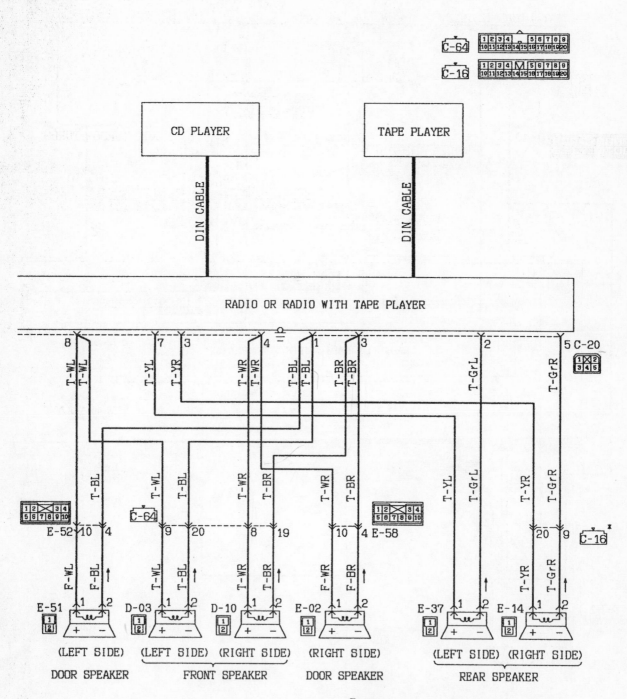

Typical audio system wiring diagram (2 of 2)

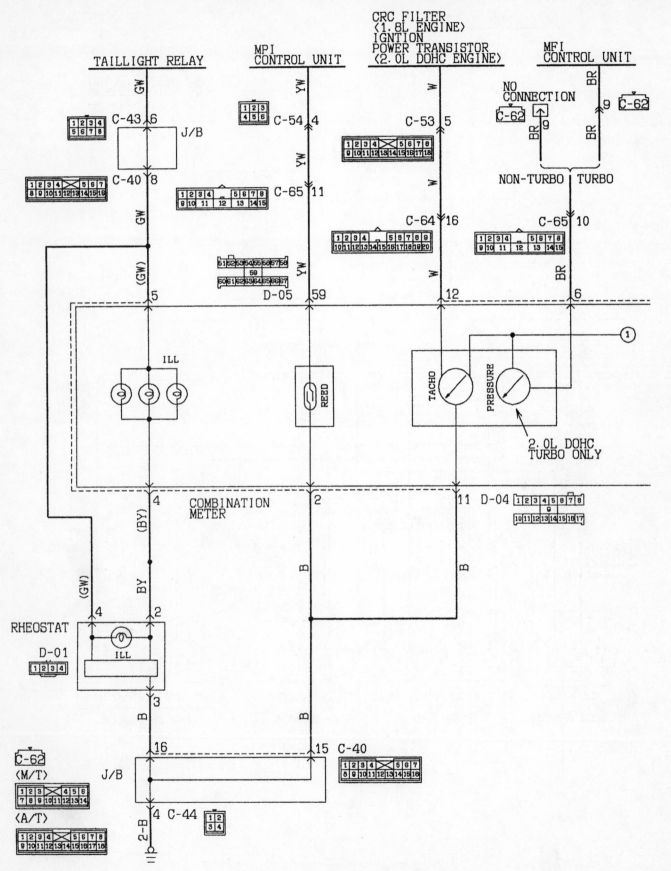

Typical instrument cluster wiring diagram (1 of 2)

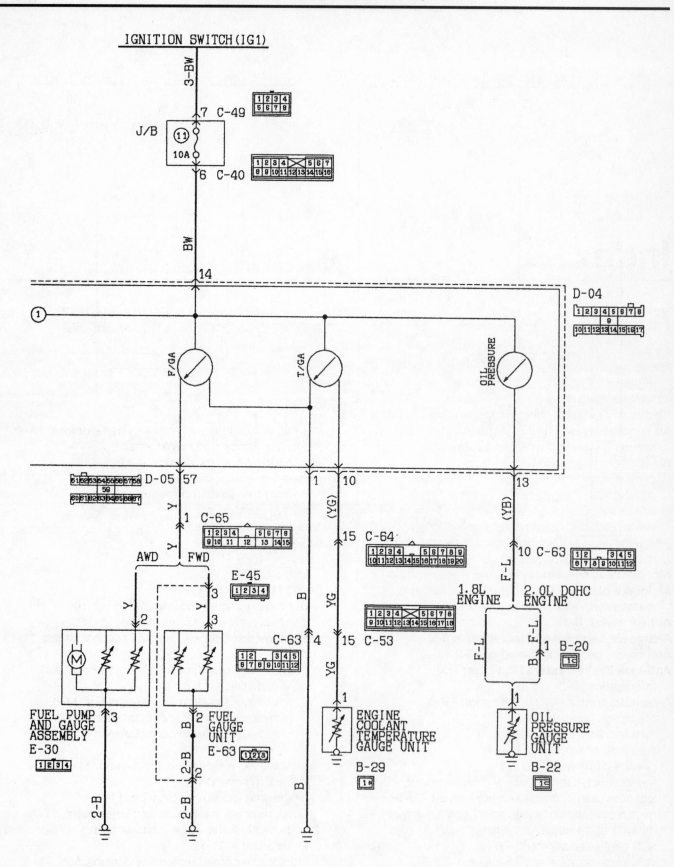

Typical instrument cluster wiring diagram (2 of 2)

Index

Haynes Automotive Manuals

NOTE: New manuals are added to this list on a periodic basis. If you do not see a listing for your vehicle, consult your local Haynes dealer for the latest product information.

ACURA
*12020 Integra '86 thru '89 **& Legend** '86 thru '90

AMC
Jeep CJ - see JEEP (50020)
14020 Mid-size models, Concord, Hornet, Gremlin & Spirit '70 thru '83
14025 (Renault) Alliance & Encore '83 thru '87

AUDI
15020 4000 all models '80 thru '87
15025 5000 all models '77 thru '83
15026 5000 all models '84 thru '88

AUSTIN-HEALEY
Sprite - see MG Midget (66015)

BMW
*18020 3/5 Series not including diesel or all-wheel drive models '82 thru '92
*18021 3 Series except 325iX models '92 thru '97
18025 320i all 4 cyl models '75 thru '83
18035 528i & 530i all models '75 thru '80
18050 1500 thru 2002 except Turbo '59 thru '77

BUICK
Century (front wheel drive) - see GM (829)
*19020 Buick, Oldsmobile & Pontiac Full-size (Front wheel drive) all models '85 thru '98
Buick Electra, LeSabre and Park Avenue; **Oldsmobile** Delta 88 Royale, Ninety Eight and Regency; **Pontiac** Bonneville
19025 Buick Oldsmobile & Pontiac Full-size (Rear wheel drive)
Buick Estate '70 thru '90, Electra '70 thru '84, LeSabre '70 thru '85, Limited '74 thru '79
Oldsmobile Custom Cruiser '70 thru '90, Delta 88 '70 thru '85, Ninety-eight '70 thru '84
Pontiac Bonneville '70 thru '81, Catalina '70 thru '81, Grandville '70 thru '75, Parisienne '83 thru '86
19030 Mid-size Regal & Century all rear-drive models with V6, V8 and Turbo '74 thru '87
Regal - see GENERAL MOTORS (38010)
Riviera - see GENERAL MOTORS (38030)
Roadmaster - see CHEVROLET (24046)
Skyhawk - see GENERAL MOTORS (38015)
Skylark '80 thru '85 - see GM (38020)
Skylark '86 on - see GM (38025)
Somerset - see GENERAL MOTORS (38025)

CADILLAC
*21030 Cadillac Rear Wheel Drive all gasoline models '70 thru '93
Cimarron - see GENERAL MOTORS (38015)
Eldorado - see GENERAL MOTORS (38030)
Seville '80 thru '85 - see GM (38030)

CHEVROLET
*24010 Astro & GMC Safari Mini-vans '85 thru '93
24015 Camaro V8 all models '70 thru '81
24016 Camaro all models '82 thru '92
Cavalier - see GENERAL MOTORS (38015)
Celebrity - see GENERAL MOTORS (38005)
24017 Camaro & Firebird '93 thru '97
24020 Chevelle, Malibu & El Camino '69 thru '87
24024 Chevette & Pontiac T1000 '76 thru '87
Citation - see GENERAL MOTORS (38020)
*24032 Corsica/Beretta all models '87 thru '96
24040 Corvette all V8 models '68 thru '82
*24041 Corvette all models '84 thru '96
10305 Chevrolet Engine Overhaul Manual
24045 Full-size Sedans Caprice, Impala, Biscayne, Bel Air & Wagons '69 thru '90
24046 Impala SS & Caprice and Buick Roadmaster '91 thru '96
Lumina - see GENERAL MOTORS (38010)

24048 Lumina & Monte Carlo '95 thru '98
Lumina APV - see GM (38035)
24050 Luv Pick-up all 2WD & 4WD '72 thru '82
*24055 Monte Carlo all models '70 thru '88
Monte Carlo '95 thru '98 - see LUMINA (24048)
24059 Nova all V8 models '69 thru '79
*24060 Nova and Geo Prizm '85 thru '92
24064 Pick-ups '67 thru '87 - Chevrolet & GMC, all V8 & in-line 6 cyl, 2WD & 4WD '67 thru '87; Suburbans, Blazers & Jimmys '67 thru '91
*24065 Pick-ups '88 thru '98 - Chevrolet & GMC, all full-size pick-ups, '88 thru '98; Blazer & Jimmy '92 thru '94; Suburban '92 thru '98; Tahoe & Yukon '98
24070 S-10 & S-15 Pick-ups '82 thru '93, Blazer & Jimmy '83 thru '94,
*24071 S-10 & S-15 Pick-ups '94 thru '96 Blazer & Jimmy '95 thru '96
*24075 Sprint & Geo Metro '85 thru '94
*24080 Vans - Chevrolet & GMC, V8 & in-line 6 cylinder models '68 thru '96

CHRYSLER
25015 Chrysler Cirrus, Dodge Stratus, Plymouth Breeze '95 thru '98
25025 Chrysler Concorde, New Yorker & LHS, Dodge Intrepid, Eagle Vision, '93 thru '97
10310 Chrysler Engine Overhaul Manual
*25020 Full-size Front-Wheel Drive '88 thru '93
K-Cars - see DODGE Aries (30008)
Laser - see DODGE Daytona (30030)
*25030 Chrysler & Plymouth Mid-size front wheel drive '82 thru '95
Rear-wheel Drive - see Dodge (30050)

DATSUN
28005 200SX all models '80 thru '83
28007 B-210 all models '73 thru '78
28009 210 all models '79 thru '82
28012 240Z, 260Z & 280Z Coupe '70 thru '78
28014 280ZX Coupe & 2+2 '79 thru '83
300ZX - see NISSAN (72010)
28016 310 all models '78 thru '82
28018 510 & PL521 Pick-up '68 thru '73
28020 510 all models '78 thru '81
28022 620 Series Pick-up all models '73 thru '79
720 Series Pick-up - see NISSAN (72030)
28025 810/Maxima all gasoline models, '77 thru '84

DODGE
400 & 600 - see CHRYSLER (25030)
*30008 Aries & Plymouth Reliant '81 thru '89
30010 Caravan & Plymouth Voyager Mini-Vans all models '84 thru '95
*30011 Caravan & Plymouth Voyager Mini-Vans all models '96 thru '98
30012 Challenger/Plymouth Saporro '78 thru '83
30016 Colt & Plymouth Champ (front wheel drive) all models '78 thru '87
*30020 Dakota Pick-ups all models '87 thru '96
30025 Dart, Demon, Plymouth Barracuda, Duster & Valiant 6 cyl models '67 thru '76
*30030 Daytona & Chrysler Laser '84 thru '89
Intrepid - see CHRYSLER (25025)
*30034 Neon all models '95 thru '97
*30035 Omni & Plymouth Horizon '78 thru '90
*30040 Pick-ups all full-size models '74 thru '93
*30041 Pick-ups all full-size models '94 thru '96
*30045 Ram 50/D50 Pick-ups & Raider and Plymouth Arrow Pick-ups '79 thru '93
30050 Dodge/Plymouth/Chrysler rear wheel drive '71 thru '89
*30055 Shadow & Plymouth Sundance '87 thru '94
*30060 Spirit & Plymouth Acclaim '89 thru '95
*30065 Vans - Dodge & Plymouth '71 thru '96

EAGLE
Talon - see Mitsubishi Eclipse (68030)
Vision - see CHRYSLER (25025)

FIAT
34010 124 Sport Coupe & Spider '68 thru '78
34025 X1/9 all models '74 thru '80

FORD
10355 Ford Automatic Transmission Overhaul
*36004 Aerostar Mini-vans all models '86 thru '96
*36006 Contour & Mercury Mystique '95 thru '98
36008 Courier Pick-up all models '72 thru '82
36012 Crown Victoria & Mercury Grand Marquis '88 thru '96
10320 Ford Engine Overhaul Manual
36016 Escort/Mercury Lynx all models '81 thru '90
*36020 Escort/Mercury Tracer '91 thru '96
*36024 Explorer & Mazda Navajo '91 thru '95
36028 Fairmont & Mercury Zephyr '78 thru '83
36030 Festiva & Aspire '88 thru '97
36032 Fiesta all models '77 thru '80
36036 Ford & Mercury Full-size, Ford LTD & Mercury Marquis ('75 thru '82); Ford Custom 500, Country Squire, Crown Victoria & Mercury Colony Park ('75 thru '87); Ford LTD Crown Victoria & Mercury Gran Marquis ('83 thru '87)
36040 Granada & Mercury Monarch '75 thru '80
36044 Ford & Mercury Mid-size, Ford Thunderbird & Mercury Cougar ('75 thru '82); Ford LTD & Mercury Marquis ('83 thru '86); Ford Torino, Gran Torino, Elite, Ranchero pick-up, LTD II, Mercury Montego, Comet, XR-7 & Lincoln Versailles ('75 thru '86)
36048 Mustang V8 all models '64-1/2 thru '73
36049 Mustang II 4 cyl, V6 & V8 models '74 thru '78
36050 Mustang & Mercury Capri all models Mustang, '79 thru '93; Capri, '79 thru '86
*36051 Mustang all models '94 thru '97
36054 Pick-ups & Bronco '73 thru '79
36058 Pick-ups & Bronco '80 thru '96
36059 Pick-ups, Expedition & Mercury Navigator '97 thru '98
36062 Pinto & Mercury Bobcat '75 thru '80
36066 Probe all models '89 thru '92
36070 Ranger/Bronco II gasoline models '83 thru '92
*36071 Ranger '93 thru '97 & Mazda Pick-ups '94 thru '97
36074 Taurus & Mercury Sable '86 thru '95
*36075 Taurus & Mercury Sable '96 thru '98
*36078 Tempo & Mercury Topaz '84 thru '94
36082 Thunderbird/Mercury Cougar '83 thru '88
*36086 Thunderbird/Mercury Cougar '89 and '97
36090 Vans all V8 Econoline models '69 thru '91
*36094 Vans full size '92-'95
*36097 Windstar Mini-van '95-'98

GENERAL MOTORS
*10360 GM Automatic Transmission Overhaul
*38005 Buick Century, Chevrolet Celebrity, Oldsmobile Cutlass Ciera & Pontiac 6000 all models '82 thru '96
*38010 Buick Regal, Chevrolet Lumina, Oldsmobile Cutlass Supreme & Pontiac Grand Prix front-wheel drive models '88 thru '95
*38015 Buick Skyhawk, Cadillac Cimarron, Chevrolet Cavalier, Oldsmobile Firenza & Pontiac J-2000 & Sunbird '82 thru '94
*38016 Chevrolet Cavalier & Pontiac Sunfire '95 thru '98
38020 Buick Skylark, Chevrolet Citation, Olds Omega, Pontiac Phoenix '80 thru '85
38025 Buick Skylark & Somerset, Oldsmobile Achieva & Calais and Pontiac Grand Am all models '85 thru '95
38030 Cadillac Eldorado '71 thru '85, **Seville** '80 thru '85, **Oldsmobile Toronado** '71 thru '85 **& Buick Riviera** '79 thru '85
*38035 Chevrolet Lumina APV, Olds Silhouette & Pontiac Trans Sport all models '90 thru '95
General Motors Full-size Rear-wheel Drive - see BUICK (19025)

(Continued on other side)

Haynes North America, Inc., 861 Lawrence Drive, Newbury Park, CA 91320-1514 • (805) 498-6703

Haynes Automotive Manuals (continued)

NOTE: New manuals are added to this list on a periodic basis. If you do not see a listing for your vehicle, consult your local Haynes dealer for the latest product information.

GEO

Metro - *see CHEVROLET Sprint (24075)*
Prizm - *'85 thru '92 see CHEVY (24060), '93 thru '96 see TOYOTA Corolla (92036)*
*40030 **Storm** all models '90 thru '93
Tracker - *see SUZUKI Samurai (90010)*

GMC

Safari - *see CHEVROLET ASTRO (24010)*
Vans & Pick-ups - *see CHEVROLET*

HONDA

42010 **Accord CVCC** all models '76 thru '83
42011 **Accord** all models '84 thru '89
42012 **Accord** all models '90 thru '93
42013 **Accord** all models '94 thru '95
42020 **Civic 1200** all models '73 thru '79
42021 **Civic 1300 & 1500 CVCC** '80 thru '83
42022 **Civic 1500 CVCC** all models '75 thru '79
42023 **Civic** all models '84 thru '91
*42024 **Civic & del Sol** '92 thru '95
*42040 **Prelude CVCC** all models '79 thru '89

HYUNDAI

*43015 **Excel** all models '86 thru '94

ISUZU

Hombre - *see CHEVROLET S-10 (24071)*
*47017 **Rodeo** '91 thru '97; **Amigo** '89 thru '94; **Honda Passport** '95 thru '97
*47020 **Trooper & Pick-up**, all gasoline models Pick-up, '81 thru '93; Trooper, '84 thru '91

JAGUAR

*49010 **XJ6** all 6 cyl models '68 thru '86
*49011 **XJ6** all models '88 thru '94
*49015 **XJ12 & XJS** all 12 cyl models '72 thru '85

JEEP

*50010 **Cherokee, Comanche & Wagoneer Limited** all models '84 thru '96
50020 **CJ** all models '49 thru '86
*50025 **Grand Cherokee** all models '93 thru '98
50029 **Grand Wagoneer & Pick-up** '72 thru '91 Grand Wagoneer '84 thru '91, Cherokee & Wagoneer '72 thru '83, Pick-up '72 thru '88
*50030 **Wrangler** all models '87 thru '95

LINCOLN

Navigator - *see FORD Pick-up (36059)*
59010 **Rear Wheel Drive** all models '70 thru '96

MAZDA

61010 **GLC Hatchback** (rear wheel drive) '77 thru '83
61011 **GLC** (front wheel drive) '81 thru '85
*61015 **323 & Protogé** '90 thru '97
*61016 **MX-5 Miata** '90 thru '97
*61020 **MPV** all models '89 thru '94
Navajo - *see Ford Explorer (36024)*
61030 **Pick-ups** '72 thru '93
Pick-ups '94 thru '96 - *see Ford Ranger (36071)*
61035 **RX-7** all models '79 thru '85
*61036 **RX-7** all models '86 thru '91
61040 **626** (rear wheel drive) all models '79 thru '82
*61041 **626/MX-6** (front wheel drive) '83 thru '91

MERCEDES-BENZ

63012 **123 Series Diesel** '76 thru '85
*63015 **190 Series** four-cyl gas models, '84 thru '88
63020 **230/250/280** 6 cyl sohc models '68 thru '72
63025 **280 123 Series** gasoline models '77 thru '81
63030 **350 & 450** all models '71 thru '80

MERCURY

See FORD Listing.

MG

66010 **MGB** Roadster & GT Coupe '62 thru '80
66015 **MG Midget, Austin Healey Sprite** '58 thru '80

MITSUBISHI

*68020 **Cordia, Tredia, Galant, Precis & Mirage** '83 thru '93
*68030 **Eclipse, Eagle Talon & Ply. Laser** '90 thru '94
*68040 **Pick-up** '83 thru '96 & **Montero** '83 thru '93

NISSAN

72010 **300ZX** all models including Turbo '84 thru '89
*72015 **Altima** all models '93 thru '97
*72020 **Maxima** all models '85 thru '91
*72030 **Pick-ups** '80 thru '96 **Pathfinder** '87 thru '95
72040 **Pulsar** all models '83 thru '86
*72050 **Sentra** all models '82 thru '94
*72051 **Sentra & 200SX** all models '95 thru '98
*72060 **Stanza** all models '82 thru '90

OLDSMOBILE

*73015 **Cutlass** V6 & V8 gas models '74 thru '88
For other OLDSMOBILE titles, see BUICK, CHEVROLET or GENERAL MOTORS listing.

PLYMOUTH

For PLYMOUTH titles, see DODGE listing.

PONTIAC

79008 **Fiero** all models '84 thru '88
79018 **Firebird** V8 models except Turbo '70 thru '81
79019 **Firebird** all models '82 thru '92
For other PONTIAC titles, see BUICK, CHEVROLET or GENERAL MOTORS listing.

PORSCHE

*80020 **911** except Turbo & Carrera 4 '65 thru '89
80025 **914** all 4 cyl models '69 thru '76
80030 **924** all models including Turbo '76 thru '82
*80035 **944** all models including Turbo '83 thru '89

RENAULT

Alliance & Encore - *see AMC (14020)*

SAAB

*84010 **900** all models including Turbo '79 thru '88

SATURN

87010 **Saturn** all models '91 thru '96

SUBARU

89002 **1100, 1300, 1400 & 1600** '71 thru '79
*89003 **1600 & 1800** 2WD & 4WD '80 thru '94

SUZUKI

*90010 **Samurai/Sidekick & Geo Tracker** '86 thru '96

TOYOTA

92005 **Camry** all models '83 thru '91
92006 **Camry** all models '92 thru '96
92015 **Celica Rear Wheel Drive** '71 thru '85
*92020 **Celica Front Wheel Drive** '86 thru '93
92025 **Celica Supra** all models '79 thru '92
92030 **Corolla** all models '75 thru '79
92032 **Corolla** all rear wheel drive models '80 thru '87
92035 **Corolla** all front wheel drive models '84 thru '92
*92036 **Corolla & Geo Prizm** '93 thru '97
92040 **Corolla Tercel** all models '80 thru '82
92045 **Corona** all models '74 thru '82
92050 **Cressida** all models '78 thru '82
92055 **Land Cruiser** FJ40, 43, 45, 55 '68 thru '82
92056 **Land Cruiser** FJ60, 62, 80, FZJ80 '80 thru '96
*92065 **MR2** all models '85 thru '87
92070 **Pick-up** all models '69 thru '78
*92075 **Pick-up** all models '79 thru '95
*92076 **Tacoma** '95 thru '98, **4Runner** '96 thru '98, & **T100** '93 thru '98
*92080 **Previa** all models '91 thru '95
92085 **Tercel** all models '87 thru '94

TRIUMPH

94007 **Spitfire** all models '62 thru '81
94010 **TR7** all models '75 thru '81

VW

96008 **Beetle & Karmann Ghia** '54 thru '79
96012 **Dasher** all gasoline models '74 thru '81
*96016 **Rabbit, Jetta, Scirocco, & Pick-up** gas models '74 thru '91 & Convertible '80 thru '92
96017 **Golf & Jetta** all models '93 thru '97
96020 **Rabbit, Jetta & Pick-up** diesel '77 thru '84
96030 **Transporter 1600** all models '68 thru '79
96035 **Transporter 1700, 1800 & 2000** '72 thru '79
96040 **Type 3 1500 & 1600** all models '63 thru '73
96045 **Vanagon** all air-cooled models '80 thru '83

VOLVO

97010 **120, 130 Series & 1800 Sports** '61 thru '73
97015 **140 Series** all models '66 thru '74
*97020 **240 Series** all models '76 thru '93
97025 **260 Series** all models '75 thru '82
*97040 **740 & 760 Series** all models '82 thru '88

TECHBOOK MANUALS

10205 **Automotive Computer Codes**
10210 **Automotive Emissions Control Manual**
10215 **Fuel Injection Manual, 1978 thru 1985**
10220 **Fuel Injection Manual, 1986 thru 1996**
10225 **Holley Carburetor Manual**
10230 **Rochester Carburetor Manual**
10240 **Weber/Zenith/Stromberg/SU Carburetors**
10305 **Chevrolet Engine Overhaul Manual**
10310 **Chrysler Engine Overhaul Manual**
10320 **Ford Engine Overhaul Manual**
10330 **GM and Ford Diesel Engine Repair Manual**
10340 **Small Engine Repair Manual**
10345 **Suspension, Steering & Driveline Manual**
10355 **Ford Automatic Transmission Overhaul**
10360 **GM Automatic Transmission Overhaul**
10405 **Automotive Body Repair & Painting**
10410 **Automotive Brake Manual**
10415 **Automotive Detailing Manual**
10420 **Automotive Eelectrical Manual**
10425 **Automotive Heating & Air Conditioning**
10430 **Automotive Reference Manual & Dictionary**
10435 **Automotive Tools Manual**
10440 **Used Car Buying Guide**
10445 **Welding Manual**
10450 **ATV Basics**

SPANISH MANUALS

98903 **Reparación de Carrocería & Pintura**
98905 **Códigos Automotrices de la Computadora**
98910 **Frenos Automotriz**
98915 **Inyección de Combustible 1986 al 1994**
99040 **Chevrolet & GMC Camionetas** '67 al '87 Incluye Suburban, Blazer & Jimmy '67 al '91
99041 **Chevrolet & GMC Camionetas** '88 al '95 Incluye Suburban '92 al '95, Blazer & Jimmy '92 al '94, Tahoe y Yukon '95
99042 **Chevrolet & GMC Camionetas Cerradas** '68 al '95
99055 **Dodge Caravan & Plymouth Voyager** '84 al '95
99075 **Ford Camionetas y Bronco** '80 al '94
99077 **Ford Camionetas Cerradas** '69 al '91
99083 **Ford Modelos de Tamaño Grande** '75 al '87
99088 **Ford Modelos de Tamaño Mediano** '75 al '86
99091 **Ford Taurus & Mercury Sable** '86 al '95
99095 **GM Modelos de Tamaño Grande** '70 al '90
99100 **GM Modelos de Tamaño Mediano** '70 al '88
99110 **Nissan Camionetas** '80 al '96, **Pathfinder** '87 al '95
99118 **Nissan Sentra** '82 al '94
99125 **Toyota Camionetas y 4Runner** '79 al '95

Over 100 Haynes motorcycle manuals also available

5-98

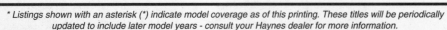